KT-549-570

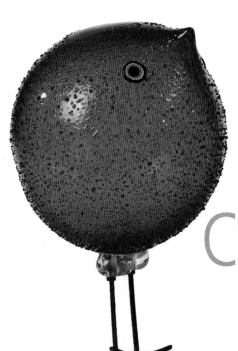

COLLECTABLES
HANDBOOK

Bromley Libraries

30128 80062 191 7

COLLECTABLES
HANDBOOK

Judith Miller
and Mark Hill

MILLER'S

Miller's Collectables Handbook 2012-2013

First published in Great Britain in 2012 by Miller's, a division of Mitchell Beazley,
imprints of Octopus Publishing Group Ltd, 189 Shaftesbury Avenue,
London, WC2H 8JY.
An Hachette Livre UK Company.
www.hachette.co.uk

Miller's is a registered trademark of Octopus Publishing Group Ltd.
www.millersonline.com

Copyright © Octopus Publishing Group Ltd 2012

All rights reserved. No part of this work may be reproduced or utilised in any form
or by any means, electronic or mechanical, including photocopying, recording or
by any information storage and retrieval system, without the prior permission of
the publishers.

———————————————

While every care has been exercised in the compilation of this guide,
neither the authors nor publishers accept any liability for any financial or
other loss incurred by reliance placed on the information contained in
Miller's Collectables Handbook.

ISBN 9781845336356

A CIP catalogue record for this book is available from the British Library.

Set in Frutiger

Colour reproduction by United Graphics, Singapore
Printed and bound in China by Toppan Printing Company

Authors Judith Miller & Mark Hill

Editorial Director Tracey Smith
Editorial Co-ordinator Katy Armstrong
Copy Editor John Wainwright
Editorial Assistants Rhea Finnie, Daniel Goode, Jessica Higgs
Indexer Hilary Bird
Advertising Sales Christine Havers
Photography Graham Rae
Design and Prepress Ali Scrivens, TJ Graphics
Production Lucy Carter

Photographs of Judith Miller and Mark Hill by Simon Upton and Graham Rae

Cover Images
Front (in rows, left to right): A tennis player troll. £5-10 PC; A Czechoslovakian Goldscheider-style terracotta wall mask. £100-150 CA; A Dinky 'HEINZ' Guy van. £120-180 VEC; A 1950s Japanese plastic chiming toy. £20-25 DSC; A 1960s Schiaparelli watch. £80-120 LHA; A rare Clarice Cliff Bizarre 'Luxor' wall plaque. £1,000-1,500 GHOU; A 1930s tinplate model of the 'Red Baron' triplane. £220-280 FRE; An early 20thC Farnell bear. £300-400 BELL; A 20thC Massachusetts goose decoy. £100-150 POOK; A Myott pottery 'Beaky' jug. £100-150 FLD; A Ferrari Old Timer plastic bird lamp. £80-120 WW
Back (in rows, left to right): A 'SUPERMAN BUMPER EDITION' annual. £90-110 CBA; A Royal Doulton 'Autumn Breezes' figurine. £10-20 CAPE; A Clarice Cliff 'Honolulu' conical sifter. £900-1,100; A Moschino 'House' bag. £180-220 LHA; A Theodore Haviland Limoge porcelain parrot. £250-300 WW; A 1930s French cameo glass vase. £250-300 FLD; A late 20thC Hermès 'Eperon' pattern scarf. £150-200 LHA; A Dinky 'ROYAL MAIL VAN'. £80-120 TOV; A Shelley Pottery 'Boo Boo' milk-jug, designed by Mabel Lucie Attwell. £60-80 WW; A 1980s John Maltby jug and bowl. £1,500-2,000 L&T; A 19thC 'King's Screw'-type corkscrew. £250-350 WW

CONTENTS

LIST OF CONSULTANTS

BOOKS

Roddy Newlands
Bloomsbury Auctions, London

CERAMICS

Beth Adams
Alfie's Antiques Market, London

Graham Cooley
Private Collector

William Farmer
Fielding's Auctioneers, Stourbridge

Kevin Graham
potteryandglass.forum andco.com

Emiel Monnink
retrominded.com

Geoffrey Robinson
Alfie's Antiques Market, London

FASHION & ACCESSORIES

Dawn Crawford
candysays.co.uk

Kerry Taylor
Kerry Taylor Auctions, London

50S & 60S

Ian Broughton
Alfie's Antiques Market, London

GLASS

Robert Bevan-Jones
Author & Private Collector

Mark Block
Block Glass, Connecticut, US

Graham Cooley
Private Collector

William Farmer
Fielding's Auctioneers, Stourbridge

Jindrich Parik
cs-sklo.cz

INUIT ART

Duncan McLean
Waddingtons, Toronto, Canada

PENS & WRITING EQUIPMENT

Simon Gray
penhome.co.uk

Hans Seiringer
hanspens.com

ORIENTAL

George Archdale
Cheffins, Cambridgeshire

SPORTING

Graham Budd
Graham Budd Auctions, London

TOYS, TEDDY BEARS & DOLLS

Leanda Harwood
leandaharwood.co.uk

Colin Lewis
The Magic Toybox, Hampshire

We are also grateful to all our friends and experts who gave us so much help and support – Beverley Adams, Richard Ball of lighter. co.uk, Al Baynham, Nigel Benson of 20thcentury-glass.com, Simon Cooper of Rosebery's, Alexander Crum Ewing, David Encill, Julie D'Arcy Evans, Jeanette Hayhurst, Kevin Harris of undercurrents. biz, Michael Jeffrey of Woolley & Wallis, Kathy Martin, Lesley McNamee of retropolitan.co.uk, Steven Moore of Anderson & Garland, Wesley Payne of Alfie's Antiques Market, Thomas Plant of Special Auction Services, Geoffrey Robinson of Alfie's Antiques Market, Adam Schoon of Tennants Auctioneers, Simon Shaw & Lloyd Farmar, Alison Snelgrove of thestudioglassmerchant.co.uk, Ron & Ann Wheeler of artiusglass. co.uk, and Nigel Wiggin of The Old Hall Club.

HOW TO USE THIS BOOK

Subcategory heading Indicates the sub-category of the main heading.

Page tab This appears on every page and identifies the main category heading as identified in the Contents List on pp.5-6.

Caption The description of the item illustrated, including, when relevant, the period, the maker or factory, medium, the year it was made, dimensions, and condition. Many captions have **footnotes** which explain terminology or give identification or valuation information.

The price guide These price ranges give a ballpark figure for what you should pay for a similar item. The great joy of collectables is that there is not a recommended retail price. The price ranges in this book are based on actual prices, either what a dealer will charge or the full auction price.

Quick Reference Gives key facts about the factory, maker, or style, along with stylistic identification points, value tips and advice on fakes.

Closer Look Does exactly that. This is where we show identifying aspects of a factory or maker, point out rare colours or shapes, and explain why a particular piece is so desirable.

The object The collectables are shown in full colour. This is a vital aid to identification and valuation. With many objects, a slight colour variation can signify a large price differential.

Source code Every item has been specially photographed at an auction house, a dealer, an antiques market or a private collection. These are credited by code at the end of the caption, and can be checked against the Key to Illustrations on pp.408-410.

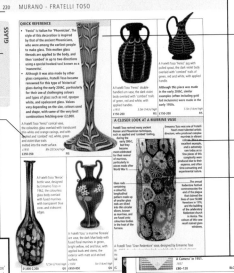

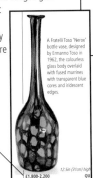

Judith/Mark Picks
Items chosen specifically by Judith and Mark, either because they are important or interesting, or because they believe that they are good investments.

INTRODUCTION

Welcome to the new edition of the Miller's Collectables Handbook. Once again we've amassed an all-new selection of thousands of collectables from across the world, each accompanied by an informative caption and a price guide. This year we've also included even more practical and helpful information than ever before. You'll notice that this edition includes more of our 'Closer Look' features, more in-depth footnotes, and more useful 'Quick Reference' sections. We've also included a new feature called 'Judith Picks' and 'Mark Picks'. In this feature we've selected a particular item for deeper discussion because we feel it's noteworthy in some way. We hope that you'll enjoy this more personal approach, as well as finding it helpful.

Two special events are taking place in 2012: the Olympic Games in London, and the diamond anniversary of the reign of Queen Elizabeth II. With this in mind, we've compiled two special sections to commemorate these events as we feel that interest in related collectables could well increase during the year and beyond.

Last year, we told you about the imminent launch of our exciting new website www.millersguides.com. We're delighted to announce that the site has been launched successfully, and has recently benefited from a complete make-over. If you haven't visited it yet, we think it'll soon become a favourite of yours.

You'll find over 190,000 items listed in our searchable database, each with a descriptive caption and a price guide. In order to help you find the information you want as quickly and as easily as possible, we've also placed each item into a simple category. An intuitive 'tag' system then allows you to search through related items, so look out for the red tags found under the caption.

You'll also find hundreds of illustrated articles, a guide to British silver hallmarks, information on caring for and repairing antiques and collectables, an illustrated dictionary of terms that also includes histories of key factories, major designers, and design movements, and much more. And the best thing? It's all free!

A 1960s Czechoslovakian Exbor glass 'Perch' fish sculpture. £200-250

On that note, the past two years have seen a continuation of the economic uncertainty and financial woes that first hit the world over five years ago. This has continued to affect the antiques and collectables markets, but it's not always as bad as it sounds. As more people experience continued instability and low interest rates for financial investments, such as pensions and savings, more of them are putting their money into tangible objects, such as antiques and collectables. For example, the prices paid for silver and gold have seen dramatic rises over the past year, and the very best pieces in any collecting category still continue to attract ever stronger prices.

Away from this higher end four important factors appear to govern the market: visual appeal, fashion, quality, and rarity. Visual appeal and fashion are tied closely together. Although many still prefer a clean-lined modern look in their homes, the current vogue for a 'vintage' look has a very positive effect on the market. In a 'vintage' home a Victorian or Edwardian tea cup and saucer may be placed next to a 1930s radio on a 1950s table. Warm, full of memories, individual, and expressive of the owner's life and loves, this mix-and-match look has caught on with many people, particularly those in their 20s and 30s. Although many disregard the trend as a passing fad, it is important, as today's vintage buyers may well continue to buy and thus become tomorrow's collectors.

Remember: quality always sells. New markets, such as post-war Czech glass, are still being discovered and developed. They, and more established markets, quickly become segregated by quality, and sometimes rarity. Whilst interest in and prices being paid for Royal Doulton figurines have fallen in general, prices for rarer pre-war figurines have held up.

We all have our own reasons for collecting, but at the root of them is a love for the piece itself. And that remains the most important reason why you should buy anything - because you love it.

A Royal Doulton original clay model of 'Vivienne'. £400-600

A 1950s Grimwades Royal Winton 'Kew' pattern chintz trio set. £65-75

ANTIQUES ARE GREEN

QUICK REFERENCE

- The advertising industry emerged in the mid-19thC and, in terms of the now much sought-after collectables it gave rise to, reached a height of diversity and brilliance during the first half of the 20thC as more and more companies vied with each other to catch consumers' eyes to sell them a product. As a result, and also becaue of the easily damaged nature of much packaging and advertising, the majority of pieces available today date from the 20thC, rather than earlier.
- Most collectors focus on one brand, or on one type of product or advertising object, such as biscuit tins. Food- and drink-related advertising and packaging are popular, and tobacco advertising has increased in desirability recently.
- Items from well-known brands, such as Guinness, and pieces with cross-market interest, such as railway advertising, tend to be the most valuable. Eye-catching, visually appealing designs will also usually be desirable and valuable.

- Tins and signs are highly sought-after, but condition is important. Examples in mint condition are preferred, and these can fetch many times the value of worn equivalents. Look for novelty tins made c1890-c1920 with unusual shapes or moving parts such as wheels. These often fetch a premium.
- Counter-top displays are often valuable. As fewer were made, and they were often damaged or discarded when a newer version arrived, they can also be rare.
- The style of a piece can help with dating. Familiarise yourself with major styles, such as Art Deco, and note the colours and styles of lettering used. Also consider the format of company names, logos, postcodes, and telephone numbers.
- Do not ignore non-tin packaging. If rare, the value of these disposable pieces can be surprisingly high. Also note, original contents do not necessarily increase value, but often indicate lack of use and therefore good condition.

A 'WHITBREAD's' 'INDIA PALE ALE' advertising sign, printed onto paper and stuck onto card, showing a bottle of Whitbread's India Pale Ale floating down on a parachute over the city of London, with some losses to the bottom left corner.

30in (76cm) high

£40-60　　　　　　　　**FLD**

A late 19thC 'Marston's BURTON ALES' reverse-cut glass sign, with gilded letters deeply cut into a black ground, within a black enamelled frame.

20in (50cm) high

£30-50　　　　　　　　**FLD**

A 'WELLINGTON INN' shield shaped painted metal pub sign, by 'THE HULL BREWERY CO., LTD.'.

33in (84cm) high

£100-150　　　　　　　　**DA&H**

A 1980s-90s 'The NAVIGATOR Ales & Porter' wooden pub sign, with arched top, in coloured paints with a sailor looking through a sextant.

Despite the brown tinted varnish and the signs of wear to the paint, this sign is modern. It's also likely that the pub doesn't even exist as the sign was probably mass-produced in the Far East. The value of such signs is purely decorative, as they're highly unlikely to become the sought-after collectables of the future.

36in (92.5cm) high

£30-40　　　　　　　　**ROS**

A 'HILL EVANS & CO's LIMITED WORCESTER PURE MALT VINEGAR' shield-shaped colour-printed tin sign, with the coat of arms of Worcester, and an image of three vinegar barrels.

11in (29cm) high

£50-80　　　　　　　　**FLD**

ADVERTISING & PACKAGING

A 1920s 'FLETCHERS TIGER & TOMATO SAUCES' printed tin sign, showing each bottle of sauce on either side of the wording.

29in (74cm) wide

£100-150   **FLD**

A 'MELLIN'S FOOD' colour lithographed cardboard shop sign, showing a baby feeding from a bottle while sitting in a bird's nest with a stork.

Mellin's Food for babies was developed in the early 1870s in an attempt to reduce the number of children who died before the age of five. At the time, one in every twelve children died around that age. Mellin improved the notable 'Liebig's Food For Infants', making it more suitable for distribution and export. Added to milk and boiling water, Mellin's was the most popular powdered infant food by the 1890s. At the time, such concoctions were even said to be more beneficial for babies than milk, being both scientific and 'modern'.

c1900   *13in (33cm) high*

£120-180   **FLD**

A CLOSER LOOK AT A TOBACCO ADVERTISING SIGN

Craven "A" were named after the 3rd Earl of Craven in 1860, and saw the height of their popularity during World War II. Owned by Rothmans, Benson & Hedges, the brand still exists today, but is only widely known in Jamaica and Canada.

Nonetheless, eye-catchingly bold and strong colours are popular with collectors today, and, give or take the dents and patch of rust, this sign is in good condition.

During the first half of the 20thC, Craven "A" frequently used scenes of sporting or outdoor pursuits to promote the health-giving factors of smoking their cigarettes, and these tend to be more popular and valuable.

The catchphrase stating that they 'will not affect your throat' was used before the dangers of smoking were known and publicised.

A large 1930s 'CRAVEN "A" WILL NOT AFFECT YOUR THROAT' red, black and yellow enamelled tin advertising sign.

40in (102cm) wide

£150-200   **GORL**

A 1920s Oxo 'IT'S 'Meat & Drink' TO YOU CONCENTRATED BEEF' enamelled tin sign, with a red Oxo cube, and white lettering, with chipped edges and corners and rusting.

Oxo is a popular and widely collected brand, but the condition of this sign reduces the value by well over 50%, particularly the large rust spots in the middle of the image.

18in (46cm) high

£80-120   **FLD**

A 'LOVELL'S TOFFEE REX THE KING OF TOFFEES' red and white enamelled tin sign.

c1920   *14in (35cm) high*

£40-60   **FLD**

A 'WILL'S "WILD WOODBINE" CIGARETTES "More Popular Than Ever"' red and white enamelled advertising sign.

36in (91cm) high

£120-180   **GORL**

A late 19thC Bull Durham Tobacco colour lithographed tin advertising sign, reading 'GENUINE "BULL" DURHAM SMOKING TOBACCO' "PRIZE WINNERS", with original wood and plaster frame.

Early American tobacco advertising pieces – including signs, packaging and more – are very popular with American collectors. This well-printed example is detailed and uses a large number of colours.

38in (97cm) high

£800-1,200   FRE

A 1920s-30s 'MIRRO, THE NEW AMAZING HOUSEHOLD CLEANSER - QUICK! EASY!' enamelled tin sign, in yellow, red, green and white on a blue background.

30in (76cm) high

£100-150   FLD

A 1920s-30s Art Deco 'AGENT FOR ROBBIALAC PAINTS' enamelled tin sign, printed to both sides in pink, white, red blue and green on a black background.

24in (62cm) high

£300-500   FLD

A late 19thC 'KEATING'S KILLS BUGS, MOTHS, FLEAS, BEETLES' enamelled tin advertising sign, with an image of a canister of Keating's, a red devil, and a line of insects.

28in (71cm) high

£70-100   FLD

A 1920s 'LENNARDS WORLD-FAMED BOOTS & SHOES' enamelled tin sign, with an image of the world with t he British Empire coloured in red, decorated in red, yellow and blue on white background.

19in (49cm) high

£70-100   FLD

A CLOSER LOOK AT AN ADVERTISING BANNER

The artwork of a man showing his son how to shoot and another man encountering a grizzly bear on a mountain pass is detailed and appealing to collectors of such memorabilia.

It is in surprisingly good condition for a printed canvas piece - most were folded up and stored away, either rotting or becoming damaged and worn over decades.

Remington was founded in 1816 and merged with Union Metal Cartridge (UMC) in 1912. Combined with the style of the font and clothing, this allows this piece to be dated to some time around 1915.

At 55in (140cm) long, it is a very large and visually impressive piece. Firearms memorabilia, particularly for major brands, is highly sought after in the US and this large piece would be very rare.

A 'COME IN AND SHOOT Remington UMC' firearms and ammunition printed canvas advertising banner, with brass grommets in each corner, with two small puncture marks and faint water stains, but in overall very good condition.

55in (140cm) long

JDJ

£3,500-4,500

An early to mid-20thC cast iron blue enamel bulldog doorstop, with moulded wording advertising 'Record Tools'.

8.75in (22cm) long

£40-60   DA&H

A Beswick 'DUBONNET' advertising group, modelled by Arthur Gredington, featuring a poodle no.1871 and a bulldog no.1872.

1963-67   *6in (30.5cm) high*

£200-300   WHP

An Ashtead Pottery 'GENOZO TOOTH-PASTE' advertising lion figurine, designed by Percy Metcalfe, glazed in mottled blue, the base with printed factory marks.

9in (24cm) wide

£350-450   WW

An early 20thC 'THE FOX TIMES' dummy board, possibly used for advertising, the wooden board hand-painted with a fox holding an edition of 'THE FOX TIMES'.

45in (114cm) high

£180-220   LC

A 'FLOWER'S KEG BITTER' painted plaster advertising bust of Shakespeare, missing the feather of his quill.

Carlton Ware produced a similar bust in ceramic during the 1960s.

9in (23cm) high

£50-80   FLD

QUICK REFERENCE - PAOLOZZI'S ELEPHANT

- By 1972, Nairn Floors had grown tired of their products being largely ignored by architects. Douglas Maxwell was asked to generate some promotional material to appeal specifically to this group. Maxwell approached the progressive sculptor and artist Eduardo Paolozzi (1924-2005) after seeing his retrospective at the Tate Gallery. Paolozzi took Nairn's idea of an elephant, which represented the strength and resilience of the flooring, and the intelligence in using it, and turned it into a 'Lego-like' sculpture, which he felt would appeal to architects. The form is modern, architectural, and typical of his unique style. Produced in a limited edition of only 3,000, it acts as a box containing colourful catalogues and brochures about Nairn's flooring and how it can be used. These are interesting themselves, and contributors included Buckminster Fuller, Peter Le Vasseur, Peter Cook, Loren Butt, Graham Tarrant, and Philip Sayer. If these are included, the price can top £1,000. Even better – for Nairn – the campaign was a success.

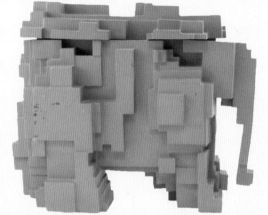

A Nairn Floors Ltd. limited edition plastic elephant, designed by Eduardo Paolozzi with Keith Powell, with removable lid, numbered 1210 from an edition of 3000.

1972   *12in (30cm) high*

£400-600   GORL

An early 20thC 'Jacoll Hats' painted advertising bust, modelled as a female.

18.5in (47cm) high

£50-80   TRI

An early 20thC automatic clockwork tobacco advertising figure, modelled as a sailor smoking a pipe, the head and hands papier mâché, raised on a wooden plinth base.

32in (82cm) high

£200-300   **BELL**

A late 19thC clockwork advertising automaton of a smoking African American, the papier mâché head with glass eyes and moving eyelids, with moving hands.

Despite the appalling condition, this fetched as much as it did for a number of reasons. Firstly, it is very early in date. Secondly automatons - effectively clockwork mechanical dolls that move to perform actions - are scarce and highly desirable. Thirdly, it features an African American, which is a scarce subject.

15in (38cm) high

£800-1,200   **DA&H**

An American 'DUFFY'S PURE MALT WHISKEY' advertising wall clock, by the New Haven Clock Co., with carved bezel frame and painted glass insert, some overpainting to back of original image and lettering.

c1900   *18in (46cm) diam*

£500-700   **DRA**

An early 20thC 'BOVRIL' advertising bottle, made from compressed paper, painted black and with three printed paper labels.

Bovril is a well known brand, and this is a comparatively large and very visual piece that would add great interest to a collection. The shape of the jar is closely related to the product.

12in (30cm) high

£250-350   **FLD**

Mark Picks

Shop countertop displays are sought-after by collectors of advertising memorabilia, particularly if the brand is well known and the style of the design and the font is typical of the period. This cabinet is a good example. Look out for brands that have cross-market interest, as these pieces will often be desirable to collectors of the products too. What collector of Britains 'Herald' Series figures wouldn't love to display them inside an original countertop cabinet? This 'cross-market' interest typically pushes prices up.

An early 20thC 'CHERRY BLOSSOM TONETTE DARK STAIN BOOT POLISH' shoe shine box, with three applied enamel advertising signs, and carved wooden shoe rest.

16.5in (42cm) high

£200-300   **GORL**

An early 20thC 'CLARK'S & ANCHOR' threads oak countertop shop display cabinet, with slim glazed front drawers.

£80-120   **FLD**

A 1950s-60s 'BRITAINS LIMITED HERALD SERIES' stained wood glass-fronted display cabinet, with sloping glass front over four glass shalves.

22in (56cm) high

£200-300   **AH**

ADVERTISING & PACKAGING

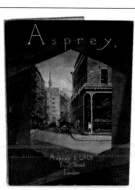

An Asprey & Co. Ltd. catalogue, with numerous black and white and colour illustrations, and pictorial hard boards.

c1930

£150-200   GORL

A CLOSER LOOK AT AN ADVERTISING CLOCK

Griswold cast iron home products are highly sought-after by collectors, particularly pieces made from the founding of the company in 1865 until 1957, when the factory closed and the brand name was sold.

Early pieces are simply marked 'ERIE', the location of the factory in Pennsylvania. The motif of the Griswold name in a cross and circle was introduced in 1897.

The spider and web trade mark dates from 1874-1905, allowing this piece to be dated.

Large, expensively made pieces such as this would have been produced in smaller numbers compared to other forms of advertising such as catalogues or cards. Survivors are rare today.

An early 20thC American Griswold cast iron skillet advertising clock, by Griswold Mfg. Co. Erie, Penn., the gold-painted skillet set with a wind-up clock, with raised moulded lettering 'ERIE UP TO TIME' and 'WE SELL HOLLOW WARE'.

14.5in (37cm) high

£3,000-5,000   SK

A large early 20thC 'Stephens' Inks' enamelled tin advertising thermometer, with some damage and wear to the base.

61in (155cm) high

£550-650   GORL

A 'ROWNTREE'S MINERS PASTILLES' colour-printed advertising card in the shape of a miner's lamp.

This is a rare advertising piece for an obscure product by a major and much loved confectionary brand. The shape also ties in closely with the product, which adds to the appeal. It's also in great condition for a card piece.

£180-220   FLD

An early 20thC '"ATORA" HUGSON'S BEEF SUET' child's pull toy, the printed tinplate cart with wheels, housing a pair of bulls.

11in (28cm) long

£450-550   GORL

A late 19thC Ashworth's Machine Cotton promotional pocket globe, composed of 24 colour-printed gores over a plaster and compostion base.

3in (7cm) diam

£250-350   TEN

A 1920s Huntley & Palmers' biscuit tin, with two hinged lids and handle, decorated with archery, minstrel and jousting scenes from the Eglinton tournament.

9in (23cm) long

£80-120   MAR

A 1960s Huntley & Palmers' 'Butlinland' biscuit tin, marked with printer's code no. 61/2649, with some fading and loss of printed image to corners.

Faded or damaged tins are usually worth very little. However, Butlins memorabilia is very collectable, hence the comparatively high price for this example.

9in (22cm) long

£25-35   SAS

A Huntley & Palmers' biscuit tin in the form of a farmhouse, printed with a farmyard scene, and with a 'brick wall' surround.

£250-350   CHT

A Huntley & Palmers' 'Cavalry' biscuit tin, printed in colour with scenes of different soldiers, with printed inscription on the bottom.

This tin was from a series of four, the others comprising 'Olden Times' and 'Gypsy' of 1893, and 'Arabian Nights' of 1894.

1894   *6in (15cm) high*

£50-70   FLD

A Huntley & Palmers' 'Lantern' biscuit tin, in the form of a railway lamp, with registered number '548328' for 1909.

This tin was also offered again in 1914.

9in (23.5cm) high

£60-80   CHT

A CLOSER LOOK AT A BISCUIT TIN

Novelty shaped tins are the most sought-after and valuable - even though this is not by Huntley & Palmer, MacFarlane, Lang & Co. tins are still widely collected.

The lid lacks the heads of half a dozen clubs. Had these still been present, and had it not been worn and dented, this tin could have fetched up to ten times as much as this.

This tin would also be desirable to collectors of golfing memorabilia. This cross-market interest forces the price up.

As well as being embossed with an appealing motif of a golfer in mid-strike, this tin is in the form of a golf bag, which is accentuated with the embossed pocket and printed 'leather' effect.

A Victorian MacFarlane, Lang & Co. 'Golf Bag' biscuit tin, the shaped tin embossed with a period red jacketed gentleman golfer and his lady golfing partner, with lid but lacking clubs, in good condition with some scuffs and dents.

1913   *9in (23cm) high*

£60-80   MM

A William Crawford & Sons Ltd. 'FAIRY HOUSE' biscuit tin and money box, produced by Barringer, Wallis & Manners, and designed by Mabel Lucie Attwell, coin slot dented, and some minor scratches.

Children's illustrator Mabel Lucie Attwell (1879-1964) is best known for her charming cherubic children and elves. She also produced designs for Shelley for their ceramics, which included tea sets, dinner ware and figurines. This piece was part of a series of three tins that could be used as money boxes after the biscuits were eaten: the other two comprised 'Bicky House' of 1933, and 'Fairy Tree' of 1935. The area around the coin slot is usually damaged, as is the finish on the lid where it was pulled off by children.

c1934   *7.5in (19cm) high*

£120-180   TOV

A 'MAZAWATTEE TEA' rectangular tin, with curved sides, printed with scenes from children's literature including 'Alice in Wonderland', 'Humpty Dumpty', 'Alice Through the Looking Glass', and 'Tweedledum and Tweedledee'.

6in (15cm) high

£220-280   FLD

QUICK REFERENCE - SAMPLE TINS

- Sample tins are miniature tins that contained a small sample of a product, such as biscuits, tea, or even makeup powder. They were given away as promotions from the late 19thC until the early 20thC, typically at events such as exhibitions.
- Often ignored due to their tiny size, early or rare examples for sought-after brands or types of products can fetch surprisingly high sums. Look out for examples that name the event, and those in the best condition possible. Many were treated badly, or just thrown away after the contents had been used. Just think how much this may have made had it not been so worn!
- As well as being for tea, this tin has appealing artwork showing the Tower of London. Hudson Scott was founded in 1799 as a paper printer, and began printing tins in c1876. It became associated with Carr's in the 1880s, and became known as Hudson Scott Ltd. in 1898, and Metal Box Co. Ltd. in 1922.

A late 19thC Hudson Scott 'TOWER GARDEN'S TEA' shaped sample tin, with a colour printed image of the Tower of London.

2.5in (6cm) long

£600-800   FLD

A 'DRINK Priory Tea' sample tin, with three illustrations comprising a cup of tea, two men drinking tea, and a tea factory, the lid printed 'Free Sample, Souvenir from Wolverhampton Exhibition'.

Wolverhampton had two large exhibitions - in 1869 and 1902. The latter was known as the 'Arts & Industrial Exhibition' and attracted Canada, who built an exhibition pavilion there.

1902   2.5in (6cm) high

£300-400   FLD

A late 19thC '"PRIMUS" INDESTRUCTIBLE LABLES' tin, complete with unused contents and instructions, containing approximately 38 labels, with rusting and loss to finish.

2.2in (5.5cm) wide

£12-18   FLD

A 'John Drummond & Sons PACKING CASE MAKERS IN WOOD AND TIN' advertising rectangular curved pocket tin.

3in (8cm) wide

£12-18   FLD

An early 20thC rugby ball shaped miniature tin, painted brown and printed 'MATCH', possibly made by Rowntrees of York.

£60-80   FLD

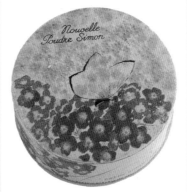

An American Snow White Products Co. 'SNOW WHITE Face Powder' printed card box, in excellent condition.

The profile of Snow White, and the choice of character, was presumably timed to coincide with the release of Disney's 'Snow White And The Seven Dwarfs' in 1937.

c1938

£20-30 PC

A 1930s French Crème Simon 'Nouvelle Poudre Simon' face powder colour-printed card box, with a motif of a butterfly on flowers.

£15-25 SH

An Anglo-American Oil Co. 'ANGLO'S TRENCH FIRES' colour-printed card box, worn and damaged, containing eight fire starting blocks.

The box explains that these are 'a boon for dug outs, tents and trenches'!

5in (12cm) wide

£35-45 FLD

A retailer's card box for Lyth & Platt 'COBRA 1 DOZEN No. 40 BLACK BOOT CREAM', containing a dozen unopened square section glass bottles boot cream, each bottle with a colour illustrated tin stopper, colour illustrated paper label around three sides and a colour neck label, with an illustrated paper label around the exterior.

each bottle 3.5in (9cm) high

£65-75 FLD

A Sutton & Sons travelling saleman's sample box, complete with 24 labelled and full glass jars of seeds, each with its metal screw-on lid, the lid bearing a label for 'Sutton & Sons, Reading, Seedsmen by Royal Warrant to HM The Queen and HRH The Prince of Wales'.

Box 11in (29cm) wide

£120-180 FLD

A 1940s bar of 'CADBURY'S Ration CHOCOLATE', in its original blue-printed grease-proof paper wrapper.

Made with powdered skimmed milk, Ration Chocolate replaced Dairy Milk from 1941 until the end of World War II.

c1942 *4in (10cm) wide*

£30-40 FLD

An early 20thC German moulded papier mâché bulldog confectionary container, with oversized head, very minor paint losses.

Germany was the world's largest producer of novelty shaped confectionary and cake related containers and decorations before World War II. Although dogs are popular subjects, particularly in as good condition as this one, Easter and Christmas related pieces tend to fetch the highest prices.

6.5in (17cm) long

£400-600 SK

QUICK REFERENCE - GUINNESS'S TOUCAN

• Guinness's famed toucan began life in 1935 as a pelican, drawn by artist John Gilroy for advertising company S.H. Benson. It was Gilroy's designs for Guinness, handled by Benson, that became celebrated across the world and kicked off their notable campaigns. Benson's copywriter, the crimewriter Dorothy L. Sayers rejected Gilroy's pelican, and the accompanying verse he had written. Instead she turned the bird into a toucan to enable her to make use of the puns based around the toucan's name. One is shown on the base of this figurine. Gilroy liked the change, and ran with it.

A large Wiltshaw & Robinson Carlton Ware Guinness advertising bar top Toucan figurine, the base reading 'How grand to be a Toucan Just think what Toucan do', the base with printed marks and 'GA /2151'.

£250-350   **A&G**

POSTERS
& Advertising Items
WANTED   COLLECTIONS OR INDIVIDUAL ITEMS
PRINTED PAPER & CARDS OF ALL KINDS
WHISKY - BEER ETC - **ENAMEL SIGNS**
CHEMISTS - FOOD ETC - BILL HEADS
SHOW CARDS - BOTTLE LABELS
PLAYING CARDS - TRADE
CATALOGUES - **PRINTERS SAMPLE**
BOOKS - **GUINNESS** - FIGURES

GORDON
25 Stapenhill Road
Burton-on-Trent DE15 9AE
Please Telephone between 9am and 7pm
Tel: 01283·567·213 Mobile: 07952·118·987

A large Wiltshaw & Robinson Carlton Ware Guinness advertising toucan figurine, the green base with 'GUINNESS' wording, with paper label to the base 'This is a Carlton Russell Product'.

27in (69cm) high

£450-550   **DUK**

A CLOSER LOOK AT A TOUCAN LAMP

At 16inches (40cm) high, it is large in size, and undamaged.

The shade, with its charming artwork, is extremely rare and in superb condition.

Watch out for reproductions, which are usually crudely modelled and decorated - the beak is a case in point as, rather than having graduated colours as here, they are usually smudged or over-delineated.

Fake toucans also typically have cream, rather than white, necks and factory marks found on the base are applied over, instead of under, the glaze.

A Wiltshaw & Robinson Carlton Ware Guinness toucan table lamp, complete with original printed shade, the base with printed mark.

As well as the points mentioned above, there are also other indicators of fakes. These include completely black tails instead of black tails highlighted in orange and red, the use of 'Ltd' after the company name, and a dirty white head on the pint instead of a more realistic creamy colour.

1952-62   *16in (40cm) high*

£350-450   **FLD**

A Wiltshaw & Robinson Carlton Ware Guinness penguin advertising figurine, with 'DRAUGHT GUINNESS' transfer to chest.

4in (10cm) high

£120-180   FLD

A Wiltshaw & Robinson Carlton Ware Guinness penguin lamp base, modelled holding a sign reading 'DRAUGHT GUINNESS', factory stamp to base, one section of base broken and reglued.

£30-40   TRI

A Wiltshaw & Robinson Carlton Ware Guinness ostrich advertising figurine, the base with 'My Goodness - My GUINNESS' and red printed factory marks.

4in (11cm) high

£80-120   FLD

A Wiltshaw & Robinson Carlton Ware Guinness kangaroo advertising figure, with 'My Goodness - My GUINNESS', and printed factory marks to base.

3.75in (9.5cm) high

£50-80   CHT

A Wiltshaw & Robinson Carlton Ware Guinness seal advertising figurine, with 'My Goodness - My GUINNESS' and printed factory marks to base.

A seal making off with a pint of Guinness on his nose, closely pursued by the zoo keeper, was the subject of the very first of Gilroy's posters, released in 1935. In 1955, the first Guinness television advert re-enacted the same scene, with a live sea lion and Charles Naughton playing the zoo keeper.

3.5in (9cm) high

£150-250   BAD

A Wiltshaw & Robinson Carlton Ware Guinness tortoise advertising figurine, with 'My Goodness - My GUINNESS' and printed factory marks to base.

3in (8cm) high

£50-70   CHT

A Wiltshaw & Robinson Carlton Ware Guinness zoo keeper advertising figurine, the base with 'My Goodness - My GUINNESS' and red printed factory marks.

Here he is - the hapless zoo keeper, whose pint of Guinness keeps being stolen by his menagerie of animals. This gave rise to the exclamatory phrase 'My Goodness - My Guinness!', even though there was a double meaning in that it also reinforced the purported health benefits of drinking Guinness.

4in (10cm) high

£50-80   FLD

AUSTRIAN BRONZES

QUICK REFERENCE

- The Industrial Revolution of the 19thC meant that, for the first time ever, it was less expensive to make bronze sculptures than marble sculptures. The improvement in manufacturing processes coincided with the rising wealth of the growing middle classes, and sculptors tapped into this new market by producing small, affordable bronze statues.
- Due to an increased appreciation of nature from the mid-19thC onwards, many of the bronzes made in France, Britain, and Austria were of animals. Away from the large, dramatic work of great French 'animalier' sculptors such as Antoine-Louis Barye (1795-1875), smaller examples are typically more affordable and more varied in subject and style.
- In the late 19thC, several bronze foundries in Vienna began to specialise in cold-painting. The technique involved painting the bronze cast with naturalistic colours while it was still warm. It was then not fired again afterwards.

- One of the best-known and most collectable makers of cold-painted bronze figurines is Franz Xavier Bergman (1861-1936). His father, also Franz Bergman (1838-1894), was a professional metalworker who founded a bronze factory in Vienna in 1860. Franz Xavier inherited his father's company, and opened a new foundry in 1900.
- A prolific maker, his factory's designs included animals, Oriental figures, and less commonly, erotic young women. Look out for his foundry's impressed signature mark of a 'B' in a vase shape (see facing page). In order not to offend his more 'proper' clients, he often marked his erotic designs 'Nam Greb', which is 'Bergman' in reverse.
- Value is affected by condition, the quality of the painting, the size, and the subject. Some animals are more desirable or rarer than others. Worn enamel and especially re-painted surfaces will reduce value considerably.

An early 20thC Austrian Bergman cold-painted bronze owl, stamped 'GESCH, 6250' and with faint stamped mark of 'B' within a vase to the underside, lacking one glass eye.

Marks incorporating the word 'GESCHÜTZT' or 'GESCH' indicate a German or Austrian (German language) patent or copyright.

5.25in (13.5cm) high

£1,200-1,800   DN

An Austrian Bergman cold-painted bronze inkwell, modelled as a short-eared owl, the naturalistically cast bird's head hinged to reveal a vacant interior, naturally painted plumage, stamped 'Bergman Geschützt'.

c1900   *5in (13.5cm) high*

£800-1,200   TEN

An early 20thC cold-painted bronze owl inkstand, the bird with hinged head, perched upon a naturalistically cast trunk base, unmarked.

5.25in (13cm) high

£380-480   AH

An early 20thC Austrian cold-painted bronze standing kingfisher, unmarked.

3.5in (8.9cm) high

£450-550   GORL

An Austrian cold-painted bronze kingfisher, with faceted glass bead eyes, raised on an integral bronze socle.

3.25in (8cm) high

£200-300   WW

An early 20thC Austrian Bergman cold-painted bronze blackbird.

4in (10cm) high

£650-850   **GORL**

A cold-painted bronze parrot, with red, green and yellow plumage, standing on an integral boulder.

4.75in (12cm) high

£250-350   **LC**

An Austrian cold-painted bronze nib cleaner in the form of a parrot, with a pad to his back, the tail feathers stamped 'Geschützt'.

3.7in (9.5cm) high

£400-600   **H&L**

A 1930s Austrian onyx 'vide poche', mounted with a cold-painted bronze budgerigar.

The lack of a cigarette well to the side of the bowl indicates this is a 'vide poche' - the French words for 'empty pocket', literally a place to put pocket change, keys and other contents of a pocket.

4.25in (11cm) long

£120-180   **DN**

Miller's Compares

This example is smaller in size, measuring only one third the size of the other.

As well as being painted in more naturalistic colours, it has its original finish.

The impressed 'B' within an urn mark shows that it is by Franz Bergman, the most notable and high quality maker of Austrian cold-painted bronzes.

Although nicely detailed, the painted colours are less naturalistic, and the brighter, less well-applied colours may indicate it has been overpainted in the past.

Overall, this bird is much better modelled with more lifelike detail - compare the claws for example.

A late 19thC Austrian cold-painted bronze curlew, standing upright.

3.25in (8.5cm) high

£180-220   **L&T**

A late 19thC Austrian Bergman cold-painted bronze woodcock, the underside impressed 'GESCH' and stamped with a 'B' within an urn mark.

10in (25cm) long

£2,500-3,500   **DN**

An early 20thC Austrian cold-painted bronze kitten, modelled with one paw playfully raised.

6.5in (17cm) long

£300-400   GORL

An Austrian cold-painted bronze reclining dog, with worn surface and damaged paintwork.

3.25in (8.5cm) long

£150-200   GORL

An early 20thC Austrian cold-painted bronze bloodhound, unmarked.

5in (13cm) long

£450-550   GORL

An early 20thC Austrian cold-painted bronze terrier, with black painted finish.

5in (13cm) long

£450-550   GORL

An Austrian cold-painted bronze reclining pug.

3in (8cm) long

£280-380   LC

An early 20thC Austrian cold-painted bronze kitten, modelled with one paw playfully raised.

6.5in (17cm) long

£300-400   GORL

An Austrian cold-painted bronze prowling cat, the underside stamped 'Geschützt'.

4.75in (12cm) long

£200-300   GORL

An Austrian cold-painted bronze fox, modelled as if ready to pounce and attack.

7in (18cm) long
£300-500   **LC**

An early 20thC Austrian cold-painted fox, holding a dead mallard in his mouth, stamped 'Geschützt'.

8in (20cm) long
£700-1,000   **GORL**

An Austrian cold-painted bronze kangaroo, with a joey in her pouch.

3in (7.5cm) high
£200-300   **LC**

An Austrian cold-painted bronze kangaroo buck, with worn painted surface.

An Austrian cold-painted bronze otter, with a fish in its mouth.

6.75in (17cm) long
£450-550   **GORL**

2.5in (6.5cm) high
£50-80   **CHT**

An early 20thC Austrian cold-painted bronze group of a fox riding a hound, the fox in a pink hunting jacket, jumping a fence, with worn paintwork.

This group combines a number of attractive features, the hunting theme, a witty choice of a well-dressed fox as the hunter, and a sense of action and movement.

An Austrian cold-painted bronze coiled snake, indistinctly marked on the base.

4.75in (12cm) wide
£300-400   **LOC**

4in (10.5cm) long
£800-1,200   **DN**

AUSTRIAN BRONZES

An Austrian cold-painted bronze model of an Arab seated upon a donkey.

5in (13cm) high

£500-700   GORL

An Austrian cold-painted bronze Nubian water seller, indistinctly signed 'I Titze', on a marble plinth.

c1900   6.5in (16.5cm) high overall

£300-500   BELL

An Austrian cold-painted bronze Arabian boy, sitting cross legged and writing on a board, the base stamped '2746'.

3.25in (8.5cm) high

£800-1,200   H&L

Judith Picks

Admittedly, this dancer is not in great condition, with damage to the original surface and some repainting. It's the main reason she sold for a comparatively small sum of money. Despite this, the subject matter is worth considering. Her almost painful looking pose is lively and brings fin de siècle fun at the Folies Bergères to mind. From her pose to her hair to her clothing, she's very much in the style of

the period she was made in. They're all positive aspects. Bergman produced a number of erotic female figurines, and exotic dancers in particular. Some have additional complex features - trigger a lever and a dress may flip open to reveal scanty underclothes. These are highly prized and can fetch thousands of pounds today. So as not to offend his more staid and customers, many are not signed with his Bergman's name or logo. Instead, many have the 'Namgreb' signature – Bergman's name in reverse, and a ploy to protect his reputation but still take credit.

An early 20thC Bergman cold-painted bronze figure of a female dancer, in blue painted costume and poised in the splits position, with impressed Bergman urn mark, and also impressed 'Geschützt', no 4133.

6in (16cm) long

£300-500   ROS

A late 19thC/early 20thC Austrian cold-painted bronze bearded gnome, humorously modelled reclining and smoking a pipe.

11in (29cm) long

£250-350   WHP

An Austrian cold-painted bronze five piece hare band, comprising a cellist, violinist, drummer, horn player and another lacking instrument.

Largest 3.25in (8.5cm) high

£600-800   GORL

A late 20thC Lalique opalescent glass 'Sparrow, Head Down' car mascot or figurine, the base with etched signature mark.

Part of a collection of three sparrows in different poses, this mascot is still sold by Lalique today.

3.5in (9cm) high

£120-180   **WHP**

A 1920s-30s British Warren-Kessler clear glass car mascot, moulded as a fan-tailed pigeon, with intaglio signature to wing.

Like the better-known Red Ashay's, Warren-Kessler's designs were inspired by Lalique's mascots. However, they are not as widely collected today as Lalique's mascots.

5.9in (15cm) high

£150-200   **WW**

A mid-late 20thC English chrome-plated car mascot, modelled as a running fox, unmarked.

6in (16cm) long

£60-90   **DN**

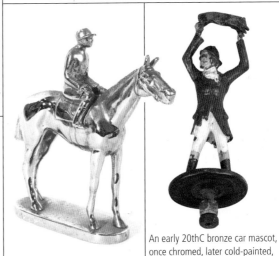

A mid-late 20thC chrome-plated car mascot, modelled as a racehorse with jockey.

4.5in (11.5cm) high

£60-80   **WHP**

An early 20thC bronze car mascot, once chromed, later cold-painted, in the form of a huntsman holding a fox aloft, titled 'Mr Yorik Goes Hunting', mounted on circular base.

6in (15cm) high

£120-180   **DA&H**

A 1920s bronze 'Old Bill' character car mascot, mounted on a wooden base, signed 'Bruce Bairnsfather' on the rim of the helmet, and with registration number '669204' for 1919 under the muffler.

British Expeditionary Force infantryman 'Old Bill' was devised by cartoonist Bruce Bairnsfather (1888-1959). Mascots of 'Old Bill' were produced by a number of makers, including the renowned Louis Lejeune, for both cars and motorcycles.

4.25in (11cm) high

£300-500   **LC**

A 1930s 'Butlins CAR CLUB' car badge, the chrome-plated casting with painted details, on a later mount.

This logo continued to be used into the 1950s.

4in (11cm) high

£120-180   **SWO**

A 1960s Heuer 'Master-Time' dashboard mounted car clock, with luminous-painted Arabic numerals on a circular black dial, with a chrome case.

1967-75   *2.25in (5.5cm) wide*

£300-500   **FLD**

A 1960s Ruddspeed Bentley chrome radiator-grill spirit flask.

8in (20cm) high

£300-400   **GORB**

A late 20thC unmarked S. S. Jaguar chrome-plated radiator-grill spirit flask, with black enamelled badge and chrome-plated wire mesh stone guard.

7in (18cm) high

£400-600   **TOV**

A 20thC Sadler racing car teapot, with a black glaze with silver highlights, and impressed marks to base.

This version, with its dramatic silver highlights contrasting against the black glaze, is very rare. Examples covered in single green or yellow glazes are considerably more common, and usually fetch under £50. The price of this example is further boosted by the excellent condition, which is unusual as the silver glaze rubs off and scratches easily.

9in (22cm) long

£400-600   **FLD**

A CLOSER LOOK AT AN AUTOMOBILE POSTER

Razzia is the pseudonym of Gerard Courbouleix Deneriaz (b.1950), who has worked for Harrod's, Macy's, and others, and is considered by some to be the finest poster artist living today.

Unlike other contemporary poster artists, he does not use computers or cameras to create his designs, but instead draws and paints the image.

His work has a strong 1980s feel to it, in terms of the colour and style of the graphics. He is also inspired by Surrealism.

As this was produced for a comparatively small event on one day, fewer examples will exist. There are also examples from similar Louis Vuitton events to collect.

A 'THE LOUIS VUITTON CLASS AT THE HURLINGHAM CLUB' poster, designed by Razzia.

2000   *31in (79.5cm) high*

$20-30   **CARS**

A menu for a banquet in honour of Sir Malcolm Campbell MBE, dated September 24th 1935, cord-bound with a brass-relief photograph cover depicting Sir Malcolm Campbell.

This dinner was held as a tribute to Campbell's achievement of a new land-speed record averaging 301.13mph at Bonneville Flats, Utah, US on September 3rd, 1935.

£150-250   **TOV**

QUICK REFERENCE

- Book collectors tend to seek out books from the very first print run of a first edition. First editions can have multiple print-runs (or impressions) in which errors are corrected, but these are typically less desirable than what is known as 'true first' editions. The number of these can be very limited, and the smaller the print run, the more valuable a book can be.
- To find out if you have a first edition, check that the publishing date and copyright date match, and that these match the original publishing date and publisher for the title. Some publishers state that a book is a first edition, or use a series of letters, or a number '1' in the series of numbers.
- First editions by popular writers from the last 150 years, such as J. R. R. Tolkien, Ian Fleming, Agatha Christie, Graham Greene, and Stephen King are hotly collected. Although iconic titles are likely to be desirable, an author's earlier books might be more valuable than their later books, since it's probable that fewer first editions were printed, making them rarer. The rule of 'supply and demand' applies here.
- The author's signature adds value, but dedications are typically less desirable, unless the recipient is famous or connected to the author.
- Check that the book is complete, and not defaced or damaged. Dust-jackets should also be clean, un-faded, and un-damaged, though they can often be restored. Check to see if the price on the inside front has been cut away or 'clipped', as this can reduce the desirability and value to some collectors. If the jacket is missing, value can fall by up to 50 per cent or more. Copies in truly mint condition will usually command a premium.

Richard Adams, 'Watership Down', first edition, published by Rex Collings Ltd., London, inked owner's name on front free endpaper, original cloth, dust-jacket, splits at corners with slight loss, tape burns to outside of jacket at spine ends.

The original title was meant to be 'Hazel and Fiver', but publisher Rex Collings disliked it and requested a new name. The book was rejected by twelve publishing companies before finding its way to Collings, who printed just 2,000 copies of the hardback first edition, which has a folding map at the end. The book sold well and won two awards in 1972. A year later, it was published by Puffin as a paperback and in America. The rest is history...

1972

£300-400   BLO

Martin Amis, 'The Rachel Papers', first edition, published by Jonathan Cape, London, with original boards in an un-clipped dust-jacket.
1973
£200-300   GORL

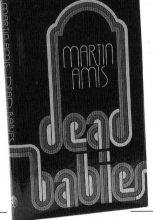

Martin Amis, 'Dead Babies', first edition, published by Jonathan Cape, London, signed by the author on the title page, faint signs of a paper-clip having been attached to first few leaves, original boards, dust-jacket, a fine copy.
1975
£500-700   BLO

Iain Banks, 'The Wasp Factory', first edition, published by Macmillan & Co., neat ownership inscription on front free endpaper, original boards, dust-jacket, a fine copy.
1984
£100-150   BLO

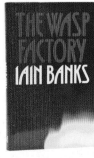

BOOKS

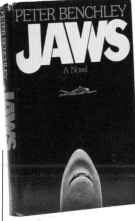

Peter Benchley, 'Jaws', first American edition, published by Doubleday, original cloth, dust-jacket, torn at head of spine, corners rubbed.
1974
£120-180   BLO

John Berger, 'G.', first edition, published by Weidenfeld & Nicholson, signed by the author on title, original boards, dust-jacket, usual slight fading to spine, slightly sunned at foot of upper panel, otherwise in very good condition.
1972
£300-500   BLO

Malcolm Bradbury, 'Eating People is Wrong', first edition, published by Secker, original boards, dust-jacket, spine very slightly sunned, otherwise in very good condition.
This was the author's first book.
1959
£60-90   BLO

A CLOSER LOOK AT A FIRST EDITION

John Benyon was one of the pseudonyms used by catastrophe and science fiction author John Wyndham (1903-69), with Benyon being one of his many middle names.

This was his first book and is very scarce, especially with its dust-jacket.

After three largely unsuccessful books, Wyndham emerged from literary obscurity in 1951 with the publication of 'The Day of the Triffids'.

This novel is unusual in that it is a detective story, rather than science fiction, the genre he is most commonly associated with.

John Beynon, 'Foul Play Suspected', first edition, published by Newnes, London, with spotting to extremities, original cloth, dust-jacket, some marking and rubbing, small tear with loss to foot of lower panel, small closed tear to head of upper panel, spine slightly sun faded.
1935
£1,000-1,500   BLO

Truman Capote, 'Breakfast at Tiffany's', first English edition, published by Hamish Hamilton, London, bookplate on front free endpaper, original boards, dust-jacket, light browning and small water-stain on lower panel, but overall a very good copy.
1958
£500-700   BLO

Truman Capote, 'Breakfast at Tiffany's', first edition, published by Random House, New York, original yellow cloth gilt, dustwrapper, coded '10/58' on front flap, fading to spine, price clipped.

The spine is frequently faded. This popular novella, made into a film starring Audrey Hepburn in 1961, was first published accompanied by three other stories. American novelist and director Norman Mailer called Capote 'the most perfect writer of [his] generation', and said that he 'would not have changed two words in 'Breakfast at Tiffany's'.
1958
£600-800   L&T

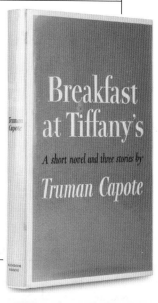

Agatha Christie, 'The Hound Of Death And Other Stories', first edition, published by Odhams Press, burgundy cloth with dust-jacket.
1933
£120-180 GORL

QUICK REFERENCE - AGATHA CHRISTIE FIRST EDITIONS

- Agatha Christie (1890-1976) was one of the world's best-known crime novelists and playwrights and is, along with Shakespeare, the best-selling author in the world. Reputedly, the Bible is the only book to sell more copies than Christie, who has sold nearly 4 billion copies of her books. This global popularity makes her first editions collectable, and often comparatively affordable as quantities printed increased as her popularity grew.
- Starring Hercule Poirot, and inspired by her travels to the Middle East with her second husband, this is one of her scarcer titles. Its popularity was bolstered when it was made into a play in 1945, interestingly lacking Poirot as Christie began to tire of the character in the late 1930s. This was followed by a Hollywood film starring Peter Ustinov in 1988, and a British television production with David Suchet in 2008.

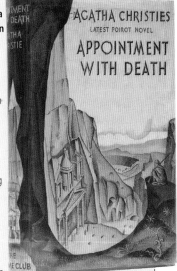

Agatha Christie, 'Appointment with Death', first edition, published by Collins Crime Club, with four pages of advertisements, original cloth, corners and spine ends slightly rubbed, spine lettering slightly dulled, dust-jacket showing a price of '7s 6d', presumably trimmed down at some point with restoration to upper and lower edges, otherwise a very good example.
1938
£1,200-1,800 BLO

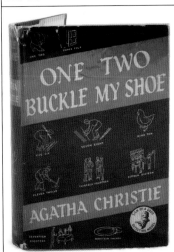

Agatha Christie, 'One Two Buckle My Shoe', first edition, published by Collins Crime Club, with un-clipped dust-jacket, original orange cloth with black lettering.
1940
£400-600 GORL

Agatha Christie, 'Evil Under The Sun', first edition, published by Collins Crime Club, with dust-jacket, orange cloth boards with black lettering.
1941
£60-80 GORL

Agatha Christie, 'Sparkling Cyanide', first edition, published by Collins Crime Club, with dust-jacket and orange cloth boards with black lettering, damage to corners and edges of dust-jacket.
1945
£50-80 GORL

Ivy Compton Burnett, 'A House and Its Head', first edition, published by William Heinemann, London, original blue cloth, dust-jacket, slightly chipped with small loss at base of spine, otherwise very good.
1935
£150-200 BLO

BOOKS

Bernard Cornwell, 'Sharpe's Company', first edition, published by Collins, London, original boards, dust-jacket, an excellent copy.
1982
£180-220   BLO

Bernard Cornwell, 'Sharpe's Gold', first edition, published by Collins, London, original boards, dust-jacket, spine slightly sunned, otherwise fine.
1981
£150-250   BLO

William Faulkner, 'Sartoris', first American edition, published by Harcourt Brace, New York, with owner's bookplate on front endpaper, original cloth and dust-jacket, spine browned, restoration to spine.

Faulkner's fourth book, this was the first of the Yoknapatawpha County titles. A heavily cut down version of his original manuscript, only 1,998 copies of the first edition were printed. The full story was reprinted as 'Flags In The Dust' in 1973.
1929
£700-900   BLO

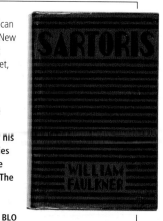

A CLOSER LOOK AT A FIRST EDITION

This is the true first edition, being the very first printing of the first American edition, which was published three years before the British edition.

This first issue can also be identified as it has six lines of printing information on the last page - these were cut to five lines in all subsequent issues.

Joseph Schindelman's original illustrations matched the text in depicting the Oompa-Loompas as African pygmies, and their service to Wonka appears almost like slavery.

Dahl did not intend to present the Oompa-Loompas as slaves and did not intend to appear racist. The famed 1971 film presented them differently and prompted Dahl to rewrite parts of the story for a second edition published in 1973.

Roald Dahl, 'Charlie and the Chocolate Factory', first issue of the first American edition, with illustrations by Joseph Schindelman, published by Alfred Knopf, New York, original cloth, dust-jacket, price-clipped, minor creasing, small split near foot of spine, overall a fine example.
1964
£2,500-3,500   BLO

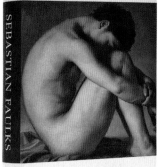

Sebastian Faulks, 'Birdsong', first edition, published by Hutchinson, London, original boards, dust-jacket, a fine copy.
1993
£250-350   BLO

Ian Fleming 'The Diamond Smugglers', first edition, published by Jonathan Cape, with original boards and dust-jacket.

This copy contains a bookplate inscribed to Eileen Cond, a keen book collector, who sent her bookplates out to authors to, hopefully, be returned signed. This is one of Fleming's few non-fiction books, and furthers Fleming's coverage for 'The Sunday Times' newspaper of the illegal smuggling of diamonds out of Africa. The first issue has gold titling on the spine.

1957
£2,000-3,000   BLO

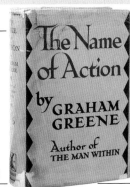

Graham Greene, 'The Name of Action', first edition, published by Heinemann, London, with original cloth and dust-jacket with some losses, some spotting.

1930
£900-1,200   **BLO**

A CLOSER LOOK AT A FIRST EDITION

Just before the book was published, fellow author J. B. Priestley threatened legal action over the character Quin Savory, whom he claimed was a defamatory representation of himself after reading a review copy - the text was changed.

It is not particularly scarce, but look out for copies in superb condition or with text mentioning 'Q.C. Savory', and 'Dickens' instead of 'Chaucer', as these are extremely rare original and unchanged versions.

The appealing jacket was designed by Philip Youngman Carter, who designed dust-jackets for many crime writers such as Georges Simenon, Carter Dickson, and his wife Margery Allingham, as well as writing over 30 crime stories himself.

This was the first of a series of books that Greene called 'entertainments' to mark them as different from his more serious literary works.

Graham Greene, 'Stamboul Train', first edition, published by William Heinemann, London, issue with 'Quin Savory', small crease to one fore-edge, minor marginal marking to fore-edge, original buckram, skilful minor restoration to dust-jacket, a very good example.

1932
£1,500-2,000   **BLO**

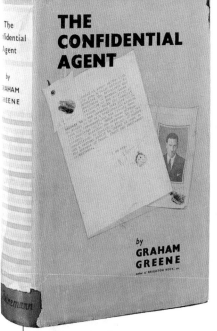

Graham Greene, 'The Confidential Agent', first edition, first impression, published by Heinemann, London, with publisher's note at end, original cloth and damaged dust-jacket, slight shelf lean, but internally very good.

1939
£3,000-5,000   **BLO**

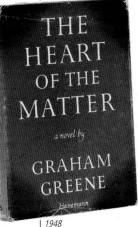

Graham Greene, 'The Heart of the Matter', first edition, published by Heinemann, London, original cloth, dust-jacket, spine faded, two corners with short splits, a few other nicks or very short tears, rubbed at extremities, still a good copy.

1948
£350-450   **BLO**

Graham Greene and Hugh Greene, 'The Spy's Bedside Book', first edition, published by Hart-Davis, with blue cloth boards and un-clipped dust-jacket, a very good copy.

1957
£150-250   **GORL**

Graham Greene, 'The Potting Shed', first edition, published by Heinemann, London, with original blue cloth boards and un-clipped dust-jacket.

1958
£50-80   **GORL**

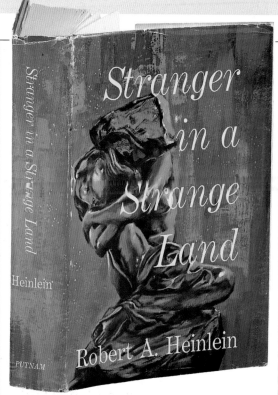

Robert A. Heinlein, 'Stranger in a Strange Land', first American edition, published by Putnam, New York, with original green cloth and dust-jacket, minor edge wear.
1961
£700-900   FRE

Jack Harvey, 'Blood Hunt', first edition, published by Headline, usual marginal browning, original boards, dust-jacket, minor creasing and bumping, small tear to one corner.

Jack Harvey was a pseudonym used by Ian Rankin so that his publisher could release more than one book by him per year, and also release books that did not include his famed Rebus character. The name is a combination of his first son's forename and his wife's maiden name.
1995
£200-300   BLO

Joseph Heller, 'Catch-22', first edition, published by Jonathan Cape, London, with original red cloth and dust-jacket.

1962
£300-500   L&T

Nick Hornby, 'Fever Pitch', first edition, first impression, published by Gollancz, London, signed and inscribed by the author on title, with original boards, dust-jacket.

This was the author's first book, which went on to sell over one million copies. Its value is pushed up as it is both a first issue and is signed by the author.
1992
£180-220   BLO

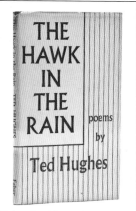

Langston Hughes, 'One-Way Ticket', first American edition, published by Alfred A. Knopf, New York, with woodcut plates by Jacob Lawrence, contemporary author's signature and later signature of the artist on front free endpaper, original cloth-backed boards, dust-jacket.
1949
£300-500   BLO

Ted Hughes, 'The Hawk in the Rain', first edition, published by Faber & Faber, London, original blue cloth, dust-jacket with Poetry Book Society wraparound band, spine slightly darkened, chipped at head of spine, edges a little darkened.
1957
£400-600   BLO

Aldous Huxley, 'Brave New World', first edition, published by Chatto & Windus, London, with original gilt stamped blue cloth, dust-jacket with some losses, and small ink inscription on front fixed endpaper.

Note the wonderful Art Deco style cover.
1932
£400-600   L&T

A CLOSER LOOK AT A BIGGLES FIRST EDITION

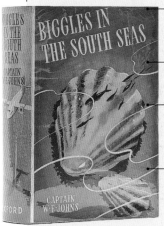

Measuring around 1.9 inches (4.8cm) in thickness across the spine, this true first edition has 255 pages and is often called the 'thick' version.

It has six full-page plain illustrations by Norman Howard, and a colour frontispiece.

As it was sold as a children's book, very few copies have survived in this fine condition - if the scarce dust-jacket is present, it is usually battered and worn, unlike this copy.

Later editions from 1940 in worn and read condition, lacking their dust-jackets, typically fetch well under £40

Captain W. E. Johns, 'Biggles in the South Seas', first edition, published by Oxford University Press, colour frontispiece, 6 full-page plain illustrations, original pictorial cloth, fine, dust-jacket, skilful and sympathetic restoration to edges, in effect a fine copy.
1940
£1,800-2,200 BLO

P. D. James, 'The Black Tower', first edition, published by Faber & Faber, original boards, dust-jacket by Errol le Cain, slight rubbing head and tail of spine, otherwise an excellent copy.
1975
£250-350 BLO

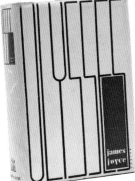

James Joyce, 'Ulysses', first American edition, first issue, published by Random House, New York, original buckram, slightly spotted, original dust-jacket with Art Deco design, slightly chipped at extremities with loss, a very good copy.

Five years earlier, in 1929, 2,000-3,000 unauthorised 'pirated' copies were printed by Adolph and Rudolph Loewinger for Samuel & Max Roth, but many were seized by The Society for the Suppression of Vice shortly after. This was the first authorised American edition, printed after the ban on this classic book was lifted. The striking jacket and the entire book was designed by German book designer Ernst Reichl, and 10,100 copies were printed.
1934
£800-1,200 BLO

Christopher Isherwood, 'Mr Norris Changes Trains', first edition, published by The Hogarth Press, London, with original cloth and dust-jacket, bookseller's small sticker on rear pastedown, slightly faded and browned in places.

This is known as 'The Last Of Mr Norris' in America.
1935
£1,200-1,800 BLO

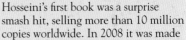

Christopher Isherwood, 'Sally Bowles', first edition, published by Hogarth Press, London, with original cloth and dust-jacket.

Although Isherwood dismissed this novel as 'trivial', it formed part of his famous 'Goodbye To Berlin' of 1939. John van Druten turned the novel into a play, 'I Am A Camera' in 1951.
1937
£80–120 BLO

Mark Picks

Hosseini's first book was a surprise smash hit, selling more than 10 million copies worldwide. In 2008 it was made into a film. First impressions of the first edition are scarce, and this example is made more desirable as it is signed, not dedicated, by the author. The extra invitation and postcard add to the desirability, and the rare original red band adds to the value.

Khaled Hosseini, 'The Kite Runner', first edition, first impression, published by Bloomsbury, signed by the author on title page in Farsi and English, with publisher's promotional postcard and Blackwell's reading invitation loosely inserted, with original boards, dust-jacket, original wrap-around.
2003
£600-800 BLO

Susannah Kells, 'The Fallen Angels', first edition, published by Collins, London, minor browning to page edges, original boards, dust jacket, overall in very good condition.

Susannah Kells is the pseudonym of Bernard Cornwell, who is best-known for his Sharpe adventure stories (see p30).

1984

£120-180   BLO

Ted Lewis, 'Jack's Return Home', first edition, published by Michael Joseph, London, original boards, dust-jacket, slight rubbing and dulling.

1970

£350-450   BLO

George Mackay Brown, 'Keepers of the House', first edition, published by The Old Stile Press, Otley, numbered 134 from a limited edition of 225 copies signed by the author, with illustrations by Gillian Martin, original cloth-backed pictorial boards, and pictorial slip case.

1986

£120–180   BLO

Bernard Malamud, 'The Assistant', first American edition, first printing, published by Farrar, Straus and Cudahy, New York, with cloth-backed brown paper boards, lettering to spine and upper cover, in dust-jacket.

1957

£200-300   BLNY

A CLOSER LOOK AT A FIRST EDITION

William Lee was the pseudonym used by William Burroughs, with 'Lee' being his mother's maiden name. This book was bound 'dos à dos' (back to back) with Helbrant's 'Narcotic Agent'.

Ace Books published inexpensive paperbacks for sale in subways and roadside stands. They were not reviewed by critics or bought by libraries. Surviving copies are scarce.

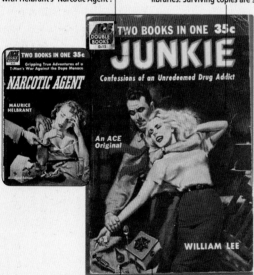

Burrough's first published book, it was produced with the help of Allen Ginsberg, who found a publisher (A.A. Wyn, owner of Ace Books) in an asylum and persuaded him to take it.

It details Burrough's life as a heroin addict, which was an unusual and challenging subject for the 1950s, but one that grew to be typical of 'pulp fiction' paperbacks.

William Lee, 'Junkie. Confessions of an Unredeemed Drug Addict', first edition, and 'Narcotic Agent' by Maurice Helbrant, published by Ace Books, New York, with original illustrated wrappers, and two spots of creasing on spine.

1953

£1,000-1,500   BLNY

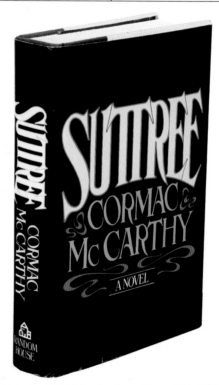

Cormac McCarthy, 'Suttree', first American edition, published by Random House, New York, with original cloth and dust-jacket with two creases.

The true first edition has a number line reading '24689753', and is stated as a first edition on the copyright page. If the price has been clipped or the jacket bears the remainder mark, the price can fall by over a third. McCarthy's fourth book, 'Suttree' is deemed his most humourous.

1979

£700-900   BLNY

A CLOSER LOOK AT A FIRST EDITION

The true and most sought-after first issue of the first edition was published in May 1936 - this date can be found on the copyright page.

Only 10,000 copies were printed, and this copy is made even rarer and more valuable as it bears Mitchell's signature on the first front-free endpaper.

If the original price is clipped off on the dust-jacket, the value can fall by up to a third.

Check that the dust-jacket is correct - the rear panel should be titled 'Macmillan Spring Novels' listing 'Gone With the Wind' as the second title in the second column. Above it should be Charles Morgan's novel 'Sparkenbroke'.

Margaret Mitchell, 'Gone With the Wind', first edition, published by Macmillan, New York, with original grey cloth and lightly creased and rubbed dust-jacket, and with very faint tidemark in lower margin of text.

The novel formed the basis for the enduringly popular Hollywood epic of 1939, starring Clark Gable and Vivien Leigh. In 2006, an example signed by over 70 members of the cast and crew fetched nearly $60,000 (£40,000) at auction.

1936
£5,000-6,000   **BLNY**

Patrick O'Brian, 'The Surgeon's Mate', first edition, published by Collins, London, original boards, dust-jacket, spine slightly sunned with small nick from foot.

1980
£400-600   **BLO**

Ellis Peters, 'A Morbid Taste for Bones', first edition, original boards, dust-jacket, an unusually good copy.

Ellis Peters was the pseudonym for Edith Pargeter (1913-95). This is the first edition of the first of the celebrated Cadfael series, subtitled 'A Medieval Whodunnit'! The series was turned into a successful TV series, which aired on ITV from 1994-96.

1977
£300-500   **BLO**

Anthony Powell, 'A Buyer's Market', first edition, published by Heinemann, London, some slight marginal browning, original cloth, dust-jacket, extremities nicked and chipped with loss to spine ends and corners.

This scarce first edition is the second in the 'A Dance to the Music of Time' series.

1952
£350-450   **BLO**

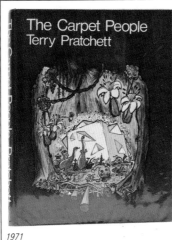

Terry Pratchett, 'The Carpet People', first edition with illustrations, published by Colin Smythe Ltd, Gerrards Cross, original cloth, dust-jacket, in original duraseal jacket, price-clipped, otherwise fine condition.

This is the author's first book, published when he was 23 years old. His first Discworld book, 'The Colour of Magic', was published in 1983.

1971
£450-550   **BLO**

Gregory David Roberts, 'Shantaram', first edition, published by Scribe, Melbourne, original boards, dust-jacket, a fine copy.

2003
£120-180   **BLO**

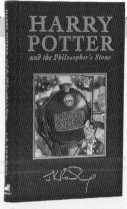

J. K. Rowling, 'Harry Potter and the Philosopher's Stone', first deluxe edition, published by Bloomsbury, London, signed by the author on half-title, original red cloth with gilt signature and mounted image, with custom cloth slip-case, a fine copy.
1999
£500-700   **BLO**

QUICK REFERENCE - HARRY POTTER DELUXE EDITIONS

- For those unable to afford, or unable to find, a true first edition, collecting Bloomsbury's deluxe editions may prove easier and more affordable. Produced from 1999, they are bound in coloured fabric-covered hard covers and have the pictorial cover of the original first edition on the front, together with Rowling's impressed facsmile signature. A ribbon bookmark is also sewn into the gilt-edged pages. This copy is worth as much as it is because it is signed by Rowling.
- 12,000 copies of the first edition of this deluxe title were printed, with '10 9 8 7 6 5 4 3 2 1' numbering on the copyright page. 17,000 copies of 'Harry Potter & The Chamber of Secrets', also shown on this page, were printed. The rarest deluxe edition is said to be Harry Potter & The Prisoner of Azkaban, with only 7,000 copies printed in conjunction with the launch of the book itself. In 2008, a full set of deluxe editions sold at auction for over £17,000.
- For more information on Harry Potter first editions in general, please see the Books section in 'Miller's Collectables Handbook & Price Guide 2010-2011'.

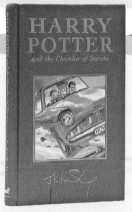

J.K. Rowling, 'Harry Potter and the Chamber of Secrets', first deluxe edition, published by Bloomsbury, London, signed by the author on dedication page, original blue cloth with gilt signature and mounted image, with custom cloth slip-case, a fine copy.
1999
£400-600   **BLO**

J.K. Rowling, 'Harry Potter and the Half-Blood Prince', first edition, published by Bloomsbury, London, publisher's bookplate signed by the author mounted on dedication page, original pictorial boards, dust-jacket, a fine copy.
2005
£350-450   **BLO**

J.K. Rowling, 'The Tales of Beedle the Bard', first trade edition, published by Children's High Level Group and Bloomsbury, London, signed by the author on leaf after title, original pictorial boards.

This book is very scarce signed by Rowling.
2008
£1,500-2,500   **BLO**

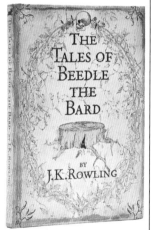

Olaf Stapledon, 'Odd John', first edition, published by Methuen, London, some spotting, original cloth, dust-jacket, price-clipped, some chips and small tears.

The dust-jacket is scarce, and this example is in overall very good condition.
1935
£400-600   **BLO**

John Steinbeck, 'In Dubious Battle', first edition published by Covici Friede, New York, signed by the author, with original yellow cloth and dust-jacket, in a custom half-morocco box.

Not only is this in good condition, albeit with a slightly rubbed jacket, but it is also signed by the author. Look out for the limited first printing of the first edition of 99 copies that were signed and numbered by the author, as examples can fetch well over double this value.
1936
£2,500-3,000   **BLNY**

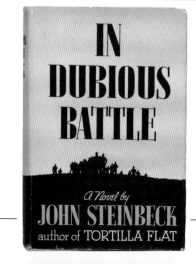

Keith Waterhouse, 'Billy Liar', first edition, published by Michael Joseph, London, with un-clipped dust-jacket and original boards.
1959
£70-100   **GORL**

Evelyn Waugh, 'Men at Arms', first edition published by Chapman, London, with original blue cloth boards and un-clipped dust-jacket, a very good copy.
1952
£250-350 GORL

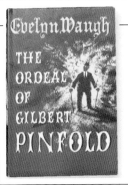

Evelyn Waugh, 'The Ordeal of Gilbert Pinfold', first edition, published by Chapman & Hall, London, with original blue cloth boards and un-clipped dust-jacket, a very good copy.
1957
£50-80 GORL

Christopher Wood, 'James Bond and Moonraker', first edition, published by Jonathan Cape, London, original boards, dust-jacket, spine slightly marked.

Fleming's original Bond novel 'Moonraker' was changed dramatically for the 11th Bond film, which launched in 1979. Due to the success of Star Wars, the villain, Hugo Drax's plot was changed from one involving nuclear missiles (a key threat in the 1950s) to one involving outer space. Christopher Wood was the film's screen writer, and was authorised to produce this modified version of Fleming's story in 1979. It quickly became a bestseller that year. In 2010, a first edition of Fleming's original book, from a print run of only 9,900 copies and signed by Fleming for well-known collector Eileen Cond (see p30), was sold at auction for over $50,000 (£30,000).
1979
£200-300 BLO

H.G. Wells, 'The Misery of Boots', first edition, published by the Fabian Society, London, with original pictorial green wrappers lettered in red, chipping to corners of wrappers, text block detaching, residue from bookplates to title and half title.

This copy was owned by John Quinn (1870–1924), a successful lawyer who was a major book and art collector.
1907
£100-150 BLNY

Peter Wright, 'Spycatcher', first edition, published by William Heinemann, Australia, and printed in Dublin, with original light orange boards and dust-jacket.

The true first edition was published in Australia and has a dust-jacket with a red band and a price reading 'IR£14.95'. Hurriedly produced to cash in on the huge publicity surrounding the British government's attempts to suppress this explosive and revealing story, there should be no illustrations or photographs inside, as there are in later editions. This book is one of the best-known and most notorious of the late 20thC, and carries an almost legendary status. Both factors mean it should continue to be popular with collectors, and may rise in value in the long term if demand continues against the limited supply. Look for true first editions, as detailed here, in as close to mint condition as possible.
1987
£100-150 BLO

Virginia Woolf, 'Monday or Tuesday', first edition, published by Hogarth Press, Richmond, four full-page woodcuts by Vanessa Bell (some offsetting), advertisement leaf at end, endpapers browned, original cloth-backed decorative boards by Vanessa Bell, a little rubbed at edges and spotted.

This is one of only 1,000 copies produced in this format. The artist Bell was Woolf's sister, and both were active in London's influential 'Bloomsbury Group' of artists, critics, intellectuals and authors.
1921
£600-800 BLO

QUICK REFERENCE

- In 1972, inspired by the natural beauty of the Scottish Borders, John Hammond founded Border Craft and Design (known as Border Fine Arts from 1974). Working with sculptor Victor Hayton and three employees, he began producing cold-cast bronze and silver animal figurines.
- In 1974 the company began producing the extremely detailed, painted moulded 'Thorianware' resin pieces it is now best-known for.
- Look out for designs by Ray Ayres (b.1952), the company's most collectable modeller. One of the original employees, Ayres has since designed over 500 models, including all of its highly desirable tractor pieces. Other notable modellers include Kirsty Armstrong (or Riley), American artist and farmer Lowell Davies, and Margaret Turner.
- Most collectors tend to focus on a type of animal, or a particular series. The popular 'James Herriot' series (based on the books by Alf Wight) is subdivided into various mini-ranges, including 'All Creatures Great and Small'. Initially, models in this series were based on subjects and characters described in the James Herriot stories, but more recent figurines are simply influenced by them. All 'James Herriot' pieces have model numbers prefixed with 'JH'.
- The most sought-after pieces are typically from limited editions. Early editions were smaller in size, but later editions have nearer to, or over, 1,000 pieces, which may include painted resin and cold-cast bronze variations, or different colourways. Model numbers usually have an 'L' prefix, unless the piece is from the 'James Herriot' series.
- Other series are identified by the modeller's initials, such as 'JB' – 'Judy Boyt Woodland Collection', or the initials of the series' name, such as 'ED' – 'Early Days'. Some exclusive figurines have also been made for the Border Fine Arts Society.

A Border Fine Arts limited edition 'All In A Day's Work' group, no.JH0593, designed by Kirsty Armstrong, from the 'James Herriott' collection, numbered 1028 from an edition of 1500, boxed with certificate.

Issued 2000   *12.5in (32cm) long*

£80-120   **CHT**

A Border Fine Arts limited edition 'Black Face Ewe and Lamb' group, style one, no.L00025, designed by Mairi Laing Hunt, numbered 77 from an edition of 750, boxed.

Two other variations of this group were produced later, but this is the most valuable.

Issued 1980   *4.5in (12cm) high*

£200-300   **CHT**

A Border Fine Arts limited edition 'Daily Delivery' group, no.JH0013, designed by Ray Ayres, from the 'Every Living Thing' series, numbered 543 from an edition of 1500, boxed with certificate, mudguard detached.

Issued 1995   *7.5in (19cm) high*

£220-280   **CHT**

A Border Fine Arts limited edition 'Bringing In The Harvest' group, no.B0735, designed by Ray Ayres, from the 'Classic Collection', numbered 391 from an edition of 850, with certificate.

Issued 2002   *6.75in (17cm) high*

£450-550   **CHT**

A Border Fine Arts limited edition 'Delivered Warm' group, no.B0040, designed by Ray Ayres, from the 'Every Living Thing' series, numbered 261 from an edition of 1500, boxed with certificate.

Issued 1997   *9.5in (24cm) high*

£180-220   **CHT**

A Border Fine Arts limited edition 'Delivering the Milk' group, no.AG01, designed by Ray Ayres, numbered 172 from an edition of 950, boxed with certificate.

Issued 1998   *6.25in (16cm) high*

£220-280   **CHT**

A Border Fine Arts limited edition 'Finishing Off' group, no.B0947, designed by Hans Kendrick, numbered 209 from an edition of 750, boxed.

10.25in (26cm) high

£120-180   **CHT**

A Border Fine Arts limited edition 'Flat Refusal' group, no.B0650, designed by Kirsty Armstrong, from the 'Classic Collection', numbered 73 from an edition of 1500, boxed.

Issued 2002   *6.5in (16.5cm) high*

£120-180   **CHT**

A Border Fine Arts limited edition 'Frontiers of Farming (Fastrac JCB)' group, no.B0273, designed by Kirsty Armstrong, numbered 11 from an edition of 1000, boxed with certificate.

Issued 1997   *6in (15cm) high*

£300-400   **CHT**

A Border Fine Arts limited edition 'Hay Cutting Starts Today' group, no.B0405a, designed by Roy Ayres, numbered 598 from an edition of 950, boxed with certificate.

Issued 2000   *5.25in (13cm) high*

£350-450   **CHT**

A Border Fine Arts limited edition 'Hedge Laying' group, no.JH0065, designed by Ray Ayres, from the 'All Creatures Great and Small' series, numbered 1027 from an edition of 1750, boxed with certificate.

Issued 1992   *7in (18cm) high*

£320-380   **CHT**

A Border Fine Arts limited edition 'Morning Exercise At Balmoral' group, no.B0814, designed by Craig Harding, from the 'Classic Collection', numbered 52 from an edition of 500, boxed with certificate.

This would also appeal to collectors of Royal memorabilia.

Issued 2003   *14.5in (37cm) high*

£250-350   **CHT**

A Border Fine Arts limited edition 'The Reluctant Pupil (Otters)' group, no.MTR008, designed by Ray Ayres, from the 'Masters of the River' series, numbered 1041 from an edition of 1500, boxed with certificate.

Issued 1995   *14in (35.5cm) high*

£150-250   CHT

A Border Fine Arts limited edition 'River Sentinel' group, no.D0302, designed by Ray Ayres, from the 'Millennium' series, numbered 402 from an edition of 1250, with certificate.

Issued 1999   *12.5in (31cm) high*

£150-200   CHT

A Border Fine Arts limited edition 'Steady Lad Steady' group, no.JH0090, designed by Ray Ayres, from the 'Every Living Thing' series, numbered 209 from an edition of 1500, with certificate.

Issued 1993   *6.25in (16cm) high*

£80-120   CHT

A Border Fine Arts limited edition 'Striking A Deal At Appleby Fair' group, no.B0664, designed by Ray Ayres, from the 'Classic Collection', numbered 436 from an edition of 600, boxed with certificate.

Issued 1999   *28in (70cm) long*

£700-900   CHT

A Border Fine Arts limited edition 'Supplementary Feeding' group, no.JH0057, designed by Anne Butler, from the 'All Things Wise and Wonderful' series, numbered 243 from an edition of 1750, with certificate.

Issued 1991   *7in (18cm) high*

£220-280   CHT

A CLOSER LOOK AT A BORDER FINE ARTS GROUP

Tractors are among the most popular subjects to feature in Border Fine Arts's sculptures.

It is from the perennially popular 'James Herriott' collection based on the much-loved stories by Alf Wright, who wrote under the name James Herriott.

This was the first sculpture to feature a tractor, and is very desirable to collectors today.

It represents a key turning point in early 20thC farming - the point where horses were replaced by machinery in the Dales, and indeed on farms across the country.

A Border Fine Arts limited edition 'New Technology Arrives (Fordson Tractor)' group, no.JH0046, designed by Ray Ayres, from the 'All Creatures Great and Small' series, numbered 193 from an edition of 1250, with certificate.

This model was designed by Ray Ayres, who was Border Fine Arts's Master Sculptor. He has been involved with the company since 1973, around the time of its inception.

Issued 1991

£1,200-1,800   CHT

QUICK REFERENCE - CAMERAS

- The daguerreotype was launched in 1839. Although arguably the first commercially viable photographic process, it was the ready availability of prepared 'dry' photographic plates and advances in camera design in the 1880s that truly opened the market to many more people. Early 19thC cameras were rare and expensive in their day and continue to be so. Meanwhile, a large number of late 19thC and early 20thC mahogany- and brass-bodied, dry-plate cameras survive today, and are usually more affordable. Look for names like Sanderson, Watson, and Lancaster.

- The Leica, made by Leitz, in Wetzlar, Germany, is perhaps the world's most collectable camera. Developed in 1913, the Leica used 35mm film and was small, light, and easy to use. Each Leica has a unique serial number on its top plate, which you can use to identify the model and year of manufacture. Prices range from around £100 for more common models to tens of thousands of pounds for rare variations and models with unusual engravings.

- With other mass-produced cameras, look for fine quality construction and well-known brand names, such as Canon and Zeiss Ikon. Variation in colour and features, such as lenses, can add value. Early digital cameras may also be worth considering.

A Sanderson tropical quarter-plate camera, with brass-mounted teak body and Dallmeyer brass lens.

Teak was used instead of mahogany for cameras destined for use in the tropics as the natural oils in the wood made it less susceptible to damage caused by heat and damp. Many, but not all, tropical cameras also have red bellows.

£180-220   ROS

An American Gundlach brass-mounted mahogany full plate camera, with rack focus, leather bellows, and a Gundlach Anastigmat F: 6.3 series IV lens and shutter, together with an associated tripod (not shown) for display purposes.

Gundlach, based in New York, are a noted maker. The value of many of these brass-mounted wood folding plate cameras depends primarily on the maker, and the quantity and type of accessories that accompany them.

Camera 14.5in (37cm) high

£200-300   SK

A 1920s Thornton Pickard 'Imperial' triple-extension brass-mounted mahogany plate camera, with black bellows and Ross lens.

Launched in 1913 and produced into the 1930s, this camera was a bestseller of its time and type.

8.5in (22cm) high

£120-180   ECGW

A Thornton Pickard 'Amber' brass-mounted mahogany plate camera, with Ross brass lens, mahogany plates, and back.

c1890-c1905

£150-200   LC

An Adams & Co. mahogany-cased plate camera, with red bellows, brass lens, and two mahogany plateholders, with an original canvas case and black velvet cover.

£200-300   LSK

CAMERAS

A Leica IIIc camera, no.387795, in grey with Leitz Elmar f=5cm 1:3.5 lens.

This camera has not been re-painted. As chrome was scarce during World War II, 3,415 Leica cameras made between 1942-44 were painted grey, rather than made in chrome.

1942

£400-600   ROS

A Leica IIIg camera, no.943743, chrome, with Leitz f=5cm 1:2 Summicron lens.

1958

£300-400   ROS

A Leica IIIc camera, no.517708, chrome, with a Summitar F 1:2 lens, and original Leitz leather carrying case and strap.

1950   *6in (15cm) wide*

£70-100   GORL

A Leica M5 'Fifty Years' Jubilee camera, no.1362636, chrome, with a Leitz 1:2/50mm Summicron lens.

Although the model M5 was deemed a failure at the time, collectors have since turned their attention to it. Of the 33,900 examples of the M5 made, this is one of the most desirable variations. 1,750 pieces with commemorative engravings were produced, of which only around 350 were in chrome.

1974

£500-700   ROS

QUICK REFERENCE - LEICA FAKES

- Although a number of camera companies, such as Reid & Sigrist of England and Muley of Japan, copied and were 'inspired by' Leitz's highly successful Leica cameras, the camera below is an out-and-out fake intended to deceive. This is how we can tell:
- The quality of the materials and manufacture are not as high as with a genuine Leica. If in doubt, pick up a Leica, note the weight, and carefully tweak a few knobs. Then do the same to the suspect piece. The difference will be clear.
- Although the overall form and layout are similar, look closely as details will differ. The frame around the viewing lens on the front of the top plate is a good example of an incorrect detail.
- Serial numbers on fakes are usually wrong for the camera. The German military only used Model III, IIIb, and IIIc cameras, not the Model A from 1928 that the '10116' serial number indicates.
- Neither Leica, nor the German military, used this logo or designation to replace the standard Leica top plate engravings.
- The value of fake Leicas depends on the market, and the age and quality of the piece itself. Many are still being made today. Some collectors like to add fakes and replicas to their collections, but most do not, as doing so encourages the market in fakes.

A 1950s Russian copy of a Leica camera, with a brass body and an authentic Leitz Summicron F1:2,8 lens, the base engraved 'Luftwaffen-Eigentum', in period leather case.

The engraving means 'Property of the Airforce', and was a mark used by the Luftwaffe during World War II. If this mark was found on an authentic Leica IIIc or IIIb camera, in superb condition and with a correct 'F1' prefixed inventory number, the camera could sell for around £2,000!

£10-50   GORB

A replica Leica camera, with engraved and gilded 'Kriegsmarine' emblem and engraved serial no.'10116' to top plate, with leather case (not shown).

£150-200   BELL

A 1950s Asahi 'Asahiflex' I 35mm SLR camera, no.26830, with Takumar 1:3.5 f=50mm lens.

This was the first Japanese 35mm SLR camera. Asahi was founded in 1919, and started to produce lenses for Molta (later Minolta) in 1931. Introduced in 1952, this was the company's first camera.

£120-180   ROS

An Ihagee 'Exakta' 66 single lens reflex camera, with Zeiss Tessar 2.8/80mm lens.

Launched at the Leipzig Fair in 1952, 'Exakta' models weren't delivered until 1954! Reputedly, only 2,000 examples were ever made, and nearly all were exported to the US.

£300-400   ROS

A CLOSER LOOK AT A MINIATURE CAMERA

Miniature, and even smaller 'subminiature', cameras are a very popular collecting area within the camera collecting field.

A triumph of engineering, it packed a vast amount of features and accessories into a tiny body. A 1938 advertisement boasted, 'Compass: the embodiment of scientific systems in miniature cameras. Built like a watch - as simple to use.'.

This camera was manufactured in Switzerland by renowned watch, clock, and precision instrument maker Jaeger Le Coultre & Cie. for the English distributor Compass Cameras Ltd.

Cased in 'Duralim' aluminium, it was designed over the space of six years by aircraft builder, pilot, politican, and businessman Noel Pemberton-Billing, and cost a staggering £30 in its day.

A Le Coultre for Compass Cameras Ltd. 'Compass' 35mm rangefinder camera, no.3341, with roll back, lacking lens cover.
c1938

£400-600   ROS

A Kodak 'Special 3A' 'Autographic' model B camera, with Compur lens housing and Carl Zeiss Tessar 1.4,5 lens, in leather case.

Although pocket folding cameras are generally very common and not at all expensive to buy, this model is more interesting than most as it was the first handheld camera with a coupled rangefinder. The 'Autographic' feature allowed the user to 'write' a date, title, or short note directly onto the film using a special stylus and a small sliding panel.
c1910-14

£40-60   GORB

A Rolleiflex twin lens reflex camera, with original leather case and strap.

5.5in (14cm) high

£60-80   GORL

A Zeiss Ikon 'Movikon' '8' wind-up movie camera, in case with 1:1.9 F=10mm lens.

£15-20   CAPE

CERAMICS

QUICK REFERENCE

- The Beswick Pottery was founded in Loughton, Staffordshire in 1894 and initially focused on ornamental vases and tableware. Animal figurines were introduced c1900, and had become a major part of production by 1930. From 1939 to 1957, the majority were modelled by Arthur Gredington. Other notable modellers include Colin Melbourne, Graham Tongue, Albert Hallam, and Alan Maslankowski.
- In 1969, Beswick was sold to Royal Doulton, but pieces continued to be produced under the name 'Beswick' until 1989 when production of Beswick and Doulton animals merged under the Royal Doulton name. The Beswick name was used again from 1999 until the factory closed in 2002.
- Collectors tend to focus on one type of animal, with dogs and cats being widely popular. Cattle, particularly bulls, are currently the most desirable, and consequently often the most valuable. Many are collected by butchers and farmers. Calves tend to be less valuable, but are still desirable, as collectors often buy calves to match their cows and bulls. Horse figurines are similarly sought-after.
- Variations in colour, types of glaze, and form (eg: a differently positioned tail) will all affect value. If you are thinking of beginning a collection, it is worth investing in a specialist guide to identify the most desirable variations. In general matt-glazed pieces tend to be more valuable than their glossy counterparts, but this is not always the case. Similarly 'rocking-horse' grey pieces are typically more valuable than those glazed in brown. Limited editions can be valuable if the edition was small, and there is demand.
- In general prices being paid for all but the rarest and most desirable Beswick animals have fallen as collections of animal figurines are currently out of fashion. Always aim to buy in the best condition possible. Examine protruding areas such as horns and hooves carefully for damage. A restored area will still be considered damaged by many collectors.

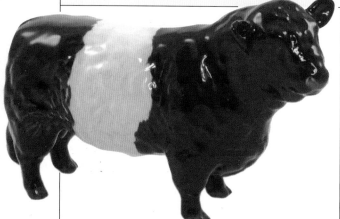

A Beswick black and white gloss-glazed Galloway belted bull, model no.1746B, designed in 1961 by Arthur Gredington.

It may look like a standard bull, but this is one of the most desirable Beswick bull models - in 2004 an example fetched £2,050 at auction. This is higher than many 18thC pottery figurines, and demonstrates the current strength of many 20thC collectables against more traditional collecting areas.

1963-69   *4.5in (12cm) high*

£2,000-2,500   **WHP**

A Beswick brown and white gloss-glazed Hereford bull, 'Ch. of Champions', model no.1363A, designed by Arthur Gredington.

This is the first version, where the horns protrude from the ears. The second version, produced from 1985-89 and usually worth around a third of this value, has horns flush to the ears - presumably as the original protruding horns were often damaged.

Introduced 1955   *4.5in (11cm) high*

£150-200   **WHP**

A Beswick brown and white gloss-glazed Hereford bull, model no.949, designed by Arthur Gredington.

1941-c1957   *5.75in*
                              (14.5cm) high

£150-200   **WHP**

A Beswick brown and white gloss-glazed Ayrshire cow, 'Ch. Ickham Bessie', model no.1350, designed by Arthur Gredington.

1954-90   *5in (13cm) high*

£150-200   **WHP**

A Beswick shaded brown and white gloss-glazed dairy shorthorn bull, 'Ch. Gwersylt Lord Oxford 74th', model no.1504, designed by Arthur Gredington.

1957-73　　*5in (12.5cm) high*

£500-700　　　　**WHP**

A CLOSER LOOK AT A BESWICK COW

This is a good example of a popular model that was produced for a long period of time, and consequently fetches a low price on the secondary market today.

The canny collector should look out for the brown Fresian, numbered 1362B and issued in 1992 in a limited edition of 130 examples, which can fetch well over ten times this value.

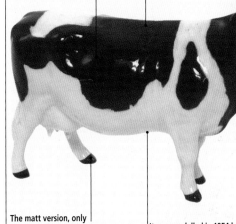

The matt version, only produced from 1985-1989, is rarer and can fetch double this value.

It was modelled in 1954 by Arthur Gredington, one of the most talented and prolific Beswick modellers.

A Beswick fawn and brown gloss-glazed Galloway bull, 'Silver Dunn', model no.1746C, designed in 1961 by Arthur Gredington.

1962-69　　　　　　　*4.5in (12cm) high*

£1,200-1,800　　　　**WHP**

A Beswick black and white gloss-glazed Friesian cow, 'Ch. Claybury Leegwater', model no.1362A, designed by Arthur Gredington.

1954-97　　　　　　　*4.5in (12cm) high*

£60-80　　　　　　　**WHP**

A Beswick tan and brown gloss-glazed Highland bull, model no.2008, designed by Arthur Gredington.

1965-90　　*5in (12.5cm) high*

£100-150　　　**WHP**

A Beswick tan and brown gloss-glazed Highland cow, model no.1740, designed by Arthur Gredington.

Unusually, the matt and gloss versions of this model are worth roughly the same amount, even though the matt version was only produced from 1985-89.

1961-90　　　　　*5.25in (13.5cm) high*

£150-200　　　　**WHP**

A Beswick brown and white gloss-glazed Hereford calf, model no.1406B, designed by Arthur Gredington.

1956-75　　*3in (7.5cm) high*

£80-120　　　**WHP**

CERAMICS

QUICK REFERENCE - BESWICK HORSES

If Beswick cattle are currently the most sought-after and valuable models, their horses must be a close second, as well as being the most familiar animal in the Beswick stable.

- The first horse was modelled in 1939 by Arthur Gredington, and over the next 50 years over 150 different models were produced - most by Gredington or Graham Tongue. As most are not marked with names or model numbers, it's essential to study the form carefully to identify the correct model.

- Colour is also important to value - rocking-horse grey is usually more valuable and rarer than brown. Combinations of colour and model must also be considered - a good example is the 818 in rocking-horse grey shown in this section. Earlier examples also tend to have better painted, shaded colour, rather than solid colour, which is more desirable to collectors.

- From 1989 to 1996, the Royal Doulton backstamp was used on all but a very few horses. The Beswick backstamp was then used until the company closed in 2002.

A Beswick palomino gloss-glazed 'Stocky Jogging Mare', model no.855, designed by Arthur Gredington.

This is the third version of this model, which was previously numbered 1090. Differences in form include a more arched tail, the off-fore leg raised, and a lowered head.

1961-89   *6in (15cm) high*
£60-80   **WHP**

A Beswick chestnut gloss-glazed pony, with head up, model no.1197, designed by Arthur Gredington.

1958-67   *5.5in (14cm) high*
£500-700   **WHP**

A Beswick gloss-glazed prancing Arab-type palomino, first version, model no.1261, designed by Arthur Gredington.

Introduced 1952   *6.75in (17cm) high*
£40-60   **WHP**

A Beswick dun gloss-glazed Highland pony, 'Mackionneach', model no.1644, designed by Arthur Gredington.

1961-89   *7.25in (18.5cm) high*
£120-180   **WHP**

A Beswick brown gloss-glazed galloping horse, model no.1374, designed by Mr Orwell.

1955-75   *7.5in (19cm) high*
£100-150   **WHP**

A Beswick brown gloss-glazed Welsh cob, rearing, model no.1014, designed by Arthur Gredington.

This is the second and later version, with the tail detached from the base. Look out for the chestnut or painted white gloss-glazed versions, which are the rarest and most valuable colourways, usually fetching over four times this value.

Discontinued 1989   *10.25in (26cm) high*
£60-80   **WHP**

A CLOSER LOOK AT A BESWICK HORSE

In gloss brown, this is almost certainly the most common horse model, and was produced in large quantities from 1940-89.

Apart from the addition of a harness, the form remained unchanged throughout the period of its production.

It was produced in fourteen different colourways, making it an ideal, yet challenging, model to collect in all its variations.

Rocking-horse grey is a scarce colour in general, but the rarest colourway for this is gloss blue, reputedly produced from c1940-54.

A Beswick 'Appaloosa' stallion, colourway no.2, model no.1772A, designed by Arthur Gredington.

The second colourway has more white areas, and less distinct roan patches than the earlier and more valuable first colourway. It was reissued in 1999 and continued to be produced until the factory closed.

Discontinued 1989   *8in (20.5cm) high*

£120-180   **WHP**

A Beswick rocking-horse grey gloss-glazed Shire mare, model no.818/H818, first version without harness, designed by Arthur Gredington.

c1940-62   *8.5in (21.5cm) high*

£400-600   **WHP**

A Beswick spotted (British) gloss-glazed 'Appaloosa' walking pony, model no.1516, designed by Arthur Gredington.

1957-66   *5.25in (13cm) high*

£300-500   **WHP**

A Beswick grey gloss-glazed Shire mare with harness and tack, model no.818/H818, designed by Arthur Gredington, from the 'Harnessed Horse' series.

1974-82   *8.5in (21.5cm) high*

£120-180   **WHP**

A Beswick dark brown gloss-glazed 'Steeplechaser' racehorse and jockey group, model no.2505, designed by Graham Tongue.

1975-81   *8in (21.5cm) high*

£300-400   **DN**

A Beswick light dapple grey gloss-glazed Lifeguard, model No.1624, designed by Arthur Gredington.

1959-77   *9.5in (24cm) high*

£400-600   **WHP**

CERAMICS

A Beswick tan and cream gloss-glazed running Afghan hound, model no.3070, designed by Alan Maslankowski.

1988-89   *5.5in (14cm) high*
£35-45   **WHP**

A Beswick brindle, tan and white gloss-glazed large bulldog, 'Basford British Mascot', model no.965, designed by Arthur Gredington.

1941-90   *5.5in (14cm) high*
£50-70   **WHP**

A Beswick cream gloss-glazed chihuahua, lying on a maroon cushion, model no.2454, designed by Albert Hallam.

1973-96   *2.75in (7cm) high*
£20-30   **WHP**

A Beswick golden brown matt-glazed labrador, model no.2314, designed by Graham Tongue, from the 'Fireside Models' series.

1970-89   *13.5in (34.3cm) high*
£200-300   **WHP**

A Beswick white and pink gloss-glazed poodle, on cushion, model no.2985, designed by Alan Maslankowski, from the 'Good Companions' series.

This is more commonly found on a turquoise cushion, and is usually worth under a third of this value. Colour counts!

1987-89   *5.5in (14cm) high*
£150-200   **WHP**

A Beswick black and tan matt-glazed Dachshund standing, model no.3103, designed by Alan Maslankowski, from the 'Good Companions' series.

This dog is worth roughly the same in black and tan, tan only, or gloss or matt glazes.

1987-89   *4.25in (11cm) high*
£50-70   **WHP**

A Beswick speckled grey gloss-glazed English setter, 'Bayldone Baronet', model no.973, designed by Arthur Gredington.

1942-89   *5.5in (14cm) high*
£60-80   **WHP**

A Beswick tan and white matt-glazed King Charles spaniel, 'Blenheim', model no.2107a, designed by Arthur Gredington.

1987-94   *5.25in (13cm) high*

£25-35   **WHP**

A Beswick white with golden tan patches gloss-glazed spaniel, running, model no.1057, designed by Arthur Gredington.

1946-67   *3.75in (9.5cm) high*

£60-80   **WHP**

A Beswick grey and tan gloss-glazed Yorkshire terrier, model no.2377, designed by Graham Tongue, from the 'Fireside Models' series.

1971-89   *10.25in (26cm) high*

£60-80   **WHP**

A Beswick tan and black gloss-glazed Cairn terrier, standing, model no.3082, designed by Warren Platt, from the 'Good Companions' series.

1988-89   *4.75in (12cm) high*

£35-45   **WHP**

A Beswick brown and tan gloss-glazed Cairn terrier, first version with ball on left leg, model no.1055A, designed by Arthur Gredington.

This model was also produced without a ball from 1946-69. That version is usually worth around 15% more.

1946-69   *4in (10cm) high*

£60-80   **WHP**

A Beswick pale tan and black matt-glazed Lakeland terrier, model no.2448, designed by Albert Hallam.

1984-89   *3.25in (8.5cm) high*

£20-30   **WHP**

Judith Picks

As the 'country cottage' look has largely fallen from fashion over the past decades, prices for all but the rarest of these quintessentially English pottery dogs have fallen too. Even well-modelled and well-painted 19thC pairs only tend to fetch under £100 today, a fraction of their price in the 1980s.

The Beswick factory made these Staffordshire mantelpiece dogs from c1898. This model number was produced in six different sizes, these being the largest and most valuable in this colourway. Even though the originals may possibly return to fashion as part of the current eclectic 'mix and match' style, it's unlikely that late examples like these will ever fetch considerably higher prices. Nevertheless, they are the most affordable way to buy into the look.

A pair of Beswick red and gold gloss-glazed Old English dogs, model no.1378/6.

1955-89   *13.25in (33.5cm) high*

£25-35   **WHP**

CERAMICS

A Beswick grey shaded gloss-glazed Persian cat, on hind legs, model no.1883, designed by Albert Hallam.

1963-71　　　　*6in (15cm) high*
£150-200　　　　　**WHP**

A Beswick ginger 'Swiss-roll' gloss-glazed Persian cat, on hind legs, model no.1883, designed by Albert Hallam.

Note the difference between the very popular striped 'Swiss-roll' and the standard ginger glaze shown below.

1964-66　　　　*6in (15cm) high*
£180-220　　　　　**WHP**

A CLOSER LOOK AT A　　　　BESWICK CAT

This example is well-painted, particularly around the neck area where the blue is nicely toned and patched.

Treasure hunters should look out for the royal blue gloss glazed variation - only one example has been found so far, making it the only cat found in this eye-wateringly rare colour!

This colourway was only produced for two years, making it hard to find as fewer examples were produced. Grey 'Swiss-roll' was produced for the same period and is also hard to find.

The ginger version, shown on the left, was produced for longer and is more characteristic of this cat, explaining why it sold in larger quantities.

A Beswick British blue (lead grey) cat, seated with head looking up, model no. 1030, designed by Arthur Gredington.

1964-66
£380-480

6.25in (16cm) high
WHP

A Beswick dark ginger gloss-glazed cat, seated with head looking up, model no. 1030, designed by Arthur Gredington.

1945-70　　　　*6.25in (16cm) high*
£60-80　　　　　**WHP**

A Beswick 'seal-point' gloss-glazed Siamese cat, seated with head up, model no.2139, designed by Mr. Garbet, from the 'Fireside Model' series.

A much rarer copper lustre-glazed version of this large cat was produced for export only in 1971. However, it generally fetches only around 25% more than this version, perhaps because it's not as appealing and the unreal colour doesn't represent the breed to cat-loving Beswick collectors.

1967-89　　　　*13.75in (35cm) high*
£100-150　　　　　**WHP**

A Beswick 'seal-point' gloss-glazed Siamese cat, seated, head forward, model no.1882, designed by Albert Hallam, from the 'Fireside Model' series.

1963-89　　　　*9.5in (24cm) high*
£30-40　　　　　**WHP**

A Beswick grey 'Swiss-roll' Persian kitten, standing, model no.1885, designed by Albert Hallam.

1964-66   4.75in (12cm) high
£150-200   **WHP**

A Beswick shaded grey gloss-glazed Persian cat, standing tail erect, model no.1898, designed by Albert Hallam.

1963-89   5in (12.5cm) high
£18-22   **WHP**

A Beswick grey 'Swiss-roll' gloss-glazed Persian cat, seated looking up, model no.1867, designed by Albert Hallam.

'Swiss-roll' is one of the most desirable and valuable colours for Beswick's cat models. It takes its name from the spiralling 'Swiss-roll' patterns on the hip and shoulder. The hip pattern can be seen on the kitten above right.

1964-66   8.5in (21.5cm) high
£220-280   **WHP**

A Beswick grey-shaded Persian cat, lying, model no.1876, designed by Albert Hallam.

1963-71   3.5in (8cm) long
£80-120   **WHP**

A Beswick 'sang de boeuf' gloss-glazed Siamese cat, lying facing right, model no.1559b (or DA 125), designed by Pal Zalmen and Albert Hallam.

The 'sang de boeuf' glaze is extremely rare and, despite being more commonly associated with Royal Doulton, is not listed on this model in either Beswick or Royal Doulton reference books.

7.25in (18.5cm) high
£180-220   **WHP**

A Beswick white gloss-glazed 'Zodiac' cat, seated, facing right, model no.1560, designd by Pal Zalmen.

This cat has a matching friend, but facing left to form a pair. The symbols on both are the signs of the Zodiac. The reason behind the development of the pattern is unknown, but was perhaps related to the ancient Egyptians' veneration of the cat as the earthly presence of a god. A number of other potteries also produced patterns inspired by or representing the Zodiac at the time - notably Arnold Machin's Wedgwood bull (see p145).

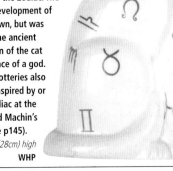

1958-67   11in (28cm) high
£100-150   **WHP**

CERAMICS

Miller's Compares

There are two different models, one facing left (no.1216) and one facing right (no.1217), which are generally worth the same.

The first versions of both models had flowers on the base - these are rarer and more valuable, but only if the flowers are not damaged.

Budgerigars are popular pets and the different variations were only produced for limited periods of time from 1951-72, so demand can be high.

Although Blue and Green are popular, Yellow was only produced from 1970-72 and is the rarest colour for any Beswick budgerigar model, hence the higher value.

LEFT: A Beswick blue gloss-glazed budgerigar, facing left, model no.1216A, first version, with flowers in high relief on base, designed by Arthur Gredington.
1967-75
£200-300
7in (18cm) high
WHP

RIGHT: A Beswick yellow gloss-glazed budgerigar facing left, model no.1216B, second version with no flowers on base, designed by Arthur Gredington.

This colour is the rarest and most valuable, as it was produced for such a short period of time.
1970-72
£800-1,200
7in (18cm) high
WHP

A Beswick turquoise and yellow gloss-glazed large cockatoo, model no.1818, designed by Albert Hallam.

The smaller version at 8.5in (21.5cm) high is model no.1180, and is usually worth around 25% less.
1962-73
£180-220
11.5in (29cm) high
WHP

A Beswick purple, green and yellow gloss-glazed Gouldian finch, with wings out, model no.1178, designed by Arthur Gredington.
1949-59
£220-280
4in (10cm) high
WHP

A Beswick blue and white gloss-glazed 'American Blue Jays' group, model no.925, designed by Arthur Gredington.
1941-65
£50-70
5in (12.5cm) high
WHP

A Beswick chestnut brown gloss-glazed 'Baltimore Orioles' group, with green claws, model no.926, designed by Arthur Gredington.

In form, colour and subject matter, these are very similar to birds produced by American company Stangl. First produced at around the same time, Stangl's birds were based on Audubon's famous 'Birds of America' publication.
1941-65
£100-150
5in (12.5cm) high
WHP

A Beswick gloss-glazed green woodpecker, model no.1218B, designed by Arthur Gredington.

Look out for the first version, produced from 1951-67, which has flowers on the base. Providing they are undamaged, a model in mint condition can fetch more than twice this.

A Beswick blue and white matt-glazed blue jay, model no.2188, designed by Albert Hallam.
1970-72   *4.5in (12cm) high*
£100-150   **WHP**

1951-67   *9in (22cm) high*
£70-100   **WHP**

A Beswick gloss-glazed bald eagle, model no.1018, designed by Arthur Gredington.
1945-95   *7.25in (18.5cm) high*
£25-35   **WHP**

A Beswick gloss-glazed pheasant on base, flying upwards, model no.849, designed by Arthur Gredington.
1940-71   *6in (15cm) high*
£70-100   **WHP**

Mark Picks

Colin Melbourne's 'CM' series of animals are unique within Beswick's production due to their stylised forms and patterns, which exemplify the Contemporary style of the 1950s. As most Beswick collectors tend to prefer animals that look realistic, the majority shunned Melbourne's style, and the range was not successful at the time.

While many Beswick collectors still feel the same today, the range does appeal to collectors of retro and mid-century design. Prices have begun to rise over the past few years after a period of being comparatively inexpensive. However bargains can still be found. The most popular models include the Bisons (no.'s 1409 and 1414), the Horse (1411) and the Lion (1419), each of which can easily fetch well over £200.

Melbourne also produced other notable designs, including 'Memphis' for Crown Devon, and values may yet rise further if there is a popular reappraisal of his work following his death in 2009.

A Beswick black, white and pink gloss-glazed Sussex cockerel, model no.1899, designed by Arthur Gredington.

Even though this is arguably the rarest and most desirable of Beswick's cockerels, apart from the Gamecock no.2059, this is a unusually high price for this model.
1963-71   *7in (18cm) high*
£800-1,000   **WHP**

A Beswick matt-glazed dove, model no.1413, series 1, designed by Colin Melbourne, from the 'CM' series.
1956-1965   *9in (23cm) high*
£120-180   **WHP**

A Beswick bronze gloss-glazed turkey, model no.1957, designed by Albert Hallam.
1964-69   *7.25in (18.5cm) high*
£500-700   **WHP**

CERAMICS

A Beswick golden brown gloss-glazed lion, facing right, model no.1506, designed by Colin Melbourne.

1957-67   *5.25in (13.5cm) high*

£25-35   **WHP**

A Beswick golden brown satin-glazed lion, without base, model no 2554B, designed by Graham Tongue.

This satin-glazed variation is usually found with a base, produced as part of the 'Connoisseur' series from 1975-84. Without the base, he is usually gloss glazed.

1987-95   *6.75in (17cm) high*

£30-50   **WHP**

A Beswick tan and black gloss-glazed tiger, model no.2096, designed by Graham Tongue.

A very rare example is known in a black satin-glaze - no pricing information is available, as none have come up for public sale.

1967-90

£70-100   **WHP**

A Beswick golden brown with black markings gloss-glazed leopard, model no.1082, designed by Arthur Gredington.

1946-75   *4.75in (12cm) high*

£50-70   **WHP**

A Beswick tawny gloss-glazed puma on rock, style 1, model no.1702, designed by Arthur Gredington.

1960-83   *8.5in (21.5cm) high*

£70-100   **WHP**

A Beswick grey and striped tan gloss-glazed elephant and tiger, model no.1720, designed by Arthur Gredington.

The elephant is the same model as model no.1770. It may be a fact of nature, but the rather gruesome subject here probably put collectors off originally, meaning this model was not popular and examples can be hard to find today.

1960-75   *12in (29.5cm) high*

£300-500   **BELL**

A Beswick dark grey with pink underneath gloss-glazed hippopotamus, model no.1532, designed by Colin Melbourne.

1958-66   *3.5in (9cm) long*

£150-200   **WHP**

A Beswick blue, yellow and green gloss-glazed golden trout, model no.1246, designed by Arthur Gredington.

The range and toning of the colours on the trout are particularly noteworthy.

1952-70 6in   (15cm) high
£100-150   **WHP**

A Beswick silver and brown gloss-glazed salmon, model no.2066, designed by Graham Tongue.

1966-75   8in (20.5cm) high
£180-220   **WHP**

A Beswick green and brown gloss-glazed perch, model no.1875, designed by Arthur Gredington.

1963-71   6.25in (16cm) long
£500-600   **WHP**

A Beswick blue, grey and green gloss-glazed marlin, model no.1243, designed by Arthur Gredington.

Beswick produced fourteen different models of fish, all of which are very well painted. Many are in dramatic poses, and all are mounted on a naturalistic base. Of all the fish, this model with its tapering protrusions is perhaps the most prone to damage. Even more than with other animals, it's essential to examine fin tips for damage, particularly as all models were discontinued around four decades ago, or longer.

1952-70   5.5in (14cm) high
£500-700   **WHP**

A Beswick black and white gloss-glazed Wessex saddleback boar, 'Fairacre Viscount', model no.1512, designed by Colin Melbourne.

1957-69   2.75in (7cm) high
£500-600   **WHP**

A Beswick black and grey gloss-glazed Berkshire boar, model no.4118, from the 'Rare Breeds' series.

c2001   2.75in (7cm) high
£40-60   **WHP**

A Beswick white gloss-glazed middle white boar, model no.4117, designed by Amanda Hughes-Lubeck, from the 'Rare Breeds' series.

2001-02   2.75in (7cm) high
£50-70   **WHP**

CERAMICS

A Beswick red-brown gloss-glazed fox, curled, model no.1017, designed by Arthur Gredington.

1945-96   1.75in (3cm) high
£35-45   WHP

A Beswick natural gloss-glazed fox, model no.2348, designed by Graham Tongue, from the 'Fireside Models' series.

1970-84   12in (31.5cm) high
£200-300   SWO

A Beswick brown gloss-glazed bear, standing, model no.1313, designed by Arthur Gredington.

1953-66   2.5in (6.5cm) high
£60-80   WHP

A Beswick grey with white face gloss-glazed Merino ram, model no.1917, designed in 1963 by Arthur Gredington.

Produced for only three years in the 1960s, this is a very rare model and is very hard to find in mint condition today. Prices rarely fall below £1,000.

1964-67   4.25in (11cm) high
£1,500-2,000   WHP

A Beswick tan gloss-glazed hare, running, model no. 1024, designed by Arthur Gredington.

1945-63   5.25in (12.5cm) high
£650-750   WHP

QUICK REFERENCE – CONDITION COUNTS

- Looking at the pieces that make up this damaged stag, it's easy to see why it sold for such a low sum. Had all the pieces of the antlers been present and carefully glued back together, it wouldnt have looked so bad displayed on a shelf - but it would still be a damaged model with an appropriately low re-sale value.
- Beswick collectors always aim to buy pieces in mint condition - any damage or restoration reduces values dramatically. This could have fetched around ten times as much as it did had it not been damaged. It's well worth noting, however, that some collectors may make an exception for the rarest and most valuable pieces, particularly if they are working on a budget. Some will feel that it's better to include a damaged and restored example in their collection than no example at all.

A Beswick golden brown satin-glazed stag, model no.2629, designed by Graham Tongue, antlers broken, some pieces present.

1978-89   13.5in (34cm) high
£8-12   WHP

QUICK REFERENCE

- Transfer-printing was developed in the mid-18thC as a cheaper and quicker alternative to hand-painting ceramics. The process involved covering an engraved copper plate with ink. The engraved design was then transferred to the ceramic body using paper, and fixed under the glaze.
- Transfer-printed wares can be distinguished from hand-painted pieces by the cross-hatching or dots created by the engraving on the copper plate. Transfer-printed patterns also lack the lines and slightly raised profile of a brushstroke applying enamel when overglazed. You may also be able to spot a join at the edge of the transfer sheet.
- The process was used by many factories and, from the 19thC onwards, pieces were mass-produced for the burgeoning middle class, and to furnish staff quarters in grand houses. Well-known names include Spode, Copeland & Garrett, and Davenport, but the makers of many pieces are not known.

- Value is primarily based on the pattern or the shape, or a combination of both. Rare and desirable shapes include baby feeders and complete tureens on stands. More common items that would have been bought in quantity, such as dinner plates, tend not be so valuable. Scarce patterns include those from Spode's 'Indian Sporting' series (see feature box) and 'The Durham Ox'. The 'Willow' pattern is perhaps the most common pattern found, and, although it is popular, values tend to be low unless the shape is rare.
- Prices have fallen over the past ten years for all but the rarest and most desirable pieces. If you like the look or want to start a collection, now if the best time to buy as pieces are affordable. The popularity of the look may return and, if it does, prices will rise. Aim to buy undamaged pieces, unless something is extremely rare and the price is right, and avoid those with brown staining, which can't be

A Staffordshire blue and white transfer-printed 'Wine Maker's' pattern 'well-and-tree' meat platter.

A 'well-and-tree' platter has troughs in the bottom, which resemble tree branches attached to a central trunk. This enabled the meat juices to drain off in the shallow well at one end.

c1820   18.5in (47cm) wide

£450-550   GORL

A Spode blue and white transfer-printed 'Antique fragments at Limisso' pattern meat platter, from the 'Caramanian' series, in medium blue, framed in S-scrolls and a border of Indian scenes including elephant and rhinoceros, the back with impressed Spode mark.

c1810   17in (43cm) wide

£600-800   ECGW

An early 19thC Staffordshire blue and white transfer-printed meat platter, decorated with a horse-drawn carriage leaving a Gothic building in a landscape.

21in (53cm) wide

£250-350   BELL

Judith Picks

Meat plates offer a lot of pattern for your pound, making a great visual impact when displayed on a dresser or wall.

The warm country cottage style should make a comeback in the future, so now is the time to buy as prices are unlikely to fall further. At around £100 each, these two attractive Staffordshire platters make a great decorative buy that is typical of the collecting area, even though the maker is unknown.

A pair of 19thC Staffordshire blue and white transfer-printed oval meat platter, showing Nuneham House in Oxfordshire within a 'Wild Rose' pattern border.

c1825-30   17.5in (44cm) wide

£150-200   GHOU

CERAMICS

An early 19thC Rogers blue and white transfer-printed 'Monopteros' pattern meat platter.

The Monopteros is the remains of an ancient building near Firoz Shah's Cotilla in Delhi. The pattern was based on Thomas Daniell's 'Oriental Scenery' aquatints. A similar version by the Swansea Pottery contains two oxen, mountains in the background and fruiting tree on the left.

21in (53cm) wide

£250-350   **GORL**

A Copeland & Garrett blue and white transfer-printed 'Hunting a Buffalo' pattern meat platter, from the 'Indian Sporting' series, the back with impressed and blue printed factory marks, and with blue printed title.

1833-47   *13in (32cm) long*

£250-350   **TOV**

A Spode blue and white transfer-printed 'Chase After A Wolf' pattern soup plate, from the 'Indian Sporting' series, with impressed and printed factory marks to reverse, with blue printed title.

c1820   *9in (24cm) diam*

£80-120   **TOV**

A Spode blue and white transfer-printed 'Death of the Bear' pattern dinner plate, from the 'Indian Sporting' series, with impressed and printed factory marks to reverse, with blue printed title.

c1820   *10in (25cm) diam*

£120-180   **TOV**

QUICK REFERENCE - THE INDIAN SPORTING SERIES

- The 'Indian Sporting' series is one of the most popular and sought-after ranges of patterns in transfer-printed ware. Produced by Spode (known as Copeland & Garrett from 1833-37) and dating from 1815-33, the designs were adapted from Thomas Williamson's book 'Oriental Field Sports, Wild Sports of the East' with drawings by Samuel Howitt, first published in 1805.
- Pattern names are usually printed on the reverse of the piece. The most commonly found pattern is the rather disturbing 'Death of the Bear', shown on this page. The most desirable pieces include meat plates in the 'Shooting at the Edge of the Jungle' pattern.
- Although values have fallen in line with the rest of the market over the past decade, the continued popularity of the series means that they are unlikely to fall further, and should rise if there is a revival of interest in the area. Look out for patterns from the series in group lots at auction, or at fairs, as they may have been overlooked. If this platter had not been cracked, it may have fetched up to double this value.

A Spode blue and white transfer-printed 'Shooting a Leopard' pattern meat platter, from the 'Indian Sporting' series, with printed and impressed marks to the reverse, cracked.

21in (52.7cm) wide

£300-500   **WW**

A Spode blue and white transfer-printed 'Common Wolf Trap' pattern dessert plate, from the 'Indian Sporting' series, with impressed and printed factory marks to reverse, with blue printed title.

c1820   *8in (21cm) diam*

£150-200   **TOV**

Mark Picks

From c1812 to1860, over 40% of Staffordshire's blue and white transfer-printed ware was exported to North America. Much was not marked with the maker's name, but may bear a pattern name. American buyers preferred a deep, inky blue, and some have heavy, almost smudgy patterns that led them to be known as 'Flow Blue'.

Look out online or at fairs or auctions for patterns with American subject matter that were specially produced for the North American market, like this, as they can fetch more in the America than in Britain or Europe. One of the most desirable ranges was Ridgway's 'Beauties of America', showing places or buildings of American historical interest. Great examples in undamaged condition can easily fetch over $1,000!

An early 19thC Wedgwood blue and white transfer-printed plate, produced for the American market to commemorate the San Fernando Rey Mission in California, with impressed mark and inscription to base, and retailer's mark for Snow and Hunt, California.

10in (25cm) diam

£25-35   ECGW

A set of twelve Don Pottery blue and white transfer-printed 'Terrace of the Naval Amphitheatre Taorminum' pattern plates, from the 'Named Italian Views' series.

The source for the scenes in this series is believed to be the 'Voyage Pittoresque ou Description des Royaumes de Naples et de Sicile' by the Abbé Jean-Claude Richard de St Non, 1781-86.

9in (23.6cm) diam

£300-500   WW

A 19thC John & Richard Riley 'Semi China' blue and white transfer-printed 'Willow' pattern dessert or fruit basket and stand, with pierced rims, the bases with printed marks.

c1827   *11in (28.5cm) wide*

£200-300   WW

An early 19thC Davenport blue and white transfer-printed ribbed oval footbath, printed with a shepherd boy playing his flute to two maidens, a river and church in the background, impressed anchor and factory mark, one handle lacking, a chip to the footrim.

21in (53cm) wide

£200-300   WW

An early 19thC Staffordshire blue and white transfer-printed jug, printed with a pastoral scene including a cottage, a river, a bridge, cows, two countrymen and two actors on a stone plinth, the top with a floral band inside and out.

6.75in (17cm) high

£60-80   ECGW

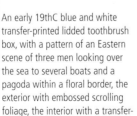

An early 19thC blue and white transfer-printed lidded toothbrush box, with a pattern of an Eastern scene of three men looking over the sea to several boats and a pagoda within a floral border, the exterior with embossed scrolling foliage, the interior with a transfer-printed pagoda design.

7.75in (20cm) high

£120-180   ECGW

An early 19thC Spode blue and white transfer-printed 'Tower' pattern feeding bottle, marked 'Spode' to the base.

Infant or baby feeders are comparatively scarce and can fetch high prices. Be sure to check the area around the hole and the stem and mouthpiece for damage or restoration. The 'Tower' pattern was made initially for export.

6.75in (17cm)

£200-300   WW

CERAMICS

QUICK REFERENCE

- Over the past four or five years prices for Chinese ceramics have risen dramatically, with millions of pounds being paid for rare, early, and important pieces, particularly those with an Imperial connection. China's rising 'cash rich' businessmen are competing over the best pieces, and it's this that is driving prices up. Motivation includes the Chinese buying back their own heritage, politics, fashion, and investment.

- Despite this, much export ware produced from the late 16thC to the 19thC is still comparatively affordable. Much of it was mass-produced, it's arguably less historically important, and competition is currently less fierce. However, as the merely rich ape the actions of the super-rich, this is starting to change in certain areas. This is certainly a market to watch.

- Chinese export porcelain includes blue-and-white, blanc-de-chine, armorial ware, and polychrome wares in the famille verte, famille rose, and other palettes. Of these, blue-and-white (white porcelain hand-painted with blue under the glaze) is most commonly found. Vases, bowls, dishes and chargers were all decorated in this style, typically with natural motifs, such as flowers, landscapes, figures, and fish. Many blue-and-white pieces have been discovered in the past few decades in the cargoes of shipwrecked vessels. Such is the range of pieces on offer that small 16thC blue-and-white ceramics can be found for as little as £50!

- Look out for decoration that is sympathetically and well applied, with a good level of detail. View museum collections and examples being sold at auction or in dealer's shops to enable you to spot fine quality pieces.

- Marks can help with identification, but remember that many early marks were applied to later pieces out of respect for, and in veneration of, ancestors. Consult a specialist guide for more information.

An 18thC Chinese famille rose bowl, delicately painted with butterflies and small insects, vases of flowers and scattered sprays, together with a carved hardwood stand.

5.5in (14cm) high

£100-150   WW

A 19thC Chinese Daoguang period famille rose bowl, painted with ladies at court, the base with a six character iron red Daoguang mark (1821-50).

7in (17.5cm) diam

£600-800   WW

One of a pair of Chinese, possibly Jiaqing period, famille rose bowls, brightly enamelled with phoenix and dragons amid flowering peony, the base of each with a six character iron red Jiaqing mark (1796-1820).

5.5in (13.5cm) diam

£450-550 pair   WW

An 18thC Chinese famille rose tea bowl and saucer, decorated with two dogs playing amid flowers and foliage, the base with Yongzheng period mark (1722-36), some enamel flaked.

4in (10.5cm) diam

£200-300   WW

A late 19thC Chinese Canton famille rose bottle vase, painted with panels of figures.

13in (33cm) high

£400-500   **WW**

A 19thC Chinese Canton famille rose bottle vase, painted with panels of figures, birds and flowers.

13in (33.5cm) high

£200-300   **WW**

A CLOSER LOOK AT A PAIR OF CHINESE EXPORT VASES

Whilst these vases look highly complex and very detailed, look closely and you'll see that they're not. The scene is typical, faces don't have expressions and the decoration was rapidly applied with little finesse, particularly on the handles.

It's good that they are a pair, and they are very decorative, but the shapes are a little clumpy, and this look is currently out of fashion.

The traditional celadon-coloured background is murky, and the other colours are brash. The effect is far from harmonious.

They have been damaged and restored, which affects value seriously, particularly for mass-produced pieces of indifferent quality.

A 19thC pair of Chinese Canton celadon ground large vases, brightly painted with panels of figures, birds, butterflies and flowers, both with restoration.

The pointers shown here give some of the reasons why these antique Chinese vases did not fetch the large sums of money that some Chinese pieces have fetched over the past few years. Late 19thC export pieces such as this were produced in vast quantities for a hungry, and rapidly expanding, market in the West. The Chinese ceramics that have fetched millions of pounds recently typically had an Imperial connection, were much earlier in date, and were of considerably higher quality. They are different things altogether.

24in (62cm) high

£500-700   **WW**

A 19thC Chinese rose medallion vase, of short baluster form with a flared mouth, enamelled in the famille rose palette with alternating panels of men in a pagoda setting or birds and flowers, within stylised foliate borders.

13.25in (34cm) high

£220-280   **FRE**

A late 19thC Chinese rose medallion punch bowl, enamelled in a typical famille rose palette with scenes of ladies in pagoda and garden settings, within a floral and foliate border including birds.

The term 'rose medallion' is more common in America, where it is applied to famille rose pieces that have been very richly decorated.

16in (41cm) diam

£400-500   **FRE**

A late 19thC Chinese Canton hexagonal section garden seat, the top and two side panels pierced with cash coin motifs, and moulded to imitate riveting, decorated with two main panels depicting numerous elegant ladies in a pavilion, against a dense foliate ground.

These large porcelain seats have become popular recently, particularly if well decorated.

18in (46.5cm) high

£600-800   **TEN**

CERAMICS

Judith Picks

Over the past 12 to 18 months, great quality early 20thC porcelains have been rising rapidly in value. As with this example, the best have a delicacy and attention to detail the majority of late 19thC mass-produced export wares do not have. Marks to look for include the Guangxu, (1875-1908), Xuantong (1909-11) and particularly some of the Republic period pieces with the Hongxian (Yuan Shikei) mark (1915-16). To demonstrate the recent price rises – which have taken place on the coat-tails of the even steeper rises very wealthy Chinese collectors have been paying for Imperial and other fine quality 14thC to 18thC wares – a similar example to this one sold at auction in 2007 for $1,400 (£900).

An early 20thC Chinese Republic period famille rose bottle vase, of globular form, a long slender neck leading to a body finely painted to show five boys playing in a garden, above a well-carved wood stand, Qianlong iron red four character mark.

c1915   *6.5in (16.5cm) high*

£3,000-5,000   **PC**

A 20thC Chinese ginger jar, decorated with bucolic lakeside scene and a poem, the decoration worn.

13.5in (34cm) high

£60-80   **DRA**

A large mid-late 20thC Chinese famille rose vase, painted with small figures in a mountainous landscape, with a house beneath, and with calligraphy to the reverse, marked 'Jing de zhen zhi', together with a carved wood stand.

The city of Jingdezhen is known as the 'capital of porcelain'. Its various factories have produced vast amounts of porcelains for over 1,700 years. Although one of the kilns there produced the 14thC Yuan vase that sold for over £15m in 2005, others also produced this vase, and many thousands like it that are still available today.

20in (50.5cm) high

£250-300   **WW**

A 20thC Republic period jardinière with underplate, with Greek key border and panels of figures in garden settings, the base with four character Qianlong mark.

1915-16   *8.25in (21cm) diam*

£1,000-1,500   **LHA**

A late 20thC Chinese famille rose dish, decorated with three figures at a table in a garden beneath a pine tree, the base with six character Yongzheng period mark (1723-35).

8in (20.9cm) diam

£100-150   **WW**

A 20thC Chinese bowl, decorated in colours and gilt with interlaced floral bands and floral sprays, within blue and gilt borders.

9.5in (24.2cm) diam

£50-80   **CAPE**

A CLOSER LOOK AT A FAKE ANTIQUE CHINESE VASE

The glaze inside the footrim does not have the pin-prick pits in it that one would expect from an early vase. It is too uniform and smooth. The wide round arch shape of the foot rim is also incorrect for the intended period.

If correct, this bottle vase shape would have been made in two or three separate pieces, which were then joined together. This, however, is one piece, and was probably slip-moulded.

The piece bears an early 15thC Xuande period mark, that was also used during the Kangxi period and later. However, the mark is too stiff and formal to have been painted by a true artist calligrapher during either period.

Mud has been applied to make it look as if this vase has been buried, thus giving the impression of age.

The cobalt blue glaze has been applied in too controlled a manner. One would expect to see some much darker areas of thickly applied glaze. This is known as a 'heaped and piled' effect.

A Chinese handpainted blue and white vase, decorated with lotus flowers and vines, the base with blue painted Xuande period mark (1426-35).

Mark bought this vase as a fake from the famous Panjiayuan flea market in Beijing in 2009 for the equivalent of £12.

7.25in (18.5cm) high

£30-40   PC

A 19thC Chinese blue and white vase, painted with a continuous lotus scroll beneath a band of ruyi heads.

14in (35cm) high

£400-600   WW

An 18thC Chinese blue and white compressed baluster vase, decorated in the Ming style, with a flower and leaf scroll above a band of false gadroons, the neck with lappets containing stylised flowers beneath short upright stiff leaves, the base with a Tianqi mark, restoration to the neck and chip to the foot.

8in (21.5cm) wide

£600-800   WW

A 19thC Chinese blue and white baluster-shaped vase, painted with small figures, pagodas and water buffalo in a mountainous river landscape.

19in (48cm) high

£700-1,000   WW

A pair of 18thC Chinese blue and white rectangular dishes, with chamfered corners, each decorated with a figure in a boat amid flowering plants.

11in (27cm) wide

£250-350   WW

A possibly 19thC Chinese blue and white bowl, painted with scaly dragons in pursuit of flaming pearls of wisdom, the interior painted with a leaping carp, the base with a six character Kangxi mark.

4.9in (12.5cm) diam

£350-450   WW

CERAMICS

QUICK REFERENCE - CHINTZWARE

- The late 19thC saw a boom in ceramics decorated with dense transfer-printed floral patterns, inspired by paisley shawls imported from India. Grimwade Brothers were the most prolific manufacturer under their 'Royal Winton' brand.
- Chintzware saw two peaks of popularity, from the 1920s-30s, and again in the 1950s. The best way of dating a piece to either period is by looking at the style of the mark (see below). The mark on the left was used from the 1920s-30s, and the mark on the right was used in the 1950s. A printed word near this mark indicates the pattern name, but not all pieces are marked with this and so you should be careful if attempting to build a set. Some patterns are very similar and it's easy to buy a different pattern by mistake.

- Value depends on the type of item, followed by the condition and the pattern. Prices for chintzware peaked during the 1990s, driven by collectors in the US. Prices then fell, but have started to climb again as chintz teawares have become popular with those who love the vintage look.

A 1920s-30s Royal Winton mark, with 'Summertime' pattern name.

A 1950s Royal Winton mark, with 'Somerset' pattern name.

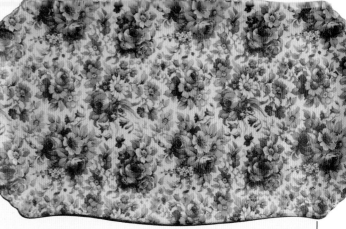

A 1920s-30s Grimwades Royal Winton 'Summertime' pattern chintz sandwich tray.

12in (30.5cm) long

£70-100   **BAD**

A 1940s-50s Grimwades Royal Winton 'Summertime' pattern chintz plate.

8in (20.5cm) wide

£40-50   **BAD**

A 1950s Grimwades Royal Winton 'Evesham' pattern chintz bowl, the back with printed factory mark, and Canadian, Australian, and New Zealand patent numbers.

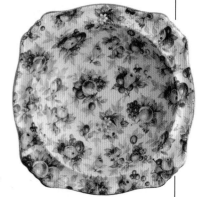

6.5in (16.5cm) wide

£20-30   **BAD**

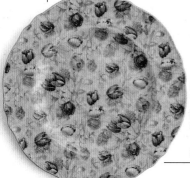

A Grimwades Royal Winton 'Stratford' pattern chintz plate, with gilt rim, printed factory mark, and Canadian registered marks.

6.75in (17cm) diam

£40-50   **BAD**

A 1950s Grimwades Royal Winton 'Julia' pattern chintz oval dish, the back printed with factory and Canadian registered marks.

6in (15cm) wide

£55-65   **BAD**

A 1950s Grimwades Royal Winton 'Kew' pattern chintz trio set, the back with printed factory mark.

Plate 6.75in (17cm) diam

£65-75 BAD

A 1930s Grimwades Royal Winton 'Chintz' pattern chintz salt and pepper set, on tray, the tray restored.

6in (15.5cm) wide

£35-45 W&L

A Grimwades Royal Winton 'Sweet Pea' pattern teapot, with gilt rims, the base unmarked.

Teapots are desirable, valuable, and much scarcer than plates as a family would have owned only one chintz teapot, but many plates. Both the handle and spout are covered with the pattern on this example, which is an additional desirable feature.

8in (20.5cm) high

£300-400 BAD

QUICK REFERENCE - AN ORIGINAL CAKE STAND OR NOT?

- **The rise in popularity of 'vintage' or 'retro' themed tea parties, and the many accoutrements that go along with them, has led to a revival in the popularity of cake stands. To take advantage of this, enterprising dealers have been converting plates into stands by drilling holes and fitting metal parts. To see if a stand is original or not, carefully unscrew the metal parts and look inside the hole. If the glaze runs inside the hole as on this example, then it's original. If it doesn't, and you can see the unglazed matte ceramic, then it's a modern conversion.**

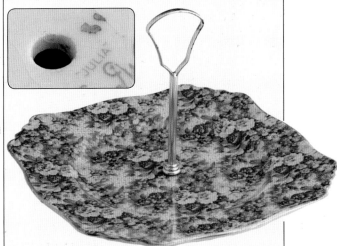

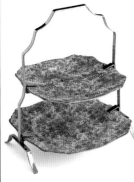

A 1930s Paragon 'Springtime' chintz butter dish and jam pot, with chrome stand and toast rack.

Grimwades are the main maker of chintzware, but other makers include Paragon, James Kent, and Crown Ducal.

5in (13cm) high

£50-80 BAD

A 1920s-30s Royal Winton 'Somerset' pattern double cake stand, with chrome-plated mounts.

8.75in (22.5cm) high

£50-70 BAD

A 1940s-50s Grimwades Royal Winton 'Julia' pattern chintz cakestand, with chrome-plated handle.

9in (23cm) diam

£55-65 BAD

CERAMICS

QUICK REFERENCE

- Clarice Cliff was born in Tunstall, Stoke-on-Trent in 1899. She started her career at Linguard Webster & Co., moving to the larger firm of A. J. Wilkinson in 1916. She was soon spotted as an emerging talent and, in 1925, owner Colley Shorter gave her her own studio in the recently acquired Newport Pottery. There she began to decorate a large number of defective blank wares with thickly applied, striking patterns in vibrant colours that disguised any damage.

- Her first range was given the name 'Bizarre', and was launched in 1928. Cliff developed a series of patterns, and trained a dedicated team of female decorators (the 'Bizarre Girls') to paint them. Pieces were produced under the 'Bizarre' heading until 1935, with numerous pattern names under the general title. The name 'Fantasque' was also used as a general title from 1928 to 1934. The dates in the captions refer to the period the pattern was produced.

- Consider the shape and size of the piece, the pattern, and the colours used when determining value. Pieces that display the pattern well, such as chargers, vases, jugs, and plates, are likely to be desirable. Geometric and stylised Art Deco shapes or patterns are particularly popular with collectors, especially when combined.

- Some patterns were produced in a range of colourways, some of which are rarer than others. Orange is a relatively common colour, while blue and purple are often rarer. Muted colours and later, less-stylised floral ranges made after the prime 1928-c1934 period tend to be the least desirable.

- Damage or wear will reduce the desirability and value, so watch out for cracks and chips. Always look at the mark, and check that it is underneath the glaze. Beware, as fakes do exist. Handle as many authentic pieces as you can, so you can learn to tell the difference.

A Clarice Cliff 'Original Bizarre' beaker, painted with blue and green triangles, between orange and blue bands, the base with printed factory marks.

3.75in (9.5cm) high

£250-350   WW

A Clarice Cliff 'Original Bizarre' stepped fern pot, shape no.368, the base with printed factory mark.

3.5in (9cm) high

£200-300   WW

A large Clarice Cliff 'Original Bizarre' beaker, painted with a broad band of yellow and red diamonds flanked by blue, black, and green triangles, between yellow and red bands, the base with printed factory mark, the yellow band overpainted.

The 'Original Bizarre' range of 1928-30 included a number of geometric patterns that don't have individual names. Although this range built Cliff's success, colours are brasher and the painting is slightly cruder than on later geometric ranges.

4.75in (12cm) high

£250-350   WW

A Clarice Cliff 'Original Bizarre' globe-shape tea cup, saucer, and side plate set, painted in shades of orange and purple, the bases with printed factory marks.

Side plate 7in (17.5cm) diam

£220-280   WW

A Clarice Cliff 'Diamonds' pattern rose bowl, shape no.234, decorated with repeat abstract panels in black, blue, orange, and yellow within conforming banding, the base with printed 'Bizarre' mark with Newport Pottery crest.

1929-30   *5in (11.5cm) high*

£700-1,000   FLD

A Clarice Cliff Bizarre 'Killarney' pattern daffodil vase, shape no.450, the base with printed factory marks, with restored handles.

Introduced in 1935, and derived from the 'Original Bizarre' range, 'Killarney' was not popular, and was withdrawn after a short period of time. It's not too popular today either, perhaps as the muted green and brown colouring and angular form doesn't appeal to collectors as much as vibrant oranges and reds, or landscape patterns.

1935   *13in (33.5cm) diam*
£250-350   **WW**

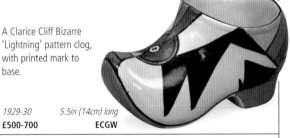

A Clarice Cliff Bizarre 'Killarney' pattern bowl, shape no.636, the base with printed factory marks.

1935   *8in (20cm) diam*
£150-250   **WW**

A CLOSER LOOK AT A CLARICE CLIFF JUG

The 'Sunspots' pattern is extremely rare. Fewer than 20 examples are known, all in red, yellow, green, and black.

At the height of the market with wealthy collectors competing to own the best pieces, a shape no.358 vase in the same pattern fetched £20,000 at auction in 2006.

It shows the influence of Cubist art, Egyptian and Aztec motifs, and even paintings by Wassily Kandinsky.

The name is not original. It was applied by the Clarice Cliff Collectors' Club in the 1990s.

The angular Art Deco conical shape echoes the geometric lines of the pattern perfectly. As well as being a popular shape with collectors, this combination of geometric shape and pattern is highly sought-after.

A rare Clarice Cliff Bizarre 'Sunspots' pattern conical jug, the base with printed marks.

c1930   *6in (15cm) high*
£3,000-5,000   **GHOU**

A 1930s Clarice Cliff Bizarre 'Liberty Band' stepped jardinière, shape no.416, painted with bands, the base with printed mark.

'Liberty Band' was introduced because it was both quick and easy to paint. As a result, larger orders could be bulked up easily. The Bizarre girl decorators had the 'liberty' to chose the colours used, and many of the bands are thickly painted.

3.5in (9cm) high
£180-220   **WW**

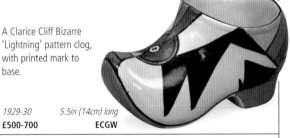

A Clarice Cliff Bizarre 'Lightning' pattern clog, with printed mark to base.

1929-30   *5.5in (14cm) long*
£500-700   **ECGW**

A Clarice Cliff Bizarre 'Swirls' pattern drum-shape preserve pot and cover, with a possibly replaced yellow, orange, and black banded cover, the base with printed 'Bizarre' mark, the base with a small chip.

c1930   *3in (8cm) high*
£150-200   **FLD**

CERAMICS

QUICK REFERENCE - CHINTZ PATTERN

- The 'Chintz' pattern depicts stylised water lily buds, leaves and flowers, and was produced in 'Orange' (comprising orange, black, tan, and red) and 'Blue' (comprising blue, green, and pink) colourways. 'Green Chintz' is also known, but is extremely rare.

- The flat pattern, which covers nearly all of the surface, is reminiscent of a fabric design, and it is known that Cliff used French Art Deco pattern books, many of them intended for fabrics, as inspiration at the time. 'Chintz' was introduced in 1932 and produced until 1933, and then again in random subsequent years during the 1930s.

A Clarice Cliff Fantasque Bizarre 'Blue Chintz' pattern Stamford-shape part tea set for two, comprising a teapot and cover, milk jug, sugar basin, and two cups, the bases with printed marks, with small chips to teapot cover and milk jug.

The strongly Art Deco Stamford-shape of this set is popular, and contrasts with the organic curving lines of the pattern.

Teapot 5in (12.5cm) high

£800-1,200

WW

A 1930s Clarice Cliff Bizarre 'Autumn Crocus' pattern meiping vase, shape no.14, painted in colours between yellow, brown and green bands, the base with printed factory marks.

As its name suggests, this form was inspired by ancient Oriental ceramics. It's a popular and comparatively scarce shape, hence the high value for this piece, which is in Cliff's most prolifically produced and best-selling pattern.

6.25in (16cm) high

£650-750   WW

A Clarice Cliff Bizarre 'Blue Chintz' pattern conical pepper pot, with stylised flowers and foliage in tonal green and blue with pink, the colours lightly oxidised.

c1932   *3in (8cm) high*

£70-100   FLD

A 1930s Clarice Cliff Bizarre 'Autumn Crocus' pattern conical sugar sifter, painted in colours between yellow and brown bands, the base with printed marks.

5.5in (14cm) high

£350-450   WW

A Clarice Cliff Bizarre 'Blue Chintz' pattern conical biscuit barrel, shape no.478, with a chrome cover and swing handle, the base with printed Bizarre mark.

c1932   *6in (15cm) high*

£200-300   FLD

A Clarice Cliff Bizarre 'Blue Crocus' pattern 'Bonjour'-shape biscuit barrel and cover, painted in colours, the base with printed factory marks, and with a restored cover.

c1934   *6in (15cm) high*

£300-500   WW

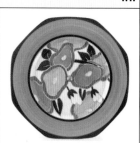

A Clarice Cliff Fantasque Bizarre 'Orange Chintz' pattern tazza, with electroplated low foot, painted in colours, the base with printed factory mark.

7.5in (22cm) diam

£80-120   WW

A Clarice Cliff Bizarre 'Hydrangea' pattern coffee set, comprising a 'Bonjour'-shape coffee pot and cover, four cups and saucers, a sugar basin, and a milk jug, the bases with printed marks.

1933
£400-600

7in (18cm) high
WHP

A Clarice Cliff Bizarre 'Latona Bouquet' pattern 'Dover'-shape jardinière, with an experimental granular glaze.

1929-31   *6.75in (17cm) high*
£250-350   **GHOU**

A Clarice Cliff Bizarre 'Petunia' pattern cup and saucer, with a band of stylised flowers and foliage over a stipple yellow and brown ground, the base with hand-painted 'Petunia' and 'Bizarre' mark.

Sharp-eyed gardeners will notice that these are not petunia flowers. The pattern is, in fact, a different colourway of 'Canterbury Bells', and the flowers aren't meant to resemble any particular flower.

c1933
£100-150   **FLD**

A Clarice Cliff Bizarre 'Rhodanthe' pattern drum-shape preserve pot and cover, with a stylised stemmed floral pattern in tonal brown and orange, the base with printed 'Bizarre' mark, with restored rim chip, light staining, and faint star crack.

1934-35   *3in (8cm) high*
£80-120   **FLD**

A Clarice Cliff Bizarre 'Solomon's Seal' pattern 'Athens'-shape cup and saucer, decorated with a hand-painted and enamelled lithograph of stylised bell flowers with green, pink, and blue banding, the base with printed script signature mark.

Introduced in 1930, this pattern was part of an early experiment to see if Cliff's designs could be applied less expensively by using a transfer outline, filled in with colour by hand. Although it wasn't very successful, perhaps because the outline gave the pattern too much regularity, it was produced for a number of years as this example shows.

c1947
£50-80   **FLD**

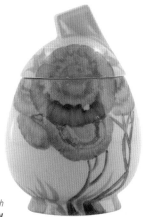

A Clarice Cliff Bizarre 'Daffodil'-shape 'Aurea' pattern preserve pot and cover, painted in colours the base with printed factory marks, with small chips to rim of cover.

'Aurea' is the blue and green colour variation of 'Rhodanthe', also shown on this page. See p.49 of 'Miller's Collectables Handbook 2010-2011' for more information.

5.3in (13.5cm) high
£180-220   **WW**

A Clarice Cliff 'My Garden' range 'Night' vase, shape no. 669, with three relief-moulded hollyhock legs in blue and purple against a black sprayed body, the base with printed 'Bizarre' mark.

Introduced in 1934, the 'My Garden' range has a variety of moulded floral parts such as handles, feet, or knobs. Plain body colours are used for the black 'Night', the pale blue 'Azure', the red 'Flame', the beige 'Mushroom', the yellow 'Sunrise', the green 'Verdant', and 'Pink'. The range sold extremely well at the time, and was produced until the start of World War II. 'My Garden' pieces don't seem to appeal to collectors today, and prices remain comparatively low, with supply being high.

5.5in (14cm) high
£80-120   **FLD**

QUICK REFERENCE - THE MELON PATTERN

- The 'Melon' pattern was introduced in 1930, and combines the curves of fruit with linear geometric lines. Lines are also used to mark out the shape or contours of the fruit, rather than just for the outline.
- The most common colourway has broad orange bands, or feet and rims, but it can also be found with red, blue, or green borders. Pastel tones, which are typically blues and greens, are also known.
- It is not too hard to find on today's market, and vibrant colour combinations tend to be the most sought-after and valuable. The pattern is also sometimes called 'Picasso Fruit' after its similarity to Cubist paintings by the artist.

A Clarice Cliff Fantasque Bizarre 'Melon' pattern crown-shape jug, painted in colours, the base with printed factory marks, damaged.

Although jugs in this form are less popular than vases or 'Lotus' jugs, the price of this example could have nearly doubled if it had been in excellent, undamaged condition.

1930-32   *7in (18cm) wide*

£120-180   **WW**

A Clarice Cliff Fantasque Bizarre 'Melons' pattern jardinière, painted in coloured enamels, the base with printed factory marks, some flaking to the orange rim.

1930-32   *8in (20cm) high*

£300-500   **L&T**

A Clarice Cliff Fantasque Bizarre 'Melon' pattern ashtray, painted in colours inside an orange rim, the base with printed factory mark.

1930-32   *4.25in (11cm) diam*

£150-200   **WW**

A large Clarice Cliff Fantasque Bizarre 'Pastel Melon' pattern circular fruit bowl, with abstract geometric fruit with blue, pink, and green banding, the base with printed 'Fantasque' and 'Bizarre' mark.

1930-32 8in (21cm) diam

£200-300   **FLD**

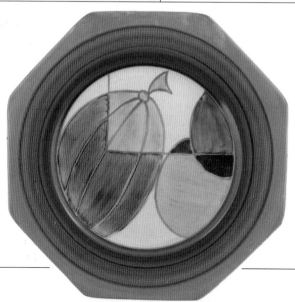

A Clarice Cliff Fantasque Bizarre 'Pastel Melon' pattern plate, painted in colours inside green, pink, and blue bands, the base with printed factory mark.

1930-32   *7.5in (19cm) high*

£200-300   **WW**

A Clarice Cliff Fantasque Bizarre 'Red Melon' pattern circular plate, the base with printed marks.

1930-32   *10in (25cm) diam*

£300-500   **GHOU**

A Clarice Cliff Fantasque Bizarre 'Berries' pattern teacup and saucer, painted in colours, the base with printed marks.

1930-31   3.3in (8.5cm) high

£200-300   WW

A Clarice Cliff Fantasque Bizarre 'Berries' pattern beaker, painted in colours, the base with printed factory mark.

1930-31   3.75in (9.5cm) high

£400-600   WW

A CLOSER LOOK AT A 'DELECIA CITRUS' BOOKEND

The distinctive dripped 'Delecia' decoration is made by applying turpentine to the glaze to thin it and then loosely painted onto the body, resulting in drips.

The combination with 'Citrus' was introduced in 1932. Look out for the rarest colour variation with silver and gold lustre fruits.

A Clarice Cliff Fantasque Bizarre 'Berries' pattern conical sugar sifter, painted in coloured enamels, the base with printed factory marks.

5.5in (14cm) high

£500-700   L&T

Introduced in 1930, and made for nearly two years, 'Delecia' was combined with a number of different patterns, and every piece is unique.

Bookends are not common, but not terribly desirable either. They were also usually damaged through use, so chips are common.

A Clarice Cliff Bizarre 'Delecia Citrus' pattern bookend, painted in colours, the base with printed factory marks, minor chips.

1932   7.5in (16cm) high

£70-100   WW

A Clarice Cliff Bizarre 'Oranges' pattern side plate, painted in colours inside an orange band, the base with printed factory mark.

1931   6in (15cm) diam

£120-180   WW

A Clarice Cliff Bizarre 'Oranges' pattern conical milk-jug, painted in colours, the base with printed factory mark.

1931   2.5in (6.5cm) high

£300-500   WW

QUICK REFERENCE - CLARICE CLIFF'S APPLIQUÉ

- Clarice Cliff's 'Appliqué' patterns were produced from 1930 until just after 1933, and were among the most labour-intensive patterns sold by the company. Requiring skill and careful attention, patterns were painted on with no outlines and covered all of the body with colour. Only a few later examples had areas of no pattern that displayed some of the honey-coloured glaze. Banding came in three variations: black, red, and black; black and honeyglaze; and black, red, black, and yellow.

- Although they form the bulk of the 'range' and tend to be the most popular, not all 'Appliqué' patterns are landscapes. Other motifs include flowers ('Appliqué Blossom'), and a bird ('Appliqué Bird of Paradise'). Some patterns are extremely rare, and only one or two examples are known, with these probably being samples.

- Priced highly at the time, 'Appliqué' pieces are still among the most valuable patterns today. This vase (both sides shown) is typical of the range, with its vibrant colours and great visual impact.

A Clarice Cliff 'Appliqué Garden' pattern bowl, painted in colours with black outlines, with Bizarre mark and facsimile signature.
c1930   *8in (21.5cm) diam*
£1,200-1,800   **L&T**

A Clarice Cliff Bizarre 365 'Appliqué Avignon' vase, painted in colours inside red and black bands, with printed and painted marks.
1930   8in (21cm) high
£2,500-3,500   WW

A small Clarice Cliff 'Autumn' pattern baluster vase, painted in coloured enamels on a green 'café au lait' ground, printed factory marks.
9in (22cm) high
£600-900   L&T

A Clarice Cliff Bizarre 'Autumn' plate, painted in colours inside orange and black bands, the base with printed factory mark.
1932   9in (23cm) diam
£350-450   WW

A rare Clarice Cliff Fantasque Bizarre 'House and Bridge' pattern conical sugar sifter, the pattern between orange bands, the base with printed mark, and a flat chip to base rim.

Although produced for three years, this pattern was sold in quite small quantities compared to 'Secrets' (see opposite page), making it hard to find today.

A Clarice Cliff 'Forest Glen' pattern conical sugar sifter, with a stylised cottage landscape below a 'Delecia'-style streaked sky in tonal brown, grey, and red, the base with large script mark, with a small chip to the foot.
c1936   6in (14cm) high
£500-700   FLD

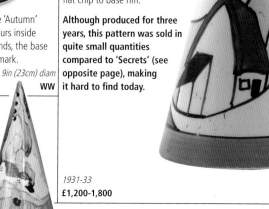

1931-33   5in (14.5cm) high
£1,200-1,800   WW

A Clarice Cliff Bizarre 'Orange Roof Cottage' pattern square stepped vase, shape no.461, painted with a landscape scene, the base with printed marks.

1932   *7.5in (19cm) high*
£1,200-1,800   **GHOU**

A Clarice Cliff Fantasque Bizarre 'Orange Roof Cottage' pattern 'Lotus' jug, painted in colours with two images between orange, yellow, and black bands, the base with printed mark.

'Lotus' jugs are a very popular, and much copied, form. Fakes are known, many in late 1920s 'Original Bizarre' patterns. The quickest and easiest way to tell if you're looking at a fake is to inspect the underside of the top of the handle. If there's a small air hole in the handle, it's a fake. For more information, see p.55 of 'Miller's Collectables Price Guide 2009'.

1932   *12in (30cm) high*
£1,500-2,000   **WW**

A Clarice Cliff Fantasque 'Orange Roof Cottage' pattern 'Stamford'-shape sugar basin, painted in colours, the base with printed factory mark.

1932   *2.6in (6.5cm) high*
£200-300   **WW**

A Clarice Cliff Fantasque Bizarre 'Orange Trees and House' pattern plate, painted in colours inside orange and black bands, the base with printed factory marks, worn.

                    8in (21.5cm) diam
£250-350   **WW**

QUICK REFERENCE - THE 'SECRETS' PATTERN

- **The charmingly pastoral 'Secrets' pattern was introduced in 1933 and sold for a number of years. Towards the end of its lifetime, it was simplified and became a 'shoulder' pattern painted onto bodies with large undecorated areas. It was one of Cliff's best-selling landscape patterns, and examples are not too challenging to find today. This vase shape is highly desirable, which raises the value of this piece. Look out for the only known colour variation, in brown, orange, and purple, as this is much rarer.**

A Clarice Cliff 'Poplar' pattern jardinière, painted in coloured enamels, the base with printed factory marks.

This pattern takes its name from the two orange and blue poplar trees in the foreground, which can only just be seen on the left hand side of this jardinière.

1932   *8in (20cm) high*
£300-400   **L&T**

A large Clarice Cliff Fantasque Bizarre 'Red Roofs' pattern beaker, painted in colours, the base with printed factory marks.

1931   *4.5in (11.5cm) high*
£600-800   **WW**

A Clarice Cliff Fantasque Bizarre 'Secrets' pattern vase, pattern no.6070, shape no.358, painted in colours below yellow and green bands, the base with printed factory mark.

                    8in (20.5cm) high
£1,000-1,500   **WW**

CERAMICS

QUICK REFERENCE - COBRIDGE POTTERY

- Cobridge Stoneware was founded in 1998 by Hugh Edwards, the owner of Moorcroft. He wanted to revive the research into complex glazes undertaken during the early 20thC by William Howson Taylor at the Ruskin Pottery, even though Taylor had taken the secrets of his complex glazes with him to his death.
- The company released a wide range of mottled, textured and high-fired glazes that would have probably made Taylor proud. Many were inspired by, and similar to, Oriental examples, just as Taylor's glazes had been at Ruskin. It also released a number of pictorial designs of natural or animal themes, some designed by notable names such as Anita Harris and Philip Gibson, both of whom also worked for Moorcroft. Many of these are similar to designs produced by Moorcroft and Sally Tuffin.
- The company's vases and bowls were widely acclaimed, and of very high quality. However, sales were not large enough to support it, and the company closed in 2005. Interest from collectors has begun to grow over the past few years, particularly for the more exotic glazes on large shapes, pictorial designs, and limited editions. Marks can be used to date a piece - the company used an apple for the first year of production, a boot for the second, and a crown for the third.

A Cobridge Stoneware shouldered baluster vase, decorated in a mottled red high-fired glaze, the base with impressed factory marks.

10in (26cm) high

£120-180   FLD

A Cobridge Stoneware tapered vase with a flared rim, with a streaked red flambé high-fired glaze over a grey ground, the base with impressed marks.

9in (22.5cm) high

£40-60   FLD

A Cobridge Stoneware elephant's-foot-shaped vase, with a high-fired tonal red flambé spotted glaze over a grey ground, with blue glazed interior, the base with impressed marks.

6.25in (16cm) high

£50-80   FLD

A Cobridge Stoneware onion-shaped vase, with a high-fired mottled and spotted tonal red flambé glaze over a buff coloured ground, the base with impressed marks.

3.75in (9.5cm) high

£30-50   FLD

A pair of Cobridge Stoneware baluster-shaped vases, decorated with stylised river plants on a graduated blue-grey ground.

£100-150   WHP

A Cobridge Stoneware limited edition 'Frog and Crown' vase, numbered 13 from an edition of 100, with impressed factory and Collector's Club marks to base, with card box.

5.5in (14cm) high

£120-180   FLD

A Cobridge Stoneware limited edition vase, designed by Philip Gibson, decorated with three mallards, numbered 8 from a limited edition 100, and signed by the artist, complete with box.

6.25in (16cm) high

£100-150   GORL

QUICK REFERENCE

- Susie Cooper (1902-1995) was one of Britain's most successful ceramic designers of the 20thC. In 1922, after studying at the Burslem School of Art, Cooper went to work for A.E. Gray and Co. as a decorator. She rose swiftly to the position of resident designer, and created a wide variety of patterns. These included stylised floral forms and jazzy, geometric Art Deco designs. Be aware that not all geometric patterns produced by Gray's were designed by Cooper. For more information see p.159.
- Cooper left Gray's in 1929 to found her own pottery, ending up at the Crown Works at Woods & Sons. She initially purchased standard shapes to decorate but, from 1932, she began designing her own forms. This was an important turning point as many of Cooper's designs rely on the unity between shape and pattern. 'Kestrel' and 'Falcon' (introduced in 1932 and 1937 respectively) are amongst her most sought-after shapes.
- Patterns were primarily inspired by the natural world, Art Deco textile designs, and modern art. Initially patterns were painted by hand, but from 1935 transfer-printed ranges were introduced, many of which are very affordable today.
- Production was discontinued during the war, and was slow to re-start as many lithographs had been damaged. Colours became more subdued, but her designs proved to be just as popular after the war as before. Today, post-war pieces are typically not as valuable as pre-war examples.
- The Susie Cooper Pottery began producing bone china in 1950, and in 1966 the pottery was acquired by the Wedgwood group. Cooper remained as a director and designer until 1972, when she resigned. The Crown Works were closed in late 1979, and she worked as a freelance designer until her death.
- Prices have fallen slightly over the past few years, but should pick up again when new collectors come to the market.

A Susie Cooper Productions biscuit barrel and cover, pattern no.E110, painted with a geometric design in yellow, 'mushroom', and black, the base with printed triangular 'Susie Cooper Productions' mark.

The unusual triangular mark was used c1930-32.

c1930 5.5in (14cm) high

£250-350 WW

A Gray's Pottery side plate, pattern no.8078 designed by Susie Cooper, painted with a geometric design in yellow, red, and black, the base with rectangular ocean liner printed mark.

c1928 5in (13cm) wide

£100-150 WW

A Gray's Pottery 'Paris'-shape milk jug, painted with the 'Cubist' pattern, no.8071 designed by Susie Cooper, the base with rectangular ocean liner printed mark.

5.25in (13cm) high

£150-200 AH

A Gray's Pottery eleven-piece coffee set, in a version of the 'Cubist' pattern designed by Susie Cooper, comprising a coffee pot, sugar bowl, cream jug, and four cups and saucers.

This jazzily coloured Art Deco set would have fetched over a third more than it did if the coffee pot (which is the most valuable piece here) had not been damaged. The spout has a few chips, and the lid is missing its knop.

Coffee pot 7.5in (19cm) high

£400-600 A&G

CERAMICS

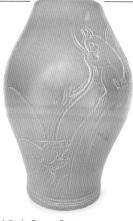

A Susie Cooper Pottery vase, decorated with repeating, stylised, multicoloured floral and foliate patterns designed by Susie Cooper.

c1932　　　　*6in (15cm) high*

£300-400　　　　**WW**

A Susie Cooper Pottery earthenware vase, decorated with incised squirrels on a matt green ground, possibly pattern no.M154, signed and dated 1933.

1933　　*12in (29.5cm) high*

£200-300　　　　**TEN**

A large Susie Cooper Pottery earthenware vase, the blue ground inscribed with a band of foliate design, the base inscribed 'Susie Cooper, ref 5/5'.

This design was exhibited at the British Industries Fair held in 1938 at Olympia and Earls Court in London, and Castle Bromwich in Birmingham.V

c1938　　*10in (25.5cm) high*

£200-300　　　　**ROS**

A CLOSER LOOK AT A SUSIE COOPER COFFEE SET

The 'Kestrel' shape was designed by Cooper herself and introduced in 1932. 'Kestrel' was made into the 1960s in a variety of different patterns.

By the early 1930s, the brightly coloured, angular, and geometric styles of the late 1920s were going out of fashion. They were replaced by stylised flowers, as here, or simple banded patterns.

A Susie Cooper Pottery earthenware bowl, the yellow matt-glazed surface carved with the 'Squirrels' pattern, no.E/345 designed by Susie Cooper.

1932　　*9.5in (24cm) diam*

£150-200　　　　**WW**

'Kestrel''s clean Art Deco form, solid and robust spout, and curving lid and handle, have made it an iconic shape in British Art Deco ceramics.

Unlike the earlier geometric set on the previous page, this set is in comparatively excellent condition, even taking into account the cracked jug. The decoration is also comparatively scarce, meaning collectors are likely to be more forgiving of damage.

A Susie Cooper Productions 'Kestrel'-shape coffee service, hand-painted with pattern no.E308 designed by Susie Cooper, comprising a coffee pot, six coffee cups and saucers, milk jug, and sugar bowl, the milk jug with a crack.

1932-33　　*Coffee pot 8in (20cm) high*

£1,200-1,800　　　　**A&G**

A Susie Cooper Productions sixteen-piece 'Kestrel'-shape coffee set, designed by Susie Cooper, decorated with graduated black bands against an orange and cream ground, comprising a coffee pot, hot water pot, milk jug, sugar bowl, and six coffee cups and saucers.

c1933　　*Coffee pot 8in (20cm) high*

£250-350　　　　**GORL**

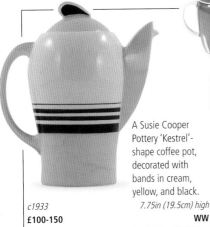

A Susie Cooper Pottery 'Kestrel'-shape coffee pot, decorated with bands in cream, yellow, and black.

c1933   7.75in (19.5cm) high
£100-150   **WW**

A Susie Cooper Productions 'Falcon'-shape coffee service, comprising a coffee pot, six cups and saucers, and a cream jug, each incised with the 'Regency Feather' pattern designed by Susie Cooper, with factory marks to the bases.

c1938   Teapot 7.75in (20cm) high
£150-200   **DUK**

A Susie Cooper Productions 'Kestrel'-shape part dinner service, hand-painted with the 'Tulip in Pompadour' pattern, no.2180 designed by Susie Cooper, comprising a vegetable tureen and cover, a sauceboat with integral stand, fruit bowl, oval meat dish, six dinner, dessert and side plates, and six fruit bowls, with brown printed marks to bases.

c1950   Tureen 10.5in (27cm) wide
£600-800   **TOV**

Judith Picks

In general, apart from 'Dresden Spray', 'Patricia Rose' and scarce variations, Susie Cooper's post-war floral designs are much less popular with collectors than her pre-war designs. This means that large sets like this are often very inexpensive, particularly compared to brand new sets on the high street.

Although an unusual combination of a modern shape and an almost traditional floral pattern, this set has a light and elegant air typical of the period. I think sets like this represent excellent value. They're functional and they make a dinner table look unique, a million miles away from the blandness of high street designs. What's more, the vintage and retro look is becoming increasingly sought-after in homes across the country, so these may rise slightly in value in the future if the look catches on. Whatever happens, prices can't go any lower!

It's also worth bearing in mind that as sets become used and pieces are damaged, as has happened here, the market for replacements might grow too.

A 1950s Susie Cooper Pottery 39-piece part dinner service, printed with the 'Magnolia' pattern, no.2284 designed by Susie Cooper, comprising a pair of 'Kestrel'-shape vegetable dishes with covers, a pair of sauce boats, ten two-handled bowls, ten saucers (two damaged), seven dinner plates (one chipped), and six side plates.

c1953   Tureens 10.5in (27cm) wide
£60-80   **CAPE**

A 1970s Susie Cooper 'Fine Bone China' 22-piece tea service, printed with the 'Wild Rose' pattern, no.C987, comprising six tea cups and saucers, six side plates, milk jug, sugar bowl, bread and butter plate, and a preserve jar and cover, each with printed marks to base.

Just like her 1950s designs, traditional designs from Cooper's later bone china ranges for Wedgwood are generally low in price, due to a tiny demand from collectors. However, values for her more abstract and modern patterns, such as 'Astral', 'Diablo' and 'Crescents', are rising. This could be an area to watch.
£50-80   **CAPE**

QUICK REFERENCE

- Since it was founded in 1815 in London's Lambeth district, the Doulton company (Royal Doulton from 1901) has produced a wide variety of ceramics, including earthy-coloured stoneware, and many thousands of collectable figurines. Unfortunately, over the past decade, values for all but the finest and rarest pieces have declined. Now may, therefore, be a good time to buy, as a potential revival in the future would cause prices to rise.
- The first decorative wares, made from 1871, were stoneware. Look for the typical motifs and artists' monograms of notable artists, such as sisters Florence and Hannah Barlow, and brothers Arthur and George Tinworth.
- Figurine production took off in 1913 under the direction of modeller, Charles Noke, who believed that Royal Doulton figurines could easily be as popular in the 20thC as those from Staffordshire had been in the 19thC. Starting with HN1,

'Darling' (1912), each figure was given an 'HN' number (HN after Harry Nixon, then manager of the painting department). This system continues today and more than 4,000 HN numbers have since been assigned, though not all refer to different figurines as different colourways were often given different numbers. It may be worth consulting a specialist guide for more information. In general, the most desirable figurines are those produced for a short time, usually before World War II. Look out for rare colourways and variations.
- Collectors tend to focus on a type, such as 'fair ladies', or historical characters, or on the work of a designer. Notable designers include Leslie Harradine and Margaret 'Peggy' Davies, both of whom are known for their 'fair ladies'.
- Condition is important, particularly with figurines, where damage will seriously reduce value. Examine all examples carefully, particularly protruding parts.

A Royal Doulton 'Victoria' figurine, HN3416, designed by Margaret Davies, from the 'Roadshow Events' series, the base with printed marks.

Produced for one year only, this is a different colourway of HN2471 'Victoria' which was produced from 1973-2000, and is generally worth under half of this value.

1992   *6.5in (16.5cm) high*

£100-150   CHT

A Royal Doulton 'Fragrance' figurine, HN2334, designed by Margaret Davies, the base with printed mark.

1966-95   *7.5in (19cm) high*

£30-50   CAPE

A Royal Doulton 'Southern Belle' figurine, HN2229, designed by Margaret Davies, the base with printed mark.

The pale blue and pink variation, HN2425, is usually worth roughly the same amount, even though it was only made from 1983-94.

1958-97   *8in (20.3cm) high*

£35-45   CAPE

A Royal Doulton 'Christmas Time' figurine, HN2110, designed by Margaret Davies, the base with printed mark.

1953-67   *7in (18cm) high*

£80-120   LOC

A Royal Doulton 'Adrienne' figurine, HN2152, designed by Margaret Davies, the base with printed mark.

This design is known in three other colourways, two with different names. Look out for the limited edition 'Joan' in yellow and green, which can fetch up to 30% more.

1964-76   *8in (20cm) high*

£50-70   WHP

Miller's Compares

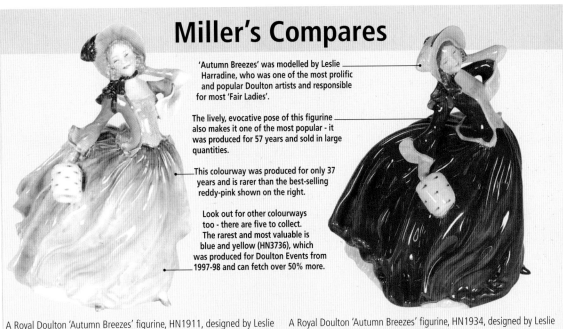

'Autumn Breezes' was modelled by Leslie Harradine, who was one of the most prolific and popular Doulton artists and responsible for most 'Fair Ladies'.

The lively, evocative pose of this figurine also makes it one of the most popular - it was produced for 57 years and sold in large quantities.

This colourway was produced for only 37 years and is rarer than the best-selling reddy-pink shown on the right.

Look out for other colourways too - there are five to collect. The rarest and most valuable is blue and yellow (HN3736), which was produced for Doulton Events from 1997-98 and can fetch over 50% more.

A Royal Doulton 'Autumn Breezes' figurine, HN1911, designed by Leslie Harradine, the base with printed marks.
1939-76   *7.5in (19cm) high*
£60-80   **CAPE**

A Royal Doulton 'Autumn Breezes' figurine, HN1934, designed by Leslie Harradine, the base with printed mark.
1940-97   *7.5in (19cm) high*
£20-30   **CAPE**

A Royal Doulton 'Rosamund' miniature figurine, M32, designed by Leslie Harradine, the base with printed marks.

Most of these figurines were produced before the outbreak of war in 1939.
1932-45   *4.25in (11cm) high*
£100-150   **CAPE**

A Royal Doulton original clay model of 'Vivienne', in a floral painted dress, modelled by Leslie Harradine, dated 1933.

This unique model was not put into production and comes with a Certificate of Authenticity from The Doulton Company. The final form of Harradine's 'Vivienne', numbered HN2073, is very different.

8in (20cm) high
£400-600   **GORL**

A Royal Doulton 'Belle O' The Ball' figurine, HN1997, designed by Roy Asplin, the base with printed mark.
1947-79   *6.75in (17cm) high*
£120-180   **LOC**

A Royal Doulton 'Carmen' figurine, HN2545, designed by E.J. Griffiths, the base with printed marks.
1974-79   *12in (30cm) high*
£100-150   **WW**

CERAMICS

A Royal Doulton 'The Old Balloon Seller' figurine, HN1315, designed by Leslie Harradine, with printed mark to base.

1929-98   7.5in (19cm) high
£60-80   **WHP**

A Royal Doulton 'The Balloon Man' figurine, HN1954, designed by Leslie Harradine, with printed mark to base.

Produced in earthenware and porcelain, 'Balloon Man' was never as popular with buyers as his female counterpart, hence his comparatively high value today.

1940-2004   7.5in (19cm) high
£70-100   **WHP**

A Royal Doulton 'Marietta' figurine, HN1341, designed by Leslie Harradine, the base with printed marks.

All three colourways of this scarce pre-war figurine are sought-after and valuable. The most valuable is HN1699 in green and red, which can fetch up to 30% more.

1929-40   8in (20.5cm) high
£700-1,000   **LSK**

A rare Royal Doulton figure 'A Chelsea Pensioner', HN689, designed by Leslie Harradine, with printed marks to base.

1924-38   6in (15cm) high
£500-700   **WHP**

A rare Royal Doulton 'A Yeoman of the Guard' figurine, HN688, designed by Leslie Harradine, with printed mark to base.

1924-38   5.5in (14cm) high
£400-600   **WHP**

A Royal Doulton 'The Potter' figurine, HN1493, designed by Charles Noke, the base with printed marks.

1932-92   7in (18cm) high
£100-150   **CAPE**

A Royal Doulton 'The China Repairer' figurine, HN2943, designed by Robert Tabbenor, the base with printed marks.

In its first year, this figurine was only available in Canada. It was then released more widely.

1982-88   6in (16cm) high
£80-120   **FLD**

A Royal Doulton 'Cocker Spaniel Lying in Basket' figurine, HN2585, with printed mark to base.

1941-1985   *2in (5cm) high*

£40-60   **WHP**

A Royal Doulton 'Terrier Puppies in a Basket' figurine, HN2588, with printed mark to base.

Dogs are among the most collectable of Royal Doulton's animal figurines, and terriers were the most popular dogs produced and sold, so there's a wide range to choose from.

1941-1985   *3in (7.5cm) high*

£30-40   **WHP**

A Royal Doulton 'Cocker Spaniel with Pheasant' figurine, HN1062, designed by Frederick Daws, with printed marks to base.

1931-1968   *3.5in (9cm) high*

£80-120   **WHP**

A Royal Doulton Springer Spaniel 'Ch. Dry Toast' figurine, HN2517, designed by Frederick Daws, with printed mark to base.

1938-1985   *3.75in (9.5cm) high*

£50-80   **WHP**

Judith Picks

Yes, he may be an 'unusual' looking pussy, even ugly, but it's often worth considering figurines that may have limited appeal to some, as they can be rarer and more valuable. They can also often be ignored by unwitting sellers, who disregard them due to their odd appearance. As ever with Doulton and other similar figurines, the devil's in the detail. If he's numbered 818 or 819, he was made from 1923-32 and could fetch over five times this amount - particularly if he's in white only. The same goes if he's in ginger or tabby.

A Royal Doulton 'Lucky' Black Cat figurine, K12, designed by Charles Noke after George Studdy's 'Ooloo' character, the base with printed mark.

1932-75   *2.5in (6.5cm) high*

£80-120   **GORL**

A very rare Royal Doulton 'Fox Seated - Style Six figurine', HN2634, from the 'Prestige' collection.

1952-92   *10in (26cm) high*

£600-800   **DN**

A Royal Doulton flambé-glazed 'Tiger, Stalking', HN2646, designed by Charles Noke, style two, from the 'Prestige' range.

1950-96   *6in (15cm) high*

£300-500   **CHT**

CERAMICS

A pair of Royal Doulton stoneware vases, slip-decorated by Harry Simeon with white Wisteria sprays and green, blue and brown glazes, the bases with impressed marks.

16in (41cm) high

£700-1,000 WW

A CLOSER LOOK AT A DOULTON ICE PAIL

This is an unusual type of decoration for Barlow who is better known for her horses and other animals.

The fact it depicts children playing also adds to its appeal, collectors of juvenalia would love to add this to their collection.

The style of the decoration, particularly the snowman, is also comparatively stylised and abstract, and recalls an etching.

Ice pails – not to be confused with smaller biscuit barrels - are scarce forms. Many became damaged or broken through use.

A Doulton Lambeth silver-mounted stoneware ice pail, decorated by Hannah Barlow, incised with children, dogs and a snowman, dated '1880', with silver plated mounts.

1880 *8in (20cm)*

£2,200-2,800 GORL

A Doulton Lambeth stoneware twin-handled vase, decorated by Frank Marshall with sgraffito diamond decoration and moulded floral cartouches, the base with impressed factory mark.

£70-100 LOC

A Doulton Lambeth stoneware vase, decorated by Hannah Barlow with green floral sprays again a brown and blue ground with raised beaded borders, the base with impressed marks, dated '1884' and with inscribed initials.

1884 *11in (28cm) high*

£120-180 DUK

A Doulton Lambeth stoneware vase, decorated by Hannah Barlow with an incised frieze of cattle resting, between panels of scrolling foliage, the base with impressed and incised marks.

13in (33cm) high

£800-1,200 WW

A Doulton Lambeth stoneware jug, decorated by Hannah Barlow with a band of incised cattle in a landscape between leaf borders, the base with impressed and incised marks and date, with a small chip to spout.

1886 *9in (23cm) high*

£150-250 DN

CERAMICS

QUICK REFERENCE - SLATER'S PATENT

- Also sometimes known as 'Chiné' wares, this manufacturing process was developed by John Slater, Doulton's decorating manager at Lambeth. Used from 1885-1939, the process involved damp lace being pressed into the exterior of a body. The lace was then burnt away in the heat of the kiln, leaving an intricate pattern, which was then painted over, typically with flowers and leaves with gilt detailing. The technique was also combined with others, producing interesting results.

- Despite the rich decorative effect, Slater's Patent pieces very rarely fetch high sums, and remain comparatively affordable, particularly for single vases. Although this is unlikely to change, they represent an affordable way to buy into a typically late Victorian look.

A Royal Doulton stoneware waisted cylindrical vase, glazed in mainly blue enamels, with a lambrequin border, with marks to base.

13in (32cm) high

£70-100   WHP

A Doulton Lambeth stoneware fish bowl, the base with impressed factory mark and inscribed 'AW'.

4in (10.5cm) high

£80-120   SWO

A pair of Royal Doulton Slater's Patent vases, with elongated glossy blue glazed necks, typically decorated with 'Chiné' bands, with mark to the base.

17in (43cm) high

£150-200   LOC

A Doulton Lambeth Slater's Patent stoneware pottery vase, of ovoid footed form with waisted neck, decorated in white and gilt with stylised flowerheads and pink lustre bands, set on a fading blue rough lace textured ground, beneath a stiff leaf border to the neck, impressed marks and painted no. '2X3904'.

12.25in (31.1cm) high

£50-70   CAPE

A Royal Doulton Slater's Patent vase, painted with flowers and gold decoration, marked 'Doulton and Slater's Patent, ET'.

16in (41cm) high

£30-40   LC

A Doulton Lambeth stoneware finial, modelled as a galleon, designed by Gilbert Bayes, with indistinct impressed mark, on a later wooden plinth, chipped.

This finial is from a series made for the washing line posts at St. Pancras Housing Association Estates in London. Other forms are known, and a dragon fetched over £12,000 at auction in late 2009 (see 'Miller's Antiques Handbook & Price Guide 2012-2013' p.496). Many of the finials sustained minor physical damage, often caused by vandalism, so condition is vital. For other examples, see Desmond Eyles, 'The Doulton Lambeth Wares', Somerset, 2002, p.231.

c1932   *17in (43cm) high*

£800-1,200   L&T

CERAMICS

A Royal Doulton Series Ware biscuit barrel, in the 'Dutch Landscape' design, produced for McVitie & Price.

1904   *7in (18cm) high*
£80-120   **TRI**

A large Royal Doulton Series Ware pottery jardinière, printed with a silhouette river landscape, the base with printed mark and stamped with pattern no. 'D3116'.

10.5in (27cm) diam
£35-45   **CAPE**

A Royal Doulton 'Titanian' vase, handpainted by Harry Allen with hooded crows, signed, and with printed, inscribed and impressed marks, no.1320a, inscribed '2.458 Hooded Crows' and impressed '8.18'.

The scarce 'Titanian' range was produced from 1915-c1930 - for more information see p.63 of 'Miller's Collectables Handbook & Price Guide 2010-2011'.

c1918   *6in (14cm) high*
£1,000-1,500   **SWO**

A Royal Doulton 'The Royal Musketeers' limited edition loving cup, designed by Charles Noke and Harry Fenton, numbered 69 from an edition of 600.

No.1 from this edition was sold at auction at Phillip's in London for £1,200 in 1999.

Introduced 1936   *9.75in (25cm) high*
£350-450   **AH**

A Royal Doulton Burslem cabinet plate, painted with a bouquet of yellow roses, signed 'Simcock', within a tooled gilded border with raised gilding, the back with retailer mark for Tiffany & Co., New York.

10.5in (27cm) diam
£100-150   **A&G**

An Art Deco Royal Doulton fifteen-piece 'Tango' pattern coffee service, comprising coffee pot, cream jug, sugar bowl, coffee cans and saucers, decorated with stylised motifs, the bases with printed mark and painted pattern no.'V1482'.

It's the high quality, renowned name of Doulton, and the appealingly modern Art Deco pattern that made this set fetch as much as it did. Floral Victorian sets are largely out of fashion and are deemed impractical, as they don't go in the dishwasher. As such, they fetch considerably less, usually well under £100.

£200-300   **CAPE**

QUICK REFERENCE

- During the 19thC and early 20thC, the Dutch town of Gouda became the centre of the Netherlands's ceramic industry, making colourful pottery that was sold around the world.
- The first major ornamental ceramics factory to open in Gouda was Plateelbakkerij Zuid-Holland (PZH or Zuid-Holland), which was founded in 1898 by Egbert Estié of Purmerend. PZH quickly became the largest and most important Gouda factory, but other notable factories include Kunstaardewerkfabriek Regina (operational 1898-1979), and Plateelfabriek Ivora (1639-1913 and 1914-1965). Several factories located outside the town, such as Arnhemsche Fayencefabriek in Arnhem, also worked in this style, and their products are grouped under the Gouda name.
- Typical Gouda pottery is Art Nouveau or Art Deco in style, decorated with brightly coloured, stylised floral or foliate patterns on a dark background. Many patterns are outlined with ochre, and feature squiggles, curlicues, or dots around the main design. Very early pieces were gloss-glazed, but PZH's matt 'Rhodian' glaze soon became the standard and most recognised Gouda glaze.
- PZH pieces are marked with a 'Gate of Lazarus' mark, which is shaped like a house. Other marks vary and can help with dating. Consult a specialist guide, such as 'The World of Gouda Pottery' by Phyllis T. Ritvo, for more information.
- Look out for large objects, with fine quality, detailed decoration. Signed pieces by recognised artists, such as Theodorus A. C. Colenbrander and Henri Breetvelt, are likely to be desirable. High gloss-glaze is generally more valuable and desirable than matt-glaze, particularly if the pattern has a white or blue background, rather than a dark ground. It may be worth watching mid-century modern designs, which are possibly under-priced and may yet increase in value.

A pair of Plateelfabriek Ivora 'Juliana' pattern vases, each high gloss-glazed with stylised flowers and foliage in colours on a cream ground, with impressed and painted marks, and repair to rim of one.

Although these are the same pattern and size as the vases to the left, note the difference in value due to damage on the rim of one.

c1920

12in (31cm) high

£200-300

WW

A pair of Plateelfabriek Ivora 'Juliana' pattern baluster vases, with tapered necks, flared rims and high gloss-glazed painted stylised floral motifs and scrolls, with hand-painted marks to bases.

12in (31cm) high

£300-500

FLD

An Art Nouveau Plateelbakkerij Zuid-Holland cylindrical vase, designed by Lendeert Johan Muller, with light and dark green, red and yellow stylised floral and foliate pattern, marked on the base 'LMB Zuid-Holland Gouda', with a long vertical hairline crack.

1899

5.75in (14.5cm) high

£500-700

QU

A Plateelbakkerij Zuid-Holland baluster vase, painted with stylised floral and foliate pattern in a high gloss-glaze in greens, yellow, red, blue, and brown on a black ground, the base with printed marks.

This is similar to Cornelius Eduard Antheunis's designs.

c1925

20.5in (52cm) high

£1,200-1,800

HERR

CERAMICS

A large Art Nouveau Plateelbakkerij Zuid Holland 'New Porcelain' range vase, model no.226, painted with flowers and foliage in colours, the base with painted marks.

The white background, high gloss-glaze and clearly demarked floral and foliate motifs in bright colours are typical features of the 'New Porcelain' range. It was designed by Wilhelmus Petrus Hartgring, and produced from his arrival at the factory in 1908 until 1923. Matt-glazed versions were also produced.

c1915   *25in (64cm) high*
£400-600   **WW**

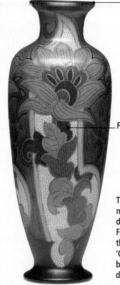

A Plateelbakkerij Zuid-Holland 'Pikan' pattern jardinière, painted with flowers, with painted marks to base.

7.5in (19cm) high
£150-200   **WW**

A Plateelbakkerij Zuid-Holland 'Pikan' pattern platter, shape 501, the back marked '1952 PIKAN GOUDA' and 'MB MADE IN HOLLAND 501'.
1952   *12.5in (30.5cm) diam*
£150-200   **QU**

A CLOSER LOOK AT TYPICAL GOUDA FEATURES

The motifs are outlined with golden ochre glaze that was painted on with a special brush to ensure a thick, even line.

Tops and bottoms are typically black, framing the designs, and horizontal black 'borders' are often used to define separate areas of a shape.

Floral and foliate patterns are strongly stylised and abstract, and are combined with dots.

The hallmark semi-matte glaze was developed by 1910. First called 'Rhodian', the range that bore it became known as 'Gouda Pottery' and the look was copied by other factories in the area and used for decades.

A pair of tall Plateelbakkerij Zuid-Holland vases, painted with a semi-matte glaze in a bold floral pattern, the bases marked 'GOUDA PLAZUID HOLLAND 4425', with factory paper labels.

These vases fetched as much as they did because they are a pair, large in size, and they are visually stunning as well as being typical of Gouda pottery in general.

18.5in (47cm) high
£1,200-1,800   **DRA**

An early 1920s Plateelbakkerij Zuid-Holland matt-glazed vase, painted with a bird amid stylised floral motifs, the base with painted marks.

16cm high
£200-300   **WW**

CERAMICS

A Dutch Gouda 'Fusian' pattern ginger jar and cover, probably by Plateelbakkerij Zuid-Holland, painted with stylised floral patterns, the base painted 'Fusian, Holland,P, 0154/4'.

20in (51cm) high

£150-200   **LC**

Mark Picks

Designs sold by prestigious London department store Liberty are interesting, important and widely collected. Some were designed by talented designer Henri Breetvelt. Produced by PZH for Liberty around 1923, this pattern was originally called 'Kaiser', but was renamed after World War I to avoid any association with Germany.

Marks on wares produced for Liberty in the early 1920s do not bear the manufacturer's name, as Liberty wanted its own name to be showcased, did not want its customers placing orders direct, and also did not want their competitors easily seeing the source of their products.

The Liberty order boosted the company, both financially and in terms of reputation, and led to a knock-on effect raising the popularity of all Gouda pottery. The company also produced another range for Liberty in the mid-1930s. Many of these later designs were spray-glazed, and some bore the company's name in addition to Liberty's.

A late 1920s-30s pair of Plateelbakkerij Zuid-Holland 'Adinda' pattern candlesticks, with alternating bands of brown and stylised motifs on a mottled yellow ground, with painted marks to the bases.

Possibly designed by Louis Bogtman or Lion Cachet, this pattern is very hard to find.

11.75in (30cm) high

£100-150   **DA&H**

A Plateelbakkerij Zuid-Holland 'Blue Pheasant' pattern ovoid vase, retailed by Liberty & Co., painted with exotic birds in blue, brown, ochre and green on a white ground, the base with printed 'LIBERTY & CO. MADE IN HOLLAND' mark.

c1922-23   *3in (7.5cm) high*

£60-80   **MOR**

A Gouda corseted vase with geometric polychromatic design, several hairline cracks to the interior only, the base marked '2073/ Futurist/8/TNT/MH/Italiano'.

6.75in (17cm) high

£120-180   **DRA**

A late 1920s Plateelbakkerij Zuid-Holland 'Collier' pattern candlestick, with barley twist stem, the brown and white ground decorated with arabesque designs, with painted marks to base.

10in (24.5cm) high

£40-60   **ROS**

CERAMICS

A 1920s-30s Plateelfabriek Schoonhoven 'Festijn' pattern baluster vase, shape 120, the base painted '120 Festijn Schoonhoven Holland +' on the base.

Schoonhoven was founded in 1920 after its founder acquired equipment from the bankrupt Plateelbakkerij De Rozeboom in the Hague. The aqua green used is distinctive, and a hallmark of the company's patterns.

9.25in (23.5cm) high
£70-90   GC

A 1920s-30s Plateelfabriek Schoonhoven 'Festijn' pattern small faceted bottle vase, shape 104, the base painted '104 Festijn Schoonhoven Holland+'.

6in (15cm) high
£30-40   GC

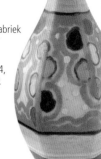

A Plateelbakkerij Flora 'Tokio' pattern vase, shape 916, the base painted '916 Tokio Flora Gouda Holland'.

The factory operated under the Flora name from 1945-1980, and is known for its production of pitchers, tableware, and unusually shaped vases. After 1980, production continued at the factory under different names.

1968-77   *6.75in (17cm) high*
£40-60   GC

An early 1970s Plateelbakkerij Flora vase, shape no.911, the base painted 'Flora HOLLAND 911'.

Although still very Dutch, the pattern is similar to some post-war West German designs, showing the impact of the popularity of these designs in the Netherlands. The lilac coloured version is known as 'Lila' and a similar pattern in glossy brown is known as 'Madrid'.

5.25in (13.5cm) high
£18-22   MTS

A 1960s-70s Koninklijke Hollandsche Goedewaagen 'Marion' pattern vase, the base with crown mark and painted '4841 Marion Koninklijke Gouda Royal Holland'.

This shows the influence of Scandinavian mid-century modern design, in both the style and colours of the leaf motifs.

5.5in (14cm) high
£30-40   GC

A 1950s-60s Plateelbakkerij Flora 'Paima' pattern shallow dish, with stylised floral design, the base marked 'Paima Flora Gouda Holland', some crazing.

8in (20.5cm) long
£12-18   TCM

A mid-20thC Royal Gouda (Plateelbakkerij Zuid-Holland) 'Chrysantheme' pattern vase, painted with stylised flower sprays on an ivory ground, painted marks.

Although produced during the same post-war time period as many of the other vases shown on this page, the style of the pattern is retrospective and traditional, showing that there was (and is) still a market for such designs.

6in (16cm) high
£35-45   FLD

QUICK REFERENCE

- Brightly coloured Italian ceramics from the 1950s, '60s, and '70s are becoming increasingly popular with collectors. Like the West German ceramics of the same era, they embody the renewed optimism of designers and buyers following World War II, and fit well into today's homes.
- Forms include vases, lamp bases, dishes, and bowls. Although some were made by hand, most were slip-moulded so they could be produced on a factory production line. They were hand-painted or carved with stylised geometric, floral, foliate, or figurative patterns that show the influence of modern art. A frequently found technique is 'sgraffito', where a design was scratched into the painted surface with a stylus. Traditional, historic designs from the 16thC and 17thC were also reproduced, and continue to be produced today.
- Many Italian ceramics were exported to design shops, department stores, and lower-end discount stores. Some distributors, such as Raymor in the US and Hutcheson & Son Ltd. in the UK, applied their own labels or marks to pieces.
- The most valuable pieces are by notable factories, such as Bitossi, or notable designers, such as Guido Gambone (1909-1969) or Marcello Fantoni (1915-2011). Gambone's work is more diverse than that of his contemporaries, but pieces can be recognised by a similar colour palette of earthy-tones, biomorphic forms and typically primitive decoration.
- Look out for large, attractive objects in good condition. Examine pieces closely as the ceramic is often fragile and easily chipped. Pieces in mint condition command a premium.
- The market for these pieces is still emerging and will develop as more information is discovered. However, it is generally good advice to look out for pieces that show skill in execution and design, as these are more likely to become valuable in the future.

A Gambone bottle-shaped vase, decorated with horses in yellow and lavender on an oatmeal ground, signed on the base with a green donkey mark and 'Italy'.

12.25in (31cm) high

£1,000-1,500　　**DRA**

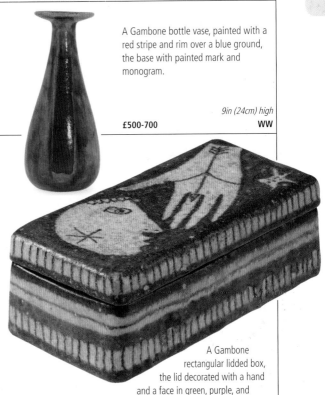

A Gambone bottle vase, painted with a red stripe and rim over a blue ground, the base with painted mark and monogram.

9in (24cm) high

£500-700　　**WW**

A Gambone rectangular lidded box, the lid decorated with a hand and a face in green, purple, and oatmeal glazes, the base signed 'Gambone Italy' and with a donkey mark.

Boxes, particularly as large as this example, are scarce forms for Gambone. The donkey mark is said to indicate that Guido Gambone decorated the piece himself, or oversaw its decoration. You'll notice that pieces with the donkey mark on this page have fetched higher prices.

8.5in (22cm) wide

£1,200-1,800　　**DRA**

A Gambone baluster-shaped vase, decorated with bands of abstract geometric motifs, the base marked 'Gambone Italy'.

7in (18cm) diam

£400-600　　**DRA**

A Bruno Gambone vase, with an ovoid neck on an elliptical body, decorated in resist with an abstract linear design, in oatmeal and bronze glazes, the base with painted marks.

8in (21cm) high

£200-300　　**WW**

CERAMICS

A Gambone bowl, decorated with a geometric design to the interior and exterior, the base with painted marks.

7.75in (19.5cm) diam

£300-400   WW

A large Gambone lamp base, decorated with geometric panels and diagonal bands in orange, blue and aubergine on a mottled midnight blue ground, the base with painted mark.

20in (52cm) high

£800-1,200   WW

A Fantoni baluster-shaped vase, with spiralling grooved decoration, glazed in vivid cobalt blue, with painted marks to base.

13in (32cm) high

£100-150   WW

A pair of Fantoni ovoid vases, with sgrafitto and painted decoration of stylised maidens each holding a flower, on a red ground, with incised signatures to bases and sides, a hairline crack to the top rim of one.

This style of decoration, using angular, almost Picasso-like figures, was widely copied by many Italian potteries from the 1950s-70s. Most of these copies were sold inexpensively as tourist souvenirs. If a piece is not signed 'Fantoni', it is unlikely to be by the company, and will be worth considerably less.

12in (31cm) high

£350-450   WW

A Fantoni Etruscan style vase, with sgraffito decoration, with a blue glazed interior, signed 'Fantoni' within the exterior pattern, the base painted 'Fantoni Italy 01174 / 18 1/2' .

7.5in (19cm) high

£300-500   DRA

A CLOSER LOOK AT A FANTONI SCULPTURE

These show a clear 'Cubist' influence in their geometric form and angular decoration, and were undoubtedly inspired by the work of Pablo Picasso, Georges Braque and Juan Gris.

They also hark back to the traditional 'harlequin' character from the Italian Commedia dell'Arte of the late 16thC.

The design may also be derived from the Italian Futurist movement, and was perhaps inspired by works by Umberto Boccioni or Giacomo Balla.

They are scarce pieces, and their modern stylisation and bright colours are very appealing.

A Fantoni abstract figural sculpture, decorated with multicoloured glazes, painted signature 'Fantoni' to underside, and remnants of painted signature 'Fantoni', 'Firenze' to reverse.

Designed c1960   17in (43cm) high

£700-1,000   ROS

Mark Picks

As prices for ceramics by Gambone and Fantoni continue to rise into the hundreds or even thousands of pounds, the plethora of Italian ceramics by unidentified potteries and designers looks incredibly good value. Most can be found for under £50, some for under £20. Designs, colours and textures are often close copies of, or inspired by, those by Fantoni and Gambone, but some are entirely unique. They were produced in large quantities for export to the rest of Europe and the US, or to be bought by tourists as souvenirs during the post-war boom after World War II. The majority bear no other marks than the 'Italy' and a mysterious number, which may indicate the pattern, shape, or even the client. Colourful and cheerful, they were cheap at the time and remain so today - but for how long?

A 1950s Italian vase, decorated with a sgrafitto pattern of a goat's head and leafy sprigs in white outlined in black, on a textured pink glazed ground, the base painted '5252 Italy'.

5.75in (14.5cm) high

£20-30   GC

A set of six mid-late 20thC Italian Fornasetti black and gilt transfer-printed small plates, depicting a chariot within a gilt surround, with printed marks on bases, and marked 'Made exclusively for Saks Fifth Avenue'.

4in (10cm) diam

£120-180   LHA

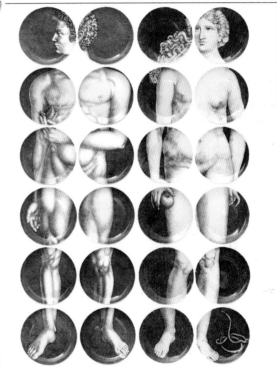

A mid-late 20thC set of twenty four Italian Fornasetti 'Adam and Eve' pattern porcelain plates, with transfer-printed decoration of Adam and Eve depicted across the plates, together with a hardcover book on the works of Fornasetti.

10.25in (26cm) diam

£2,000-3,000   LHA

An Italian Società Ceramica Italiana Laveno Art Deco 'Monza'-shape vase, in pattern No '1297' designed by Guido Andlovitz, featuring handpainted dancers, small vignettes and gilded stars on 'Giallo 2' ground, the base impressed 'SCI', printed 'Lavenia', and with date mark for 1928.

For more information, see p.98 of 'Italian Art Ceramics 1900-1950' by Valerio Terraroli. The neck on this vase is cracked, hence the low price. Had it been in undamaged condition, it could have fetched over three times as much. The market for such modern takes on traditional folk scenes is still young, but is likely to grow.

1928   *20.5in (52cm) high*

£200-300   A&G

A 1960s-70s Italian waisted cylindrical vase, glazed green with an all-over sgrafitto design of figures within a forest, the base with painted marks.

15in (37.5cm) high

£150-200   WW

QUICK REFERENCE

- While the market for Chinese ceramics has risen, the Japanese market has mostly remained stable, even declining in certain areas. This is partly due to the respective states of the Chinese and Japanese economies.
- The most popularly collected styles include the vibrant blue, red, and white Imari, and the intricately decorated cream and gilt Satsuma. Imari porcelain was made from the late 17thC at Arita on Kyushu. It was shipped from the port of Imari (from which it takes its European name) to the West.

- Satsuma wares take their name from a feudal province in southern Kyushu. As with Imari ware, the subject, motifs, and detail, and how well these are executed are the main indicators to value.
- Marks are inconsistent. As well as the family name of the potter and, sometimes, a place name, many pieces are marked with the adopted name of the workshop (its 'art-name'). Cyclical dates and Japanese period-names (nengo) were used on some pieces made before the 18thC.

An early 20thC Japanese Imari charger, painted with fan-shaped segments of flowers and shrubs on a blue and white floral ground.

17.5in (44cm) diam

£80-100   DA&H

A Japanese Meiji period Imari bowl, decorated with feathers and flowers, with lotus-shaped reserves of shells.

10in (26.5cm) diam

£100-150   DN

A Japanese Meiji period Imari vase and cover, of ribbed ovoid form with domed cover, decorated with shaped panels, containing flowering leafy foliage, on a floral ground.

14.25in (36.2cm) high

£80-100   CAPE

A late 19thC Japanese Imari vase, typically decorated with blossom and flowering shrubs in a fenced garden.

9in (23cm) high

£60-80   WHP

A 20thC Japanese Imari vase, of baluster form with a frilled border, decorated with flowers and foliage.

18in (46cm) high

£70-90   ECGW

Miller's Compares

The clothes and faces are comparatively very simply painted - they do not have expressions or individuality, like those on the other pair do.

The rest of the decoration was painted on without complex detail and probably in a hurry - compare the bands of decoration around the bases and rims of the two pairs.

These are more interesting shapes than simple cylinders, and they bear a signature mark for Unzan on the base.

There is a better sense of perspective to the pattern, and the subject matter is also more unusual and meaningful than standard ladies in a garden.

The decoration is much richer, being three-dimensional, and very complex and detailed.

A pair of early 20thC Japanese Satsuma vases, of cylindrical form, decorated with panels containing figures in an interior setting, with sprays and borders of flowers and butterflies.

5in (13cm) high

£120-180   DA&H

The vases on the left may be smaller than those on the right but it's not really the difference in size that counts here - it's the difference in quality.

A pair of Japanese Meiji period Satsuma trumpet-form vases, moulded in relief with the eighteen Lohan, the base with blue Shimazu mon, and gilt Satsuma yaki, Unzan.

c1880.   *12in (30cm) high*

£1,200-1,800   SWO

A late 19thC Japanese Satsuma vase, typically heavily decorated with numerous immortals seated in a landscape, signed on the base.

9.5in (24cm) high

£200-300   GORB

A large Japanese Meiji period Satsuma vase and cover, of tapering ovoid form and twin handles, the cover with shi-shi finial, the body decorated with warriors and geometric and floral borders.

26in (66cm) high

£600-800   L&T

A Japanese Meiji period Satsuma koro and cover, by Kinkozan, painted and gilt with variously shaped figural panels against a ground of flowers, on tripod feet, signed 'Kinkozan zo' in gilt to base.

Kinkozan was a family of ceramicists who owned a factory, rather than an individual artist. The workshop (later, a factory) was active from 1645-1927, with production peaking from 1875 until the 1920s.

A Japanese Meiji period Satsuma miniature vase, decorated with spiralling bands of chrysanthemums.

3.5in (9cm) high

£180-220   GORL

3in (8cm) high

£500-700   TOV

CERAMICS

QUICK REFERENCE - LORÉ

• For many years, the maker of these vases has been unknown. Research by Emiel Monnink of www.retrominded.com has revealed their origins. Loré Ceramic Industries was founded in 1954 by Louis Thijssen and René Peeters in Beesel, the Netherlands. The name was taken from the first two letters of their forenames.

• Loré produced utilitarian wares such as tiles, decorative wares, and unique artist works. Designs were produced by Peeters and a small number of artists including Joe Thissen, Jules Rummens, Peter Schoenmakers, and Mathieu Camps. Camps's forms are highly modern, largely architectural, and sometimes austere. Many have a shape number with the prefix 'B', which possibly indicates a series, or a glaze type as they are found in similar types of graduated glaze in blues, greens, and browns. This jug vase is one of the more commonly found shapes, and is in the largest of three sizes, as indicated by the '/3' suffix after the shape number.

• Over-expansion and the economic problems of the late 1970s caused the company to close in 1981. Since Monnink's discovery of this information, values for Loré ceramics have risen.

A 1970s Dutch Loré double-handled vase, shape no.B46, designed by Mathieu Camps, with graduated green and brown glaze.

6.5in (16.5cm) high

£25-35   RM

A 1970s Dutch Loré double-handled vase, shape no.B156, designed by Mathieu Camps, with graduated blue and brown glaze.

6in (15cm) high

£120-180   RM

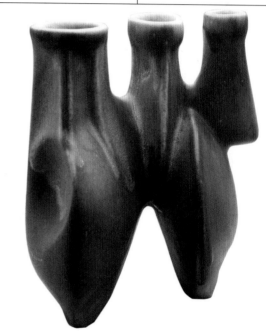

A 1970s Dutch Loré triple-welled vase, shape no.B75, designed by Mathieu Camps, with graduated blue and cream glaze.

9.5in (24cm) high

£200-300   RM

A 1970s Dutch Loré jug vase, with two apertures, shape no.B111, designed by Mathieu Camps, with graduated blue and cream glaze.

8in (20.5cm) high

£250-350   RM

A 1970s Dutch Loré double-welled footed bowl, shape no.B72, designed by Mathieu Camps, with graduated blue and cream glaze.

9.75in (24cm) wide

£80-120   RM

A very rare Dutch Loré advertising vase, with two feet and single hole, with graduated, mottled blue glaze, impressed 'Loré'.

5in (12.5cm) high

£80-120   RM

QUICK REFERENCE

• In 1897 William Moorcroft (1872-1945) joined James MacIntyre & Company's ceramics factory as a designer. There he created his first major ranges 'Florian' and 'Aurelian', which met with great success. Their curving, often symmetrical, floral designs were inspired by Moorish and Art Nouveau patterns. Inherent to Moorcroft's work was the tube-lining process whereby liquid clay would be piped onto the surface of the body, outlining the desired pattern, forming enclosed 'cells' that were filled with liquid glaze.

• Moorcroft left MacIntyre in 1912 to set up his own company with the backing of London retailer Liberty & Co. Moorcroft's high quality hand-thrown shapes and hallmark stylised floral designs soon struck a chord with consumers. He was awarded the Royal Warrant in 1929.

• William died in 1945 and his son Walter took over the business. Old designs were continued or refreshed in different colours or styles, and new ranges designed by Walter were introduced. Colours were rich and deep, and patterns were inspired by the natural world.

• The most highly sought-after examples tend to be from the earlier ranges, such as 'Florian', or limited production designs, such as 'Claremont'. However, more recent collections from key designers such as Sally Tuffin (see pp.132-8) are also proving popular.

• Ranges can be dated according to colours, marks on the base, and the pattern. Examples from ranges produced for long periods of time tend to be the least valuable, particularly smaller pieces.

A James Macintyre & Co. 'Poppy' pattern vase, no.401753, designed by William Moorcroft, the base with painted signature reading 'W. Moorcroft, Des.' and printed factory marks.

The elegant, attenuated shape is not only highly appealing, but is also typical of the period, and works with the design extremely well.

10in (25cm) high

£2,000-3,000   DUK

A James Macintyre & Co. 'Florian Ware' 'Poppy' pattern baluster vase, designed by William Moorcroft, the base with brown printed mark and green painted 'W. Moorcroft des.' mark.

7in (17.5cm) high

£1,200-1,800   DN

A James Macintyre & Co. 'Florian Ware' 'Peacock' pattern twin-handled vase, designed by William Moorcroft, the base with printed mark, green painted signature, and no.'1693'.

5in (12.5cm) high

£1,000-1,500   DN

A late 20thC Moorcroft 'Anemone' pattern ovoid vase, designed by Walter Moorcroft, with a mottled green ground, the base with original paper label, blue signature, and impressed factory marks.

'Anemone' was originally drawn by William, and was used by Walter from 1945 until 1975 when he re-drew it. The new version was initially produced on a blue or 'Woodsmoke' ground, with yellow grounds being used from 1978, and green or ivory from 1984.

9.5in (24cm) high

£350-450   GHOU

A late 20thC Moorcroft 'Anemone' pattern squat baluster vase, designed by Walter Moorcroft, on a green ground, the base with impressed factory mark and 'Potter to H. M. The Queen', with blue-washed incised signature.

3.25in (8cm) high

£120-180   CAPE

CERAMICS

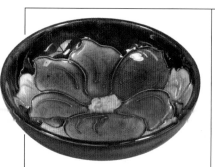

A small Moorcroft 'Clematis' pattern dish, designed by Walter Moorcroft, with a blue ground and a circular foot, the base with impressed and painted marks.

4.5in (11.5cm) diam

£60-80   DA&H

A Moorcroft flambé 'Freesia' pattern bowl, designed by William Moorcroft, the base with impressed signature and 'Potter to H. M. The Queen' mark, with blue painted initials and paper label.

12.5in (32cm) diam

£1,000-1,500   DN

A Moorcroft 'Leaf and Berry' pattern shouldered vase, designed by William Moorcroft, with a graduated green ground, the base with impressed marks and blue painted signature.

c1930   *10in (25cm) high*

£800-1,200   L&T

A late 1940s-50s Moorcroft 'Orchids' pattern vase, designed by William Moorcroft and developed by Walter Moorcroft, with a blue ground, the base with impressed mark, facsimile signature, and blue painted signature.

7in (17.5cm) high

£200-300   TOV

A CLOSER LOOK AT A BISCUIT BOX

Poppies were first used by William Moorcroft in his landmark 'Florian' wares for Liberty, and remained a mainstay in his choice of flowers for many decades.

Although they don't have the elegance of a vase, biscuit barrels are extremely rare and sought-after.

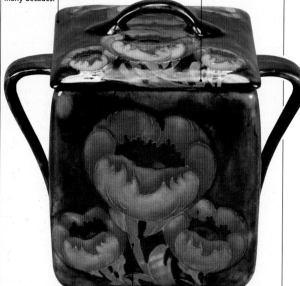

A Moorcroft 'Pomegranate' pattern vase, designed by William Moorcroft, with a mottled green-blue ground, the base with green signature and printed marks.

Early poppies from the 'Florian' range are smaller and more stylised. Later versions produced during the 1920s and '30s are larger and more natural in appearance.

Always check the lid, the inside rim, and the elegantly curved handles for damage, such as chips or cracks, as these were practical objects made to be used. Fortunately this example is undamaged.

A 1920s-30s Moorcroft 'Big Poppy' pattern twin-handled square biscuit box and cover, designed by William Moorcroft, with a shaded blue ground, with impressed mark and blue painted initials.

4.25in (11cm) high   *6.75in (17cm) high*

£280-320   GORB   £2,800-3,200   DN

CERAMICS

SPRING SUMMER WINTER

Antiques for Everyone

THE NEC BIRMINGHAM

HALLS 17-19

Free Car Parking • Vetted for Authenticity

For ticket bookings call: 0844 581 0827
or Book Online

www.antiquesforeveryone.co.uk

All bookings are subject to a single transaction fee
Rights of admission reserved. Security searches in operation. Visitors are not permitted to bring antiques into the fair.

CLAR**ION**
ARTS **HOMES** &ANTIQUES

CERAMICS

QUICK REFERENCE

- In 1921, the Carter & Co. Pottery in Poole, Dorset acquired a subsidiary pottery and became known as Carter, Stabler & Adams. Renowned for its hand-thrown and hand-decorated domestic and decorative art ceramics, the company was widely known as the 'Poole Pottery'.
- Early pieces were decorated with traditional floral and striped patterns. These were largely replaced in the mid-1920s by a new Art Deco style range designed by Truda Carter, which dominated production until the 1950s. Stylised floral and foliate patterns in a recognisable palette of colours are typical. Look out for geometric patterns and those featuring animals, as these are often rarer, and are more likely to be desirable. Large, highly decorated pieces that display the pattern well tend to be the most valuable.

- Modern, curving pieces were introduced following World War II, and kept Poole Pottery at the forefront of design. The 'Contemporary' and 'Freeform' ranges were primarily designed by Guy Sydenham, and decorated with linear or stylised foliate patterns by Alfred Read and Ruth Pavely.
- The Poole Studio was founded in the 1960s by Sydenham and Robert Jefferson. This led directly to the creation of ranges like 'Delphis', 'Aegean', and 'Atlantis', which are much sought-after today. Abstract patterns in bright oranges, reds, browns, and greens are typical of these ranges.
- Many of Poole's more recent designs are also collectable. Indeed, several of its most notable designers, such as Sally Tuffin (see pp.132-138) and Janice Tchalenko, only joined the company during the 1990s. Look out for limited editions, many of which are sought-after today.

A 1920s-30s Poole Pottery vase, shape no.966, pattern 'BX' designed by Truda Carter, the base with impressed and painted marks and decorator's mark for Marjorie Batt.

Batt worked at Poole from 1925 to 1935, and used a painted three line 'III' mark.

10in (24.5cm) high

£400-600   WW

A 1930s Poole Pottery ovoid vase, shape no.152, pattern 'SK' designed by Truda Carter, featuring a deer among flowers, the base with impressed and painted marks.

10in (26cm) high

£150-200   MOR

A Poole Pottery baluster vase, shape no.337, pattern 'ZW' designed by Truda Carter, the base with impressed and painted marks.

The style of the pattern indicates that this is probably from the 1940s-50s when patterns became simplified with more open space between the elements.

10in (25cm) high

£150-200   DN

A tall 1940-50s Poole Pottery vase, shape no.83, with a variant of pattern 'SK' designed by Truda Carter, the base with impressed and painted marks.

16in (39.5cm) high

£200-300   DN

QUICK REFERENCE - POOLE MARKS

Poole Pottery used over 120 different marks between c1900 and c2000. Some of the more frequently seen marks are shown here. In general, numbers equal a shape number, letters equal a pattern, and strange motifs, monograms or stylised double initials are a decorator's mark. Always consider the layout, format and wording of a mark as differences can often be small. The form and style of the pattern should also back-up the date suggested by a mark.

The printed factory mark on the right was used 1952-55. The painted 'E/YFC' mark indicates the pattern, and the x's are a decorator's mark.

This printed or stamped mark was used 1955-59. A taller and more rounded version was used 1959-67.

This impressed mark (far left) was used 1925-34. Versions without the 'Ltd.' after the company name also date from the 1920s-30s. The incised '897' is the shape number, the 'EP' is the pattern name, and the 'H'-like symbol is a decorator's mark for Anne Hatchard.

The Poole Studio mark was impressed or printed onto bases of 'Studio' wares 1962-64.

This impressed mark was used from 1930 until the 2000s. A similar mark with chamfered corners was used 1924-50. A raised border and letters indicate a date of production from 1922 to 1934.

This unframed printed mark was used 1966-80. The '79' beneath is the shape number, and the three line mark above it is a decorator's mark for Shirley Campbell. A range name, such as 'Aegean', is sometimes printed beneath.

A 1920s-30s Poole Pottery ovoid vase, shape no.440, pattern 'V' designed by Truda Carter, painted with stylised flowers in colours, with impressed and painted marks.

7in (17.5cm) high

£120-180   **WW**

A 1920s-30s Poole Pottery vase, pattern 'NT' decorated by Ann Hatchard, the base with impressed and painted marks, with restoration and hairline to neck.

This is an unusual pattern, which almost takes the form of an abstract 'Willow' pattern in terms of its layout and the bird.

10in (26cm) high

£120-180   **WW**

A small late 1920s Poole Pottery vase, shape no.384, pattern 'TY' designed by Truda Carter, the base with impressed mark and chip to footrim.

5.25in (13.5cm) high

£25-35   **CAPE**

A Poole Pottery wall charger, made for W. T. Lamb & Sons, painted with a spray of flowers in shades of blue, yellow, and ochre, on a white ground, with impressed and printed marks.

13in (33cm) diam

£120-140   **WW**

CERAMICS

Mark Picks

In some ways, the 'Contemporary' range has become more sought-after than Poole's 1920s-30s 'Traditional' range over the past few years. The cool colours, and clean, modern forms fit perfectly into today's interiors, and sum up the design aesthetic of the 1950s perfectly. Examples can often still be found in charity shops and flea markets, so keep your eyes peeled, particularly for classic patterns, or shapes from the popular 'Freeforms' range.

This piece, from the collection of Roy Holland, managing director of Poole Pottery, features a vibrant pattern that may have been a trial of Ruth Pavely's 'HOL' harlequin pattern in different colours. This rarity explains its higher value.

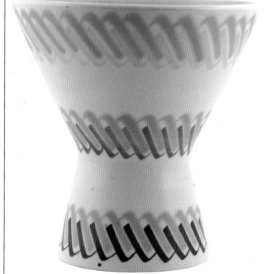

A 1950s Poole Pottery 'Contemporary' carafe vase, shape no.690 designed by Guy Sydenham and Claude Smale, the base with printed and impressed marks, and painted '28'.

12in (30cm) high

£550-650   **WW**

A 1950s Poole Pottery 'Contemporary' carafe vase, shape no.690 designed by Guy Sydenham and Claude Smale, in pattern 'YES' designed by Alfred Read, the base with printed and painted marks.

12in (31cm) high

£250-350   **WW**

A late 1950s Poole Pottery 'Contemporary' vase, shape no.266 probably designed by John Adams, pattern 'X/PKC' designed by Alfred Read in 1954, the base with printed and painted marks.

10in (25cm) high

£350-450   **WW**

A Poole Pottery 'Contemporary' jardinière, shape no.180 designed by Guy Sydenham and Alfred Read, pattern no.'X/PLC' designed by Alfred Read, the base with printed and painted marks.

7in (19cm) high

£120-180   **WW**

A Poole Pottery 'Freeform' vase, shape no.352 designed by Guy Sydenham and Alfred Read, pattern 'PV' designed by Ruth Pavely, the base with printed and painted marks.

7.75in (19.5cm) high

£100-150   **WW**

A Poole Pottery 'Contemporary' waisted vase, shape no.725 designed by Guy Sydenham and Alfred Read, pattern 'X/HYT' designed by Alfred Read, the base with printed and painted marks.

8in (20.5cm) high

£300-500   **WW**

A Poole Pottery 'Freeform' bowl, shape no.338, pattern 'X/PV' designed by Ruth Pavely, the base with printed and painted marks.

17in (44cm) wide

£80-120   **WW**

A Poole Pottery 'Studio' charger, painted with a geometric floral design in orange over a pitted orange ground, the base with printed marks.

1.75in (4.5cm) diam

£250-350 WW

A small Poole Pottery 'Studio' plate, decorated in resist with a geometric design in red, black, and ochre, the base with printed marks.

8in (20.5cm) diam

£80-120 WW

A Poole Pottery 'Studio' 'Delphis' dish, decorated in shades of orange, yellow, and black with an abstract design, with blue factory stamp to base.

10.75in (27cm) diam

£100-150 TRI

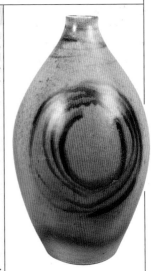

A Poole Pottery 'Studio' charger, no.B22, decorated by Tony Morris with a seagull flying out to sea, the back with printed and painted marks.

16in (41cm) diam

£350-450 WW

A CLOSER LOOK AT A POOLE CHARGER

Tony Morris joined Poole Pottery in 1963 and began by developing experimental glazes with Robert Jefferson. His work is highly sought-after today.

Decorators and designers were encouraged to experiment freely during the 1960s, and their designs summed up the look and feel of the period perfectly.

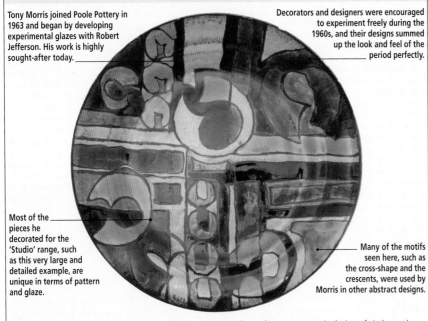

Most of the pieces he decorated for the 'Studio' range, such as this very large and detailed example, are unique in terms of pattern and glaze.

Many of the motifs seen here, such as the cross-shape and the crescents, were used by Morris in other abstract designs.

A Poole Pottery 'Studio' charger, decorated by Tony Morris with an abstract geometric design of circles and rectangles, in shades of green, yellow, and blue, the back with printed 'Studio' mark.

14in (35.5cm) diam

£1,200-1,800 WW

A Poole Pottery 'Studio' 'Delphis' ovoid vase, potted by Guy Sydenham, decorated with a mottled orange glaze with black circles, the base with impressed factory mark and impressed potter's mark of a 'G' within an 'S'.

1966-67 *13in (32cm) high*

£350-450 DN

CERAMICS

QUICK REFERENCE - ATLANTIS

- The 'Atlantis' range was developed by innovative and progressive designer and potter Guy Sydenham from 1965-66. It was given its name in 1969, and was produced into the mid-1970s. Each piece followed a design, but was unique as it was hand-carved and decorated. Typical features include a sparse use of a limited range of earthy glazes, which left the red or grey clay body exposed, and deeply carved patterns. These are typically geometric, appear like fungus or stylised wheat sheaves, or have stone-like textures. The resultant look is very close to studio pottery, which was increasing in popularity at the time.

- 'Atlantis' pieces were made by other throwers and decorators, including Jenny Haigh, Beatrice Bolton and Susan Dipple, but Sydenham was the leading light for the range, and his work tends to be most sought-after. Look out for his rare 'Helmet' or 'Mermaid' lampbases, which can fetch over £2,000. For examples, see 'Miller's Collectables Price Guide 2009', p.89.

A Poole Pottery 'Atlantis' vase, by Guy Sydenham, with incised vertical decoration, the base with impressed and incised marks.

20cm (8in) high

£180-220   SWO

A Poole Pottery 'Atlantis' vase, by Guy Sydenham and Susan Dipple, model 'A9/1', incised with columns, and glazed blue, white, and black, the base with impressed and incised marks.

7in (17cm) high

£150-250   WW

A Poole Pottery 'Atlantis' lamp base, by Carrol Kellett, with incised bands, and glazed in oatmeal and olive green/brown, the base with impressed and incised marks.

11in (29cm) high

£120-180   WW

A Poole Pottery 'Atlantis' vase, by Susan Dipple, with incised columns and lines, the base with impressed and incised marks.

3.75in (9.5cm) high

£80-120   SWO

A Poole Pottery 'Atlantis' vase, by Jenny Haigh, with incised bands of decoration, glazed in black and cream, the base with impressed marks and incised artist cyphers.

4.25in (11cm) high

£150-250   WW

A Poole Pottery redware 'Atlantis' vase, by Guy Sydenham, the base with impressed marks.

4.5in (11.5cm) diam

£150-250   SWO

A 1970s Poole Pottery 'Delphis' charger, shape no.54, painted with a stylised sunburst in shades of blue and yellow on a lime green ground, the base with printed and painted marks.

16in (41cm) diam

£100-150   **WW**

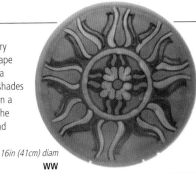

A Poole Pottery 'Aegean' charger, shape no.54, decorated by Carolyn Wills (Walters) using a resist with an owl on a light grey ground, the base with printed and painted marks.

1972-79   16in (41cm) diam

£150-200   **DN**

A CLOSER LOOK AT A POOLE CHARGER

The 'Aegean' range was developed by decorator Leslie Elsden, and launched in 1970. It was hoped that the range would become the successor to 'Delphis', but it was never as popular and was withdrawn in 1980.

The 'Aegean' range was made using many different decorating techniques, including sgraffito, sprayed glazes, and resists, in which a waxy substance repels the glaze and marks out the design once fired.

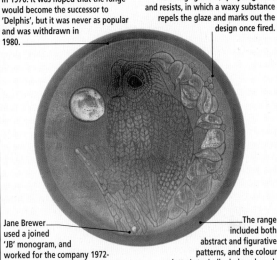

Jane Brewer used a joined 'JB' monogram, and worked for the company 1972-75, allowing this piece to be accurately dated to a small time period.

The range included both abstract and figurative patterns, and the colour palette is typically dark and much less vibrant than 'Delphis'.

A Poole Pottery 'Aegean' charger, shape no.54, decorated by Jane Brewer, with a resist and sprayed pattern of an owl perched before the full moon, the base with printed and painted marks.

1972-75   *16in (41cm) diam*

£180-220   **WW**

A Poole Pottery limited edition 'Christ on the Cross' cathedral plate, shape no.6, with pattern no.479 designed by Tony Morris, decorated by Carolyn Wills, numbered 912 from an edition of 1,000, in fitted box.

This was part of a series of limited edition plates inspired by stained glass windows. Issued in 1973, this design was inspired by the 12thC lancet windows in Notre Dame cathedral in Chartres, France.

1973   *13in (32cm) diam*

£120-180   **WW**

A mid-late 1970s Poole Pottery 'Delphis' waisted vase, shape no.85, decorated in green, yellow, and red, the base with printed factory mark.

15.75in (40cm) high

£80-120   **GORL**

A modern Poole Pottery limited edition 'Kink' vase, decorated with the 'Red Daisy' pattern designed by Karen Ford, numbered 6 from an edition of 250, the base with printed and painted marks, and with certificate.

c2000   *14in (36cm) high*

£70-100   **DA&H**

CERAMICS

QUICK REFERENCE - CHARLOTTE RHEAD

- Charlotte Rhead (1885-1947) came from a long line of ceramics designers based at the Staffordshire potteries. After studying at the Fenton School of Art, she learnt the tube-lining technique at Wardle & Co. in Hanley. She then worked for Keeling & Co. and tilemaker T. & R. Boote, before joining Wood & Sons, where her father was art director, in 1913. From 1926 to 1931, she worked for Burgess & Leigh, where she trained a team of tube-liners. Her most prolific period was 1931-43, when she worked for A. G. Richardson under the brand name 'Crown Ducal'. After that, she returned to Wood & Sons as art director.

- Although an innovative woman designer in her own right, her work has never been as popular as that of her contemporary Clarice Cliff. Even her scarcest and most desirable designs rarely fetch over £1,500, although this may change if more collectors are drawn to her

A Crown Ducal 'Primula' pattern ribbed ovoid vase, shape no.161, pattern no. unknown and designed by Charlotte Rhead, enamelled and tube-lined in green and yellow, and with a 'stitch' rim line, the base with factory and signature marks.

c1934   *9in (22.5cm) high*

£50-70   **MOR**

A Crown Ducal 'Persian Rose' pattern flower jug, pattern no.4040 designed by Charlotte Rhead, enamelled and tube-lined with a floral and foliate pattern, with yellow rim, base, and handle, the base with factory and signature marks.

8in (20.5cm) high

£70-100   **MOR**

A Crown Ducal 'Golden Leaves' pattern ribbed ovoid vase, shape no.212, pattern no.4921 designed by Charlotte Rhead, tube-lined and painted in orange, green, and brown lustre glazes against a cream ground, the base with factory and signature marks.

8in (19.5cm) high

£60-90   **MOR**

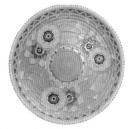

A Bursleyware 'Trellis' pattern jug, pattern no.TL3 designed by Charlotte Rhead, enamelled and tube-lined in shades of orange and brown, the base with factory marks.

8in (21cm) high

£30-50   **MOR**

A Crown Ducal 'Rhodian' pattern plaque, pattern no.3272 designed by Charlotte Rhead, enamelled and tube-lined in shades of yellow, orange, and mocha, the reverse with factory and signature marks.

14in (36.5cm) diam

£100-150   **MOR**

A Crown Ducal 'Blue Peony' pattern charger, pattern no.4016 designed by Charlotte Rhead, painted in shades of blue, with factory and signature marks to base.

The inspiration for this striking floral pattern may have come from Iznik tiles.

c1935   *13in (32cm) diam*

£150-200   **MOR**

CERAMICS

QUICK REFERENCE - ROOKWOOD

- In 1880 heiress Maria Longworth Nichols founded the Rookwood Pottery, transforming her ceramic-painting hobby into a commercial venture. The company did not turn a profit until William Watts Tyler joined as production manager in 1883. When Nichols moved abroad in 1890 Tyler took over the pottery, and turned it into an award-winning success.
- The company is best-known for its very high quality glazes, which were often heavily influenced by Japanese ceramics. Of these glazes the best-known is perhaps the first to be developed, the graduated yellow-brown Standard Glaze (1884). Pieces in this glaze were typically decorated with flowers. Portraits are known, but are much rarer, and consequently more desirable.
- Two more glazes were introduced in 1894. Iris was clear and glossy, while Sea Green was green-tinted, and often used for images of fish. Vellum, which creates a misty, almost-Impressionistic appearance, was introduced in 1900, and Matte glazes in 1901. Tyler was keen to experiment, and strove to rediscover ancient techniques or create new ones by hiring specialist glaze technicians. Due to the importance of the glaze to Rookwood collectors any crazing or damage on a piece will significantly reduce its value and desirability.
- The company employed several famous artists throughout the course of its history including Matthew Daly, Albert Valentien, and the revered Kataro Shirayamadani. Signed pieces by such artists tend to be the most valuable and sought-after, so look out for their marks. The company's post-1905 mass-produced pieces, known as 'Production' ware, are not artist-signed and tend to be less desirable. Rookwood closed in 1964.

A Rookwood Standard Glaze ovoid vase, decorated with flowers by Irene Bishop, the base with Rookwood marks, numbered '534D', and with artist's cypher.
1903   *6.75in (17cm) high*
£300-500   LHA

A Rookwood Standard Glaze footed vase, of flattened ovoid form, decorated with flowers by Sara Elizabeth Coyne, the base with Rookwood marks.
3.75in (9.5cm) high
£220-280   LHA

A Rookwood Vellum glaze ovoid vase, decorated with shore birds and cattails by Kataro Shirayamadani, the base with impressed marks and drilled hole.

Kataro Shirayamadani (1865-1948) was a highly skilled Japanese ceramics decorator who worked at Rookwood from 1887 to 1948. His work is highly prized, particularly if the decoration is finely detailed or embellished with silver. His masterpieces can fetch tens of thousands of pounds. However, the decoration is relatively simple on this example, and a hole has been drilled into the base so that it can be used as a lampbase, which reduces the value. As such it represents a more affordable way to include the work of this great decorator in a collection.

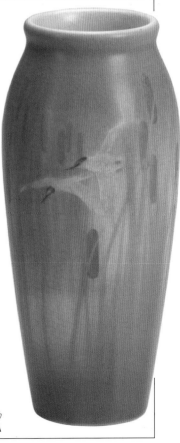

10in (25cm) high
£500-700   DRA

A Rookwood Standard Glaze two-handled vase, decorated with holly leaves and berries by Jeannette Swing, the base with impressed marks including model number '459 D', and 'SJ' artist's initials.
1904   *6in (15cm) high*
£300-500   FRE

A Rookwood Wax Matte glaze ovoid vase, decorated with daisies by Elizabeth Lincoln, the base with impressed marks including the 'flame' mark.
1932   *4in (10cm) high*
£300-400   DRA

QUICK REFERENCE - ROOKWOOD MARKS

- The impressed tree-shape mark that can be found on the bottom of nearly all Rookwood pottery made between 1886 and 1967 is known as the 'flame' mark. The precise format will allow you to date a piece to a particular year. The 'trunk' is formed from a stylised monogram made up of a reversed 'R' for Rookwood, and a 'P' for 'pottery'. Every year after 1886 saw the addition of another curving 'flame' mark to the canopy of 'branches'. By 1900, the canopy had gained fourteen 'flame' marks and no more were added. Instead, in 1901, the Roman numeral 'I' was added below the tree-like mark, and this changed every year. So the 'XV' shown here would indicate fifteen years from 1900, indicating 1915, the year this pot was made.

- The '1812' beneath it is the shape number, and beneath that there's usually an inscribed artist's monogram, which is not present on this example.

A Rookwood hexagonal tapered vase, with a dripped all-over mottled deep blue glaze, the base with impressed 'flame' mark and numbered '1812', lacks artist's mark.

1915   *7.5in (19cm) high*

£150-250   **DMC**

A Rockwood Matte glaze ovoid vase, moulded with a grape and vine leaf pattern with a light blue glaze, the base with impressed 'flame' mark and numbered '2604'.

1925   *6.25in (16cm) high*

£200-300   **FRE**

A pair of Rookwood 'Production' bookends, in the form of rooks, covered in brilliant majolica glazes, restored.

1928   *6.5in (17cm) high*

£200-300   **DRA**

A pair of Rookwood 'Production' bookends, in the form of baskets of flowers, covered in brilliant majolica glazes, with some scratches.

1929   *5.75in (15cm) high*

£150-200   **DRA**

A Rookwood 'Production' cat paperweight, covered in slate and amber crystalline glazes, the base with 'flame' mark.

1928   *4in (10cm) high*

£350-450   **DRA**

A Rookwood green faïence tile, moulded with a stag in low relief, the reverse with impressed mark.

8in (20cm) wide

£120-180   **DRA**

QUICK REFERENCE

- Established in 1890 in the 'pottery state' of Ohio, USA, the Roseville Pottery company initially made utilitarian wares. The company grew quickly, acquiring other factories and, by 1910, production was centred in Zanesville, Ohio.
- Roseville produced its first art pottery range, 'Rozane' in 1900. It was similar to Rookwood's popular 'Standard Glaze', and its success led to more art pottery ranges. By 1908, demand for expensive hand-decorated pottery had declined and Roseville turned to mass-produced moulded ranges with quicker and easier designs. An artist who might have spent a day decorating a piece could now paint over 300 in the same time. The company had great success with many of these ranges. The pottery closed in 1954.
- The noted designer Frederick H. Rhead worked at Roseville from 1904 to 1908. During this time he introduced many of the ranges that are most sought-after today, such as 'Della

Robbia', as well as the widely-used squeeze-bag technique.
- Roseville's moulded designs are often based around natural motifs. Important names from this period include Frank Ferrell, who designed patterns and shapes from 1917 to 1954, and George Krause who devised glazes from 1915 to 1954.
- The moulding of any mass-produced piece should be clear and crisp, and glazes should be well and correctly applied to the pattern. Shapes affect value, and colours also count – blue is often more desirable than brown. Although easily found, early ranges such as 'Pine Cone' and 'Dahlrose', are widely collected and desirable. Ranges in popular styles, such as Art Nouveau and Art Deco continue to be sought-after.
- Condition is extremely important, with chips or cracks devaluing a moulded piece by at least 50 per cent. Fakes and reproductions also exist, so make sure you closely examine marks on the base.

A Roseville 'Blackberry' jardinière and pedestal set, the base unmarked.

Introduced in 1932, 'Blackberry' was used on nearly 30 different shapes and is a popular pattern with collectors today. Most pieces are unmarked, although some may have originally had foil labels or hand-written shape numbers.

28in (71cm) high

£1,200-1,800   DRA

A Roseville 'Dahlrose' bud vase, shape no.78-8, with angled handles, the base unmarked.

8.25in (21cm) high

£200-300   BEL

A Roseville 'Dahlrose' jardinière and pedestal, the base with moulded marks.

Jardinière 13in (33cm) diam

£400-600   FRE

A Roseville 'Florentine' bowl, of shouldered form, with square handles and plain glazed interior, the base stamped 'Rv' in blue ink.
c1924-38   *8in (20cm) diam*
£60-90   FRE

A Roseville 'Fuchsia' twin-handled vase, on a deep blue ground, the base with impressed factory marks.

7.5in (20cm) high

£40-60   WW

CERAMICS

A Roseville 'Futura' handled jardinière, decorated with leaves, the base unmarked.

This bowl was painted green at some point, although the seller has managed to remove nearly all of it. Always be extra careful when buying anything that has been painted over, as the paint can hide a multitude of sins. Also make sure the paint can be removed, and that removing it won't cost too much, before you buy.

14.5in (37cm) diam

£300-500   DRA

A Roseville 'Futura' wall pocket, with crack to the bottom point, the base with Roseville sticker.

8.25in (21cm) high

£120-180   DRA

A Roseville blue 'Magnolia' teapot, the base marked 'USA 4'.

7.75in (19.5cm) high

£150-200   BEL

A Roseville 'Pinecone' vase, shape no.712, with a brown ground.

12in (30.5cm) high

£350-350   DRA

Miller's Compares

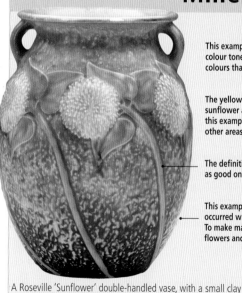

This example has much more variation in its colour tones, and features deeper and richer colours than the other.

The yellow and green glazes used on the sunflower and leaves are better applied on this example, and have not dripped into other areas.

The definition of the moulded details is not as good on this example.

This example has an imperfection that occurred when the vase was being moulded. To make matters worse it's on one of the flowers and so is very visible.

A Roseville 'Sunflower' double-handled vase, with a small clay imperfection to one bloom, the base unmarked.

A Roseville 'Sunflower' double-handled vase, the base unmarked.

8in (20cm) high

£300-500

DRA   £600-800

9in (23cm) high

DRA

QUICK REFERENCE - VELMOSS

- The name 'Velmoss' applies to at least three different designs. The earliest, dating from c1917 to c1922, is known correctly as 'Velmoss Scroll' and has an impressed pattern of highly stylised pink roses and sinuously curving green stems. The pattern shown here, which features vertical stylised leaves, came later, but is known as 'Early Velmoss'. This pattern was superseded in 1935 by a similar pattern, in which the leaves overlap and curve. A final pattern has a small sprig of curving leaves and berries that resemble mistletoe placed near, or issuing from, the rim.
- Colours are muted and comprise pinky-red, beige, blue, green, and blue-green. Some patterns were only produced in certain colours, for example, this variant was not produced in pinky-red.

A Roseville early 'Velmoss' flaring vase, with two small burst-glaze bubbles on the inside rim, the base unmarked.

12in (30.5cm) high

£300-500　　DRA

A Roseville 'Early Velmoss' two-colour umbrella stand, with unmarked base.

The pattern shown here is strongly Arts and Crafts in style, and is similar to art pottery pieces by Grueby. Umbrella stands are scarce forms as so many were broken or damaged through use.

20in (51cm) high

£600-900　　DRA

A tall 1920s Roseville 'Vista' vase, the base unmarked.

Introduced in c1920, 'Vista' is typically unmarked, although some examples have an ink-stamped shape number and size on the base. It's scarce compared to more common ranges such as 'Pine Cone' or 'Dahlrose', and tends to fetch higher prices as a result of this and because of its decorative appearance.

15in (38cm) high

£450-550　　DRA

A Roseville 'Windsor' vase, shape no.547-6, with a mottled blue ground and geometric decoration around the rim, the base unmarked, in mint condition.

'Windsor' was introduced in 1931, and can be found with mottled blue or orangey-red glazes.

6.25in (16cm) high

£300-400　　BEL

A Roseville 'Wisteria' double-handled vase, with graduated blue-brown ground, the base unmarked.

7in (18cm) high

£250-350　　DRA

A Roseville 'Woodland' twisted faceted vase, painted with poppies in amber glazes, the base unmarked.

Sometimes known as 'Rozane Woodland', this range was introduced in 1905 and was inspired by Japanese designs. Patterns are enamelled onto a bisque body in colours. Sixteen different shapes are known from factory pattern books.

6.5in (16.5cm) high

£500-700　　DRA

A Roseville 'Zephyr Lily' jardinière, with a green ground, with minor glaze fleck to a petal, the base with factory marks.

8in (20.5cm)

£80-120　　DRA

QUICK REFERENCE - ROYAL BAYREUTH

- The factory now widely known as 'Royal Bayreuth' was founded with special royal permission from King Friedrich Wilhelm II in Tettau, Thuringia, Germany in 1794. This fact is indicated by its official name 'Königlich Privilegierte Porzellanfabrik Tettau', which means 'a porcelain manufacturer in Tettau by privilege of the King'.

- The mainstay of production was tableware and figurines, but during the last years of the 19thC the factory became well-known for a wide and varied range of highly decorative jugs, tobacco jars, teapots, and similar wares in the shapes of animals, leaves, or fruits. Fashionable in Victorian and Edwardian homes, many were exported to the US, where the main body of collectors can still be found today.

- Values depend on the shape, size, age, and quality of decoration of a piece. Among the most sought-after and valuable pieces are jugs or other vessels in the form of playing cards with the devil as a handle or other motif. Other shapes, such as squirrel jugs, can also be valuable. Always examine a piece carefully for damage such as cracks, as this reduces value.

A Royal Bayreuth water buffalo cream jug, painted in tones of red, the base with blue printed factory mark.

c1900   5.75in (14.5cm) long

£30-40   DMC

A Royal Bayreuth alligator cream jug, the base with green printed factory mark

4.5in (11.5cm) high

£40-50   DMC

A Royal Bayreuth cockerel water jug, the base with blue printed factory mark.

c1905   8in (20.5cm) long

£100-150   DMC

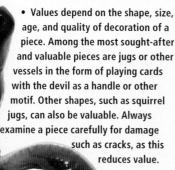

A Royal Bayreuth black crow cream jug, with a brown beak, the base with blue printed factory mark.

4.75in (12cm) high

£60-80   DMC

A Royal Bayreuth Saint Bernard dog water jug, unmarked.

8.5in (21.5cm) long

£50-70   DMC

A Royal Bayreuth fish head creamer, the base with blue printed factory mark.

4.5in (11.5cm) high

£30-40   DMC

QUICK REFERENCE - ROYAL BAYREUTH MARKS

• Over 25 different marks are known for Royal Bayreuth. The style of mark below is the most commonly seen and indicates that a piece was made after 1900. If the lions are facing away from each other, the piece dates from after 1968. As well as blue, as here, both marks can be found in grey, red, or gold. The mid-late 19thC mark of a single lion holding a shield with a 'T' in it was re-introduced during the mid-1940s. This is usually accompanied by the words 'US Zone', indicating the piece was made in the American governed zone of post-WWII Germany 1945-c1949.

A Royal Bayreuth kangaroo cream jug, the base with blue printed factory mark and marked '17'.
c1910   *4.75in (12cm) high*
£40-60   **DMC**

A Royal Bayreuth ladybird cream jug, the base with blue printed factory mark.
c1910   *3.75in (9.5cm) high*
£100-150   **DMC**

A Royal Bayreuth orange-red lobster water jug, the base with blue printed factory mark.
c1910   *9in (23cm) wide*
£80-120   **DMC**

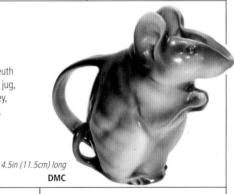

A Royal Bayreuth mouse cream jug, painted in grey, with red eyes, unmarked.
4.5in (11.5cm) long
£60-80   **DMC**

A Royal Bayreuth parakeet milk jug, painted in green and orange, the base with blue printed factory mark.
5in (12.5cm) long
£60-80   **DMC**

A Royal Bayreuth red pig cream jug, the base with blue printed factory mark.
c1905   *4.5in (11.5cm) high*
£40-60   **DMC**

A Royal Bayreuth coiled snake milk jug, the base with blue printed factory mark.
8.5in (21.5cm) long
£80-120   **DMC**

CERAMICS

QUICK REFERENCE

- The Derby Crown Porcelain Co. was established in 1878 in Derby, England, by William Litherland and Edward Phillips. The company rose quickly to prominence, and in 1890 it became Royal Crown Derby Porcelain after being awarded the Royal Warrant. The company is still producing high quality porcelain and pottery today.
- Early wares were hand-painted, with printed wares being added in 1891. Pieces decorated by a noted artist, such as Désiré Leroy, Albert Gregory, or Cuthbert Gresley, are likely to be desirable.
- Although the company has produced ceramics in many styles, Royal Crown Derby is best-known for its 'Imari' patterns, inspired by the Japanese export ware of that name. Royal Crown Derby's Imari ranges currently include the dinnerware ranges 'Old Imari', 'Traditional Imari', 'Blue Mikado', and 'Olde Avesbury'.

- Royal Crown Derby paperweights were introduced in 1981. Designed by Robert Jefferson, the first range comprised six pieces in the shape of animals and birds. The range has since expanded featuring new editions by John Abilitt and some remodelled versions of Jefferson's originals. Designs began to be withdrawn from production annually from 1987.
- Early examples were filled with sand and were functional, but they soon became entirely ornamental as sand hindered production and increased postage costs. All paperweights have a stopper, typically gold-coloured. Silver-coloured stoppers indicate a 'second' quality piece. A hexagonal stopper was used during the Millennium. Look out for rare pieces produced for short periods of time, in mint condition.
- From c1890, pieces are generally marked with a crown above a monogram. Mark variations include 'Made in England' and 'Bone China'. Year marks were used from 1882 to 1958.

A late 19thC Royal Crown Derby 'Imari' tea tray, decorated in pattern no.3788, stamped to base with date code for 1895 and registration number '204893'.

1895   *18in (46cm) wide*

£80-120   **TRI**

A Royal Crown Derby 'Old Imari' oval meat plate, in pattern no.1128, with burnt orange mark.

15in (38cm) diam

£150-200   **AH**

A Royal Crown Derby 'Imari' commemorative Christmas plate for 1991, numbered 431 from a limited edition of 1,500, with printed marks to back.

1991   *8.5in (22cm) diam*

£30-40   **TRI**

A late 20thC Royal Crown Derby 'Old Imari' fruit bowl, in pattern no.1128, of steep sided octagonal form, the base with printed marks.

8.25in (21cm) wide

£200-300   **CAPE**

A Royal Crown Derby 'Old Imari' soup tureen and cover, in pattern no.1128, with two acanthus leaf sheathed handles and acorn knop, the base with iron red mark.

11.5in (29cm) diam

£450-550   **AH**

A late 20thC Royal Crown Derby 'Old Imari' plant pot holder, in pattern no.1128, with slightly flared rim, and printed mark to base.

4.5in (11.4cm) high

£100-150   **CAPE**

A 20thC Royal Crown Derby 'Imari' ovoid vase, with printed marks to base.

5in (12.5cm) high

£60-80   **WHP**

A CLOSER LOOK AT A DERBY LOVING CUP

Cuthbert Gresley (1876-1963) trained under artist J. P. Wale, and became a notable, although not top-tier, artist at Derby.

Although he executed a wide range of designs, he was skilled at landscapes and flowers, which became his specialities.

Cuthbert was part of a well-known family of painters. His father Frank was a noted watercolour painter, as was his grandfather James Stephen. His brother Harold also decorated porcelain at Derby and painted.

The simple yet elegant design of the rest of the decoration indicates that it was made in the early 20thC when Regency styles were revived.

A Royal Crown Derby loving cup, hand-painted with a loch scene by Cuthbert Gresley against a cobalt blue and gilded striped ground, with printed marks to base.

4.25in (11cm) high

£300-400   **GORL**

A Royal Crown Derby baluster-form vase, painted by W. Dean with fishing boats at dusk within a gilt tooled cartouche on a cobalt blue ground, signed, the base with printed marks and date cypher.

1942   *4.25in (11cm) high*

£150-200   **AH**

A pair of late 20thC Royal Crown Derby 'Old Imari' candlesticks, in pattern no.1128, with panelled tapering columns on shaped square bases, with moulded mythical fish to the corners, with printed marks to base.

10.5in (27cm) high

£500-700   **CAPE**

CERAMICS

A Royal Crown Derby 'Honey Bear' paperweight, designed by Robert Jefferson and decorated by Jo Ledger.

A more complexly gilded version was produced from 1997 to 2006 for retailer Govier's of Sidmouth. Look out for examples from the 'pre-sale' limited edition of 500 designed by Sue Rowe, which have a special backstamp. These can fetch over three times as much as this earlier design.

1994-97   *4in (10cm) high*

£40-60   **CHT**

A Royal Crown Derby 'Beaver' paperweight, designed by Robert Jefferson and decorated by Jo Ledger.

A version with a dark blue back and head-top designed by Sue Rowe and known as 'Riverbank Beaver' was sold in a limited edition to Collectors' Guild members in 2002. It is worth slightly more than this example.

1994-   *97 3in (7.5cm) high*

£35-45   **CHT**

A CLOSER LOOK AT A PAPERWEIGHT

This 'Bull' was released to the Collectors Guild in 1991 before being released generally a year later.

This 'Bull' shape has also been produced in two limited editions, one in red and gold in an edition of 400 for Harrod's, and one in green and gold in an edition of 750 for Connaught House. Both can be worth over 50% more than this example.

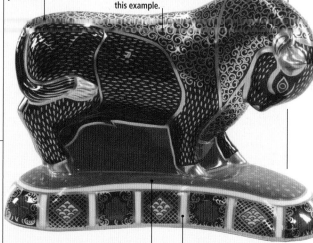

Costing between £225 and £315 across its ten year lifetime, it was an expensive purchase. This meant fewer were sold compared to other less expensive models like 'Pheasant', also shown here, which cost £26.95-£70 across its lifetime.

The crescent shaped base is decorated with the company's famous 'Old Imari' pattern, no.1128, harking back to the company's fine heritage.

A Royal Crown Derby 'Imari' 'Bull' paperweight, designed by Robert Jefferson (modeller) and Jo Ledger (decorator).

1992-2002   *5in (13cm) high*

£150-200   **WHP**

A Royal Crown Derby 'Bulldog' paperweight, designed by Robert Jefferson and decorated by Jo Ledger.

1991-97   *3.25in (8.5cm) high*

£50-70   **CHT**

A Royal Crown Derby 'Camel' paperweight, designed by John Ablitt.

Like the 'Bull', this was an expensive purchase, costing from £245-380 across its twelve year lifetime.

1996-2008   *7in (17cm) high*

£150-200   **CHT**

A Royal Crown Derby 'Hummingbird' paperweight, designed by John Ablitt.

A 'Bee-Eater' version with a dark blue chest was sold from 2003 to 2008, and is now worth around the same amount as this example. Jo Ledger, then art director of Royal Doulton, owner of the Royal Crown Derby brand, wanted a more colourful bee-eater hummingbird, so the later model was produced.

1983-2000   *5in (10cm) high*

£40-60   **CHT**

Mark Picks

It's not just the originally expensive paperweights that are worth large sums today. As with many antiques and collectables, once demand exceeds supply, prices rise. 'Deer' was the first model available to Royal Crown Derby Collectors' Guild members only, and it was only available to them in 1994. This makes it a comparatively hard to find and sought-after model for collectors today. At the time it cost £150, so it has more than doubled in value. As with so many 20thC collectables, it pays to learn which ones are rare! Always aim to buy an example in mint condition, which also retains its box and 'first quality' gold stopper, as these are likely to hold their value, or rise further in value, in the future.

A Royal Crown Derby limited production 'Deer' paperweight, designed by John Ablitt.

1994   *6in (15cm) high*
£300-400   **CHT**

A Royal Crown Derby 'Imari' 'Pheasant' paperweight, designed by Robert Jefferson and Brian Branscombe.

This best-selling form was revived in 1999, and called 'Woodland Pheasant'. Produced for the Collectors' Guild, the colours of the top of the head and back were changed from blue to green, and other details were painted differently.

1983-98   *2.5in (6.5cm) high*
£30-50   **WHP**

A Royal Crown Derby 'King Charles Spaniel' paperweight, designed by Donald Brindley and Sue Rowe.

2003-06   *3.75in (9.5cm) high*
£50-70   **CHT**

A Royal Crown Derby 'Tiger Cub' paperweight, designed by Robert Jefferson and decorated by Jo Ledger.

1993-96   *3in (7.5cm) high*
£30-50   **CHT**

A Royal Crown Derby 'Bengal Tiger' paperweight, designed by John Ablitt.

1994-99   *5in (12.5cm) high*
£120-180   **CHT**

A Royal Crown Derby 'Zebra' paperweight, designed by John Ablitt.

1995-98   *5in (13cm) high*
£100-150   **CHT**

CERAMICS

A Ruskin Pottery vase, with everted rim, covered in a rich purple lustre glaze, the base with impressed marks, and dated.

1922   *7.5in (22cm) high*

£450-550   **WW**

A Ruskin Pottery vase, of shouldered form, covered in a lavender lustre glaze, the base with impressed marks, and dated.

Although the Chinese-inspired form of this vase is pleasing, its streaked glaze could be better and more detailed. The price is therefore considerably lower than the price paid for more interestingly glazed pieces.

1910   *10in (24cm) high*

£120-180   **WW**

A Ruskin Pottery stoneware urn-shaped vase, with three handles, modelled in low relief with a Tudor rose motif, glazed with a matt blue glaze, dripped yellow to the shoulder and handles, the base with impressed marks.

                          10in (25cm) high

£120-180   **WW**

A Ruskin Pottery pedestal bowl, covered in an ochre-mottled strawberry-pink lustre glaze, the base with impressed marks, and dated.

1924   *7.5in (20cm) high*

£200-300   **WW**

A Ruskin Pottery high-fired stoneware ovoid vase, with long cylindrical neck and everted rim, covered in a sang de boeuf and lavender glaze with mint-green speckles, the base with impressed marks and dated.

The Ruskin pottery was founded in Birmingham in 1898 by Edward R. Taylor. Named after the famed art critic and artist John Ruskin, the pottery saw its golden years under Taylor's son, William Howson Taylor. Taking Chinese forms and glazes as inspiration, he devised the many complex and unique glazes for which the company is known. Ruskin closed in 1935 and all the glaze recipes were destroyed, which means they have never been repeated.

1909   *10in (23.5cm) high*

£600-800   **WW**

A Ruskin Pottery high-fired stoneware bowl, covered in a mottled sang de boeuf and silver glaze under a mint-green glaze, the base with impressed marks, and dated.

1933   *10in (24.5cm) diam*

£250-350   **WW**

QUICK REFERENCE

- The term 'studio pottery' is applied to pottery made by independent potters in their own studios, or by a small team of assistants working under a potter's guidance. Although the movement began in the 19thC, it really took hold in the early 20thC, and then boomed after World War II.
- As studio pottery is all handmade, or hand-decorated, each piece is unique. Although typically decorative, most pieces are also functional, and include vases, bowls, and tableware. Each potter's work is also defined by its individualistic and expressive artistic elements.
- The most desirable and valuable work was made by potters who are considered pioneers of the movement. These include Bernard Leach (1887-1979) and his colleague Shoji Hamada (1894-1978), Lucie Rie (1902-1981) and her colleague Hans Coper (1920-1981), Charles Binns (1857-1934), and Otto (1908-2007) and Gertrude (1908-1971) Natzler. Pieces made by them can fetch many hundreds, or thousands, of pounds.
- Work from important students (or descendents, in the case of Leach) of such forerunners is often more affordable and equally important when placed in context. Pottery by Michael Cardew is a good example.

- As this second generation of potters continues to be studied, many collectors are also beginning to turn to the work of their students, many of whom are still living. Over the past three decades, greater attention has been paid to studio pottery as an art form capable of conveying a message, and artists have responded by enhancing this quality in their pots. As a result, studio pottery is now considered as one of the most vibrant art forms on the market today.
- Apart from the maker and date, key points to consider include quality in terms of form, glaze, and overall design. Innovation is also an important indicator to value, with pieces that led the way towards new styles or embodied the 'look' of the day tending to be more desirable. Look out for large objects, as these are often scarcer and highly desirable.
- Always examine the base for an impressed or inscribed mark. Investing in a reference guide showing potters' marks is essential. There are still bargains to be had, both among currently unrecognised potteries and with those pieces whose marks have not been recognised by the seller. Be sure to check thoroughly for damage such as chips or cracks as this usually has a dramatic effect on the value.

A David Leach porcelain bowl, with sliced decoration, covered in a gun-metal glaze, the base with impressed seal mark.

7.5in (19cm) diam

£350-450   WW

A David Leach stoneware ovoid vase, with a collar rim, and decorated with a foxglove motif in rust over a tenmoku glaze, the base with impressed seal mark and paper label reading 'DL1'.

A similar example of this Oriental-inspired form in a dolomite and tenmoku glaze can be seen on p.305 of 'David Leach', by Emmanuel Cooper and Kathy Niblett, published by Richard Dennis Publications.

A Lowerdown Pottery porcelain vase, by David Leach, with sliced exterior decoration, covered in a copper reduction glaze, the base with impressed seal marks.

5.25in (13.5cm) high

£500-700   WW

A large David Leach stoneware vase, painted with abstract forms in a tenmoku glaze, the base with impressed seal mark.

14in (35cm) high

£450-550   L&T

10in (26cm) high

£1,200-1,800   WW

CERAMICS

QUICK REFERENCE - THE LEACH FAMILY

- The Leach family are almost certainly the most important and influential family of studio potters in the world. Primarily influenced by Oriental ceramics, Benard Leach promoted functionality over decorative or artistic aspects. Following his teachings, style and lead, nearly all members of the family were or became potters, including his wife, sons and grandsons. Each of them used different impressed marks, which are shown here.

An impressed seal mark for the Leach Pottery
The Leach pottery was founded in St. Ives by Bernard Leach and Shoji Hamada in 1920. As well as being influential to studio potters across the world, it became an important training ground. This mark can be used on its own, or accompanied by the personal impressed seal of a particular potter. The pottery is still open today, and also houses a museum covering the Leach tradition.

An impressed seal mark for Bernard Leach
The 'father of studio ceramics' Bernard Leach (1887-1979) used a number of marks, with this mark being the most commonly found. It has two dots near the 'L'. From 1913 to the 1920s he used a 'BHL' impressed mark, and after 1940 he often also painted his initials on the back or base of a piece.

Impressed seal marks for the Lowerdown Pottery and David Leach *The Lowerdown Pottery was founded by Bernard's son, David Leach (1911-2005) in 1956, after he left St. Ives. Other mark variations include the 'LD' mark with two dots to its right, and a mark combining the 'LD' closely in a circle. David's sons Jeremy (b.1941) and Simon (b.1956) now pot at Lowerdown.*

An impressed seal mark for Janet Leach
Texan potter Janet Darnell (1918-1997) married Bernard Leach in 1956, after meeting him in 1952 and studying in Japan. Pursuing her own working methods and aesthetic, she is known for her bottle vases and randomly applied steaks or patches of glaze that add movement.

A Leach Pottery stoneware unomi, decorated with a foliate stem in tenmoku glaze, with indistinct personal seal and a Leach Pottery seal mark.

An unomi is a Japanese tea bowl.
3.75in (9.5cm) high
£180-220   WW

A Leach Pottery stoneware unomi, resist-decorated with a flowerhead motif in an ash glaze, with indistinct seal marks, and a small nick to top rim.
3.5in (9cm) high
£60-80   WW

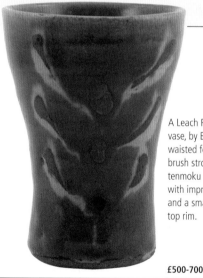

A Leach Pottery stoneware vase, by Bernard Leach, of waisted form, with simple brush stroke design in tenmoku on a blue ground, with impressed seal marks, and a small bruise to the top rim.
5.5in (14cm) high
£500-700   WW

A late 20thC Bernard Leach stoneware charger, the well incised with a rice plant motif, and glazed in pale blue, with painted 'BL' monogram to reverse.
11in (28cm) diam
£700-900   WW

A Leach Pottery porcelain vase, by Janet Leach, of slender form with everted rim, with applied lug handles, and covered in a pale celadon glaze with tenmoku brush design, the base with impressed seal marks.
5.75in (14.5cm) high
£400-600   WW

QUICK REFERENCE - MICHAEL CARDEW

- Michael Cardew (1901-1983) is considered to be Bernard Leach's most important and influential student. He founded a number of potteries, the first of which was the Winchcombe Pottery, established in 1926, where he worked until 1939, and then again 1942-44. He founded the Wenford Bridge Pottery in 1939, before moving to Africa where he taught and founded a pottery at Abuja in 1950. Travelling between Africa and the UK during the late 1940s-50s, he founded the Kingwood Pottery in 1948, and later returned to Wenford Bridge. Unsurprisingly, his influence was wide, and he taught and developed many important potters, as well as developing his own style. His pupils included the prolific Sidney Tustin, Ray Finch, his son Seth Cardew (whose mark is an 'S' inside a 'C'), Svend Bayer, and Danlami Aliyu.

A Winchcombe Pottery Mark.

A Wenford Bridge Pottery mark.

Michael Cardew's personal seal mark.

Sidney Tustin's personal seal mark.

An early Winchcombe Pottery slip-decorated earthenware plate, by Michael Cardew, the rim decorated with a wavy trail design, the back with impressed seal marks.

10in (24.5cm) diam

£200-300   WW

A Winchcombe Pottery earthenware plate, by Michael Cardew, decorated to the well with an olive-green glaze and trailed in brown, the base with impressed seal marks.

7.5in (19cm) diam

£250-350   WW

A Winchcombe Pottery slip-decorated dish, by Sidney Tustin, glazed to the foot in a green glaze with a brown combed design to the well, the back with impressed seal marks.

10in (25cm) diam

£200-300   WW

A Winchcombe Pottery single-handled jug vase, by Michael Cardew, with green glaze and slip decoration, the base with impressed seal marks, and a hairline to the rim.

5.25in (13.5cm) high

£250-300   WW

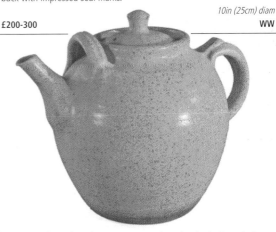

An oversized Winchcombe Pottery teapot, in a pitted ash glaze, the base with impressed seal mark.

10.75in (27.5cm) high

£100-150   WW

A Winchcombe Pottery terracotta wall pocket, by Michael Cardew, the deep brown-black glaze incised with a grass stem design, the base with impressed seal marks.

9in (23cm) high

£180-220   WW

A large Wenford Bridge Pottery stoneware platter, by Seth Cardew, painted with a standing bird, the back with personal seal mark and Wenford Bridge Pottery mark.

Seth Cardew (b.1934) joined his father at Wenford Bridge in 1971 after a career in film-set construction and design. He began potting in earnest in 1974, and ran Wenford Bridge Pottery until 2004 when he relocated the pottery to Spain. Many of his designs include painted motifs of animals or people, some of which are similar to his father's designs, such as this bird design.

c1975   *13in (34cm) diam*

£200-300   L&T

A Winchcombe Pottery hand-thrown coffee pot, by Michael Cardew, with pulled loop handle and shallow cover, decorated with a hand-painted sprig motif over the buff glazed ground, with impressed marks.

10in (24cm) high

£300-400   FLD

A Wenford Bridge Pottery 'Gwari' casserole and cover, by Michael Cardew, with incised decoration under a tenmoku glaze, the base with impressed seal marks.

13in (33cm) diam

£350-450   WW

An African Abuja Pottery 'Gwari' stoneware casserole and cover, by Peter Gboko, with incised band of decoration, incised 'PKG' to base, with glaze faults.

The Gwari are a Nigerian ethnic group, known for their openness and love of peace and order.

10in (25cm) wide

£80-120   WW

A Kingwood Pottery bowl and cover, by Michael Cardew, painted with a foliate motif in black and rust on a cream ground, the base with impressed marks.

4.75in (12cm) diam

£450-550   WW

An African Abuja Pottery stoneware bowl, by Asibo Ido, decorated to the well with a stylised anteater, and glazed in shades of blue, the base with impressed seal marks, with chips and hairline crack to top rim.

11in (27cm) diam

£80-120   WW

A small Aldermaston Pottery pottery bowl, by Alan Caiger-Smith, painted in red copper lustre.

4.25in (11cm) diam

£120-180   SWO

An Aldermaston Pottery bowl, painted in flambé red and bronze on an off-white ground with foliate brushstroke design, the back with painted marks and 'CFA' monogram.

7in (17.5cm) diam

£100-150   WW

An Aldermaston Pottery plate, by Alan Caiger-Smith, painted to the well with copper swirls, the back with painted marks.

11in (28cm) diam

£380-420   WW

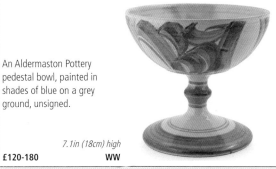

An Aldermaston Pottery pedestal bowl, painted in shades of blue on a grey ground, unsigned.

7.1in (18cm) high

£120-180   WW

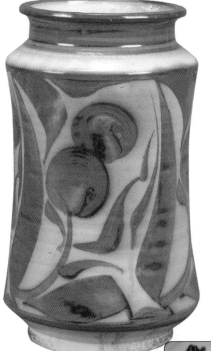

An Aldermaston Pottery amber lustre-glazed albarello jar, by Alan Caiger-Smith, with stylised fruit in panels, the base with painted 'AW' mark in red lustre and indistinct date mark.

This distinctive form is known as an albarello jar, an ancient Middle Eastern tin-glazed earthenware medicine jar, which was also produced in Italy from the 15thC onwards. The style of the decoration on this piece recalls Hispano-Moresque motifs.

9in (23cm) high

£100-150   DN

A CLOSER LOOK AT AN ALDERMASTON JUG

This jug was item 13 in the 'Past, Present & Future: Alan Caiger-Smith & Nick Caiger-Smith' catalogue and exhibition, held from 23rd September to the 3rd October 1998.

The painted tin-glazed motif is complex and unusual, which is typical of Caiger-Smith's distinctive style.

This is Alan Caiger-Smith's painted mark, showing he made and decorated this jug.

The three dots are a date mark for 1963, making this an early example. Caiger-Smith used a different motif for each year from 1959 to 2003.

An Aldmermaston Pottery 'Cat' pattern jug, by Alan Caiger-Smith, painted in mid-brown and yellow tin glazes, the base with painted marks and date mark.

The Aldermaston Pottery was founded by Alan Caiger-Smith (b.1930) and Geoffrey Eastop (b.1921) in Berkshire, England in 1955. Caiger-Smith specialised in wheel-thrown earthenware functional items, decorated with tin glazes or reduction-fired lustre glazes. A large number of potters worked at the Aldermaston Pottery until it closed in 2006 with the retirement of Caiger-Smith. Interest in the pottery's production is rising rapidly.

1963   *11in (28cm) high*

£350-450   DN

CERAMICS

A large Rose Cabat 'Feelie' pottery vessel, with unglazed ceramic base and nearly closed neck, covered with a 'dripping' mustard-yellow glaze, signed and inscribed 'UMCAOIO'.

American studio potter Rose Cabat (b.1914) is best-known for her ovoid 'Feelies', which are vessels that suggest sensuality in their form, colour, and feathery-textured glazes, and which seem to invite you to touch and handle them.

5in (13cm) high

£600-800   **FRE**

A Fulham Pottery plate, by Quentin Bell, incised and painted with a mythical creature in coloured glazes, the back with incised marks.

Quentin Bell (1910-1996) was the son of Bloomsbury Group artist Vanessa Bell and art critic Clive Bell. He lectured in Art History at Durham University, and became the Slade Professor at Oxford University. He potted at Fulham from the 1930s to the 1980s.

10in (25.5cm) diam

£350-450   **WW**

Two Walter Keeler graduated salt-glaze stoneware jugs, of slightly angular form with applied strap handles, glazed in a mottled blue/green, the bases with impressed marks.

Tallest 6.25in (16cm) high

£200-300 pair   **WW**

A Michael Casson wood-fired stoneware pedestal bowl, painted in blue with a frieze to the interior, the base with painted monogram.

7in (18cm) diam

£200-300   **WW**

A Gordon Cooke porcelain teapot and cover, of flatted form with looped handle, and sprayed glaze, the base with stamped 'GC' monogram.

6.25in (16cm) high

£400-600   **WW**

A CLOSER LOOK AT A KATE MALONE VASE

Kate Malone (b.1959) is known for her sculptural vases, which resemble 'super-charged' fruits, vegetables, flowers, or berries, and cross the line between functional and decorative items.

She uses a white industrial clay, which makes her vibrant colour palette appear even brighter.

Her choice of forms reflects her love of nature and her interest in the exuberant fecundity of the natural world.

She is also inspired by the colours and forms of Victorian majolica and Staffordshire creamware.

A Kate Malone 'Pineapple' earthenware vase, glazed in yellow and green, the base with incised signature.

7.25in (18.5cm) high

£750-850   **WW**

A John Maltby stoneware dish, painted with abstract flowers and a cross design in red, green, and brown slips, the base painted 'Maltby', with repair to one corner.

11in (27.5cm) square

£500-600   **WW**

A large John Maltby stoneware platter, of rounded square section, the well with painted numbers and geometric design, the base painted with 'Maltby'.

14in (34.5cm) diam

£500-700   **WW**

QUICK REFERENCE - JOHN MALTBY

- John Maltby was born in 1936 and studied with David Leach from 1962 to 1963. Since 1974, he has only made unique, individual pieces. He is inspired by the abstract sculptural paintings of the St. Ives school artists, such as Ben Nicholson, Christopher Wood, and the naïve painter Alfred Wallis. Like them, he draws inspiration from the environment of the harbour town, with familiar boats, nets, ropes, buildings, and the sun reduced to geometric or linear elements that echo his forms. Pablo Picasso and Paul Klee are further influences, and similarities can be found in Maltby's use of simple symbols, such as the cross. His figural sculptures are similar in style, and often draw on kings, queens, nature, and family groups. His marks vary from his inscribed or painted surname, to an impressed 'M' seal with one or two dots within. His work is found in many public and private collections, and interest in his work has been surging over the past five years.

A John Maltby stoneware cup-form, slip-decorated with sailing boats, the reverse with slip splash decoration, the base painted 'Maltby'.

4.5in (11.5cm) high

£450-550   **WW**

A large 1980s John Maltby jug and bowl, each painted with abstract forms, bases painted with 'Maltby'.

Jug 11in (29cm) high

£1,500-2,000   **L&T**

A John Maltby 'King, Bird and Fish' stoneware figure, with textured surface, the base with impressed seal mark.

22in (55cm) high

£500-700   **WW**

A Mortlake Pottery ovoid vase, by George J. Cox, of shouldered form, covered in a 'dripping' purple and violet glaze, the base with incised marks and dated '1912'.

1912   *11in (27cm) high*

£350-450   **WW**

CERAMICS

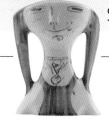

A Richard Parkinson Pottery 'Schoolgirl' bust, designed by Susan Parkinson, painted in shades of blue, with original paper retail label.

8in (20cm) high

£500-700   **WW**

A 1970s Purbeck Pottery slip-moulded vase, designed by Robert Jefferson, with textured surface, decorated with brown and beige brushed glazes.

Robert Jefferson is best-known for his innovative design work for Poole, where he co-developed the 'Delphis' and 'Studio' ranges, among others.

10in (25cm) high

£80-120   **GC**

A large Mary Rich cylindrical porcelain vase, of shouldered form with flaring rim, glazed in blue and lavender, with gilt decoration, the base with impressed seal mark.

16in (40.5cm) high

£200-300   **WW**

Judith Picks

With the growth of interest in craft and studio pottery, the contemporary market is looking ever more vibrant. Certain names are standing out as innovative or remarkable, or both. Mary Rich's finely potted porcelain works are unique in terms of their style, with richly gilded and coloured geometric designs. Rich (b.1940) trained under Harry and May Davis at the Crowan Pottery, and with David Leach in the early 1960s before founding her own pottery. She is inspired by Islamic and Far Eastern ceramics and art, and has a particular interest in gold works and lustre glazes. Although she is still producing ceramics, her work seems to be fetching increasingly strong prices on the secondary market at auction and from dealers. As such, she certainly seems be one to watch for the future. Look out for large sizes, as much of her work is small.

A large Mary Rich flaring porcelain bowl, glazed in purple and blue, with gilt banded decoration, the base with impressed seal mark.

10in (26cm) diam

£200-300   **WW**

A Lucie Rie stoneware bowl, glazed to the foot in a matt bronze glaze over pale blue and buff, the foot with impressed seal mark.

Provenance: From Doreen and Ted Appleby, who were neighbours of Hans Coper, Rie's close collaborator. Rie (1902-1995) was a great innovator in studio pottery, and most often used the impressed mark shown here, sometimes with variations indicating a year of production. Hotly sought-after, her work typically fetches high hundreds, or thousands, of pounds.

5.25in (13.5cm) diam

£1,800-2,200   **WW**

A 1970s Bernard Rooke 'Totem Pole' lamp base, comprised of moulded sections assembled on a metal pole, each with beige and green glazes, and unglazed textured areas.

30in (76cm) high

£150-200   **WHP**

An American Mary and Edwin Scheier glazed low bowl, decorated in grey, cream, and pink glazes with a primitive portrait, the base inscribed 'Scheier'.

The Scheiers' primitive, almost tribal style was developed after they went to Puerto Rico in 1946. Inspired by themes such as birth and protection, they believed that vessels could portray 'some aspect of the human spirit'. As well as being decorated with inscribed sgrafitto techniques, some motifs are moulded in relief.

12.75in (32cm) diam

£500-700   DRA

A small American Stahl Pottery pitcher, with impressed and inscribed bands, the base inscribed 'Made by rr stahl 1/10/48'.

1948   *3in (7.5cm) high*

£200-300   ANT

A Canadian Otto Wichman baluster vase, in a lustrous grey-blue glaze with random spots of a crystalline cobalt-blue glaze, the base with impressed 'OW' monogram and inscribed 'X'.

Little is currently known about Wichman, apart from that that he was born in 1934 and immigrated to Canada from Germany in the late 1940s, settling in White Rock, British Columbia, and presumably returning to Germany later. His well-potted, balanced forms were inspired by classical European and Oriental shapes. He typically used complex crystalline glazes in a variety of colours, which he presumably created himself. In 1982 he entered a vase into the annual Westerwald ceramics competition.

6.5in (16.5cm) high

£50-70   DODA

A Coldrum Pottery earthenware vase, by Reginald Wells, covered with an unusual volcanic pitted brown-grey glaze, with a wide neck, the base with impressed marks.

c1920   *7.75in (20cm) high*

£120-180   GORL

An Alan Young pottery group, modelled as two smugglers or fishermen sitting on a settle, signed on the base.

Alan is the son of William Young, who produced similar humorous figures at the Runnaford Pottery in Devon.

5.25in (13cm) high

£60-80   GHOU

A Paul Young earthenware candleholder, with branches, leaves, and birds, gloss-glazed in colours, the base with impressed seal mark.

11in (28.5cm) high

£100-150   WW

CERAMICS

QUICK REFERENCE

- The Tremaen Pottery was founded by artist Peter Ellery in 1965. Initially the pottery was based in Marazion, Cornwall, but, as success grew, it moved to larger premises in the nearby town of Newlyn in 1967.
- Ellery had trained in art and ceramics at Bath College, and took an unusual approach to studio pottery. He was inspired by the Cornish landscape, and by the art being produced in Cornwall at the time by artists such as Barbara Hepworth.
- Some early pieces were pressed into moulds by hand, but the majority of production was made by pouring liquid clay (or slip) into moulds. Forms typically mimic the rounded pebbles found on beaches, but can also be figural, in the shape of stylised fishing boats or seaside towns.
- His designs typically feature moulded motifs, such as ancient runic symbols or cow parsley, or bear abstract brushstrokes. Both are painted or highlighted with earthy, muted colours.
- Many pieces are marked with an impressed logo (see p.128), or a rectangular label bearing the name of the pottery, but not all are. It's worth familiarising yourself with typical forms, colours, and patterns to aid with identification.
- Although vases and other forms were produced, lamp bases were Tremaen's biggest output. These were made in a wide range of sizes, colours, and glazes, and were given Cornish names, such a 'Canyon', 'Jizal', 'Boscawen', and 'Zennor'. Lampshades were usually of earthy coloured Hessian, although few original lampshades have survived.
- During the 1970s designs became less innovative, with more and more focus being given to novelty forms intended for the tourist market. The recession of the 1980s created increasing economic difficulties, and in 1988 Ellery left to focus on painting. The pottery closed soon afterwards. His work has been reappraised recently, and is rising in value.

A large Tremaen Pottery 'Bowjey' moulded lampbase, with curved and runic motifs.
1973-78   *12.5in (32cm) high*
£100-150   **GC**

A Tremaen Pottery moulded 'Jizal' lampbase, with curving and runic pattern, and impressed factory mark.
1973-78   *12in (31cm) high*
£70-90   **M20C**

A Tremaen Pottery 'Bowjey' white glazed moulded lampbase, with curving and runic symbols highlighted in a green glaze.

This light, but still naturally inspired colour is very unusual.
1973-78   *8.5in (21.5cm) high*
£100-150   **GC**

A 1970s Tremaen Pottery moulded lampbase, with randomly applied trails of slip, glazed with cream and brown glazes, with green baize covered base.

The pattern is similar to those found on 'Gwarra' lampbases, even though the shape is 'Bowjey'.
16.5in (41.5cm) high
£100-150   **M20C**

A large 1970s Tremaen Pottery 'Bowjey' lampbase, with impressed parsley design, and blue paper factory label to base.

18in (45.5cm) high

£80-120   M20C

A Tremaen Pottery 'Cow Parsley' moulded lampbase, with gold foil 'Tremaen Pottery Cornwall' sticker to the brown baize covered base.

Ellery used real cow parsley to create the mould. A smaller 7.5in (19.5cm) high 'Cow Parsley' lampbase was also produced, as was a very rare large vase. All three have different patterns.

1984-88   *14.25in (36cm) high*

£80-120   GC

A Tremaen Pottery 'Moon' vase, with abstract storm-like dripped, brushed, and sgrafitto pattern, with blue 'Tremaen Newlyn' sticker.

c1968-72   *12in (31cm) high*

£120-180   GC

A Tremaen Pottery 'Ruan' moulded lampbase, with runic symbols and brown-orange glazes.

11.5in (29cm) high

£80-120   GC

A small Tremaen Pottery 'Ruan' moulded lampbase, with hieroglyphic or runic symbols.

1978-80   *9.5in (24cm) high*

£70-100   GC

A late 1970s Tremaen Pottery moulded lampbase, with impressed Chinese style symbols, and blue 'Tremaen Pottery Newlyn' sticker.

11.5in (29cm) high

£70-90   GC

A small Tremaen Pottery moulded 'Boscawen' lampbase, with swirling design, and blue paper factory label.

1973-75   *11in (27.5cm) high*

£70-90   M20C

CERAMICS

WWW.KCSCERAMICS.CO.UK

Contact us for Top Offers before any house clearance

special price £8500.00 (rrp £16,000.00)

Specialist in Lladro, Troika, Copenhagen
We Buy and Sell all Antiques and Collectables

Credit & Debit Cards Accepted
Professional packing & shipping worldwide

Email: karen@kcsceramics.co.uk
Phone/Fax 0208 384 8981
Mobile: 07969 572208

Valid Insurance Certificate with all purchases

Visit our secure on-line shop

www.KCSCERAMICS.co.uk

QUICK REFERENCE

- The Troika Pottery was founded in 1963 by potter Benny Sirota, painter Lesley Illsley, and architect Jan Thompson (who left in 1965). The pottery was initially based at Wheal Dream in St. Ives, Cornwall, but the company soon became very successful and expanded, moving to Newlyn in 1970.
- Designs evolved through the 1960s, although the production techniques used remained consistent. Shapes were slip-moulded using liquid clay poured into moulds to ensure uniformity and ease of production. Early pieces tended to have smooth and glossy surfaces, and were often glazed in white, with the characteristic matt, textured glaze becoming the main decorative treatment around 1974.
- Influences included Scandinavian ceramics, and the work of Paul Klee and Constantin Brancusi. Colours tend to be earthy and muted in tone, and shapes are frequently geometric. Many new shapes were introduced in the late 1960s.

- Although it can be recognised from its style, Troika is usually marked on the base. These marks can be useful in dating a piece, and identifying who decorated it. See the next page for information on Troika marks, and what they mean.
- Consider the style of decoration, size, colour, and style, as these typically affect value. 'Anvil' vases, plaques, and 'Head Masks' are examples of rarer pieces that tend to be desirable, while practical rectangular vases are the most common.
- When considering common shapes, it's worth bearing in mind that the work of certain designers, particularly those who became head designers, tends to be the most desirable.
- In general, look for well-made, complex geometric patterns, particularly with figural or pictorial images, as they tend to be the scarcest. Always examine pieces carefully for chips and cracks as these can reduce the price significantly. The company closed in 1983.

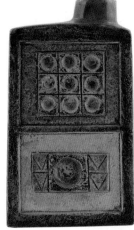

A 1970s Troika Pottery 'Chimney' vase, modelled in low relief with geometric panels, painted in shades of ochre and blue, the base with painted pottery marks.

8in (20.5cm) high

£300-500   WW

A Troika Pottery 'Chimney' vase, decorated by Anne Lewis, in low relief with geometric panels, painted in shades of ochre and blue, the base with painted pottery marks and 'AL' monogram.

Lewis worked at Troika from 1966 until 1972.

1970-72   7.5in (20.5cm) high

£350-450   WW

A 1970s Troika Pottery 'Chimney' vase, modelled in low relief with geometric panels, painted in blue with a bronze shoulder, the base with painted pottery marks.

8in (20cm) high

£350-450   WW

A 1970s Troika Pottery square jardinière, on square feet, modelled in low relief with geometric panels, painted in shades of ochre and blue, the feet glazed bronze, the base with painted pottery mark, and with re-sprayed panel to interior.

7.5in (18cm) high

£250-300   WW

A 1970s Troika Pottery 'Slab' vase, modelled in low relief with geometric panels, painted in shades of ochre and blue, the base with painted pottery marks.

7.5in (17.5cm) high

£200-300   WW

CERAMICS

QUICK REFERENCE - TROIKA MARKS

The hand-painted marks on the base of a piece of Troika can help with identification and dating, particularly if used in combination with the finish and the shape.

Mark 1   *Mark 2*   *Mark 3*

Marks 1-3 (above) include 'St. Ives', the name of the town where Troika was founded. These are the earliest marks and date from 1963 to 1970. The 'trident' motif in Mark 3 was only used in the first few years, and could be printed, painted, or impressed into the base, meaning its shape can vary.

Mark 4   *Mark 5*

If 'St. Ives' is not included in a mark, it should be assumed that the piece dates from 1970-83 while the pottery was located in Newlyn. From this time most pieces were simply signed 'Troika', as in Mark 4. Variations include 'Troika Cornwall' as in Mark 5, 'Troika England', or 'Troika Cornwall England'. The town name Newlyn does not appear in marks.

The monograms or motifs used by individual decorators are also useful. Some decorators are more important and sought-after than others, particularly if they became head decorators. The years a decorator was at Troika can also be compared to the dates a shape was in production to nail down a more precise date for a piece. The 'SB' monogram in Mark 1 is for Stella Benjamin (working 1963-67), the 'LJ' monogram in Mark 4 is for Louise Jinks (1976-81), and the reversed 'CC' mark in Mark 5 is probably for the fettler and decorator Colin Carbis (1976-77). Some artists are still unknown, and three decorators had the initials S. B., so it's well worth getting to know individual monograms. However, not all pieces were signed in this way, and some simply bear the Troika name.

A Troika Pottery 'Coffin' vase, of tapered rectangular form, decorated by Louise Jinks with abstract panels picked out in tonal brown and green, the base with hand-painted 'Troika Pottery Cornwall' marks with 'LJ' artists monogram

Jinks was head decorator from 1979 to 1981.

1976-81   *7in (17.5cm) high*
£120-180   **FLD**

A large Troika Pottery 'Rectangle' vase, decorated by Simone Kilburn with geometric decoration on a blue ground, the base with painted pottery marks and initialled 'SK'.

1975-77   *12.25in (31cm) high*
£220-280   **GORL**

A large Troika Pottery 'Cylinder' vase, decorated by Honor Curtis with bands of alternating blue and white discs over a white glazed ground, the base with painted pottery marks and initialled 'HC'.

1970-73   *14in (36cm) high*
£150-200   **FLD**

A Troika Pottery 'Urn' vase, decorated by Louise Jinks with a band of alternate blue and white circles with sgrafitto lines over a blue ground, the base with painted pottery marks and initialled 'LJ'.

1976-81   *10in (25.5cm) high*
£120-180   **DN**

A 1970s Troika Pottery 'Urn' vase, decorated with two bands of circles, the base with painted pottery mark and decorator's monogram.

10in (25cm) high

£150-200   GHOU

A 1970s Troika Pottery 'Spice Jar', relief-moulded with various geometric motifs, glazed in greens and browns, the base with painted pottery marks.

£150-200   ECGW

A Troika Pottery 'Wheel' vase, decorated by Louise Jinks, moulded in low relief with geometric panels, glazed in ochre and blue, the base with painted pottery marks, and 'LJ' monogram.

1976-81   *7.5in (16cm) high*

£300-500   WW

A small 1970s Troika Pottery 'Wheel' vase, modelled in low relief, painted in shades of green and brown, the base with painted pottery mark.

4.5in (11.5cm) high

£80-120   DA&H

Mark Picks

Most collectors aim to find vases, or perhaps a rare mask, but those in the know also look out for the very rare wall plaques made at St. Ives from 1963 to 1970. These plaques were among the earliest shapes made at St. Ives, and could be as large as five feet high. As well as abstract motifs, decoration included the three stages of marriage (these plaques were known as 'Love Plaques'), or the river Thames. Many of these plaques were designed by co-founder Benny Sirota, although others, such as Roland Bencem also made them. Those made by Sirota often bear his thumb- or fingerprints, as well as his monogram.

Such is their scarcity that Troika plaques have been known to sell for more than £3,000 at the height of the market. This example has great visual impact, and shows the influence of modern art and sculpture in its geometric design. Each one is a unique artwork that is also important to the history of British studio pottery. As such, they should hold their current values, even as the Troika market continues to settle.

A rare Troika Pottery wall plaque, by Benny Sirota, the long rectangular form with raised geometric panels, glazed black and ochre, the reverse with painted pottery mark.

15in (38.5cm) long

£1,800-2,200   WW

A Troika Pottery rectangular table lamp, decorated by Jane Fitzgerald with a geometric pattern in grey-green, blue, and cream glazes, the base with painted pottery marks and 'JF' monogram.

1976-83   *9in (22cm) high*

£150-200   DN

A 1970s Troika Pottery rectangular lamp base, one side decorated with a female figure, the other side with two circles against a blue ground, the base with painted pottery marks.

12in (30cm) high

£200-300   GORB

CERAMICS

QUICK REFERENCE

- Sally Tuffin (b.1938) studied at the Walthamstow Art School and at the fashion department of the Royal College of Art. She founded her first business with fellow fashion graduate Marion Foale in 1962. 'Foale & Tuffin' soon became renowned for its youth-orientated clothing, which epitomised the popular Carnaby Street look in 1960s 'Swinging London'. Despite their success, the pair split in 1972 and the business closed.
- In 1986, Tuffin's husband, legendary publisher and collector Richard Dennis, acquired a stake in the historic ceramics company Moorcroft. Tuffin consequently became the company's art director. Although she did not profoundly alter the look that characterised the company's designs, she refreshed their approach and her new designs met with great success. 'Finches', 'Cluny', and 'Penguins' are among her most celebrated ranges.
- Tuffin left Moorcroft in 1993 to focus on the Dennis China Works, a pottery she and her husband had founded in 1985.

- Dennis China Works is run from a converted Gothic rectory and chapel in Somerset, England. All the pottery is thrown and decorated in-house, by hand, by a small team working closely with Tuffin. Designs remain close to those she produced for Moorcroft, focusing on natural subjects such as plants and animals. Many designs are produced in limited editions of varying sizes.
- Collectors hotly anticipate the annual auction of unique and trial pieces, which is held at Bonhams in London, and the annual Collectors' Day at the Dennis studio.
- Look out for trial pieces, designs produced in small limited editions (often under 50), and classic or complex patterns.
- Designs produced by Tuffin for her own pottery, which is still active, tend to be more desirable than those produced for Moorcroft.

A Moorcroft 'Ochre Finches' pattern lamp base, designed by Sally Tuffin, with printed and painted marks to base.

A Moorcroft 'Finches' pattern jug, designed by Sally Tuffin in 1988, with a blue ground, the base with printed and painted marks.

6in (14.5cm) high

£180-220   CHT

A small Moorcroft 'Finches' pattern baluster vase, designed by Sally Tuffin, with a green ground and impressed and painted marks to the base.

4.25in (11cm) high

£80-120   TRI

Despite this vase being rarer in ochre than other colours (it was only produced in 1989 and 1990 with an ochre ground), ochre is a less sought-after colour with collectors. Lampbases also tend to be less desirable shapes in general than vases.

1989-90   *7in (18.5cm) high*

£150-200   CHT

A Moorcroft 'Plum' pattern vase, designed by Sally Tuffin, the base with impressed and painted marks.

1988-90   *4in (11cm) high*

£70-100   LSK

A Moorcroft 'Sunflower' pattern vase, designed by Sally Tuffin, with a coral red ground, the base with painted and impressed marks.

This pattern is usually found with a light blue background.

11in (28cm) high

£400-600   WW

A CLOSER LOOK AT A SALLY TUFFIN VASE

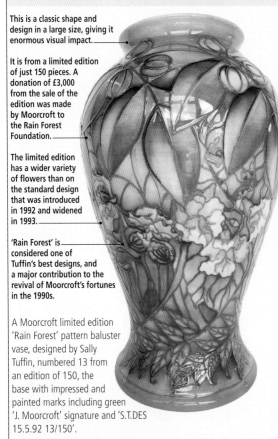

This is a classic shape and design in a large size, giving it enormous visual impact.

It is from a limited edition of just 150 pieces. A donation of £3,000 from the sale of the edition was made by Moorcroft to the Rain Forest Foundation.

The limited edition has a wider variety of flowers than on the standard design that was introduced in 1992 and widened in 1993.

'Rain Forest' is considered one of Tuffin's best designs, and a major contribution to the revival of Moorcroft's fortunes in the 1990s.

A Moorcroft limited edition 'Rain Forest' pattern baluster vase, designed by Sally Tuffin, numbered 13 from an edition of 150, the base with impressed and painted marks including green 'J. Moorcroft' signature and 'S.T.DES 15.5.92 13/150'.

See 'Moorcroft: A Guide to Moorcroft Pottery 1897-1993', by Paul Atterbury, p.190, pl.3 for similar vase.

1992   *17in (43cm) high*
£800-1,200   **TEN**

A Moorcroft 'Bramble' pattern ginger jar and cover, designed by Sally Tuffin in 1991, the cream ground shading to dark blue, dated and with impressed marks.

1998   *6.5in (17cm) high*
£100-150   **AH**

A Moorcroft 'Violet' pattern charger, designed by Sally Tuffin in 1987, shape no.783/10, with a light green background, with impressed and painted marks to underside.

1987-90   *10in (25.5cm) diam*
£200-300   **ROS**

A large Moorcroft limited edition 'Temptation' bowl, designed by Sally Tuffin, numbered 79 from an edition of 500, with impressed and painted marks.

1990   *10in (26cm) diam*
£250-350   **TEN**

A pair of 1990s Moorcroft 'Finches' candlesticks, designed by Sally Tuffin, on a blue ground, with impressed and painted marks.

The blue ground was used for this pattern from 1988. Ochre was used 1989-90.

8in (21cm) high
£250-300   **TEN**

Judith Picks

Moorcroft are best-known for producing Art Nouveau style patterns and designs inspired by the natural world. This small vase appears almost Art Deco in style and form. The design was produced in a variety of colours as part of an experimental range in 1987, shortly after Tuffin and her husband Richard Dennis joined Moorcroft. Even though it is very different from the style loved by collectors, I think the scarcity of these vases, their unique style, and the inclusion of the Moorcroft name make them a good bet for the future.

A Moorcroft globe vase, with an experimental pattern designed by Sally Tuffin, the base with impressed mark, and green painted 'WM' and 'ST'.

1987   *7in (17cm) high*
£150-200   **DN**

CERAMICS

A Dennis China Works 'Cornflower' pattern vase, designed by Sally Tuffin, the base marked 'Dennis China Works, S T Des, No 3, 2000'.

This vase is a second. Seconds are typically sold direct from the studio at special collectors' events.

2000   *6.5in (16cm) high*

£60-90   LC

A Dennis China Works 'Datura' pattern vase, designed by Sally Tuffin, with a black ground, the base marked, 'Dennis China Works, 2004, RMc, S.T.Des, No 9'.

2004   *12in (30cm) high*

£150-200   LC

A Dennis China Works 'Bluebell' pattern lidded box, designed by Sally Tuffin, with dome topped lid and finial, 'CW' artist's monogram for thrower Chris Wright, and also marked 'Dennis China Works, CW, 2002, S.T.Des, No 26'.

2002   *3.75in (9cm) high*

£60-90   LC

A Dennis China Works 'Clover' pattern lidded box, designed by Sally Tuffin, with a dome topped lid and finial, with 'CW' mark for thrower Chris Wright, also marked 'Dennis China Works, 2002, S.T.Des, No 13'.

2002   *3.75in (9cm) high*

£60-90   LC

A Dennis China Works 'Split Lily' vase, designed by Sally Tuffin, marked 'Dennis China Works, S T Des, No 67, 2000'.

2000   *4.5in (12cm) high*

£100-150   LC

A large Dennis China Works limited edition 'Navy Magnolia' pattern ovoid vase, designed by Sally Tuffin, numbered 4 from an edition of 20 for Mary Whettem, the base marked with 'CW' monogram for thrower Chris Wright, also marked 'Dennis China Works, 2005, S.T Des, NO 4/20'.

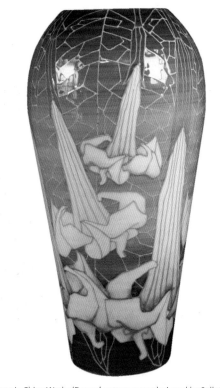

A Dennis China Works 'Datura' pattern vase, designed by Sally Tuffin, with a green background, the base marked, 'ST des, Dennis China Works, No 11, 2002', and with impressed 'RMc' mark for thrower Rory McLeod.

2002   *12.25in (31cm) high*

£200-300   LC

2005   *13.5in (34cm) high*

£300-500   LC

CERAMICS

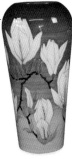

A Dennis China Works 'Bees and Snowdrop' pattern vase, designed by Sally Tuffin, with a graduated blue and white ground, marked 'Dennis China Works, 2002, S.T. Des, No 44'.

This range was devised in response to collectors who had loved a previous snowdrop range that also included a few bee motifs.

2002   *6.25in (16cm) high*
£100-150   **LC**

A Dennis China Works 'Magnolia' pattern vase, designed by Sally Tuffin, with a graduated blue background, marked 'Dennis China Works, 2004, S.T. Des, No 23'.

2004   *8.25in (21cm) high*
£120-180   **LC**

A Dennis China Works 'Primrose' pattern vase, designed by Sally Tuffin, the top and interior painted in a purple glaze, marked 'ST des, No 5, Dennis China Works', and with 'RMc' mark for thrower Rory McLeod.

c1998   *9.5in (24cm) high*
£180-220   **LC**

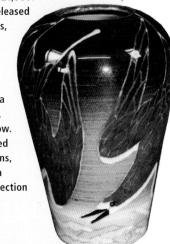

A Dennis China Works 'Tulips' pattern vase, designed by Sally Tuffin, the vase painted with flowers on a dark green ground, marked 'ST des, Dennis China Works, no 26', and with impressed 'RMc' mark for thrower Rory McLeod.

9.75in (25cm) high
£100-150   **LC**

A small Dennis China Works 'Sunflower' pattern cylindrical vase, designed by Sally Tuffin, decorated with flowers on a green ground, with impressed inscription reading, 'As the Sunflower turns to its God when it sets' the base marked 'ST des, Dennis China Works', with impressed 'RMc' mark for thrower Rory McLeod.

6in (15cm) high
£200-300   **LC**

QUICK REFERENCE - MINIATURES

- **Tuffin's miniature vases are an affordable way to start collecting her distinctive ceramics. The range the miniature vase below came from also included a large version of this shape, which originally cost over £1,000!**
- **It is interesting that Moorcroft released a range of miniatures in the 1970s, echoing the tiny salesmen's samples of the earlier 20thC.**
- **Each miniature is a unique, tiny work of art.**
- **As space can be, or can become, a serious issue for many collectors, the appeal of miniatures may grow. Although not every range included a miniature version of the patterns, it would be possible to build up a beautiful and representative collection that could comfortably live on a single shelf!**

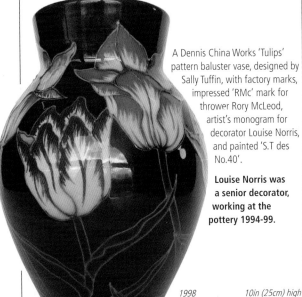

A Dennis China Works 'Tulips' pattern baluster vase, designed by Sally Tuffin, with factory marks, impressed 'RMc' mark for thrower Rory McLeod, artist's monogram for decorator Louise Norris, and painted 'S.T des No.40'.

Louise Norris was a senior decorator, working at the pottery 1994-99.

1998   *10in (25cm) high*
£150-200   **TEN**

A Dennis China Works 'Sooty Terns' miniature vase, designed by Sally Tuffin, the base with 'CW' mark for thrower Chris Wright, and also marked 'DCW, 2004, S.T.Des, No 31'.

2004   *3.25in (8cm) high*
£100-150   **LC**

CERAMICS

A Dennis China Works limited edition 'Albatross' pattern vase, designed by Sally Tuffin, a 'second' from an edition of 20, with scrolling 'MS' decorator's mark for Michelle Sutton, and 'CW' thrower's mark for Chris Wright, also marked 'Dennis China Works, S T Des, 2005'.

The edition was produced for retailer Mary Whettem.

2005   *12.5in (32cm) high*

£250-350   LC

A Dennis China Works 'Toucan' pattern vase, designed by Sally Tuffin, with a dark green ground, marked 'ST des, Dennis China Works, 2000'.

'Toucan' (1997-2000) is a very popular range with many collectors.

2000   *6.25in (16cm) high*

£200-300   LC

A Dennis China Works 'Owl' vase, designed by Sally Tuffin, the base marked 'DCW, 2003, S.T.Des, No 42' and with with 'CW' mark for thrower Chris Wright.

Tuffin often uses the natural markings on animals as inspiration for the backgrounds behind them. She also chooses or adapts shapes to suit each animal. The full-bodied owl vase here is an excellent example.

2003   *3.75in (9cm) high*

£120-180   LC

A Dennis China Works trial 'Pelican' pattern ovoid vase, designed by Sally Tuffin, decorated with three Pelicans on a blue ground, marked 'ST des, Dennis China Works, 2000, Trial'.

2000   *10.5in (27cm) high*

£450-550   LC

A Dennis China Works 'Polar Bear' lidded pot, designed by Sally Tuffin, the lid with a polar bear finial modelled by Alan Pepper, and with with 'CW' mark for thrower Chris Wright, the base also marked 'Dennis China Works, 2003, S.T.Des, No 5'.

2003   *5.75in (14cm) high*

£180-220   LC

A CLOSER LOOK AT A SALLY TUFFIN CHARGER

This is a second. Had it been first quality, the price could have nearly doubled.

The penguin figures were individually modelled by Alan Pepper, who trained at Poole Pottery and is responsible for all the three-dimensional figural knops or additions to patterns.

Loved by Tuffin, penguins are also sought-after by collectors. 'Penguin Huddle', a unique box with a lid covered with over 140 penguin figures, fetched £21,000 at auction at Bonhams in 2007.

Note the naturalistic colouring and shapes, and the heads of swimming penguins near the edge. It's this attention to detail that Tuffin's collectors love.

A Dennis China Works 'Penguin Mountain' charger, designed by Sally Tuffin, with 'HW' and 'CN' decorators' marks for Heidi Warr and Natasha Chapman, marked, 'Dennis China Works, S T Des, 2006'.

2006   *11.5in (29cm) diam*

£350-450   LC

A Dennis China Works 'Egyptian Head' lidded vase, designed by Sally Tuffin, with 'AW' decorator's monogram for Adam White, marked 'Dennis China Works, ST Des, 2007'.

This piece is marked as a second. Adam White joined the Dennis China Works as a trainee decorator in 2003. This very apt and suitable turquoise colourway was introduced in 2006.

2007   *7.75in (19cm) high*

£180-220   **LC**

A Dennis China Works trial 'Lily' lidded head vase, designed by Sally Tuffin, with scrolling 'TP' decorator's monogram for Tania Pike, also marked 'Dennis China Works, S T Des, Trial 2, 2008'.

Pike joined the Dennis China Works in 1998 and specialises in roundels. The colours are somewhat bolder on this trial than the final range.

2008   *7.75in (19cm) high*

£180-220   **LC**

A CLOSER LOOK AT A HEAD POT

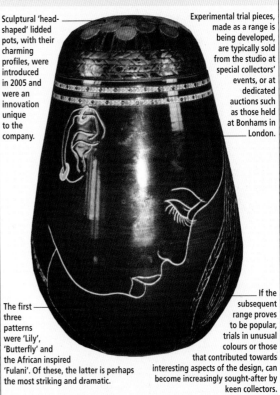

Sculptural 'head-shaped' lidded pots, with their charming profiles, were introduced in 2005 and were an innovation unique to the company.

Experimental trial pieces, made as a range is being developed, are typically sold from the studio at special collectors' events, or at dedicated auctions such as those held at Bonhams in London.

The first three patterns were 'Lily', 'Butterfly' and the African inspired 'Fulani'. Of these, the latter is perhaps the most striking and dramatic.

If the subsequent range proves to be popular, trials in unusual colours or those that contributed towards interesting aspects of the design, can become increasingly sought-after by keen collectors.

A Dennis China Works trial 'Fulani' pattern lidded head vase, designed by Sally Tuffin, with 'CN' decorator's mark for Natasha Chapman-Cox, also marked 'Dennis China Works, S T Des, Trial 3, 2004'.

Natasha Chapman-Cox joined the company in 2003 as a trainee decorator.

2004   *8.75in (22cm) high*

£200-250   **LC**

A Dennis China Works limited edition 'Gabriel' pattern vase, from the 'William Morris Angels' range designed by Sally Tuffin, numbered 2 from an edition of 50, the base marked 'ST des, No 2/50, Dennis China Works, 2002' and with impressed 'RMc' mark for thrower Rory McLeod.

The pattern was inspired by a design by William Morris. The limited edition set also included the angels Raphael and Uriel.

2002   *9.75in (25cm) high*

£120-180   **LC**

A Dennis China Works limited edition 'Holden Wood Spring' vase, designed by Sally Tuffin, numbered 24 from an edition of 25, also marked 'Dennis China Works, S T Des, 2003'.

2003   *7.75in (19cm) high*

£120-180   **LC**

A Dennis China Works limited edition 'Holden Wood Summer' vase, designed by Sally Tuffin, numbered 67 from an edition of 100, also marked 'Dennis China Works, S T Des, 2002'.

This vase was a special commission for specialist retailer Holden Wood Antiques. Celebrating the company's first five years in business, it was limited to 100 vases, decorated with incised drawing, painting and slip-trailing techniques. Most of this series were decorated by Michelle Sutton, who has a BA in graphic design and joined the pottery in 2000.

2002   *7.75in (19cm) high*

£120-180   **LC**

CERAMICS

A Dennis China Works limited edition 'Cedrus Libani' pattern vase, designed by Sally Tuffin, tubeline decorated with pine trees in a sunset setting, with impressed and painted marks, numbered 7 from an edition of 25, with painted marks to base.

This is a rare vase. Not only was the edition size very small, but it was expensive due to the amount of work involved.

1995   *10in (26cm) high*
£600-800   **WW**

A Dennis China Works 'Strawberry' baluster vase, designed by Sally Tuffin, the base marked 'Dennis China Works, 2002, S.T.Des, No 3'.

2003   *3.75in (9cm) high*
£80-120   **LC**

A Dennis China Works 'Strawberry' pattern fluted vase, designed by Sally Tuffin, with 'CW' mark for thrower Chris Wright, also marked 'Dennis China Works, CW, 2003, S.T.Des, No 9'.

'Strawberry' was introduced in 2003. The range included a teapot, two sizes of jar, a charger, and the vases shown on this page.

2003   *6.5in (16cm) high*
£100-150   **LC**

A Dennis China Works 'Pineapple' bottle vase, designed by Sally Tuffin, on a green ground, the base marked 'ST des, No 1, Dennis China Works', and with impressed 'RMc' mark for thrower Rory McLeod.

15.75in (40cm) high
£500-700   **LC**

Mark Picks

Sally Tuffin worked for Poole Pottery from 1995 to 1998. Her primary purpose there was to revive the aims of their previously very popular 'Studio' range. All the pieces in the range were intended to be prestigious limited editions, many targeted at collectors.

Much of her inspiration for her 'Studio' work came from the quayside setting of the pottery, so many have a strong marine feel. Surprisingly, 'Parasol' did not prove popular at the time, so can be harder to find today. However, it is typical of both Poole's and Tuffin's much-loved styles, so may become sought-after as more collectors are drawn to her work there. This trial piece may prove even more interesting than the standard range to the right collector.

A Poole Pottery trial 'Parasol' pattern vase, designed by Sally Tuffin, with an accompanying letter of authentication.

British Airways used one of Tuffin's designs for Poole on the tail fins of some of their planes in the late 1990s.

1996   *8.5in (22cm) high*
£150-200   **GORL**

A Dennis China Works 'Hornet' pattern vase, designed by Sally Tuffin, painted with aeroplanes on a graduated green and blue ground, the base with 'CW' mark for thrower Chris Wright and also marked 'Dennis China Works, 2004, S.T Des, No 11'.

This is the only motif and pattern designed by Tuffin that does not feature, and was not inspired by, the natural world. Tuffin says that the pattern was inspired by a photograph 'of American winged planes 'mothballed' in geometric formation' in the desert in Arizona.

2004   *12.5in (32cm) high*
£400-500   **LC**

QUICK REFERENCE - VAN BRIGGLE

- The Van Briggle pottery was opened in Colorado Springs, Colorado, in 1901 by Artus Van Briggle (1869-1904). As well as studying and working at Rookwood (see pp.105-106), Van Briggle had studied in Paris. There he first saw the ancient Chinese Ming dynasty matt glazes that he later devoted his life to recreating. His organic forms were inspired by the Art Nouveau and Arts and Crafts movements.
- Van Briggle died in 1904, and his wife ran the pottery until 1912 when she sold it. The company changed ownership, moved location a number of times, and is still operational today. The most collectable and valuable pieces generally date from when Artus Van Briggle ran the pottery. Pieces produced under his wife are also highly sought-after. Inscribed marks on the base, the shape, and the glaze are all factors used to date and value a piece. This vase has a superb Art Nouveau style design, and is also reticulated.

A mid-20thC Van Briggle Pottery 'Lorelei' vase, with blue-patched matt pink glaze, the base with inscribed marks.

11in (28cm) high

£80-120   **FRE**

A large 1920s Van Briggle moulded vase, embossed with papyrus leaves under a graduated 'Persian Rose' glaze, the base marked 'AA VAN BRIGGLE 20'.

10.5in (26.5cm) high

£600-800   **DRA**

A Van Briggle reticulated vase, embossed with papyrus motifs under a 'Persian Rose' glaze, with a vertical hairline crack from the rim.

1916   *6.5in (16.5cm) high*

£800-1,200   **DRA**

A Van Briggle bowl-vase, with swirling trefoils under green and blue matt glaze, the base marked 'AA VAN BRIGGLE COLO SPGS 695', with a hairline crack to base, possibly from firing.

1908-11   *4in (10cm) high*

£200-300   **DRA**

A Van Briggle 'Lotus' centrepiece-bowl, with raised foliate-form rim, and blue-green crackle glaze, the base signed 'Van Briggle / Colo. Spgs' with trademark conjoined A's mark and capital 'D'.

c1950   *6in (15cm) diam*

£80-120   **FRE**

A pair of Van Briggle 'Bird of Paradise' bud vases, with blue-green crackle glaze, the base signed 'Van Briggle / Colo. Spgs.' with trademark conjoined A's mark.

9in (23cm) high

£100-150   **FRE**

CERAMICS

QUICK REFERENCE

- Wedgwood was founded by Josiah Wedgwood in Staffordshire in 1759. In 1762 he met his future partner Thomas Bentley, a Liverpool merchant who instilled o Wedgwood a love of the Classical that would strongly influence the company's designs from then on. The famous Jasperware range was developed in c1774-75. It was initially produced in blue, black, and green with applied white low-relief friezes of Classical scenes. With its increasing popularity, new colour combinations were developed.

- In c1762 Wedgwood also perfected creamware, a popular form of earthenware. It became known as 'Queensware' after the firm secured the patronage of Queen Charlotte in 1765.

- Wedgwood continued its 18thC styles and patterns into the 19thC, and retained its prominence in the 20thC by employing key designers to develop new ranges.

- One of the most important is New Zealand architect and designer Keith Murray (1892-1981), who joined Wedgwood in 1932. His forms are typically simple and unembellished, and bear matt glazes. Colours include 'Moonstone' white, 'Straw Yellow', and the most commonly found 'Green'. Production peaked during the 1930s, but continued into the 1950s.

- Illustrator and war artist Eric Ravilious (1903-1942) designed nursery and tableware from c1936 to 1940. He produced many notable and sought-after designs, including a coronation mug, the 'Alphabet' mug, and the 'Afternoon Tea', 'Travel' and 'Garden Implements' china sets. Other notable 20thC designers include Daisy Makeig-Jones (1881-1945), who designed the complex 'Fairyland Lustre' range of the 1910s and 1920s (see p.141), Norman Wilson (1902-1980), John Skeaping (1901-1980), and Millicent Taplin (1902-1980).

A Wedgwood blue 'Jasperware' campana urn vase and cover, with typical Classical figures within anthemion and palmette sprigged borders, the base with impressed mark.

13in (33cm) high

£600-800

AH

A late 19th/early 20thC Wedgwood blue 'Jasperware' baluster table urn, with circular sectional column supporting globular top, encrusted with portraits and grape and vine swags, lacking cover, unmarked.

17in (43.5cm) high

£250-350   MAR

A Wedgwood 'Caneware' urn vase, with applied sprigged blue floral decoration including passion flowers below a border of anthemions.

3.5in (8.5cm) high

£80-120   LHA

A Wedgwood blue 'Jasperware' cache pot, applied with a continuous sprigged band of Classical figures, the base with impressed mark.

8.25in (21cm) diam

£80-120   LC

A late 19thC Wedgwood majolica tripartite shell-dish, painted with coloured glazes, the base with impressed marks.

11in (27cm) wide

£70-100   **DN**

A late 19thC Wedgwood majolica circular bowl, the base rim with an applied silver-plated mount, and with stamped factory marks.

10in (25cm) diam

£50-70   **GHOU**

A late 19thC Wedgwood majolica ewer, decorated with dogs, with pewter lid, unmarked.

10.5in (27cm) high

£200-300   **GORL**

Judith Picks

This is an excellent example of how fashion has affected desirability and prices. This pattern was produced from 1961 until 1986, and would have been very expensive in its day, as one would expect from such a high quality maker. Because it was expensive, it became the sort of 'china' that would have been brought out for special occasions, and treated very carefully.

As more people turned to a more relaxed and less formal manner of drinking tea made with tea bags from mugs, the popularity of these sets fell dramatically. It has never fully recovered, but there is hope for the future. Original owners who treasure their sets will often need replacements for broken or worn pieces. In addition it is becoming increasingly fashionable to drink tea from 'harlequin' sets made up of many different individual pieces with 'old fashioned' patterns. Cups and saucers, and maybe an accompanying side plate, are usually the easiest part to sell, but teapots are typically the most valuable.

A late 20thC Wedgwood 27-piece 'Gold Florentine' porcelain tea service, pattern no.W4219, with Renaissance inspired gilt-printed borders of dragons and scrolling designs, comprising eight cups and saucers, eight side plates, a milk jug, sugar bowl, and a square bread and butter plate, with printed marks.

£120-180   **CAPE**

A Wedgwood dressing table set, printed and painted in the 'Imari' palette with floral borders, comprising a pair of candlesticks, a ring tree, a trinket dish, and a hexagonal box and cover, on tray, the bases with printed mark and painted pattern no.'23879D'.

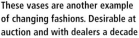

Unlike the tea sets, dressing table sets seem unlikely to return to fashion. Few people have dressing tables now, and fewer would want to 'clutter them up' with a set like this. Some do want replacement pieces, and individual objects, such as the candlesticks, may be of interest, so it's likely this set would be split up for re-sale, unless a buyer wanting a 'retro-antique' look in their bedroom can be found!

Tray 12.5in (32cm) wide

£55-75   **CAPE**

A set of three late 20thC Wedgwood vases and covers, painted with pheasants, cattle, and deer by M. Harnett, on a gilded black ground, each titled and numbered to base.

These vases are another example of changing fashions. Desirable at auction and with dealers a decade ago, popularity has sadly dropped. These skilfully and beautifully hand-painted vases, produced by one of Britain's most legendary potteries, are also too late in date for many collectors. However, at under £100 each, they'd give an immediate taste of 19thC style if displayed on a mantelpiece or in a cabinet.

10.25in (26cm) high

£220-280   **GORL**

CERAMICS

QUICK REFERENCE - WEDGWOOD'S LUSTRE RANGES

- Most of Wedgwood's early 20thC lustre ranges were designed by Daisy Makeig-Jones (1881-1945), who was one of the first female ceramics designers to gain recognition in the 20thC. After showing considerable talent in art, she applied to and joined Wedgwood in 1909. By 1914, she had become a designer and had been given her own studio. Her first patterns were based on nursery rhymes and applied to nursery ware. After seeing an exhibition of lustre ware, and observing the development of the powder-blue glaze at Wedgwood, she began to pursue complex lustre ranges.

- The 'Ordinary Lustre' range was launched in 1915, and was inspired by Oriental ceramics. More elaborate patterns based on fairy tales, fables, and myths, seen through a child's vivid imagination, came shortly after. Known as 'Fairyland Lustre', many of these patterns strongly resemble book illustrations by artists such as Arthur Rackham. Labour-intensive to create, 'Fairyland Lustre' was expensive to buy but sold well to wealthy clients. Its success led to other companies such as Carlton Ware and Crown Devon imitating, but never matching, the extravagant look.

- 'Leapfrogging Elves' is one of her most notable patterns, with 'Dana, Castle on a Road', 'Candlemas' and 'Fairy Gondola' also being popular. New patterns were launched in the early 1920s, but many were discontinued in 1929 and during the Great Depression. Further cutbacks led to Makeig-Jones retiring in 1931, and the 'Fairyland Lustre' range was discontinued in 1941.

- The first digit of the painted model numbers on bases is a 'Z', not a '2', and was the company code for 'china ornaments'. You should also be aware that the same pattern numbers were used for many variations.

- Prices have mushroomed over the past five years, particularly in the US. This is especially true for large pieces in complex patterns, which can fetch over £10,000. Damage reduces value considerably, as the examples on this page show. Although prices may now be peaking, this is still a market to watch.

A Wedgwood 'Fairyland Lustre' Empire-shape bowl, in the 'Leapfrogging Elves' pattern, pattern no.Z4968 designed by Daisy Makeig-Jones, printed and painted in colours and gilt on a black lustre ground, the base with printed and painted marks.

5.25in (13cm) wide

£1,000-1,500   **A&G**

A Wedgwood 'Fairyland Lustre' bowl, in the 'Poplar Trees' pattern, pattern no.Z4968 designed by Daisy Makeig-Jones, the interior with a central 'Mermaid' medallion surrounded by the 'Woodland Bridge' pattern, the base with Portland Vase mark and painted 'Z4968', with a cracked rim.

This could have fetched up to 50% more had it not been cracked.

c1920   *11in (28cm) diam*

£1,000-1,500   **TEN**

A Wedgwood 'Fairyland Lustre' octagonal bowl, in the 'Butterfly' pattern, pattern no.Z4832 designed by Daisy Makeig-Jones, with a mottled orange lustre interior, and printed and painted marks to base, the pattern worn.

c1920   3.5in (9cm) wide

£70-100   **CHT**

A Wedgwood 'Ordinary Lustre' covered bowl, in the 'Flying Humming Birds' pattern, pattern no.Z5294, designed by Daisy Makeig Jones, with a figural finial and printed and painted marks to base.

c1917   6.25in (16cm) diam

£200-300   **LHA**

A 1920s Wedgwood 'Fairyland Lustre' lily tray, in the 'Fairy Gondola' pattern, no.Z4968 designed by Daisy Makeig-Jones, the base with painted and gilt Portland Vase mark and impressed 'W' (star crack to base).

Chargers are usually among the most sought-after forms as they display a lot of pattern and have enormous and immediate visual impact. This example could have fetched around twice this price had it not had a star crack in the base.

13in (33cm) diam

£600-800   **TEN**

A Wedgwood 'Ordinary Lustre' meiping-shaped vase and cover, decorated with the 'Dragon' pattern, pattern no.Z4829 designed by Daisy Makeig-Jones, with printed and painted marks to base.

c1915   9in (23cm) high

£350-450   **RW**

A Wedgwood matt green shoulder vase, shape no.3805 designed by Keith Murray, the base impressed 'Wedgwood' and with printed signature mark.

11in (29cm) high

£300-500   DS

A Wedgwood matt green vase, shape no.3842 designed by Keith Murray, the base with printed mark and with unfinished rim.

This appears to be the body part of a shape no.3805 shoulder vase (shown left), but without the top, leaving an unfinished rim. If so, and given the shorter height, this could have been a trial piece for a third, smaller size of shoulder vase.

4.5in (11.5cm) high

£120-180   BEV

A Wedgwood matt green vase, shape no.3868 designed by Keith Murray, the base with printed 'KM' monogram mark.

6.75in (17cm) high

£120-180   RW

A Wedgwood 'Moonstone' white spherical vase, shape no.3765 designed by Keith Murray, the base with printed marks.

6in (15cm)

£200-250   GORL

A 1930s Wedgwood matt blue spherical vase, shape no.3802 designed by Keith Murray, with banding and collar rim.

Despite the clear similarities, this shape is different to shape no.3765 (also shown on this page). This vase has a taller neck and different carved banding than no.3765, and is scarcer, particularly in blue.

9in (24cm) high

£500-700   WHP

A 1940s Wedgwood 'Moonstone' white shoulder vase, shape no.3805 designed by Keith Murray, the base with printed 'KM' mark.

This style of mark was introduced in 1940, when earthenware production moved to Barlaston, Staffordshire. Be aware that some pieces produced after this date were printed with earlier style marks.

7.25in (18.5cm) high

£750-850   BEV

A small 1930s Wedgwood 'Black Basalt' vase, shape no.3888 designed by Keith Murray, with a shallow collar foot and ovoid body, with incised chevron pattern, the base with later red painted mark.

4in (10cm) high

£400-600   FLD

CERAMICS

A CLOSER LOOK AT A WEDGWOOD VASE

Wedgwood 'Black Basalt' ware designed by Keith Murray is very rare. Only bronze is rarer.

This is a large piece, and the design is strongly Modernist and very rare.

The simple form and cut bands are typical features of Murray's designs, but the step between the cylindrical body and the curving base, which gives this form a machine-like feel, is unusual.

'Black Basalt' wares designed by Murray usually have red printed marks, as here.

A 1930s Wedgwood 'Black Basalt' vase, shape no.3891 designed by Keith Murray, with fluted top band and step to lower body, the base with printed signature mark.

9in (22.5cm) high

£800-1,200   PC

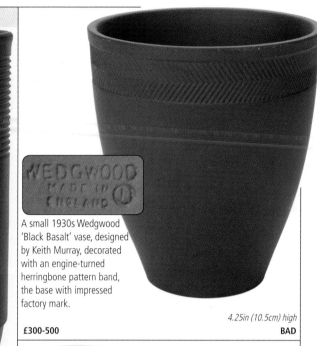

A small 1930s Wedgwood 'Black Basalt' vase, designed by Keith Murray, decorated with an engine-turned herringbone pattern band, the base with impressed factory mark.

4.25in (10.5cm) high

£300-500   BAD

A Wedgwood 'Straw' yellow mug, shape no.3810 designed by Keith Murray, the base with printed signature mark.

5in (12.5cm) high

£70-90   BEV

A Wedgwood footed bowl, shape no.3994 designed by Keith Murray, the body with grey glaze, the foot and rim with applied silver leaf, the base with printed signature mark.

With its silver details and grey glaze, this is a rare design on a hard-to-find shape. Unfortunately, the interior is stained, reducing the value slightly.

11.75in (30cm) diam

£350-450   WW

A small rare 1930s Wedgwood white cocktail cup, shape no.3999 designed by Keith Murray, with painted silver banding, the base with printed 'KM' mark, painted '66149 N', and impressed '8'.

3.25in (8cm) high

£50-80   BEV

A Wedgwood matt green cigarette box, shape no.3871 designed by Keith Murray, with a ribbed body and plain rectangular handle, the base with printed signature mark.

7.25in (18.5cm) long

£120-180   FLD

QUICK REFERENCE - ART DECO ANIMAL FIGURINES

- Animal figurines are collected by thousands across the world, and form one of the most common themes for collectors. Charming and realistic depictions are the most widely collected, but those produced in distinct styles add a dramatic sense of period style to a room, and make a novel alternative theme. The Art Deco style is particularly suited to today's tastes in interior design, and many period examples are perhaps under-appreciated.

- Wedgwood's best-known animal figures were modelled by John Skeaping (1901-80). He studied at the Central School of Art, the Royal Academy Schools and, later, in Rome. He married the famed sculptress Barbara Hepworth who profoundly influenced his work, in that it became simpler in form and detail, and primitive in a Modern manner.

- In 1926, upon his return to England, he was commissioned by Wedgwood to design a series of fourteen animals, only ten of which appear to have been produced. These were made in 'Black Basalt' and a variety of matt colours. Skeaping's animals were popular and most were produced into the late 1930s, with some continuing to be made into the 1950s. Their simplified, angular, and distinctly Modern forms

reflect the Art Deco style perfectly and suit the homes of today as much as the homes of the period. Skeaping's choice of animals also follows the style, ranging from deer and antelopes to a polar bear.

- If you like the look, look out for the sculptural work of Alan Best, particularly his figurines of athletes, from the same period.

A Wedgwood glazed earthenware figure of a lion attacking a gazelle, designed by John Skeaping, with impressed marks to base.

7in (19cm) high

£100-150　　　　　　　　**LSK**

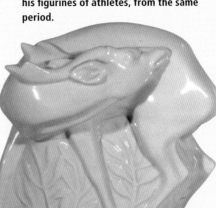

A Wedgwood 'Fallow Deer' figurine, designed by John Skeaping, covered in a 'Straw' yellow glaze, impressed 'Wedgwood' and 'J Skeaping' to side of plinth.

7in (19cm) high

£180-220　　　　　　　　**WW**

A Wedgwood 'Duiker Lying' glazed earthenware figure, designed by John Skeaping, impressed 'Wedgwood' and 'J Skeaping' to the side of the base, printed marks to base.

This cost 8s 9d during the 1930s. The range was reasonably priced and became popular with middle-class buyers with an eye for modern design.

5in (13cm) high

£70-100　　　　　　　　**LSK**

A Wedgwood glazed earthenware figure of a mountain goat, designed by Roy Smith, impressed 'Roy Smith' to the side of the base, with printed marks to base.

7in (18.5cm) high

£100-150　　　　　　　　**LSK**

A Wedgwood glazed earthenware figure of a bison, designed by John Skeaping, impressed 'Wedgwood' and 'J Skeaping' to the side of the plinth, with printed marks to base.

8in (19.5cm) high

£150-200　　　　　　　　**LSK**

A Wedgwood 'Queensware' 'Taurus the Bull' figurine, designed by Arnold Machin in c1945, printed with signs of the Zodiac, with date code apparently for October 1950.

16in (41cm) long

£250-350　　　　　　　　**A&G**

CERAMICS

QUICK REFERENCE - ALFRED & LOUISE POWELL

- Architect and painter Alfred Powell (1865-1960) submitted his first designs to Wedgwood in 1903. He had become associated with the Arts and Crafts movement, and Wedgwood, aware of the growing importance of the movement, were consequently keen to put his designs into production.
- Working from a studio in Bloomsbury, London, Powell's relationship with Wedgwood lasted over 40 years, although the quantities of his designs declined after 1930. Alfred's wife Louise (1882-1956) also contributed designs after their marriage in 1906.
- One of the couple's regular visits to the company led to the revival of some hand-painted designs by Josiah Wedgwood, which in turn lead to the establishment of the handcraft department during the 1920s. Run by Millicent Taplin, the department produced the Powells' designs, as well as Taplin's own designs, which were strongly influenced by the Powells. Handcraft designs fall into two broad categories: simple, stylised floral and foliate designs, which are usually applied to tableware, or complex, richly coloured patterns, inspired by Islamic, Moorish, Renaissance, or armorial designs. The piece below is a good example of this second type of pattern, which was typically applied to decorative wares.

A Wedgwood charger, decorated with the 'Rhodian' pattern designed by Alfred Powell, painted with scrolling flowers and foliage in shades of blue, green, purple, and silver lustre, the base with impressed factory marks and painted mark '5731'.

c1925   *14in (36cm) diam*

£500-700   **L&T**

A Wedgwood dinner plate, from the 'Garden' range designed by Eric Ravilious, transfer-printed and painted with a seated lady in a garden feeding birds, within a wave border, picked out in pale yellow wash, the base with printed marks.

10in (25cm) wide

£120-180   **FLD**

A Wedgwood pottery charger, designed by Louise Powell, model no.3057, painted in shades of blue and 'mushroom' with a foliate design over a white ground, with impressed and painted marks.

12in (30cm) diam

£400-600   **WW**

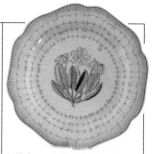

A Wedgwood plate, designed by Louise Powell, painted to the well with cowslips, the base with impressed marks and painted monogram.

9in (23cm) diam

£300-400   **WW**

A Wedgwood circular soup bowl, from the 'Travel' range designed by Eric Ravilious, transfer-printed with a stylised steam train emerging from a tunnel within a wave line border, all on a grey ground, the base with printed marks.

9in (23cm) wide

£180-220   **FLD**

Mark Picks

Much of the memorabilia produced for the landmark Festival of Britain exhibition in 1951 was of poor quality, but this mug is quite different. Printed onto Wedgwood's 'Queensware', Makinson's pattern captures the excitement and modern look of the exhibition perfectly. As well as the famous festival logo, the pattern includes people looking at the Skylon, and a scene of the 1851 Great Exhibition, held a century earlier. Stylish and appealing to Wedgwood and Festival of Britain collectors, this mug makes a great buy.

A Wedgwood commemorative '1951 Festival of Britain' mug, designed by Norman Makinson, with printed marks to base.

2.75in (7cm) high

£150-200   **TRI**

CERAMICS

A Weller 'Hudson Scenic' ovoid vase, decorated by Sarah Timberlake with a summer landscape, with glaze flake to base and heavy crazing, the base signed 'Weller Pottery' and 'Timberlake'.

9in (24cm) high

£300-500   DRA

A Weller 'Hudson Perfecto' baluster vase, decorated with purple irises on a graduated green to cream-yellow ground, the base with partial factory mark.

14in (36cm) high

£350-450   DRA

A Weller 'Hudson Perfecto' ovoid vase, decorated with clusters of grapes on a lavender ground, with restored chip at rim, the base stamped 'Weller'.

15.5in (39cm) high

£350-450   DRA

QUICK REFERENCE - WELLER

- Weller was founded by Samuel Weller (1851-1925) in 1871 in Fultonham, Ohio, and initially produced utilitarian wares. It moved to the 'pottery city' of Zanesville in 1888 and began to expand, introducing high quality hand-decorated art pottery in the 1890s, and becoming the world's largest art pottery by 1904.
- Weller bought the nearby Lonhuda Pottery in 1894. He then learned its decorative glazing techniques for use on Weller's 'Louwelsa' range, which was also similar to Rookwood's 'Standard Glaze' (see p.105). Other well-known Weller ranges included 'Aurelian' (c1897), 'Eocean' (1898), and 'Hudson' (c1917).
- By the 1920s, the popularity of expensive hand-decorated wares was declining, and the pottery introduced moulded 'production' ranges. During the early 1930s, hand-decorated wares were discontinued entirely, as the pottery suffered badly in the Great Depression. Although new life was injected in the 1930s, the decline was set, and Weller closed in 1948.
- Notable designers included Charles Upjohn, Jacques Sicard, and Frederick Rhead. Early hand-decorated wares tend to fetch the highest prices, particularly if the pattern is appealing and by a notable artist, such as Sarah Timberlake.

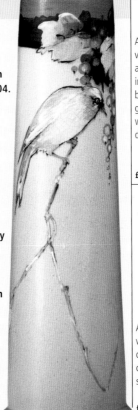

A Weller 'Glossy Hudson' tapering cylindrical vase, decorated with a bird on a grape branch, with short underglaze firing line to base, chip on foot-ring and underglaze chip to rim, the base with factory marks and illegible artist's signature.

13in (33cm) high

£700-1,000   DRA

A Weller cylinder vase, decorated with a blue and pink iris on a graduated blue and green ground, the base with factory marks, damaged.

8.5in (22cm) high

£250-350   DRA

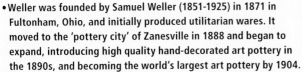

A Weller 'Hudson Light' flaring vase, decorated with Virginia creeper on a graduated blue to cream ground, crazed, the base signed 'Weller'.

10.5in (27cm) high

£120-180   DRA

CERAMICS

A CLOSER LOOK AT A WELLER VASE

The 'La Sa' range was introduced in 1920. It was devised by John Lessell, who was Weller's art director from 1920 to 1924.

Designs for the range typically included a tree and expanses of water and land, as here.

It was a significant range for the company, who reacted against the decline in sales of hand-decorated, high-end art wares by introducing stunning new designs.

The use of a rich lustre glaze on the 'La Sa' range often leads to confusion between this range and Jacques Sicard's earlier 'Sicardo' line (1902-12) for Weller. However, 'Sicardo' patterns are more stylised, and generally don't include landscapes.

A Weller 'La Sa' baluster vase, decorated with a lake landscape, with shallow spider-line crack to the interior only, and wear to glaze inside rim and around the base, the base signed 'Weller La Sa'.

14in (36cm) high

£300-500   DRA

A small Weller 'Jewelled Cameo' ovoid vase, decorated with seahorses outlined in green, on a graduated mottled pink ground, with tight hairline to rim, the base with factory marks.

4in (10cm) diam

£100-150   DRA

A Weller 'Flemish' tulip-shaped vase, with scrolling stem and leaf support, the base with stamped mark.

8.75in (22cm) high

£200-300   DRA

A Weller 'Forest' footed jardinière and pedestal, the jardinière with multiple hairline cracks throughout, both stamped 'Weller Ware'.

This piece could have sold for up to five times more had it not been so damaged. Multiple cracks are costly to restore and repair.

28in (71cm) high

£60-80   DRA

A Weller wall hanging, with large pink blossoms and blue birds nesting in branches, repair to one beak, a few firing flaws, the back with impressed factory mark.

Even though moulded 'production' wares are generally less sought-after and valuable than earlier Weller pieces, this is a large, detailed, and very scarce piece, which makes it desirable. Visually impressive, it also only has one area of damage.

15in (38cm) high

£1,000-1,500   DRA

A life-size Weller 'Garden Ware' running rabbit, the base with ink kiln stamp.

12in (30cm) long

£800-1,200   DRA

QUICK REFERENCE

- The distinctive, brightly coloured Wemyss ware was first made in 1882 at the Fife Pottery. The pottery (established in c1790 by Robert Methven Heron) had initially produced ceramics in muted colours until Czech-born decorator Karel Nekola began to paint pieces with flowers and leaves.
- Production grew quickly, and a wide range of shapes were produced. These included the large ceramic pigs and cats for which the firm is best known today. Some were sold through the London firm of Thomas Goode & Son, whose marks can often be found on Wemyss pieces.
- Patterns are typically hand-painted depictions of flowers, particularly cabbage roses, plants, fruit, birds, and other animals. Most patterns were designed by Nekola, who trained a team to reproduce his work. He also decorated some pieces

- himself, and these are highly sought-after. Other key decorators include James Sharp and Edwin Sandland.
- Most people collect by pattern, some of which are more desirable than others. Shape may also affect value, with rare shapes commanding a premium. Look out for original sleeping piglets, as these can be worth over £10,000!
- The rights to Wemyss ware were sold to the Bovey Tracey Pottery, Devon in 1930. Karel Nekola's son, Joseph moved with the pottery, taking the moulds with him, and continued to paint Wemyss ware until his death in 1952. Esther Weeks then took over until the pottery closed in 1957.
- Pieces produced at Devon have a cleaner white 'glassy' glaze, and are lighter than examples from Fife. They tend to be less valuable than earlier pieces.
- Modern Wemyss ware is now made at the Griselda Hill pottery, Fife, which was established in 1985.

A pair of early 20thC medium-sized 'Japan' shape vases, decorated with cabbage roses, both with painted and impressed marks 'Wemyss' to the bases.

8in (21cm) high

£500-700   L&T

A pair of early 20thC 'May' shape vases, each decorated with yellow cabbage roses on a black ground, the bases with impressed 'Wemyss' marks.

Black grounds are scarce.

6.5in (16.5cm) high

£350-450   L&T

A large Wemyss preserve jar and cover, decorated with apples, the base with impressed 'Wemyss Ware R. H. & S.' mark.

The 'R. H. & S.' mark is for Robert Heron of the Fife Pottery in Scotland. By the 1880s, Robert Heron & Son were branding their range of decorated earthenware 'Wemyss ware' in honour of the local Wemyss family who were avid and lucrative patrons.

c1900   5.9in (15cm) high

£300-500   L&T

A small early 20thC 'Grosvenor' shape vase, decorated with carnations, the base with impressed 'Wemyss' mark.

5.5in (14cm) high

£250-350   L&T

A Wemyss tea kettle, decorated with cabbage roses, the base with printed 'T. Goode & Co.' retailer's mark.

Tea kettles are very rare shapes. This example was sold by high-end central London retailer, Thomas Goode.

c1900   6.25in (16cm) high

£1,200-1,800   L&T

CERAMICS

QUICK REFERENCE - EDWIN SANDLAND

- Edwin Sandland was a talented decorator who worked at the potteries in Hanley, Staffordshire. He left to join the army pay corps in 1915, only to be invalided out a year later. He then went to work at the Fife pottery, and succeeded Karel Nekola as artist director on his death in 1915. Sandland stayed and worked at Fife until 1928. Apart from continuing Wemyss's much-loved designs, he also brought in new designs and new spins on old designs, including the use of black grounds, as seen on the 'May' vases on the previous page.

A large Wemyss plate, decorated with hairy gooseberries, the base with impressed 'Wemyss Ware R. H. & S.' mark.

c1900   *8in (21.5cm) diam*

£600-800   **L&T**

A Wemyss flower bowl, decorated by Edwin Sandland with cabbage roses, the restored base with painted 'Wemyss T. Goode & Co.' marks and with impressed mark 'Wemyss' mark.

12in (31cm) diam

£250-350   **L&T**

A medium Wemyss plate, decorated with tulips, the base with impressed 'Wemyss R. H. & S.' mark.

5.5in (14cm) diam

£200-300   **L&T**

A Wemyss quaich, decorated with apples, the base with impressed 'Wemyss' mark, and printed 'T. Goode & Co.' retailer's mark.

10in (26.5cm) diam across handles

£400-600   **L&T**

A Wemyss low quaich, decorated with red plums, painted mark 'T. Goode & Co. London Wemyss', and with impressed 'Wemyss Ware R. H. & S.' mark.

10in (26cm) diam across handles

£400-600   **L&T**

A 1920s-30s Wemyss 'Jazzy' comb tray, decorated with cabbage roses, the base with painted 'Wemyss 213' mark.

10in (25cm) long

£150-200   **L&T**

A Wemyss match box cover, decorated with cherries, the base with printed 'T. Goode & Co.' retailer's mark.

3in (8cm) long

£220-280   **L&T**

QUICK REFERENCE

- Over the past five to seven years, after a period of being unfashionable, West German ceramics produced during the 1950s-70s have become highly collectable and sought-after.
- This period witnessed an explosion of innovation and design, which changed considerably across each decade. Companies such as Bay Keramik, Dümler & Breiden, and Ruscha underwent a revival, and were joined by newer companies such as Scheurich and Otto Keramik. Although shapes were mass-produced on production lines, glazes were applied by hand. The results were exported internationally.
- During the 1950s forms were generally curving and asymmetric, often with angled handles and rims. Patterns were made up of clearly delineated, often geometric, forms in bright, primary colours. Typical forms include jugs, which were intended for use as display objects or vases rather than pouring. Currently affordable, this style may yet see its day.

- The 1960s and '70s saw a complete change in style, with the order of structured patterns giving way to glazes that were trailed, dripped, or daubed over simple forms. The colour and texture of the glaze became the most important factor. Many of these were bubbling 'fat lava' glazes in vibrant colours such as orange, red, and blue.
- Makers can be identified by considering the marks on the base, the form, and the type and colour of glaze used. As this area is still new, discoveries are still being made, and there is much to learn as many companies' archives were destroyed.
- At the present time examples with bolder and wilder 'fat lava' glazes are the most popular and valuable. Many were produced in smaller quantities than the 'tamer' designs in browns or beiges on simple forms, making them rare. Size is also important, with larger 'floor vases' being highly sought-after and commanding the highest prices on today's market.

A 1950s-60s West German Bay Keramik jug, with scrolling dark brown lines and yellow and blue rectangles on a brushed cream glaze, with silver foil factory label, the base moulded '249-40'.

16in (40.5cm) high

£70-100   GC

A 1950-60s West German Bay Keramik jug, with black-lined banded pattern in red, yellow, and blue, with silver foil factory label, the base moulded 'WEST-GERMANY 1142-30'.

12in (30.5cm) high

£50-80   GC

A 1960s West German Bay Keramik conical jug with angled handle, designed by Bodo Mans, with silver foil factory label, the base moulded 'WEST-GERMANY 1111-20'.

8in (20.5cm) high

£60-80   GC

A 1960s West German Bay Keramik conical vase, designed by Bodo Mans, the base moulded 'WEST-GERMANY 1012-17', with original silver foil factory label.

6.75in (17cm) high

£50-70   GC

A 1950s West German Bay Keramik asymmetric oval tray, designed by Bodo Mans, with yellow and white glossy mottles, resist lines, and ellipses, and blue lines and orange dots, the base moulded 'WEST-GERMANY 1210'.

10.5in (26.5cm) long

£60-80   GC

CERAMICS

A small late 1950s-60s Bay Keramik jug, shape no.282/20, decorated with the 'Florenz' pattern introduced in 1955, the base impressed 'GERMANY 03' and printed '30'.

8in (20.5cm) high

£25-35   W&L

A 1960s West German Carstens cylinder vase, painted with yellow, turquoise, and red circular motifs with black lines, with gold foil factory label, the base moulded 'W.GERM.683-18'.

7in (18cm) high

£40-60   GC

A 1950s-60s Fohr waisted vase, painted with red and green rectangles in black squares, with gold foil factory label, the base moulded 'MADE IN GERMANY 330 20'

8in (20.5cm) high

£30-40   GC

A 1960s-70s West German Jasba vase, shape no. 563/12, with creamy white glaze and resist pattern of stylised plants, highlighted in green and red, the base with indistinct moulded marks.

This design is also available in a (more commonly found) monochrome variation without the green and red decoration.

5in (12.5cm) high

£70-100   GC

A 1950s West German Ruscha 'Marocco' pattern ovoid vase, shape no. 849/1, the form and pattern designed by Hans Welling in 1956, with sgrafitto lines and glossy glazed panels of abstract geometric motifs, the base with inscribed marks.

8.5in (21.5cm) high

£70-100   GC

A CLOSER LOOK AT A RUSCHA DISH

The curving form, with its asymmetric handle, is typical of the 1950s, and was partly inspired by Scandinavian Modernism of the time.

The pattern and form are both by the artist Hans Welling (b.1924), who worked at Ruscha 1956-59 and produced some of their best-selling and (today) most desirable designs.

An influential name in West German ceramic design at the time, Welling also produced designs for Keto, Schlossberg, Rosenthal, Hutschenreuther, and Cortendorf. He also helped to found Ceramano in 1959.

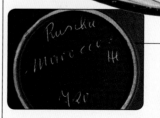

Along with most Ruscha designs produced in the 1950s and early 1960s, the base is hand-inscribed with the company's name, the pattern name, the shape number (720), and the glazer's initials (HH).

A late-1950s Ruscha 'Marocco' pattern asymmetric handled dish, the form and pattern designed by Hans Welling in 1956, the base inscribed 'Marocco HH 720'.

13.5in (34cm) long

£50-70   MA

A 1970s West German Dümler & Breiden 'Polar' range vase, designed in 1972, from the 'Relief' series, with green circle and grey-white glaze, the base impressed 'D&B RELIEF 22/15 GERMANY'.

6.25in (16cm)

£40-60   **GC**

A 1970s West German Dümler & Breiden 'Polar' range handled bucket vase, designed in 1972, from the 'Relief' series, the base with factory crossed sword motif and moulded '22/30'.

12in (30.5cm) high

£35-55   **GAZE**

QUICK REFERENCE - GRÄFLICHE ORTENBURGSCHE

- Gräfliche Ortenburgsche was founded in Tambach in 1946, and closed in 1968. As 'lava' glazes only became widely popular in the early 1960s, this makes its examples comparatively scarce.
- The company's two key designers were Irene Pasinski and Ursula Beyran. Beyran studied with a number of notable potters, including Otto Lindig, and began working for Gräfliche Ortenburgsche in 1967. After the company closed, she set up her own studio.
- Polish artist and industrial designer Pasinski studied at the Carnegie Tech, USA, before going on to École du Louvre and the Institut D'Art Appliqué à L'Industrie in Paris. She produced many shape and glaze designs for Gräfliche Ortenburgsche, and returned to the US to found her own design consultancy in the same year.
- Gräfliche Ortenburgsche used the moulded mark shown above, but many pieces are unmarked so it's best to identify them from shapes, glazes, or preferably both. Red lava glazes like this one tend to be the most desirable and valuable. The '1' suffix after the 605 shape number indicates that this was part of a series of the same shape in different sizes.

A 1960s West German Gräfliche Ortenburgsche low jug vase, form no.619 designed by Irene Paskinski, with light blue volcanic lava glaze over a matt dark grey glaze, unmarked.

4.75in (12cm) high

£80-120   **GC**

A 1960s West German Gräfliche Ortenburgsche jug vase, designed by Irene Pasinski, with black-mottled glossy red lava glaze, the base moulded with the company logo and '605/1'.

9in (23cm) high

£120-180   **GC**

A 1970s West German Kreutz Keramik footed cylinder vase, with red and black bubbled lava glaze under a satin-matt cream glaze, with gold and silver foil factory label, unmarked.

This band of lava glaze 'bubbling up' through the glaze that covers the rest of the body is typical of Kreutz pieces from the 1970s. Note the addition of a red glaze towards the bottom of the band.

6in (15cm) high

£50-70   **GC**

A 1970s West German Otto Keramik conical footed vase, the form designed by Kurt Tschörner, the thick red volcanic lava glaze designed by Otto Gerharz, the base covered with felt.

9.5in (24cm) high

£150-200   **GC**

CERAMICS

A 1970s West German P-Keramik triple-holed vase, the matt brown glazed body decorated with splodgy orange glazes, unmarked.

Many of these are found with labels for the distributor Riffarth.

4in (11cm) high

£30-50   GC

A 1970s West German Roth Keramik jug vase, with matt black volcanic lava glaze dripped over a glossy orange glazed body, the base impressed 'W.GERMANY 101'.

7.5in (19cm) high

£70-100   GC

A 1970s West German Silberdistel tapering vase, probably designed by Uwe Kerstan, covered with a thick cobalt blue matt bubbled lava glaze, the base inscribed '42/10'.

5in (12.5cm) high

£40-60   GC

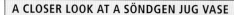

A CLOSER LOOK AT A SÖNDGEN JUG VASE

Söndgen were founded in Adendorf in 1893, and are still producing ceramics today under the guidance of the grandson of the founder.

Until recently, the company was not known for its 'Fat Lava' products, as many pieces were attributed to other makers. Recent research, however, has proved otherwise.

The company mainly used a white clay.

Impressed marks take this format, or simply have the three or four digit shape number over a line and the size in centimetres, as in the centre.

Commonly-used decorative techniques are slightly raised bands, zig-zags, or lines applied by tube-lining. These are not unique to Söndgen.

A 1970s West German Söndgen jug vase, designed by Walter Gerhards, with dark grey tube-lined lava glaze motifs under a striated orangey-red glossy ground, the base impressed 215/25.

10in (25cm) high

£55-65   GC

A 1970s West German Söndgen jug vase, with disc rim, the satin-matt dark brown glaze with a dripped graduated red, yellow, orange, green, and brown band, the base impressed 'Made in W.Germany Foreign 240/25'.

10.75in (27cm) high

£55-65   GC

A 1970s West German Söndgen baluster vase, featuring orange and yellow bands with think bubbled lava glaze outlines, the base impressed 'Made in W-Germany Foreign 220/25'.

Many of Söndgen's designs were originally produced by Walter Gerhards for Kera Keramik. When Kera closed, Gerhards brought his designs with him to Söndgen, as well as continuing to design others.

13.5in (34.5cm) high

£60-80   GC

A Royal Worcester dessert plate, painted with fruit by Horace H. Price, with solid gilded gadrooned rim, signed, the back with blue printed factory mark and date mark.

1936   *11in (26.9cm) diam*

£600-700   **TEN**

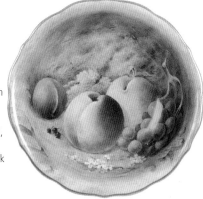

A Royal Worcester bowl, painted with fruit by William Albert Ricketts, with gilded rim, misted gilded exterior and angled foot, signed, the back with puce printed factory mark and year mark.

1923   *9in (23.1cm) diameter*

£650-850   **TEN**

A Royal Worcester sugar bowl, painted with fruit by Albert Shuck, with undulating rim and flared foot, solid gilded exterior, the back with brown printed factory mark, and year mark.

c1923   *4in (10.2cm) diam*

£300-500   **TEN**

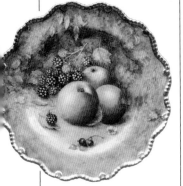

A Royal Worcester plate, painted with fruit by Richard Sebright, with gilded gadroon moulded undulating rim, the back with printed puce factory mark.

c1942   *9in (22cm) diam*

£550-650   **DN**

A mid-20thC Royal Worcester cabinet plate, painted with fruit by Harry Ayrton, with gadroon-moulded undulating gilded rim punctuated by shells, signed, the back with black printed factory mark, and 'C55' gilder's mark.

Harry Ayrton (1905-1976) began working at Royal Worcester in 1920, and trained under William Hawkins, who was foreman of the men's painting department. He became one of the company's most celebrated fruit painters, and continued to paint them after his retirement in 1970.

£1,200-1,800

9in (22.6cm) diam

TEN

A 1970s Royal Worcester vase and cover, painted with fruit by Stephen Ward, with pierced cover, within gilt borders, signed, the base with black printed crown and wheel mark, shape number 'H/169 A'.

6in (16cm) high

£400-600   **TEN**

A Royal Worcester pot-pourri vase and cover, painted with peaches and grapes by Frank Roberts, with gilded ground and panels.

c1900   *5.5in (14cm) high*

£180-220   **ECGW**

CERAMICS

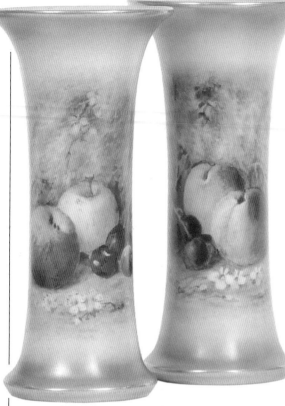

A pair of Royal Worcester spherical vases, with pierced gilt rims and moulded bases, painted with pink roses on fading grounds, set between moulded gilt borders, the bases with puce printed factory marks, shape number '278', 'H 15.54', and date marks for 1936 and 1937.

c1936   *3.75in (9.5cm) high*

£300-400   **CAPE**

A late 20thC Royal Worcester tea cup and saucer, painted with fruit by Arthur Lewis, with gilded interior and trim, the bases with printed black factory mark.

£350-450   **FLD**

A pair of small Royal Worcester trumpet vases, painted with fruit by William Albert Ricketts, with gilt-misted flared necks and bases, with differing designs, both signed, the bases with green printed factory mark, year mark, and shape number 'G923'.

1924   *5in (12cm) high*

£400-600   **TEN**

A Royal Worcester circular footed bowl, with ruffled spray gilded rim, decorated with flowers with gilt highlights.

7.5in (20cm) diam

£40-60   **LHA**

A Royal Worcester blush porcelain jug, the basket weave moulded body applied with a lizard, decorated in enamel, with simulated bamboo handle, the base with printed factory mark and date mark.

1910   *6in (16cm) high*

£100-150   **FLD**

QUICK REFERENCE - HARRY DAVIS

- As well as the shape and size, much of the value of Royal Worcester depends on the painted decoration, and who painted it. Harry Davis (1885-1970) is considered one of the company's foremost painters.

- He started working for the company when he was 13 and trained under the talented landscape artist Ted Salter until 1902. He loved nature, and became highly skilled at painting landscapes, sometimes with animals. Fish were a particular speciality. He undertook many prestigious commissions including painting dinner services for a Maharajah and Mr Kellogg, of cereal fame. He was also a talented teacher, and succeeded William Hawkins as foreman of the men's painting department in 1928. With all this in mind, it's not surprising that Davis is a favourite of Henry Sandon, the world's foremost Worcester specialist, and a colleague of ours on the BBC 'Antiques Roadshow'.

- This piece is typical of Davis's evocative, misty style and is on a complex and highly decorative shape. Although prices have declined in general, prices for the best pieces remain strong.

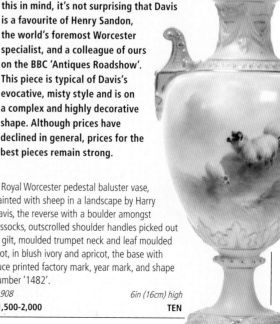

A Royal Worcester pedestal baluster vase, painted with sheep in a landscape by Harry Davis, the reverse with a boulder amongst tussocks, outscrolled shoulder handles picked out in gilt, moulded trumpet neck and leaf moulded foot, in blush ivory and apricot, the base with puce printed factory mark, year mark, and shape number '1482'.

c1908   *6in (16cm) high*

£1,500-2,000   **TEN**

A 1920s-30s Austrian Amphora baluster vase, with a sgrafitto and resist pattern of birds and foliage on a mottled beige ground, the base with printed factory mark, and hairline crack to foot rim.

13in (33cm) high

£50-70   GHOU

A Pearl Pottery Art Deco bachelor's three piece tea set, with green and yellow striped decoration on a cream ground, the base printed 'Edna Best Art Pottery Exclusive to Lawley's'.

Edna Best (1900-1974) was a highly popular actress during the mid-20thC. She didn't design these homewares, but lent her name to them in an early form of celebrity endorsement. Another pattern is known, which is even closer to Clarice Cliff's designs as it features orange and yellow banding and a stylised fruit design.

Teapot 4.25in (10.5cm) high

£100-150   FLD

A 1970s Canadian Blue Mountain Pottery footed ovoid vase, with the 'Mocha' glaze, with an abstract glaze dripped pattern.

10.5in (26.5cm) high

£60-80   TWF

A CLOSER LOOK AT A BLUE MOUNTAIN VASE

The Blue Mountain pottery was active from the 1940s until 2004 and produced decorative wares that were exported all over the world. Such wares are becoming increasingly valuable today.

Dominic Stanzione was a potter at Blue Mountain for around five years before leaving in 1971. This orange glaze is typical of his work, as is a fabulous deep blue.

This hard-to-find studio piece was made in the display area of the pottery, where a real 'studio pottery' had been set up to show factory visitors how pots were made.

A smaller travelling pottery also toured department stores and major events with the same aim.

A late 1960s Canadian Blue Mountain Pottery 'Studio' vase, designed and made by Dominic Stanzione, with a dripped and mottled orange glaze, thin neck, and flared rim.

12in (30.5cm) high

£150-200   TWF

A pair of C. H. Brannam baluster vases, decorated with panels of sgraffito birds on branches, on a tan ground, the bases with incised marks, and dated.

1890   *15.75in (40cm) high*

£350-450   GORL

A mid-1920s Brush-McCoy 'Jewel' vase, with glossy green, pink, and blue triangular motifs and dots arranged in bands.

Introduced in 1922, the 'Jewel' range used the squeeze-bag technique to create three-dimensional motifs that resemble jewellery. Bodies are shaded and bisque-like. The range included twelve vase shapes, three candlesticks, a bowl, and a jardinière.

6in (15cm) high

£500-700   DRA

CERAMICS

A Burmantofts majolica spoon warmer, modelled as a seated crocodile, covered in a yellow glaze, the base impressed '1898'.

6.75in (17cm) high

£200-300   AH

A late 19thC Burmantofts turquoise faience 'grotesque' crocodile, with an open mouth and curly tail, the base impressed with factory marks including '1906', with a few chips to edges.

6in (15cm) high

£300-500   TOV

A mid-20thC French Roger Capron 'VERMOUTH' bottle vase, decorated with sandy yellow, white, orange, and blue bands, and with painted marks to base.

Roger Capron (1922-2006) studied Applied Arts in Paris during World War II. In 1946, he moved to Vallauris, where he founded a pottery called 'L'Atelier Callis' that helped to bring about a renaissance of this well-known pottery town. He then bought a factory in 1952, which became successful, exporting its products internationally and employing over 100 people during the 1970s. The economic crisis caused the pottery to close in 1982, and Capron returned to making unique pieces, some of which were shown in international expositions. Always popular, his work has become increasingly valuable over the past few years.

14in (36cm) high

£100-150   WW

A Fieldings Crown Devon vase, handpainted with pattern A84 comprising orange, yellow, and grey diamonds and brown triangles, the base with printed and painted marks.

10in (25cm) high

£180-220   WW

A 1920s Fieldings Crown Devon bottle vase, with a lustre glaze pattern of butterflies, columns of gold dots, and bands of ivy leaves to the neck, the base with gold printed factory mark.

9in (23cm) high

£80-120   BAD

A pair of Fieldings Crown Devon Art Deco geometric design plates, handpainted with pattern A20, and with printed and painted marks to the bases.

7.5in (19cm) wide

£200-300   WW

A pair of 1950s Foley Bone China candleholders, with a white stencil-painted pattern of stylised fountains, the bases with printed marks.

3in (7.5cm) diam

£30-50   BAD

A 1950-60s German Goebel bee-shaped jam pot, the base with printed blue 'C by W. Goebel W. Germany' mark, and impressed 'H6'.

4.5in (11.5cm) high

£80-120   **BAD**

A 1920s-30s Grimwades Royal Winton lustre bowl, with brown-mottled yellow exterior, and banded pattern with stylised fruit to the interior, the base with black printed factory mark.

7.25in (18.5cm) diam

£60-80   **BAD**

A rare Gray's Pottery ball vase, hand-painted with a geometric floral design in shades of blue, yellow, and brown on a cream ground, the base with printed clipper mark, with minor hairline crack to base rim.

Not all Art Deco patterns produced by Gray's Pottery were by Susie Cooper. She worked there from 1923 to 1929, and pattern numbers prefixed with the letter 'A' were not designed by her.

7in (18cm) high

£220-280   **WW**

A 1920s-30s Grimwades Royal Winton tazza, hand-painted with an Art Deco geometric pattern, the base with printed 'Ivory England' mark and 'Handcraft 10024' painted mark.

This 'Handcraft' range is unusual for Grimwades, whose name at this time is more commonly associated with transfer-printed floral chintz wares. Examples of these can be seen on pp.64-65.

3.75in (9.5cm) high

£60-80   **BAD**

A Grueby vase, with tooled and applied full-height leaves alternating with buds, under a fine matt green glaze, with circular pottery stamp.

The bug and leaf design and green glaze are typical of both Grueby and American Arts and Crafts pottery.

An A. G. Harley Jones Wiltonware Art Deco lustre vase, decorated with a stylised Oriental landscape on a crimson ground, highlighted in gilt, with printed mark, and gilt painted no. '1611/5375'.

Carlton Ware was not the only company to produce lustre wares after the success enjoyed by Daisy Makeig Jones's ground-breaking work at Wedgwood. Designer Horace Wain left Carlton Ware in the 1920s to join the Harley Jones factory. It is likely this pattern was by him, hence its similarity to Carlton Ware.

13.75in (34cm) high

£70-100   **CAPE**

A small early 20thC French Longwy pin dish, of octagonal form, enamel decorated with stylised flowers and foliage over a turquoise ground, with printed mark.

4.75in (12cm) wide

£50-70   **FLD**

8.5in (21.5cm) high

£1,200-1,800   **DRA**

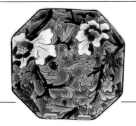

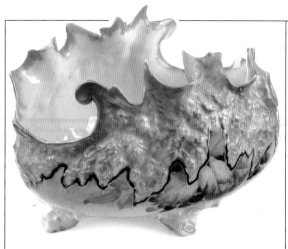

A Scottish Possil Pottery 'Nautilus' porcelain shell-form jardinière, of scrolling form, decorated with leaves and fruit, on log shaped feet, with gilt highlights.

c1900   *9.75in (25cm) wide*

£80-120   L&T

A Peters & Reed 'Landsun' vase, decorated with tree-lined hills, minor grinding around base.

9.5in (24cm) high

£350-400   DRA

A French Pierrefonds stoneware twin-handled vase, covered in a dripped and mottled crystalline glaze, the base with impressed mark.

16.5in (42cm) high

£350-450   WW

A CLOSER LOOK AT A RIDGWAYS VASE

Ridgways, active from 1838 to 1964, produced good quality ceramics in the prevalent styles of the day. Many are sought-after by collectors today.

This design is close to the Aesthetic style that was popular during 1860s-90s. The movement was known for favouring exotic decoration and Oriental ornament.

The registered design mark gives clues to the date of this piece. The 15 indicates the day of the month, the 'H' indicates April, and the 'J' indicates the year 1880.

Be aware that a design may have been made for a long period of time after the date the design was registered.

A late 19thC Ridgways Aesthetic style blue and white transfer-printed urn vase, with gilt scrolling vines to handle, the base with printed factory marks and diamond registration mark for 15th April 1880.

For more blue and white transfer-printed wares, please see pp.57-59.

12.5in (32cm) high

£60-80   BAD

A Robj 'Cusenier Prunellia' porcelain decanter and stopper, modelled as a woman gathering fruit, the base with printed marks, hairline crack to base rim.

Cusenier is a type of liqueur produced in France, and Prunellia is the flavour. Robj are a very high quality and sought-after maker.

11in (28cm) high

£250-350   WW

A Royal Cauldon 'Cairo Ware' footed bowl, hand-painted with stylised flowers and leaves, and with a stylised bird to centre.

9in (23cm) diam

£50-70   FLD

CERAMICS

A CLOSER LOOK AT A STONELAIN DISH

New York-based Associated Artists produced a limited range of ceramics decorated by leading artists of the day including Gwen Lux, Arnold Blanch, J. C. Diego, and Alexander Archipenko.

The blank bodies were potted by William Sioni and Frances Server, whose 'SS' monogram can be found in the company's impressed ewer mark.

These bowls were only produced from the early 1940s until 1952, and examples are hard to find, particularly in this large size.

This is a complex pattern and represents the styles of the day in terms of its curving, asymmetric form and series of stylised biological motifs.

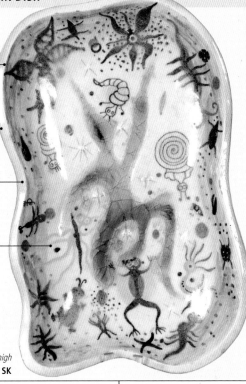

An American Stonelain Pottery and Associated Artists of New York bowl, decorated by J. G. Diego with an abstract aquatic scene, marked 'Diego' and with impressed Stonelain mark, tight crack, and some glaze chips.
c1942-52   19in (48.5cm) high
£700-1,000   **SK**

A 1970s Taunton Vale Industries transfer-printed storage jar, with printed mark to base.

In the 1970s Taunton Vale was acquired by Staffordshire Potteries Ltd., who were based at the Keele Street Pottery and owned a number of other potteries.
6in (15cm) high
£15-20   **RET**

An A. J. Wilkinson Art Deco shouldered vase, designed by John Butler, the base with blue printed Wilkinson back stamp.

John Butler and Fred Ridgway were designers at Wilkinson's, which later became known for producing the designs of Clarice Cliff. Cliff worked with Butler to produce 'Tibetan' and 'Oriflamme' ware, and was asked by Butler to produce a special piece of 'Tibetan' ware for an exhibition. A skilled artist, Butler was impressed by Cliff's skills at hand-painting, and nurtured her development.
12in (30cm) high
£150-200   **GHOU**

A late 19thC Continental majolica vase in the form of a dancing crocodile, with head and three legs up and tail curled, painted naturalistically, with indistinct shield mark.

8.25in (21cm) high
£200-300   **GORL**

A 1930s Czechoslovakian Art Deco vase, hand-painted with a colourful pattern of stylised flowers on a glossy yellow ground, the base with printed gilt 'Czechoslovakia Hand-Painted' mark.
7.25in (18.5cm) high
£70-90   **BAD**

A pair of small 1970s transfer-printed ceramic octopus place-card holders.
2in (5cm) high
£15-20   **RET**

A small early 20thC lady's silver and green guilloché enamelled powder compact, with indistinct Birmingham hallmarks.

1.5in (4cm) diam

£40-60   **CAPE**

A silver and pale blue guilloché enamelled powder compact, of octagonal form, the lid applied with the RAF logo, with hallmarks for Birmingham.

1947   *3in (7.5cm) wide*

£80-120   **WHP**

An enamelled silver power compact and Ronson lighter set, both decorated with a pair of Mallard ducks in flight over reeds, with maker's mark 'Hcd', hallmarks for Birmingham, with original fitted presentation box.

1948

£250-350   **TEN**

A circular 9ct gold powder compact, with engine-turned barleycorn decoration, in excellent condition.

2.5in (6cm) wide

£300-400   **WW**

A silver and guilloché enamelled circular compact, the lid enamelled with a riverscape scene, with 'R & S' maker's marks and hallmarks for Birmingham.

1928   *2.25in (5.5cm)*

£150-200   **GORB**

A CLOSER LOOK AT A PAIR OF COMPACTS

The maki-e (literally 'sprinkled picture') process requires great skill and is very time-consuming.

These compacts were probably produced for luxury goods retailer Dunhill, which had an agreement to market Namiki lacquered pens, lighters, and other accessories in Dunhill shops in the West.

Namiki maki-e lacquer on materials other than the hard rubber used for pen bodies is rare. Furthermore very few compacts are known and an original pair is even rarer.

Shobi is a noted lacquer artist. He was on the founding committee of the Kokkokai school of lacquer artists, and on the staff of the late Prefecture High School in 1905. From 1907 he was an independent artist.

Although goldfish and pond weed are the most common motifs for Namiki lacquer ware, the very good condition, rarity of the base material, and the type of object make these outstanding.

A rare pair of 1930s Japanese Namiki coromandel wood powder compacts, of disc form, each gilt decorated and maki-e lacquered with carp and pond weed, with 'Namiki kan' characters and artist's signature for Maizawa Shobi.

Other pieces decorated by Shobi include a cigarette case, which bears a similar design.

4.25in (11cm) diam

£800-1,200   **WHP**

QUICK REFERENCE

- Costume jewellery is becoming increasingly popular as more and more people recognise the high quality design and craftsmanship of some of these fake gems. Some iconic pieces by well-known makers are now commanding prices close to those paid for precious jewellery, and even unsigned pieces are rising in value. Most collectors buy costume jewellery with the intention of wearing it, so the style, eye-appeal and 'sparkle factor' of a piece is very important. Beautifully designed jewellery will generally be desirable, even without a renowned maker's name. However, much costume jewellery is still comparatively affordable.
- Sought-after makers include Trifari, Miriam Haskell, Chanel, Kenneth Jay Lane, and Hattie Carnegie. Copies are becoming more common, particularly at the upper end of the market, so learn to recognise their styles and marks – names are usually marked on the back of their pieces. Both the style of the piece and the style of the mark can help to date a piece.
- As well as the design and the designer name, the quality of the materials and craftsmanship will affect value. During the 1930s and 1940s, many pieces of costume jewellery were made from solid silver (set with glass stones) and marked 'Sterling' to the reverse. As well as the material having a value of its own over the more commonly used base metal, these pieces are usually well-designed and well-made.
- Look out for large and multi-faceted 'stones'. Look, too, at the way the stones are set – the best examples are held in place with metal prongs, with work done by hand. Others are simply glued in place. Much costume jewellery has three-dimensional effects that may be hand-wired onto the frame, and these are particularly sought-after. In general, any piece that took considerable skill or time to manufacture will be desirable and valuable.
- Missing stones will reduce value considerable. Although replacements can be found, it is often hard to find an exact match of size or colour tone. Some beads and faux pearls used by designers like Miriam Haskell are even more difficult to find as they were exclusively supplied, and are typically no longer made, let alone to the same quality.

A Hattie Carnegie gold-plated owl brooch, with inset blue rhinestone eyes, the back stamped 'Hattie Carnegie'.

£70-100   LHA

A Hattie Carnegie gold-plated elephant and mouse brooch, the back stamped 'Hattie Carnegie'.

£50-80   LHA

A Hattie Carnegie clown brooch, with red enamel, inset rhinestones and faux pearls, the back stamped 'Hattie Carnegie'.

£120-180   LHA

A 1950s Hattie Carnegie blue and cream plastic 'Aztec Warrior' brooch, with inset rhinestone details, the back stamped 'Hattie Carnegie'.

£150-200   LHA

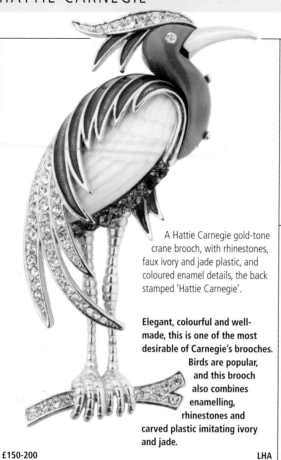

A 1960s Hattie Carnegie blue and green plastic toucan brooch, with rhinestone details, the back stamped 'Hattie Carnegie'.

£80-120   LHA

A Hattie Carnegie faux ivory plastic flower brooch, with rhinestones accents, the back stamped 'Hattie Carnegie'.

£80-120   LHA

A Hattie Carnegie gold-tone crane brooch, with rhinestones, faux ivory and jade plastic, and coloured enamel details, the back stamped 'Hattie Carnegie'.

Elegant, colourful and well-made, this is one of the most desirable of Carnegie's brooches. Birds are popular, and this brooch also combines enamelling, rhinestones and carved plastic imitating ivory and jade.

A 1960s Hattie Carnegie faux coral and turquoise fish brooch, with rhinestone details, the back stamped 'Hattie Carnegie'.

The animal form, and bold and brash colours are typical of Carnegie's instantly recognisable 'fabulously fake' look.

£150-200   LHA

£100-150   LHA

Miller's Compares

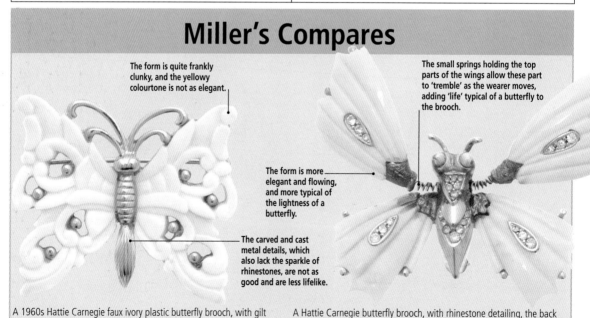

The form is quite frankly clunky, and the yellowy colourtone is not as elegant.

The small springs holding the top parts of the wings allow these part to 'tremble' as the wearer moves, adding 'life' typical of a butterfly to the brooch.

The form is more elegant and flowing, and more typical of the lightness of a butterfly.

The carved and cast metal details, which also lack the sparkle of rhinestones, are not as good and are less lifelike.

A 1960s Hattie Carnegie faux ivory plastic butterfly brooch, with gilt details, the back stamped 'Hattie Carnegie'.

£40-50   LHA

A Hattie Carnegie butterfly brooch, with rhinestone detailing, the back stamped 'Hattie Carnegie'.

£150-200   LHA

A Trifari rhinestone and enamel bird brooch, the back stamped 'Trifari'.

£50-80   LHA

A pair of Trifari male and female figural brooches, with red glass cabochon faces and rhinestone detailing, the backs stamped 'Trifari', with wear to the gold finish.

£100-150   LHA

A CLOSER LOOK AT A TRIFARI BROOCH

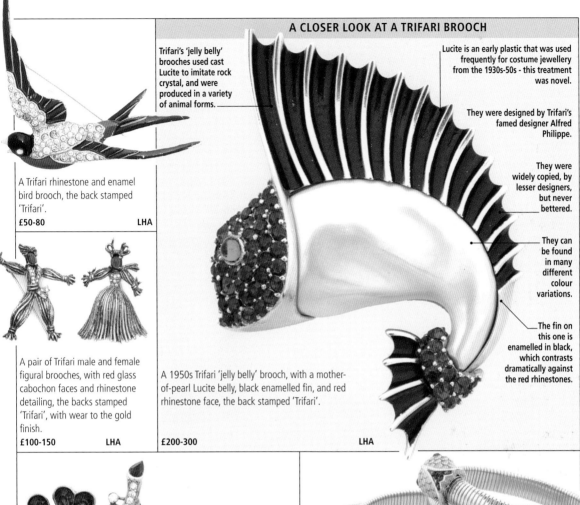

Trifari's 'jelly belly' brooches used cast Lucite to imitate rock crystal, and were produced in a variety of animal forms.

Lucite is an early plastic that was used frequently for costume jewellery from the 1930s-50s - this treatment was novel.

They were designed by Trifari's famed designer Alfred Philippe.

They were widely copied, by lesser designers, but never bettered.

They can be found in many different colour variations.

The fin on this one is enamelled in black, which contrasts dramatically against the red rhinestones.

A 1950s Trifari 'jelly belly' brooch, with a mother-of-pearl Lucite belly, black enamelled fin, and red rhinestone face, the back stamped 'Trifari'.

£200-300   LHA

A 1940s Trifari rhinestone floral brooch, set with red and colourless faceted rhinestones and with teardrop-shaped pendants, the back stamped 'Trifari'.

£200-300   LHA

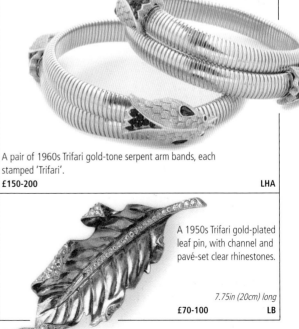

A pair of 1960s Trifari gold-tone serpent arm bands, each stamped 'Trifari'.

£150-200   LHA

A 1950s Trifari gold-plated leaf pin, with channel and pavé-set clear rhinestones.

7.75in (20cm) long

£70-100   LB

COSTUME JEWELLERY

A late 20thC Chanel gold-tone oversized cuff, with alternating panels of clear rhinestones and faux cabochon pearls, unmarked.

£400-600   LHA

A late 20thC Chanel resin and gold-tone metal bracelet, in a chainlink motif, the inside stamped 'Chanel'.

£180-220   LHA

A Chanel and Maison Gripoix cross pendant necklace, with a long chain and poured glass cabochons, stamped 'Chanel'.

Maison Gripoix (founded c1870) worked for a number of costume jewellery designers, beginning with Chanel in the mid-1920s and followed by Dior in the 1950s, and YSL in the 1980s. They are known for their pâte-de-verre glass 'stones', and those made by pouring glass into a mould surrounded by a metal frame to resemble plique-à-jour enamel. Colours are typically strong and vibrant.

£400-600   LHA

QUICK REFERENCE - CHANEL

- **Gabrielle 'Coco' Chanel (1883-1971) was a pioneer of 20thC costume jewellery from the 1910s onwards, and many even attribute the coining of the term to her. Her intentionally 'faux' designs looked striking and lavish, but were affordable to those who wanted to accessorise their Chanel couture outfits. Bold cuff designs with Maltese crosses were designed by Coco herself during the 1920s and 30s, with many featuring poured glass 'stones' made by Maison Gripoix. The popularity of her brand and the integrated look she developed is still very strong today, and her high quality costume jewellery designs can fetch as much as some jewellery made from precious stones and metals.**

A Chanel black Lucite oversized cuff, with multi-coloured stones and small colourless rhinestones forming a Maltese cross, the interior stamped 'Chanel'.
1995
£800-1,200   LHA

A pair of mid-1950s Chanel turquoise glass brooches, with rhinestones accents, the back of one stamped 'Chanel'.

These brooches can be seen on page 98 of 'Jewelry by Chanel' by Patrick Mauries.
1954
£800-1,200   LHA

A 1970s Chanel Paris gold-plated brooch, with petal-like rim of coin forms.

2in (5cm) high
£80-120   PC

Judith Picks

Lane has become famous for his bold and extravagant jewellery designs, mainly due to the enormous following he has built up via TV sales channel QVC. However, the quantity of his designs produced has expanded along with the growth of his following.

His vintage pieces, particularly from the 1960s, probably represent the best bet for the future due to their quality, workmanship, and the fact that fewer pieces from this period are likely to exist. As his following is so strong, it is likely that the popularity of his name and the market for his designs will continue, and may even grow. Elaborate collar necklaces like this are typical of his 1960s designs, and are already fetching high prices. Marks can help date a piece. Before the 1970s, his work was signed 'KJL', and then after the late 1970s 'Kenneth Jay Lane' or 'Kenneth Lane'.

A 1960s Kenneth Jay Lane turquoise blue glass and clear rhinestone bib necklace.

Bib 18cm (7in) long

£1,000-1,500 CRIS

A 1960s Kenneth Jay Lane eagle brooch, with clear rhinestones, green cabochons, and enamelled feathers, the back stamped 'KJL'.

£60-80 LHA

A 1960s Kenneth Jay Lane gold-tone snake hinge-bracelet, with clear rhinestones and coral and green glass cabochons, the back stamped 'KJL'.

£120-180 LHA

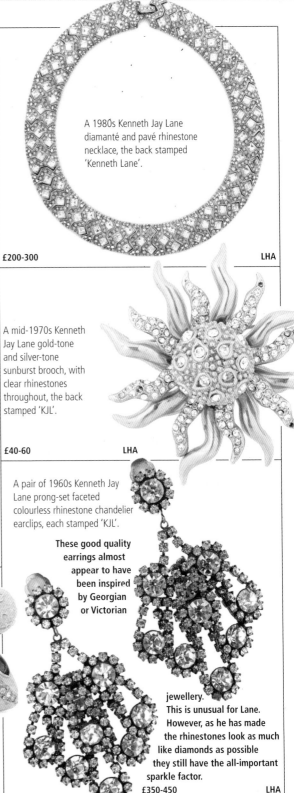

A 1980s Kenneth Jay Lane diamanté and pavé rhinestone necklace, the back stamped 'Kenneth Lane'.

£200-300 LHA

A mid-1970s Kenneth Jay Lane gold-tone and silver-tone sunburst brooch, with clear rhinestones throughout, the back stamped 'KJL'.

£40-60 LHA

A pair of 1960s Kenneth Jay Lane prong-set faceted colourless rhinestone chandelier earclips, each stamped 'KJL'.

These good quality earrings almost appear to have been inspired by Georgian or Victorian jewellery. This is unusual for Lane. However, as he has made the rhinestones look as much like diamonds as possible they still have the all-important sparkle factor.

£350-450 LHA

A 1940s Marcel Boucher gold-tone bird brooch, with turquoise and red cabochons, clear rhinestones throughout, the back stamped 'Boucher'.

£60-80　　　　　　　　　　　　LHA

A Ciner black enamelled horse's head bangle, with rhinestones throughout, the inside stamped 'Ciner'.

£100-150　　　　　　　　　　　　LHA

A 1950s Ciner turtle brooch, with a green enamel shell surrounded by tiny faux pearls, the underside stamped 'Ciner'.

The value would have been over 50% higher had it not been so worn.

£50-80　　　　　　　　　　　　LHA

A CLOSER LOOK AT A MIRIAM HASKELL BRACELET

Each piece of Miriam Haskell is made by hand, and is of excellent quality.

Woven strings of faux pearls or coloured glass beads are a hallmark element of her designs.

A 1950s pair of Christian Dior purple and blue faceted rhinestone earclips, each stamped 'Chr Dior'.

£80-120　　　　　　　　　　　　LHA

A 1950s Exquisite gilt and carnival glass flower brooch, the back marked 'Exquisite Regd'.

£20-30　　　　　　　　　　　　TDG

This piece is unusual for Haskell as the red is so vibrant. All her glass beads were specially commissioned from factories on Murano.

Many of her pieces have a very strong three-dimensional construction.

A 1950s Miriam Haskell red-beaded and hand-wired floral wrap bracelet, the back with a panel stamped 'Miriam Haskell'.

£250-350　　　　　　　　　　　　LHA

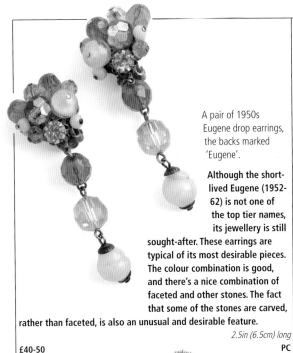

A pair of 1950s Eugene drop earrings, the backs marked 'Eugene'.

Although the short-lived Eugene (1952-62) is not one of the top tier names, its jewellery is still sought-after. These earrings are typical of its most desirable pieces. The colour combination is good, and there's a nice combination of faceted and other stones. The fact that some of the stones are carved, rather than faceted, is also an unusual and desirable feature.

2.5in (6.5cm) long

£40-50   PC

A pair of 1990s Christian Lacroix baroque-style gold-tone earclips, set with glass cabochons, stamped 'Christian Lacroix'.

£100-150   LHA

A 1970s Jomaz gold-tone sunburst demi-parure, comprising a brooch and earclips, with turquoise and dark blue cabochons and clear rhinestones, the backs stamped 'Jomaz'.

£80-120   LHA

A 1970s Jomaz gold-tone peacock brooch, with green, blue, and clear rhinestones, and blue and green enamel, the back stamped 'Jomaz'.

£150-200   LHA

A 1980s Karl Lagerfeld chainlink and resin pendant necklace, the back stamped 'Karl Lagerfeld'.

£100-150   LHA

A 1960s Lanvin green faux jade and gold-tone disc pendant, on a snake chain, the back stamped 'Lanvin'.

£200-300   LHA

A 1960s Lanvin gold-tone and red enamel pendant necklace, on a snake chain, the back stamped 'Lanvin'.

Produced during the 1960s and 70s, these almost 'futuristic' metal and plastic geometric pendants are the best-known of Lanvin's vintage costume jewellery designs.

£250-300   LHA

COSTUME JEWELLERY

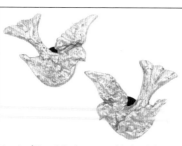

A pair of Yves Saint Laurent gold-plated dove earclips, the backs stamped 'YSL'.

Look closely, the gold-plating is very worn, showing the silvery-coloured base metal underneath. This reduces desirability and value as most costume jewellery is bought to be worn.

£70-100   LHA

A pair of Moschino black cuffs, designed by Sharra Pagano, one cuff with a brass question mark and the other with a heart, unmarked.

This pair was accompanied with an original line drawing of the design by Sharra Pagano, hence the higher price. Without this, they would be worth around £300-400.
1988

£500-600   LHA

A 1970s Panetta organic textured brooch, set with a large oval brown rhinestone and smaller colourless rhinestones, stamped 'Panetta'.

£30-40   LHA

A 1970s Emilio Pucci geometric enamelled suite, comprising a long necklace with circle pendant, a bangle bracelet, and matching earclips.

£250-350   LHA

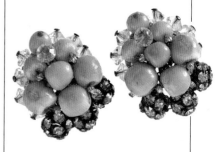

A pair of 1950s Vendôme silver-tone and faux turquoise earrings, with clear crystal beads and pavé-set rhinestones, marked 'Vendôme'.

1.25in (3cm) long

£60-80   PC

Judith Picks

Vendôme was a brand introduced by major maker Coro in 1944 to capitalise on the trend for Parisian styles. By the 1960s it had become a byword for elegant French fashions in costume jewellery. Although this isn't one of their best high-end pieces, it is excellent value for money. The Vendôme name is growing in popularity among collectors, and this piece combines enamelling with high quality rhinestones in a deep, three-dimensional design. The style and predominantly light blue colour is also popular, fashionable, and very wearable.

A 1950s Vendôme brooch and earclip set, claw-set with blue rhinestones and with green enamelled leaves, the backs stamped 'Vendôme'.

£60-80 set   LHA

A 1930s-40s diamanté brooch, set with aurora borealis and colourless rhinestones.

This is better quality than many of the similar pins produced at this time - look how the stones are set to maximise the glittery effect on the left hand curl.

2in (5cm) wide

£30-40   PC

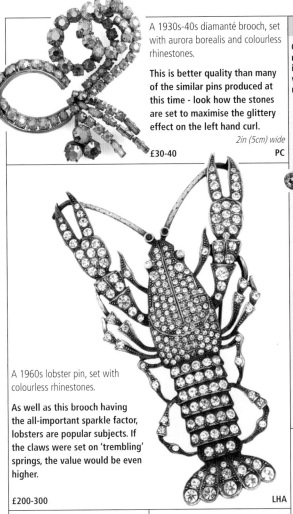

A 1960s lobster pin, set with colourless rhinestones.

As well as this brooch having the all-important sparkle factor, lobsters are popular subjects. If the claws were set on 'trembling' springs, the value would be even higher.

£200-300   LHA

A CLOSER LOOK AT A CROWN BROOCH

Crown pins were initially produced to commemorate royal events. From the 1930s-50s they were produced in greater quantities to coincide with a series of popular romantic-historical movies.

Look out for the sterling silver pieces designed by Alfred Philippe during the 1940s - these can fetch up to £300.

Although this is early in date, the most sought-after and valuable costume pieces are by Trifari.

Crown pins form a collecting area of their own. This one has a ring at the bottom, which would have originally held a safety chain and catch

A late 1910s silver crown brooch, set with white and red rhinestones.

If you're lucky enough to find a Trifari crown brooch, make sure it's not a 1980s re-issue. Considerably less valuable, they were made from different materials and are much lighter in weight than original 1940s examples.

£100-150   PC

A pair of unsigned earrings, almost certainly by Regency, with yellow, brown and aurora borealis rhinestones in claw settings.

Although unmarked, the choice of stones, and the way they are cut and set almost certainly indicates that they are by Regency. They were probably part of a parure (a set comprising a necklace, earrings, brooch and bracelet), and it was typical for a company to not mark each piece with their name. Major pieces, such as the necklace, are more likely to be marked, but smaller pieces like earrings are often not. Marks are important - if these were marked Regency, they could fetch up to double this price.

1in (2.5cm) long

£30-40   PC

A pair of 1920s French cast-metal earrings, set with green glass watermelon-cut drops.

2in (5cm) long

£30-50   PC

A 1950s monkey novelty brooch, with mink covered gold-tone body and googly eyes.

£40-60   PC

COSTUME JEWELLERY

A CLOSER LOOK AT A BAKELITE BROOCH

Martha Sleeper (1910-83) was a successful silent movie star and comedienne during the 1920s, and a Broadway actress during the 1940s.

She also made jewellery, and her business expanded to incorporate handmade clothes and jewellery after she moved to Puerto Rico in 1950. Identification is hard as there are no catalogues.

Most of her jewellery designs were made in colourful plastic, and took novelty shapes including animals, African tribal art, and fruit. School related themes, such as this one, were also a favourite of hers.

This appealing piece is made up of a number of different components and has great charm.

A 1930s bakelite and gilt metal 'school books' pendant brooch, probably by Martha Sleeper.

£100-150   LHA

A late 1930s mottled green and yellow cast and carved phenolic bracelet and dress-clips set, with applied brass detailing.

£350-450   PC

A pair of Lea Stein ladybird striated red and black Rhodoid brooches, the pins stamped 'Lea Stein'.

£40-60   LHA

A 1920s Egyptian style resin and early plastic necklace, the pendants with applied cast Pharaoh's head and stylised scarab.

Howard Carter's discovery of Tutankhamen's tomb in 1922 led to 'Egyptomania', with Egyptian style motifs being used across the decorative arts. This fad also contributed to the development of the Art Deco style, which was popularised from 1925 onwards.

£70-100   LHA

An early 1920s cicada brooch, probably in cast Galalith, set with rhinestones and metal studs, the wings highlighted with gold paint.

£30-50   PC

A 1930s reverse-carved Lucite brooch, the borders hand-carved and with painted highlights, with metal-backing.

£80-120   PC

QUICK REFERENCE

- Cufflinks as we know them evolved during the 18thC. Cuffs on shirts first appeared as ruffs in the early 16thC, and were tied together with ribbons. By the early 18thC fashionable men had replaced 'cuff strings' with pairs of identical buttons joined by a short chain. Often acting as a display of wealth, such 'links' became common by the end of the century, and were ubiquitous by the Victorian period.

- Most early to mid-19thC cufflinks were of simple design, conforming to the tastes of the middle-classes. Early examples were usually made from gold, silver or ivory, with electroplating becoming more common from c1860. Designs became more complex and decorative towards the end of the century, and became more flamboyant from the early 20thC.

- As most people buy cufflinks with the intention of wearing them, style and eye-appeal are very important to value. Those with witty designs, or in Art Nouveau or Art Deco styles tend to be popular. Naturally, the materials used will also affect the value considerably.

- Engraved initials will only be of interest and value to buyers with the same initials. 19thC or 20thC gold or silver links with simple repetitive designs are usually only worth their weight. A connection to a famous individual or story increases value.

A pair of 18ct gold plain oval cufflinks.

0.6oz (17g)

£400-600   LC

A pair of 18ct gold oval cufflinks, engraved with initials, together with three dress studs, in original fitted case.

Despite being solid 18ct gold, these cufflinks are considerably less desirable than others on this page as they are engraved with initials. Polishing the initials away would damage the look of the cufflinks and be expensive. Unless your initials are 'GHC', these do not have appeal or make a great investment. They are literally only worth their 'weight in gold'.

£60-80   LC

A pair of 18ct gold oval cufflinks, engraved with a crest.

Although heraldic family crests were made for a particular person, these motifs are not as immediately personalised as initials and are more wearable. Hence prices are typically higher.

0.6oz (17g)

£300-400   LC

A pair of 9ct gold T-bar cufflinks, with large square panels displaying the Sheffield 1973 hallmarks.

Although large hallmarks are sometimes used for decorative purposes today, these were produced to commemorate the bicentenary of the founding of the Sheffield assay office in 1773.

approx 0.6oz (17g)

A pair of 18ct gold oval concave cufflinks, inscribed with 'LUF' initials.

0.5oz (13g)

£100-150   LC

A pair of mid-late 20thC 9ct gold cufflinks, engraved with a crossed-hatch design.

£35-45   WHP

£150-200   CAPE

Mark Picks

Drinking-related cufflinks are incredibly popular with both collectors and those looking for something more unusual to wear on their cuffs. Although these were undoubtedly not produced by Moët & Chandon themselves, that doesn't really matter. The fact that they show 'extravagant' champagne, and a major brand at that, make them very desirable. They're also double-sided, solid 18ct gold, and enamelled rather than being set with painted panels. Moreover, the enamelling is of good quality.

A pair of early 20thC 18ct gold oval cufflinks, enamelled with 'Moët' and the neck of a champagne bottle, stamped '18'.

£1,200-1,800   **DN**

A pair of early to mid-20thC Continental 18ct gold and reverse-painted crystal cufflinks, decorated with four game or water birds and set over mother-of-pearl backings, the gold stamped '750u'.

These fetched more than the others on this page due to three reasons - they are 18ct gold, the birds are comparatively very well painted, and the crystal is unusually set over a mother-of-pearl ground.

0.45oz (13.3g)

£1,500-2,000   **DOR**

A pair of American 14k gold reverse-painted glass cufflinks, with a motif of a Scottish terrier on grass.

Scottie dogs are one of the most popular breeds among the many who collect dog-related antiques and collectables. They reached the height of their popularity in the 1920s-50s, when a number of famous people had Scotties, including Shirley Temple, and US Presidents Eisenhower and Roosevelt.

c1910

£300-400   **FRE**

A late 19thC/early 20thC Austrian silver cufflink and shirt stud set, with reverse-painted crystals showing game birds and animals over mother-of-pearl backings, each stamped with the Austrian government hallmark for 1872-1922.

overall 1.15oz (32.7g)

£1,200-1,800   **DOR**

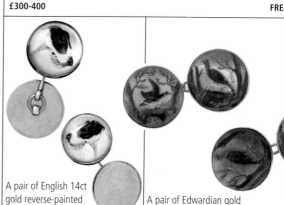

A pair of English 14ct gold reverse-painted glass cufflinks, one panel on each decorated with the profile of the head of a schnauzer.

c1910

£400-600   **FRE**

A pair of Edwardian gold reverse-painted crystal game bird cufflinks, with panels depicting two cock pheasants, a duck, and a woodcock.

£800-1,200   **WW**

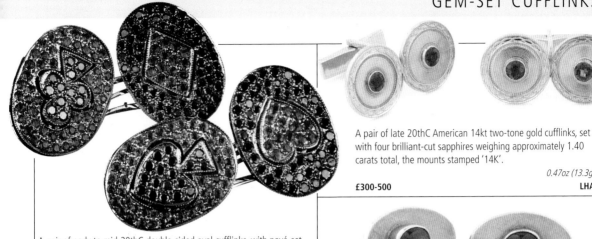

A pair of early to mid-20thC double-sided oval cufflinks, with pavé-set black diamonds and circular-cut pink sapphires in the design of a suite of playing cards, with figure of eight connections.

Gambling themes are almost as popular as those relating to drinking. The most popular and valuable cufflinks are known as 'The Four Vices', where each panel bears a design related to the four vices of men - gambling (cards), betting (horse racing), women (a can-can dancer) and drinking (a cocktail glass or champagne bottle). Perfect for the professional poker player, this set also hides a secret - the figure of eight chain links. In China '8' is an auspicious and lucky number.

£800-1,200   DN

A pair of late 20thC American 14kt two-tone gold cufflinks, set with four brilliant-cut sapphires weighing approximately 1.40 carats total, the mounts stamped '14K'.

0.47oz (13.3g)

£300-500   LHA

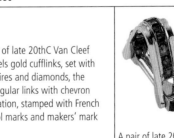

A pair of late 1960s-70s American 14kt gold cufflinks, containing two oval cabochon cut-star rubies weighing approximately 3.00 carats total, the mounts stamped '14K JK'.

Large, oval or egg-shaped, cufflinks are typical of the late 1960s, particularly if they have textured surfaces. The shape was also popular for wristwatch cases at the time.

0.77oz (21.8g)

£250-350   LHA

A pair of 1970s American 14kt white gold cufflinks, containing two round cabochon cut-star sapphires weighing approximately 8.00 carats total, and four round brilliant cut diamonds weighing approximately 0.64 carat total, the mounts stamped '14K'.

0.66oz (18.7g)

£300-500   LHA

A pair of 1970s-80s American 14kt yellow gold cufflinks, set with two round brilliant-cut diamonds, weighing approximately 0.05 carat, stamped '14k'.

0.29oz (8.2g)

£100-150   LHA

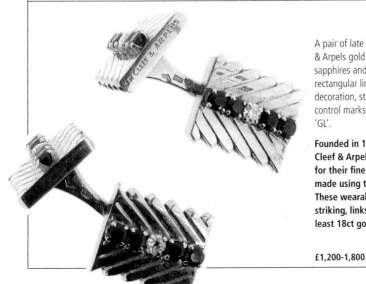

A pair of late 20thC Van Cleef & Arpels gold cufflinks, set with sapphires and diamonds, the rectangular links with chevron decoration, stamped with French control marks and makers' mark 'GL'.

Founded in 1896 in Paris, Van Cleef & Arpels is world-renowned for their fine quality jewellery made using the best materials. These wearable and simple, yet striking, links are likely to be at least 18ct gold.

£1,200-1,800   WW

A pair of late 20thC Continental 18ct gold sapphire 'stirrup' cufflinks, set with square-cut sapphires and sapphire cabochons with a total weight of 3ct, with safety fastening and stamped '750'.

This popular style is still being produced today.

0.6oz (17.2g)

£600-800   DOR

CUFFLINKS

A pair of mid-late 20thC Danish Georg Jensen silver cufflinks, each stamped 'Georg Jensen Sterling Denmark' and '67'.

0.85in (2.16cm) wide

£300-500   **DRA**

A pair of silver cufflinks, in the style of Henning Koppel for Georg Jensen, with maker's marks for George Tarratt Ltd. of Leicester, and Birmingham hallmarks for 1967.

£35-45   **DN**

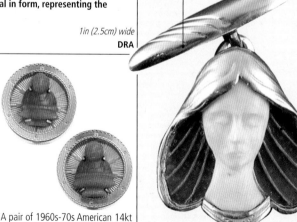

A pair of late 20thC Tiffany & Co. 14kt gold button-shaped cufflinks, stamped 'Tiffany & Co'.

0.76oz (21.5g)

£400-600   **FRE**

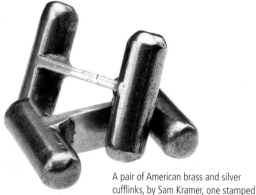

A pair of American brass and silver cufflinks, by Sam Kramer, one stamped with a mushroom cypher.

Sam Kramer (1913-64) was an eccentric jeweller who sold his Modernist style jewellery from a shop in New York. He also often incorporated unusual materials into his work, including taxidermists' glass eyes, moose teeth and random bits of quartz. These are comparatively simple and traditional in form, representing the Modernist side of his work.

1in (2.5cm) wide

£250-350   **DRA**

A CLOSER LOOK AT A PAIR OF CUFFLINKS

The materials comprise solid gold, ivory and enamel, so are fine and add to the value.

The woman's hair is picked out in plique-à-jour enamel, which has no back, allowing the light to shine through and brightening up the green.

The overall shape is reminiscent of a moth or butterfly - both were almost commonly used as motifs in the Art Nouveau movement.

Ladies in a calm, sleep-like pose with long flowing hair and dresses are typical of the Art Nouveau movement. The faces are beautifully carved.

A pair of 9ct gold cufflinks, enamelled with a school or college crest and stripes.

0.25oz (7.6g)

£80-120   **GHOU**

A pair of 1960s-70s American 14kt gold cufflinks, set with carved and dyed-green jade Buddhas, stamped '14K'.

0.96oz (27.2g)

£220-280   **LHA**

A pair of Art Nouveau gold and ivory cufflinks, designed as a woman's head in ivory with a surround of plique-à-jour enamel, fluted torpedo shaped backs.

£1,500-2,000   **WW**

QUICK REFERENCE

- Placed in water by wily hunters, duck decoys attract live ducks to a chosen spot by making them believe the area is safe. Ducks are not the only waterfowl depicted as decoys, but they are the most commonly found.
- The earliest decoys were made from bound twigs and reeds by Native Americans before the arrival of European settlers. Decoys were produced on a much larger scale throughout the 19thC and into the early 20thC until commercial bird hunting was outlawed in the 1920s. Many regions, particularly states or parts of states in the US, developed their own styles and body forms during this era. For example, New Jersey and Delaware decoys are typically hollow, while duck decoys made in Maryland are usually solid.
- Most duck decoys found today date from the end of the 19thC onwards. The main

- indicators to value are the form, the presence or lack of original paint, and the level of detail.
- A well-known maker, such as A. E. Crowell, William Bowman, or Obadiah Verity, will also add value. Some decoys are marked on the base with the maker's name, but others are only marked with the name of the original owner, so consult reference books to distinguish the two.
- Apart from decoy collectors, decoys appeal to folk art collectors, interior decorators, and those looking for an individual statement piece for a room. Condition is important, but wear and tear caused by water, gunfire, or poor storage, can be appealing.
- While commercial decoy production dwindled in the 1920s, folk artists have continued to create duck decoys. Pieces by notable artists can be highly prized and valuable, and are worth looking out for, as some already fetch high prices.

A 1920s American Evans factory Canvasback drake duck decoy.

Inspired by Mason decoys, Walter Evans ran a small factory in Ladysmith, Wisconsin from 1921 to 1932, and is said to have made well in excess of 1,000 decoys. Bodies were hollow, and heads were hand-carved with glass eyes. The paint he used was very durable, meaning the surfaces of many have survived in good condition.

18in (46cm) long

£700-1,000　　　　　　　　　　　　　　　　POOK

An early 20thC American standard-grade Redhead duck decoy, attributed to the Mason factory.

Based in Detroit from 1895 to 1924, the Mason factory's decoys are among the most celebrated in the collecting community. Their standard-grade decoys have glass eyes, no bill carving, and painted details. They're also smaller than the 'premium' Challenge- or Premier-grade decoys.

14in (36cm) long

£120-180　　　　　　　　　　　　　　　　POOK

A mid-20thC American black duck decoy, attributed to Harry M. Shourds of Ocean City, New Jersey.

16.5in (42cm) long

£220-280　　　　　　　　　　　　POOK

An early 20thC American Mason factory standard-grade Oldsquaw duck decoy.

13.5in (34cm) long

£120-180　　　　　　　　　　　　POOK

A mid-20thC American Pintail drake duck decoy, attributed to R. Madison Mitchell.

Mitchell (1901-1993) produced decoys from 1924 onwards. It is believed that he made and sold over 100,000 decoys, making him one of the most prolific makers in the US.

17.5in (44cm) long

£150-200　　　　　　　　　　　　POOK

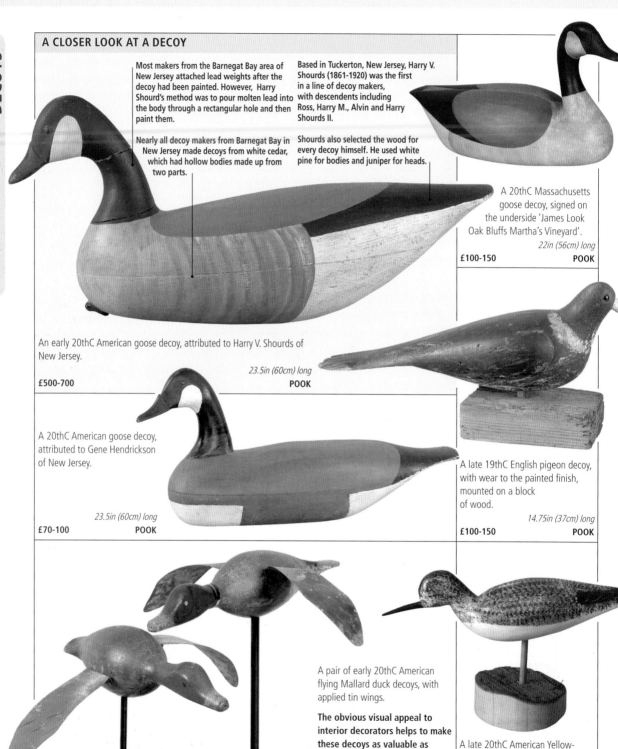

A CLOSER LOOK AT A DECOY

Most makers from the Barnegat Bay area of New Jersey attached lead weights after the decoy had been painted. However, Harry Shourd's method was to pour molten lead into the body through a rectangular hole and then paint them.

Nearly all decoy makers from Barnegat Bay in New Jersey made decoys from white cedar, which had hollow bodies made up from two parts.

Based in Tuckerton, New Jersey, Harry V. Shourds (1861-1920) was the first in a line of decoy makers, with descendents including Ross, Harry M., Alvin and Harry Shourds II.

Shourds also selected the wood for every decoy himself. He used white pine for bodies and juniper for heads.

A 20thC Massachusetts goose decoy, signed on the underside 'James Look Oak Bluffs Martha's Vineyard'.

22in (56cm) long

£100-150   POOK

An early 20thC American goose decoy, attributed to Harry V. Shourds of New Jersey.

£500-700

23.5in (60cm) long

POOK

A 20thC American goose decoy, attributed to Gene Hendrickson of New Jersey.

23.5in (60cm) long

£70-100   POOK

A late 19thC English pigeon decoy, with wear to the painted finish, mounted on a block of wood.

14.75in (37cm) long

£100-150   POOK

A pair of early 20thC American flying Mallard duck decoys, with applied tin wings.

The obvious visual appeal to interior decorators helps to make these decoys as valuable as they are, as does the addition of hand-painted tin wings.

Largest 16.75in (43cm) long

£600-900   POOK

A late 20thC American Yellow-legged Shorebird decoy, attributed to Hurley Conklin of New Jersey.

14.25in (36cm) long

£150-200   POOK

QUICK REFERENCE - DOLLS

- The doll industry saw its first real boom in France and Germany during the mid-late 19thC. Makers such as Armand Marseille, Heubach, and Kammer & Reinhardt mass-produced dolls made with bisque heads. Finer quality dolls were made by factories such as Bru, and these tend to be the most valuable.
- Look for impressed or incised marks on the back of the head as these typically show the mould number, and sometimes indicate the maker. Lively, well-painted, and characterful features, and clean, undamaged bisque are likely to make a bisque-head doll desirable.
- Hard and soft plastic dolls from the second half of the 20thC are becoming increasingly desirable today as the children who played with them grow into nostalgic collectors. The most desirable and valuable dolls are likely to be by major makers, such as Mattel (creators of Barbie), Ideal, and Pedigree. A premium is usually paid for the earliest or scarcest models.
- However old the doll, the highest prices will always be paid for those in mint condition. They should ideally have their original clothes and hairstyles (cut hair greatly reduces value). Modern plastic dolls should be in clean, unplayed-with condition, and ideally come with their original clothes, boxes, and tags.

An Ernst Heubach bisque girl doll, mould no.250, with blue sleeping eyes, open mouth, blonde wig, and new clothes, the head incised 'Heubach Köppelsdorf 250 3 Germany', together with a cane armchair.

22.5in (57.5cm) high

£250-350   KAU

A small 1920s Simon & Halbig bisque doll, mould no.15, with fixed eyes, painted mouth and jointed composition body, back of the head marked 'S.H' and 'K*R', with blonde wig and original clothes.

Simon & Halbig, established in 1869, supplied Kämmer & Reinhardt with most of its doll heads from 1902 onwards. The company was acquired by Kämmer & Reinhardt in 1920, hence the additional 'K*R' marks on this doll.

6in (15cm) high

£100-150   GORL

A Gebrüder Knoch bisque doll, mould no.185, with fixed brown eyes, painted eyebrows, open mouth with five teeth, ceramic hands and lower legs, and composition body, wearing a turquoise dress.

11.5in (29cm) high

£40-60   SAS

A Schützmeister & Quendt bisque baby doll, mould no.201, with sleeping eyes, open mouth, and jointed composition body, the head incised with the 'SQ' monogram and mould number.

c1900   *17in (43cm) high*

£80-120   GORL

A Simon & Halbig bisque head doll, with sleeping brown eyes, open mouth exposing four teeth, blonde wig, and composition body, the head incised 'SH PB * 1906'.

1906   *25in (62.5cm) high*

£80-120   CHT

DOLLS

A Gebrüder Heubach bisque character child, with moulded hair, brown side-glancing eyes, open closed-mouth, jointed arms, and blue painted shoes, wearing a period trimmed cotton dress and underwear.

c1910   8in (20cm) high

£200-300   SK

A Gebrüder Heubach bisque figurine of a child wearing an Easter bunny outfit, with an eggshell-shaped match holder behind.

c1890   5.5in (14cm) high

£100-150   BEJ

A C. F. Kling & Co. bisque crawling boy, with swivel neck, painted and moulded features with blond hair, brown glass eyes, closed smiling mouth, and moulded night clothes.

Provenance: Mary Merritt Doll Museum.

c1890   6in (15cm) high

£650-750   SK

QUICK REFERENCE - PIANO BABIES

- German doll makers began producing dolls or figurines made entirely from moulded bisque in the late 19thC. Larger examples like this are often known as 'piano babies' as they were placed on top of pianos, often to hold down decorative fabric covers in Victorian or Edwardian parlours.

- Although a number of factories produced them, one of the best-known makers is Gebrüder Heubach. Identified by a printed or impressed sunburst mark on the base, Heubach's dolls are typically of very high quality with many realistic and fine hand-painted details. The quality of the moulding is also very high, particularly the drapes of clothing, and the face and hair.

- During the 1920s-50s, a number of piano babies were made in Japan. These are typically of poorer quality, and are made from a bisque that feels rougher to the touch. They have less well-executed details, particularly around the eyes and mouth, and are also often lighter in weight. Air holes on the base from the production process are also larger on these later examples. Genuine examples have tiny holes.

A German glazed bisque 'Frozen Charlie', the seated child with painted and moulded features, in an oval bath tub.

c1860   3.25in (8.5cm) high

£300-400   SK

A C. F. Kling & Co. bisque crawling girl, with swivel neck, painted and moulded features, blonde hair with black headband, blue glass eyes, open smiling closed-mouth with painted teeth, and moulded night clothes.

c1890   6in (15cm) high

£700-1,000   SK

An early 20thC French bisque reclining nude lady, with brown wig, and painted face and ballet shoes.

Found in many different poses and sizes, these highly collectable figurines are often known as 'Bathing Beauties'. The largest, which have more detailed moulding and clothing than this example, are the most valuable.

2in (5cm) high

£120-180   CHT

A CLOSER LOOK AT BARBIE

Although she is in excellent condition and retains her box, she lacks her red shoes and pearl earrings.

Both Barbie no.5 and no.6 were available with more hair colours than previous models, such as titian (red hair). They can be distinguished as no.6 generally has a broader face.

Although she has no greening on her ears caused by the metal rods in the earrings, and her painted facial features are in excellent condition, her hair needs re-styling.

The colour of her lips and eyebrows were changed depending on her hair colour.

A Mattel Barbie 'Ponytail' doll, no.6, with brunette hair, original red swimsuit, and card picture box.

1962-66   *12in (30.5cm) high*
£120-180   **MTB**

A Mattel 'Talking Stacey' talking doll, with original striped two-piece swimsuit, and original box, in mint condition but lacking her foil tag.

Stacey is Barbie's best British friend, and is a challenge to find as she was never as popular as Barbie. Pulling the ring at the back of her neck operates her voice.

c1969   *13in (33cm) high*
£300-400   **MTB**

A Mattel '30th Anniversary' 'Francie' doll, with outfits, original packaging, and window box.

Introduced in 1965, Francie is Barbie's 'modern cousin'. This reproduction model was introduced in 1996 to celebrate her 30th anniversary.

1996   *14in (35.5cm) high*
£40-60   **MTB**

A 1990s Hornby 'Cassy Getting Ready' doll, in mint condition, complete with outfit and plastic box.

Introduced in 1991, the 'video cassette case'-like boxes were a special feature that opened up to form a room-set. As a girl's collection grew, room-sets could be combined to form an entire house.

10in (25.5cm) high
£20-30   **MTB**

A 1990s Hornby 'Cassy Coffee Morning' doll, complete with original outfit, packaging and plastic box, all in mint condition.

10in (25cm) high
£20-30   **MTB**

A 1970s Flair Toys Ltd. 'Dizzy Daisy' doll, from the 'Fashions by Mary Quant' series, with early small head, in mint condition, complete with original stripy outfit and window box.

'Dizzy Daisy' was the budget doll from the 'Daisy' range. She didn't have bendable legs or a twisting waist. This red, white, and blue leotard was the first version of this outfit. It sold very well, and is therefore much more common than later, differently coloured outfits.

9.5in (24cm) high
£80-120   **MTB**

A CLOSER LOOK AT A 'DUSTY' DOLL

Released by Kenner as a competitor to Barbie, Dusty's outfits focused on sports rather than fashion. Unfortunately for fashion-conscious girls, Dusty was larger than Barbie, and so they couldn't share clothes.

Like many dolls of the 1970s, she had a tanned skin tone. She also had a twisting waist and jointed wrists enabling her to 'use' her sporty accessories.

Her sporting theme, size, and shape gave her an almost tomboyish air, which was not very popular with little girls. Dusty was consequently withdrawn by the end of the 1970s.

Her instantly recognisable face was either loved or loathed by children.

A 1970s Kenner 'Dusty Tennis Champ' doll, with stand, in excellent condition, complete with racquet, stand, original outfit, and card box.

12in (30.5cm) high

£100-150   MTB

A mid-1980s Hornby 'Flower Fairies Garden Ballet' doll, the back of her head marked 'Hornby 1983', in mint condition, complete with outfit and box.

12in (30.5cm) high

£40-60   MTB

A Kenner 'Strawberry Shortcake Orange Blossom' vinyl doll, complete with 'Marmalade' pet, in mint condition with original box.

'Strawberry Shortcake' is a rapidly growing collecting area, particularly in the US. Although not necessarily rare, black dolls are popular with collectors.

1979-1982   *8in (20.5cm) high*

£18-22   MTB

An early 1960s Ideal 'Tammy Telephone Booth' doll, in mint condition complete with rigid blue plastic telephone booth, original outfit, and presentation box, one hinge damaged on the booth door.

12in (30.5cm) high

£120-180   MTB

A 1960s Ideal 'Pepper' doll, in mint condition, with original outfit, and original triangular window box.

Pepper is Tammy's little sister. This example has a very pale head as the plastic components have degraded over time. This emits a gas that collects in the head if it cannot escape from the packaging.

12in (30.5cm) high

£100-150   MTB

A mid-late 1960s American Character 'Tressy' doll, with 'growing hair', in mint condition, complete with original outfit, brochure, and presentation box.

14in (35cm) high

£100-150   MTB

A 1950s Linda hard plastic doll, with floral printed dress and bonnet, the back moulded 'MADE IN HONG KONG', in original and excellent condition.

Sold in corner shops, these were less expensive copies of the popular British 'Miss Rosebud' dolls. The halo-like upturned bonnet and the style of dress are typical features. A 'Miss Rosebud' doll in similar condition might fetch just over twice the value of this one.

8in (20.5cm) high

£15-20   DSC

A CLOSER LOOK AT A LENCI DOLL

Lenci was founded in Turin, Italy in 1918. By the 1920s it was renowned for its charming moulded felt dolls.

The 'Lenci' name is an acronym of 'Ludus Est Nobis Constanter Industria', the Latin for 'To Play is Our Constant Work'.

Series 149 dolls were of children older than babies or toddlers, but younger than the teenagers that made up series 400.

Always check that the moulded felt is clean and bright, and that the delicately painted blushing cheeks and other facial features are intact, as this maximises value.

Look out for character or costume Lenci dolls, as these can fetch the highest sums.

An Italian Lenci felt girl doll, from series 149, with painted features and pigtails, wearing a turquoise blue dress and orange bonnet.
c1926-30   *16in (40cm) high*

£450-550   FLD

A 1950s 'Roddy' hard plastic miniature doll, with swinging arms, lacking clothes.
3.5in (9cm) high
£5-8   DSC

A 1930s American sprayed composition 'Topsy' doll, with cotton babygro, unmarked.
9in (23cm) high
£30-40   DSC

A late 1950s Palitoy 'Archie Andrews' ventriloquist doll, in excellent condition with instructions and tissue, in original box in good condition.

15in (38cm) high
£60-90   SAS

A novelty cotton reel doll, made up of various reels of cotton, with painted composition face, and a cotton and lace dress, holding baby with porcelain shoulder head.
9in (23cm) high
£35-45   AH

A 1930's Lenci-style felt 'Shirley Temple' doll, with painted features and blonde ringlets, wearing a green, yellow, pink, and black dress, unmarked.
17in (44cm) high
£80-120   FLD

FASHION

QUICK REFERENCE - FASHION

- Vintage fashion has become increasingly mainstream over the past few years with many people choosing to buy vintage pieces to create an individual look. As a result of this widening of interest, prices have risen considerably across the board.
- The highest prices are paid for the work of well-known designers who were pioneers of a look or style. Learn to identify different labels, as most had or have a less sought-after diffusion range as well as a haute couture collection.
- The 1950s, 1960s, and 1970s continue to be the most desirable and practical periods of costume design to collect, however, typically bright, brash and bold pieces from the 1980s are beginning to see a significant rise in value. The work of innovative designers of the period, such as Gianni Versace and Vivienne Westwood, is highly sought-after, particularly those pieces from well-known and iconic collections.
- The most desirable pieces of any decade or designer will sum up the age and have 'eye appeal'. This will include the colour, pattern, and shape of a piece. Other important indicators to value include the quality of the material, the cut, and the stitching. Avoid stained or torn items (unless that was intentional!), as these will be unpleasant to wear, and both collectors and wearers of vintage fashion shy away from them.
- Keep an eye on magazines and celebrities to spot what might be 'the next big thing', but remember that while trends may lose popularity, good style never goes out of fashion.

A 1960s Pierre Balmain bright-green tailored suit, no. 154 892, the jacket inset with elliptical panels that carry the chunky buttons, labelled.

Chest 36in (91cm)

£500-700   KT

A 1980s Jean-Charles de Castelbajac yellow wool coat, straight fit, with all-over 'washing instructions' embroidery, with 'JC de Castelbajac' label.

£350-450   LHA

A 1990s Chanel sea-foam green skirt suit, the jacket trimmed in black patent leather, with a notched collar, flower detailed buttons, four front pockets, fully lined, the pencil skirt with patent leather trim at hem, fully-lined, labelled 'Chanel Boutique'.

£450-550   LHA

A 1980s Jean-Charles de Castelbajac multicoloured linen 'Bear' sleeveless swing dress, with a bear and 'tout est dit Bear' painted on front, with on-seam pockets, and 'JC de Castelbajac' label.

Jean-Charles de Castelbajac (b. 1949) crosses Pop Art with haute couture in his brightly coloured printed or painted designs. As well as bold geometric patterns, he reproduces characters or icons from popular culture, such as Mickey Mouse, Bambi, politicians, celebrities, and, here, the teddy bear. In this way his flamboyant designs are inspired by greats such as Andy Warhol and Keith Haring. Although not yet in the 'top tier' of sought-after names, this may change as time passes, and this era and his distinctive look is reappraised.

Size 0

£300-500   LHA

A 1960s Chanel couture cobalt-blue bouclé wool tweed suit, the jacket with braided trim and a straight skirt, fully lined, with 'Chanel' label, numbered label removed.

£350-450   LHA

A Courrèges lavender vinyl Mod ensemble, comprising a jacket with white snap closures and logo at front, and a matching mini skirt with white belt, together with a matching vinyl purse, all labelled 'Courrèges'.

Culminating in man landing on the moon, the 1960s was obsessed with the world of the future and the space race. This obsession permeated through into fashion, and André Courrèges (b.1923) was the style leader. Often using 'futuristic' plastic over natural materials such as wool and cotton, his designs were simple, often unisex, and typical of the 1960s take on what we might be wearing in space in the future. For a populist take on the look, think of the uniforms from popular TV series 'Space: 1999'.

Size 40

£550-750 LHA

A mid-1960s Courrèges white wool single-breasted coat, no.1116, with top-stitched detailing to the shoulders and to the large curved triangular patch pockets, with back belt, labelled.

Chest 34in (86cm)

£1,000-1,500 KT

A Christian Dior couture ribbed red silk 'cocoon' coat, with oversized black beaded buttons and 'Christian Dior/102610' label.

This coat was released as part of Dior's autumn 1959 collection, designed by Yves Saint Laurent. The collection wasn't generally well-received due to the knee-length and tightly belted waists on skirts and dresses.

£1,500-2,000 LHA

A CLOSER LOOK AT A THEA PORTER KAFTAN

Israeli-born designer Thea Porter (1927-2000) began by importing Turkish and Middle Eastern home furnishings and clothing to sell in her shop in Soho, London in 1966.

Along with the entire ethnic look, kaftans became fashionable in the late 1960s and '70s and, as demand grew, Porter began to design her own, which were made in opulently embroidered, luxurious fabrics.

With shops in London, New York, and Paris, her clients included Elizabeth Taylor, Barbra Streisand, and members of royalty, who loved the combination of exoticism and individuality tinged with the allure of the harem.

The best examples, like this one, were always expensive and few were made. Her work fell out of fashion in the 1980s, but, following a reappraisal in the early 2000s, prices have risen dramatically.

A Thea Porter multicoloured silk and cotton evening kaftan, with gold embroidery and sequins throughout, with 'Thea Porter Couture' label.

Overall length 70in (118cm)

£3,500-4,500 LHA

A late 1980s Moschino 'Popeye' jacket and dress ensemble, the quilted jacket with 'Popeye' cartoon to the torso and chequerboard sleeves, together with a fitted chequerboard dress, both with 'Moschino Pret-a-Porter' labels.

1989

£200-300 LHA

A 1970s Thea Porter 'Orientalist' ensemble, comprising a jacket and trousers in emerald-green silk woven with bamboo, with a braided belt, the jacket and trousers labelled 'Thea Porter Couture'.

Size 10

£400-600 LHA

QUICK REFERENCE - GIANNI VERSACE

- Italian designer Gianni Versace (1946-1997) began his career in fashion by assisting his mother, who was a dressmaker. He presented his first collections of knitted, leather, and suede clothing for Florentine Flowers, Callaghan and his own label 'Complice' in the mid-1970s. In 1978, he founded a new label 'Gianni Versace' and opened his first boutique in Milan. He soon became known for his provocative, extroverted, and almost vulgar style. His youth-oriented quasi-diffusion lines 'Versus', 'V2 by Versace', and 'Signature' were launched 1989-91, and were joined by the 'Istante' line in 1995.

- As indicated by his Medusa head logo, Versace's influences include Classical Greek and Roman motifs, but Pop Art was also important. This suit is typical of that theme, with its clear inspiration from the art of Andy Warhol. Versace also became known for unusual combinations of materials, such as coarse jute fabric and gold thread, and his use of unusual materials, such as neoprene.

- Versace was murdered in 1997, and the business was taken over by his sister Donatella who continues to develop his highly individual look. Regardless of your opinion of his work, he was one of the greatest fashion designers of the late 20thC.

An early 1990s Gianni Versace multicoloured printed corset pouf dress, with a fitted bodice with removable straps, and full pleated skirt with crinoline, labelled 'Versace Jeans Couture'.

Size 42

£300-500   LHA

An early 1990s Gianni Versace 'Betty Boop' jacket, with multicoloured printed Harley Davidson and Gumby motifs, labelled 'Versace Jeans Couture'.

£150-200   LHA

A Gianni Versace 'Warhol' suit, with all-over printed portraits of Marilyn Monroe and James Dean, with rhinestone buttons, labelled 'Gianni Versace Couture'.

1991

£800-1,200   LHA

A Gianni Versace graphic print sequin cocktail dress, strapless and very fitted, and with a low back, labelled 'Versus'.

This dress sums up the Versace look in terms of its bold colours, tropically-inspired Pop Art style print, and the atypical use of sequins, which have been printed to create the design.

Size 40

£800-1,200   LHA

A Gianni Versace couture blue and red silk evening gown, with a low back and rhinestone ornamentation at the straps, labelled 'Gianni Versace Couture'.

The form, colours, and pattern hark back to 1960s styles, but don't really shout Versace. This explains the price, which you might think would be higher considering it's a couture piece.

£200-300   LHA

A Gianni Versace couture black and printed jersey dress, with a leather neckline and belt, labelled 'Gianni Versace Couture'.

Size 44

£150-250   LHA

A late 1960s Cathy McGowan Boutique purple crepe dress, backed with nylon, with ruched collar, faux-buttoned front and belt, labelled.

Known as the 'Queen of the Mods', TV-presenter Cathy McGowan shot to fame in 1963 when she was selected to present the legendary 'Ready Steady Go!'. Her role led to her becoming a fashion guru in the 1960s, and a boutique was founded to build on this reputation.

38.25in (97cm) long

£60-80   **CANS**

A 1960s lime green cotton dress, with striped collar and waist, and white plastic buttons, unlabelled.

37.5in (95cm) long

£35-45   **CANS**

A 1960s Mod-style Liza Peta 'Jerseyware' woven black dress, with red and white stripe.

40.5in (103cm) long

£60-80   **CANS**

A 1960s French cotton mini dress, the waist with cut circles and with beige and brown grosgrain trim, with label for 'PIERRE 156 Rue de Neuilly'.

Along with the red and white striped black dress shown on this page, this simple, almost futuristic dress was undoubtedly influenced by the designs of Pierre Cardin and André Courrèges.

36.75in (93cm) high

£50-70   **CANS**

A 1960s tartan printed cotton and white polyester stretch A-line mini-dress.

31.25in (79cm) high

£35-45   **CANS**

A 1960s Elgee of London green and red tartan belted coat with kilt pin, with 'Made In England' label.

35.5in (90cm) high

£70-100   **CANS**

A late 1960s Canadian Irving Posluns woven chenille tapestry coat, with hood, with rope fastenings to front and black faux fur trim.

41in (104cm) long

£80-120   CANS

A 1960s French GEB Mod-style leather-look PVC coat, with white trim and chunky white plastic zips, with 'GEB (Modèle Dépose)' label to inside.

This material was sometimes known as 'pleather'. Without any regard to how hot it might be to wear, manmade materials like this were deemed fashionable, practical, and stylish in the '60s.

32in (81cm) long

£60-80   CANS

A 1970s Peters Brothers for Harrod's woven rayon suit, with check- and diamond-pattern, and wide collar.

This suit is very Sybil Fawlty. You can almost hear the shrill cry 'Basiiillll!'.

41.5in (105cm) high

£50-70   CANS

A 1970s C&A navy blue cotton belted dress, printed with white birds and donkeys with carrots in their mouths.

It's the crazy pattern that leads to the value here. Similar unprinted examples fetch a maximum of £40.

36.75in (93cm) long

£60-70   CANS

A late 1970s St. Michael cotton strapless dress, printed with umbrellas and with white piping.

Labels on 1970s Marks & Spencer clothing are useful for dating. The '3/77' on the second label indicates this was made in March 1977.

1977   *30.5in (77.5cm) long*

£35-45   CANS

A 1970s rayon maxiskirt, printed with brightly coloured geometric patterns and ladybirds, unlabelled.

44.5in (113cm) long

£20-30   CANS

A 1970s Ben Sherman printed cotton lady's long-sleeved shirt, with stripe and diamond pattern.

Ladies shirts by Ben Sherman are unusual.

£28-32   CANS

A 1970s Cavalier 'Styled By Sumroni' blue paisley printed cotton long-sleeved men's shirt, with rounded tab collar.

£25-30   CANS

A 1970s Tootal orange paisley printed cotton short-sleeved men's shirt.

£35-40   CANS

Mark Picks

The trade in vintage top hats is strong, particularly with those wishing to invest in a hat for weddings or events such as Royal Ascot, as they are much less expensive than new hats. Size matters and, although standard sizes are the most commercial, it's worth keeping an eye out for very large or very small sizes as they may command a premium from those they fit.

Also keep an eye out for hats that come in their original fitted cases, like this one, as the cases can fetch as much as, or more than, the hat itself. Quirkily shaped and often covered with beautifully patinated leather, they're popular with interior decorators who display them on piles of vintage luggage, or place them neatly in a hallway or dressing room to suggest the bygone age of the gentleman, or the revived dapper dandy.

An early 20thC Kendal Milne black silk top hat, in tan leather fitted case.

£120-180   RW

An early 20thC Ridgmont straw boater hat, with a red band, marked inside 'The Ridgmont Make, Gold Medal, Paris'.

12.25in (31cm) diam

£20-30   LC

A 1980s Gianni Versace silk gentleman's tie, printed with black and white leopard skin effect and butterflies fluttering around strawberry plants.

£25-35   LHA

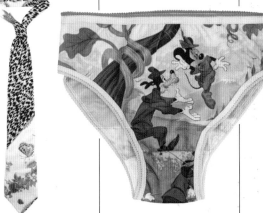

A pair of 1970s polyester Mickey Mouse underpants, with Mickey, Goofy, and other Disney characters on the front and back.

10.75in (27cm) wide

£10-15   CANS

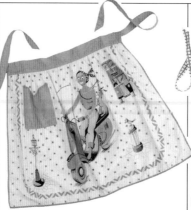

A 1960s printed paisley nylon slip, with black piping and straps.

23.25in (59cm) long

£15-20   CANS

A 1950s cotton apron, printed with a girl on a scooter, a streetlamp, London bus, and fire hydrant, with a pink strap and pocket.

19.25in (49cm) long

£10-15   CANS

A 1950s cotton apron, the large blue pocket printed with Scottie dogs.

Along with poodles, Scottie dogs are very typically 1950s, and it's the presence of these cute dogs that pushes the value up slightly.

19.25in (49cm) long

£12-18   CANS

A late 20thC Chanel black leather belt, with a gold-tone shaped adjustable buckle, stamped 'Chanel'.

£100-150   LHA

A large Chanel black leather biker belt, with gold-tone buckle and chain, the interior stamped 'Chanel' in gilt.

1993   *Waist 32in*

£100-150   LHA

A pair of 1950s-60s Schiaparelli black and white laminated sunglasses, with black and white three-dimensional plastic stripes at the top and sides, and carved plastic floral embellishments at each corner, stamped 'Schiaparelli'.

£800-1,200   LHA

A late 20thC pair of Chanel 'Cuvée Cork' shoes, printed 'Chateau Chanel' on the back heel, and stamped 'Chanel'.

Size 37

£100-150   LHA

An Edwardian silver-mesh lady's evening bag, with hallmarks for Birmingham.

1916

£50-70   **WHP**

A 1950s bright pink felt handbag, with an applied wavy violet fabric band mounted with red fabric roses, rhinestones, beads, and faux pearls.

This pink is very close to Elsa Schiaparelli's famous 'Shocking Pink' used on the box of her 1937 perfume 'Shocking'.

8.5in (21.5cm) wide

£70-100   **GCHI**

A 1950s Nettie Rosenstein black lizard skin box bag, with a studded amber Lucite handle and closure, stamped 'Nettie Rosenstein'.

9in (23cm) high

£150-250   **LHA**

A 1950s-60s Nettie Rosenstein brown crocodile skin trapezoidal bag, with two matching shoulder straps, stamped 'Nettie Rosenstein'.

9in (23cm) wide

£80-120   **LHA**

A 1980s Chanel quilted black patent leather bag, with a logo pocket at front, long chainlink shoulder strap, and tassel zipper closure, stamped 'Chanel'.

This design is based on Coco Chanel's famous '2.55' quilted handbag, which has been a design classic since its release in 1955.

9in (23cm) wide

£800-1,200   **LHA**

A 1980s Chanel fuchsia quilted silk evening bag, with a pearl and rhinestone strap, and a Gripoix glass cross motif at front closure, stamped 'Chanel'.

For more information about Gripoix, please see p.166.

6in (15cm) high

£400-600   **LHA**

A Moschino red and purple suede tote, with floral appliqués at front, and lacey edges, stamped 'Moschino'.

14in (36cm) wide

£150-200   **LHA**

FASHION

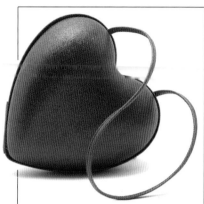

A 1980s-90s Moschino red glitter covered hard-sided heart-shaped bag, stamped 'Moschino'.

7in (18cm) high

£250-350   LHA

A 1990s Kathrine Baumann heart-shaped American flag minaudière, with a hidden gold-tone chain shoulder strap, stamped 'KB Beverly Hills'.

Ex-model and actress Baumann founded her handbag company in 1988, and has become known as the 'Beverly Hills Bag Lady'. Her designs have been sported by many top Hollywood names.

4in (10cm) high

£80-120   LHA

A Moschino red and yellow 'House' bag, with a red metallic roof, floral felted sides, and snakeskin trim, stamped 'Moschino'.

9in (23cm) high

£180-220   LHA

A Moschino red black and white leather 'Present' handbag, with a long black leather shoulder strap, and label stamped 'HAPPY 2000!', the interior stamped 'Moschino'.

2000   6in (15cm) high

£120-140   LHA

A Moschino pink leather guitar case-shaped bag, with a long matching shoulder strap and handle, stamped 'Moschino'.

19in (48cm) long

£450-550   LHA

A CLOSER LOOK AT A JUDITH LEIBER HANDBAG

Hungarian-born handbag designer Leiber (b.1921) emigrated to the US in 1947, and worked for costume jeweller and handbag designer Nettie Rosenstein before founding her own company in 1963.

She is best-known for her cast metal 'minaudière' evening bags, which are inspired by purses made by Van Cleef & Arpels during the 1930s. They have attracted numerous Hollywood stars and almost every First Lady since 1963.

Produced in a huge variety of different novelty shapes, including animals, the bags are cast, and then labour-intensively studded by hand with hundreds of glittering Swarovski crystals.

Her bags are expensive to buy and are highly exclusive. As such the most desirable discontinued designs can fetch more than they cost originally.

A Judith Leiber watermelon rhinestone-studded minaudière, with hidden chain shoulder strap, the interior stamped 'Judith Leiber'.

Minaudière is taken from the French word for 'to charm'.

6in (15cm) wide

£2,000-2,500   LHA

An Hermès printed silk 'Persepolis' pattern scarf, designed by Sophie Koechlin in 2000, in bright jewel tones on a black ground.

c2001   *35in (89cm) wide*

£150-200   **FRE**

An Hermès printed silk 'Grand Fonds' pattern scarf, designed by Annie Faivre in 1992, with tropical fish on a royal blue background.

Meaning 'Great Depths', and inspired by the sea, 'Grand Fonds' is one of the company's best selling designs. In 2002, a 'Grand Fonds Detail' version was released, featuring one of the fish designs enlarged.

35in (89cm) wide

£180-220   **FRE**

A late 20thC Hermès printed silk 'Eperon' pattern scarf, designed by Henri D'Origny in 1974, printed in green, navy blue, and gold.

35in (89cm) wide

£150-200   **LHA**

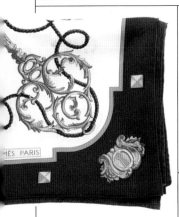

A Gucci printed silk scarf, with a floral motif within a broad green border, labelled 'Gucci'.

35in (89cm) wide

£60-90   **LHA**

A late 20thC Hermès printed silk 'Les Clefs' pattern scarf, designed by Cathy Latham in 1965, with gold key motifs.

35in (89cm) wide

£220-280   **LHA**

A 1970s-80s Yves Saint Laurent printed silk scarf, with a multicoloured geometric pattern, branded 'YVES SAINT LAURENT' within the print.

35in (89cm) wide

£100-150   **LHA**

A 1960s-70s Emilio Pucci blue, beige, and brown geometric print scarf, with 'Emilio Pucci' label, and 'Emilio' brand printed within the design.

50in (127cm) wide

£120-180   **LHA**

QUICK REFERENCE

- Reacting to the privations and horrors of the war, designers in the 1950s and 1960s turned to bright colours and new asymmetric shapes in a forward thinking, positive manner. Young couples moved into newly-built houses and decorated them with cheap and cheerful, but fashionable, furniture.
- Often tagged 'Contemporary', the look was modern and miles away from the austere and dull designs of the 1940s. It was also very different from the angular, geometric style of the Art Deco period, although some stylisation did continue. New developments in science, technology, and atomic power also influenced design in terms of form and pattern.
- Designers took advantage of numerous new man-made materials, many developed for the war, such as vinyl, Formica, Draylon, and nylon. These could be easily coloured and moulded into a range of forms, which made them well-suited to the new design aesthetic.

- During the early 1950s, surplus wartime aluminium was widely used for domestic products. Both plastic and aluminium objects were also easy to mass-produce, making them affordable for the manufacturer and the buyer.
- Many pieces were not intended to last, but they were so inexpensive that people could afford to throw away worn out things and replace them with new. In some cases this can mean that mint condition examples are rare and desirable.
- Popular motifs include poodles, Parisian scenes, exotic Far Eastern subjects, polka dots, geometric of abstract patterns, atomic structures, and elegant, elongated women, including risqué pin-up girls. The 1950s also saw the beginning of celebrity endorsement and rock and pop music.
- In general good condition pieces that are colourful, appealing, and typical of the 1950s and 1960s are likely to be desirable. A known designer will almost certainly add value.

FOCUS on the PAST

25 Waterloo St, Clifton Village,
Bristol BS8 4BT
Tel: 0117 9738080
www.focusonthepast.org

OPEN EVERY DAY

Established for more than 30 years in the heart of Clifton Village, Bristol, near the Suspension Bridge, Focus on the Past is an Antique Centre on 2 floors for 12 dealers selling a wide variety of affordable antiques, furniture and collectables from traditional to quirky, and classic to kitsch. Stock includes antique, pine and painted furniture, kitchenalia, beds, silver, china, jewellery, advertising and packaging, and Retro.

A 1950s Duron black, pink, and yellow painted plaster 'Banana Girl' figurine, with pink split-skirt.

10.75in (27.5cm) high

£70-100   MA

A pair of 1950s black, red, yellow, and white painted plaster African musician figurines, in mint condition.

6.25in (16cm) high

£50-70   MA

A 1950s painted plaster bust of a stylised African girl, in mint condition.

8.5in (21.5cm) high

£30-50   MA

A pair of 1950s American polychome painted plaster Oriental busts, impressed 'WWAS' on the back.

7.25in (18.5cm) high

£70-100   MA

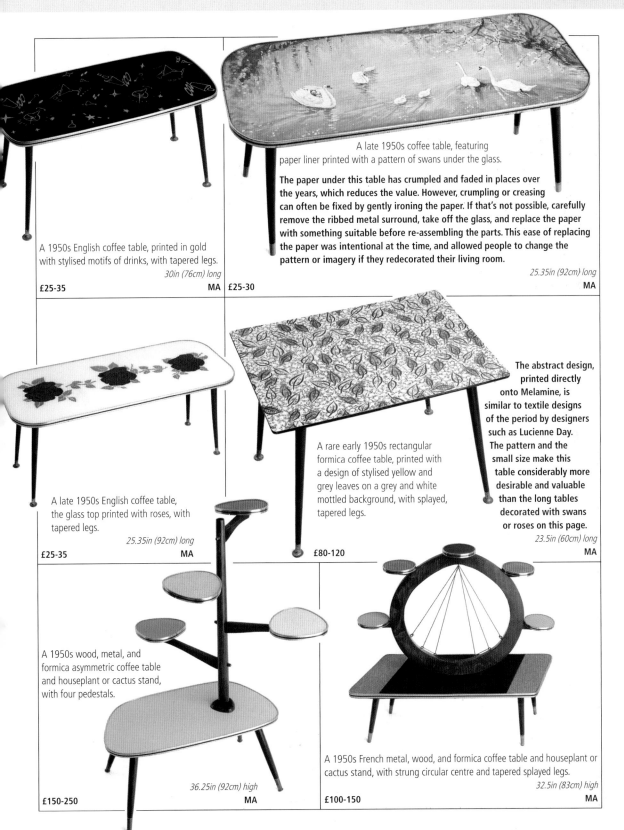

A late 1950s coffee table, featuring paper liner printed with a pattern of swans under the glass.

The paper under this table has crumpled and faded in places over the years, which reduces the value. However, crumpling or creasing can often be fixed by gently ironing the paper. If that's not possible, carefully remove the ribbed metal surround, take off the glass, and replace the paper with something suitable before re-assembling the parts. This ease of replacing the paper was intentional at the time, and allowed people to change the pattern or imagery if they redecorated their living room.

25.35in (92cm) long

MA

A 1950s English coffee table, printed in gold with stylised motifs of drinks, with tapered legs.

30in (76cm) long

£25-35   MA

£25-30

A late 1950s English coffee table, the glass top printed with roses, with tapered legs.

25.35in (92cm) long

£25-35   MA

A rare early 1950s rectangular formica coffee table, printed with a design of stylised yellow and grey leaves on a grey and white mottled background, with splayed, tapered legs.

£80-120

The abstract design, printed directly onto Melamine, is similar to textile designs of the period by designers such as Lucienne Day. The pattern and the small size make this table considerably more desirable and valuable than the long tables decorated with swans or roses on this page.

23.5in (60cm) long

MA

A 1950s wood, metal, and formica asymmetric coffee table and houseplant or cactus stand, with four pedestals.

36.25in (92cm) high

£150-250   MA

A 1950s French metal, wood, and formica coffee table and houseplant or cactus stand, with strung circular centre and tapered splayed legs.

32.5in (83cm) high

£100-150   MA

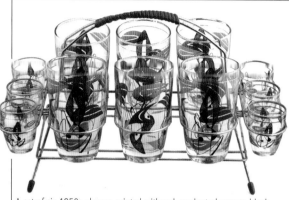

A set of six 1950s glasses, printed with red, graduated orange, black, and sky blue abstract motifs, together with a set of six shot glasses with matching patterns, all contained in an original gilt-wire stand.

Complete sets of these jauntily printed mass-produced glasses can be very hard to find, particularly with their original wire stands. Typical themes and motifs include abstract geometric forms, cocktails, dice, playing cards, glamourous girls, and exotic foreign locations.

Stand 14in (36cm) long

£60-80   **MA**

Two of a set of six late-1950s-60s drinking glasses, printed with a red, green, white, and yellow pattern of bottles, soda siphons, and glasses.

4.5in (11.5cm) high

£50-70 set   **MA**

Two of a set of eight 1950s glasses, printed with a pattern of abstract music notes, marked 'FOREIGN' within the pattern.

4in (10cm) high

£35-45 set   **MA**

Two of a set of six 1950s American high ball tumblers, printed with textured blue, pink, and black patterns.

With their concrete-like texture and geometric pattern, they recall the windows and walls of skyscrapers. These themes have been brought back into fashion by TV shows such as 'Mad Men'.

5.5in (14cm) high

£25-35 set   **MA**

One of a set of four early 1950s tapered glasses, printed with playing cards and lines.

3in (8cm) high

£20-30 set   **MA**

A 1950s 'Glamour Girl' pressed glass mug or beer tankard, the interior with 'reversed' transfer showing the same girl topless.

Collectors tend to pay more for examples with the more appealing and brightly coloured beach ball style cushion, as seen here. Watch out for modern reproductions: transfers are printed in a different manner and tend to be scratched off easily.

5in (12cm) high

£32-38   **MA**

One of a set of six late 1950s tapered glasses, printed with stacks of playing cards and embellished with gold lines.

Apart from being larger, this is more valuable than the other playing card glass on this page because it has a more detailed and better printed design, it's waisted, and has gilt detailing.

4.5in (11cm) high

£35-45 set   **MA**

QUICK REFERENCE - SINGLE BOXES

- The 1950s saw the emergence of the cult of the teenager, and rock 'n' roll. 45s with the latest tunes were all the rage, and these cases were mass-produced to store them in. Colourful examples with rock 'n' roll themes such as young jiving or dancing couples tend to be more desirable. Avoid buying examples that are stained, split, or torn.

A 1950s printed vinyl 'Rock N Roll' single box, printed with a design of musical instruments, jiving couple, roses, stars, fashionable cities, and the forenames of jazz musicians.

8in (20.5cm) high

£30-35   MA

A 1950s printed vinyl 'Twist with Ken' single record case, with colourful pattern of musical instruments, with integral handle .

This has nothing to do with Barbie's boyfriend Ken, who arrived on the scene sometime after this case was introduced!

8in (20.5cm) high

£22-28   MA

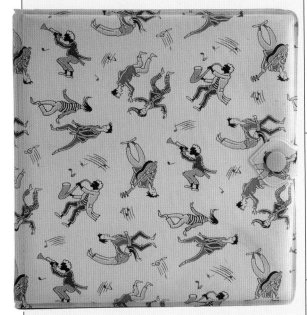

A 1950s printed vinyl 'Rock N Roll' single case, printed with a design of jiving couples and musicians.

8in (20.5cm) high

£30-35   MA

A 1960s German printed vinyl single case, printed with various bottles of alcohol.

8in (20.5cm) high

£20-25   MA

A 1960s printed vinyl single case, with psychedelic circles and lines.

The design recalls the 1960s Op Art movement championed by artists such as Bridget Riley.

8in (20.5cm) high

£20-25   MA

A 1950s German printed vinyl single case, with a stylised design of postal services.

8in (20.5cm) high

£22-28   MA

A 1950s printed vinyl single box, with abstract pattern of pink, light blue, yellow, and beige splotches on a fawn background with random black lines.

As with the table on the previous page, this single box mimics fashionable textiles of the day, such as those designed by Lucienne Day.

8in (20.5cm) high

£25-35   MA

A 1950s painted plaster 'Exotic Lady with a Drum' table lamp, with original glass, in mint condition.

Like the statues on the first page of this section, the paint and indeed the plaster of these lamps is easily damaged, which reduces the value considerably. Be careful of the head, which can often become detached at the neck, despite the wire armature concealed in the plastic. These unusually exotic lamps have become increasingly expensive over recent years, mainly as examples in mint condition have become so rare.

16.5in (42cm) high

£100-150   MA

A 1950s American TV lamp, in the shape of a seated girl gazing upwards, with original paper shade (not shown), in mint condition, the back impressed 'M. FIELACK C'.

Produced in a huge variety of shades and themes, these were placed on top of a newcomer to the 1950s home - the television.

13.5in (34cm) wide

£200-250   MA

A 1950s yellow plastic-coated wire letter rack, with black plastic ball terminals.

6in (15cm) wide

£8-12   MA

A very rare 1950s black finished wire letter rack, modelled as a seated man reading a book, with coloured plastic ball finials.

4.5in (11.5cm) high

£20-25   MA

A 1950s British Dibro 'Fairy Princess' table or tree decoration, lacks pin to fit to stand, with instructions.

5.25in (13.5cm) high

£20-25   MA

A 1950s black-painted cast-metal 'Zulu' bar accessory, the head fitted with a bottle opener, the spears as cocktail sticks, impressed 'MADE IN ENGLAND'.

6.75in (17cm) high

£60-80   MA

A late 1960s Evers pineapple-shaped plastic ice bucket, with glass liner, unmarked.

Without the glass liner, the value of this ice bucket plummets to about half the value of this example.

10.5in (27cm) high

£30-50   MA

QUICK REFERENCE

- The Skrdlovice Glassworks was founded at Skrdlovice, Czechoslovakia, by Emanuel Beránek (1899-1973) in 1942. Early designs were produced by Beránek and his brothers, together with Vlasta Lichtagová and Milena Velísková.
- The company was nationalised by the Communists in 1948. Despite this control, it produced a unique body of work that is of great significance to Czech glass design. Between the 1950s and the 2000s it worked with almost all the talented and important glass designers of the period, including Frantisek Zemek, Pavel Hlava, Jan Kotík, and Vladimír Jelínek.
- From 1962 to 1967, the chief designer was Miloslava Svodobová, with František Vízner taking over until 1976, and Jaroslav Svoboda holding the position from 1969 to 1986.
- All the glass produced was blown and formed by hand at the furnace, (known as 'hutní sklo' in Czech) and a beneficial close bond was fostered between the blowers and the designers.

- Pieces are unsigned, and were marked with a factory or export label only. This has usually been washed away, making identification problematic. Over 4,000 different designs were produced until the factory closed in 2008 as a result of the rise of inexpensive imports from the Far East.
- The market is still very new, and there is much research still to be done. Pieces by the most important designers in the industry, particularly Vízner, are currently the most valuable. However, hallmark designs in typical colours used by the company (such as topaz) are also sought-after by collectors. Size counts, with larger pieces often fetching more.
- Production quantities varied depending on the design and some designs may eventually prove to be scarce as information is uncovered. Once more is known and designs can be firmly attributed many believe that interest in the factory and prices for its works will mushroom.

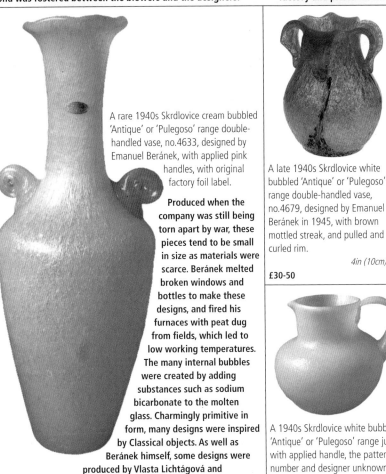

A rare 1940s Skrdlovice cream bubbled 'Antique' or 'Pulegoso' range double-handled vase, no.4633, designed by Emanuel Beránek, with applied pink handles, with original factory foil label.

Produced when the company was still being torn apart by war, these pieces tend to be small in size as materials were scarce. Beránek melted broken windows and bottles to make these designs, and fired his furnaces with peat dug from fields, which led to low working temperatures. The many internal bubbles were created by adding substances such as sodium bicarbonate to the molten glass. Charmingly primitive in form, many designs were inspired by Classical objects. As well as Beránek himself, some designs were produced by Vlasta Lichtágová and Milena Velísková.

11in (28cm) high

£100-150   RBJ

A late 1940s Skrdlovice white bubbled 'Antique' or 'Pulegoso' range double-handled vase, no.4679, designed by Emanuel Beránek in 1945, with brown mottled streak, and pulled and curled rim.

4in (10cm) high

£30-50   RBJ

A 1940s Skrdlovice white bubbled 'Antique' or 'Pulegoso' range jug, with applied handle, the pattern number and designer unknown.

£70-100   RBJ

A rare 1940s Skrdlovice cream bubbled 'Antique' or 'Pulegoso' range double-handled vase, no.4641, designed by Vlasta Lichtágová.

4in (10cm) high

£60-80   RBJ

A 1960s Skrdlovice colourless and green cased triform bowl, no.5991, designed by Emanuel Beránek in 1959, with original 'Bohemia Glass' foil label.

7in (18cm) wide

£25-35   RBJ

GLASS

A CLOSER LOOK AT A SKRDLOVICE VASE

Made for over 30 years, this is a classic Skrdlovice design that can be found in many different colourways and sizes. This particular colourway is distinctively Czech.

It takes its 'Propeller' name from the production process. Jets of compressed hot air were fired at the hot body as it was turned. These jets pushed the glass to form the characteristic 'fins'.

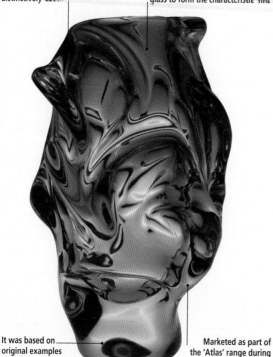

It was based on original examples designed by the artist and teacher Jan Kotík and produced by Emanuel Beránek. These are squatter and have more pronounced fins.

Marketed as part of the 'Atlas' range during the 1960s, it was sold around the world and the look inspired a number of factories including Sweden's Aseda.

A 1950s-80s Skrdlovice amber and green-cased 'Propeller' vase, no.5503, designed by Jan Kotík in 1955.

8.25in (22cm) high

£80-120   RBJ

A 1960s Skrdlovice blue, green, and colourless glass cased 'Andromeda' range vase, no.5346, designed by Jaroslav Beránek in 1953.

Although designed in the 1950s, the 'Andromeda' range was sold primarily during the 1960s. Larger examples currently fetch over £150. Other colours include topaz, rose pink, amethyst, and green. Colourless glass is scarce.

7in (18cm) high

£40-60   RBJ

A 1960s Skrdlovice vase, no.5909, designed by Emanuel Beránek in 1959, with asymmetric blue and pink wells in a rose tinged body.

This sculptural vase shows Beránek's exploration of the 'steam pin' technique and biomorphic forms, which were developed by Timo Sarpaneva for his prize-winning 'Orchid' vases, designed for littala in 1953. The effect is produced by inserting a wet piece of wood into the glass while it is still molten and part-formed. The heat turns the water to steam, which creates a void as it escapes.

10.5in (27cm) high

£70-90   RBJ

A 1960s Skrdlovice green and colourless-cased 'Blanka' range vase, no.5980, designed by Emanuel Beránek in 1959.

8.5in (22cm) high

£50-70   RBJ

A 1960s Skrdlovice blue and colourless-cased basket, no.6239, designed by Jan Beránek in 1962.

This was also made using the 'steam pin' technique described on this page.

6.25in (16cm) high

£50-70   RBJ

A 1960s Skrdlovice triple-cased rose-pink, green, and colourless large vase, no.5988, designed by Jan Beránek in 1959.

Designed by Emanuel's son Jan, this is one of the company's most recognisable designs. It can be found in many different sizes and colours. Examples may be made in a single colour, or be double- or triple-cased. The hallmark swirling body is created using tools to 'pull' the surface into shapes. Jan worked with many Czech glass designers at Skrdlovice for over three decades.

12in (30.5cm) high

£150-200   RBJ

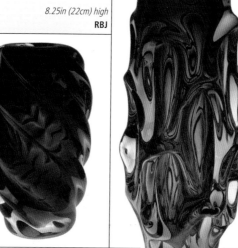

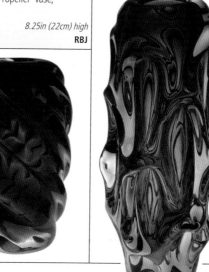

A 1960s-70s Skrdlovice amber-cased light blue 'Galaxy' range vase, no.6532, designed by Miloslava Svobodová in 1965, with golden-amber chips to the exterior.

Larger sizes, which stand around 14in (35.5cm) high, are considerably scarcer than these smaller sizes, and can fetch over five times this price. The textured surface is gained by rolling the core body in glass chips, which are then partially melted into the body in the furnace. This combination of colours is scarce. The colourway of the example on the top right is more common.

8.25in (22cm) high

£100-150   **JPC**

A 1960s-70s Skrdlovice green 'Galaxy' range vase, no.6534, designed by Miloslava Svobodová in 1965, with blue chips to the exterior.

7in (18cm) high

£80-120   **JPC**

A CLOSER LOOK AT A SKRDLOVICE VASE

The technique, developed with Jan Beránek, involved winding a thin thread of hot glass around the core, then immersing it in clear liquid glass. This caused the air to expand and create hundreds of spiralling bubbles of different sizes.

The 'Whirlpool' can also be found in different sizes and colours, and in bowl forms. Large vintage examples are worth the most.

This sought-after design was produced for around three decades. Later examples from the late 1980s-90s tend to be made in brasher colours, and are generally worth under half the value of older examples.

František Vízner (b.1936) is perhaps the most notable and famous glass designer and maker of the late 20thC, and this is one of his hallmark designs.

A 1970s-90s Skrdlovice light green 'Whirlpool' vase, no.6823, designed by František Vizner in 1968, with spiralling pattern of trapped internal air bubbles.

11in (28cm) high

£150-250   **RBJ**

A 1970s-80s Skrdlovice vase, no.7117, designed by František Vízner in 1971, the cylindrical light-brown core with applied colourless prunts.

This design was only available in one size, although precise heights do vary slightly as each piece was handmade.

6.5in (16.5cm) high

£100-150   **RBJ**

A 1970s-80s Skrdlovice colourless-cased cobalt-blue bottle vase, no.7346, designed by František Vízner in 1973, with textured surface.

7in (18cm) high

£150-200   **JPC**

A 1970s-80s Skrdlovice amber-cased colourless vase, no.7610a, designed by Karel Wünsch in 1976, with asymmetric form and well.

Larger versions can fetch around £50-80.

5.5in (14cm) high

£30-40   **RBJ**

GLASS

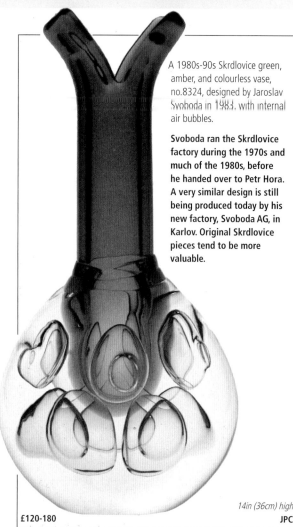

A 1980s-90s Skrdlovice green, amber, and colourless vase, no.8324, designed by Jaroslav Svoboda in 1983, with internal air bubbles.

Svoboda ran the Skrdlovice factory during the 1970s and much of the 1980s, before he handed over to Petr Hora. A very similar design is still being produced today by his new factory, Svoboda AG, in Karlov. Original Skrdlovice pieces tend to be more valuable.

14in (36cm) high
£120-180   **JPC**

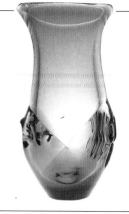

A 1970s-90s Skrdlovice colourless, green, and amber cased vase, no.7633, designed by Ladislav Palecek in 1976.

10.25in (26cm) high
£50-70   **RBJ**

A 1980s Skrdlovice blue and amber-cased vase, no.7919, designed by Ladislav Oliva in 1979, with ribbed sides.

12in (30.5cm) high
£80-120   **JPC**

A 1980s-90s Skrdlovice blue and colourless-cased vase, no.7913, designed by Jan Juda in 1979.

11in (28cm) high
£40-60   **RBJ**

A 1970s-80s Skrdlovice green, blue, and colourless cylindrical vase, no.7233, designed by Jaroslav Svoboda in 1972.

As with the vase above, this design is still made today by Svoboda's new factory.

12.5in (31.5cm) high
£100-150   **JPC**

A 1970s-80s Skrdlovice blue and colourless-cased vase, no.7104, designed by Karel Wünsch in 1971, with tapering body, flared rim and internal random air bubbles.

8.25in (22cm) high
£40-60   **RBJ**

A 1980s-90s Skrdlovice moulded brown and colourless-cased vase, no.8622, designed by Petr Hora in 1986, with textured surface.

7.5in (19cm) high
£40-60   **JPC**

A 1970s Czechoslovakian Chlum u Trebone glassworks ruby red mould-blown textured vase, designed by Jan Gabrhel in 1969.

These can be found in a number of different sizes and shapes along the same theme, with internal air bubbles or this textured finish. The ruby red colour is scarce.

7.5in (19cm) high

£120-180   **GAZE**

A 1950s Czechoslovakian Harrachov Glassworks 'Harrtil' vase, with an internal mesh of fibre devised by Milos Pulpitel, with an asymmetric pulled rim.

8in (20.5cm) high

£120-180   **GC**

A 1960s-70s Czechoslovakian Harrachov Glassworks 'Harrtil' ashtray or bowl, designed by Milan Metelak, the blue body with internal mesh devised by Milos Pulpitel.

4in (10cm) high

£80-100   **GROB**

A CLOSER LOOK AT A PAVEL HLAVA VASE

Pavel Hlava (1924-2003) is one of the most important Czech glass designers of the second half of the 20thC, and his work is slowly being reappraised.

As well as designs for tableware and serial production, Hlava produced a series of progressive and unique hand-blown and -worked 'studio glass' pieces throughout his career.

These were innovatively blown into a variety of objects and materials, including wire cages, bags or sacks, and moulds.

Many were also given internal protrusions, which is a hallmark of his designs.

They were typically produced in a heat-sensitive glass that changed colour from yellow to red, and sometimes red to green to blue, when parts were reheated.

A Czechoslovakian Pavel Hlava studio glass vase or art object, hand-blown and worked in heat-sensitive graduated red-to-orange-to-yellow glass, the base inscribed 'PHlava Czechoslovakia 1969'.

1969   *23in (58cm) high*

£5,000-7,000   **FIS**

A 1960s-70s Czechoslovakian Exbor cased vase, designed by Pavel Hlava in 1957, the tapered facet-cut form cased in a graduated brown-to-colourless glass over an internal pink core, the base with circular acid stamp.

Although this award-winning vase was produced in comparatively large quantities over a couple of decades, the recent market has seen more examples than are likely. Most are probably of recent manufacture. They are typically in brighter colours than the originals, and do not bear the Exbor acid stamp on the base. Most also have minor flaws such as visible 'creases' in the cased layers, or trapped air bubbles.

8.5in (22cm) high

£250-350   **FIS**

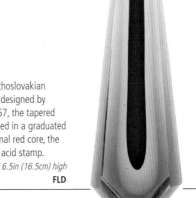

A 1960s-70s Czechoslovakian Exbor cased vase, designed by Pavel Hlava in 1957, the tapered facet-cut form cased in a graduated blue over an internal red core, the base with circular acid stamp.

6.5in (16.5cm) high

£150-250   **FLD**

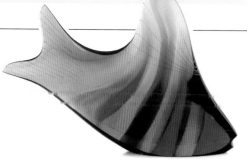

A 1960s Czechoslovakian Exbor cased, cut, and polished 'Perch' fish sculpture, no.70295, designed by Josef Rozinek and Stanislav Honzík from 1958, unmarked.

Glassmaker Rozinek and glass cutter Honzík were inspired to design this stunning range after seeing a series of fish sculptures designed by Vera Lisková for Moser at the 1958 Brussels Exposition. Rozinek was also a keen angler! Introduced in 1959 and promoted heavily during the late 1960s, the range comprised ten different fish in five sizes.

10.5in (27cm) long

£200-250   GC

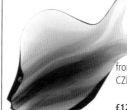

A 1960s Czechoslovakian Mstisov Glassworks or Moser Glassworks vase, designed by Hana Machovska in c1961, from the 'Romana' range, with applied pink and blue side trails on a colourless cased yellow body.

9in (23cm) high

£100-150   FLD

A 1960s Czechoslovakian Exbor cased, cut and polished 'Carp' fish sculpture, no.70293, designed by Josef Rozinek and Stanislav Honzik from 1958, the base with circular 'EXBOR CZECHOSLOVAKIA' acid-etched mark.

6.5in (18cm) long

£120-180   GC

A 1990s Czechoslovakian Crystalex mould-blown black glass vase, designed by Marcela Vosmikova in 1988, with machine-cut rim and printed blue and red lines.

This vase appears almost Postmodern, echoing the work of Ettore Sottsass, Alessandro Mendini, and others for the Studio Alchimia or Memphis groups.

4.5in (11cm) high

£30-40   GC

A 1960s Czechoslovakian Exbor cased, cut, and polished 'Trout' fish sculpture, no.70297, designed by Josef Rozinek and Stanislav Honzik from 1958, the base with circular 'EXBOR CZECHOSLOVAKIA' acid-etched mark.

8in (20cm) high

£200-300   PC

A late 1960s Borské Sklo cylinder vase, from the 'Dual' range designed by Karel Wünsch from 1962, the graduated yellow core cased in a thin layer of red and cut with geometric designs and a flat facet to the front and back, unsigned.

Karel Wünsch (b.1932) is known for his cut works, which he still produces today using high quality blanks made in the 1960s and '70s. His 'Dual' range, with its angular and modern cuts, is highly sought-after. Colours include green, yellow, purple, red, and dark blue. The large cut facets allow light into the forms.

8in (20.5cm) high

£250-300   GC

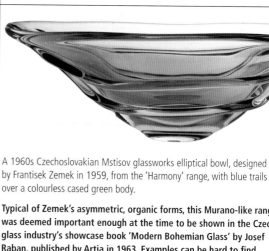

A 1960s Czechoslovakian Mstisov glassworks elliptical bowl, designed by Frantisek Zemek in 1959, from the 'Harmony' range, with blue trails over a colourless cased green body.

Typical of Zemek's asymmetric, organic forms, this Murano-like range was deemed important enough at the time to be shown in the Czech glass industry's showcase book 'Modern Bohemian Glass' by Josef Raban, published by Artia in 1963. Examples can be hard to find today.

11.5in (29.5cm) long

£100-150   PC

QUICK REFERENCE - ITALIAN GLASS

• Not all Italian glass was made on Murano. Other factories, including a number based in and around the town of Empoli near Florence, mass-produced primarily mould-blown glass.
• Many pieces are very similar to famous designs by other factories. These long thin decanters are often attributed to US maker Blenko, particularly if they are in red or yellow. However, if you look closer, the colours and type of glass are different to Blenko's.
• Italian examples are also typically blown into a mould, and may possibly bear mould lines.
• Necks are sometimes lined with plastic, or stoppers are very loose. Most Italian pieces do not bear the pontil marks on the base that indicate a hand-finish.

A 1950s-60s Italian purple vertically ribbed mould-blown floor decanter, with optical effect and shaped stopper.

24.5in (62cm) high

£35-45   RET

A 1950s-60s 'Kingfisher' blue mould-blown floor decanter, with moulded vertically ribbed design and teardrop-shaped stopper.

25.25in (64cm) high

£40-50   RET

A 1950s-60s Italian purple spiral-moulded footed floor decanter, with mould lines and teardrop-shaped stopper.

24.5in (62cm) high

£40-50   RET

A 1950s-60s Italian purple mould-blown floor decanter, with swirling wave design.

22in (55.5cm) high

£20-25   RET

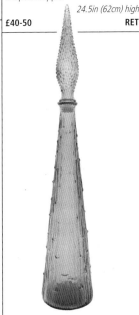

A 1950s-70s Italian Empoli yellow mould-blown floor decanter, the base moulded 'MADE IN ITALY'.

22.5in (57cm) high

£15-20   M20C

A 1950s-60s Italian red conical mould-blown bottle, with elongated teardrop stopper.

25.5in (65.5cm) high

£30-40   RET

GLASS

A 1950s-60s Italian green mould-blown floor decanter, with mould lines and hobnail pattern, with teardrop-shaped stopper.

21.75in (55cm) high

£28-32   **RET**

A 1950s-70s Italian orange-cased opaque white mould-blown baluster vase.

10.75in (27cm) high

£20-25   **RET**

A CLOSER LOOK AT A STOPPERED BOTTLE

- Red-cased opaque-white examples are more desirable and valuable than transparent examples. This large piece has great decorative appeal.

- At first glance, the form of the body is very similar to Otto Brauer's 'Gulvvase', designed for Kastrup-Holmegaard, which suggests a Danish origin.

- The proportions are different, the neck is taller, and the over-sized stopper was not part of Brauer's design. These facts all indicate this piece was made elsewhere.

- The glass is more thinly blown than that of Kastrup-Holmegaard examples, resulting in a lighter weight.

A 1970s probably Italian red-cased opaque white glass bottle, with over-sized stopper, with colourless outer layer.

13in (33cm) high

£80-120   **RET**

A 1950s-70s purple-cased opaque white urn-shaped vase, with applied colourless handles.

14in (35.5cm) high

£40-50   **RET**

A 1950s-60s Italian teal-blue cased opaque white waisted display goblet.

12.5in (31.5cm) high

£32-38   **RET**

A 1950s-60s Italian orange-cased opaque white urn-shaped vase, with applied colourless handles.

8.5in (21.5cm) high

£40-60   **RET**

QUICK REFERENCE

- Mdina Glass was founded in Malta by Michael Harris in 1968. Harris, a former tutor at the Royal College of Art, had become proficient in the new studio glass techniques that had been developed in the USA. At Mdina he began adapting these techniques to commercial production, making unique handmade pieces of art glass. Production was initially aimed at the tourist market, but soon also included valuable export sales in the UK, US, and Germany.
- Pieces are typically chunky, thick-walled, and cased in clear glass. Forms include vases, bowls, dishes, paperweights, and sculptural forms, such as the 'Fish', which is Harris's most characteristic and desirable design. Colours are reminiscent of the Maltese landscape, and include sea greens and blues, and sandy ochres, and browns.
- Although Harris left Mdina in 1972, the company continues to produce his designs today. He founded Isle of Wight Studio

- Glass in the same year, and began to produce new designs. His first ranges, including 'Aurene', were developments of his work at Mdina, and were decorated with broad swirls of mottled colour in deep blues, ochres, browns, and pinks.
- This changed in 1978 with the introduction of the new range 'Azurene', which was flecked with gold or silver leaf. It went on to become a hallmark of the studio's designs. Other popular ranges include 'Kyoto' and 'Golden Peacock'. It's also worth looking out for ranges that were experimental or produced for small periods of time, as these may be valuable.
- Most Mdina pieces are signed with the studio name, and many Isle of Wight pieces bear a sticker. Pieces from either factory signed by Harris are scarce and highly sought-after. Large pieces also tend to fetch a premium.
- Michael Harris died in 1994, but Isle of Wight Studio Glass continues today under his son Timothy and widow Elizabeth.

A mid-1970s to 1980s Mdina Glass 'Lollipop' vase, the interior with two blue and green spheres with silver chloride and a trapped air bubble to either side, covered in a layer of colourless glass, the base inscribed 'Mdina'.

6.75in (17cm) high

£40-60   **FIS**

A 1980s Mdina Glass 'Fish' vase, the mottled translucent pink core covered with transparent blue 'wings', with attenuated neck, the base inscribed 'Mdina'.

7in (18cm) high

£70-100   **FLD**

A large mid-late 1970s Mdina Glass 'Fish' vase, with mottled and striated brown core, with angled 'wings' with traces of silver chloride, and attenuated neck, the base inscribed 'Mdina'.

The angled form indicates that this piece was not made by Michael Harris. Along with the colour, this means the piece must have been made after Harris left Mdina Glass in 1972.

9in (23cm) high

£150-200   **FLD**

A late 1970s Mdina Glass 'Cut Ice Lollipop' vase, from the 'Tiger' range, the marbled blue, green, and brown core covered with a layer of colourless glass and cut with two facets on one side, unmarked.

8in (20cm) high

£120-180   **WHP**

A mid-1970s to 1980s Mdina Glass footed bowl, from the 'Ming' range, with vertical stripes of blue-green and silver chloride to the sandy-coloured interior, the base inscribed 'Mdina'.

5.25in (13cm) diam

£30-40   **FIS**

GLASS

A Mdina Glass bowl, from the 'Tiger' range designed by Joseph Said or Eric Dobson, with random trails of green and brown on a mottled sandy background, the base inscribed 'Mdina 90', with factory plastic label.

1990   *4in (10.5cm) high*

£80-120   FIS

A mid-late 1970s Mdina Glass mould-blown bark-textured mottled brown and amber glass vase, with flared rim, the base inscribed 'Mdina'.

5in (12.5cm) high

£15-20   CAPE

A late 1970s-1980s Mdina Glass bottle vase, the mottled sandy core with a marbled blue, green, and brown band, with an outer layer of colourless glass, unmarked.

6in (15cm) high

£80-100   SWO

An Isle of Wight Studio Glass charger, from the 'Tortoiseshell' range, designed by Michael Harris, the base inscribed 'Michael Harris Isle of Wight'.

Large chargers like this were probably made by Harris himself, as he was one of the few people at the studio with sufficient physical height, strength, and skill to 'spin' the molten gob of glass out into a charger. This piece is also signed by Harris, and it is therefore almost certain that it was made by him.

A 1980s Mdina Glass stoppered bottle, of square section, with applied blue-green trails over a mottled orange body, the base inscribed 'Mdina'.

12in (30cm) high

£50-70   FLD

1973-c1982   *15in (38cm) wide*

£350-450   FLD

Miller's Compares

Mdina Glass versions are typically much thicker and heavier in weight than Isle of Wight Studio Glass examples.

Isle of Wight Studio Glass cylinder vases do not have a tapered foot as this does.

Mdina Glass tortoiseshell objects have flat polished bases, which may or may not be inscribed 'Mdina'. Isle of Wight Studio Glass examples do not have polished bases and typically bear the studio's impressed 'flame' mark shown here.

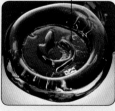

The patterning is very different on Isle of Wight Studio Glass examples, and the banding tends to be more regular. Early examples can have a sandy cream tone to parts of the decoration.

Although Harris may have experimented with the colouring and design of the range before 1972, Mdina's tortoiseshell glass was introduced after he left. The Isle of Wight Studio Glass range designed by him is typically more desirable and valuable.

A late 1970s Mdina Glass footed cylinder vase, with mottled and swirling tonal brown and sandy decoration, with slight iridescent effect, unsigned.

6.75in (17cm) high

£35-45   FLD

A large 1970s Isle of Wight Studio Glass globe vase, from the 'Tortoiseshell' range, designed by Michael Harris, the base with impressed 'flame' pontil mark.

1973-c1982   *7in (18cm) high*

£100-150   FLD

A small Isle of Wight Studio Glass globe vase, from the 'Seaward' range, designed by Michael Harris, the base with plain 'broken' pontil mark and inscribed 'Michael Harris Isle of Wight'.

This was one of the first ranges introduced by Harris after he founded Isle of Wight Studio Glass in 1972. This rare piece was almost certainly made by him.

1973   *4.25in (10.5cm) high*
£180-220   TGM

A CLOSER LOOK AT AN ISLE OF WIGHT VASE

The 'Fish' vase is Harris's most iconic and celebrated design, and is highly desirable to collectors.

It was only produced in this large size and this deep blue colourway for two years.

This example was almost certainly made by Harris, due to the skill it required, and his signature to the base. This makes the piece scarce and desirable, and increases the value.

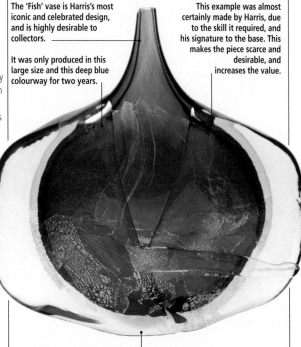

The numbering on the base does not imply a limited edition. Instead it indicates that this piece was sold as part of a group of 500 different shapes and sizes to American retailers such as JC Penney in 1987.

A rare large Isle of Wight Studio Glass 'Fish' vase, from the 'Azurene Blue' range, designed and made by Michael Harris, the cobalt blue core with applied gold and silver leaf, the whole thickly cased in colourless glass, the base signed 'Michael Harris 36/500 England'.

1985-87   *9.5in (25cm) high*
£800-1,200   FLD

A large Isle of Wight Studio Glass 'Lollipop' vase, from the 'Pink Azurene' range, designed by Michael Harris, with 22ct gold and silver leaf decoration, with polished unmarked base.

c1979-94   *10in (24cm) high*
£70-100   FLD

An Isle of Wight Studio Glass cylinder vase, from the 'Nightscape' range, designed by Michael Harris, with randomly swirled trails melted into the body and an iridescent finish, and a polished, unmarked base.

1988-93   *6in (16cm) high*
£150-200   CHT

A small Isle of Wight Studio Glass vase, from the 'Fondant' range, designed by Timothy Harris in 1981, the colourless body overlaid with layers of thin shards of pink and blue glass, with triangular black label to base.

From one of Timothy Harris's first production ranges for his father's studio, this vase is extremely rare. The range was discontinued within a year or so of its introduction as it did not sell well. Buyers incorrectly deemed the bubbles trapped under the shards to be faults.

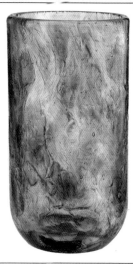

3.5in (9cm) high
£70-90   PC

An Isle of Wight Studio Glass 'Allsorts' perfume bottle, from the 'Bon Bon' range, designed by Michael, Elizabeth, and Timothy Harris, with applied spots and dark iridescent ground.

1989-93   *3.75in (9.5cm) high*
£40-60   TGM

GLASS

QUICK REFERENCE

- Monart glass was produced in Perth, Scotland between 1924 and 1961. The Moncrieff glassworks factory had initially only produced scientific items until the factory's owner's wife, Isobel Moncrieff, persuaded Salvador Ysart, a prominent Spanish glassblower, to develop art glass for the company. The name 'Monart' is thus a hybrid of the names 'Moncrieff' and 'Ysart'.
- Between 1924 and 1933 Salvador and his sons designed over three hundred shapes for vases, jars, and lamps. Much inspiration was drawn from Chinese ceramics, with simple forms displaying rich mottled and swirled patterns.
- Each piece was handmade and is therefore unique in patterning and precise form. Patterns were made with coloured glass chips that were melted into the body and often manipulated into swirls with tools. Tiny metal 'aventurine' flecks may also be included.

- Production of Monart glass ceased in 1939 and resumed on a smaller scale following World War II under Salvador Ysart's son, Paul. Production in this period only ever amounted to around 10% of the company's overall output.
- In 1946 Salvador and his two other sons set up Ysart Brothers Glass where they produced the similar 'Vasart' glass. This is generally slightly less desirable than Monart glass. This company was acquired by Teacher's Whisky in 1964, and the name changed to Strathearn Glass.
- Substantial pieces of Monart can command around £300, but this can rise for particularly scarce decorative effects and forms, such as lampbases. Always examine pieces for cracks, chips, and damage as this can have a detrimental effect on value. Prices reached a peak in the early 2000s, but have suffered somewhat more recently. A revival of interest, and hopefully values, is widely anticipated.

A Monart glass vase, shape SA, cased in colourless glass over a graduated purple and jade green mottled body, with three central purple and bronze aventurine swirls, the base with polished pontil mark.

7in (18cm) high

£180-220   FLD

A Monart glass vase, shape SA, cased in clear crystal over a white and jade green mottled interior with three central purple and bronze aventurine swirls, with polished pontil mark.

7in (18cm) high

£180-220   FLD

A Monart vase, shape SA, decorated with pale blue and green mottles, and with pink and aventurine swirls, the base with polished pontil mark bearing a paper label.

7in (18cm) high

£150-250   L&T

A Monart vase, possibly shape JA, cased in colourless glass over a marbled and streaked shoulder in green, purple, red, and blue, over a mottled lilac ground.

6in (15cm) high

£350-450   FLD

A large Monart vase, colour 42b, of baluster form with a flared mottled blue rim and mottled pink body, the base with ground pontil mark.

8.75in (22cm) high

£120-180   GORL

A Monart footed and shouldered vase, with a shallow collar neck, possibly shape C, cased with colourless glass over a graduated golden amber to red marbled ground.

8in (21cm) high

£300-400   FLD

A Monart glass vase, shape FA, decorated in mottled orange graduating to brown at the shoulder, with aventurine inclusions, the base with polished pontil mark.

9in (22cm) high

£180-220   WW

A CLOSER LOOK AT A MONART VASE

Red is a very rare colour for Monart, particularly in vibrant tones such as this. Red can easily become dark brown if reheated too frequently or for too long in the furnace.

Although traditional, this urn-shaped form is a desirable classic.

The 'Paisley Shawl' pattern is also rare and highly sought-after. It takes its name from the spiralling swirls that almost look like paisley patterns.

Unlike much Monart, the bright colours here are typical of the 'Jazz Age' of the 1930s when the piece was made.

A rare Monart vase, shape JA, with a 'Paisley Shawl' pattern red body, and blue and white mottles and swirls.

9in (22cm) high

£1,200-1,800   L&T

A Monart glass shouldered vase, shape F, with mottles in green graduating to blue, and internally decorated with pulled white columns and air bubbles, cased in colourless glass, the base with polished pontil mark.

This vase was decorated with coloured powdered enamels and glass chips, before the body was blown into a vertically ribbed 'optic' mould, and twisted slightly, to give the near-spiralling vertical lines. As well as this unusual extra step, the colours are also bold and appealing.

9in (23cm) high

£700-1,000   WW

A Monart vase, shape FB, in mottled green graduating to blue, with silver aventurine inclusions, cased in colourless glass, the polished pontil mark with applied paper label.

13in (34cm) high

£350-450   WW

A Monart beaker vase, shape OE, in mottled pale blue with internal bubbles.

9in (23cm) high

£200-300   L&T

GLASS

A Monart vase, shape HB, with a trefoil rim, in mottled graduated green glass cased in colourless glass.

Another example of this vase can be found on p.61 of 'Ysart Glass', the landmark book on the subject by Frank Andrews, Ian Turner, and Alison Clarke, published by Volo in 1990.

10in (24.5cm) high

£80-120   WW

A Monart vase, shape UG, the mottled blue body with internal air bubbles and green swirls, the polished pontil mark with a paper label.

The swirls are made by twisting the hot, decorated glass using glassmaker's tools. Think of how you get the iced decoration on the top of a Bakewell tart - it's the same type of technique, except you twist rather than drag through the streaks.

11in (27.5cm) high

£200-300   CHT

A Monart vase, shape LD, with graduated green to black (dark purple) mottles, with aventurine inclusions.

8in (20cm) high

£120-180   CHT

A Monart vase, in mottled grey and purple with aventurine inclusions, cased in colourless glass, the polished pontil mark with a paper label reading 'Special 435'.

10in (25.5cm) high

£200-300   L&T

A rare Monart jar and cover, shape R, the mottled green body and lid with internal air bubbles and aventurine inclusion, with original paper label to base and retailer's label for 'Watsons China Hall, High Street, Perth'.

7in (17cm) high

£400-600   MAR

QUICK REFERENCE - GLASS BOWLS

- Monart bowls tend to be less desirable to collectors, and so less valuable, than vases. However, there are exceptions. Some scarce bowls, especially if they are very large in size, can be very desirable.
- Applied pattern on glass bowls is nearly always on the underside, due to how such pieces are made and decorated. A glassmaker will apply decoration to the outside of the gob of glass as usual, then blow it slightly, open it up and spin it out into a bowl form. In doing this, the decorated exterior of the gob becomes the bottom side of the bowl. The body has to be transparent, or at least translucent, for the decoration underneath to be seen from the top.

A Monart bowl, shape YE or DF, with combed pink threads and silver aventurine inclusions, cased in colourless glass, the base with polished pontil mark.

17in (42.5cm) diam

£150-200   WW

QUICK REFERENCE - MONART, VASART OR STRATHEARN?

- Although colours, shapes, and patterns can indicate which factory (or period) a piece belongs to, the simplest general way to identify it is to look at the marks on the base.
- Monart pieces bear a concave, polished pontil mark. Bear in mind that this is a standard glass-making technique, so the presence of this feature alone does not mean your piece was by Monart. The colours, pattern, and shape have to match too. The concave area also sometimes holds a circular paper label, as shown above, however most of these labels have been washed away. Any handwritten digits on a label usually indicate the shape and pattern.
- Vasart pieces made from 1946-56 usually bear the word 'Vasart' acid-etched into the base in a script-like font. A black circular label with the company's name may also be found.
- Strathearn pieces, which were made until 1973, are typically marked with an impressed pontil mark of a stylised salmon leaping out of water, as shown above right.

A Vasart beaker vase, the mottled pink body with internal air bubbles and a band of darker pink swirls, the base with etched mark.

7.5in (19.5cm) high

£50-80   PC

A Vasart beaker vase, with orange, white, and brown mottled and swirled decoration, the base with etched mark.

7.5in (19cm) high

£50-80   PC

A Vasart waisted vase with a flared rim, the mottled pink and green body with a band of spiralling inclusions, the base with etched marks.

7.75in (19.5cm) high

£60-80   PC

A Vasart vase, with a flared rim, the mottled pink and green body with a band of spiralling inclusions, the base with etched marks.

7.5in (19cm) high

£70-100   PC

A Vasart ovoid vase, with graduated pink mottles and a prominent band of two-tone green and brown mottled spiralling swirls, the base with etched mark.

1947-64   *10in (25cm) high*

£120-180   PC

GLASS

Judith Picks

It's well worth looking out for glass lamps as they are rarer than vases and consequently tend to fetch higher prices. This is particularly true of lamps made by Monart, and especially those with complex and appealing forms. In 2003, Ysart glass researcher, author, and collector, Ian Turner, sold his private collection at Christie's, London. A rare, tall Monart lamp with a matching shade and a strong Art Nouveau feel to the curving form and serpentine mottled pattern sold for over £3,500.

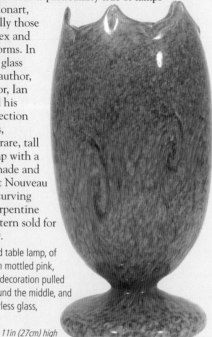

A Vasart footed table lamp, of tulip form, with mottled pink, grey, and blue decoration pulled into swirls around the middle, and cased in colourless glass, unmarked.

11in (27cm) high

£300-500   **WW**

A 1970s Strathearn yellow and brown mottled waisted vase, the central twisted band of brown, red, and blue, the base with impressed leaping fish mark.

7.25in (18.5cm) high

£70-100   **BAD**

A Strathearn mottled brown and yellow vase, with a ring of swirls and multicoloured swirls to waist, cased in colourless glass, the base with leaping salmon pontil mark.

8in (20.5cm) high

£50-70   **PC**

A Strathearn thistle-shaped speckled lime, red, and green posy vase, with paper Strathearn label to base.

3.75in (9.5cm) high

£15-20   **TGM**

A Strathearn glass vase, of footed flared form, with mottled powder blue over jade green with a central band of multicoloured spirals, the base with impressed leaping salmon mark.

9in (23cm) high

£80-120   **FLD**

A Vasart basket, with graduated teal-blue mottles above translucent white mottles, with additional multicoloured chips.

4in (10cm) high

£20-30   **PC**

QUICK REFERENCE

- During the 1950s glass made on the Venetian island of Murano underwent a style revolution. Historic techniques were updated, revived in different methods, and brought forward into the 20thC. Although traditional designs were still made, bright, vibrant colours and stylish modern forms brought Murano glass to the forefront of fashion once again. Modern, abstract art, and sculpture were strong inspirations.
- Factories who led this movement included Venini (founded 1921), Seguso Vetri D'Arte (1933-92), Barovier & Toso (founded 1942), and A.V.E.M (founded 1932). Many employed notable designers to produce their new ranges. These designers included Paolo Venini, Fulvio Bianconi, Flavio Poli, Ercole Barovier, and Dino Martens.
- Value is primarily based on the name of the company and the name of the designer. Some ranges are also scarce, which can add value. Although some pieces are marked, many

are not and original labels have often been removed. Visit museums, collections, and auctions to learn which are the most desirable and valuable designs. Pay close attention, and handle as many verified pieces as possible, as other factories frequently copied successful designs.
- The style revolution continues to this day, and it is worth looking out for designers and makers who became known from the 1970s onwards, such as Pino Signoretto, Vittorio Ferro, Laura Diaz de Santillana, and Dale Chihuly.
- Away from leading designs and designers, appealing and representative pieces can be found for under £100. Look for key themes such as bright colours and modern forms. Also consider technique and size. The larger and more complex a piece is, the more likely it is to be valuable. Examine pieces carefully as chips, scratches and flaws such as bubbles (unless they were intended) will decrease desirability and value.

A Venini 'A Fasce' stoppered attenuated bottle, designed by Fulvio Bianconi in c1953, the colourless body cased in grey, with an orange band over an opaque white ground, with factory paper label numbered '447.9'.

15in (36cm) high

£550-650   QU

A Venini 'A Fasce' stoppered bottle, designed by Fulvio Bianconi in 1956, the colourless body covered with red, and with a turquoise band over an opaque white ground, the base with circular acid-etched 'venini murano Italy' mark.

12.5in (31cm) high

£550-650   QU

A Venini 'A Fasce' cylinder vase, designed by Fulvio Bianconi from 1951-55, the deep violet body overlaid with a red band on an opaque white ground, the base with three line 'venini murano ITALIA' mark.

6in (15cm) high

£250-350   FIS

A Venini 'A Fasce' cylinder vase, designed by Fulvio Bianconi in c1950, the transparent smoky brown glass, internally decorated with a wide orange band, the underside with three line acid-etched 'venini murano italia' factory mark .

7.5in (19cm) high

£800-1,200   DOR

A Venini 'A Fasce' square-section vase, designed by Fulvio Bianconi in c1953, the colourless mould blown body overlaid with cobalt blue, with a yellow band over an opaque white ground, with factory paper label.

This is a very unusual shape for this range.

10in (24.5cm) high

£800-1,200   QU

GLASS

A large Venini 'A Canne' flared vase, designed by Gio Ponti, the colourless body overlaid with red and green vertical canes, the base with engraved signature, and dated '2001'.

At the time this book went to press, this colourway was still available in the Venini catalogue, along with versions in blue and green, red and yellow, and yellow and blue.

2001   *11in (27.5cm) high*
£300-400   **FLD**

A small Venini 'A Canne' flared vase, designed by Gio Ponti in 1955, the colourless glass body overlaid with multicoloured glass rods.

5in (10cm) high
£450-550   **QU**

A small Venini 'A Fasce Verticali' bowl, designed by Fulvio Bianconi in 1951, the colourless glass body overlaid with panels of green, light blue, red and golden-brown glass.

4in (10cm) diam
£350-450   **FIS**

A Venini 'incalmo' vase, designed by Tapio Wirkkala in 1966, with green rounded base and broad grey rim, the base with acid-etched 'venini murano Italia' mark.

7.5in (19.2cm) high
£650-850   **QU**

A Venini 'Tuuli' range 'incalmo' flask, designed by Timo Sarpaneva in 1989, with three fused bands of overlaid glass in blue over opaque white, pale blue, and deep purple, the base engraved 'venini 90 Sarpaneva' and with factory plastic label.

'Incalmo' is a challenging technique, and involves two differently coloured, separate sections of hot glass being joined. Each section must be at a similar heat and of the same size, and the colours must 'work' with each other as the piece cools to avoid cracking. Here the glassmaker joined three separate sections in different colours.

1990   *12.5in (30.5cm) high*
£800-1,200   **QU**

A CLOSER LOOK AT A HANDKERCHIEF VASE

The strong colour is good, and iridescent surfaces are comparatively scarce on Murano glass. Giorgio Ferro's 'Ansa Volante' range for A.V.E.M. is among the most notable examples.

This now iconic form of a falling handkerchief frozen in time and space is typical of the witty and whimsical nature of many post-war designs on Murano.

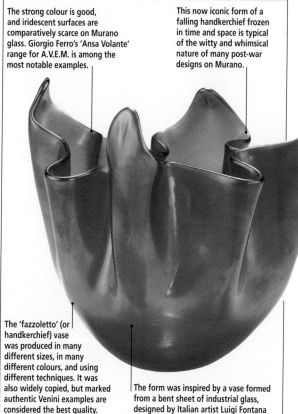

The 'fazzoletto' (or handkerchief) vase was produced in many different sizes, in many different colours, and using different techniques. It was also widely copied, but marked authentic Venini examples are considered the best quality.

The form was inspired by a vase formed from a bent sheet of industrial glass, designed by Italian artist Luigi Fontana

A Venini handkerchief vase, designed by Fulvio Bianconi and Paolo Venini from 1948-49, the deep blue body with an iridescent exterior, the base with 'venini murano Italia' acid-stamp.

5in (10.5cm) high
£450-550   **QU**

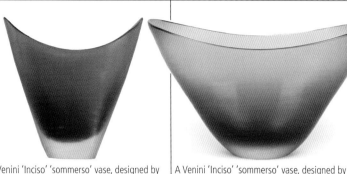

A Venini 'Inciso' 'sommerso' vase, designed by Paolo Venini in 1956, the purple base overlaid with blue and colourless layers, the exterior cut with fine lines, the base with 'venini murano ITALIA' acid-stamp.

5in (15.5cm) high

£800-1,200   QU

A Venini 'Inciso' 'sommerso' vase, designed by Paolo Venini in 1956, the orange body cased in colourless glass, the exterior cut with a series of fine lines.

17in (42cm) long

£1,000-1,500   DOR

A Venini 'Pulegoso' stoppered bottle, designed by Napoleone Martinuzzi in c1930, the diagonally-ribbed translucent green body with random differently sized internal bubbles, the ribs with internal gold foil inclusions, with diagonally-ribbed colourless stopper.

5in (11cm) high

£600-800   QU

Mark Picks

The Diaz de Santillana family are integral to the later history of Venini. In 1959, founder Paolo Venini died, and was succeeded by Venini's widow and their daughter's husband Ludovico Diaz de Santillana as directors. Ludovico's daughter, Laura designed this piece and others from 1976, becoming the artistic director of the company from 1980 to 1985. From 1986 she continued to design for Venini, as well as for her father's new company, EOS Design nel Vetro (est.1986).

This bottle is from a series of six, each with stoppers influenced by organic forms. Many of them resemble cacti or similar simplified plants. Her hallmark use of bold and contrasting colours is shown, as is the Postmodern-feel typical of the period. Although they may be deemed too modern for today's market, her importance to the company and design of the period mean that this (in my opinion) should become an important series in the future.

A Venini 'Monofiori' stoppered bottle, designed by Laura Diaz de Santillana in c1996, the emerald green body with red organic form stopper, the base engraved 'Venini '96'.

1996   *4.5in (11.5cm) high*

£150-250   FRE

A Venini ovoid vase, designed by Laura Diaz de Santillana in 1987, the colourless body cased in violet and with a layer of fragmented gold leaf under an outer layer of colourless glass, the base engraved 'venini 87'.

Fragmented gold foil was used in this manner on Murano during the 1930s. After it is applied, the fragmentation occurs as the body is blown and expanded outwards.

1987   *12.5in (29.5cm) high*

£800-1,200   DOR

A Venini 'Folto' bowl, designed by Mary Ann 'Toots' Zynsky, the turquoise-blue body overlaid with a random network of pink canes with opaque white cores, the base engraved 'Zynsky x venini 1984'.

Mary Ann 'Toots' Zynsky (b.1955) is a well-known American studio glassmaker. Her hallmark designs are made from a large number of extremely thin, vibrantly multicoloured glass rods, fused together to form vessels. Here, coloured rods are used in a different manner. As the application of the rods differs from piece to piece, each piece is effectively unique, thus combining studio and factory glass.

1984   *9in (23cm) diam*

£800-1,200   FIS

GLASS

A Barovier & Toso 'Moreschi' ashtray, designed by Ercole Barovier, the colourless glass body overlaid with 'tiger's eye' panels of honey-brown and brown bordered with golden-brown stripes, the base cut and polished.

The pattern is very similar to Bianconi's c1950 'Pezzato' design for Venini, where alternating panels of rectilinear glass are overlaid onto a colourless glass body.

6.25in (15cm) diam

£300-500   **FIS**

A Barovier & Toso 'Cordonato Oro' vase, designed by Ercole Barovier, the colourless glass ribbed body with pulled and curled rim, and barley-twist columns of gold leaf fragments.

9.5in (25cm) high

£250-350   **FIS**

A Barovier & Toso 'Cordonato Oro' vase, designed by Ercole Barovier in 1950, the colourless cased body with vertical external ribs, and diagonal internal ribs with applied gold leaf inclusions, with cut and pulled neck and rim.

The distinctive 'Cordonato Oro' range is one of Barovier's best-known. Typified by its twisted gold-flecked ribs and pulled rims, it was launched to great acclaim at the Venice Biennale in 1950.

10in (23.5cm) high

£550-750   **QU**

A CLOSER LOOK AT A MURANO VASE

The name is derived from the 'fossilised wood'-like appearance of the design, and refers to the prehistoric Neolithic period.

Historic and traditional techniques, such as threading, had been abandoned during the Novecento movement of the 1920s and 30s, but were revived and reinterpreted during the 1950s as part of a return to crafts.

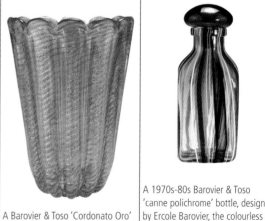

The pattern is made by applying threads of opaque white and brown glass around the body, and then pulling (or 'combing') them into the pattern, a technique used frequently during the Art Nouveau period.

Ercole Barovier experimented widely with 'primitive' and archaic forms and patterns, more so than any other designer and glassmaker on Murano at the time.

A Barovier & Toso 'Neolitico' vase, designed by Ercole Barovier in 1954, the clear glass body cased in colourless glass and internally decorated with brown and opalescent white threads combed into curves, the underside with incised signature.

c1960   *7.5in (22cm) high*

£600-800   **DOR**

A Barovier & Toso 'Cordonato Oro' vase, designed by Ercole Barovier in 1950, the colourless cased body with applied diagonal pink threads and gold leaf inclusions, with scalloped rim.

10in (22.5cm) high

£700-900   **QU**

A 1970s-80s Barovier & Toso 'canne polichrome' bottle, designed by Ercole Barovier, the colourless glass body overlaid with vertical multicoloured bands, and with a blue stopper, the base engraved 'Barovier & Toso murano', and with plastic factory label.

10in (25.5cm) high

£500-700   **FIS**

GLASS

QUICK REFERENCE - SOMMERSO GLASS

- If Murano is best-known for one type of glass, it's the multicoloured, multi-layered cased glass known as 'sommerso'. The term literally means 'submerged', and describes the technique whereby contrasting coloured layers of glass are laid over each other.
- Although the technique of casing glass is historic, it was revived with verve and panache by Flavio Poli during the 1930s, after he became artistic director at Seguso in 1934. The post-war period saw an explosion of rainbow colours being used on clean-lined modern forms.
- In 1950, Poli's 'sommerso' designs for Seguso met with great acclaim at the Venice Biennale and, in 1954, they won the prestigious 'Compasso D'Oro' award, which sealed their popularity. This success led to imitation, and many companies copied the look from the 1950s onwards, but rarely matched the quality. Other notable names include Cenedese and Arte Nuova, but many of the factories and designers remain unidentified. Look out for large examples with a number of different, appealing, coloured layers that have flawless demarcations.

A Seguso Vetri D'Arte 'sommerso' vase, designed by Flavio Poli in c1955, in colourless, green and amber-coloured glass.
7.5in (17.5cm) high

£500-700   QU

A Seguso Vetri D'Arte 'sommerso' vase, designed by Flavio Poli in c1955, in colourless, amber-coloured and yellow glass.
17.5in (44cm) high

£2,000-3,000   QU

A late 1960s-70s Seguso Vetri D'Arte 'sommerso' ovoid footed vase, the blue core overlaid with light green.
15in (39cm) high

£200-300   FIS

A Seguso Vetri D'Arte tapering vase, designed by Archimede Seguso, the colourless body overlaid with translucent white and brown spiralling bands.
c1950 8.75in (22cm) high

£400-600   QU

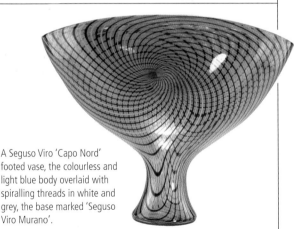

A Seguso Viro 'Capo Nord' footed vase, the colourless and light blue body overlaid with spiralling threads in white and grey, the base marked 'Seguso Viro Murano'.

Seguso Viro was founded by one of Archimede Seguso's two sons, Giampaolo in 1993. In turn, he was joined by his three sons, Gianluca, Pierpaolo, and Gianandrea, thus continuing the family's long-standing connections with Murano glass. The company continues to produce glass using classic techniques today. This spiralling design, featuring 'filigrana' threads, is a hallmark of the company.
c1995   *12.5in (30cm) high*

£1,000-1,500   QU

An Archimede Seguso 'Canne Traversale' dish, the colourless asymmetric body with overlaid alternating dark violet and white zanfirico rods.
c1960   *7in (18cm) wide*

£200-300   FIS

QUICK REFERENCE

- 'Fenici' is Italian for 'Phoenician'. The style of this decoration is inspired by that of the ancient Phoenicians, who were among the earliest people to make glass. Thin molten glass threads are applied to the body, and then 'combed' in up to two directions using a special hooked tool known as a 'maneretta'.

- Although it was also made by other glass companies, Fratelli Toso became renowned for this type of 'historical' glass during the early 20thC, particularly for their use of challenging colours and types of glass such as red, opaque white, and opalescent glass. Values vary depending on the size, colours used and shape, with some of the very best combinations fetching over £2,000.

A Fratelli Toso 'Fenici' conical vase, the colourless glass overlaid with translucent thin white and orange casings, and with applied and 'combed' red, white, green and violet-blue trails melted into the matt surface.

c1910   *8in (20.5cm) high*

£250-350   **FIS**

A Fratelli Toso 'Fenici' double-handled urn vase, the dark violet body overlaid with 'combed' trails of green, red and white, with applied handles.

c1910   *5.5in (14cm) high*

£150-200   **FIS**

A Fratelli Toso 'Fenici' jug with pulled spout, the dark violet body overlaid with 'combed' trails of green, red and white, with applied handle.

Although this piece was made in the early 20thC, similar examples (often including gold foil inclusions) were made in the early 1950s.

5.5in (14cm) high

£150-200   **FIS**

A CLOSER LOOK AT A MURRINE VASE

Fratelli Toso revived many ancient Roman and Phoenician techniques, such as applied and 'combed' trailing, during the early 20thC, but they became most celebrated for their revival of murrines, particularly in pieces made after World War II.

Ermanno Toso was one of Fratelli Toso's most talented artistic directors, who produced complex murrines in vibrant colours. This is an excellent example, and is extremely rare today as so few pieces of this complexity were produced due to their expense, and often time-consuming and experimental nature.

Glass rods containing a colourful, longitudinal pattern made up of smaller glass rods are sliced into thin circular slivers, known as murrines, and are fused onto colourless bodies in the heat of the furnace.

The annual Redentore Festival commemorates the end of the plague that claimed the lives of over 50,000 Venetians in 1576, and the building of the celebratory Redentore church in Venice. The colours of this vase recall stained glass windows.

A Fratelli Toso 'Gran Redentore' vase, designed by Ermanno Toso in c1960, the colourless glass body overlaid with fused polychrome murrines of different shapes, with a matt surface, with two factory paper labels, one handwritten with 'Redentore L/C'.

12.5in (33cm) high

£20,000-30,000   **QU**

A Fratelli Toso 'Nerox' bottle vase, designed by Ermanno Toso in 1962, the colourless glass body overlaid with fused murrines with transparent blue cores and iridescent edges.

12.5in (31cm) high

£1,800-2,200   **QU**

A Fratelli Toso 'a murrine floreale' urn vase, the dark blue body with fused floral murrines in green, bright yellow, red and blue, with applied buds and stems, the exterior with matt acid-etched surface.

c1920   *5in (14cm) high*

£650-850   **QU**

A large 1960s Cenedese flared 'sommerso' vase, designed by Antonio da Ros, with yellow and red layers, and internal trapped air bubble near the base.

15in (39.5cm) high

£3,000-4,000   **QU**

A 1960s Cenedese 'sommerso' attenuated bottle, designed by Antonio da Ros, with colourless glass over a red core. 2

7.5in (70cm) high

£1,000-1,500   **QU**

A Vittorio Ferro glass vase, made at Vetreria de Majo, the colourless glass body overlaid with fused murrines in marbled turquoise and grey, with iridescent veins, the base inscribed 'Vittorio Ferro'.

c2000   *10in (27cm) high*

£1,200-1,800   **QU**

Mark Picks

Despite being made so recently, murrine vases by Venetian maestro Vittorio Ferro (b.1932) have been strong sellers at auction. The best examples can fetch more than their original price, depending on where and when they were bought, which is very unusual for such contemporary glass on the secondary market.

Ferro was perhaps the most talented glassmaster at Fratelli Toso. He worked there for over 30 years until the 1980s, producing many of their most desirable works. After leaving, he went on to design and make his own murrine works at the De Majo and Fratelli Pagnin factories. His vibrant colours (typical of postwar Murano glass), his unique iridescent veined murrines, and the respect he commands within the Muranese glass community mean that values are sure to remain stable, if not rise further.

A Vittorio Ferro glass vase, made at the Vetreria de Majo, the colourless glass body with fused murrines in marbled red, green and blue, the base engraved 'Vittorio Ferro'.

c2000   *12.5in (29.8cm) high*

£800-1,200   **QU**

An A.V.E.M. 'Bizzantina' or 'Tutti Frutti' bowl, the interior with sections of multicoloured rods, gold and silver foil inclusions, and murrines, and red exterior.

7in (17.5cm) diam

£30-40   **WW**

A Yoichi Ohira 'A Canne' 'incalmo' vase, made by De Majo, the colourless lower body with applied colourless, turquoise, yellow and black canes, the neck and rim in smoke-grey glass with an applied turquoise rim, the base engraved 'de Majo Murano Y.Ohira 1990'.

Unlike Vittorio Ferro, Japanese-born Yoichi Ohira designs glass, rather than making it. As well as working with the De Majo factory, he has also worked with maestro Andrea Zilio at Anfora. His deceptively complex designs are held in high regard by glass collectors globally.

1990   *10in (25.7cm) high*

£800-1,200   **QU**

GLASS

A large 1960s-70s Murano glass 'sommerso' vase, with green core, yellow layer and colourless outer layer.

18in (46cm) high

£200-300   **FLD**

A 1960s-70s Murano glass 'sommerso' vase, with pulled neck, aubergine-grey core, turquoise glass layer, and colourless outer layer.

13in (33.5cm) high

£100-150   **WW**

A 1960s-70s Murano glass 'sommerso' vase, after a design by Flavio Poli for Seguso, the blue core overlaid with a darker blue layer, a brown-pink layer, and an outer colourless layer.

Although the rim and aperture are different, the form is very similar to Poli's designs, such as the 'Valva' range of the 1950s.

8in (21cm) high

£120-180   **WW**

QUICK REFERENCE - COPYING ON MURANO

- **Murano has been home to many glass factories since the 13thC. Even though the number during the mid-late 20thC 'golden age' was lower than in previous centuries, and has declined since, there were still enough to ensure strong competition in a limited market. Factories that could not employ the most talented designers often relied on copying the styles of others to become commercially successful.**

- **The 'sommerso' style was perhaps the most prolifically copied (see p219), but this vase is another great example. The avant garde style of the decoration was devised by artist Dino Martens (1894-1970) for Aureliano Toso around 1948-52. Named 'Oriente', these 'painterly' pieces were all unique and created a stir at the time. Highly priced, and highly sought-after, other companies soon attempted to copy them. Although the choice of colours are right on this piece, the tones and application are not, and it lacks the large star-like murrines and additional colours found on authentic examples. The form is also not as well-made or balanced as those by Martens.**

- **The best authentic Aureliano Toso pieces by Martens can fetch over 20 times the price this example fetched! So, given that modern fakes are becoming harder and harder to spot, it's important to buy from a reputable source.**

A 1960s-80s Murano glass 'sommerso' ovoid bowl, the deep pink core overlaid with a blue layer and a colourless outer layer.

5.9in (15cm) high

£40-60   **WHP**

A 1950s-60s Murano glass ovoid vase, with pulled and curled rim, the colourless glass body applied with copper aventurine, melted chips in orange, yellow, turquoise and black, unsigned, but with Murano glass label to base.

10in (25.5cm) high

£350-450   **ROS**

A late 20thC Murano glass tricorn dish, the colourless body decorated with melted chips in brown, red, blue, white and copper aventurine, almost certainly from the 'Oriente' range by Aureliano Toso, and designed by Dino Martens.

8in (21cm) wide

£800-1,200   **FLD**

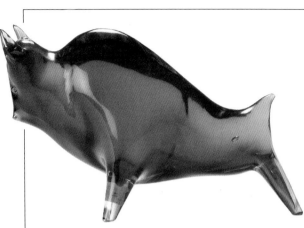

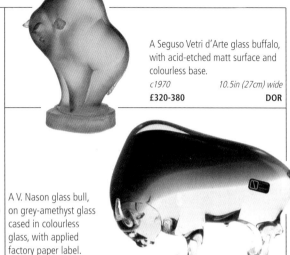

A Seguso Vetri d'Arte glass buffalo, with acid-etched matt surface and colourless base.

c1970   *10.5in (27cm) wide*

£320-380   **DOR**

A V. Nason glass bull, on grey-amethyst glass cased in colourless glass, with applied factory paper label.

11in (28cm) wide

£70-100   **WW**

A Seguso Vetri D'Arte 'Toro Giallo, Blue, Violetto' 'sommerso' glass bull, designed by Flavio Poli, with green, violet and blue body.

c1962   *7in (17.5cm) high*

£850-950   **VZ**

A Seguso Vetri D'Arte 'Pesce Rosso Blu' 'sommerso' glass fish, model no.9824, designed by Flavio Poli, the blue core cased in red and an outer layer of colourless glass, with factory label and inscribed '117'.

19.5in (49.5cm) long

£800-1,200   **VZ**

A Cenedese 'sommerso' fish, designed by Antonio da Ros in c1960, with pink and blue internal layers and hotworked features.

13.5in (34cm) long

£400-600   **FIS**

A 1950s-60s Murano glass dolphin table lamp, the red glass body with applied clear glass details with aventurine inclusions, and applied glass cane eyes, unsigned, but with applied 'Murano Glass' paper label.

19in (49cm) high

£60-90   **WW**

A large late 20thC Murano glass stylised whale, the grey-tinted colourless body graduating to opaque white, with internal grey stripes, the base engraved 'P.Salvatore'.

14in (35cm) long

£200-300   **FLD**

GLASS

A CLOSER LOOK AT A PAIR OF ANIMAL FIGURINES

Artist, caricaturist, illustrator and designer Fulvio Bianconi produced his first figurines for the 1948 Biennale, with ranges such as 'Grotteschi' and 'Commedia del'Arte' including carnival characters, such as musicians, acrobats and masked guests.

Most were produced in witty, heavily stylised forms with white bodies thoughtfully embellished with coloured glass details, which are time-consuming to apply. They arguably avoid the 'kitsch' nature of many other Murano glass figurines.

A pair of Venini 'Gallo E Gallini' figurines of a rooster and a hen, designed by Fulvio Bianconi in c1950, the opaque white glass bodies decorated with multicoloured threads, applied stripes, and pulled features.

7.25in (18cm) high

£1,000-1,500　　　　　　**LHA**

The earliest examples were made with great care by maestro Arturo 'Boboli' Biasutto. Many designs were produced for decades. Early examples usually have the Venini acid-stamp on the base, but this is not always the case. Always look for quality of manufacture and signs of age.

His human characters are more popular with most collectors than his animals. These unmarked examples are probably later re-issues.

A Seguso Vetri d'Arte glass cat, with graduated grey body, grey head and curled opaque grey bow, colourless ears, and applied grey and white eyes.

As well as being by a notable factory, the eccentric and amusing form also contributes to the value. Animals like this are not easy to make, with each feature formed using different tools to manipulate the molten glass.

c1960　　　　*9.5in (24cm) high*

£1,200-1,800　　　　　　**DOR**

A pair of Mazzega dark green opaque glass elephants, with raised trunks and applied opaque white tusks and eyes.

These would have been challenging to make, given the number of pulled features. Elephants with their trunks raised are a symbol of good luck.

1940　　*Largest 8.75in (22.5cm) high*

£650-750　　　　　　**DOR**

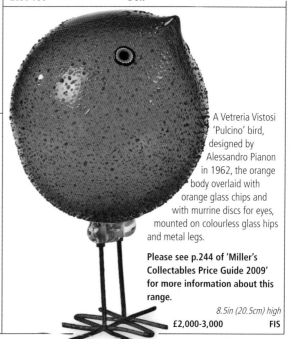

A Vetreria Vistosi 'Pulcino' bird, designed by Alessandro Pianon in 1962, the orange body overlaid with orange glass chips and with murrine discs for eyes, mounted on colourless glass hips and metal legs.

Please see p.244 of 'Miller's Collectables Price Guide 2009' for more information about this range.

8.5in (20.5cm) high

£2,000-3,000　　　　　　**FIS**

A Cenedese glass dog, designed by Antonio da Ros in c1960, the neodymium glass body with applied murrines in red, blue and green, with hotworked face and paws.

7.25in (18.5cm) high

£100-150　　**FIS**

A Barovier & Toso 'Efeso' dove, designed by Ercole Barovier in 1964, the dark cobalt blue glass containing a network of random tiny bubbles.

4.75in (12cm) high

£180-220　　**FIS**

MILLER'S

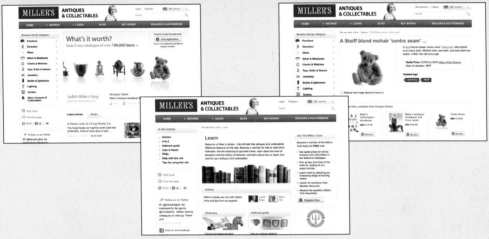

Check out the brand new website at
www.millersonline.com

Miller's Antiques Price Guide
2012-2013

Miller's Costume Jewellery

Whether you're buying or selling,
take Miller's with you

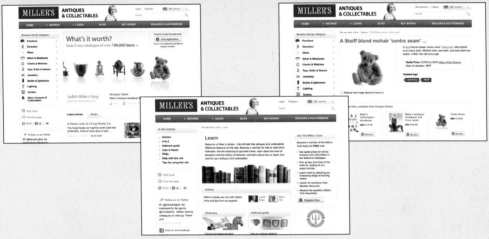

GLASS

A Pino Signoretto 'corroso' glass figurine, designed and made by Pino Signoretto, in the form of a crouching man wearing a hat, the base signed 'Pino Signoretto, Murano'.

Pino Signoretto (b.1944) is one of the most notable living glass designers and maestri on Murano today. He opened his first studio in 1978, and has travelled the world working with artists such as Dale Chihuly and Jeff Koons. The matt 'corroso' effect, which looks here like heavily weathered stone, is gained by treating the surface with acid. The stone-like colours on this would have been added using powdered coloured enamel.

8in (20cm) high

£350-450   **TRI**

A pair of 1950s-70s Murano glass figurines of a flamenco dancer and matador, in white, red and black glass with colourless glass gold aventurine trim.

Compare the style of these to the chickens on the previous page. Many collectors who like Bianconi's chickens and similar characters find these types of figurines 'kitsch' and unappealing. Even though they were largely mass-produced, they nevertheless require skill to make and they do have their fans. Are you among them?

15in (39cm) high

£200-300   **FLD**

A Murano glass 'Diana' statue, inspired by Karl Hagenauer, probably designed by Guido Balsamo Stella and produced by S.A.L.I.R.

This dainty statue was created using the 'lampworking' technique where a small burner is used to melt glass rods so they can be manipulated and joined together. Practised around the world, it is most often associated with the Bimini factory and the town of Lauscha in Germany.

1930-32   *8.75in (22cm) high*

£500-700   **DOR**

A 1990s Murano lampworked red, black and blue glass figurine of a devil playing a guitar, by Lucio Bubacco, the base engraved 'BL'.

1990   *8.25in (21cm) high*

£300-400   **FIS**

A late 20thC Venini 'Costume Regionale' figurine, designed by Fulvio Bianconi in c1950, with green millefiori style murrines, and vertical rods of alternating pink filigrana and white circular murrine designs, unmarked.

8in (20cm) high

£300-400   **WW**

A pair of 1950s-70s Murano glass figurines of a lady and gentleman, in elaborate red costumes with applied white borders and amber glass frills.

16.5in (42cm) high

£120-180   **DUK**

QUICK REFERENCE

- Over the past few years, increased media coverage outside of specialist publications combined with a reappraisal by collectors has caused a surge of interest in Scandinavian glass, and a corresponding rise of prices paid.
- The style of Scandinavian glass has evolved significantly since World War II, but nature has been a strong inspiration throughout. 1950s designs typically feature curving forms, asymmetric styles, and cool, sometimes austere colours.
- The 1960s saw an era of clean lines, bright colours, and a geometric Modern style that gradually gave way towards the end of the decade to the more textured forms of the 1970s.
- A number of factories were at the forefront of production including Orrefors, Kosta Boda, Riihimäen Lasi Oy, and Holmegaard. Also look out for the work of designers who defined, influenced, and embodied the movement, such as Tapio Wirkkala, Sven Palmqvist, and Vicke Lindstrand.

- Examine the base as engraved marks can help with identification and dating. With a little experience, designer and maker are also easily distinguished by colour, technique, and the overall style of the piece. It may be worth researching secondary factories, designers, or ranges that are not currently as popular as some of the 'greats', as, if the quality is there, these may prove to be wise investments.
- As well as the maker and designer, 'eye appeal' is also important. Appealing designs that represent the era should be desirable. Consider also how a piece has been made as hand-blown vases are generally worth more than mould-blown examples, particularly if the techniques used are complex. Examine pieces thoroughly for chips, cracks, and water damage as this will have a detrimental effect on the value.

A 1960s Kosta vase, designed by Vicke Lindstrand, the blue core cased in colourless glass, with original paper label, the base engraved 'Kosta 41825 V Lindstrand'.

6in (16cm) high

£120-180   MAR

A Kosta 'Dark Magic' cased vase, designed by Vicke Lindstrand, the base inscribed 'KOSTA LH 1605'.

The 'L' in the 'LH' prefix indicates it was designed by Lindstrand, the 'H' indicates hand-formed glass. The numbers can help to identify the period when the piece was designed.

c1959   *5in (12.5cm) high*

£250-300   PC

A 1950s-60s Kosta tapering ovoid vase, designed by Vicke Lindstrand in 1955, with internal spirals of burgundy threads, the base inscribed 'KOSTA LH 1405'.

6.25in (16cm) high

£120-180   MHT

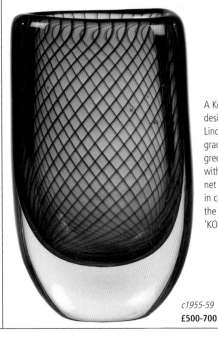

A Kosta glass vase, designed by Vicke Lindstrand, the graduated blue and green glass core with an overlaid net of lines, cased in colourless glass, the base engraved 'KOSTA LH 1589'.

c1955-59   *9in (23cm) high*

£500-700   FIS

A Kosta Boda 'Mirage' series green and blue glass vase, designed by Göran Wärff, the base inscribed 'Kosta Boda GWTH 1040103'.

Note how Wärff has updated Kosta's well-known cased and coloured curving forms for the 21stC.

c2008   *7in (18.5cm) high*

£80-120   CHT

GLASS

A Kosta 'Vår' (Spring) ovoid vase, designed by Vicke Lindstrand, with dark burgundy-brown vertical trails representing trees and applied orange, green, brown, and red spots resembling leaves, the base with 'LINDSTRAND KOSTA' acid stamp and inscribed 'LU 2010'.

The 'LU' prefix here shows that this was from Lindstrand's 'Unica' (Unique) series of the early to mid-1950s. Despite the name, many examples were made, and they are only unique in the slight variations that occur between entirely handmade pieces. The series included 'Vår', 'Sommer', 'Höst', and 'Vinter' vases, each representing a season, and the 'Abstracta' range.

c1950-51   *7in (18cm) high*

£1,000-1,500   **FIS**

A 1980s Kosta Boda 'Artist's Collection' glass bowl, no.58137, designed by Bertil Vallien, the colourless core with a green mottled rim, and a lightly iridescent deep-brown mottled body, the base with etched marks.

7.5in (18cm) wide

£60-80   **WW**

A 1980s Kosta Boda 'Artist's Collection' bottle vase, designed by Bertil Vallien, with powdered enamel decoration and moulded abstract celestial motifs, signed 'Boda Artist B. Vallien 48330'.

5.75in (14.5cm) high

£70-100   **PC**

A CLOSER LOOK AT A KOSTA BODA VASE

Stockholm-born Ulrica Hydman-Vallien (b.1938) studied glass and ceramics at the Stockholm College of Art under Stig Lindberg, and joined Kosta Boda in 1972.

She is also a talented artist, and this influence can be seen clearly in her works, which often feature Expressionist painted designs.

She is inspired by nature, Classical themes, mythology, and human existence in a contemporary and unique way.

Her work is arguably yet to be properly appreciated by many collectors.

Djurgården is an island in central Stockholm with extensive forests and meadows, which acts as a place of relaxation and escape for city-dwellers, a 'Garden of Eden' perhaps. Hydman-Vallien hints at this in her depiction of Adam and Eve on this vase, which was produced for the island.

A Kosta Boda 'Unik' vase, designed by Ulrica Hydman-Vallien in 1986, the colourless glass body with a matt surface, with melted-in amber and claret-red powder inclusions, and stylised figures of Adam, Eve, and the devil painted in coloured enamels, the base inscribed 'Kosta Boda Unik 310860128 Ulrica H.V, För Djurgården 1986', and with maker's label.

1986   *10in (23.3cm) high*

£300-400   **QU**

A 1990s Kosta Boda 'Can Can' footed bowl, no.59147, designed by Kjell Engman in 1991, with mottled powdery lustre body on an aquamarine base with orange banding, the base with engraved marks.

10in (26cm) high

£120-180   **L&T**

A Kosta Boda 'Boat' cast-glass sculpture, designed by Bertil Vallien, with polished surface, internal stripes, and powdered enamel decoration, signed 'KOSTA BODA B. Vallien ATELIER 305869003 800053', on a wooden base.

It's worth comparing this example to the one shown on p.291 of 'Miller's Collectables Price Guide 2009' (N.B. different in US. p.260). The sculpture shown here is much smaller and much less detailed, which explains why it's worth a little over a tenth of the price of the one featured in the previous guide. It's also an 'Atelier' design, meaning it was produced in quantity, rather than as a one-off.

6.75in (17.5cm) long

£200-250   **FIS**

Miller's Compares

The Graal technique was developed in 1917 by glassmaster Knut Bergqvist and designer Simon Gate. The pattern is etched, cut, or engraved onto the core body.

The body is then cased in colourless glass and blown outwards to its final form. As no or very little air is captured in the design, lines and details tend to be finer and more definite.

The sandblasted body is then cased and blown like Graal, but the trapped air bubbles in the sandblasted cavities create a more rounded, fluid form.

The Ariel technique was developed later, in 1937, by Vicke Lindstrand. The pattern is created by sandblasting the design into the core body.

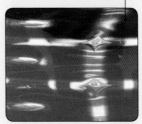

An Orrefors 'Fiske-Graal' bowl, designed by Edward Hald, with wavy border and internally decorated with fish swimming among seaweed, engraved to the base 'Orrefors, Sweden, Graal, 16886, Edward Hald'.

The 'Fiske-Graal' (Fish Graal) design was designed by Hald and produced 1937-88. Values vary depending on the complexity of the design, and the date. Earlier examples are generally more valuable.

5.25in (13cm) wide

£450-650   DUK

An Orrefors 'Ariel' bowl, designed by Edvin Öhrström, the thick glass wall with radiating burgundy and clear square patterns, with central trapped air bubble, the base inscribed 'Orrefors Ariel No.500M Edvin Öhrström'.

7.25in (18.5cm) diam

£450-650   TEN

A Swedish Orrefors 'Slip-Graal' pear, designed by Edward Hald, with an internal network of blue threads, amber tinting, and a colourless ribbed glass casing, the base engraved 'ORREFORS S. Graal 1879 E5 Edward Hald'.

1975   *9.5in (25cm) high*

£250-350   FIS

A late 1960s Orrefors 'Graal' bowl, designed by Gunnar Cyrén, the blue body with opaque lime green bands and spots below a stylised foliate band, the base with inscribed marks.

Gunnar Cyrén (b.1931) designed for Orrefors 1959-70, and introduced bright, opaque colours to the factory in 1966. His designs, particularly the 'Pop' glasses, created quite a stir at the time, partly as the company was known for transparent glass in cool and sober colours.

9in (23cm) diam

£200-300   DRA

An Orrefors 'Ariel' bowl, designed by Edvin Öhrström in c1952, with alternating columns of burgundy glass and trapped air bubbles, cased in colourless glass, the base with etched marks.

5in (12cm) diam

£200-300   WW

A 1980s Orrefors 'Expo' collection vase, designed by Anne Nilsson, the base inscribed 'Orrefors 100 Expo 5034-25'.

Nilsson (b.1953) worked at Höganäs 1980-82, Orrefors 1982-99, Kosta Boda 2001-05, and now designs for Swedish furniture giant IKEA. This piece is accompanied by an original Expo certificate.

13.5in (34cm) high

£100-150   FRE

GLASS

A Holmegaard olive-green 'Gulvvase' vase, designed by Otto Brauer in 1962, with original Holmegaard paper label.

17.5in (42cm) high

£70-100   **WW**

A Holmegaard green ovoid vase, no.15469, designed by Per Lütken in 1955, the base inscribed with factory marks and '19PL61'.

Always examine these forms carefully when buying. Flaws such as creases or bubbles indicate a second and will reduce the value considerably, particularly with experienced or dedicated collectors. Perfect examples of the largest size, 15-16in (38-41cm) high, can exceed £1,000 if in mint condition.

1961   *9.5in (24.5cm) high*

£250-300   **PC**

A Holmegaard smoky-grey 'Thule' vase, no.16949, designed by Per Lütken in 1957, with asymmetric rim, the base engraved with factory marks and '19PL60'.

9in (23cm) diam

£70-100   **DUK**

A Holmegaard Sapphire blue 'Selandia' asymmetric glass bowl, no.14595, designed by Per Lütken, with engraved marks to the base.

Introduced 1955   13in (33cm) wide

£50-70   **WW**

A late 1970s Holmegaard 'Neck Glass', no.3211004, designed by Christer Holmgren in c1975, with original leather cord and box.

The box states: 'Neck-glass. The glass that hangs round your neck. This glass solves an old problem - where to put your glass at a party or a reception and then remember which glass is yours. With the new Holmegaard neck-glass you need never say no to a drink because you'll always have a glass to hand - or rather a glass round your neck. Our neck-glass also leaves you a hand free to smoke, eat, shake hands - or even hold another drink. It's quality. It's handblown. It's a lot of fun.'.

7.25in (18.5cm) high

£30-50   **ZI**

A small Danish Holmegaard handled frigger bowl, from the 'Cascade' series designed by Per Lütken in c1975, with multicoloured melted-in glass chips on an opaque white ground

A 'frigger' is a (usually) unique piece made by a glassmaker either at the end of a day, or to use up the very last remains of a batch of glass. They were often given as gifts, and may be functional or decorative. Their value depends on their size and complexity, and, where applicable, the demand for the range to which they relate.

3.75in (9.5cm) high

£150-200   **ZI**

QUICK REFERENCE - OIVA TOIKKA

- It's easy to see that Oiva Toikka's designs don't follow the usual themes of Scandinavian glass. If anything, their iridescent, trailed designs hark back to Art Nouveau glass, although the forms and often 'rustic' feel are entirely unique to him. This difference is something he seems to revel in as, when asked about this, he describes his work as 'baroque...an irregular pearl'.
- Born in 1931, he trained at the Helsinki design school as a ceramicist from 1953-60, while also producing designs for Arabia. He has also produced theatrical set designs, and textile designs for Marimekko. He joined Nuutajärvi Notsjö in 1963, and introduced his most famous range, these stylised birds, in 1973.
- This range is now hotly collected around the world. Look out for limited editions, those in unusual colours, or those that were only produced for short periods of time. Later examples of this bird, which was produced for a number of years, have silvery-iridescent glass heads, rather than colourless. A range of birds continues to be produced by Iittala, Nuutajärvi's new owner, today. Every year a new design is released.

A Nuutajärvi Notsjö glass 'Alli' bird, designed by Oiva Toikka in 1980, with alternating bands of cream mottled green, 'pulled in' at the wing, the base with inscribed factory and artist's marks.

Introduced 1980   *5in (13cm) high*
£100-150   **TRI**

A Nuutajärvi Notsjö glass 'Pheasant', designed by Oiva Toikka in 1981, the iridescent body with pulled trailed threads, with original factory label, the base with inscribed factory and artist's marks.

Introduced 1981   *10in (23cm) wide*
£100-150   **WW**

A Nuutajärvi Notsjö vase, designed by Oiva Toikka c1965, the colourless glass body with combed applied threads in opaque white, blue, green, and brown, with a heavy iridescence, the base inscribed 'O. Toikka Nuutajärvi Valio', and with maker's plastic label.

7.5in (16.5cm) high
£200-300   **QU**

A Nuutajärvi Notsjö glass display goblet, designed by Oiva Toikka in c1974, with an off-white bowl on a brown and cream bulbous glass stem and foot, the base with engraved manufacturer's marks.

1975-78   *12in (30.5cm) high*
£250-350   **PC**

A Nuutajärvi Notsjö 'Prism' cut cased glass vase, designed by Kaj Franck in 1954, the burgundy core overlaid with colourless and light blue glass, the base engraved 'K. Franck Nuutajäärvi Notsjö'.

The stark, minimalist shape is typical of Franck's work.

c1960   *6.5in (16.5cm) high*
£300-400   **FIS**

A Nuutajärvi Notsjö colourless-cased yellow 'Saturnus' (Saturn) vase, designed by Jaakko Niemi in 1962, the base with engraved marks.

c1962   *9.25in (23cm) high*
£150-200   **PC**

GLASS

A 1960s Ekenäs green glass vase, designed by John Orwar Lake, with an applied band of moulded knobbles.

5.5in (14cm) high

£30-50   PC

A large Flygsfors 'Coquille' range vase, designed by Paul Kedelv, of flared cylindrical form with four oval apertures below four pulled points, cased in clear crystal over pink and white, with engraved signature.

17in (42cm) high

£150-200   FLD

A CLOSER LOOK AT A GLASS BOWL

This piece appears in the Iittala catalogue from 1951 to 1960. This piece is therefore scarcer than other Wirkkala designs that were produced for many years, such as the 'Ultima Thule' range.

Wirkkala (1915-1985) was heavily influenced by nature, often by forms seen on walks through the Finnish countryside. This curving form is clearly inspired by an open flower or a toadstool.

The piece is very practical, and shows Wirkkala's keen understanding of the elements of design the post-war Scandinavians became renowned for.

It is from a series of similar vases and bowls finely cut with lines. Look out for the 'Kantarelli' (Chantarelle) vase, which is taller and has only one peak in the rim. Original examples made from 1948 to 1957 can fetch around £2,000!

A 1950s Iittala glass footed bowl, no.3523, designed by Tapio Wirkkala in 1951, the one-piece foot, stem, and bowl with finely cut vertical lines, the base inscribed 'Tapio Wirkkala Iittala 3523'.

9in (23cm) diam

£400-600   FRE

Mark Picks

Ekenäs was founded in 1917, and closed in 1976. From 1953 until 1976, its chief designer was John Orwar Lake. Although Ekenäs is a very small company in the story of post-war Scandinavian glass, and very little else is known about Lake, these mottled ranges have been increasing in value over the past few years, probably due to their appealing colours.

Forms tend to be very simple and are unornamented. Vases usually fetch more than bowls, particularly if they display a good range of colours and colour tones. Look out for the mottled orangey-red version, which is much scarcer, and can often fetch twice the price of this bluey-green range. If you're lucky enough to pick up one of these pieces for a good price, sit it on a windowsill and let the light flood through it. The range of colours is quite eye-popping!

A 1960s Swedish Ekenäs glass bowl, designed by John Orwar Lake, with a graduated blue to mottled-green ground and inverted rim, the base with engraved factory marks and 'J. O. Lake' signature.

6.5in (16.5cm) wide

£50-70   FLD

A 1970s Norwegian Hadeland colourless-cased cinnamon glass bowl, probably designed by Willy Johansson, with machine-cut rim, with factory gilt foil label.

2.5in (6.5cm) high

£15-20   WHP

A mid-late 1980s Iittala 'Claritas' black and opal glass vase, no.3620, designed by Timo Sarpaneva in 1983, the base with inscribed factory and designer marks.

This design was re-introduced with burgundy, amber-yellow, or steel-blue cores to commemorate the 130th anniversary of Iittala in 2011. The new range also included this original colour, as well as some variations to the disc and air bubble design.

10in (26.5cm) high

£800-1,200   SWO

A Riihimäen Lasi Oy colourless-cased red mould-blown 'Tulppaani' (Tulip) vase, no.1516, designed by Tamara Aladin in 1971.

1971-76   8in (20.5cm) high

£70-100   PC

A Riihimäen Lasi Oy mould-blown 'Ruusu' (Rose) vase, no.1477, designed by Tamara Aladin in 1966.

This was also available in a 12in (30cm) high size, which is usually worth around £50-80.

1967-76   7.75in (20cm) high

£40-60   PC

A Riihimäen Lasi Oy colourless-cased green mould-blown 'Tulppaani' (Tulip) vase, no.1512, designed by Tamara Aladin in 1971.

1971-76   8in (20cm) high

£25-35   PC

A Riihimäen Lasi Oy orange mould-blown 'Quadrifolio' vase, designed by Nanny Still in 1967, with textured exterior.

1968-72   8in (21cm) wide

£100-150   LSK

A late 1960s Riihimäen Lasi Oy mould-blown and cut neodymium glass 'Terälehdet' (Petals) bowl, no.6573, designed by Aimo Okkolin in 1965, the base inscribed 'Aimo Okkolin Riihimaen Lasi Oy'.

This is an unusual and comparatively scarce design. Also sometimes known as 'Alexandrite', neodymium glass is not commonly used by Scandinavian factories, and is more commonly associated with Czech and Central European factories. It changes colour from a pale, icy blue (see inset) in fluorescent light to the colour shown here under incandescent light. This design is also unusual for Riihimäen Lasi Oy (often known as Riihimaki) as it is cut.

8in (20.5cm) diam

£150-200   PC

A 1960s-70s Ruda mould-blown glass vase, probably designed by Göte Augustsson, with textured decoration of a Viking warrior to one side and a maiden to the other.

c1965   8.5in (21.5cm) high

£40-60   PC

A Swedish Strömbergshyttan freeform glass vase, designed by Gunnar Nylund, the base inscribed 'Strömbergshyttan G. Nylund'.

Gunnar Nylund (1904-1997) was a designer and art director at Strömbergshyttan from 1954 to 1967. He is better-known for his ceramic designs for Rörstrand.

4.25in (11cm) high

£80-120   PC

GLASS

QUICK REFERENCE

- During the early 1960s Harvey Littleton (b.1922) and Dominick Labino (1910–1987) developed a process by which individuals could melt, form, and blow glass outside of the factory environment. The resulting 'studio glass' movement spread from America to the UK and Europe in the late 1960s and 1970s. Artists developed and shared their skills and, as a result, pieces became more complex and more appealing.
- During the 1980s top museums and collectors around the world started adding studio glass to their collections, signifying a world-wide shift in thinking about glass as an art form, rather than as a craft.
- Date is not always a good indicator of value. Some early examples of studio glass styles are crude, though they do represent important developments. Collectors tend to focus on complex designs, or the work of pioneers.

- Pioneers whose works are sought-after include Sam Herman (b.1936), Peter Layton (b.1937), and Dale Chihuly (b.1941). As the work of these first generation artists becomes scarcer and more expensive, many collectors are turning to the second and third generations of glassmakers, many of whom studied under these pioneers and are still active today. Pauline Solven (b.1943) is a good example (see p.238).
- As well as learning about important names, it's a good idea to learn about the different glass-making techniques. Complex pieces were often time-consuming to make and these are generally sought-after and valuable. Large pieces, which were challenging to make, are also worth looking for.
- Although much studio glass is signed, it can be difficult to read signatures. Some pieces are not signed at all. Visit museums and galleries to learn how to recognise hallmark styles and techniques used by different glassmakers.

A Sam Herman glass vase, of compressed ovoid form with cylindrical neck, the mottled cream, yellow, blue, and green body cased in colourless glass, and with an overlaid trail of cobalt-blue trails, the base engraved 'Samuel J. Herman 1971'.

Samuel J. Herman (b.1936) is one of Britain's most important and influential studio glassmakers, and is credited with kick-starting the studio glass movement in the UK. Early pieces such as this are highly sought-after.

1971   *6.75in (17cm) high*
£550-750   FLD

A Sam Herman bottle vase, the mottled ochre body cased in colourless glass and overlaid with randomly applied purple trails, the base inscribed 'Samuel J. Herman 1972'.
1972   *8in (20.5cm) high*
£200-300   FIS

A Sam Herman glass bottle vase, the striated amber body decorated with silver chloride and iridescent mottles on a colourless glass exterior, the base inscribed 'Samuel J. Herman 1971'.
1971   *11in (27.5cm) high*
£150-250   WW

A Val St. Lambert conical glass vase, designed by Sam Herman, the flared form with green, blue, sandy beige, and brown mottles and silver chloride, the base inscribed 'SJH 1979' and with other indistinct inscribed numbers.

Sam Herman worked as a consultant designer at Val St. Lambert from 1990, having previously designed glass for the company during the 1970s. Not all pieces bearing his initials or name were made by him.
1979   *13in (32cm) high*
£300-400   WW

A Sam Herman glass vase, with cloudy and streaked light-blue and purple glass over a translucent white ground, cased in colourless glass, and with applied purple rim, the base inscribed 'Samuel J. Herman 1970'.

1970   *10in (25cm) high*
£500-700   WW

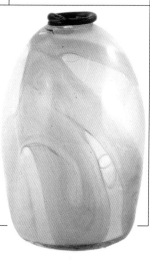

A Peter Layton 'Kimono' ovoid glass vase, decorated with a mottled black spiralling pattern on a white ground.

This 1980s range is similar to a more recent range called 'Glacier', except the latter has a coloured interior.

5in (12.5cm) high

£250-350   PC

A 1980s Peter Layton 'Kimono' flattened ovoid glass vase, decorated with a random network of yellow mottles on a blue ground, the base with inscribed signature.

6.75in (17cm) high

£300-400   DN

A Peter Layton glass vase, the pink glass body with pulled and swung rim, and white and black surface decoration, unsigned.

7.5in (21cm) high

£80-120   WW

A CLOSER LOOK AT A PETER LAYTON VASE

Peter Layton (b.1937) is one of Britain's leading studio glass artists, and his work is becoming increasingly sought-after, particularly vintage examples of his best-loved designs.

Layton is largely self-taught. His studio in South London has acted as a training ground for many up-and-coming glassmakers and designers, firming up his importance in the world of studio glass.

He is known for his use of vibrant colours in various patterns. Each piece is handmade and thus unique.

Rounded, pebble-like forms with areas of colourless casing that magnify the internal design, as in this example, are another hallmark of his designs.

An early 21stC Peter Layton 'Spirale' ovoid vase, with a narrow circular aperture, the alternating broad red and thin light-blue stripes cased in clear crystal, with engraved signature to base.

For more information on Layton, please see pp.252-253 of 'Miller's Collectables Handbook 2010-2011'.

7in (17.5cm) high

£300-500   FLD

An Ed Iglehart striated glass stoppered bottle, with 'kicked up' base and hollow stopper.

Born in the US in 1941, Ed Iglehart has worked in Scotland since 1972. He is best-known for his lighting, and for his small glass mushrooms and toadstools. All are finely blown like this highly unusual bottle. Note how the addition of silver chloride causes the colour to change when light passes through it. Although Iglehart's works are often largely affordable when re-sold on the 'secondary market', he may be a name to watch in the future.

8in (20.5cm) high

£60-80   PC

A Peter Layton glass vase, of pulled irregular mottled green glass with lustre finish, the base inscribed 'Peter Layton 1980'.

1980   *7.5in (21cm) high*

£350-450   WW

GLASS

QUICK REFERENCE - LOTTON GLASS

- American Charles Lotton (b.1935) is a self-taught glassmaker who first encountered glass in 1965. He was working as a cosmetologist at the time, and a client brought in a collection of vintage carnival glass. This event inspired Lotton to collect glass, and then attempt to make his own.

- In 1970, he set up his first studio behind his house to produce his own iridescent glass, much of it inspired by Art Nouveau examples. He experimented with numerous formulae until he found success. The results attracted the attentions of top Art Nouveau dealer Lillian Nassau. Selling a range of glass exclusively through her for five years made his name, and he continued to develop his burgeoning reputation throughout the 1970s and '80s. His three sons David, Daniel, and John followed him into the business, and produced their own similar glass in various glass studios in Illinois.

- Charles's work can be found in many private and public collections, including the Smithsonian Institute, and the Corning Museum of Glass. Large 'hallmark' works with many complex layers of floral and foliate designs are highly sought-after. If they are iridised and in the style of Louis Comfort Tiffany or other well-known Art Nouveau predecessors, so much the better.

A Charles Lotton 'Multi Flora' glass vase, the blue ovoid body decorated with applied burnt orange blossoms and green heart-shaped leaves, the base inscribed 'Multi Flora Charles Lotton 1980'.

1980   *20.75in (22cm) high*

£500-700   WES

A Charles Lotton 'Multi Flora' bulbous glass vase, the body decorated with applied burnt orange and white blossoms and shaded yellow and green heart-shaped leaves on dark blue stems, the base inscribed 'Multi Flora Charles Lotton 1982'.

1982   *6.25in (16cm) high*

£350-450   WES

A Charles Lotton 'Multi Flora' iridescent glass vase, the iridescent gold ovoid body with applied blue and white blossoms and shaded green heart-shaped leaves, the base inscribed 'Multi Flora Charles Lotton 1979'.

1979   *15.25in (16cm) high*

£400-600   WES

A Daniel Lotton 'Anthurium Floral' glass vase, the iridescent colourless-cased blue bulbous body decorated with applied pink, white and yellow blossom and yellow heart-shaped leaves, the base inscribed 'Anthurium Floral Daniel Lotton 1994'.

Note the depth in the pattern here. The complex Anthurium flowers appear to 'float' over the leaves, with both elements floating over the deep blue body. This effect is time-consuming to create, and requires great skill.

1994   *18.25in (19.5cm) high*

£650-750   WES

A John Lotton iridescent cylindrical glass vase, with applied stylised foliate decoration, the base signed and dated 1989.

1989   *8.5in (22cm) high*

£450-550   LHA

A Charles Lotton vase, the gold iridescent body with applied silvery stylised leaves and stems, the base inscribed 'Charles Lotton 1987'.

1987   *7.25in (18cm) high*

£300-400   FRE

A Charles Lotton beaker-shaped vase, the iridescent gold glass body with applied and combed Art Nouveau style trails, with matt iridescent surface, the base inscribed 'Lotton 1973'.

1973   *8in (20.5cm) high*

£300-400   FIS

A CLOSER LOOK AT A LABINO SCULPTURE

Along with Harvey Littleton, scientist and glass technician Dominick Labino (1910-87) was one of the founders of the studio glass movement. In 1965, working at the famed Toledo workshops in Ohio, US he formulated and provided the special glass recipe that allowed glass to be melted and made in a small furnace.

Although this is an early example, it is also simple compared to other examples which can have many more layers of internal veiling and can sell for over twice the value of this one.

Pieces from his 'Emergence' series of the 1970s-80s, with their internal veils of purpley-pink glass and trapped air bubbles, comprise his best known works and were made using a process that he developed himself.

Due to the importance of both Labino and this iconic series of sculptural works, values are very unlikely to fall and may well rise as more attention is paid to the development of the movement.

A Dominick Labino glass sculpture, from the 'Emergence' series, the base inscribed 'Labino 6-1972'.

1972   *7.75in (20cm) high*
£2,000-3,000   **DRA**

A Charlie Meaker glass ovoid vase, the colourless body overlaid with broad red and blue trails, the base inscribed 'CHARLIE MEAKER BADEN 1980'.

This was made at the Lobmeyr studio in Studio Franzenbad in Baden, Austria. Meaker graduated from the Royal College of Art, worked briefly under Michael Harris at Isle of Wight Studio Glass, and has lived and worked in Denmark and the US.

1980   *7in (18cm) high*
£200-300   **FIS**

A Charlie Meaker glass bell vase, the dark blue glass body overlaid with opaque white trails.

c1980   *6.5in (16cm) high*
£100-150   **FIS**

A German Albin Schaedel lamp-worked glass cylindrical vase, the colourless glass body overlaid with applied panels of multicoloured glass, the base engraved 'S 77'.

Albin Schaedel (1905-1999) came from a family of glassmakers based around Lauscha, Thuringia, Germany. The area is known for its lamp-worked laboratory glass, small Christmas and other decorations, and animals, made using similar techniques. Schaedel worked in his father's bead studio from 1924 until 1934 when he became an independent glassmaker. After being a soldier during World War II, he returned to making glass in Communist East Germany where he became a recognised glassmaster and influential teacher during the 1960s and '70s. His first international recognition came when he participated in the 1959 international glass exhibition at the Corning Museum of Glass, NY, US. By the time he retired due to health reasons in 1980, he had become widely known for his finely blown lamp-worked designs executed in vibrant colours.

1977   *10.5in (26cm) high*
£800-1,200   **FIS**

A German Volkhard Precht 'Drawing Up the Clouds in the Mountains' glass bell vase, the colourless glass body with blue mottles and applied randomly sized sections of multicoloured glass, the base signed 'V. Precht 1978 Aufziehende Wolken Im Gebirge'.

1978
£400-600   **FIS**

A German Albin Schaedel flattened-globe lamp-worked glass vase, the thin colourless body with applied sections of violet, green, yellow, and blue glass, the base engraved 'S'.

c1985   *5in (10cm) high*
£300-400   **FIS**

GLASS

A Pauline Solven 'Onion' vase, the globular form with flared rim, with amber-brown streaks, trapped internal air bubbles, and silver chloride streaks, the base inscribed 'Pauline Solven 1970'.

1970   *7.5in (16cm) high*

£150-200   **WW**

A 1970s Pauline Solven globular vase, with applied mottled orange, purple, and yellow chips melted into the surface.

4.5in (11.5cm) high

£50-70   **GORL**

A Pauline Solven cylindrical vase, with an opaque white interior and applied sections and bands in different tones of green and blue, the base signed 'Pauline Solven RH 351 1979'.

1979   *10.25in (26cm) high*

£200-300   **FIS**

QUICK REFERENCE - PAULINE SOLVEN

- Pauline Solven (b.1943) studied glass under Sam Herman and Michael Harris at the Royal College of Art before joining 'The Glasshouse' studio and gallery collective as manager. She continued to make and sell her own glass while there, and left to found her own studio in 1975. Within a few years, she and her husband Harry Cowdy had expanded this to include a gallery that would later also showcase the work of other glassmakers. Her works can be found in many collections from the Corning Museum of Glass, NY, US, to the Victoria & Albert Museum, London, UK, and numerous important private collections.

- Working entirely alone, her abstract works are usually inspired by the natural and man-made environment around her. The title and design of this work hints at a building. From the late 1990s onwards, she began to cut up and reassemble blown works, playing with the dimensionality of the designs she created, which can appear flat even though they are not. Most recently, this has developed into entirely flat panels of fused glass in geometric patterns that can suggest perspective.

A Pauline Solven 'Red/White Elevation' vase, comprised of blown, cut, and glued sections of glass decorated with coloured enamels, with a matt surface, the base engraved 'Pauline Solven 1993'.

1993   *12in (30.5cm) high*

£400-600   **FIS**

A Norman Stuart Clarke iridescent glass vase, with randomly applied and melted-in straps, signed to the base.

Norman Stuart Clarke's work is becoming increasingly desirable among collectors, although most pieces can still be found for less than £500.

5.5in (14cm) high

£100-150   **GORL**

A German Kurt Wallstab lamp-worked glass bottle vase, the violet-black body with an applied translucent chequerboard panel of yellow, green, and blue bands, the base engraved 'Wallstab 84'.

1984   *6.75in (17cm) high*

£150-200   **FIS**

A German Roderich Wohlgemuth lamp-worked glass vase, the colourless globular body decorated with applied concentric rings of colour and spiralling white thread, signed 'W'.

1976   *3.75 (9.cm) high*

£200-300   **FIS**

QUICK REFERENCE - BURMESE & QUEEN'S BURMESE

- Recognised by its graduated pink-to-yellow colouring, Burmese glass was developed by American glassmaker Frederick Shirley in 1881, and patented in 1885. In 1886, Thomas Webb & Sons of Stourbridge, England, acquired the British license to produce it.

- Bodies are translucent and, in addition to pink-to-yellow, may also be found in pink or yellow. The graduated tone was made by adding uranium to the glass mix and reheating it in the furnace, which turned it pink. The surface was then treated with acid, which gave a matt finish.

- Pieces with enamelled decoration are often known as 'Queen's Burmese' because some samples from Shirley's Mount Washington Glassworks were sent to, and admired by, Queen Victoria and Princess Beatrice. However, that name is also sometimes applied to undecorated pieces by Webb.

- Values depend on the type of object, size, and quality of the decoration.

- As many glass collectors currently focus on 20thC glass, prices have suffered in recent years, but they have remained more stable than other Victorian glass.

A late 19thC Thomas Webb & Sons 'Queen's Burmese' ovoid posy vase, the graduated pink-to-yellow body enamelled with a band of ivy branch, the base with factory acid-stamped mark.

4.75in (12cm) high

£250-350   FLD

A pair of late 19thC Thomas Webb & Sons 'Queen's Burmese' posy vases, the graduated pink-to-pale yellow compressed ovoid bodies with square section necks, enamelled with stylised flowers and foliage, unmarked.

3in (8cm) high

£250-350   FLD

A Thomas Webb & Sons 'Queen's Burmese' vase, the yellow ground enamelled with a butterfly amid sprays of a thorny flowering shrub.

4.75in (12cm) high

£250-350   WW

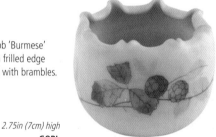

A Thomas Webb 'Burmese' glass pot, with frilled edge and decorated with brambles.

2.75in (7cm) high

£100-150   GORL

An S. Clarke 'Burmese' glass fairy night light, with ruffled tray, the shade painted with fruiting maples, cracked.

Clark is well-known for his fairy lights.

6.25in (16cm) high

£250-350   GORL

A Czechoslovakian Moser enameled glass vase, the egg-shaped yellow body raised on three blue legs, enamelled with gilt-outlined white floral and foliate sprays, decorated with trailed blue zig-zags and with a zig-zag rim.

c1900   13.75in (35cm) high

£200-300   IMC

A late 19thC Stourbridge 'Autumnal' range ovoid vase, the deep pink body cased in white opal glass, with a folded frill rim, three yellow legs, and three applied green, yellow, and pink stylised leaves.

These vases, which may be an acquired taste, are surprisingly complex to make. Manufacturers include Walsh Walsh and Boulton & Mills.

6.25in (16cm) high

£50-80   FLD

A pair of moulded cranberry glass vases, of ribbed and bulbous form.

c1900   *6.25in (16cm) high*

£50-70   **WHP**

A pair of Victorian cranberry glass 'Jack in the Pulpit' vases, with crimped rims and applied clear shell spirals.

9in (23cm) high

£80-120   **LOC**

An early 20thC cranberry crackle glass lemonade jug, with applied colourless handle.

10.5in (27cm) high

£35-45   **WHP**

A pair of Victorian vases, the mould-blown pink bodies overlaid in opaque white, enamelled with birds on flowering branches and butterflies, with frilled rims.

10.5in (27cm) high

£80-120   **DA&H**

A late 19thC iridescent glass vase, the dimpled body with applied green rim and applied pink thistle with green spiky leaves.

5.5in (14cm) high

£60-80   **GORL**

A 19thC yellow satin glass vase, of bulbous form with slender neck and frill rim, with allover quilted pattern.

7.25in (18cm) high

£80-120   **DA&H**

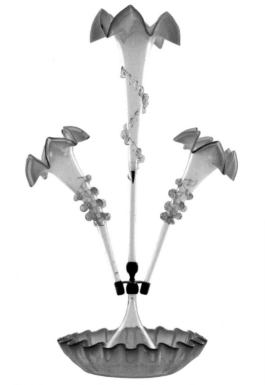

A late 19thC épergne, comprising one tall trumpet and two short trumpets with flared and frilled rims, trailed with pinched decoration and rising from a circular scalloped base.

Épergnes were placed at the centre of Victorian tables and held fruit, sweetmeats, or flowers. Some épergnes may have more stems than this example. Exuberant, yet delicate and elegant, épergnes have seen a drop in value as they are of limited practical use, and have little decorative appeal to many today.

22in (55.5cm)

£120-180   **WW**

GLASS

QUICK REFERENCE

- Whitefriars was founded in 1680, near Fleet Street in London. In 1834 it was acquired by James Powell. Under Powell and his descendents, the company thrived and grew during the 19thC. Although correctly called Powell & Sons, most collectors refer to the company, and the glass it made, as 'Whitefriars' - a name that was officially adopted in 1962.
- During the late 19thC, the company emerged at the forefront of British glass design with its Art Nouveau style ranges inspired by Venetian and European designs. These, and some early 20thC designs, are currently not as desirable as before, and many think they are under-appreciated and under-valued.
- Instead, designs from the second half of the 20thC are the most popular today. Most of these were produced by Royal College of Art graduate Geoffrey Baxter (1922-95), who joined the company in 1954. William Wilson, James Hogan, and Peter Wheeler are other important designers.
- Baxter is known for his modern, Scandinavian-inspired designs. These range from gently curving forms in muted colours and bold reds in the late 1950s, to the strongly coloured, textured ranges of the late 1960s and 1970s. Shapes were innovative, and drawn from the natural world and geometry.
- It's these designs, released as the 'Textured' range from 1967 onwards, that are considered the pinnacle of his success, and are the most sought-after designs today.
- Colour, form, and size are all important factors to consider, as these can affect the value significantly. Iconic designs such as the 'Drunken Bricklayer' or the 'Banjo' can nearly double in price if in a rare colour such as meadow green. Look for crisply moulded details as moulds wore down over time.

A Whitefriars golden amber ribbon-trailed lamp base, no.9055, designed by Barnaby Powell in 1935.

1938-40   *13in (32cm) high*

£200-300   **WW**

A large 1930s Whitefriars 'Minoan' graduated blue to sea-green vase, no.1211, designed by Harry Powell, with applied deep blue threads.

The form was designed by Harry Powell in c1903, and was based on an ancient Minoan vase. Powell also designed a similar form (no.1258) with a taller neck, based on a Bronze Age vessel. Values are roughly the same for 1258s, as they are for equivalent 1211s, because it's the colour that counts. Ruby is much rarer than blue and sea-green and more valuable.

8in (20cm) high

£300-400   **FLD**

A Whitefriars amethyst wave-ribbed tumbler vase, no.8473, designed by Marriott Powell c1930.

This design was produced until the early 1970s, but was only produced in amethyst until 1949.

1938-1949   *10in (25.5cm) high*

£60-80   **FLD**

A 1920s-30s Whitefriars sapphire-blue wrythen-fluted footed bowl, designed by either William Wilson or James Hogan, with folded rim.

12in (30cm) wide

£50-70   **FLD**

GLASS

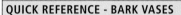

A Whitefriars pewter 'bark' vase, no.9690, from the 'Textured' range, designed by Geoffrey Baxter in 1966.

1969-72   *7.5in (19cm) high*
£70-100   **WHP**

QUICK REFERENCE - BARK VASES

- Textured surfaces were popular in the decorative arts during the early 1960s, so it was inevitable that they would be applied to glass at some point. The earliest textured glass production range was the bark-textured 'Finlandia' range designed by Timo Sarpaneva for Iittala in 1964, but, despite the similar bark-theme of Baxter's vases, it is unlikely that Baxter directly copied Sarpaneva. It's more likely that there was something 'in the air' in the 1960s, not least nature and the landscape acting as inspiration. It was certainly the landscape that influenced Baxter with this design. Metal moulds were made from moulds lined with real bark he had collected at weekends.

- Highly popular and successful, the resulting design was made from 1967 to 1980 and is common today. However, production dates vary depending on the colour and size. The examples shown here are listed with the production years for that colour and size combination. Four sizes were produced in total, and the smallest and the next size up are shown in this box. The next size up from these (no.9691) was only produced until 1974. The very largest size (no.9734, which stood 10.5in (27cm) high) is much rarer, as it was only produced for a few months in 1969. Recognised by its tapered, fluted base, it was only produced in kingfisher, pewter, ruby, and tangerine. A handful of 'experimental' meadow green examples are known. These represent the rarest of the rare of this design, and are a real challenge to find!

Two Whitefriars ruby 'bark' vases, no.9689 and no.9690, from the 'Textured' range designed by Geoffrey Baxter in 1966.
1967-80
Largest 7.75in (18.5cm) high
£100-150 both   **FLD**

A Whitefriars kingfisher 'bark' vase, no.9691, from the 'Textured' range, designed by Geoffrey Baxter in 1966.
1969-74   *7.5in (19cm) high*
£50-80   **FLD**

A Whitefriars tangerine 'bark' vase, pattern no.9691, from the 'Textured' range designed by Geoffrey Baxter in 1966.
1969-74   *7.5in (19cm) high*
£40-60   **WHP**

A Whitefriars indigo 'Cucumber' vase, no.9679, from the 'Textured' range designed by Geoffrey Baxter in 1966.
1967-72   *11in (29cm) high*
£150-200   **DS**

A Whitefriars kingfisher 'Aztec' vase, no.9816, from the 'Late Textured' range, designed by Geoffrey Baxter in 1972.
1972-74   *7in (18cm) high*
£60-80   **TGM**

QUICK REFERENCE - WHITEFRIARS FAKES

- This example is an authentic 'Hoop' vase, but, over the past few years, fakes have become widespread due to the high sums Whitefriars vases are fetching. Fakes are commonly found in red, but in a different tone to ruby, and have a differently patterned textured finish.

- Upon its release in 1967, the 'Hoop' vase was only produced in cinnamon, willow and indigo. Kingfisher and Tangerine versions were released in 1969, and the aubergine colour was added in 1972, which was the final year of production.

- For a full review of the current crop of fake Whitefriars vases, see p.260 of 'Miller's Collectables Handbook 2010-2011'.

A Whitefriars cinnamon 'Bamboo' vase, no.9669, from the 'Textured' range designed by Geoffrey Baxter in 1966.

1967-70　　　*8in (20cm) high*

£180-220　　　**DS**

A Whitefriars indigo 'Basketweave Slab' vase, no.9667, from the 'Textured' range designed by Geoffrey Baxter in 1966.

1967-69　　*11in (27.5cm) high*

£100-150　　　**WW**

A Whitefriars tangerine 'Hoop' vase, no.9680, from the 'Textured' range designed by Geoffrey Baxter in 1966.

1969-72　　　*12in (30cm) high*

£500-700　　　**DS**

A Whitefriars kingfisher 'Nuts & Bolts' or 'Hobnail' vase, no.9668, from the 'Textured' range designed by Geoffrey Baxter in 1966.

1967-70　　　*10.5in (27cm) high*

£200-300　　　**CAPE**

A Whitefriars pewter 'Coffin' vase, no.9686, from the 'Textured' range designed by Geoffrey Baxter in 1967.

Although the 'Coffin' vase is one of the most common shapes, look out for rarer examples in sage or lilac.

1969-80　　　*5in (13cm) high*

£60-80　　　**FLD**

A Whitefriars cinnamon 'Pyramid' or 'Triangle' vase, no.9674, from the 'Textured' range designed by Geoffrey Baxter in 1966.

1967-69　　　*7in (18cm) high*

£100-150　　　**SAS**

GLASS

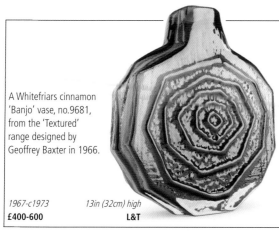

A Whitefriars cinnamon 'Banjo' vase, no.9681, from the 'Textured' range designed by Geoffrey Baxter in 1966.

1967-c1973   *13in (32cm) high*

£400-600   **L&T**

A Whitefriars pewter 'Banjo' vase, no.9681, from the 'Textured' range designed by Geoffrey Baxter in 1966.

Along with the 'Drunken Bricklayer', the 'Banjo' is the most sought-after and valuable design from the 'Textured' range. Look out for examples in indigo or meadow green, which are rarer and can fetch around a third more than this example in pewter.

1967-c1973   *12.75in (32cm) high*

£700-1,000   **GORL**

Mark Picks

One of the factors that differentiates Baxter's textured designs from those of his early Scandinavian contemporaries is the 'urban' nature of many pieces. Although nature was a clear inspiration, man-made themes (see the 'Drunken Bricklayer' vase) and purely geometric forms (such as this vase) were also key.

Designs from the first 'Textured' range issued in 1967, such as the 'Banjo', are the most sought-after, but I'd recommend looking at some of the designs from the 'Late Textured' range, introduced from c1970 onwards. Although small, this great design is typical of the period and represents so many of the themes behind Baxter's range. Furthermore, it was only made for a few years, making examples of this shape harder to find than others from the range. Considering these two points, the 'Double Diamond' looks almost undervalued when compared to other designs in the 'Late Textured' range.

A Whitefriars willow 'Banjo' vase, no.9681, from the 'Textured' range designed by Geoffrey Baxter in 1966.

1967-c1973   *13in (32cm) high*

£400-600   **L&T**

A Whitefriars tangerine 'Guitar' vase, no.9675, from the 'Textured' range designed by Geoffrey Baxter, this piece designed in 1967.

'Guitar' vases were made by spiralling and stapling a bent wire into the inside of a mould. They were made in eight colours, of which ruby is the rarest, being possibly only experimental.

1969-70   *7in (18cm) high*

£180-220   **DA&H**

A Whitefriars sage 'Long Neck Bottle' vase, no.9818, from the 'Late Textured' range designed by Geoffrey Baxter in 1972.

1972-1980   *7in (18cm) high*

£40-60   **DS**

A Whitefriars aubergine 'Double Diamond' vase, no.9759, from the 'Late Textured' range designed by Geoffrey Baxter in 1971, with a factory paper label.

1971-74   *6.25in (16cm) high*

£180-220   **DS**

A Whitefriars 'Old Gold' globe vase, from the 'Studio' range designed by Peter Wheeler, unsigned.

1969-70 5in (12cm) high

£150-200   **WW**

A Whitefriars orange vase, from the 'Studio' range designed by Peter Wheeler, unsigned.

For more information about the shortlived 'Studio' range, inspired by the growth of the 'Studio' glass movement, see p.279 of the 'Miller's Collectables Price Guide 2009'.

5in (11.5cm) high

£150-200   **WW**

A CLOSER LOOK AT A WHITEFRIARS VASE

By the mid-1970s, textured glass had become stale, with many other factories copying the successful look. Another innovation was required.

This piece was part of a series of vases randomly decorated with unique patterns. Sketches by Baxter are known, but examples are very rare.

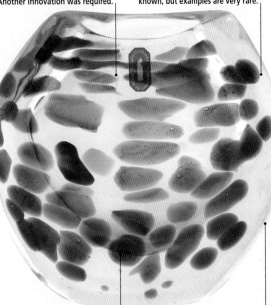

Whitefriars reacted to the growing importance of the studio glass movement with a range designed by Peter Wheeler and a limited series of unique pieces, such as this vase.

Despite their rarity and importance to the Whitefriars story, prices for these experimental pieces are generally lower than those for the best 'Textured' designs. This is because fewer collectors feel the need to own one compared to, say, a 'Banjo' vase.

A Whitefriars experimental elliptical vase, designed by Geoffrey Baxter, of clear glass internally decorated with blue spots, with factory paper label.

6in (15cm) high

£400-600   **WW**

A Whitefriars kingfisher 'Knobbly' vase or lampbase, no.9612 designed by William Wilson and Harry Dyer in 1963.

9.5in (24.1cm) high

£20-30   **CAPE**

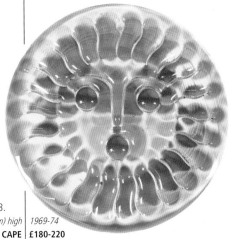

A Whitefriars yellow 'Sunspot' sun-catcher window decoration, designed by Geoffrey Baxter in 1969.

1969-74

7.5in (19cm) diam

£180-220   **WHP**

A 1960s-70s Whitefriars ruby duck, with original factory label to base.

This form was made in various different styles between 1955 and 1980. See www.whitefriarsducks.co.uk for more information.

5.75in (15cm) high

£50-60   **TRI**

QUICK REFERENCE - WMF IKORA

- Württembergische Metallwarenfabrik's (WMF) glass factory was built in 1883, and began to experiment with art glass in 1925. Their 'Ikora' range was developed by works manager Karl Weidmann in 1926, a year after their lustre 'Myra' range. 'Ikora' was mould-blown or free-blown, and used coloured enamels and chemicals on a colourless or transparent coloured body. The crackle effect was gained by dipping the hot part-blown body into cold water, causing the exterior to shatter and the chemicals to run into the cracks. The body was then reheated, which sealed the cracks, and cased with a layer of colourless glass.

- Look out for unusual decorative effects, such as a web of bubbles, glittering metal powder inclusions, heat-reactive opalescent, or iridescent finishes.

- The range was produced until the mid-1950s, and bowls and baluster shape vases (both shown here) were the most common forms.

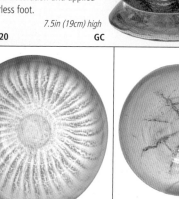

A WMF 'Ikora' baluster vase, with orange and amber toned mottled decoration and applied colourless foot.

7.5in (19cm) high

£80-120   GC

A German WMF 'Ikora' glass 'Dexel Egg' vase, designed by Walter Dexel, with a dark-blue network of crackle veins and internal bubbles on a light-blue ground.

c1938   *7in (17.5cm) high*

£120-180   VZ

A WMF 'Ikora Kristall' baluster vase, designed by Karl Wiedmann in 1951, the colourless glass body with applied graduated red-orange and opaque white powdered enamel with a craquelure effect, cased in an outer layer of colourless glass.

9.5in (25cm) high

£100-150   FIS

A 1960s German WMF squat ovoid vase, with short neck, with deeply cut hemispherical lenses with central nodules, the top with blue powder inclusions, fading to green at the base, the whole with heavy gold iridescence.

10.25in (26cm) high

£300-500   VZ

A German WMF 'Ikora' glass bowl, of clear glass with 'crackle' green and red radiating ribs.

14.5in (37cm) diam

£60-100   WW

A German WMF 'Ikora' glass dish, with brown and beige mottling and veining on a graduated grey to blue ground.

c1930   *9in (23 cm) diam*

£180-220   VZ

A late 1990s Caithness globe vase, the colourless body with opaque white layer, and an exterior colourless layer with applied and melted-in graduated green and blue chips, and random blue-grey trails, with machine-cut and polished rim.

Rather than being from the 'Xanadu' range as stated in previous editions of this book, this piece was from what was probably a trial range, produced around the same time as 'Xanadu'. It doesn't appear to have been given a name, and it's likely only a small quantity of pieces were made for sale in factory shops. This is a particularly unusual form.

4in (10.5cm) high

£30-40   GROB

A CLOSER LOOK AT A CHANCE GLASS ASHTRAY

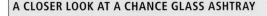

Introduced in 1929, 'Orlak' was Chance Glass's first domestic glass range. It was made from a heat-resistant borosilicate glass similar to Pyrex.

The ice blue colour and geometric form are typically Art Deco.

The cigarette or pipe rests on the 'wings' make the piece functional as well as decorative.

Found in transparent glass or opaline glass, the design was by Robert Goodden (1909-2002), a key and influential British designer and architect.

Different marks can be found moulded on bases, including Parker (smoking accessories, not fountain pens) and Chance. This example is confusingly moulded 'Orlik', the brand of a Scandinavian pipe maker.

A rare Chance Glass light blue pressed glass ashtray or pipe rest, pattern no.ID13, designed by Robert Goodden in c1935, from the 'Orlak' range, the base moulded 'Orlik'.

c1936   *5.8in (14.8cm) wide*

£15-20   GROB

A 1990s-2000s Dartington orange ovoid vase, from the 'Studio' range, with frosted exterior and depression cut with repeated oval facets, with polished base and plastic factory label.

14.5in (37cm) high

£50-80   GC

A set of four 1970s Davidson coloured and cased mould-blown textured vases, from the 'Luna' range.

Pay close attention to both the shape and the design of the texturing. These vases are not by Whitefriars, but were produced to 'cash in' on the popularity of textured glass during the late 1960s and '70s. This, originally inexpensive, range was introduced in 1971.

£25-35   WHP

A Durand baluster vase, the opaque white body with combed green Art Nouveau style decoration, and applied iridescent gold trailing, the base inscribed 'Durand 1912-7', with breaks in the threading at the neck.

7.5in (19cm) high

£250-350   DRA

A Durand baluster vase, the kingfisher blue iridescent body with applied iridescent gold glass trails.

Durand glass was made at the Vineland Flint Glass Works in New Jersey, America, from c1912 to 1924. Owner Victor Durand Jr (1870-1931) was a French emigré, and his glass was an attempt to imitate the highly popular (and expensive) iridescent glass by Steuben and Tiffany.

c1920   *7.25in (18cm) high*

£500-700   LHA

GLASS

A 1930s Haden, Mullett & Haden 'Cloudy' vase, of footed flared form, in graduated yellow to colourless glass over a white veined ground, unmarked.

6in (15cm) high

£100-150   FLD

A 1930s (or later) Hartley Wood double gourd vase, with multicoloured streaks and striations, the base with broken pontil mark.

7.5in (19cm) high

£80-120   GC

A Leerdam asymmetric cased vase, model AM2059 designed by Floris Meydam, from the 'Unica' series, in green and opaque pink glass with pulled rim, the base with etched marks and date mark for 1956.

1956   5in (14.5cm) high

£100-150   WW

A Leerdam colourless and deep blue ovoid vase, designed by Sybren Valkema, with large internal air bubbles.

c1964   10.5in (27cm) high

£300-400   QU

A CLOSER LOOK AT A MAASTRICHT VASE

Max Verboeket (b.1922) was chief designer at Maastricht from 1954 to 1972, and is arguably an overlooked name in 20thC glass.

His cased, swirling Kristaluniek (Unique Cristal) glass was influenced by Muranese designs. It is often misattributed to Murano, or a Scandinavian maker such as Kosta or Holmegaard.

Some pieces, like this one, are signed. Unsigned pieces can be identified by looking closely at their forms, as Maastricht shapes are subtly different from those by other companies.

This tone of green is also a good identifying feature. It was unique to the company and is known as 'vert du chine'.

A mid-late 1950s Dutch Kristalunie Maastricht vase, designed by Max Verboeket, the thick colourless glass with aubergine and green internal swirls, and the base with etched marks.

10in (24cm) high

£150-200   WW

A Dutch Kristalunie Maastricht vase, designed by Max Verboeket, the bulbous body with slender neck and splayed rim, internally decorated with a blue and green trailed design, signed to base 'Max Verboeket AE59 Maastricht'.

1959   10.5in (27cm) high

£80-120   SAS

A 1930s-50s Nazeing cylindrical vase, shape no.36/7 from the 'Ruskin Ware' range, with everted rim, the colourless glass body with a combed blue and white spiralling 'Lattice' design with trapped airbubbles, cased in colourless glass, the base unsigned.

6in (15.5cm) high

£80-120   **WW**

A Japanese OTK mould-blown textured glass vase, fading from light green to colourless.

Little is currently known about OTK, but it is possible that the company was a distributor rather than a manufacturer. Its glass was exported, hence the English language label, and is commonly found in Australia. This vase was inspired by the form of bamboo. Whitefriars 'Haemorrhoid' vase, designed by Geoffrey Baxter, was probably also a strong influence. All other examples of OTK glass found to date are textured, and many have the same use of graduated colour.

10.5in (26.5cm) high

£40-50   **M20C**

A large 1920s-30s French Schneider spherical vase, with machine-cut and polished collar rim, with cloudy orange decoration, the base with acid-etched Schneider signature.

10in (26cm) high

£300-500   **WW**

A 1960s-70s French Sèvres organic-form vase, with swung out rim, flattened side 'wings', and oval 'Sèvres' acid mark to base.

This vase changes colour under different types of light. The designers for Sèvres glass during this period are unknown, but most designs have curving, organic forms.

7.5in (19cm) high

£20-30   **PC**

A 1920s-30s Steuben 'Gold Aurene' baluster vase, the iridescent gold body with applied foot and everted rim, the base inscribed 'Steuben Aurene' and numbered '2908'.

7.75in (20cm) high

£400-600   **LHA**

A Stevens & Williams 'Bottle Green' vase, shape no.1024A designed by Keith Murray, the swollen fluted form with a heavy applied foot, the base with acid-etched mark and facsimile signature.

c1938   *10in (24.5cm) high*

£300-500   **WW**

A 1930s Stevens & Williams horizontally ribbed vase, with internal light blue and green swirls, the base with polished pontil mark.

The two-colours of spirals combine with the horizontal ribbing to give a pleasing optical appearance as the piece is viewed from different angles.

8in (20.5cm) high

£120-180   **GROB**

GLASS

A 1930s Stuart & Sons cocktail glass, the bowl enamelled with a huntsman, and with an applied amber conical foot and ball knop, unmarked.

4.7in (12cm) high

£20-30 **FLD**

A French Verlys dish, with three modelled pinecone feet, and moulded pattern of pine needles and branches, the base moulded 'Verlys'.

Along with Sabino, Verlys was a company that produced designs in imitation of Lalique.

6.25in (16cm) diam

£100-150 **FRE**

A 1990s-2000s Irish Waterford tapering square section vase, from the 'Metra' range, the amethyst body overlaid with colourless glass, cut with four facets and with corner wedge cuts near the rim.

10in (25cm) high

£80-120 **CHT**

A 1970s-80s Polish Zabkowice amber pressed glass vase, designed by Jan Sylvester Drost in 1972, the base with flat machine-cut and polished rim.

The optical effect of this vase is gained by the vertical fluting to the interior contrasting with the horizontal fluting to the exterior. The type of base on this range of vases is similar to those used by the Sklo Union group of factories in Czechoslovakia, often leading to misattributions.

7in (18cm) high

£40-60 **GC**

An Art Deco glass vase, enamelled with Egyptian lotus flower decoration, unsigned.

7.5in (18.5cm) high

£70-100 **WW**

A probably French Art Deco enamelled glass vase, enamelled with geometric design in black, red, and white.

10in (26.5cm) high

£250-350 **WW**

A Bimini or Lauscha red and opaque white liqueur glass, with figural stem.

4.25in (11cm) high

£25-35 **GROB**

MARBLES

QUICK REFERENCE

- The earliest marbles were handmade, predominantly in Germany, from the 1860s to the 1920s. These can be identifed from the remains of their pontil marks where they were broken away from the glass rod to form a sphere.
- The most desirable handmade marbles are those that are in mint condition, particularly large or rarer models such as the opaque Indians and 'sulphides', which have internal white porcelain-like forms.
- In 1905 M. F. Christensen developed a marble-making machine in the US and the centre of production moved to that continent. Handmade marbles tend to be the most sought-after but, because of high prices and scarcity, many collectors now focus on early- to mid-20thC machine-made marbles.
- From the 1950s on, South American and Far Eastern factories began producing marbles on a vast scale. Most were 'cat's eye' type marbles, which are of no real interest to collectors.

- Always consider pattern, colour, symmetry, and size as they dramatically affect price. Signs of wear, or chips, scuffs, and marks all have detrimental effects on value. A marble in mint condition can be worth up to double that of a worn example.
- The late 20thC saw a boom in the production of 'art glass' marbles and (larger) spheres that were not for use in games. Made by independent studio glass artists, they require great skill and a mastery of challenging techniques to make. Although some update traditional designs, boundaries are often pushed to create intricate and innovative designs. Colour, popular culture, and the reflective, refractive, or magnifying properties of optical glass are recurrent themes.
- As well as considering the technique and size, look out for the work of certain artists such as Paul Stankard, Jesse Taj, and Daniel Benway, as their work is very desirable.

A James Alloway 'Gaffer's Revenge' multicoloured ribbon and latticinio decorated marble, with sections of swirling canes and threaded components encased in a clear glass body.

2000-10   *2.5in (6.5cm) diam*
£100-150   **BGL**

A Keith Baker 'Onionskin' marble, with elongated spattered decoration over a black core.

2000-10   *1.25in (3cm) diam*
£25-35   **BGL**

A Brett Christian 'Flora with Ladybug' marble, with lamp-worked flower and a ladybug murrine above.

2000-10   *1.5in (4cm) diam*
£60-80   **BGL**

A Rajesh Kommineni 'Vortex' marble, with multicoloured millefiori borosilicate glass cane swirls, and star murrine set lamp-worked flowers, on a black ground.

2in (5cm) diam
£60-80   **BGL**

A Kevin O'Grady multicoloured vortex borosilicate glass marble, with rake-pull reverse set with murrines, with a dated signature murrine.

The image shows both sides of this marble. As well as the pulled and combed floral design, note the insertion of the specially-made murrines. O'Grady developed vortex marbles in borosilicate glass, and is also known for his inventive and complex murrines.

2004   *1.5in (4cm) diam*
£120-140   **BGL**

MARBLES

A CLOSER LOOK AT A MARBLE

Benway is known for embellishing the surface of his marbles, here with coloured prunts.

The 'rake-pull' technique involves dragging coloured molten glass into a shaped and swirling pattern with a tool, and is commonly used by contemporary marble and glass sphere makers.

Cut facets are another hallmark feature of his work. Here they serve as lenses, adding optical interest by magnifying or reducing the various internal designs.

Combining many complex techniques, Benway's marbles are virtuoso displays of appealing art glass techniques, rather than functional 'toys'.

A large Daniel Benway 'Scope 05' marble, with multicoloured rake-pull interior and reverse exterior design, with surface embellishment of applied red prunts on white bases, and a ring of six cut facets, one to the top.

2005   *3.25in (8.25cm) diam*
£200-300   **BGL**

A Kris Parke 'Onionskin' marble, with pulled red, blue, and white 'onionskin' lobe overlaid with 'blizzard' dichroic glass fragments, encased in colourless glass.

Like the elongated spattered techique used on the 'Onionskin' marble on the previous page, this 'blizzard' technique was practised by glass marble makers from the late 19thC onwards.

2000-10   *2in (5cm) diam*
£60-80   **BGL**

A Joshua Sable 'Floral' marble, with multicoloured pulled dots, with a rake-pull equator line around a central blue, green, yellow, orange, and red lamp-worked flower.

2000-10   *1.5in (4cm) diam*
£100-150   **BGL**

A Steve Sizelove 'Dichroic Galaxy' marble, the multicoloured centre made up of dichroic glass threads arranged in a swirling design, and surrounded by black borosilicate glass

1.5in (4cm) diam
£60-80   **BGL**

A Beth Tomasello floral marble, with lamp-worked blue-spotted white flowers on a foliate ground.

1.5in (4cm) diam
£100-150   **BGL**

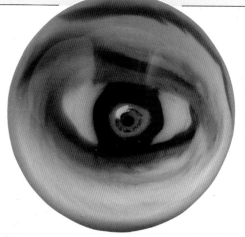

A Beth Tomasello 'Eye' marble, the swirling pink ground set with an eye murrine with green iris and pupil, with multicoloured reverse design.

2000-10   *1.25in (3cm) diam*
£100-150   **BGL**

A Brett Young and Larry Zengel 'Onionskin' marble, the lobed design filled with green, blue, yellow, and orange tartan patterns.

2000-10   *2in (5cm) diam*
£100-150   **BGL**

An Old Hall 'Alveston' range stainless steel stemless bud vase, no.45661, with conical foot, designed by Robert Welch.

Two short-stemmed versions of this shape were also produced. Similar forms with a thick, short stem and a domed foot are not by Old Hall.

1971-84   *6in (15.5cm) high*

£20-30   **GC**

A pair of Old Hall 'Campden' range stainless steel triple candlesticks, no.44221, with teak disc footpads, designed by Robert Welch in 1957, with etched marks to one leg.

The candlesticks represent one of Welch's most iconic designs. Always examine the feet as missing or badly damaged pads devalue the set by over a half.

1958-76   *9in (23cm) high*

£100-150   **GC**

A pair of 1960s Old Hall 'Campden' range stainless steel milk and coffee pots, designed by Robert Welch in 1957, with teak handles and finials.

Look out for the rare matching sugar bowl, which was made from the same tooling as a pot, but cut down.

1958-74   *7.25in (18.5cm) high*

£80-100   **M20C**

An Elkington silver-plated teapot, from the 'Pride' range designed by David Mellor in 1955, stamped '53722' to the base.

Look out for solid silver examples of this Design Council award winning design as they can fetch over £400.

1957   *9in (23cm) long*

£40-60   **PC**

A 1970s-80s Danish Stelton 'Cylinda Line' stainless steel coffee pot, designed by Arne Jacobsen in 1967, the base stamped 'Lauffer Stainless Stelton Denmark'.

A 1980s Alessi 9090 chrome-plated coffee pot, designed by Richard Sapper in 1979.

The first object made by the company's new Crusinello factory, this coffee pot won an award at the prestigious 11th Golden Compass Awards.

A 1960s-70s Portuguese Copral copper coffee or chocolate set, with coffee pot, milk jug, and lidded sugar bowl on a tray, with elongated conical wooden handles, the base marked 'COPRAL MADE IN PORTGUAL'.

8in (20cm) high

£80-120   **GC**

7in (18cm) high

£40-60   **SAS**

Coffee pot 9in (23cm) high

£50-60   **RET**

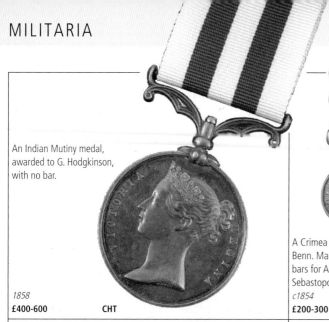

An Indian Mutiny medal, awarded to G. Hodgkinson, with no bar.

1858

£400-600   CHT

A Crimea medal, awarded to Corpl. Benn. Manning S.F.GDS., with three bars for Alma, Inkermann, and Sebastopol, partially renamed.

c1854

£200-300   TEN

A Queen's South Africa medal, awarded to Pte H G Ricketts, of the 26 Coy Imperial Yeomanry, with three bars, for Transvaal, and South Africa 1901 and 1902.

c1902

£180-220   CHT

A gold-coloured brooch of the 31 Squadron R.A.F., marked 'Silver 9ct', in good condition.

£120-180   W&W

An officer's gilt and silver-plated cap badge of The Duke of Wellington's Regiment, in very good condition.

£100-150   W&W

A Falklands War South Atlantic medal, awarded to R01 (G) D. M. Bargh D181777M on H.M.S. Coventry, with rosette, together with job description and certificate of qualifications.

Medal value and desirability is dependant not only on the type of medal, but also who it was awarded to. If the serviceman was particularly brave or notable, or played a key role in an important campaign, the price can rise.

£1,200-1,800   GORL

A red enamelled gold-coloured brooch of The West Yorkshire Regiment, with silver Prince of Wales feathers, in very good condition.

£100-150   W&W

A World War II British paratrooper's helmet, with traces of black and green camouflage paint, padded lining, 'BMB' maker's mark, name 'Andrew McMillan', webbing straps, and chin piece, in good condition.

This helmet was sold with a letter from the vendor explaining that it was worn by a friend of his father's who was flown into action in 'Operation Market Garden' by a glider as he was too young to be parachuted in.

£400-600   W&W

A late 19thC brass fireman's helmet, with embossed dragon crest, lacking chin strap.

A regimental drum for the 6th Bn. Grenadier Guards, decorated with Royal coat of arms and battle honours, lacking drum skin and converted for use as a waste paper bin.

£700-1,000   DN   £400-600   GORL

A US military officer's woollen jacket, with 13th Air Force and other badges, in very good condition.

£70-100   ECGW

A World War II R.A.F. military woollen uniform, comprising jacket and trousers, in very good condition.

£180-220   ECGW

A Royal Marines officer's navy blue dress jacket, with four stripes to the right arm, brass buttons, and gold braid, in excellent condition.

£60-90   ECGW

A Prussian Garde Infantry Regiment pickelhaube, with mounts and steel Garde eagle with superimposed star centre, the inside of the skull with maker's stamp, and BA XVII regimental stamp, with chinstrap and repainted rosettes, in good condition.

1914

£350-450   W&W

ORIENTAL

QUICK REFERENCE

- Interest in and prices paid for Chinese works of art have increased dramatically in line with those being paid for Chinese ceramics (see pp.60-63). The Chinese economy is booming, allowing a small percentage of the population to spend extravagantly to re-acquire its cultural history. Meanwhile, the Japanese economy remains comparatively depressed, and this has affected prices being paid for Japanese works of art, which remain comparatively low.
- As such, now could be a good time to buy if you like Japanese art. This is particularly true of the higher end of the market. Many believe that good quality pieces from the Meiji period (1868-1912) are currently undervalued.

- Japanese netsuke remain one of the most popular collecting areas. They were originally carved as toggles for the sash (obi) on a kimono, and supported cords strung with containers (sagemono).
- After the wearing of kimonos fell out of fashion, netsuke continued to be produced as artistic objects representing ideas and characters from Japanese culture and mythology. Most are carved in ivory, but wood and bone were also used.
- Larger figurative carvings (similar in style to netsuke) are known as okimono. These were placed in traditional Japanese display alcoves known as tokonoma.
- In both instances, the carver, age, detail, subject, and sense of humour or expressiveness all contribute towards value.
- From the late 19thC to the early 20thC, both China and Japan exported wares to the West in vast quantities. Whatever you are interested in, focus on the best quality you can afford.

A Japanese Meiji period carved marine ivory netsuke of an elderly couple, the man with a stick and lantern, inscribed 'Tomochika'.

Marine ivory comprises the front two teeth (or tusks) of the walrus. It is commonly used by those living near the Arctic, including the Inuit and some north Russian groups. It is typically very hard.

c1870   2.5in (6cm) high
£400-600   SWO

A 19thC Japanese Meiji period carved ivory okimono of an Immortal, with a gourd at his feet.

5in (13cm) high
£400-600   SWO

A 19thC Japanese Meiji period carved ivory okimono figure group, in the form of a hunter killing an eagle.

3in (7cm) high
£100-150   TOV

A late 19thC Japanese Meiji period carved ivory figure of a seated Buddha.

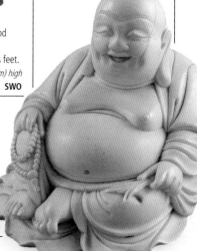

3.75in (9.5cm) high
£350-450   GORL

A 19thC Japanese Meiji period carved ivory netsuke of Daruma, seated with his mouth wide open.

Also known as Dharma, this netsuke represents Bodhidharma, the founder of the Zen sect of Buddhism. Although typically a form of toy, he represents good luck and perseverance, and is often given as a gift of encouragement.

1.5in (4cm) high

£100-150 **SK**

A Japanese Meiji period carved ivory netsuke of a nio, making music with a broom using a pipe as a plectrum.

A nio is a guardian and travelling companion of the Buddha, according to Japanese tradition. Muscular in build and often armed, they are usually seen guarding the entrance to Buddhist shrines.

c1900 *2in (4.5cm) high*

£300-400 **SWO**

A late 19thC Japanese carved ivory netsuke of a fledgling, with horn-inlaid eyes and frilled wings, inscribed 'Masanao'.

Masanao is a known carver, and the dumpy form of this charming baby bird is appealing.

c1880 *2.2in (5.5cm) wide*

£1,000-1,500 **SWO**

DODO
ANTIQUES

COME EXPERIENCE US...

NEW SHOP
with a
NEW APPROACH
on
HOW ANTIQUE CENTRES SHOULD BE

DODO ANTIQUES
THE OLD COCK INN
(JUST OFF MARKET PLACE TO THE RIGHT OF TAYLOR'S ESTATE AGENTS)
SILVER END, OLNEY, BUCKINGHAMSHIRE MK46 4AL

OPEN 7 DAYS A WEEK.

CONTACT US FOR FURTHER INFORMATION ON
T: 01234 240 505
INFO@DODOANTIQUES.CO.UK   WWW.DODOANTIQUES.CO.UK

A late 19thC Chinese export carved ivory card case, each side densely carved with numerous figures in pavilions amid willowy trees, with later replaced hinge.

Cantonese card cases are highly collectable. The age and the symbols shown are important factors when determining value. This example is late 19thC with a fairly typical scene and is well-carved and detailed, thus its high value. Many late 19thC examples are not as well-carved.

3.75in (9.5cm) high

£700-900 **IMC**

ORIENTAL

A pair of Chinese turquoise and yellow cased Peking glass vases, of baluster form, carved in relief with birds among blossoming branches.

7.5in (19cm) high

£100-150 **DN**

A pair of Chinese white and blue cased Peking glass vases, of baluster form, carved in relief with a pair of birds in a blossoming magnolia tree growing from rocks, with solid blue bands to the rim and foot.

c1940 *14in (35.5cm) high*

£700-900 **TEN**

A Chinese white and red cased Peking glass bowl, with a light opalescent effect, carved with a pattern of three birds among flowering branches.

2.75in (7cm) high

£800-1,200 **LHA**

A probably 20thC Chinese green and white cased Peking glass brushwasher, carved with a frieze of storks standing amid waves and rocks.

This bowl is very well-proportioned and very well-carved, with a sense of perspective and a good level of detail. White casing over coloured glass is also more difficult than casing a colour with a colour, as white and coloured glass contract at different rates as they cool, often leading to the body cracking. The stork is a symbol of longevity in Chinese mythology.

3in (8cm)

£2,000-3,000 **WW**

A CLOSER LOOK AT A FAKE PEKING GLASS VASE

The Qianlong emperor (reigned 1735-95) was the last Chinese emperor to insist the Imperial mark was only used on pieces for him or his palaces. The Qianlong reign mark on the base is too poorly applied for this to be an Imperial piece.

There is a large bubble in the footrim, and other large bubbles elsewhere in the body. These are not signs of a piece of Imperial quality.

The colours are far too bright and vivid, and the raised decoration has been applied in blobs and then carved back, rather than having been applied in many layers and then cut bacl.

The mud on the exterior is suspicious, and has been applied to suggest age.

A late 20thC fake Peking glass vase, of baluster form, the bubbly colourless body overlaid with red, green and blue, and carved with ducks, birds in flight, leaves and water lilies, the base with inscribed mark.

5.75in (14.5cm) high

£20-30 **PC**

A Chinese opaque pink Peking glass bowl, carved with branches, flowers and leaves, raised on a carved floriform wood stand.

6in (15cm) diam

£180-220 **LHA**

QUICK REFERENCE - PEKING GLASS

- Chinese glass from before the Qing dynasty (1644-1912) is scarce. primarily as it was used as a less costly and more easily worked version of hardstones such as turquoise. After the accession of the Kangxi Emperor in 1662, the import of European glass changed the situation. From then on, Jesuit missionaries led a growth in the popularity of glass, with techniques developing under later Emperors.

- Three types of glass were produced: enamelled, overlaid cameo glass, and coloured glass. 18thC and early 19thC Peking enamelled glass followed porcelain in terms of decoration, but had an added luminosity only available with glass. Detail is everything. Dating from the 18thC to the 20thC, cameo-cut overlaid glass often combined colours, and was intended to imitate natural materials such as hornbill, or manufactured materials such as blue and white porcelain. Coloured glass dates from the same long period, and took the appearance of the hardstones (such as lapis lazuli) that inspired it. Song Dynasty ceramics were also imitated by glass with copper inclusions.

- Marks generally comprise reign marks, which are compromised in format by the vertical lines of a cutting wheel. Complexity, age, and visual or symbolic appeal are all factors that count towards value. Many reproductions and fakes exist (see box, left).

A late 19thC/early 20thC Chinese Peking glass waterpot, formed as a lotus flower head with pink, green and white overlays, one side carved with a small flowering lotus plant.

4in (10.5cm) high

£1,200-1,800 WW

A late 19thC Chinese Peking glass five colour snuff bottle, with yellow, green, blue, black and red carved overlay in the form of leaves and flowers on an opaque white glass bottle.

3.5in (9cm) high

£400-500 LHA

A late 19thC Chinese opaque white Peking glass vase, decorated with polychrome enamelled scenes depicting young boys at play.

5.5in (14cm) high

£1,000-1,500 LHA

A 20thC Chinese colourless and yellow cased Peking glass snuff bottle, carved with yellow rings, lacking stopper.

2in (5cm) high

£35-45 WW

A Chinese turquoise Peking glass bottle vase, with a cylindrical neck and ovoid body.

c1800   *7.25in (18.5cm) high*

£600-800 WW

A small 19thC Chinese amethyst Peking glass bowl, with plain exterior.

Provenance: Acquired by a teaching missionary in Amoy, China in 1906, and brought back to Britain in 1941.

4.25in (11cm) diam

£220-280 DN

ORIENTAL

QUICK REFERENCE - SOAPSTONE

- Soapstone, also known as steatite, is a comparatively soft rock composed primarily of the mineral talc. As such, it is easy to carve and has been used for centuries by sculptors across the world to produce small to medium sized compositions. It comes in a variety of colours ranging from cream to amber through to brown and green. As such, it is often mistaken for jade, however, unlike jade, it is possible to scratch soapstone with a knife or even a finger nail. The vast majority of soapstone sculptures produced for the past hundred years have been for the tourist industry, which began to peak during World War II and the Korean war, and grew further with the increase of less expensive international holidays in the late 20thC.
- When looking at a sculpture, consider the colour, size, age, quality, and the level of detail or stylisation. Most mass-produced tourist pieces have forms that are blocky, lumpen, and poorly conceived. Most of these will have been carved quickly and basically. Genuine examples can be extremely hard to date, so a strong provenance for 18thC and early 19thC pieces will add value. Look at the best examples in museums and galleries to learn how to recognise the style

and appearance of truly antique pieces. However, there's nothing wrong with buying a 20thC soapstone carving (many of these now being 'antiques' themselves!) if you like it. Many examples can be found for under £100, and will form a great collection. The rule here is buy it if you like it, as prices for such tourist pieces are unlikely to rise in the future.

A 20thC Chinese soapstone carving of three shi-shi dogs.

9in (23cm) long

£50-80   GORL

A late 18thC/early 19thC Chinese soapstone group, carved as a mother and two young chilong.

5.3in (13.5cm) long

£100-150   SWO

A 20thC Chinese green soapstone desk seal, in the shape of a seated Buddhistic lion, on a square base carved with calligraphy.

Soapstone seals with rectangular bases carved with Chinese characters usually indicating a name are still produced in China today. A street artist can carve characters onto a small seal already carved with an animal, measuring around 2.75in (7cm) high, for less than £10.

4in (11cm) high

£40-60   ROS

A pair of 20thC Chinese carved soapstone figures of stylised crouching dragons, with horns and ribbed chests.

5.5in (14cm) long

£100-150   TEN

A pair of late 19thC Chinese carved soapstone dragons, on square plinths with incised decoration.

8in (20.5cm) high

£60-80   ROS

A 20thC Chinese carved cream coloured soapstone model of a horse, with a carved hardwood stand, and a fabric covered and lined fitted box.

2.25in (6cm) high

£30-40   GORL

An 18thC Chinese soapstone carving of Shoulao, standing holding a branch over his shoulder, his robes finely incised with cloud scrolls, and with polychrome details, damaged.

Provenance: This was purchased by Sackville George Pelham, 5th Earl of Yarborough from top London dealer John Sparks Ltd., and is recorded in their archive. It's the movement in the cloak, the fine quality, and this provenance that marks this out as desirable and valuable.

8in (21cm) high

£2,000-3,000　　　　　　　　　　　　　　　　**WW**

A late 19thC Chinese carved soapstone figure of an Immortal, holding a ju-i sceptre, on a carved wooden rockwork base.

14.5in (37cm) high

£80-120　　　　　　　　**CAPE**

An early 20thC Chinese carved soapstone figure of Guanyin, holding a vase, adapted into a lampbase.

12.5in (32cm) high

£50-80　　　　　　　　**LC**

An early 20thC carved soapstone baluster vase, decorated with lotus blossom details to a stained carved stand, slightly damaged.

11in (27cm) high

£25-35　　　　　　　　**FLD**

An early 20thC Chinese soapstone vase, carved in the form of a lotus plant.

12in (29.5cm) high

£150-200　　　　　　　　**DN**

A 20thC Chinese soapstone boulder group, carved with two sages holding a scroll, a crane and a deer among bamboo, prunus and pine, on a pierced stand.

15in (39cm) high

£180-220　　　　　　　　**DN**

A 19thC Chinese soapstone brushwasher, carved with eight figures issuing from clouds, with a stork and a deer to the base.

5in (13cm) high

£800-1,200　　　　　　　　**WW**

ORIENTAL

A pair of mid-20thC Chinese cloisonné ovoid vases, decorated with red capped cranes among pine and blossoms on a blue ground, beneath a ruyi head band and a flared neck.

15in (39cm) high

£500-700   **TOV**

A pair of 19thC Chinese cloisonné candlesticks, with hexagonal bases, decorated with dice, hammers, tongs, and other implements.

8in (20.5cm) high

£700-1,000   **WW**

QUICK REFERENCE - THE IMPERIAL DRAGON

- Unlike in the West, the dragon is a blessed, lucky and benevolent beast in Chinese mythology. It is also powerfully symbolic. When shown with five claws, it is known as the Imperial Dragon, and was used by the Emperor only. As on this dish, the dragon is usually shown flying through the clouds, or swimming through the waves, while chasing the sacred pearl (tama). This pearl is symbolic of wisdom, rebirth and qi, the creator of all energy and life. It is usually shown emitting flames that look like sprouting seeds.

- It is important to remember that the presence of a five-clawed dragon on a piece does not mean that it was owned by a Chinese Emperor, or is even based on a piece that was. This dish is one of many hundreds of thousands of similar pieces made in the late 20thC for Chinese and Western tourists, as indicated by the comparatively simple design, brash colours and light-toned brassy metal. True pre-20thC Imperial pieces are both extremely rare and of the very finest quality.

An early 20thC Chinese cloisonné shallow bowl, decorated with Imperial dragons on a black ground.

8.25in (21cm) diam

£25-35   **DN**

A Chinese cloisonné dish, decorated with a crane and a deer beneath a pine tree, the border with lotus, chrysanthemum, prunus and songbirds.

c1900

10in (25cm) diam

£500-700   **WW**

A 20thC Chinese cloisonné jar and cover, of orbicular form with domed cover and peg feet, decorated with floral panels on an iron red, scrollwork ground.

3.75in (9.5cm) high

£20-30   **CAPE**

A Japanese cloisonné ovoid vase, decorated with cranes, with a silvered base ring and rim.

6.5in (17cm) high

£150-200   **LHA**

A pair of Japanese Meiji period cloisonné vases, each slender shouldered ovoid body decorated with a pair of eagles perched on rocky outcrops above a waterfall, pool and blossom on a sage green ground, (one with minor faults).

6in (15cm) high

£180-220   **TOV**

A CLOSER LOOK AT A CLOISONNÉ VASE

Master cloisonné worker Ando Jubei established his workshop in Nagoya, Japan in 1881, employing a number of skilled craftsmen to produce his designs.

He is known for a number of technical innovations including a repoussé ground covered with clear enamel, and transparent 'plique à jour' inspired by French designs.

His company's marks include 'Ando Made' in Japanese kanji characters within an oval, and a 'mon' comprising four small petal shapes within a circle. Pieces marked 'Japan' or 'Made in Japan' are 20thC, even if they have other marks.

An early 20thC Japanese Ando Jubei cloisonné vase, decorated with a flowering prunus tree, bamboo and other flowers on a red ground, with stamped mark to the footrim.

11in (27.5cm) high

£150-250   **WW**

A small Japanese late Meiji period cloisonné jar and cover, the domed cover with foliate openwork button finial within an arcade, a further arcade to the shoulder over diverse mon roundels containing Buddhistic precious objects, flowers and birds, against a dense scroll ground, a lappet band to the base, on four tri-lobed out-swept feet.

3.9in (10 cm) high

£300-500   **TEN**

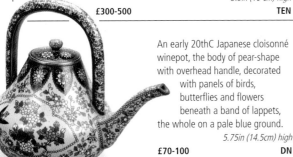

An early 20thC Japanese cloisonné winepot, the body of pear-shape with overhead handle, decorated with panels of birds, butterflies and flowers beneath a band of lappets, the whole on a pale blue ground.

5.75in (14.5cm) high

£70-100   **DN**

A large 20thC Japanese cloisonné charger, decorated with a basket of flowers.

25in (64cm) diam

£200-300   **LHA**

PAPERWEIGHTS

QUICK REFERENCE

- The first glass paperweights were made in 1843 on the Venetian island of Murano. Notable makers included Pietro Bigaglia, who was known for his paperweights with patterns made up of tiny sections of coloured glass canes known as millefiori (Italian for 'a thousand flowers'). They caught on with the rising middle clases and factories vied to learn the skills of their creation, and take advantage of the trend
- The 'golden age' of the paperweight followed, and lasted until the mid-1850s. Production was centred in France where factories such as Baccarat (est.1764), Clichy (1837-1885) and Saint Louis (est.1767) produced glass weights of different sizes. As well as complex millefiori patterns, they also produced intricate lamp-worked designs of flowers or fruit.
- When the fashion waned in the mid-1850s, many French paperweight makers moved to the US, and continued their work at factories such as the Boston & Sandwich Glass Co.
- Paperweights were also made in the UK by Richardsons, Whitefriars, and Bacchus & Sons, and in Bohemia.

- Collectors tend to focus on mid-19thC French paperweights, or those made elsewhere from the mid-20thC onwards. This later period is dominated by American and Scottish makers. Notable makers include Emil Larson, Charles Kaziun, and Paul Stankard in the US, and Paul Ysart, John Deacons, and William Manson in Scotland. The Scottish Caithness factory produced many paperweights from 1969 onwards. Designed by a small team of specialist designers, these are widely collected
- 19thC French weights can be identified by the colours, the pattern, and the elements that make up the pattern, such as the 'Clichy Rose' (see facing page). Most 20thC paperweight makers signed their work on the base or include a 'signature cane' (see facing page) in the design.
- As well as the maker, the size and complexity of a weight will affect value. Very large (magnum) weights and miniature weights can be rare. You should also consider the design. Those with more complex, time-consuming to produce patterns are more likely to have a higher value.

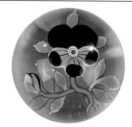

A mid-19thC Baccarat pansy paperweight, with lamp-worked pansy, and leafed stem, with an extra bud, the polished base cut with a star.

2.75in (7cm) diam

£250-350   FIS

A mid-19thC Baccarat pansy paperweight, with a lamp-worked purple and yellow flower, a bud, and green stem and leaves.

2.75in (7cm) diam

£300-500   DN

A mid-19thC St. Louis paperweight, containing two lamp-worked pears, an apple, and four cherries on stems with green leaves, over a double swirl lattice white thread ground.

2in (5cm) high

£700-1,000   DOR

An 1850s Baccarat anemone paperweight.

2.25in (6cm) diam

£800-1,000   BGL

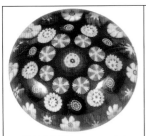

A mid-19thC Clichy paperweight, set with concentric circles of coloured canes on a green ground.

3in (7.5cm) diam

£650-850   SWO

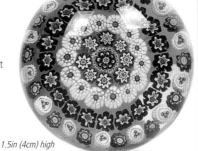

A mid-19thC Baccarat paperweight, with multicoloured and white millefiori canes set in concentric circles.

1.5in (4cm) high

£700-1,000   DOR

A mid-19thC Baccarat paperweight, with concentric rings of multicoloured millefiori and star canes on a colourless ground, the base with polished pontil mark.

2.5in (6.5cm) diam

£200-250   FIS

A mid-19thC St. Louis paperweight, with concentric circles of blue, red, green and white millefiori murrines.

2in (5cm) high

£120-180   FIS

A mid-19thC Clichy millefiori crown paperweight, with central Clichy rose.

3in (7.5cm) diam

£700-1,000   GORL

QUICK REFERENCE - PAPERWEIGHT TERMINOLOGY

SILHOUETTE CANE

A cane with the profile of an animal, person or flower, made up of many thin rods compacted together. The ancient Romans were the first to use them for coloured portraits. During the 19thC they were used by many Venetian companies, particularly Baccarat. Its manager Jean-Baptiste Toussaint is credited with introducing the technique in paperweight production after seeing his nephew Emile Gridel making paper cut-outs of animals, as a result these are often known as 'gridels'.

UPSET MUSLIN

A background made up of randomly placed sections of tubular cane cut into different lengths. The cane is made up of a spiralling white thread in colourless glass. This background is also sometimes referred to simply as 'muslin'.

MILLEFIORI

The Italian word for 'a thousand flowers'. Thin glass rods (known as canes) are made up of many much thinner coloured rods arranged longitudinally together to form a flower-like pattern when cut in cross-section, like pixels on a screen. These canes are then sliced into short sections to reveal the internal floral pattern, a little like a stick of seaside rock, which are then stood on end and arranged in a group to form a 'set up'. If the canes cover the entire 'ground' of the base of a weight, this is known as a 'carpet-ground' weight. The 'set up' is picked up on a gather of glass and covered with a dome of colourless glass to form the paperweight. During this latter process, the maker must be careful not to trap any air bubbles under the dome.

LAMP-WORKING

Thin rods and sections of glass are heated with a small blow torch until they become pliable. They are then pulled, cut, bonded to each other, and worked with tools into different forms, such as leaves, stems and flowers. Once constructed, the three-dimensional glass piece is applied to a base and then covered with a colourless glass dome.

DATE CANE

A series of canes, showing a date, usually from the 1840s. They were commonly used in French canes made by the major companies. A letter 'B' before the date indicates the weight was made by Baccarat. The year is not always the year that the weight was made, and fakes are known.

CLICHY ROSE

A trademark cane used by French company Clichy to identify some of its paperweights. It can be found in different colours and sizes, but always resembles a tight, but opening rosebud. The company also used a cane containing the letter 'C'.

SIGNATURE CANE

Made in a similar way to date canes and millefiori, signature canes usually contain the initials, or the first letter of the surname or company of the maker. The 'PH' here indicates Peter Holmes, 'PY' is Paul Ysart, 'H' is Ysart's Harland factory, 'WM' is William Manson, 'JD' is John Deacons, and 'P' Perthshire Paperweights.

PAPERWEIGHTS

A CLOSER LOOK AT A BACCARAT PAPERWEIGHT

Tightly packed carpet-ground weights like this, featuring many different types of canes, are highly desirable, especially if they are by major companies such as Baccarat.

There are many different type of silhouette cane, including an elephant, reindeer, horse, dog, butterfly, and a walking man, some of which are scarce.

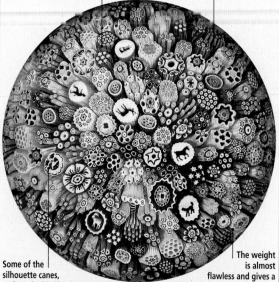

Some of the silhouette canes, such as the bird here, are particularly complex in terms of their composition and construction.

The weight is almost flawless and gives a superb sense of colour, almost appearing to 'explode' at the viewer due to the dome's magnification.

A Baccarat closepack millefiori paperweight, with various silhouette canes including an elephant, reindeer, horse, dog, butterfly, and a man, and with an '1848' date cane.

1848   *3in (7.5cm) diam*
£4,500-5,500   **DCP**

A mid-19thC Baccarat paperweight, with colourful millefiori canes, and with devil, dog, horse and pheasant silhouette canes, and '1848' date cane.

1848   *2in (4.5cm) high*
£700-1,000   **DOR**

A mid-19thC Clichy millefiori paperweight, with a clear ground.

2.75in (7cm) diam
£300-500   **GORL**

A mid-19thC Clichy paperweight, with colourful millefiori canes including two green and pink and one white Clichy rose canes, some scratches.

2in (4.5cm) high
£700-1,000   **DOR**

A mid-19thC Clichy chequer 'scramble' paperweight, decorated with millefiori and twist canes.

'Scramble' paperweights contain a random selection of sections of different canes and tend not to be as valuable as more organised patterns. However, the sections on this example are arranged in a chequerboard pattern, which makes this weight more desirable than typical 'scramble' weights.

3.25in (8.5cm) diam
£250-350   **GORL**

A mid-19thC St. Louis jasper-ground paperweight, enclosing a roundel of three colours of concentric canes around a central quatrefoil, on a blue jasper-ground, with a small bruise to one side.

2.25in (5.5cm) diam
£100-150   **WW**

QUICK REFERENCE - CAITHNESS PAPERWEIGHTS

- Caithness Glass was founded in 1961 and officially released its first abstract paperweights in 1969. Paul Ysart had produced some weights after joining the company in 1962, but these had largely been traditional forms.

- Ysart, Terris and Peter Holmes continued to produce innovative paperweights during the 1970s, with production expanding rapidly during the 1980s and '90s. By 1993, 44 people made paperweights at Caithness under Terris's direction, including a team of designers such as Helen MacDonald, Gordon Hendry, and Alastair MacIntosh. Over 2,300 different designs have been produced in limited and unlimited editions, and they have become collected across the world.

- Look out for the work of notable designers, small edition sizes, and complex designs. Some editions included in this section were closed before the run was completed, and this is indicated in the footnote. 'Admiration' was only issued in this large, 'magnum' size, and originally cost £300.

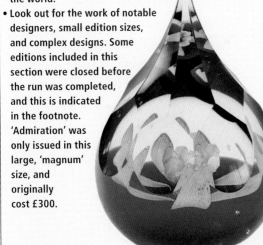

A Caithness Glass limited edition 'Ammadora' paperweight, no.CT1410, designed by the Caithness Design Studio, from the 'Modern Design' series, the base with factory marks and numbered 21 from a limited edition of 50.
1997
£120-180   CHT

A Caithness Glass limited edition 'Auld Lang Syne' paperweight, no.CT1398, designed by Helen MacDonald, from the 'Modern Design' series, the base with factory marks and numbered 43 from a limited edition of 125.

This edition was closed at no.96.
1997
£40-60   CHT

A Caithness Glass limited edition 'Admiration' magnum paperweight, no.CT1399, designed by Colin Terris, from the 'Modern Design' series, the base with factory marks and numbered 41 from an edition of 75.
1997
£150-200   CHT

A Caithness Glass limited edition 'Butterfly' paperweight, no.CT1019, designed by William Manson, from the 'Traditional' collection, the base with factory marks and numbered 15 from a limited edition of 150.

This edition was closed at no.141. There are at least four different designs bearing the name 'Butterfly'.
1993
£35-45   CHT

A Caithness Glass limited edition 'Camelot II' paperweight, no.1471, designed by Colin Terris, from the 'Colin Terris Designer' collection, the base with factory marks and numbered 31 from a limited edition of 250.

The edition was closed early at no. 228.
1997
£60-80   CHT

A Caithness Glass limited edition 'Dahlia' paperweight, no.CT1204, designed by William Manson, from the 'Traditional' collection, the base with factory marks and numbered 64 from a limited edition of 150.

Only 124 examples had been made by the time the edition was closed. In the same year Helen MacDonald designed a different weight bearing the same name in an edition of 50, which can fetch over three times the value of this example.
1995
£35-45   CHT

PAPERWEIGHTS

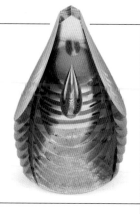

A Caithness Glass limited edition 'Debut' paperweight, no.CT1149, designed by Helen MacDonald, from the 'Modern Design' series, the base with factory marks and numbered 3 from an edition of 50.

1995

£50-80   **CHT**

A Caithness Glass limited edition 'Delphinium & Ladybird' paperweight, no.CT1253, designed by William Manson, from the 'Traditional' collection, the base with factory marks and numbered 45 from a limited edition of 150.

This edition was closed at no.90.

1995

£60-80   **CHT**

A CLOSER LOOK AT A PAPERWEIGHT

This is a 'magnum' sized paperweight, which is the largest size of paperweight made at Caithness.

The dome has been cut with facets to add sparkle and movement, and to reflect the flower inside in a lively manner.

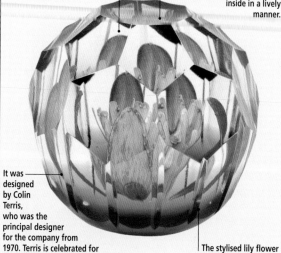

It was designed by Colin Terris, who was the principal designer for the company from 1970. Terris is celebrated for his progressive abstract weights, which launched an entirely new category of paperweights and art glass.

The stylised lily flower and leaves inside were lamp-worked to give them three-dimensional form.

A Caithness Glass limited edition 'Enchantment' magnum paperweight, no.CT1299, designed by Colin Terris, from the 'Modern Design' series, the base with factory marks and numbered 65 from a limited edition of 75.

1996

£180-220   **CHT**

A Caithness Glass limited edition 'Fairy Land' paperweight, no.CT1173, designed by Helen MacDonald, from the 'Modern Design' series, the base with factory marks and numbered 25 from a limited edition of 100.

1995

£120-180   **CHT**

A Caithness Glass limited edition 'Imprint' paperweight, no.CT1407, designed by Alastair MacIntosh, from the 'Modern Design' series, the base with factory marks and numbered 64 from a limited edition of 200.

This edition was closed at no.107.

1997

£30-50   **CHT**

A Caithness Glass limited edition 'Innocence' paperweight, no.CT1396 designed by Colin Terris, from the 'Modern Design' series, the base with factory marks and numbered 62 from a limited edition of 75.

1997

£50-70   **CHT**

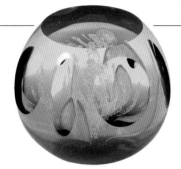

A Caithness Glass limited edition 'Iris' paperweight, no.CT-488, designed by Colin Terris, from the 'Watercolours' series, with surface decoration of irises and a band of millefiori canes, the base with factory marks and numbered 176 from a limited edition of 750.

This was the first of three designs called 'Iris', with the others containing lamp-worked flowers. This edition was closed at no.239. The original retail price was £37.95.

1986   *3in (8cm) high*

£25-35   **WHP**

A Caithness Glass special edition 'Jubilee Orchid' paperweight, no.CT1062, designed by Colin Terris, from an edition of 1,833, with factory marks to the base.

This was the Collectors' paperweight for 1994, with the edition being completely sold out at a retail price of £99 or $275.

1994

£30-50   **CHT**

A CLOSER LOOK AT A PAPERWEIGHT

Shown in the 2006 catalogue, this weight originally cost £425.

Caithness Glass acquired the Whitefriars brand name (along with its remaining moulds) in 1981, and used it for a range of paperweights.

The Whitefriars range comprises weights with traditional millefiori patterns or lamp-worked motifs, often in bright colours and with cut facets.

Whitefriars weights produced by Caithness usually contain a 'signature cane' showing the famous logo of a hooded monk in blue.

A Caithness Glass limited edition 'Lilac' paperweight, designed by Alan Scott, from the 'Whitefriars Love Flowers' collection, with a cut circle, cut facets, and internal lamp-worked flowers and foliage, with engraved signature, numbered 45 from a limited edition of 50.

2006   *3in (7.5cm) high*

£280-320   **FLD**

A Caithness Glass limited edition 'New World' paperweight, no.CT740, designed by Stuart Cumming, from the 'Modern Design' series, the base with factory marks and numbered 228 from a limited edition of 750.

1990   *3in (7.5cm) diam*

£30-50   **PC**

A Caithness Glass limited edition 'Norman Conquest' paperweight, no.1402, designed by Colin Terris, from the 'Modern Design' series, the base with factory marks and numbered 12 from a limited edition of 100.

1997

£100-150   **CHT**

A Caithness Glass limited edition 'Paper Chase' paperweight, no.CT1144, designed by Alastair MacIntosh, from the 'Modern Design' series, the base with factory marks and numbered 504 from a limited edition of 750.

692 examples of this design were produced.

1995

£30-50   **CHT**

A CLOSER LOOK AT A SET OF PAPERWEIGHTS

The other planets, 'Uranus', 'Jupiter', 'Neptune' and 'Earth', were released in a limited edition of 500 in 1970, numbered CT4 A-D, and are known as 'Planets, Set Two'.

This set was a design reinterpretation of the original 'Planets' set, which was released in a limited edition of 500 in 1969.

A set of four Caithness Glass limited edition 'Planets, Set Three' paperweights, comprising clockwise from left no.CT1158C 'Saturn', no.CT1158D 'Mars', no.CT1158A 'Mercury', and no.CT1158B 'Venus', designed by Colin Terris, the bases with factory marks and each numbered 106 from a limited edition of 350.
1995

£150-200   CHT

The original set was a landmark design for the company and for 20thC paperweight design in general, due to its theme and abstract design.

This edition, produced to mark the 25th anniversary of the original set, was closed with 232 sets having been issued.

The original set, numbered CT1 A-D, originally cost £40 per set. Today it can fetch over £1,000.

A Caithness Glass limited edition 'Seahorse' paperweight, no.CT1198, designed by William Manson, from the 'Traditional' collection, the base with factory marks and numbered 34 from a limited edition of 50.

This was the second Caithness paperweight design to include a lamp-worked seahorse. The first, released in 1986, is not spherical, and is worth around the same amount. 208 pieces were produced from an edition of 250.

1995
£150-200   CHT

A Caithness Glass limited edition 'Seascape' paperweight, no.CT1118, designed by William Manson, from the 'Traditional' collection, the base with factory marks and numbered 12 from a limited edition of 50.
1994
£120-180   CHT

A Caithness Glass limited edition 'Stingray' paperweight, no.CT1120, designed by William Manson, from the 'Traditional' collection, the base with factory marks and numbered 6 from a limited edition of 50.
1994
£150-200   CHT

A Caithness Glass limited edition 'Tranquil Pool' paperweight, no.CT1344, designed by Colin Terris, from the 'Modern Design' series, the base with factory marks and numbered 34 from an edition of 50.
1996
£120-180   CHT

A Caithness Glass unique 'Tropical Delight' paperweight, designed and made by Sarah Peterson and Martin Murray, the base with engraved signatures and numbered 1 of 1, complete with box and certificate.
c2009
£250-350

4in (10cm) high
FLD

QUICK REFERENCE - PERTHSHIRE PAPERWEIGHTS

- **Perthshire Paperweights was founded in Crieff, Scotland in 1968 by Stuart Drysdale after he left Strathearn Glass. He employed five skilled glassmakers from Strathearn, including John Deacons (who left c1978) and Peter McDougall. As well as making paperweights, they helped to train locals in the skills of glass-making.**
- **Quality was extremely high, and many different types of weight were produced, typically in limited editions. Nearly all their weights include a 'P' signature cane, often with the year of manufacture.**
- **After Stuart Drysdale's death in 1990, his son Neil took over until his untimely death in 2001. The factory closed in the same year, with McDougall setting up his own company in Crieff the year after.**
- **Perthshire's paperweights are highly collectable across the world.**

A Perthshire Glass limited edition millefiori paperweight, the five petalled floral form made up of variously coloured canes, the centre of each petal with a cane containing a bicycle, hot air balloon, car, boat, and train respectively, with 'P1980' date cane.

1980   *3in (7.5cm) diam*
£200-300   **ROS**

A Perthshire limited edition paperweight, with millefiori and silhouette canes on a pink latticinio ground, with 'P1976' date cane, numbered 179 from an edition of 400, in original presentation box with certificate.

1976   *2.75in (7cm) diam*
£120-180   **ECGW**

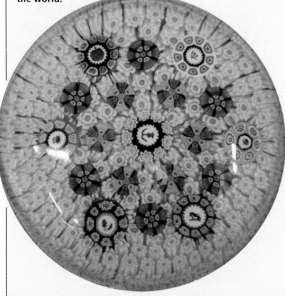

A Perthshire limited edition carpet-ground paperweight, containing seven coloured silhouette canes of flowers, animals, and birds on a carpet of light coloured canes, with 'P1977' date cane to base, numbered 45 from an edition of 400, in original presentation box with certificate.

1977   *3.25in (8.5cm) diam*
£250-350   **ECGW**

A Perthshire limited edition 'Christmas 1985' crown paperweight, containing ten red, green and, white twisted canes alternating with white latticinio canes, with central cane with candle and holly, with 'P1985' date cane and paper label to base, numbered 87 from an edition of 300, in original presentation box with certificate.

1985   *2.75in (7cm) diam*
£200-300   **ECGW**

A Perthshire limited edition 'Christmas 1986' paperweight, containing a lamp-worked red candle with holly and berries floating on a basket of fifteen green canes alternating with red and white latticinio canes, with signature cane 'P' in one of the green canes, numbered 52 from an edition of 300, in original presentation box with certificate.

1986   *3in (7.5cm) diam*
£150-200   **ECGW**

A Perthshire limited edition 'Christmas 1983' paperweight, containing a lamp-worked holly wreath with red berries tied with a green and red ribbon on a white latticinio ground, 'P1983' date cane and paper label to base, numbered 252 from an edition of 350, in original presentation box with certificate.

1983   *2.75in (7cm) diam*
£150-200   **ECGW**

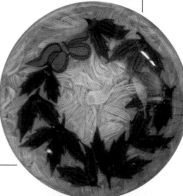

A Paul Ysart floral paperweight, the lamp-worked flower with red petals and green stem surrounded by millefiori canes, with a 'PY' signature cane near the base of the stem.

'PY' signature canes were typically used for weights exported to the US. Ysart was approached by Paul Jokelson, the President of the American 'Paperweight Collectors Association', in around 1955 and from then on, many of Ysart's weights were distributed to keen collectors in the US.

2.5in (6.5cm) wide

£180-220   **L&T**

A Paul Ysart paperweight, with an orange and red lamp-worked fish over a mottled powder pink ground within an air bubble ring, with 'H' cane to underside and partial original paper label.

The 'H' stands for Harland, where Ysart founded his own studio after leaving Caithness in 1970.

2.75in (7cm) diam

£100-150   **FLD**

Mark Picks

Late 20thC Scottish paperweights are hotly collected across the world. Look out for those by key makers such as Paul Ysart, William Manson, John Deacons, or Peter MacDougall. Peter Holmes is another leading maker who is still active today, over four decades after he started making paperweights. He studied under the master designer and maker Paul Ysart, and carries on many of the techniques and traditional styles he learnt from him. Over the past decade, the traditional paperweight industry has shrunk. As people stop making or die, finely-honed historic skills are lost. The best craftworks of today become the antiques of tomorrow, so it's well worth supporting the skilled craftsmen and artists producing them. This unique weight is an excellent example of its kind. If you need any more persuasion, just compare the price to that of many older weights.

A Scottish Borders Art Glass paperweight, designed and made by Peter Holmes, with 'PH' signature cane near the base of the stem, the base signed 'Scottish Borders Art Glass Peter Holmes 2007'.

2007   *3.5in (9cm) diam*

£120-180   **SBA**

A Paul Ysart floral paperweight, the lamp-worked flower with red and yellow petals and green stem on a green ground, surrounded by latticino and aventurine canes, the base with a 'PY' paper label.

2.5in (6.5cm) wide

£180-220   **L&T**

An American Lundberg Studios 'White Crane' paperweight, the lamp-worked crane in flight over a cobalt blue ground with a lighter blue swirl.

2in (5cm) diam

£200-250   **SWB**

An American David P. Salazar 'paperweight style' sphere, with a hotworked butterfly over a pink hibiscus flower, signed on the base.

Salazar is the most widely recognised exponent of the Californian 'painting with glass' technique. The facet cuts are an unusual feature.

2in (5cm) diam

£150-200   **BGL**

A CLOSER LOOK AT A STANKARD PAPERWEIGHT

Paul Stankard (b.1943) is one of the world's most important and skilled contemporary paperweight artists, with examples in many top museums across the world.

He also incorporates forms, such as root people, and words to encourage the viewer to consider the deeper mystical and poetic themes of the progress of life and nature, fertility and decay.

He is celebrated for his exquisitely lamp-worked floral arrangements, which are so realistic that some people have thought they were real flowers.

Inspired by a deep love of nature and botany, his arrangements are complex and contain many different, carefully crafted elements.

A Paul Stankard 'Botanical' paperweight, containing a bee hovering over a floral arrangement including flowers, leaves, an ant, a beetle, moss, and berries, the roots below containing two root spirits and the words 'dew', 'nectar', 'fertile', 'seeds', and 'scent', the base inscribed 'Paul J. Stankard T4 1999'.

1999   *3.25in (8.5cm) diam*
£1,800-2,200   **LHA**

A Stourbridge millefiori paperweight, with blue, red, white, and green cut canes around a central white star.

Provenance: J. F. Blood & Sons, Antique Dealers, Manchester, and with the remains of a Sotheby's lot label for the sale of the collection of Mrs Applewhaite-Abbott, on February 24th 1953. Applewhaite-Abbott (d.1938) was one of the earliest important 20thC collectors of paperweights and a major influence in the revival of the collecting area from the 1930s onwards.

c1850-60   *4in (10.5cm) diam*
£350-450   **TEN**

A Paul Stankard 'Paphiopedilum Orchid' paperweight, with a burgundy spotted pink and white orchid flower, green stems and leaves, buds and roots, signed 'Paul J. Stankard EGW3 1989'.

1989   *3in (7.5cm) wide*
£650-850   **DRA**

A late 20thC Okra Glass paperweight, designed by Richard Golding, decorated with stylised flower heads and hearts over a silver iridescent ground with combed lines, unmarked.

£80-120   **FLD**

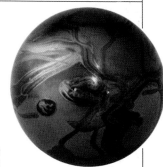

A late 20thC Glasform iridescent paperweight, decorated with stylised motifs in a gold colourway, signed 'J Ditchfield-Glasform no.PW135', with original paper label to base.

3in (8cm) high
£70-90   **MAR**

A Whitefriars paperweight, designed by Geoffrey Baxter, the faceted form inset candle cane.

3in (8cm) diam
£70-80   **WW**

QUICK REFERENCE

- Vintage fountain pens began to be more widely collected in the 1970s, and peaked in interest and value in the 1990s and early 2000s. Like many collecting areas, the name of the maker is everything, and most collectors focus on the biggest brands. These include Parker, Waterman, and Montblanc, but, over the past few years smaller brands, such as Conway Stewart, have risen in desirability and value.

- Although brand is often the most important consideration, rarity and quality affect value considerably, as does a pen's visual impact and eye-appeal. Pens with gold-plated overlays, lacquerwork designs, or those in unusual, brightly coloured celluloids tend to be the most valuable. Certain models, such as Parker's Duofold or 51, also tend to be more popular. Modern limited edition pens can also be valuable. Size is also a consideration, as many pen collectors are men and therefore favour larger pens that fit their hands. Common,

standard pens are often worth under £30, even with their original gold nibs. However, these can make practical and interesting 'everyday' writing instruments.

- The 'golden age' of the fountain pen dates from the late 1910s-30s although, as many have now become scarce and expensive, collectors have turned to lesser brands and later pens from the 1960s onwards. The advent of the internet has meant that collectors from different countries can learn about and collect pens from countries other than their own.

- Earlier writing equipment is also desirable. This includes steel nibs, the pen holders that held them, inkwells, and propelling pencils. Most pieces found will date from the early 19thC onwards. Earlier examples can be rare but not always valuable. Although makers' names such as Bramah or Mordan & Co. are very desirable, the materials used and the complexity of the decoration effect value the most.

A Sampson Mordan and Gabriel Riddle silver 'Everpointed' propelling pencil, with alternating panels of lines and dots, and engine-turned decoration, the terminal, sliding collar, and nozzle with gilt foliate casting, stamped with 'SM GR' makers' marks and 'Patent G.Riddle', and with London hallmarks for 1836.

1836 3.75in (9.5cm) long
£150-200 WW

Mark Picks

The earliest of Mordan's celebrated 'Everpointed' pencils are usually simply, yet elegantly, decorated, and it's easy to pass over them as they all look the same. Early examples produced under Mordan and Riddle's partnership can be scarce. It's always worth checking the hallmarks as any piece produced before 1825 would be extremely rare, highly desirable, and potentially very valuable to a collector. An example from this period could fetch over £1,000! Furthermore, some early Mordan examples were not hallmarked, meaning some sellers price them less expensively as they do not think they are silver. Keep your eyes peeled!

A Sampson Mordan and Gabriel Riddle reeded silver 'Everpointed' propelling pencil, with an intaglio seal terminal, with 'SM GR' makers' marks and London hallmarks.

1831 3.5in (9cm) long
£150-250 WW

An early 19thC unmarked silver-inlaid tortoiseshell-overlaid propelling pencil, with flowering vine and piqué work decoration, and inset amethyst terminal.

c1835 3.5in (9cm) long
£350-450 WW

A Sampson Mordan for Lund reeded pen and pencil combination, with decorated shaped sliders and screw-off domed top for lead storage, with 'SM' hallmarks for London 1857, stamped 'LUND - CORNHILL LONDON'.

1857 3.5in (9cm) long
£120-180 PC

A Lund ivory propelling pencil, stamped 'LUND PATENTEE LONDON', with a spiralling silver collar to propel the lead.

Based in Cornhill in the city of London, Lund was a stationer and retailer of finely made, often mechanical, objects.

c1840 3.75in (9.5cm) long
£50-70 PC

A W. Thornhill & Co. gold three-colour twist-action propelling pencil, with three coloured enamel bands, with hand-engraved initials 'C. B.'.

£100-150 **SWO**

A white metal cased three-colour twist-action propelling pencil, with suspension ring, marked 'Lockwood, New Bond Street'.

As indicated by its location on one of London's most prestigious shopping streets, Lockwood would have been the retailer, rather then the manufacturer.

£80-120 **CAPE**

A late 19thC Sampson Morden & Co. three-colour sterling silver propelling pencil, with coloured stone mounted sliding buttons, and 'S.MORDAN & CO' mark.

3in (7.5cm) long

£180-220 **GORL**

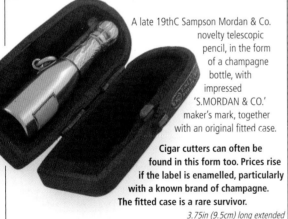

A late 19thC Sampson Mordan & Co. novelty telescopic pencil, in the form of a champagne bottle, with impressed 'S.MORDAN & CO.' maker's mark, together with an original fitted case.

Cigar cutters can often be found in this form too. Prices rise if the label is enamelled, particularly with a known brand of champagne. The fitted case is a rare survivor.

3.75in (9.5cm) long extended

£150-200 **WW**

A late 19thC Thornhill & Co. novelty propelling pencil, in the form of a tennis racket, with registration diamond for 1878, with suspension loop.

This pencil would also appeal to collectors of tennis memorabilia, hence the high price.

1878 *3in (8cm) long*

£450-550 **SWO**

A CLOSER LOOK AT A NOVELTY PENCIL

Blossoming from the 1880s-90s, and shown in their 1897 catalogue, Mordan's novelty pencils are highly sought-after by collectors today.

Made from silver and marked with Mordan's name, they are all of very high quality, with superb and fine detailing.

The more unusual the form, the more valuable it is likely to be. Owls, pistols and crosses are more common than boars or squirrels.

The mechanisms are well-engineered and costly to repair. The mechanism on this example is still working. By pulling the squirrel's head up, the pencil extends outwards.

A rare late 19thC Sampson Mordan & Co. silver novelty telescopic pencil, in the form of a squirrel holding a nut, with 'S.MORDAN & CO.' impressed marks.

1.5in (3.5cm) high

£1,200-1,800 **LC**

A late 19thC Sampson Mordan & Co. novelty telescopic pencil, in the form of a hand with a garnet-set ring on one finger, with intaglio bloodstone seal terminal.

This form was also used for a dip pen nib-holder, which is scarcer than the pencil and can fetch up to £500 or more. Beware of dented examples as these can be expensive and difficult to repair.

Closed 1.5in (4cm) long

£180-220 **WW**

PENS & WRITING

A CLOSER LOOK AT A PEN & PENCIL COMBINATION

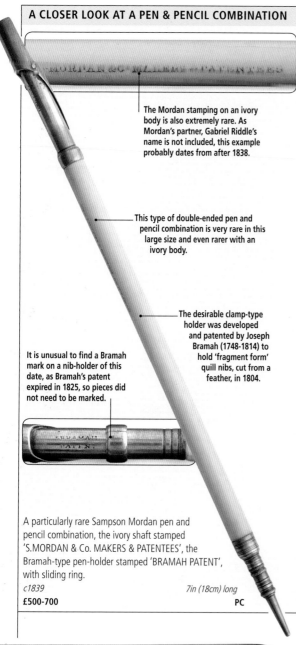

The Mordan stamping on an ivory body is also extremely rare. As Mordan's partner, Gabriel Riddle's name is not included, this example probably dates from after 1838.

This type of double-ended pen and pencil combination is very rare in this large size and even rarer with an ivory body.

The desirable clamp-type holder was developed and patented by Joseph Bramah (1748-1814) to hold 'fragment form' quill nibs, cut from a feather, in 1804.

It is unusual to find a Bramah mark on a nib-holder of this date, as Bramah's patent expired in 1825, so pieces did not need to be marked.

A particularly rare Sampson Mordan pen and pencil combination, the ivory shaft stamped 'S.MORDAN & Co. MAKERS & PATENTEES', the Bramah-type pen-holder stamped 'BRAMAH PATENT', with sliding ring.

c1839   *7in (18cm) long*

£500-700   **PC**

A very rare late 18thC ivory dip-pen-holder, with later tubular gold nib and chased gold bands, cleaned and uncracked.

The chased gold bands are similar to those attached to a late 19thC French penner illustrated in the seminal book 'Western Writing Implements In The Age Of The Quill Pen', by Michael Finlay, published by Plains Books in 1990.

4.25in (11cm) long

£250-350   **PC**

A rare George III presentation silver dip-pen, in the form of a quill, with maker's marks for John Jago and London hallmarks for 1794.

These were often given as school prizes to scholars or pupils for their achievements in handwriting, and often bear an inscription relating to the owner or event. John Jago is a notable and sought-after maker.

1794   *8.25in (21cm) long*

£350-450   **LC**

An 1820-1840s Bramah-type pen-holder, with turned mother-of-pearl shaft, with acorn finial, the silver collar and clamp marked 'BRAMAH PATENT'.

6in (15.5cm) long

£100-150   **PC**

A Joseph Gillot spring-ground 'Mammoth Quill' no.1001 pen-holder, the spiral fluted oak handle with large brass tubular nib.

It's the collectable Gillot name, and the rarity and large size of this nib that makes this pen-holder as valuable as it is.

c1885

£80-120   **BLO**

A late 19thC wooden novelty pen-holder, the terminal carved with a dog's head.

The material used, and the quality and level of detail on the carving affect value. This is relatively well-carved, but could be better. Had it been by a major maker, its value would be higher.

£30-40   **AMER**

A CLOSER LOOK AT A PEN SET

Waterman's used a numbering code on the end of the their pens' barrels up to c1930. With this 'No.0552', the 0 indicates gold-filling, the first 5 a full overlay, the second 5 a lever-filler, and the 2 a No.2 size pen and nib.

The addition of the original fitted presentation box makes the set more desirable, but not necessarily much more valuable.

An original matching set is very desirable to collectors, but the value would have been higher had the gold finish not been worn away through use at the pen's extremities.

Collectors call this wear 'brassing' as the underlying brassy base metal is showing through. Although this can be polished to improve its appearance, it would need to be re-plated to fix the damage permanently.

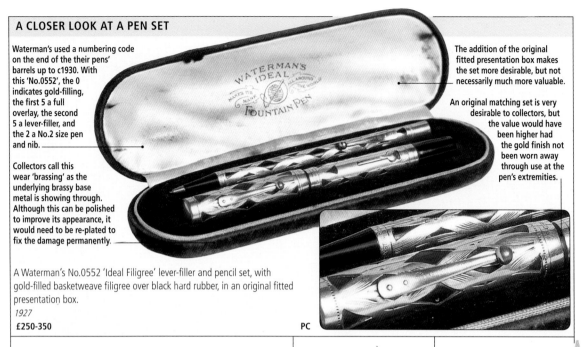

A Waterman's No.0552 'Ideal Filigree' lever-filler and pencil set, with gold-filled basketweave filigree over black hard rubber, in an original fitted presentation box.
1927
£250-350   **PC**

A Waterman's brown pearl 'Lizard' celluloid no.92 lever-filler, with Waterman's Ideal no.2 nib.
c1935
£100-150   **PC**

An English Waterman's light and dark rose pearl striated W3 lever-filler, with gold-filled trim and Waterman's W2-A nib, with a 1950s card box.
c1946
£30-50   **BPH**

An English Waterman's light and dark blue pearl W5 lever-filler, with Waterman England 14ct W-2A nib.

These pens were sold into the 1950s. Button-filling examples are much rarer and can fetch up to twice the value of this example.
c1946
£50-70   **HSR**

A French Waterman's sterling silver 'Crocodile' CF converter- or cartridge-filler and ballpoint pen set, with gold-filled trim and medium Waterman's 18K integral nib, in mint condition.

The 'CF' was the first commercially successful cartridge-filling fountain pen. Designed by car designer Harley J. Earl, it was introduced in 1953. After the American Waterman's factory closed in 1957, the 'CF' was made in a variety of finishes for nearly three decades in France. Always examine the gold-plated areas on either side of the nib as these were often corroded by the ink, and any damage reduces the value dramatically. This 'Crocodile' finish is sought-after, particularly in solid gold.
c1976
£140-180   **BPH**

A French Waterman's 'Man 100' 'Opera' converter- or cartridge-filler, with engine-turned body, gold-plated trim, and two-colour Waterman 18K Ideal nib.

Large, modern pens that were landmarks in their day, such as the 'Man 100', have become more sought-after than many vintage models over the past decade. The 'Man 100' was released in 1983 to commemorate the centenary of the company.
c1987
£150-200   **BPH**

A 1950s Burnham black-veined blue and grey pearl marbled no.60 lever-filler, with Burnham medium 820 nib.

Burnham pens tend to fetch under £100 unless they are very large, colourful, early in date, and in mint condition.
£20-30
AMER

A 1920s Conklin 'Lapis' blue Pyroxylin celluloid 'Endura Junior' lever-filler and twist-action pencil set, with red hands and ring-top caps, pen with Conklin 'Toledo' medium crescent nib.
c1928
£100-150
PC

A late 1920s American Carter's no.9125 'Jade' green Coralite celluloid lever-filler and propelling pencil set, the pen with Carter 'Inx Pen' nib.

Carter were best-known for their ink and office-related products, and only produced pens from c1926 to 1932. Their 1927 range was the first to use colourful celluloids. This example shows light discolouration of the 'Jade' green, caused by the internal rubber ink sack degrading.
£350-450
AMER

A 1930s Conway Stewart No. 540 'Dinkie' blue marbled celluloid lever-filler.
£50-70
AMER

A 1950s Conway Stewart No. 60 'Cracked Ice' celluloid lever-filler, with a medium no.58 Conway Stewart nib.

For more information about the sought-after 'Cracked Ice' series, please see 'Miller's Collectables Handbook 2010-2011' p.294.
1952
£100-150
PC

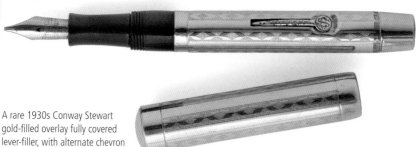

A rare 1930s Conway Stewart gold-filled overlay fully covered lever-filler, with alternate chevron and smooth panel patterns, with a medium 14ct Conway Stewart nib.

Conway Stewarts with original factory marked metal overlays are very rare, hence the high price for this small pen. The engine-turned pattern is also very crisp on this example.
£120-180
HSR

A late 1920s American Diamond Point 'Fill-E-Z' oversized red hard rubber lever-filler, with Artcraft nib.

This pen was produced in imitation of Parker's highly successful 'Big Red' 'Duofold Senior' (introduced 1921).
£120-180
AMER

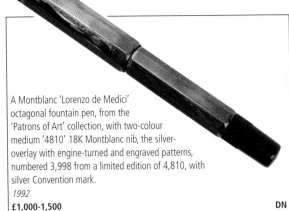

A Montblanc 'Lorenzo de Medici' octagonal fountain pen, from the 'Patrons of Art' collection, with two-colour medium '4810' 18K Montblanc nib, the silver-overlay with engine-turned and engraved patterns, numbered 3,998 from a limited edition of 4,810, with silver Convention mark.

1992

£1,000-1,500   DN

A Montblanc 'Octavian' fountain pen, from the 'Patrons of Art' collection, with silver spider's web filigree over black resin, with two-colour medium 4810 18K Montblanc nib, numbered 3,958 from a limited edition of 4,810, with silver Convention mark.

This design is based on very rare 'spider's web' pens from the 1920s. Examples of the original could fetch well over £3,000.

1993

£600-800   DN

A Montblanc 'Agatha Christie' black resin fountain pen, from the 'Writer's Edition', with a silver-gilt clip modelled as a snake, the head inset with sapphires as eyes, with two-colour medium '4810' 18K Montblanc nib, numbered 3,554 from a limited edition of 4,810, the clip stamped '925'.

The snake motif was intended to hint at the 'creeping tension' of Christie's novels. This design was produced on a variety of different pens, with differing edition sizes. There were 4,810 fountain pens with gold-plated and sapphire-set clips, 23,000 fountain pens with silver ruby-set clips, 18,000 ballpens, and 7,000 fountain pen, ballpen, and pencil sets. This is the most valuable single piece.

£300-500   DN

A 1920s Parker 'Jade' green celluloid Duofold Senior button-filler, with replaced later Parker 'Arrow' nib.

£100-150   AMER

Miller's Compares

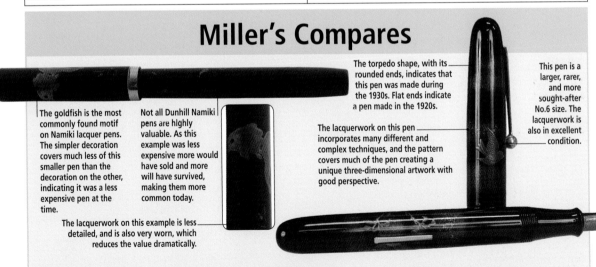

The goldfish is the most commonly found motif on Namiki lacquer pens. The simpler decoration covers much less of this smaller pen than the decoration on the other, indicating it was a less expensive pen at the time.

The lacquerwork on this example is less detailed, and is also very worn, which reduces the value dramatically.

Not all Dunhill Namiki pens are highly valuable. As this example was less expensive more would have sold and more will have survived, making them more common today.

The torpedo shape, with its rounded ends, indicates that this pen was made during the 1930s. Flat ends indicate a pen made in the 1920s.

The lacquerwork on this pen incorporates many different and complex techniques, and the pattern covers much of the pen creating a unique three-dimensional artwork with good perspective.

This pen is a larger, rarer, and more sought-after No.6 size. The lacquerwork is also in excellent condition.

A Dunhill Namiki maki-e lacquer lever-filler, with a fan-tailed goldfish design, and Namiki no.2 nib, with worn artist's signature, and factory marks.

5in (13cm) long

£150-200   WW

Namiki's maki-e lacquer designs can take many months to produce, please see p.162 for more information. Both these examples are comparatively slim. The largest pen Namiki produced was the No.50 'Giant'. In 2000, a 'Giant', decorated with a dragon by Iijima Genroku, fetched a world-record price of £183,000.

A Dunhill Namiki No.6 maki-e laquer lever-filler, size 6, decorated with two birds in flight on the cap, and a fruiting and flowering branch on the barrel, with nashiji gold-powder bands, a six character signature, and a Dunhill Namiki No.6 nib.

5.4in (13.8cm) long

£3,000-5,000   TOV

A scarce 1940s English Parker Duofold 'herringbone' celluloid button-filler.

£200-300

PC

A 1950s Esterbrook grey striated full-size 'J' series lever-filler, with chrome-plated trim and medium Esterbrook '9314-M Relief' steel nib, in near mint condition.

£20-30

PC

A 1910s Frank Swan's chased red hard rubber 'Red Stylo' ink pencil, with some damage to the section threads.

An ink pencil has a fine tube instead of a standard nib. Leading from the ink supply in the barrel to the tip of the tube is a small wire. The ink runs around the wire and down the tube to the paper. This model is rare in red hard rubber. Frank Swan's pens were not produced by Mabie, Todd & Co., which is known for its 'Swan' pens.

£30-40

PC

A French Parker 180 'Barleycorn' converter- or cartridge-filler, with two-sided medium gold nib.

Introduced in 1977, this pen is distinguished by its 'unique' double-sided spear-like nib.

c1980

£70-100

HSR

A 1920s Montblanc enamel-overlay 0-size miniature safety pen, with some chips to the enamel.

The chips to the enamel reduce the value, as it is expensive to repair. In perfect condition, this pen might have fetched over £1,000, as enamelled Montblancs are very rare.

3.25in (8.5cm) long

£300-500

GORL

A 1920s Parker Duofold Senior 'Jade' green pencil.

Without degrading rubber ink sacks inside, pencils did not discolour, and are, therefore, very useful for determining the original colours of plastics. Even though they are not fountain pens, and thus have lower values, large size pencils are prized because collectors can complete a set. This pencil matches the 'Jade' Parker Duofold also shown on this page.

£40-60

BPH

A 1920s Japanese Namiki maki-e lacquer lever-filler, decorated with a Ho-Ho bird and foliage on a nashiji gold dust ground, with 14ct Namiki No.2 nib, artist's signature, and gold-plated cap band and clip.

4.75in (12cm) long

£1,500-2,000

GORL

A 1920s Mabie Todd & Co. Swan 'Jade' green celluloid fountain pen and pencil set, with original fitted case.

£150-200 GORL

A 1940s Wahl-Eversharp 'Skyline' 'Executive' lever-filling pen, with green striped cap and Eversharp 14K nib, in good condition with some wear.

£40-60 AMER

A Pelikan no.140 burgundy piston-filler, with transparent green ink window, and fine 14ct Pelikan nib.
c1952-55

£100-150 HSR

A Pelikan no.400NN black and green striped piston-filler, with export imprint on barrel, with medium 14ct Pelikan nib.
c1956-65

£80-120 HSR

A very rare 1920s Wyvern chased black hard rubber 'Selfil & Safety' no.43 syringe-filler, with 14ct Warranted nib, in good condition.

This pen is exceptionally rare due to its highly unusual filling mechanism, which cannot have been a success. To date no other examples have come to light. One might imagine that its great rarity would make it valuable - not so. It is by a comparatively minor British maker, isn't of the greatest quality, and is pretty boring to behold, despite the unusual mechanism. As such, only a few collectors would compete to own it, and even then the price would have to be right. Items like this prove that rarity does not always indicate high values.
c1920

£50-80 PC

A Wyvern no.101 snakeskin-covered button-filler, with medium Wyvern 14ct nib, and some wear to the skin.

The 101 was also available with a leather covering, but exotic snake, lizard, and crocodile skin is much rarer. The condition of the skin is intrinsic to the value.
c1950

£80-120 PC

A 1930s English Unique mauve 'Snakeskin' celluloid lever-filler, with Art Deco stepped chrome-plated clip and Unique 14ct medium nib.

£30-40 AMER

A 1930s Wahl-Eversharp turquoise pearl and black swirl celluloid Bantam bulb-filler, with Wahl 14K no.0 nib.
c1933

£20-30 AMER

A rare late 18thC French silver travelling writing set, the shaped silver inkwell with cover closed by a butterfly wing-nut, with three silver pen nibs, each with threaded end to screw into a short handle, in a purple plush-lined wooden case with black fishskin cover and sprung button-catch.

1.75in (4.5cm) wide

£500-600 BLO

A 19thC French Tonnel of Paris silver travelling inkwell, the cover with a band of foliate decoration and blue cabochon finial, the lid with button release mechanism, the gold-washed interior with further cover and glass well.

1.75in (4.5cm) high

£150-200 ECGW

An early 20thC novelty 'cricket ball' travelling inkwell, with red leather cover enclosing a further brass cover and glass well.

2.5in (6.5cm) high

£150-200 ECGW

An Elkington & Co. plain silver capstan desk inkwell, with Birmingham hallmarks for 1910.

The missing glass liner can be replaced, and so this does not reduce the value too much. If the inkwell was dented or split, value would have been affected more seriously.

1910 *4in (10cm) diam*

£40-60 CAPE

A pewter 'grotesque' bird inkwell, in the Martin Brothers style, the internal ceramic inkwell with a 'sang-de-boeuf' glaze, unmarked.

c1900-10 *4in (10.5cm) high*

£300-400 BELL

An early 20thC German Bittmann novelty desk set, each piece modelled as a curling implement, comprising an inkwell, a caster, a seal, a dip pen, and a paper knife.

Like the cricket inkwell also on this page, the sporting theme contributes to much of the value of this piece, as it is not made from precious metals or by a major maker. Curling items are also very rare, even if only collected by a comparatively small number of collectors.

£400-500 WW

A 1920s-30s brown Bakelite box, with hinged lid, unmarked.

The stepped form of the box shows the influence of Art Deco architecture.

7.5in (19cm) long

£80-120   P&I

An Eloware semi-spherical footed Bakelite box, with cloudy mottled yellow, green, red, and brown patches, the exterior faded, the base with moulded 'ELOWARE' mark.

This cloudy effect was achieved by throwing raw pigment into the mix of molten plastic. Linsden used the same technique, but usually with less dramatic colours.

6.25in (16cm) diam

£65-75   P&I

A brown Bakelite coffer-type box, with moulded beaded edges, unmarked, damaged.

8.5in (21.5cm) wide

£40-60   P&I

QUICK REFERENCE - BEATL & BANDALASTA

- Bandalasta is the tradename of a type of moulded and marbled plastic devised by chemist Edmund Rossiter in 1924, comprising a mixture of thiourea formaldehyde and cellulose pulp. The first samples were sold in bottles marked with a beetle logo. The company name was soon modified to BEATL, which was a contraction of 'Beat All' as well as a reference to the bug logo.
- A number of companies took up Bandalasta, including Brookes & Adams and Linga Longa. From 1926 until the early 1930s, a 'BEATL Shop' on Regent St, London, exclusively sold products made from the resin. Lighter in weight and less fragile than ceramic, it became widely popular in picnic sets.
- In terms of desirability, the stronger the colour, and the more colours in the marbling, the better. Some shapes and colours are also scarcer than others, and may therefore be more sought-after.

CANDLESTICK & BAKELITE

TELEPHONES FROM THE 1920s to 70s,
for candlestick and classic

Above: a red pyramid telephone

www.candlestickandbakelite.co.uk
Call or email for a free catalogue, or download it from our website.
020 8467 3743
candlestick.bakelite@mac.com

9, Chesham Avenue, Petts Wood, Orpington, Kent, BR5 1AA.

A 1920s-30s Brookes & Adams 'Bandalasta' orange and cream marbled plastic 'Tea For Two' doll's or child's tea set, comprising a (cracked) teapot, two teacups and saucers, a sugar bowl, a milk jug, and two side plates, with moulded marks to the bases.

Teapot 5in (12.5cm) long

£55-65   P&I

A rare 1920s-30s brown Bakelite combination clock and bedside table lamp, the revolving shade with numbers and fixed marker to indicate the time, with indistinct registration number to the base.

13in (32.5cm) high

£80-120   DN

A CLOSER LOOK AT A BAKELITE LAMP

The streamlined, sculptural design has been attributed to the Hungarian-born avant garde, Cubist sculptor Gustave Miklos (1888-1967), however this has not been confirmed.

The lamp's nickname 'Bolide' is a French word applied to racing cars, and is also descriptive of a type of an explosive fireball-like meteorite.

It is a piece of ingenius design, with its compact folding form and ability to be angled at different heights.

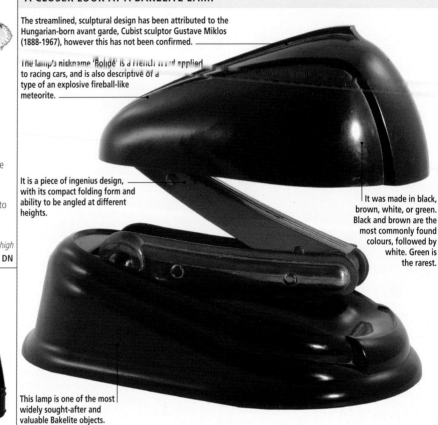

It was made in black, brown, white, or green. Black and brown are the most commonly found colours, followed by white. Green is the rarest.

This lamp is one of the most widely sought-after and valuable Bakelite objects.

A 1930s Philco black Bakelite and chrome electric fan heater.

16in (39.5cm) high

£100-150   DN

A late 1940s French Société Jumo black Bakelite 'Bolide' folding desk lamp, designed in 1945, reputedly by Gustave Miklos, with Bakelite base and shade, and internal extending metal arm, the base with factory stamp.

11in (28cm) wide

£700-1,000   WW

A 1930s-40s Codeg Ltd. brown Bakelite model of a streamlined car, with a celluloid windscreen, the underside moulded 'Made in England'.

These large and stylish toy cars are rare, particularly in undamaged condition and complete with the windscreen. The form is similar to the Cord sports car of the period, and so these models also appeal enormously to collectors of automobilia.

13in (34cm) wide

£700-1,000   WW

A mottled brown Bakelite 'Speed Fix Handroller' sticky-tape roller, with serrated metal cutting edge, moulded 'British Patent No.477418'.

3.5in (8.5cm) long

£25-35   P&I

One of a pair of 1930s orange Catalin or cast-phenolic elephant-shaped napkin rings, with inset beige phenolic eyes.

3in (7.5cm) wide

£28-32 pair   P&I

QUICK REFERENCE

- Most posters are bought to be displayed. This means that a striking design is likely to attract interest, and that condition is of paramount importance. Folding, tears, and stains reduce value, particularly if the surface of the image is affected. However, some damage can be restored. Many posters have been professionally backed onto linen for preservation. This does not reduce value and can, in fact, enhance desirability.
- Posters for popular films, and classic or cult favourites, are usually desirable, while posters for lesser-known films are generally only sought-after if designed by famous artist, such as Robert Peal, Giuliano Nistri, or Saul Bass.
- The most desirable sizes are those which are easiest to display. For example, the US one-sheet 27in (68.5cm) by 41in (104cm) and the UK quad 30in (76cm) by 40in (84cm).
- Product posters are still sought today due to their visual appeal and their importance to 20thC poster and graphic design. The style and font can help to date them.
- Always consider the brand and the item depicted. Posters for popular brands or products are usually worth more. Look out for striking images with bold, bright colours, and designs that are typical of a period. As with film posters, a strong design by a notable designer, such as Jean Carlu, Paul Colin or Bernard Villemot, will usually prove desirable.
- Travel posters saw their 'golden age' from the 1920s to the 1960s. The earliest and most prolifically produced were ocean-liner and railway company posters, and these tend to be the most popular and valuable types today. Airline posters are rising in value and desirability. Again, look for major brands such as White Star, BOAC, Air France, and Canadian Pacific. Notable designers here include Cassandre (Adolphe Mouron), Terence Cuneo, and Tom Purvis.

'ANDY WARHOL'S BLOOD FOR DRACULA', British quad poster, printed by W. E. Berry Ltd., unmounted.

1974 42in (105cm) wide
£450-550 WW

'VIVA JAMES BOND' 'BONS BAISERS DE RUSSIE' (From Russia with Love), French one sheet poster, illustration by Yves Thos., printed by Ets St. Martin Imp., with folds.
1963 63in (160cm) high
£300-500 DS

'LIVE AND LET DIE', American two sheet poster, copyright United Artists Corporation, with folds.
1973 77in (196cm) high
£300-400 DS

'CASINO ROYALE', original Spanish poster, in near mint condition, linen-backed.
1967 39in (99cm) high
£400-600 BLNY

'THE MAN WITH THE GOLDEN GUN', American poster, copyright United Artists Corporation.
1974 77in (196cm) high
£300-500 DS

'MOONRAKER', American one sheet poster, published in the USA, with folds.

1979   *41in (104cm) high*

£120-180   **WW**

'JAWS', UK one sheet poster, printed by W. E. Berry Ltd., unmounted.

    60in (152cm) high

£250-350   **WW**

A CLOSER LOOK AT A FILM POSTER

Although the designer is not known, this poster recalls the Saul Bass designs (particularly for 'Vertigo') where a man seemingly falls into a spiralling abyss.

While he may not have designed this poster, Bass did produce the startling opening credits to this Hitchcock directed film. The credits also include strong lines that eventually form the squares of a window on a New York office block.

The British version of this poster has four red and black rectangles with Hitchcock's face staring out at the viewer over the falling man, while designs for other countries usually include the famous biplane.

Released during the Cold War, the film covers themes such as espionage, mistaken identity, national security, and the power of governments.

'NORTH BY NORTHWEST', American one sheet poster, linen-backed.

1959   *41in (102cm) high*

£800-1,200   **BLNY**

'Niagara', starring Marilyn Monroe, a British half sheet poster, with two folds.

1953   *28in (71cm) wide*

£200-300   **GORL**

'PUTTIN' ON THE RITZ', American one sheet poster, linen-backed.

1930   *41in (104cm) high*

£300-400   **BLNY**

'QUATERMASS AND THE PIT', British quad poster, unmounted.

1967   *40in (101.5cm) wide*

£250-350   **WW**

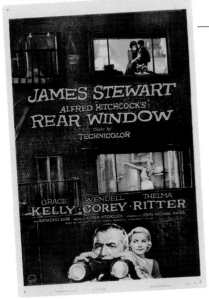

'REAR WINDOW', American one sheet poster, in very good condition, linen-backed.

'Rear Window' is considered one of Hitchcock's best and most tense suspense thrillers. This classic poster captures the film's setting brilliantly.

1954 *41in (104cm) high*
£2,200-2,800 **RTC**

'REBECCA OF SUNNYBROOK FARM', American one sheet poster, in near mint condition, linen-backed.

Shirley Temple has a large following. This film includes a number of notable Temple songs, including 'On The Good Ship Lollipop', and a memorable dance scene finale, where Temple dances with a toy soldier.

1938 *41in (104cm) high*
£500-700 **RTC**

'The Thomas Crown Affair', Australian one sheet poster, style A, in near mint condition, linen-backed.
1968 *40in (102cm) high*
£200-300 **BLNY**

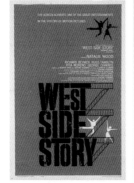

'WEST SIDE STORY', designed by Joseph Caroff, American one sheet poster, linen-backed.
1961 *41in (104cm) high*
£350-450 **BLNY**

Judith Picks

It's been almost impossible to forget about Spider-man in the last few years. Having just finished three incredibly popular movies, starring Tobey Maguire, he's about to be re-launched into a new series of films, with an entirely new cast and a new director. The new movie will undoubtedly bring more fans to this already successful franchise, which could mean prices for classic memorabilia will go up. This poster, advertising the 'movie release' of a two-part live-action television special, 'The Deadly Dust' (now re-named 'Spider-man Strikes Back'), is a good example of something I think will increase in value. Although linked to the comparatively unpopular television series, it features a dynamic image of Spidey bursting out of the background, and would look great on any fan's wall

'SPIDER-MAN STRIKES BACK', American one sheet, copyright Marvel Comic Books and Columbia Pictures Industries.
1978 *39in (99cm) high*
£150-250 **DS**

'LE MAGICIEN D'OZ' ('The Wizard of Oz'), Belgian poster, in near mint condition, linen-backed.

Original posters for this legendary film, produced and released on the eve of the outbreak of the Second World War, are very rare and highly sought-after.

1939 *22in (56cm) high*
£2,000-3,000 **RTC**

'VINS CAMP ROMAIN', designed by Claude Gadoud, printed by Camis, Paris, lithograph in colours, in near mint condition, linen-backed.

c1930   *62.5in (159cm) high*
£800-1,200   **BLNY**

'CHATEAU ROUBAUD VIN ROSÉ', designed by Leon Dupin, printed by Joseph Charles, lithograph in colours, linen-backed.

55in (150cm) high
£1,200-1,800   BLNY

QUICK REFERENCE - MICHEL LIEBEAUX

• Michel Liebeaux (pseudonym Mich) (French, 1881-1923) designed this advertisement for the le Fakyr drink. The drink's powder is used in the making of tonic wines such as the Taillan 'grand vin du quinquina'. Quinquina was a name used collectively for bitters having quinine as one of their main ingredients. Jack Rennert – the undisputed king of American poster knowledge – calls Mich a 'master humorist'. Mich's main clients were the bicycle and automotive industries. At the 1912 Salon des Humoristes, he exhibited 50 sporting designs. His drawings also filled the pages of 'La Vie Parisienne', 'Le Rire', and 'L'Écho de Paris'.

'LE FAKYR', designed by Mich (Michel Liebeaux), printed by Publicité Wall, Paris, lithograph in colours, linen-backed.

c1915   *62in (157cm) high*
£1,500-2,000   BLNY

A CLOSER LOOK AT A POSTER

Quina, produced by Maurin, was a French apéritif, which went on to be banned by the government. The elephant on the label suggests the power of the drink.

Cappiello designed posters for many French companies. Designed in 1906, this is considered to be his finest poster and is highly sought-after.

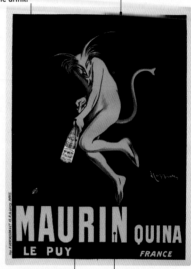

The green devil both hints at the alcoholic strength of the drink and at the 'fée verte' (green fairy), which was the nickname for the equally noxious absinthe.

Cappiello (1875-1942) helped move poster design out of the Art Nouveau style and into a more modern age with his humour and use of bright and bold colours on black backgrounds.

'MAURIN QUINA', designed by Leonetto Cappiello, printed by P. Vercasson, Paris, lithograph in colours, linen-backed.

The best-known appearance of the 'green fairy' over the last few years was played by Kylie Minogue in Baz Luhrmann's 2001 blockbuster 'Moulin Rouge'.

1906   *62.5in (156cm) high*
£1,000-1,500   **BLNY**

'KINAGIN', designed by E. Patek, printed by A. Marsens, Lausanne, lithograph in colours, in near mint condition, not linen-backed.

1943   *50in (127cm) high*
£1,000–1,500   BLNY

'SCHICK'S COCKTAIL', designed by an anonymous designer, printed by Gouweloos, Brussels, lithograph in colours, linen-backed.

c1925   *61in (155cm) high*
£800-1,200   BLNY

A CLOSER LOOK AT A BALLY POSTER

Jacques and Pierre Bellenger were twin brothers who studied at the Académie Julian, and then worked together their whole lives. They produced posters for a number of major companies of the time including Quinquina Bourin and the bicycle and automobile company, Favor.

Bally was an innovator in advertising, using posters as early as 1910. They went on to use many major artists, such as Bernard Villemot, to create eye-catching, modern poster designs.

This design borrows heavily from Leonetto Cappiello's famous 1929 poster for Nitrolian paints in its use of someone descending stairs (see 'Miller's Collectables Price Guide 2009', p.367).

The strong diagonal line is powerful, and the choice of vibrant colours and modern, clean-lined style are typical of Bally's poster designs.

The Bellengers cleverly allowed both the women's and the men's shoe ranges to be showcased in this design.

The blank space at the bottom of the poster could be printed with a retailer's name.

'BALLY', a shoe advertising poster, designed by Jacques and Pierre Bellenger, printed by Chateaudun, Paris.

c1950   *62in (157.5cm) high*

£500-700   **SWA**

'Floris', a French soap powder poster, designed by Herbert Leupin, printed for Steinfels by J.C. Müller, Zürich, torn and with wrinkled margins.

The bold colours, use of shadows behind the images, simple font, and stylised pegs are all very modern, and typical of one aspect of the 'mid-century modern' movement that was developing at this time.

1949   *50.25in*
                          (127.5cm) high

£500-800   **SWA**

WANTED
1960's and 1970's
CONCERT POSTERS

FLYERS, HANDBILLS, PROGRAMMES, TICKETS, PERSONAL EFFECTS, SIGNED ITEMS, DOCUMENTS, ANYTHING UNUSUAL OR ASSOCIATED 1960's AND 1970's ROCK AND POP MEMORABILIA.

WE PAY
THE BEST PRICES

We will pay up to **£6,000** for an original concert poster for **THE BEATLES**, **£4,000** for **THE ROLLING STONES** and **THE WHO**, **£2,000** for **LED ZEPPELIN** and **JIMI HENDRIX**, as well as very high prices for other 1960's and 1970's Rock and Pop Memorabilia.

FREE VALUATIONS
CASH PAID INSTANTLY

Tel: 01494 436644 or 07890 626840

Email: music@usebriggs.com

BRIGGS ROCK AND POP MEMORABILIA
Loudwater House,
London Road, Loudwater,
High Wycombe,
Buckinghamshire, HP10 9TL

'Zonophone Record GRAND PEACE RECORD', a poster promoting a recording to celebrate the end of World War I, lithograph in colours.

Registered in 1899, Zonophone was a brand applied to records and record players by Frank Seaman of Camden, New Jersey, USA. He had worked for Emile Berliner's Gramophone Company, and legal action resulted in that company owning Zonophone from 1903. The 'Zonophone' name was used until 1931, when the company merged with the Columbia Gramophone Company to form Electrical & Musical Industries, best-known as EMI.

1919   *18in (45cm) high*
£70-90   **FLD**

'GOOD PERFORMERS USE HENLEY'S STITCHLESS AND SEALED HENLEY TENNIS BALL', designed by an unknown designer, with scuffed surface and other wear.

This poster would appeal to three types of collector: poster collectors, tennis memorabilia collectors, and collectors who like seals.

c1920   *30in (76cm) high*
£300-500   **FLD**

'PÉTROLE STELLA', a petrol advertising poster, designed by Henri Boulanger Gray, published by Imp. Courmont Frères, Paris, linen-backed, framed.

51in (130cm) high
£600-900   **WW**

'Harley Davidson', a record and celebrity promotion poster, featuring Brigitte Bardot, printed by J. Press Ltd, with creases and abrasions.

Sex symbol Brigitte Bardot's best-known song was composed in 1967 by her one-time lover Serge Gainsbourg. The cover of the single had an image of Bardot astride a motorcycle wearing a mini skirt and high boots, which became immensely popular, and led to the release of this mass-produced poster. Despite the large quantity printed, the vast majority did not survive being hung in teenage boys' rooms, dorm rooms, or student flats, making this example particularly rare today.

1968   *39.5in (100cm) high*
£200-300   **SWA**

'CARTERS GIANT FLOWERED SWEET PEAS', a seed advertising poster, designed by E. Whatley, with folds.

30in (76cm) high
£220-280   **FLD**

'CORSETS LE FURET', designed by Roger Perot, printed by Etab Lts Delattre, Paris, signed in the print, linen-backed, framed.

1933   *55in (140cm) high*
£600-800   **WW**

'MIT DEM RHEINGOLD VON DER NORDSEE ZU DEN ALPEN', designed by Ivo Fallax, for German Railways.

23.75in (60cm) high

£200-300   ON

A CLOSER LOOK AT A RAILWAY POSTER

This poster art was taken from a 1947 oil painting by Sir Terence Cuneo (1907-96), a celebrated artist who is widely considered to be the best painter of railways and trains in the world.

Most of Cuneo's paintings contain a 'trademark' small mouse hidden amid the action, which can be a challenge to spot. Here a satisfied looking cat can also be seen.

Cuneo's paintings are renowned for their realism and the way they capture the grandeur of the locomotive. Initial sketches for this image were made in front of the Sir Reginald Matthews in Doncaster.

'Giants Refreshed' is widely held to be one of Cuneo's finest paintings, and the streamlined A4 'Pacific' shown is a much-loved LNER locomotive.

'GIANTS REFRESHED "PACIFICS" IN THE DONCASTER LOCOMOTIVE WORKS', with artwork by Terence Cuneo, printed for the London & North Eastern Railways by Waterlow and Sons Ltd., the bottom border printed with British Railways totems.

1947   *40in (102cm) high*

£2,500-3,500   ON

'VALLÉE DE JOUX', designed by Louis Koller, printed by A. Trub & Cie., lithograph in colours.

40in (102cm) high

£350-450   BLNY

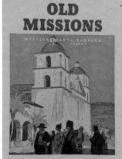

'Southern Pacific' 'OLD MISSIONS' 'SANTA BARBARA', designed by Maurice Logan, for the Southern Pacific route, lithograph in colours.

23.25in (59cm) high

£200-300   ON

'RAPIDE', designed by an unknown designer, printed by Perin-Dufour for the French state railways and the Southern Railway, lithograph in colours, linen-backed.

1932

39in (99cm) high

£400-600   BLNY

'WAGON RESTAURANT', by Dom, a French railway poster, printed by S. C. I. P., in excellent condition, lithograph in colours, linen-backed.

c1930   *39in (99cm) high*

£600-800   BLNY

POSTERS

'EUROPE International Mercantile Marine Lines AMERICAN RED STAR WHITE STAR', designed by Fred Hoertz, minor losses.

41in (104cm) high

£350-450   WW

'LLOYD SABAUDO GRANDI ESPRESSI "CONTE ROSSE"-"CONTE VERDE"', a cruise liner poster, lithograph in colours, parts of the edges restored and over-coloured, the top border with adhesive and ink stamps, linen-backed.

Founded in 1906, the Lloyd Sabaudo line began to carry passengers in 1907. Linking Italy to Asian and American ports, it merged with a number of other Italian shipping lines in 1932, becoming part of the Italian Line.

c1933   *39.25in (100cm) high*

£1,800-2,200   SWA

QUICK REFERENCE - AIRLINE POSTERS

• The 707 was the first mass-produced civilian jet aircraft in the US, and ushered in the 'Jet Age'. As civilian air travel began to grow into the mature industry it is today, the whole nature of air travel changed, with the expansion of airports, the development of ticketing and reservation systems, and even the much maligned airline food! It took its maiden voyage in December 1957, and was put onto the transatlantic service by Pan Am in 1958. American Airlines began using 707s in 1959.

• Airline posters have become increasingly sought-after over the past decade, and could eventually increase to the same levels of desirability and value as cruise posters. This poster is a good bet as it is typical of the styles of the day, and clearly focuses on the most important aspect of the 707, the large and powerful jet engine.

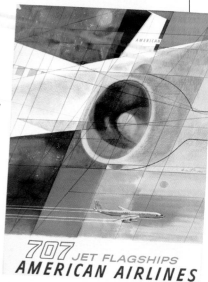

'AMERICAN AIRLINES' '707 JET FLAGSHIPS', an airline poster, lithograph in colours, some minor losses, tears and wrinkles.

c1958   *40in (101cm) high*

£1,200-1,800   SWA

A 1930s Imperial Airways lithographed poster/brochure, promoting air travel and describing the 'Heracles' and 'Hannibal' classes.

31in (78cm) high

£300-400   FLD

'M. E.A. liban', a Middle Eastern Airlines tourist poster for Lebanon, designed by Jacques Auriac, in excellent condition, linen-backed.

c1960   *31.5in (79.5cm) high*

£800-1,200   BLO

'LEYSIN', a Swiss Alps tourism poster, designed by Jacomo, printed by Marci, Bruxelles, lithograph in colours, in excellent condition, linen-backed.

c1948   *39in (100cm) high*

£350-450   BLO

'Skis BADAN', a Swiss skiing poster, printed by M. Collet, Genève, in excellent condition, linen-backed.

39in (99cm) high

£500-700   **BLO**

'Ski, André JAMET', a French skiing poster, designed by Marsin, printed by Affiches et Publicité, Paris, in excellent condition, linen-backed.

c1960   *63in (160cm) high*

£800-1,200   **BLO**

QUICK REFERENCE - SKIING POSTERS

- Exciting, glamorous, and even romantic, it's not surprising that skiing is a favourite sport of many. And what better way to celebrate your favourite sport out of season that by displaying a skiing poster in your home?
- A number of factors contribute towards value. Bold, strong images are preferred, particularly if they date from the 'golden age' of the poster from the 1930s to 1950s. Vivid colours and a 'bright' feeling reflecting the Alpine sunshine are also good features. Combine these with a strong sense of drama and speed, and a poster becomes even more desirable, particularly if it is in good condition, as these posters are bought to be framed and put on display. The resort is also important, with the most exclusive being generally more sought-after.
- Prices have risen faster and higher than for many other types of poster for one reason: many ski fans are wealthy, and as money competes against money prices have risen considerably. Related, but less dynamic imagery, such as alpine scenes, or later posters from the 1970s-80s, which tend to be photographic, are usually more affordable.

'PONTRESINA' 'DIAVOLEZZA', a skiing poster, designed by three times Olympic award winning poster artist Alexander Diggelmann, printed by Und Verlag, Chur, in excellent condition, linen-backed.

1933   *40in (102cm) high*

£2,000-3,000   **BLO**

'Winter in Germany', a German skiing poster, designed by L. Hueu, printed by Jilert & Ewald, Steinheim am Main, linen-backed.

c1955   *40in (102cm) high*

£150-200   **BLO**

'DARTMOUTH WINTER CARNIVAL FEBRUARY 1993', a skiing, surfing and carnival poster, in excellent condition, not backed.

Dartmouth is a popular resort, and a micro-collection of posters promoting the resort can be built up.

1993   *34in (87cm) high*

£70-100   **BLO**

'ROCHERS DE NAYE', a skiing poster, designed by Otto Ernst, printed by A. Trub & Cie., lithograph in colours, linen-backed.

Although produced to advertise the train that took skiers up to the rocks of Naye mountain, which towers over Montreux, the interest and real value of this poster lies in the fact it depicts skiers, is by a known artist, and is early in date.

1924   *39.5in (100cm) high*

£3,000-4,000   **BLNY**

'DICK WHITTINGTON', a theatrical production poster, printed by Taylor's Printers, Wombwell, Yorks, in excellent condition.

The blank space at the top could be printed with the name of the theatre that was putting on the play, meaning that any group, from amateur through to professional, could afford to display a professionally designed, eye-catching poster.

c1960

£80-120   **FLD**

'BABES IN THE WOOD', a theatrical production poster, designed by Hegofs, printed by Taylor's Printers, Wombwell, Yorks, in excellent condition.

c1960

£70-100   **FLD**

'The Trial of Mary Dugan,' a theatrical poster for the Savoy Theatre, designed by Ian Emmerson, printed by A. E. King Ltd.

Although the theatre is well-known and the design is appealing and typical of its time, the price of this poster is low as neither the play nor the actors are well-known.

1958   *30in (76cm) high*

£30-50   **WW**

'BA.TA.CLAN', a Swiss operetta/ cabaret poster, designed by Aslan, printed by Roto-Sadag, in near mint condition, linen-backed.

1973   *50in (127cm) high*

£500-700   **BLNY**

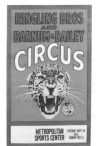

'RINGLING BROS AND BARNUM & BAILEY CIRCUS', an American circus poster, with roaring leopard.

c1965   *43in (109cm) high*

£100-150   **DS**

'1ER SALON DU CINEMA', a French film festival poster, designed by Hervé Moran, printed by Bedos & Cie., Paris, in excellent condition, lined-backed.

1989   *23in (58cm) high*

£120-180   **BLNY**

'REDHILL ART SCHOOL', an art exhibition poster, unsigned. Despite being very decorative and typical of the 1930s, it isn't quite Art Deco enough to appeal to most collectors. Judging by the slightly wobbly wording and design, it was probably designed by one of the students at the art school, and isn't of the greatest quality. Furthermore, although it must have been wealthy and large enough to print its own posters, the Redhill Art School isn't the most famous art college in the world, with no famous graduates, and so it's unlikely to attract the attention of many collectors. If you like this piece, don't let me put you off buying it, but just don't expect it to rise in value!

Rarity doesn't always indicate a high price, which is unfortunate for this poster because it's certainly rare, being produced for a single event lasting only three hours in a country town.

c1930   *30in (76cm) high*

£5-8   **FLD**

Mark Picks

As the social experiment that was Communism in Russia has crumbled, so collectors and scholars are turning their attention to the products of the régime. Propaganda and other posters are rapidly becoming sought-after, particularly those produced in avant garde, abstract and modern styles, such as Constructivism. This poster was used by the Bolsheviks to attract support from a largely illiterate population. The new styles represented the new age and government.

Look out for visually striking work produced by notable artists such as Alexander Apsit (who developed the hammer and sickle motif), Viktor Deni, and Dmitri Moor. Desirable later names include Alexander Rodchenko, El Lissitzky, and Gustav Klutsis. Although most Russian posters of this era were issued in runs of up to 50,000, they are rare today as many were lost or destroyed, being intended only as momentary political tools, rather than historical or graphic documents to be kept. I personally believe that Soviet design of the 1920s-70s is under-rated and is certainly an area to watch for the future. Although most Russian and other collectors focus on finely-made pre-revolutionary objects, this may change as this important part of world history is re-evaluated. Prices being paid for similar Chinese, Czech, and Polish film posters from the same period are already rising rapidly.

['Workers of the World Unite'], a two sheet political poster, designed by Dmitri Moor (1883-1946), lithograph in colours, backed on Japan paper.

1931   *40.75in (103.5cm) high*

£600-900   **BLNY**

['We Will Carry the Flag Towards the Final Destination!'], printed by Poligrafkombinat, Kalinin, with fold creases and minor edge tears.

The banners read 'Towards the festivity of Communism! For Socialism! For the Rule of Soviets!'.

1963   *33in (83.5cm) high*

£300-500   **SWA**

['Trevozhnyi Signal'], a Russian film poster, designed by Mikhail Dlugach, lithograph in colours, linen-backed.

1925   *28.75in (72cm) high*

£500-800   **BLNY**

['Under Naval Fire'], designed by Vladimir and Georgii Stenberg, lithograph in colours, in near mint condition, linen-backed.

10,000 copies of this poster were printed.

1928   *42in (107cm) high*

£3,000-4,000   **BLNY**

'VIST THE USSR THE COUNTRY OF THE WORLD'S FIRST COSMONAUT', a Soviet tourism poster, published by Intourist, in excellent condition, with repaired creases and tears.

The Soviet Union was the first country to put a satellite and a man into space. They were rightly proud of this enormous achievement, and even promoted it in travel agencies as a form of propaganda.

c1965   *39in (99cm) high*

£1,000-1,500   **SWA**

POSTERS

'LEND TO DEFEND HIS RIGHT TO BE FREE BUY DEFENCE BONDS', designed by Tom Purvis, printed for H. M. Stationery Office by Fosh & Co. Ltd.

The National Savings Movement was established in 1916 to reduce borrowing and raise funds for the war effort. The War Savings Committee was founded in 1939 to encourage the same during World War II. The charming image of a boy and his Meccano set means this poster also appeals to Meccano and toy collectors.

c1942   15in (38cm) high
£250-350   FLD

'Put Your Trust in the Navy & Your Money in SAVINGS CERTIFICATES', designed by an anonymous designer, printed for H. M. Stationery Office by Gilbert Whitehead & Co.

c1942   30in (76cm) high
£120-180   FLD

'WAR SAVINGS ARE WARSHIPS', designed by Norman Wilkinson, printed by J. Weiner for National Savings.

c1942   30in (76cm) high
£200-300   FLD

'THIS IS YOUR COUNTRY' 'LIVE TO HONOR IT', an American wartime poster, designed by an anonymous designer, printed by Mather & Co., Chicago, linen-backed.

1924   48in (122cm) high
£800-1,200   BLNY

'WHAT THEY CARRY... WAR SAVINGS - your fighting equipment', designed by an anonymous designer, printed for H. M. Stationery Office by W. R. Royle & Son Ltd. WFP 357.

c1917   20.5in (51cm) high
£50-70   ON

'I need your RAGS', a British wartime poster, printed for H. M. Stationery Office, in good condition, with some losses and tears to corners and edges.

c1941   20in (51cm) high
£15-25   FLD

'I Don't Care' 'We Care For Those Who Care', an American poster promoting care at work, lithograph in colours, printed by Mather & Co., Chicago, linen-backed.

1925   47.5in (120cm) high
£500-800   BLNY

QUICK REFERENCE - RADIOS

- The 'golden age' of radio design lasted from the 1930s until the 1950s, and pieces from this time tend generally to be the most sought-after. Shape, colour, and style are more important to most collectors than the internal mechanism itself.
- Much radio design of the 1930s was strongly influenced by period architecture such as skyscrapers, and a feeling for modernity and the future, so defining features include strong geometric lines, and stepped forms. During the 1950s, shapes generally became more streamlined and curved, and new influences included automobile design of the period.
- Material is also a key factor, and the emergence of plastics such as Bakelite and cast pheonlic (Catalin) revolutionised radio production. Most early radios were cased in wood, but as plastic took over radios began to appear in vibrant reds, blues, and greens. Look out for models made by manufacturers such as EKCO, Emerson, and FADA as these tend to be the most desirable and occupy the upper echelons of the market. In 2007 a very rare baby blue 'Air King' fetched $51,000 at auction.
- In general, Art Deco models in bright colours tend to command the highest prices, but 1930s wood-cased or brown Bakelite radios occupy the majority of the market, and prices for the most stylish examples remain strong.

A late 1920s American Freshman 'Masterpiece' radio, in a mahogany case with carved panels and borders, the lid interior with gilt-transfer name, with instruction booklet and original card.

Charles Freshman's 'Masterpiece' was a landmark radio in that it was considerably less expensive than the radios that preceded it. It consequently sold in vast quantities, truly becoming the 'people's radio'. The 'Masterpiece' can be housed in a number of different cases. This mahogany case was one of the higher-end and more expensive variations.

1927   *31in (79cm) wide*
£150-200   **DRA**

An Art Deco novelty satinwood and ebonised wood radiogram, modelled as a miniature grand piano, the hinged lid opening to reveal a radio and turntable, the keyboard lid enclosing a sound box, raised on square tapering legs with block feet and castors.

34in (86cm) high
£250-350   **AH**

An RCA Victor valve radio, model no.66X8, in a red marbled Catalin case, in excellent condition.

The model 66X radio came in a number of different cases, each with their own number. The 66X9 was cased in marbled black Catalin, the 66X2 in ivory painted Bakelite, and the 66X3 and 66X4 had wooden cases. Nicknamed 'tuna boats', the Catalin versions (66X8 and 66X9) were said to be the largest Catalin radios made.

1946   *9in (23cm) high*
£200-300   **DN**

An Etronic portable valve radio, model no.EPZ 4213, in a cream and black Bakelite case with top handle over the register.

1951   *11in (28cm) high*
£100-150   **DN**

An American Evans Products for Emerson Radio Co. valve radio, model no. 578A, designed by Charles Eames in 1946, with an ash-veneer case, a matching plastic face, and Bakelite knobs.

1946-52   *9.25in (23cm) wide*
£450-550   **DRA**

An American Crosley 'Dynamic' valve radio, model no.11-103 U, with red-sprayed Bakelite body and bull's eye style dial.

1949-1955   10.25in (26cm) wide

£150-250   **CAT**

A late 1950s Kolster-Brandes 'Toaster' radio, model no.FB10FM, with a cream Bakelite case.

This is the later FM only version, which was released in 1955 (five years after the standard 'FB10') at a cost of £10.16s.8d.

7in (18cm) high

£50-80   **RW**

A CLOSER LOOK AT A RADIO

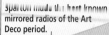

Art Deco mirrored furniture is highly fashionable at the moment, particularly in blue.

Sparton made the best known mirrored radios of the Art Deco period.

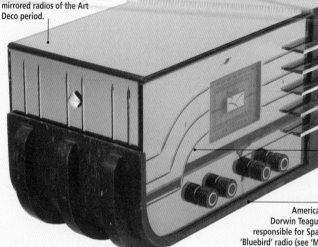

The geometric lines are typical of the period, imparting a feel of speed and movement. The curved form gave rise to the radio's nickname, the 'Sled'.

It was designed by notable American industrial designer Walter Dorwin Teague (1883-1960), who was also responsible for Sparton's circular, blue mirrored 'Bluebird' radio (see 'Miller's Antiques Handbook & Price Guide' 2012-2013 p.587), and the eye-wateringly rare 'Nocturne' radio of 1935.

Model '558' was an improvement on model '557', with better electronics. The re-design of the mirrors also gave a multi-layered impression. It was also available in pink, which is rarer but less widely desirable.

A late 1930s American Sparton valve radio, model no.558, designed by Walter Dorwin Teague in 1937, with four knobs, a square dial, blue mirrored covered case, chromed horizontal slats, and ebonised wood base, lacking back.

£1,500-2,000

17.5in (44.5cm) wide

EG

A 1970s Italian Brionvega orange plastic folding-cube radio, model no.TS522, designed by Richard Sapper and Marco Zanuso in 1964, with chromed handle and trim.

£60-90   **WHP**

A 1970s German Nordmende 'Spectra Futura' radio, designed by C.E.I. Raymond Loewy in 1968, with orange, red, and white plastic rectangular case.

This radio can also be found with panels in other colours.

8in (20cm) high

£250-350   **A&G**

A 1970s Sarleen plastic pocket radio, model no.38334, boxed.

£5-10   **GAZE**

QUICK REFERENCE - RAILWAYANA

- The allure and romance of the steam train ensure that railwayana remains popular with collectors. Signs, particularly the nameplates of well-known locomotives or station totem signs, occupy the top of the market. A premium is paid for those in original condition, as well as those that are fresh to the market. Carriage prints, tickets, timetables, and handbills are much more affordable and plentiful.

- Railwayana from before 1924 is extremely rare, and does not have a wide collecting base. Most collectors focus on the 'big four' railway companies from the 'golden age' of steam: London, Midland & Scotland (LMS), London & North-Eastern Railway (LNER), Great Western Railway (GWR), and the Southern Railway (SR). All four operated from 1924 until 1948 when the railways were nationalised. Memorabilia associated with the smaller companies in this period is likely to be rarer, and will be highly sought-after (see Mark Picks on p.301).

- Pieces dating from 1948 until The Beeching Report of 1963 (which lead to the closure of a number of stations and lines) are also popular, but may not be as valuable as memorabilia from the 'golden age'. If you have an eye on the future market, it might be worth considering later items from the period of diesel and electric traction as these may increase in value.

- Be aware that, due to the popularity of the field, some items, particularly signs, have been reproduced. Make sure you buy from reputable dealers or auction houses.

A Southern Railways 'EASTLEIGH' totem sign, flanged.

36in (91cm) wide

£1,000-1,500   CHT

A British Rail (Southern) 'SALISBURY' totem sign.

36in (91cm) wide

£1,200-1,800   CHT

G. W. Railwayana Auctions Ltd

The Worldwide Specialist Auctioneers of Railway, Transport & Advertising Memorabilia

Bredon Office Tony Hoskins 01684 773487 / Evesham Office Simon Turner 01386 760109

W: www.gwra.co.uk   *E: simon@gwra.co.uk*

A British Rail (Southern) 'ANDOVER TOWN' target sign, with some enamel losses and corrosion damage.

36in (92cm) wide

£700-1,000   CHT

A British Rail (Southern) 'TISBURY' target sign, with minor enamel losses.

20in (66cm) wide

£400-600   CHT

An 'L. & S. W. R.' painted cast iron railway information sign, reading 'NEITHER MATCHES NOR LIGHTS MUST BE TAKEN NEAR STORED PARAFFIN', with original paint.

17in (42cm) high

£150-250   CHT

A 'LONDON & NORTH WESTERN RAILWAY' (LNWR) cast iron line side sign, with moulded 'BEWARE OF THE TRAINS LOOK BOTH UP & DOWN THE LINE BEFORE YOU CROSS.' white painted lettering on a black ground.

29in (74cm) wide

£100-150   CHT

A 'BRITISH RAILWAYS' enamelled sign, reading 'WARNING IS HEREBY GIVEN TO PERSONS NOT TO TRESPASS UPON THE RAILWAY PENALTY NOT EXCEEDING 40/-', with minor losses to the enamel.

12in (31cm) high

£60-90   CHT

A 'HIGHLAND RAILWAY COMPANY' coat of arms, on a green painted shield-shaped wooden plaque.

The Highland Railway Company operated in the remote northernmost counties of Scotland. It was formed when a number of smaller railways merged in 1865, and was amalgamated into the London, Midland & Scottish Railway in 1923. As with many smaller railways, Highland Railway Company has an enthusiastic band of collectors keeping its memory alive.

£350-450   TEN

SHEFFIELD RAILWAYANA AUCTIONS

"Britain's leading Railwayana Auction House"
Steam World

Nameplates, Posters, Postcards, Clocks, Totems, White Star, Cast Iron Signs, Signalling Devices, Tickets, Lamps, China, Silver Plate, Antiquarian Railway Books, Anything related to Railways

DATES FOR 2012

March 10th, June 16th, September 8th, December 15th

Commission rate to vendors only 10% plus VAT (i.e. 12%) on single items, no other hidden charges. Illustrated catalogue in full colour £6 available 2-3 weeks prior to each auction. Free telephone valuations. Free collection of nameplates or collections. Why not telephone now?

SHEFFIELD RAILWAYANA AUCTIONS
4 The Glebe, Clapham, Bedford MK41 6GA
Tel/Fax: +44 (0)1234 325341
Email: SheffRailwayana@aol.com
Website: www.sheffieldrailwayana.co.uk

Mark Picks

The high price of this lamp shows that it's well worth keeping an eagle eye open for railway memorabilia away from the 'greats' such as the GWR, GNER, and LMS. The Furness Railway Company operated independently from 1846 until 1923, and was a major contributor to the development of the Lake District tourist industry, and Barrow-in-Furness. In December 1922, it was absorbed into the London, Midland & Scottish Railway.

Pieces actually used on the railway, particularly in good and complete condition, are highly sought-after. The Furness Railway Company has a very strong following and a dedicated charity that looks after its various assets, including the earliest working standard-gauge locomotive in Britain. This charity and other collectors will compete to own pieces like this, which are easy to display and look great.

A rare Furness Railway Company Messengers Patent signalling lamp, the corrugated body set with a brass name plaque and two other brass plaques stamped 'FRC Coniston No.1' and 'Park Road Crossing', with bevelled-edged clear glass lens, the inner casing with original blue glass lining and original burner.

£3,800-4,200   **TEN**

A Great Northern Railway black-finished tinplate signalling lamp, with bull's eye lenses, coloured filters, clear side lenses, and original tinplate burner, with brass plaques reading 'GNR No.15759' and 'Gedling'.

£150-200   **TEN**

A Staffordshire transfer-printed pottery pint mug, of tapered form, printed in brown and hand-coloured with a steam tender 'EXPRESS' train pulling two carriages and a flatback trunk with phaeton, the base with transfer-printed 'B&L' mark.

c1850-60   *4in (10.5cm) high*

£150-200   **TEN**

A London, Midland & Scottish Railway iron wages cup, with brass plaque numbered '629', and stamped to the front 'L(M)S'.

£20-30   **CHT**

A Furness Railway Company copper two-handled hot water urn and cover, used in the Coniston Dormitory, the shallow domed lid with arched handle stamped 'FRC', the front stamped 'F.R.C. CONISTON. DORMITORY' over a brass tap.

This was used in the dormitory by the drivers and staff of the railway's Coniston Water steam boat 'Gondola'.

c1870   *15in (37cm) high*

£1,000-1,500   **TEN**

A Midland Railways mahogany-cased 'Block Instrument', the dial with 'TRAIN ON LINE', 'LINE CLEAR', and 'LINE BLOCKED' indicator panels.

19in (48cm) high

£70-100   **CHT**

A British Railways (Midland) 'Smiths Empire' wall clock, with Roman numerals and seconds dial, with oak surround and box containing clockwork mechanism, with key, and in full working order.

£300-500   **VEC**

QUICK REFERENCE

- Rock and pop memorabilia continues to make news headlines with items worth thousands or even hundreds of thousands of pounds coming up for sale across the world. Despite this, the market is varied, and there's something for every pocket, including records, tickets, posters, autographs, and even items owned by the stars themselves.

- It's that latter category that tends to attract the most interest and the highest prices. Clothing worn or instruments used by an artist are always sought-after, and a connection to a major event or concert will typically add a premium. If a star was photographed with it, and it's typical of their style or music, so much the better.

- Apart from the object itself, the most important consideration here is provenance, which must be cast-iron.

- The most popular bands and artists tend to lead the way in terms of value, as they have such a large and diverse fan base. Good examples are Elvis Presley and the Beatles. Less widely-loved artists may still have a dedicated following but, with less competition for pieces, values tend to be lower.

- Artists such as the Beatles and Elvis Presley had their image attached to a vast array of merchandise. The more mass-produced a piece was, and the more examples that have survived, the more affordable it is likely to be. Collectors will always prefer to buy examples in the best condition possible.

- With an eye to the future, it may be worth looking at artists who appeal to a younger generation that might look back and collect nostalgically when they grow up. Good examples could include Oasis, Blur, Madonna, and Kylie Minogue.

- In all instances look for eye-catching and appealing memorabilia that shows the stars at their best.

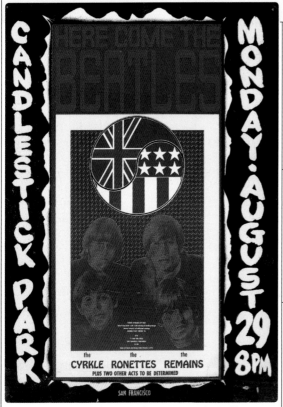

'HERE COME THE BEATLES', rare original concert poster, designed by Wes Wilson, for the concert at Candlestick Park, San Francisco, on August 29th 1966, featuring The Beatles, The Cyrkle, The Ronettes, and The Remains.

This poster was produced for The Beatles's last ever live, ticketed performance. Watched by a crowd of around 25,000 people, The Beatles performed eleven songs and were on stage for 33 minutes. Later unauthorised reprints of this poster are generally worth under £30.

1966   *26.5in (67.3cm) high*

£1,200-1,800   **FRE**

A very rare Watermark for ABC 'RINGO'S YELLOW SUBMARINE, A VOYAGE THROUGH BEATLES MAGIC' five LP box set, with original stapled sleeve note, in original case.

This rare set features Ringo narrating 'A Voyage Through Beatles Magic' as aired across 25 programmes on the ABC FM Radio Network from June 4th to November 26th 1983.

1983

£200-300   **GORB**

A Beatles 'Let It Be' deluxe box set, the 160pp 'Get Back' book and album in good condition, with original inner tray.

1970

£150-200   **GORB**

'Die Beatles in Yellow Submarine', German language film poster, with wear at the folds, and creases.

1968   *33in (84cm) high*

£35-45   **ROS**

A Beatles 'Reveille Special' advertising poster, showing the group on a beach in old fashioned swimming costumes, with facsimile signatures down the right hand side.

59in (150cm) wide

£80-120   **GORB**

A rare out-take photograph of The Beatles from the 'Sgt. Pepper's Lonely Hearts Club Band' album cover shoot, by photographer Michael Cooper.

1967   *20in (51cm) wide*

£300-500   FRE

A set of four Beatles autographs, signed by the four band members in blue biro on an autograph album page, framed and glazed.

8.25in (21cm) wide

£1,200-1,800   GORB

Mark Picks

I see a fair few 'Beatles' autographs at the 'Antiques Roadshow'. Most of them, sadly, turn out to be printed. Look for variations in the lines that ink (even a biro) takes when the signature is signed by hand. Also look on the back of the paper, as the pressure of signing can leave an indentation matching the signature.

Provenance is the next issue. How were the signatures obtained, and did the owner actually see the band signing their autographs? Sometimes a wonderful and memorable story of meeting the band is revealed! These questions are very important, as many autograph books or photos were taken and signed out of sight by roadies or secretaries. Sometimes one or two Beatles would sign for the rest of the band, as well as for themselves. Check that the style of each signature matches authentic examples. Also look for naturally free-flowing signatures. If they look too studied or have tell-tale shakey 'pauses', you should be suspicious.

Finally, you should ask, what are the signatures on? Autograph books are great, but this photograph of the band with their characteristic hairstyles and clothes would make a collector's heart sing. Add to that the fact that each autograph is near the right band member, and not over the faces or over each other's signatures, and you have one of the best examples of Beatles autographs that this amount of money can buy.

A signed Beatles group photograph portrait, signed in biro and marker pen by the four band members, with pencil marks to rear, aquired by the vendor following a concert at the Glasgow Odeon in December 1965.

1965   *8in (21cm) high*

£3,000-5,000   L&T

BEATLES & POP MEMORABILIA WANTED

Up To £2000 PAID FOR BEATLES AUTOGRAPHS ON ONE PAGE

Up To £5000 PAID FOR BEATLES CONCERT POSTERS

Any Pop Memorabilia Considered - Free Quotations
Beatles, Hendrix, Stones, Zeppelin, Who, Floyd, 60's, 70's

Autographs, Lyrics, Concert Posters, Handbills Programmes, Tickets, Personal Effects, Set Lists & More

FREE QUOTATIONS

TOP PRICES PAID!

TRACKS LIMITED

PO BOX 117, Chorley, Lancashire, PR6 0QR
TEL: 01257 269726 - FAX: 01257 231340
e-mail: sales@tracks.co.uk
we-buy-beatles.com

A 'Beatles Hummer' musical instrument, with cardboard tube, printed with a portrait of the band, with facsimile signatures and plastic end and top cap, made by Louis F. Dow & Co, copyright 1964 NEMS.

c1965   *11in (28cm) long*

£60-80   GORB

ROCK & POP

A CLOSER LOOK AT A BEASTIE BOYS MEDALLION

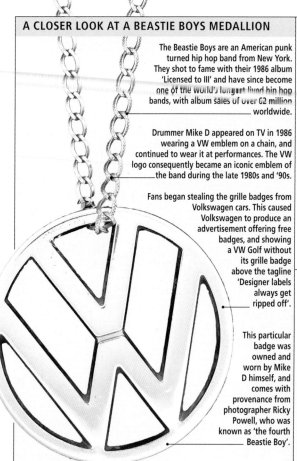

The Beastie Boys are an American punk turned hip hop band from New York. They shot to fame with their 1986 album 'Licensed to Ill' and have since become one of the world's longest lived hip hop bands, with album sales of over 62 million worldwide.

Drummer Mike D appeared on TV in 1986 wearing a VW emblem on a chain, and continued to wear it at performances. The VW logo consequently became an iconic emblem of the band during the late 1980s and '90s.

Fans began stealing the grille badges from Volkswagen cars. This caused Volkswagen to produce an advertisement offering free badges, and showing a VW Golf without its grille badge above the tagline 'Designer labels always get ripped off'.

This particular badge was owned and worn by Mike D himself, and comes with provenance from photographer Ricky Powell, who was known as 'the fourth Beastie Boy'.

A Beastie Boys metal VW medallion and chain, worn by Mike D (Diamond) of the Beastie Boys during the mid-1980s.

Medallion 3.5in (9cm) diam

£1,200-1,800   **FRE**

A David Bowie autographed 'Hunky Dory' English pressing, by RCA Victor, boldly signed by Bowie to the reverse and dated '79'.
1979
£80-120   **GORB**

An 'ELVIS SINGS' 45rpm record sleeve, no.47-8100 featuring the songs 'Return To Sender' and 'Where Do You Come From', signed by Elvis in blue ink.
1962   *7in (18cm)*
£700-1,000   **FRE**

A very rare Elvis Presley autographed 'Girls! Girls! Girls!' English pressing, by RCA Victor monopressing, boldly signed by Elvis to the front.
1962
£400-600   **GORB**

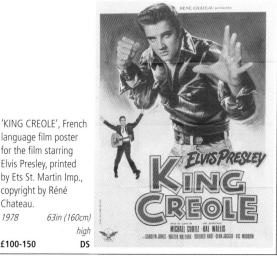

'KING CREOLE', French language film poster for the film starring Elvis Presley, printed by Ets St. Martin Imp., copyright by Réné Chateau.
1978   *63in (160cm) high*
£100-150   **DS**

A rare Jimi Hendrix Experience white label Track Records promotional 'are you experienced' LP album, the artwork designed by Bruce Fleming.
1967   *12.25in (31cm) wide*
£150-250   **FRE**

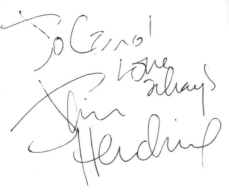

A Jimi Hendrix autograph, inscribed 'To Carol, Love always, Jimi Hendrix' in black ink on an autograph album page.

4.75in (12cm) wide

£800-1,200   **FRE**

A Buddy Holly autographed album page, signed and inscribed by Holly in blue ink on a pink page 'To Marilyn, Buddy Holly'.

c1958   6in (15cm) wide

£250-350   **FRE**

A Mattel 'Donny & Marie Osmond' doll gift set, in mint and boxed condition.

1977   Box 13in (33cm) high

£70-100   **MTB**

A Rolling Stones autographed programme, signed by all five members of the band in red ink, also with signatures of Inez and Charlie Foxx, with wear from folds and creases.

1963

£700-1,000   **GORL**

WANTED

1960's and 1970's CONCERT POSTERS

FLYERS, HANDBILLS, PROGRAMMES, TICKETS, PERSONAL EFFECTS, SIGNED ITEMS, DOCUMENTS, ANYTHING UNUSUAL OR ASSOCIATED 1960's AND 1970's ROCK AND POP MEMORABILIA.

WE PAY THE BEST PRICES

We will pay up to **£6,000** for an original concert poster for **THE BEATLES**, **£4,000** for **THE ROLLING STONES** and **THE WHO**, **£2,000** for **LED ZEPPELIN** and **JIMI HENDRIX**, as well as very high prices for other 1960's and 1970's Rock and Pop Memorabilia.

FREE VALUATIONS CASH PAID INSTANTLY

Tel: 01494 436644 or 07890 626840

Email: music@usebriggs.com

BRIGGS ROCK AND POP MEMORABILIA
Loudwater House,
London Road, Loudwater,
High Wycombe,
Buckinghamshire, HP10 9TL

ROYAL MEMORABILIA

QUICK REFERENCE

- Although it had been produced before, the popularity of Royal commemorative ware boomed during the 19thC. Transfer printing meant that ceramics could be quickly and cheaply produced, and railways ensured a wide distribution.
- Popularity peaked during the late 19thC and the early 20thC. Even though it is still produced today, it enjoyed its last major hurrah with the coronation of Elizabeth II in 1953.
- Collectors tend to focus on one monarch, with Queens Victoria and Elizabeth II being the most popular. This is partly due to the number and variety of pieces produced during their long reigns. In 2012, Elizabeth II joins Victoria as the only British monarch to have celebrated a Diamond Jubilee.
- Interest in pieces celebrating the lives of younger members of the current Royal family is currently growing. Look out for small limited editions (ideally less than 500). Keep all paperwork and boxes as these increase value.

- Other collections are built around a single event. Look out for those that generated less merchandise as fewer pieces may be more desirable. For example, fewer pieces were produced for Prince William's birth than for his wedding.
- Ceramics were the first and still the most popular form of Royal memorabilia, but a wide variety of other commemoratives have been made. These include objects, such as biscuit tins, that were specially decorated everyday items, or objects produced especially for the event, such as reproductions of Princess Diana's engagement ring (recently worn by Kate Middleton).
- Apart from the monarch and event, value is mainly dependant on rarity, good craftsmanship, a notable maker, eye-appeal, and condition. Some wear on 19thC pieces is understandable. However, cracks and chips reduce desirability, while damage on recent pieces reduces value considerably.

A Staffordshire '1840 Queen Victoria and Prince Albert Marriage' commemorative blue and white transfer-printed jug, with a titled portrait of Victoria and Albert and 'MARRIED FEB 10 1840' inscription.

3.5in (9cm) high

£400-600   **TEN**

A Doulton '1897 Queen Victoria Diamond Jubilee' commemorative mug, the trumpet-shaped body with a sepia printed portrait within a coloured floral cartouche, lined in gilt, with factory marks to base.

£120-180   **H&C**

HISTORICAL & COLLECTABLE
Specialist Auctioneers and Valuers Since 1991

For the only regular specialist auctions of

COMMEMORATIVES

including

Royalty, Political, Exhibition & War

POT LIDS & PRATTWARE
Fairings, Goss & Crested China
Baxter & Le Blond Prints

Forthcoming auction dates:
10th September 2011
3rd December 2011
3rd March 2012
2nd June 2012

(Please check prior to each auction for exact details).

For further information or a free sample catalogue please contact Andrew Hilton

Telephone: **0118 971 2420**

Email: **commemorative@aol.com**

HISTORICAL & COLLECTABLE

Kennetholme, Midgham, Reading RG7 5UX

(North side of the A4, 8 miles west of junction 12 on M4/A4)

www.historicalandcollectable.com

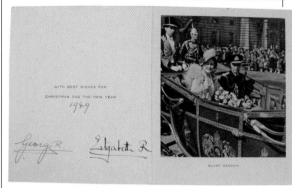

A Royal presentation photograph of George V, Queen Mary, and Edward, Prince of Wales, signed by all three on the mount, and indistinctly signed by the photographer, framed and glazed.

It is believed that this photograph was taken on the steps of Royal Naval College, Dartmouth.

14in (35.5cm) high

£400-600   SWO

A Royal Doulton '1936 George V In Memoriam' commemorative loving cup, with sepia printed portrait and wording, and printed factory marks to the base.

1936

£50-70   H&C

A Royal Christmas card, signed by George VI and Queen Elizabeth to the Archbishop of Canterbury in 1949, featuring a photograph of the couple on their silver wedding anniversary.

£120-180   GORL

A Crown Ducal '1937 Edward VIII Coronation' commemorative pint mug, decorated in colours with the Royal cypher and date set between gilt lined chequered borders.

1936   *4.5in (11.5cm) high*

£30-40   CAPE

A Bretby '1937 Edward VIII Coronation' commemorative souvenir musical character jug, the handle formed as an 'E', and the base with impressed marks.

1936   *8.5in (22cm) high*

£120-180   GORL

A CLOSER LOOK AT A PAIR OF COMPORTS

These high quality comports were designed for sale by Herbert Goode, who worked for London retailer and Royal Warrant holder Thomas Goode & Sons. They were made by the highly skilled glassmaker William (Billy) Swingewood Snr.

The intention was to produce an exclusive limited edition of 50 pieces with coloured crowns, but, perhaps due to cost, only two comports were made with coloured crowns, of which this is one.

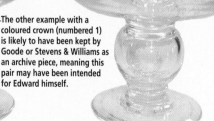

The wording cut into the feet reveals that they are both numbered '2' from the edition of 2 (coloured) and 50 (colourless), and that they were made on the 28th December 1936, eighteen days after Edward VIII abdicated.

The other example with a coloured crown (numbered 1) is likely to have been kept by Goode or Stevens & Williams as an archive piece, meaning this pair may have been intended for Edward himself.

A pair of Stevens & Williams glass comports, the feet and bowls engraved with wording commemorating the coronation and abdication of Edward VIII, the knops containing lampworked crowns, and the base of each bowl containing an Edward VIII coin.

1936   *6in (15cm) high*

£2,000-2,500   MDM

A pair of Crown Ducal transfer-printed bone china mugs, commemorating the births of Princess Elizabeth (left) in 1926, and Princess Margaret (right) in 1930, lined in gilt and with factory marks to bases.

These mugs, featuring portraits taken by photographer Marcus Adams, were produced on the event of George VI's and Queen Elizabeth's (Elizabeth and Margaret's parents) coronation. Memorabilia featuring key members of the Royal family as children is particularly popular with collectors.

c1937   *3in (7.5cm) high*

£120-180   **H&C**

A Royal Doulton '1937 George VI and Queen Elizabeth Coronation' commemorative mug, with transfer-printed portrait of Princess Elizabeth, and E-shaped handle, with gilt highlights and printed factory marks to the base.

1937

£120-180   **H&C**

A small Crown Ducal '1937 George VI and Queen Elizabeth Coronation' bowl, showing a likeness of the young Princess Elizabeth within a gilt, red, and black border, the base with printed factory marks.

4.5in (11.5cm) diam

£40-60   **H&C**

Judith Picks

Paragon produced its first commemorative wares in 1911 for the Coronation of George V. The company is best-known for its very high quality loving cups. Typically richly decorated in gilt and vibrant colours, they have enormous appeal to collectors. As they were produced in limited editions of comparatively few pieces, they can be hard to find and are usually priced accordingly. Look out for the largest sizes, as different sizes were produced for some events, and larger pieces are rarer and more desirable.

One of the pieces at the 'top of the tree' of Royal memorabilia, such mugs should appreciate over time, providing the market remains popular.

A Royal Crown Derby '1953 Queen Elizabeth II Coronation' commemorative bone china pin tray.

c1953   *4.25in (10.5cm) long*

£30-50   **H&G**

An Arthur Wood '1953 Queen Elizabeth II Coronation' earthenware lion-handled mug, with factory marks to the base.

c1953   *4.75in (12cm) high*

£50-70   **H&G**

A Wedgwood '1953 Queen Elizabeth II Coronation' commemorative Queensware mug, pattern no.CL 6487, designed by Richard Guyatt, with pink and black stylised animal and foliate design with gilt highlights.

1953   *5.75in (14.5cm) wide*

£80-120   **PC**

A Paragon '1953 Queen Elizabeth II Coronation' commemorative bone china loving cup, with lion handles, with certificate, numbered from a limited edition of 1,000.

c1953   *4.75in (12cm) high*

£300-400   **PC**

A '1953 Queen Elizabeth II Coronation' commemorative silver thimble, embossed with a scene of the Queen's carriage travelling to Westminster Abbey, with Birmingham hallmarks, in a fitted red leather case, retailed by Asprey.

1953   *1in (2.5cm) high*

£180-220   **WW**

A Le Rage '1953 Queen Elizabeth II Coronation' commemorative souvenir compact.

1953

£50-80   MGT

A '1953 Queen Elizabeth II Coronation' commemorative silver letter knife, with Sheffield hallmarks.

1952   *8.5in (21.5cm) long*

£120-180   PC

A '1953 Queen Elizabeth II Coronation' commemorative Union Jack printed card shield.

1953

£25-35   PC

A '1953 Queen Elizabeth II Coronation' commemorative scarf, printed in colours, with card tag, in near mint condition.

1953   *28in (71cm) wide*

£30-40   PC

A '1953 Queen Elizabeth II Coronation' commemorative metal and printed plastic badge.

1953   *1in (2.5cm) diam*

£8-12   PC

A Crescent diecast and plastic Queen Elizabeth II 'Royal State Coach' model, mounted on a wood-effect plastic base, with card information tag, and in original hard plastic case, in excellent condition.

Look out for the lead version by Britains, as this can fetch over £100 in good condition, and even more if it's in better condition and retains its box.

c1953

£15-20   SAS

Miller's Compares

The screen or transfer-printing on this example is very poor by comparison to the Spode mug. It has brash colours and poor details, and no additional gilding.

The shape is standard, indicating this is a mass-produced mug, probably made in the Far East. The Spode mug has a much more pleasing shape.

This example is made by Spode, one of Britain's finest and most historic makers, renowned for its quality production.

Made from fine bone china, a type of porcelain perfected by Spode around 1800, this mug would have been produced in far smaller numbers, and is therefore rarer today.

A Spode '1977 Queen Elizabeth II Silver Jubilee' bone china tankard, the front with monogram, the back with Royal coat of arms, both beneath a border of intertwined thistles, clovers, leeks, and roses.

1977   *4in (10cm) high*
£30-50   **PC**

A '1977 Queen Elizabeth II Silver Jubilee ' transfer-printed earthenware mug, the back decorated with other 20thC monarchs.

c1977   *3.5in (9cm) high*
£5-8   **PC**

A Poole Pottery '1977 Queen Elizabeth Silver Jubilee' limited edition charger, decorated by Julie Williams with the lion and unicorn in bright enamels simulating stained glass within a black border, numbered 93 from an edition of 250, with original box and certificate.

1977   *12.25in (32cm) diam*
£150-200   **GORL**

A Loughton Hall '1977 Queen Elizabeth II Silver Jubilee' bone china two-handled vase and domed cover, painted with a view of Windsor Castle, verso with a Royal coat of arms, on a midnight blue and gilt ground, numbered 21 from a limited edition.

1977   *14in (35.5cm) high*
£40-60   **CAPE**

A Royal Worcester '1977 Queen Elizabeth II Silver Jubilee' relief portrait plaque, designed by Arnold Machin OBE RA, numbered 149 from a limited edition of 1,000, in a parcel-gilt mahogany frame.

1977   *14in (35.5cm) high*
£120-180   **DN**

A Whitefriars '1977 Queen Elizabeth II Silver Jubilee' commemorative engraved glass goblet, designed by Geoffrey Baxter, in original presentation box with certificate.

Even though Whitefriars is one of the most popular and sought-after names in 20thC glass, its commemorative pieces often only appeal to Royal memorabilia collectors, rather than Whitefriars collectors.

1977   *6.75in (17cm) high*
£70-100   **WW**

A '1977 Queen Elizabeth II Silver Jubilee' silver goblet, with four applied motifs and engraved with a crown, date, and initials, with Sheffield Jubilee hallmarks, and presentation box.

1977   4.25in (11cm) high 5oz (142g)

£70-100   CAPE

QUICK REFERENCE - FALLEN OUT OF FASHION

- Fashion and utility play large parts in collecting and the value of items. Just as Georgian and Victorian dining tables have taken a hit now very few use or want such furniture, the desirability and value of letter knives has fallen too. This is because we receive far fewer letters today, thanks to the digital age that brought us the mobile phone and email. Not only that, but many also saw letter knives as fussy and fiddly to begin with.

- This example fetched its high value as the retailer is high-end, the maker is good, it's from a small-ish limited edition, and the price of silver is very high (at the time of writing in late Summer 2011). Other examples without these advantages would fare less well. Unless nostalgia-driven letter knife collecting becomes widespread, this situation is unlikely to change.

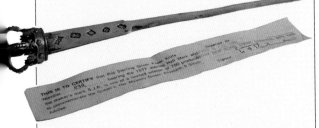

An Asprey '1977 Queen Elizabeth II Silver Jubilee' limited edition silver and parcel-gilt paper knife, with a Royal crown finial, with original certificate numbered 232 from an edition of 750, 'SJR' makers' mark for S.J. Rose, and London Jubilee hallmarks.

1977   10in (25.2cm) long 2oz (57g)

£100-150   LC

A pair of '1977 Queen Elizabeth II Silver Jubilee' moulded glass goblets, the interiors with printed monogram, wording, and crown on a silver ground, with original display box.

1977   5in (12.5cm) high

£10-15   GAZE

A '1977 Queen Elizabeth II Silver Jubilee' limited edition silver letter opener, the terminal embossed with the Royal coat of arms, with maker's mark for Roberts & Belk, and Sheffield hallmarks.

1977   11in (28cm) long 5oz (142g)

£70-100   GORL

A pair of '1977 Queen Elizabeth II Silver Jubilee' chromium-plated teaspoons, with moulded and enamelled finials including a profile portrait.

1977   4.75in (12cm) long

£7-10   GAZE

A '1977 Queen Elizabeth II Silver Jubilee' commemorative match tin, with printed portrait and wording on a stylised foliate ground.

1977   2in (5cm) high

£7-10   PC

A '1977 Queen Elizabeth II Silver Jubilee' home-made tapestry footstool, on an early 20thC turned oak base.

c1977   13.25in (33.5cm) wide

£20-30   GAZE

QUICK REFERENCE - AN 'ANNUS HORRIBILIS'

• In her anniversary speech, Queen Elizabeth stated that 1992 was her 'annus horribilis' due to a number of events. Those included Prince Andrew's divorce from Sarah Ferguson, Princess Anne's divorce from Captain Mark Phillips, Windsor Castle catching fire, and the publication of Princess Diana's 'tell-all' book, 'Diana: Her True Story'. One month after her November speech, it was announced that Prince Charles and Princess Diana were to separate. Prices for much memorabilia from this anniversary are still comparatively low, but this may change as Her Majesty's reign is reappraised and re-assessed, as the 'annus horribilis' was an important, if unpleasant, year.

A Royal Crown Derby '1992 Queen Elizabeth II 40th Anniversary of Accession' limited edition cup and cover, commissioned by Goviers of Sidmouth, numbered 39 from an edition of 100.

1992   *8.75in (22cm) high*

£40-60   **TRI**

A Royal Worcester Imari patterned '2002 Queen Elizabeth II Golden Jubilee' plate, with coat of arms to centre, surrounded by iron red, gilt, and cobalt blue panels.

2002   *8in (21cm) diam*

£30-40   **TRI**

A Halcyon Days '2002 Queen Elizabeth II Golden Jubilee' limited edition enamel box, with coat of arms and wording to central panel, surrounded by flags, from an edition of 50.

3.25in (8.5cm) wide

£200-300   **PC**

A Royal Doulton 'Her Majesty Queen Elizabeth' limited edition figurine, HN2878, designed by E. J. Griffiths, from a limited edition of 2,500.

1983   *10.75in (27cm) high*

£80-120   **L&T**

A set of twenty-five Canadian Franklin Mint Ltd silver ingots celebrating 'Elizabeth Our Queen', each moulded with scenes, contained in a fitted case, with booklet and certificate of authenticity.

At the time of writing, the price for silver is extremely high, which accounts for much of the value of this set.

25oz (710g) approx

£400-600   **WW**

A mid-late 20thC Queen Elizabeth II banner, depicting the Royal coat of arms, hand-worked in gold thread, silks, and velvet against a red baize ground.

42in (107cm) high

£800-1,200   **GORL**

QUICK REFERENCE

- The basis for modern scientific enquiry was laid in the Italian Renaissance, and it was consequently in this period that scientific instruments took off. Christopher Columbus's discovery of America in 1492 created a demand in fellow explorers for navigational instruments. Nicolas Copernicus announced that the sun was the centre of the solar system in 1543, and this revolutionary idea sparked a desire for better observational astronomy instruments. Galileo Galilei famously improved and popularised the telescope in 1609.

- Pieces from this era are extremely rare and are mostly of museum quality, but there is a wide range of late 18thC and 19thC instruments to choose from on the market today.

- Most collectors tend to focus on one category of instrument, such as navigational, medical, or optical, or on one specific type, such as telescopes or microscopes. Most instruments from this period were finely engineered from lacquered brass, but other materials, such as mahogany and occasionally precious metals, were used, depending on the instrument.

- Apart from the type of instrument, the most important indicators to value are the date, the maker, the quality, and the condition. Look for dates, names, and other marks inscribed on the instrument. 20thC examples are rarely collectable, unless finely constructed by a notable maker.

- The style and function of the instrument can also help to date it. Generally speaking, navigational backstaffs were superceded by octants, which were then superceded by sextants as technology and understanding developed.

- Beware of modern reproductions, particularly telescopes. Many were made in the Far East or India, usually from very 'yellow' brass, and have poor mechanical movements. Examine authentic examples to learn how to spot them.

- Over the last decade values for scientific instruments have fallen, as the area has been unfashionable. Medical instruments are more sought-after. In general complex, finely made examples are likely to be desirable, particularly if they have their original accessories and box.

An early 20thC brass military compass, finished in black, with mother-of-pearl dial, numbered graduation around the case, with folding brass sight, and hinged brass and glass cover, in leather case.

2in (5cm) diam

£25-35 ECGW

An early 20thC Sampson Mordan & Co. military brass compass, with graduated dial, black finish, scales around the case, military arrow mark, and original leather case.

2in (5cm) diam

£60-80 ECGW

A 19thC Chinese wood geomantic compass, inscribed with Chinese characters and symbols in segments arranged in nine concentric rings, with compass to centre.

Geomantic compasses have been made since the 18thC for use by sailors. Replicas are still being produced today, and are unfortunately often sold as genuine antiques. Both replica and original models are found with lids.

1.75in (4.5cm) diam

£100-150 DOR

A 19thC Mauchlineware-cased compass and cover, with paper register dials to the interior.

Mauchlineware pieces were typically sold as souvenirs, and usually bear a transfer of a location or building on the exterior.

2.5in (6cm) diam

£100-150 WHP

SCIENTIFIC INSTRUMENTS

An American Brown & Hunt of New York brass surveying vernier compass, the silvered-brass engraved dial signed and with fleur-de-lys at North, other cardinal points in block lettering, needle ring engraved '0-90' in four quadrants, and limbs with vernier adjustment dial and thumb screw, 'T' vials, screw-on sights, and ball head tripod attachment.

15in (38cm) long

£450-550   SK

A late 19thC Stanley brass surveyor's level, no.8590, signed 'Stanley, Gt Turnstile Holborn, London, W.C.', in a fitted teak case.

13in (33cm) long

£70-100   WW

An early 20thC Casella black-finished and lacquered brass theodolite, with sighting tube, silvered vernier scale, spirit level, rack and pinion movement, on triform base with levelling screws, lacking eye pieces and magnifiers.

15in (38cm) high

£200-300   DN

An American lacquered brass sextant, by D. Eggert & Son of New York, with vernier scale, thumb-screw adjustment, inset bone scale marked 'U.S. Navy 13126', sun shades, telescope attachments, and original walnut bob, with printed paper label reading, 'Nautical Instrument, D. Eggert & Son, 239 Pearl Street, New York'.

8in (20cm) wide

£400-600   SK

A CLOSER LOOK AT A SEXTANT

A sextant is used for nautical navigation, and provides the angle between a celestial object (such as the sun) and the horizon. Combined with the time the elevation was taken, this can be used to chart a position on a map or chart.

The box sextant was developed by instrument maker William Jones in 1797. It is smaller, more portable, and less prone to damage than the standard sextant's exposed arc.

It was so-named as it is the equivalent of one sixth of a 360 degree circle.

It superseded the octant which was developed by John Hadley and Thomas Godfrey c1730.

This late Victorian example does not bear a maker's name. If it did and the maker was notable, it could have fetched significantly more.

A 19thC brass drum or box sextant, with silvered vernier scale and screw-fitting sighting telescope, contained in a fitted mahogany box.

£600-800   TEN

An American 12in (30.5cm) ebony octant, by Gedney King & Son, Boston, Massachusetts, the black-finished brass frame with inset bone vernier scale, with thumbscrew adjustments and lock, vacant inset plaque, brass sighting tube, horizon and index mirrors, sun shades, wooden handle and brass feet, in its original fitted case.

Octants are usually found with ebony or (earlier) mahogany frames, whereas sextants are usually made from a metal, such as brass.

£300-500   SK

A Victorian brass mining-angle measuring instrument, in the form of a hanging demi-circle, with scales from 90–0–90, with two brass plummets, in an original velvet-lined, leather-covered wood case.

13in (32cm) wide

£180-220   DOR

SCIENTIFIC INSTRUMENTS

QUICK REFERENCE – THE IMPORTANCE OF THE MAKER

- The maker, and thus the quality and date, of an optical or scientific instrument makes an enormous difference to value. The work of good quality makers or retailers, particularly from the late 18thC and early 19thC, will always fetch more. Look out for names such as George Adams, J. Cuff, J. B. Dancer, W. & B. Jones, Benjamin Martin, R. & J. Beck, Jesse Ramsden, and Dollond. Broadhurst Clarkson & Co. are a well-known and prolific maker, but not quite in the top league, even though this is a good quality telescope.

- It's worth paying attention to any address details given in an inscription or label, as makers sometimes moved location, and this can be a means of dating an instrument to a more precise period.

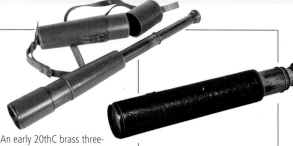

An early 20thC brass three-draw naval-issue telescope, by Broadhurst Clarkson & Co., with impressed 'B. C. & Co. Ltd' maker's mark, also stamped 'Tel Sct.Rect MKII', with brown leather clad body and extending-hood brown leather case and strap.

£80-120   CAPE

A 19thC brass and leather mounted four-draw brass-bodied telescope, unmarked.

30.5in (77cm) long

£60-80   ECGW

A 19thC three-draw day or night brass telescope, by Thomas Harris & Son, the mahogany sleeve stamped on the first draw 'T Harris & Son, London, Improved Day or Night'.

Extended 32.5in (82cm) long

£120-180   LC

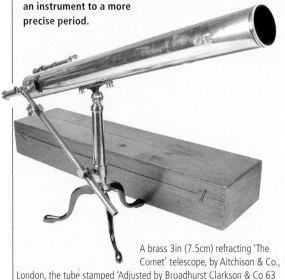

A brass 3in (7.5cm) refracting 'The Comet' telescope, by Aitchison & Co., London, the tube stamped 'Adjusted by Broadhurst Clarkson & Co 63 Farringdon Road, London E.C.', the end stamped 'The Comet Aitchison & Co London and Provinces', on a folding tripod base with two eye pieces, in a fitted mahogany case.

36.5in (93cm) long

£500-700   WW

A 19thC ivory and brass pocket telescope, by 'Wm Watkins of St James St, London', with two brass draws, and an ivory sleeve and eyepiece, contained in a cylindrical leather case.

Extended 3.5in (9cm) long

£120-180   LC

A pair of early 20thC gilt-brass lorgnette-type opera glasses, with mother-of-pearl covered faceted body and telescopic folding handle.

£30-40   CAPE

A pair of late 19thC Negretti and Zambra ivory and brass opera glasses, with ivory sleeves and eyepieces.

Avoid examples where the ivory is split or stained, or where panels of mother-of-pearl are missing, as this reduces values dramatically.

£150-200   ECGW

SCIENTIFIC INSTRUMENTS

A 19thC lacquered-brass monocular microscope, by Pastorelli & Co. of London, with fine and coarse focus adjustment above a stage with X and Y adjustment, with pivoted plano-concave mirror below, the whole pivoted between two shaped uprights with Y-shaped baseplate signed 'Pastorelli & Co. 208 Piccadilly, London', in original mahogany box, with some original accessories including objective lenses and a small selection of slides.

Pastorelli & Co. operated from 208 Piccadilly, London 1859-75. A 'monocular' microscope has one viewing tube, and a 'binocular' microscope has two viewing tubes leading to one. The maker, complexity, brass construction, and inclusion of some accessories makes this as valuable as it is.

Box 17in (42cm) high

£400-600   DN

A late 19thC lacquered-brass monocular microscope, by Mottershead and Co. of Manchester, with rack and pinion, and fine screw focusing, on a triform base applied with retailer's plaque, together with three objectives in brass storage cases.

As well as manufacturing scientific instruments, Negretti & Zambra were a well-known retailer, operating out of their large shop in Holborn.

15in (38cm) high

£200-300   CAPE

A late 19thC lacquered-brass travelling microscope, by J. Swift & Son, with folding tripod stand, rack and pinion focusing, and ebonised stage, two objectives, concave mirror, and leather fitted carry case.

£300-400   BELL

A CLOSER LOOK AT A   MICROSCOPE

The wooden base is a box. This small microscope unscrews into numerous parts, which can be securely stored inside for travelling.

This 'type' was designed by Charles Gould in 1820, hence the name. They are sometimes called 'Cary-types' as they were retailed by William Cary among others.

It was designed to satisfy the growth of interest in natural history, enabling people to observe small bugs and botany out 'in the field'.

It is important that all the parts are still there, particularly those that make up the microscope, such as the column, stage, tube, and eyepieces.

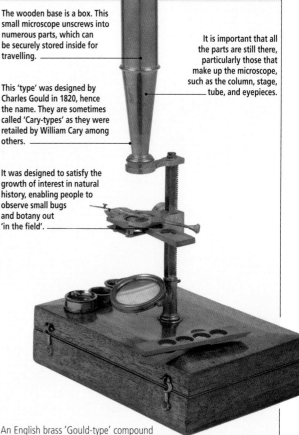

A German lacquered-brass and cast iron monocular microscope, by Ernst Leitz of Wetzlar, numbered '175913', with four objectives and four eyepieces, in its original wood case.

c1915   14in (34.5cm) high

£200-300   DOR

A lacquered-brass monocular microscope, by Carl Zeiss of Jena, with cast iron stand, numbered '12640', and with three objectives ('AA', 'DD' and 'a2'), and two eyepieces Nos.2 and 4, condensor, and original fitted mahogany case.

c1888   15in (38cm) high

£350-450   DOR

An English brass 'Gould-type' compound microscope, with three objectives, an eyepiece, three boxwood slides, and other accessories, contained in a fitted velvet-lined mahogany case.

c1830   6.5in (16.5cm)

£1,000-1,500   DOR

A 19thC mahogany and brass magic lantern, by Reynolds & Branson Ltd. of Commercial Street, London, bearing an ivorine label stamped 'Stroud & Rendel's Science Lantern'.

24in (61cm) long

£250-350   GHOU

A lacquered brass pantograph, signed 'W. & S. Jones 30 Holborn London', other limbs with graduated scales and marked in block letters 'B', 'C' and 'D' with corresponding adjustable pen holders, six neatly turned ivory rollers and central weighted support, and fitted dovetailed mahogany box.

Reputedly devised by Christoph Scheiner in 1603, the pantograph was used for enlarging or reducing drawings or maps. William and Samuel Jones are recorded as being at 30 Holborn from 1800 to 1860.

c1820   *30in (76cm) long*

£400-600   SK

A CLOSER LOOK AT A STEREOGRAPHOSCOPE

The large lens on a graphoscope was used for viewing text, maps, photographs or prints in detail.

This example also has a small lens allowing stereographic slides to be viewed.

A card with two seemingly identical images side-by-side was placed on the sliding holder and moved into focus until a three-dimensional image could be seen through the two eyepieces.

Most fold down into a compact box. This example is of very good quality, with walnut burr veneer, ebonised eyepieces, and ebony stringing to the edges.

A late 19thC burr walnut veneered stereographoscope, with three lenses and ebonised mounts above a positionable, angled base.

£300-400   L&T

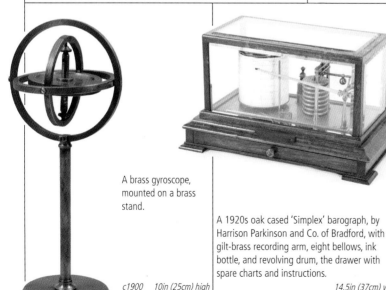

A brass gyroscope, mounted on a brass stand.

c1900   10in (25cm) high

£150-200   DOR

A 1920s oak cased 'Simplex' barograph, by Harrison Parkinson and Co. of Bradford, with gilt-brass recording arm, eight bellows, ink bottle, and revolving drum, the drawer with spare charts and instructions.

14.5in (37cm) wide

£300-400   CAPE

A set of Victorian postal scales, with incomplete set of weights, on serpentine wooden base.

Look out for precious materials, more decorative designs, or good maker's names (such as Sampson Mordan), as this can increase the price.

£30-40   CAPE

SCIENTIFIC INSTRUMENTS

A botanical model of a cockchafer, made of painted carved wood, plastic, and fabric, mounted on a wood and metal stand, with light damage and wear.

Originally inhabiting dusty corners of college or university laboratories, these often complex models were used for demonstrations in lectures. The best examples are realistically modelled and painted, and come to pieces in layers, showing internal details such as a skeleton, organs, or parts of either. Each important part was numbered or indicated with a paper label. Look out for examples bearing a maker's name, and examples from before the late 19thC, which are rare. Over the past decade, these models have become fashionable interior accessories for those looking for a unique, eccentric look. This has meant that prices have risen, as decorators compete with collectors to own the best, most complex, and often bizarre examples. This cockchafer is an excellent example.

c1950   *21in (54cm) high*
£1,500-2,000   **DOR**

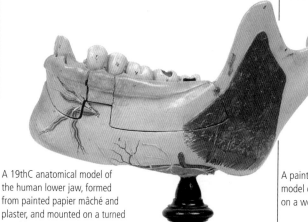

A 19thC anatomical model of the human lower jaw, formed from painted papier mâché and plaster, and mounted on a turned wood base, with light damage and wear.

11in (27cm) high
£600-800   **DOR**

A painted papier mâché and plaster model of a molar tooth, mounted on a wood and metal stand.

c1910   *13in (32cm) high*
£750-850   **DOR**

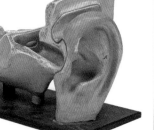

A painted papier mâché and plaster anatomical model of a human ear, mounted on a rectangular wooded base, with wear and damage, and lacking some parts.

12in (30cm)
£150-200   **DOR**

A painted plaster anatomical model of the human inner ear, mounted on a turned wood stand.

Although relatively plain, aural models, such as this, are sought-after by medical collectors. For others, the appeal lies in its almost sculptural quality.

c1890   *14in (36cm) high*
£750-850   **DOR**

A painted plaster anatomical model of the human heart, on a turned wood base, with some damage.

c1920

11in (28cm) high
£500-700   **DOR**

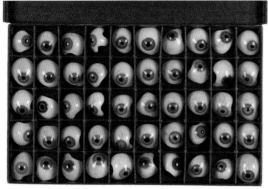

A set of fifty prosthetic handmade glass eyes, contained in an original fitted card box.

19thC and early 20thC glass eyes are surprisingly hard to find and valuable, particularly in quantity and in original fitted cases.

c1910   *Box 10in (25.5cm) wide*

£2,500-3,000   **DOR**

QUICK REFERENCE - PHRENOLOGY HEADS

- Phrenology was a 'science' that was said to be able to indicate the emotions, intelligence and psychological character of a person from the shape of, and the bumps on, their head. Popular from c1810 to c1840, it was developed by the German doctor Franz Gall in the early 1800s. Heads like this were produced, usually bearing the name Fowler, with labels showing which part of the head each emotion or character trait corresponded to. They have been reproduced many, many times over the past thirty years, usually in a lightweight, white ceramic with blue and black transfers. Original examples can fetch a few hundred pounds, with later examples fetching only a few pounds.

- George Dutton was a Fellow of the British Phrenological Society who moved to Lumley Avenue, Skegness in 1890. Alas, by that point, the income from his phrenological practice was not enough to keep his family, so he also turned to selling books, printing, and operating a library.

A moulded white plaster phrenology head, painted in cream, with paper labels detailing the different qualities of the brain, the back with a paper label reading 'GHJ Dutton, Phrenologist, Author and Bookseller, Skegness', with wear and damage.

c1895   *6in (15cm)*

£30-50   **FLD**

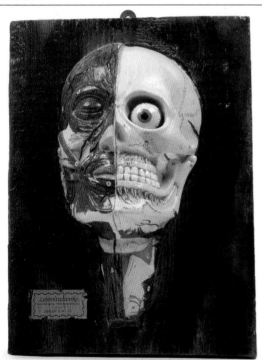

A German painted papier mâché and plaster anatomical model of the human head, by Lehrmittelwerke Berlinische Verlagsanstalt, with applied numbering, on a wall-mounted wooded plaque.

c1910   *13in (34cm) high*

£1,000-1,500   **DOR**

A 19thC lacquered brass and ivory enema set, in its original fitted mahogany case, unlabelled.

12in (30cm) wide

£120-180   **GORB**

A wood and lacquered-brass sliding pill-making machine, for producing pills in two different sizes.

c1900

£120-180   **DOR**

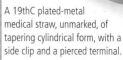

A 19thC plated-metal medical straw, unmarked, of tapering cylindrical form, with a side clip and a pierced terminal.

6in (15.2cm) long

£120-180   **WW**

SCOUTS & GUIDES

QUICK REFERENCE

- In 1903 Robert Baden-Powell (1857-1941), a Lieutenant General in the British Army, discovered that his military training manual, 'Aids to Scouting', was being widely used by teachers and youth organisations. He decided to re-write the book so that it was specifically applicable to young people, and in 1907 tested his ideas by holding the first 'Scout' camp for some local boys at Brownsea Island in southern England.
- The resulting movement, which emphasised practical outdoor activities and mental, phsyical, and emotional development, developed rapidly. Scout groups were formed spontaneously across the country, and then the world, from 1910 onwards.
- In 1910, a new organisation, the Girl Guides, was created for girls by Baden-Powell and his sister Agnes. In 1920, the first World Scout Jamboree was held in London. In 2011, Scouting and Guiding together had over 41 million members worldwide. Despite this, it is still considered a niche market.

- The Scout uniform, featuring a neckerchief and campaign hat, has become iconic. Distinctive uniform insignia include the fleur-de-lys and the trefoil, as well as merit and other fabric badges. Such badges are one of the most popular collecting areas, due to the nostalgia they conjure up in buyers, and the wide and appealing collection that can be built up. Handbooks, pamphlets, magazines, stamps, camping equipment, and other items are also collected.
- When determining value consider a number of criteria, including the quality, the material, the date, and the scarcity of a piece. If the piece is appealing and representative of the movement, then so much the better. In general, early pieces from the first two or three decades of the 20thC are the most desirable, particularly if they are connected to Baden-Powell. Cross-market interest (from toy collectors, for example), can increase prices paid due to increased demand.

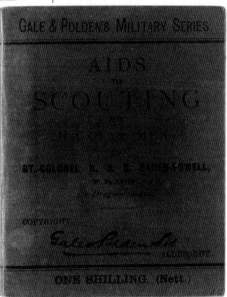

BT.-Colonel R. S. S. Baden-Powell, 'Aids to Scouting for N.-C. Os. & Men', published by Gale & Polden Ltd, Aldershot.,with original red wrappers, backstrip sun faded.

1899
£150-200   **L&T**

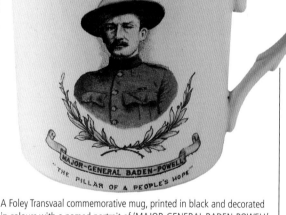

A Foley Transvaal commemorative mug, printed in black and decorated in colours with a named portrait of 'MAJOR-GENERAL BADEN-POWELL', the reverse inscribed in black for the siege and relief of Mafeking with dates, and with a pair of circular plaques with colour portraits of General Sir Redvers Henry Buller and Major-General John French, cracked.
£180-220   **SAS**

A Boer War commemorative badge, with printed portrait of 'COL. BADEN POWELL'.

1in (2.5cm) diam
£15-25   **PC**

An Elliot Pottery stoneware jug, commemorating the relief of Mafeking, incised and decorated in blue, and applied with monograms of Queen Victoria and Robert Baden-Powell, the handle shaped as a hound.
1900   *6.75in (17.5cm) high*
£120-180   **FLD**

An English Boer War commemorative plaque, featuring an unusual portrait of Lord Baden-Powell, with gilt trim.
c1900   *8in (20cm) high*
£90-100   **RCC**

Six of a set of 50 C.W.S. Cigarettes 'Boy Scout Badges' cigarette cards.

Although only six cards are shown, the price range is for the complete set of 50 cards in excellent condition.

c1939

£40-60 set   CWD

A set of Britains 'Boy Scouts' lead figures, no.161, comprising a Scout master with eight various Scouts marching, with poles, very good condition but two Scouts missing arms, contained in a good condition box with illustrated label, lid paper lifting.

1925-37

£180-220   VEC

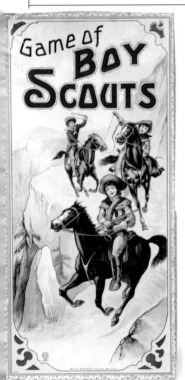

An American Milton Bradley 'Game of BOY SCOUTS' game, the box lid with colour lithographed paper label, the interior depicts camp scenes, with several wood markers.

Milton Bradley (1836-1911) is widely credited with establishing the board game in the US after he founded the Milton Bradley Company in 1860. Bradley also studied and mastered colour lithography (printing), and it's the fabulous printed artwork that makes this game valuable and desirable. Rather than the game itself, the condition and subject matter of the colourful label is the most important aspect.

22in (56cm) wide

£200-300   BER

A CLOSER LOOK AT A VESTA CASE

Vesta cases are a highly collectable area in their own right. The serrated strip at the bottom was used for striking the match.

Probably produced to commemorate the relief of Mafeking in May 1900, the portrait of Baden-Powell makes this vesta case desirable and expensive. Scouting and Baden-Powell collectors would compete against militaria and vesta case collectors.

Enamelled vesta cases are among the most sought-after produced, particularly if the enamelling is well-painted, detailed and realistic.

Although not the very best, Saunders & Shepherd (founded in 1869) is a good quality Birmingham maker, which was also active in Holborn, central London from 1873 to 1902.

A Victorian silver vesta case, with enamelled portrait of Lord Baden-Powell, with maker's marks for Cornelius Desormeaux Saunders & James Francis Hollings Shepherd, and with hallmarks for Birmingham.

1900   *2in (5cm)*

£1,200-1,800   A&G

An American 'FORT ORANGE COUNCIL - BOY SCOUT POW WOW JUNE 1, 2, 1935' badge.

c1935   *0.75in (2cm) diam*

£50-60   PC

An American woven fabric New York World's Fair 'BOY SCOUTS OF AMERICA SERVICE CAMP' badge.

c1939   *4in (10cm) wide*

£30-40   PC

SCOUTS & GUIDES

A silver figurine of a Girl Guide leader, standing on an ebonised plinth with a presentation plaque, with maker's marks for David Hollander & Sons Ltd., and hallmarks for Birmingham.

The plaque reads 'PRESENTED TO MRS D. BEVINGTON SMITH AS AN APPRECIATION FROM PAST AND PRESENT GUIDES AND BROWNIES 12.4.1937'.

1936   *6in (15cm) high*
£200-300   DN

A mid-late 20thC American Boy Scouts of America short-sleeved shirt, with 'Official Blouse' label and other badges to the sleeves and front.
£10-15   BR

A 1930s American Johnson & Johnson 'GIRL SCOUTS OFFICIAL FIRST AID KIT' tin, with printed lid, lacking contents.
6in (15cm) high
£20-30   BH

A 1930s Girl Guides 'COMPACTOID' printed-tin first aid case, complete with contents.
4.25in (11cm) wide
£30-50   PC

A Royal Doulton 'Brownie Bunnykins' figurine, DB61, designed by Graham Tongue and modelled by Warren Platt.
1987-93   *4in (10cm) high*
£30-50   PSA

A CLOSER LOOK AT A SET OF BRITAINS GIRL GUIDES

The Girl Guide Movement was founded in 1910, the same year that Britains introduced lead figures of Scouts. Guides weren't produced until the 1930s.

As they are scarce, reproductions and fakes are known. Reproductions should cost around £15. Originals are hollow-cast and a Guide should have an air exit-hole in the crown of her hat.

This is a group, rather than a set, as indicated by the unusual number of leaders and Guides.

Guides and their leaders are hard to find, perhaps because lead figures were primarily boys' toys, and a set of Girl Guides wasn't as appealing to a young boy as a set of Scouts or soldiers.

Guides are generally rarer than their leaders, and there are no colour variations known, so beware of repainted figures.

A group of Britains 'Girl Guide' lead figures, comprising four Girl Guides and five leaders, all in excellent condition, and another larger leader in worn condition.
c1930-39
£500-700   VEC

QUICK REFERENCE

- Sculpture has arguably always taken a firm second place in popularity and value behind 'flat art' such as paintings, prints, and drawings, but this appears to be changing. Similarly, although 18thC and 19thC examples remain desirable, more attention is now being paid to 20thC pieces.
- As a new generation of collectors comes to the fore, many 20thC sculptors are beginning to see the recognitition they deserve as their work is revisited and reappraised.
- Many collectors are beginning to buy pieces that complement the Mid-century Modern look that is currently so popular. In such cases the look of a piece is often more important than the identity or importance of the sculptor.
- Learn about the background of a sculptor including where they studied, when and where they worked, and who they studied under. Catalogues from major educational institutions and exhibitions at key galleries are good places to start.
- Although the work of major names such as Henry Moore and Barbara Hepworth may be beyond most people's budgets, there are plenty of second or third tier sculptors whose work may grow in desirability as more is discovered and their names become more widely recognised.
- Always look for quality in execution and material, and a reflection of the look of a period. An interesting story behind a sculptor or their work can often add value and interest.
- Collectable sculpture includes many pieces from all over the world that are not necessarily deemed 'fine art'. Away from African and other tribal art, which has its own market, Inuit art has risen in desirability and value over the past decade.
- Produced in Northern Canada from the 1950s, Inuit sculpture is predominantly carved from soapstone. Look for the work of notable artists, and interesting pieces that illustrate myths and stories from Inuit life and culture.

A 'Clatt Stone Forms' abstract sculpture, by Kathleen Haldane, of two stones mounted on a wooden plinth.

13in (33cm) wide

£60-90   **SHAP**

A 'Guardian' carved and assembled mahogany sculpture, by Kathleen Haldane.

Haldane was a member of the Scottish Society of Woman Artists (SSWA), founded in 1924.

27in (69cm) high

£100-150   **SHAP**

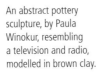

An abstract pottery sculpture, by Paula Winokur, resembling a television and radio, modelled in brown clay.

7in (18cm) high

£250-350   **FRE**

A mid-late 20thC Austrian walnut, brass-washed metal, and wire abstract sculpture, unsigned, the body reminiscent of the top of a stringed musical instrument.

13.75in (35cm)

£250-350   **DRA**

SCULPTURE

Mark Picks

Some names bubble around the market on the verge of becoming major and important for years. Studio potter Bernard Rooke is one, and sculptor Brian Willsher is another. Born in 1930, Willsher studied engineering at Woolwich Polytechnic 1946-49, and did a number of differing jobs before qualifying as a dental technician. His first sculptures were created in 1954, after he had a motorcycle accident. While in plaster himself, he began to experiment with small plaster sculptures, eventually moving to wood.

His career as a sculptor took off after exhibitions at Dunn's of Bromley in 1965, and at prestigious retailer Heal's in 1966 and 1967. Further exhibitions followed but, in 1968, his work was still not classified as sculptural art by Customs & Excise, despite support from renowned sculptor Henry Moore, and art critic, poet and author Herbert Read. As a result, they were taxed heavily when they were sold and exported, which caused major problems. From then, Willsher chose to market and largely sell his work personally, appearing in only select exhibitions. This is perhaps the reason his work is not more widely recognised today. Finely machined, his complex, geometric, abstract, and organic forms are quintessentially of their time. I believe that they are certainly worth watching closely over the coming years.

An 'Approaching Scarlett' abstract mahogany sculpture, by Brian Willsher, composed of concentric interlocking elements, signed and titled by the artist to underside.

c1980   14in (34.5cm) high
£150-250   **ROS**

An abstract Brazilian-mahogany sculpture, by Brian Willsher, of concentric curvilinear form, mounted on a mahogany base, signed and dated '1991' in pen to underside.

1991   *17in (43cm) high*
£250-350   **ROS**

A large abstract Brazilian-mahogany sculpture, by Brian Willsher, of concentric curvilinear form, mounted on a poplar base, signed and dated '1989' in pen to underside.

1989   *29in (73cm) high*
£400-600   **ROS**

A large abstract Brazilian-mahogany sculpture, by Brian Willsher, of tall flared fan-shaped form, mounted on a mahogany base, signed and dated '1991' in pen to underside.

1991   *29in (74cm) high*
£250-350   **ROS**

A large abstract Brazilian-mahogany sculpture, by Brian Willsher, of flared fan-shaped form rising to a point, mounted on a mahogany base, signed and dated '1997' in pen to underside.

1997 27in (69.5cm) high
£300-400   **ROS**

A wooden abstract sculpture, attributed to Neville Bertram (1901-1995), with incised 'NB' monogram.

Neville Bertram trained under Tyson Smith in Liverpool.

14in (35cm) high
£150-200   **WW**

An Inuit stone, skin, horn, and antler 'Drummer' figure, by Nelson Takkiruq (b.1930), E4-120, from Gjoa Haven.

9in (23cm) wide

£1,500-2,000   **WAD**

An Inuit stone and antler 'Drummer' figure, by George Tataniq (1910-1991), E2-179, from Baker Lake, signed in syllabics.

7in (18cm) high

£2,500-3,500   **WAD**

A CLOSER LOOK AT AN INUIT SCULPTURE

More stylised, almost abstract, Inuit sculptures tend to be the most desirable, and Ullulaq's work is typical of that.

Bulging, distorted forms with grotesque, exaggerated expressions typify Ullulaq's distinctive work, as do the inset horn and antler teeth and eyes.

He was influenced by his nephew, the renowned Karoo Ashevak. Both were among the founders of the important Netsilik School of carvers, which became known for these bizarre styles.

This sculpture was executed when Ullulaq had become a full-time and recognised artist. By 1994, the best Inuit art had already become increasingly valuable and sought-after.

An Inuit stone, musk ox horn, and antler 'The Fiddler' figural sculpture, by Judas Ullulaq (1937-1998), E4-342, from Gjoa Haven, signed in syllabics.

1994   *12.5in (32cm) high*

£6,000-8,000   **WAD**

An Inuit stone 'Shaman Drummer with Wings' figure, by Iyola Kingwatsiak (1933-2000), from Cape Dorset, signed in Roman.

16.5in (42cm) high

£1,200-1,800   **WAD**

An Inuit stone 'Woman Drinking' figure, by Qavaroak Tunnillie (b.1928), E7-929, from Cape Dorset, signed in syllabics.

19in (48.5cm) high

£600-800   **WAD**

An Inuit stone 'Owl Sheltered Her Young' figure, by an unidentified artist, from Cape Dorset.

c1950   *11in (28cm) wide*

£4,000-5,000   **WAD**

SCULPTURE

An Inuit green soapstone recumbent seal figure, by Timothy Kitishimik (b.1938), E9-1675, with inset carved ivory tusks (one damaged), signed in syllabics and disc number.

10.5in (27cm) long

£400-600   **TAC**

An Inuit soapstone 'Seal and Pup' figure, by Lucassie Ikkidluak (b.1949), signed in syllabics.

10.5in (26.5cm) high

£1,500-2,000   **WAD**

An Inuit stone and antler 'Musk Ox' figure, by Martha Apsaq (b.1930), E2-282, from Baker Lake, disc number inscribed, signed in syllabics.

10in (25.5cm) long

£1,200-1,800   **WAD**

An Inuit stone 'Dancing Bear' figure, by George Arluk (b.1949), E3-1049, from Arviat, signed in Roman.

12in (30.5cm) high

£400-600   **WAD**

An Inuit stone and ivory 'Bashful Walrus' figure, by Kananginak Pootoogook (1935-2010), E7-1168, from Cape Dorset, signed in syllabics.

As well as the importance of the artist, and the abstraction and stylisation of the sculpture, a sense of humour can also attract buyers. This charming sculpture of a walrus trying to hide behind his flipper, is charming, amusing, and would have been highly appealing to buyers no matter who had carved it.

13in (33cm) high

£3,000-4,000   **WAD**

An Inuit soapstone 'Polar Bear' figure, by an unidentified artist.

The vast majority of Inuit art found on the market is by sculptors who are unknown because they did not sign the piece, or have not yet become known if they did. Most will probably remain unknown, and much of their work will probably not rise in value, particularly more ordinary looking, simply carved examples like this bear. However, they do form a more affordable starting point for a collection, and if you buy well, you may just be lucky!

5in (12.5cm) high

£100-150   **WAD**

A late 20thC carved wood sculpture, in the form of a stylised torso, unsigned.

23.5in (60cm) high

£120-180   **DRA**

A Cubist-style black-glazed ceramic sculpture, by Peter Hayes, mounted on a slate base, the base inscribed 'Peter Hayes 1986'.

Born in 1946, Hayes is a leading contemporary British sculptor. He studied at art school in Birmingham, and went to work as a ceramicist with African tribes until his return to the UK in 1982.

1986   *13in (32cm) high*

£350-450   **WW**

A mid-late 20thC Danish rosewood 'Lovers' figural sculpture, by 'Simone', with impressed signature to base.

15in (39cm) high

£250-350   **WW**

A 20thC unusual carved limestone abstract sculpture of two figures wrestling, unsigned.

10.5in (27cm) high

£120-180   **GORL**

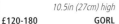

A 'mother and child' lead wall sculpture, by Tom Whalen R.S.A. (1903-1975), mounted on a wooded plaque.

17in (44cm) high

£300-400   **SHAP**

A small bronze figural sculpture, by Rudolf Svoboda, mounted on a red veined marble base, unsigned.

6in (15.5cm) high

£70-100   **WW**

A cast bronze head sculpture with two faces, by Gertrude Hermes, mounted on a black slate plinth.

Painter, engraver, and sculptor Gertrude Hermes (1901-1983) was a graduate of Leon Underwood's Brook Green School of Art. She was a member of and taught at the Royal Academy until 1976, and examples of her work are in many collections, including London's Tate Gallery.

7.5in (19cm) high

£500-700   **GORL**

SCULPTURE

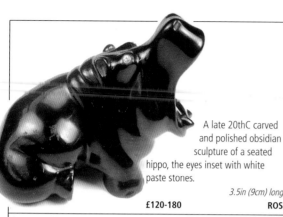

A late 20thC carved and polished obsidian sculpture of a seated hippo, the eyes inset with white paste stones.

3.5in (9cm) long

£120-180   ROS

A carved Connemara stone sculpture of a frog, by Sven Berlin, highlighted with gilding.

Sven Berlin (1911-1999) was a painter and sculptor who was also known for his writings, particularly his controversial fictionalised biography 'The Dark Monarch', which was banned two weeks after it was published in 1962.

8.25in (21cm) wide

£1,200-1,800   DUK

A CLOSER LOOK AT A SCULPTURE

François Pompon (1855-1933) worked with Auguste Rodin and inspired Constantin Brâncu i. In his day some said he was the greatest animal sculptor since the legendary Antoine Louis Barye

He stripped away detail and reduced the form to essentials, thereby capturing the true spirit of a polar bear and creating a sculpture that fitted seamlessly into the Art Deco style.

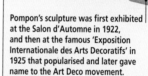

Pompon's sculpture was first exhibited at the Salon d'Automne in 1922, and then at the famous 'Exposition Internationale des Arts Decoratifs' in 1925 that popularised and later gave name to the Art Deco movement.

The popularity of Pompon's sculpture led it to be reproduced in large quantities. This example is carved rather than cast, which makes it more desirable.

A carved plaster maquette of 'L'Ours Blanc' (the white bear), from a model by François Pompon, naturalistically modelled walking, and incised 'Pompon' to foot.

As a result of Pompon's sculpture being exhibited at the 1925 exhibition, the polar bear joined the gazelle as a popular animal of the Art Deco style.

12in (31cm) wide

£1,200-1,800   WW

A Zimbabwean carved and polished stone sculpture of a stylised owl, by Ernest Chiwaridzo, signed on the back.

14in (36.5cm) high

£400-600   DN

A Slovenian cast-bronze sculpture of a bull, by Jánez Bóljka, part polished, part dark patinated, signed with a monogram, and stamped 'Bóljka'.

11in (28cm) long

£450-550   DN

A cast-bronze sculpture of a charging bull, indistinctly signed 'Cossio', and marked in gilt.

9in (23cm) long

£600-800   DUK

QUICK REFERENCE

- Although sewing is no longer a fashionable hobby, antique sewing tools remain extremely desirable. Most items available to the collector today date from the 19thC. At this time sewing was seen as a popular and virtuous pastime for girls and ladies, and a huge expansion of production ensured that there was a wide variety of tools for them to use.
- Earlier sewing tools are typically very rare, as far fewer were produced and most of these were worn, damaged, or lost. The spread of affordable sewing machines in the early 20thC meant a decline in demand for many hand-held sewing tools.
- Victorian sewing tools were made from variety of materials. Wooden pieces, particularly Mauchlineware, and Tartanware, are common, as are pieces in metals such as silver and brass. Many tools were made from silver during the Edwardian period, as the price of silver had dropped. Ivory, bone, and mother-of-pearl were also used frequently.

- Collectors typically focus on a single type of item, such as thimbles. Desirable thimble makers include James Horner, Charles Iles, and James Fenton. Gold thimbles are rare and even plain examples are usually valuable. Silver examples are also sought-after, with base metals being less so. The steel-lined 'Dorcas' range is an exception, with examples often being highly sought-after.
- Other collectable sewing items include needlecases (including 'Averys'), pincushions, thread winders, scissors, tape measures, and sewing boxes. French compendia or boxes with 'Palais Royale' marks are usually valuable. The larger they are and the more tools they contain, the better.
- Homemade pieces can be found, and are often more charming than factory-made pieces. In general look out for finely crafted pieces in precious materials, as these are likely to be the most valuable.

An early 18thC silver thimble, with stamped scroll mark around the skirt, engraved with scrolled initials and dates 'SM 1690-1720', with maker's mark comprising 'JI' with a key.

Note the irregular punched indentations in the top. These are indicative of thimbles made by hand before the development of the 'nose machine' in the 1750s, which allowed for indentations to be punched regularly. The form is also early. From the mid-18thC onwards, tops became less domed, and thimbles were generally less squat.

0.75in (1.5cm) high

£300-500   WW

A late 17thC gold thimble, engraved with reserves of flowers between floral straps, with scratched initials 'M M', unmarked.

Many silver or gold thimbles made before the 1870s are unmarked, as their weight was under the statutory five penny weight.

c1690   *0.75in (2cm) high*

£350-450   WW

An extremely rare George III gold thimble, marked 'Piercy's PATENT', with a row of trellis piercing around the base, and an oval cartouche with script initials 'EH', lacking liner.

John Piercy is recorded as working in the Snowhill area of Birmingham around 1818. His patent relates to the use of tortoiseshell, missing on this example, to line a thimble or be used for the body.

1815-1820   *1.75in (2cm) high*

£800-1,200   WW

A late 18th/early 19thC gold thimble, with a 'mushroom' dome, wriggle engraved band, the cartouche engraved 'ELVIRA', unmarked.

0.75in (2cm) high

£150-200   WW

An early 19thC Dutch silver thimble, with reserves of putti in relief and applied flowers, with a Dutch duty mark.

0.75in (2cm) high

£250-300   WW

A CLOSER LOOK AT A GOLD THIMBLE

The fitted case, covered with Morocco leather, is high quality and of the period. Its survival is rare, and adds desirability and value.

Lambert, based in London, were a high quality jeweller, and merged with competitor Harman & Co. in 1916.

The contrast between punched matt and polished surfaces, hand-worked high relief leaves, flowers, and dotted basal band, and inset coral and pearls, indicates that this is a very high quality thimble that would have been expensive in its day.

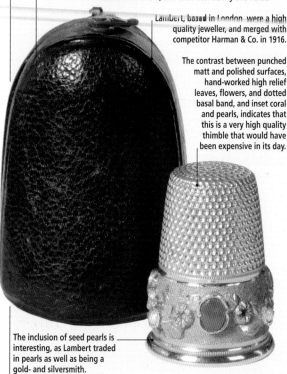

The inclusion of seed pearls is interesting, as Lambert traded in pearls as well as being a gold- and silversmith.

A mid-19thC gold thimble, with a basal band of raised floral swags inset with four coral cabochons and punctuated by tiny split seed pearls, in a period fitted case marked 'Lambert Jewellers, 12 Coventry Street'.

1in (2.5cm) high

£400-600   TEN

A mid-19thC 15ct gold thimble, initialled 'J. B.' among foliate engraved decoration, with maker's mark 'C. M.' with hallmarks for London.

1858

£250-350   H&L

A late 19thC 15ct gold thimble, with applied wirework and beaded decoration with plain escutcheon, with makers mark 'H. G. & S.', and hallmarks for Birmingham.

A good proportion of mid- to late Victorian gold jewellery was 15ct. Very yellow in tone, 15ct gold was introduced in 1854 and discontinued in 1932.

1889

£280-380   H&L

A gold thimble, with applied band of scrolled decoration, set with four yellow stones, and engraved 'E. S.', in a fitted case marked 'Heming & Co. 28 Conduit St London W.'.

£120-180   WW

A late 19thC French silver thimble, stamped around the lower body with a shepherdess and her sheep.

1in (2.5cm) high

£200-300   WW

A late 19thC silver thimble, of tapering circular form, with scrolling filigree and blank cartouche, unmarked.

1in (2.5cm) high

£40-60   WW

An early 20thC Norwegian enamelled silver thimble, decorated with pink roses on a striped white ground.

£50-70   CAPE

An early 19thC Austro-Hungarian silver-gilt sewing necessaire, the tapering tubular case engine-turned to give a woven lattice effect, the screw-cover revealing a combined needle case, bobbin, and a sectional box, no apparent maker's mark but struck several times with census marks for Salzburg 1807/08.

1897/8   *3.75in (9.5cm) long 1.25oz (35g)*
£450-550   LC

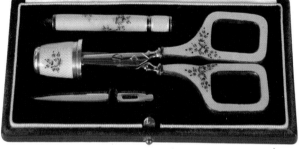

An early 18thC silver-gilt sewing etui, in the form of a mace, with chased and engraved scrollwork against a matt ground, with turned finials, the base and cover hinging open, with push-button releases, unmarked.

c1720   *4in (11cm) long 1.5oz (43g)*
£800-1,200   LC

An early 20thC Asprey & Co. four piece sterling silver and floral enamelled sewing set, comprising scissors, thimble, needle case and stitch un-picker, in a later blue plush lined and fitted case bearing Asprey PLC marks.

The colour and style of enamelling here is typical of the 1920s-1950s but the case is later.

£200-300   CAPE

A 19thC silver sewing set, comprising a pair of scissors, a pen knife, a thimble, a bodkin, and a crochet needle, with foliate scroll decoration, in a fitted velvet lined case.

5in (12.7cm) long
£150-200   WW

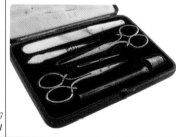

A sewing necessaire, in a fitted case comprising a pencil, a thimble, a mother-of-pearl and steel knife, a mother-of-pearl mounted steel piercer, a needle, and two pairs of steel scissors.

£100-150   WW

A late 19thC sewing set, the ivory oval case containing a gold thimble and gold handled scissors, the lock cartouche and thimble engraved 'H. M.'.

3.5in (9cm) long
£200-300   LC

A Victorian silver novelty sewing case, in the form of a hinged suitcase, containing three fitted bobbins, with maker's marks for Sampson Mordan & Co., and hallmarks for London.

This combines a fine and desirable maker with a novelty form and a collecting area (travel) that has strong and wide interest.

1874   *2in (5.5cm) long*
£800-1,200   WW

SEWING

A 19thC carved bone thimble case, modelled as a house, with hinged roof.

2in (5cm) high

£200-300　　　　　　　　　　　　GORB

An early 19thC rosewood cotton reel stand, with two pincushions, one thimble holder, base drawer, and carrying handle.

6in (15cm) wide

£220-280　　　　　　　　TRI

A CLOSER LOOK AT A SEWING COMPENDIUM

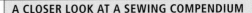

Architect and designer John Nash's remodelling of the famous Brighton Pavilion was completed in 1822, allowing this piece to be dated relatively accurately.

Novelty shapes are highly sought-after. Not only is this piece large, very well turned and -painted, and proportionate, it's also incredibly charming.

Painted 'whitewood ware' is the earliest form of Tunbridgeware, so it also appeals to collectors of this souvenir ware too, widening the market.

Despite being a functional item, with its pincushion and sewing tools, it is in superb condition, with a good patina and very little wear to the painted design.

A Regency Tunbridge hand-painted 'whitewood ware' sewing compendium, modelled as a Brighton Pavilion dome, the screw-off onion dome revealing a pincushion above a further compartment containing sewing implements.

c1825　　　　　*9in (23cm) high*

£6,000-8,000　　　　　　GORL

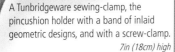

A Tunbridgeware sewing-clamp, the pincushion holder with a band of inlaid geometric designs, and with a screw-clamp.

7in (18cm) high

£250-350　　　　　　TRI

A Victorian turned ebony sewing-clamp, with a pincushion and screw-thread fixing.

4.75in (12cm) high

£30-50　　　　　　SWO

A pressed-brass quadruple needle case, by R. Turner of Redditch, of oblong form with rising needle holders.

Made to hold different sizes of needles, these cases are often known as 'Averys' after William Avery of Redditch, who designed and made the first one in 1868. Production exploded during the 1870s, when most 'Averys' were made. Look out for figural examples, as these are the most valuable.

c1880　　　　　*2.75in (7cm) long*

£50-70　　　　　　DA&H

QUICK REFERENCE

- The value of an ounce of silver rose dramatically from late 2009, which has affected the silver market considerably. In April 2011, an ounce reached a high of £30.16. Price has fluctuated widely since. Consequently common and unexceptional early 20thC silver teasets, which once fetched low to mid-hundreds of pounds, are now worth high hundreds of pounds for the value of their silver weight only.
- This has strengthened, but not necessarily affected, the price of small silver novelties produced from the mid-19thC onwards. As these pieces tend to be small in size, and light in weight, their 'scrap value' is still low, so the maker, date, type of item, and condition apply more to value.
- Learn how to recognise the makers' marks of notable makers, such as Sampson Mordan, Walker & Hall, and Nathaniel Mills, as their work tends to be highly sought-after. Certain collecting categories also tend to be more desirable than others, and these include, notably, writing equipment, and card and vesta cases.

- In all instances, the quality of a piece counts towards value. The finer and more detailed the work is, the higher the value is likely to be. Enamelling will typically add value, especially if it is well-executed, and has an appealing theme.
- Also look out for items that have cross-market appeal. Themes related to sports, well-known places, and famous people can appeal to fans of that sport, place, or person. This widening of the market often leads to higher values.
- Many of these small novelties were made to be used, and can show signs of wear. Silver is a comparatively soft metal, and functional items that were carried around have often been left with dents and splits from accidental impacts, and a loss of detail caused by rubbing. Although dents and splits can be repaired, it can be costly, and the 'ghostly' remains of damage is often still apparent.
- Beware that when cleaning a dirty silver piece one is effectively removing an (oxidised) layer of silver. As such, excessive cleaning will eventually reduce levels of detail.

A Victorian silver card case, maker's mark 'HA', of lobed oblong form, with bright-cut engraved decoration surrounding a cartouche with a monogram, with remains of gilding, with hallmarks for Birmingham.

1862   *3.75in (9.5cm) high*

£100-150   **AH**

A Victorian silver card case, maker's mark 'CC', of lobed oblong form, with bright-cut engraved pattern of ivy leaves and foliage surrounding a cartouche with monogram, with remains of gilding, with hallmarks for Birmingham.

1885 3.75in (9.5cm)

£80-120   **AH**

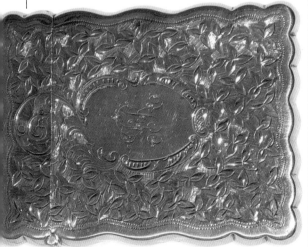

A late Victorian silver card case, of lobed oblong form, with gilded bright-cut engraved leaves surrounding a gilded cartouche containing a monogram, with indistinct maker's mark, with hallmarks for Birmingham.

1901   *3.75in (9.5cm) high 1.7oz (48g)*

£180-220   **AH**

A Victorian silver card case, engraved with floral and scrolling decoration, with hallmarks for Birmingham.

1868

£120-180   **BELL**

SILVER

A CLOSER LOOK AT A CARD CASE

Snuff boxes, vinaigrettes, and card cases decorated with this style of architectural subject matter are known as 'castle tops', even though they often depict other types of building.

The building and the surrounding pattern are embossed from the reverse into the silver and then chased from the front. Extra details are then engraved into the outer surface using a sharp tool known as a burin.

Nathaniel Mills (1746-1840) was the best maker of this type of box, being renowned for quality and detail. He was succeeded by his sons, Nathaniel, William, and Thomas, who continued the family tradition.

All of Mills's work is sought-after, but interest from alumni of this esteemed college adds to competition from card case and 'castle top' collectors, raising the price.

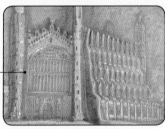

A Victorian silver 'castle top' card case, maker's marks for Nathaniel Mills, of shaped rectangular form, with chased view of King's College, Cambridge, with hallmarks for Birmingham.

'Castle tops' reached the height of their popularity between the 1830s and the 1870s. They were often sold as scenic souvenirs to those travelling on Britain's new and expanding railway network.

1847   *4in (10cm) high 2.3oz (65g)*

£1,200-1,800   **TEN**

A Victorian silver 'castle top' card case, maker's marks for Yapp & Woodward, chased on one side with York Minster within a textured ground and raised scrolls and flowers, the reverse with further floral decoration, with hallmarks for Birmingham, with original fitted case.

Yapp & Woodward are known for their fine quality card cases. Despite this their work is not as collectable as that of Nathaniel Mills or Joseph Willmore.

1845   *4in (10cm) high*

£650-750   **TEN**

An early Victorian silver double-sided 'castle top' card case, maker's marks for Taylor & Perry, with a view of Kenilworth Castle in relief on one side and Warwick Castle on the other, each view bordered by engine-turned 'tartan' decoration, with hallmarks for Birmingham.

1838   *3.75in (9.5cm) high 2oz (57g)*

£600-800   **LC**

A Victorian silver rectangular card case, maker's mark 'T.H.', with presentation cartouche inscribed 'K.B. a present from John Blake', with a foliate scrolling ground, with hallmarks for Birmingham, cased.

1896   *4.25in (11cm) long 3oz (85g)*

£150-200   **AH**

A Continental white-metal card case, with engine-turned decoration, the cover with blank cartouche.

'White metal' is the British term for metals containing silver made outside the United Kingdom. Such metal does not bear official British hallmarks denoting the level of purity of silver.

3.25in (8.5cm) wide

£80-120   **A&G**

An Edwardian silver card case, in the form of an envelope, the exterior with engraved decoration, with hallmarks for Birmingham.

1906

£120-180   **BELL**

A CLOSER LOOK AT A VESTA CASE

The railway theme makes this desirable to collectors of railwayana as well as to collectors of vesta cases and small silver objects. This increased competition raises the price.

Thornhill were a notable retailer of fine luxury objects, ranging from silver items to cut glass, luggage, games compendia, and more.

It is perfectly proportioned, extremely well-made, and, despite being just 2in (5cm) high, has a wealth of tiny details, which were all made by hand.

The mark here is a registered diamond used for protecting designs. The number and letter combination allows the design to be dated to 23rd August 1873, though this piece may have been made later.

A Victorian silver novelty vesta case, in the form of a railwayman's lamp, with a clear lens, hinged cover, and striker plate on the base, stamped 'Thornhill' and with a registered design diamond, with indistinct hallmarks.

2in (5cm) high 1oz (28g)

£800-1,200   **LC**

A late Victorian silver and enamel vesta case, maker's marks for Cornelius Desormeaux Saunders and James Shepherd, the front enamelled with a panel depicting a soldier and inscribed 'A GENTLEMAN IN KHAKI', with hallmarks for Birmingham.

1899   *2in (5cm) high*

£400-600   **TOV**

A Victorian vesta holder, in the form of a mug, maker's marks for F. Edmonds and E. Johnson, the ribbed handle with striking strip, with hallmarks for London, also stamped with the retailer's name of 'W.Thornhill & Co, 144 Bond St'.

1890   2in (5cm) high 1.25oz (35g)

£100-150   **LC**

A Victorian silver vesta case, with applied head of a Scottie dog, maker's mark 'J.W.', with hallmarks for Birmingham.

Although this is not of the best-quality, pieces depicting Scottie dogs (especially in fine materials) are highly collectable. This is also of an early date. Most Scottie dog memorabilia dates from the 1920s-30s, or the 1950s.

1897   1.75in (4.4cm) high

£180-220   **AH**

An Edwardian silver vesta case, maker's marks for William Henry Leather, inset with Scottish agate in the form of thistles, surrounded by hand-engraved foliate motifs, with hallmarks for Birmingham.

The quality of the design is not as fine as that of other vesta cases, and there are signs of wear.

1907   1.75in (4.5cm) high

£20-30   **A&G**

A silver and enamel vesta case, maker's marks for John William Kirwan, enamelled with the Sedbergh Public School crest and motto, with engraved initials 'J.A.C.T.' to reverse and dated 'November 30th 1911', with hallmarks for Birmingham.

J.A.C.T. are the initials of John Alexander Chisholm Taylor, who had a distinguished military record in World War I. Such provenance raises interest, and often the value of a piece.

1910   2in (5cm) high

£320-380   **A&G**

SILVER

QUICK REFERENCE - PEPPERETTES

- Silver pepper shakers in novelty forms have been popular since the late 19thC, and peaked in popularity during the early 20thC. They are keenly sought-after by collectors, and prices can be high. Damage such as dents to the thin metal can be repaired, although this is typically expensive, and splits are more serious.

- Look for unusual and amusing shapes, and popular themes such as railwayana, hunting, and sports. Animals can also be highly desirable, particularly if they are widely-collected, such as dogs, cats, and frogs. If the animal or person has a strong and appealing 'character', this can only increase the value, as can a wealth of fine and realistic details. The maker is also very important, and a combination of these key elements can bring amazing results. In 2010 a rare, characterful, and animated standing frog pepperette made by the highly-rated maker James Barclay Hennell in 1880 fetched over £4,000 at auction, despite being only 4.5in (11cm) high (See 'Miller's Antiques Handbook & Price Guide 2012-2013' p.335).

A pair of Continental silver novelty pepperettes, modelled as a Dutch boy and girl in traditional costume, with 'RL' sponsor's mark and English import marks for 1911/12.

c1911   *3.5in (8.5cm) high 5oz (142g)*
£300-500   LC

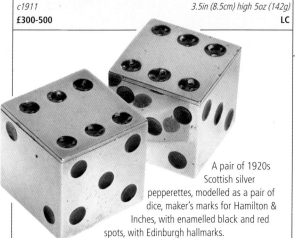

A pair of 1920s Scottish silver pepperettes, modelled as a pair of dice, maker's marks for Hamilton & Inches, with enamelled black and red spots, with Edinburgh hallmarks.

Suggestive of louche yet exciting nights of glamorous gambling, dice were a popular and recurrent motif in the 1920s-30s and during the 1950s.

1920 and 1925   *each 1in (2.5cm) high 2.8oz (79g)*
£550-650   TEN

A pair of silver pepperettes, in the form of artillery shells, with maker's marks for Hamilton & Inches, with pierced and engraved points and screw-off bases with reeded rim, with hallmarks for Edinburgh.

1914   *3in (8cm) high*
£400-600   L&T

A pair of Edwardian silver pepperettes, in the form of hunting horns, with engraved monograms, with hallmarks for London.

1906 4.75in (12cm) high
£280-320   WHP

A pair of Victorian silver-gilt novelty pepperettes, in the form of champagne bottles, with pull-off caps, maker's mark mis-struck but probably by E. S. Barnsley, with hallmarks for Birmingham.

1888   *3.5in (9cm) high 1oz (28g)*
£350-450   LC

An Edwardian novelty pepperette, in the form of a kitten with a bow around its neck, with maker's marks for W. Vale & Sons, with hallmarks for Birmingham.

1909   *1.5in (4cm) high 0.1oz (2.8g)*
£150-250   LC

A 1920s silver novelty pepperette, in the form of a fighting cock, with maker's marks for F.B. Thomas, with hallmarks for London.

1927   *3in (8cm) high 2.4oz (68g)*
£600-800   TEN

A set of eight 1930s Danish sterling silver-gilt and guilloche enamel coffee spoons.

Colourful sets, such as this, can be valuable if in solid silver, primarily due to the value of the weight of the silver. If the enamel is undamaged, this also raises value, as such pieces were functional items and many are damaged through use.

3.5oz (99g)

£80-120   CAPE

A set of six silver coffee spoons, maker's mark 'HA', with heart-shaped bowls, with hallmarks for Sheffield.
1916.
£100-150   WHP

One of a pair of late 20thC silver egg cups, maker's mark 'CSAC', with hammered body and faceted feet, with hallmarks for London.
1977   *4oz (113g)*
£50-80   WHP

A pair of George III silver salts, maker's marks for Samuel Meriton, on three shell-shaped feet, monogrammed, with blue glass liners, with hallmarks for London, 1767, with a pair of George II Hanovarian saltspoons, marks rubbed
c1750.   *Salts 2.5in (6.4cm) diam*
                          5oz (142g)
£300-500   LC

A novelty sugar sifter ladle, maker probably George Bowen & Sons, with a bowl in the form of a snail shell, with patent-registered design number, with hallmarks for Birmingham.
1900   *1oz (28g)*
£70-100   LC

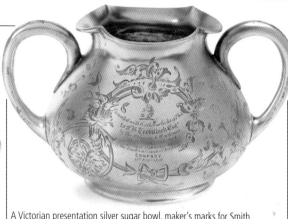

A Victorian presentation silver sugar bowl, maker's marks for Smith, Nicholson & Co., engraved with foliate sprays and twin cartouches, one engraved with a railway goods wagon, the other inscribed 'Presented with 6 other articles of Plate to F. H. Trevithick Esqr. by the Officers & Workmen of the Locomotive and Carriage Department of the Eastern Counties Railway COMPANY 11th Feb-y 1856', with hallmarks for London.

Francis was the son of the famous engineer Richard Trevithick, and his career spanned many branches of railway management. This sugar bowl, among other items of silver, was presented to him on his retirement. It's this connection and provenance that makes it as valuable as it is.

1854   *7.5in (19cm) wide 11.5oz (325g)*
£400-600   TEN

Mark Picks

Fruit knives form a niche collecting area all of their own. They can be found in many different sizes and forms, and with different decorative details - variety abounds. Many are covered with carved mother-or-pearl panels, like this example.

They were typically used during the Victorian and Edwardian periods, after dinner, to peel and cut fruit. Little used and wrongly unfashionable today, they make a great budget collectable as they are usually much more affordable than many other silver items. Most unboxed examples fetch around £20 or less, although prices can rise depending on the maker, size, and quality.

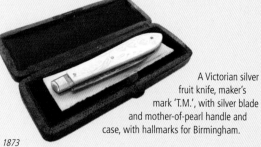

A Victorian silver fruit knife, maker's mark 'T.M.', with silver blade and mother-of-pearl handle and case, with hallmarks for Birmingham.

1873
£35-45   WHP

SILVER

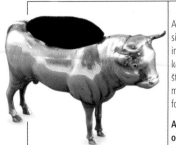

An Edwardian novelty silver pincushion, modelled as a bull, maker's mark for Cohen & Charles, with hallmarks for Birmingham.

1906	*2.5in (6.5cm) long*
£500-700	**GORL**

An Edwardian novelty silver pincushion, in the form of a kangaroo, with mis-struck 'II?' maker's mark, with hallmarks for Birmingham.

Although birds, pigs, and other domestic animals are more widely collected, kangaroos are rare, hence the high price. Unfortunately this example is rather worn or it might have fetched more.

1908	*2.75in (7cm) high*
£600-800	**LC**

An Edwardian novelty silver pincushion, in the form of a crouching frog, maker's marks for Henry Matthews, with hallmarks for Birmingham, damaged.

1908	*2.5in (6cm) long*
£200-300	**TEN**

An Edwardian novelty silver pincushion, in the form of a bear, marks probably for H. V. Plithey and Co., with moving arms and legs, a muzzled ringed nose, with hallmarks for Birmingham.

Small silver items in the form of bears are highly sought-after by teddy bear lovers, who are known as 'arctophiles'. This rare example was made at the same time as the earliest true 'teddy bears', and takes their characteristic shape, albeit with a bigger back hump!

1908	*2.25in (6cm) long*
£800-1,200	**WW**

A George V novelty silver pincushion, in the form of a swan, maker's marks for Adie & Lovekin Ltd., with hallmarks for Birmingham.

1924	*2.75in (7cm) long*
£200-300	**GORL**

A novelty silver pincushion, in the form of a boot, maker's marks for S. Blanckensee & Son Ltd., with a wooden base, with hallmarks for Birmingham.

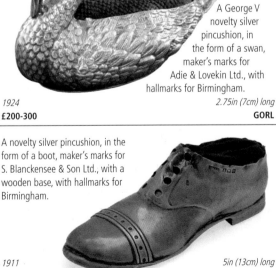

1911	*5in (13cm) long*
£120-180	**WW**

A CLOSER LOOK AT A PINCUSHION

Pincushions in the form of nursery rhyme or fairy tale characters were not always aimed at children. They are extremely rare today, as few were made and many of these were lost.

Levi & Salaman were founded in 1870 and are a highly desirable maker, known for their detailed work on small silver objects, such as nécessaires, spoons, pepperettes, and pincushions.

The egg-shape is typical of Humpty, and his face, lock of hair, arms, and bow are full of detail and character.

The embossed silver is very thin, but it has remained in undamaged, excellent condition.

An Edwardian novelty silver pincushion, in the form of Humpty Dumpty, maker's marks for Levi & Salaman, embossed 'HUMPTY DUMPTY', with hallmarks for Birmingham.

1910	*1.5in (4cm) high*
£1,200-1,800	**WW**

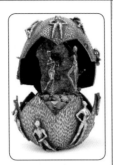

A Stuart Devlin 'Adam & Eve' silver-gilt egg, the textured exterior with applied silver male and female figures, hinged and opening to reveal a silver male and female figure standing beneath a tree beside a rough, bright-green crystal on a naturalistic base, with hallmarks for London.

1974   *3in (7.5cm) high*

£500-700   **L&T**

A Stuart Devlin limited edition silver-gilt and enamel 'Prince Charles and Lady Diana Spencer' commemorative egg, numbered 68, the textured egg revealing Prince of Wales feathers above a green and white foliate enamel ground, with hallmarks for London, together with a textured silver-gilt egg stand also by Stuart Devlin, with matching hallmarks.

This egg was popular and sold well at the time, meaning examples aren't too hard to find. While royal memorabilia is strongly collected, the theme makes this egg less appealing to many Devlin collectors.

1981   *2.75in (7cm) high, 2.85oz (89g)*

£300-500   **DN**

A CLOSER LOOK AT A PAIR OF CANDLEHOLDERS

Australian born Stuart Devlin (b.1931) is one of the best-known silver- and goldsmiths in Britain today. He has designed coins for a number of countries, and was awarded the Royal Warrant in 1982.

He is known for designs that contrast textured gold against plain silver. Such designs broke away from the clean-lined Modernist look popular in the first half of the 20thC with their extravagance and almost 'space age' appearance.

Over the past five years, Devlin's work has been re-appraised and has risen enormously in value. This is particularly true of rarer items, such as boxes and covered dishes set with semi-precious gems.

Although his 'surprise' eggs are collected, it's his candlesticks, candelabra, and drinking goblets that typically have the widest appeal.

A pair of Stuart Devlin silver-gilt candlesticks, of cylindrical form with flaring conical drip-pan, textured silver-gilt openwork filigree cylinder shades, with hallmarks for London.

1971   *10.75in (27.5cm) high 23.5oz (730g)*

£1,200-1,800   **DN**

A Stuart Devlin limited edition silver-gilt 'Silver Jubilee' commemorative egg, numbered 24, opening to reveal a model of the Imperial State Crown, with original box and the original bill of sale.

1977   *3.5in (8cm) high 8.15oz (230g)*

£300-500   **DN**

A Stuart Devlin 18ct gold box, of oval section, with a straight back and granulated textured exterior, the hinged cover mounted with an amethyst-crystal formation, with hallmarks for London.

1970   *2.25in (6cm) high 5oz (151g)*

£3,500-4,500   **DN**

A Stuart Devlin silver parcel-gilt circular flared bowl and cover, the cover of cast openwork mesh design with an amethyst-crystal cluster finial, with hallmarks for London.

1975   *8.25in (20.5cm) diam*
     23oz (716g)

£1,500-2,000   **DN**

QUICK REFERENCE - MODERN BRITISH SILVER

- Previously, there was very little interest in silver or gold work by designer silversmiths such as Gerald Benney, Stuart Devlin (see previous page), David Mellor, Louis Osman, and Christopher Lawrence. But, over the past five years, interest in (and consequently prices paid for) post-war British silver has been mushrooming. All the designers named above studied at the Royal College of Art under noted pre-war silversmiths, such as Robert Goodden, Leslie Durbin, and Eric Clements. This innovative new generation completely changed the style of British silver and gold during the 1950s-70s.
- Forms tend to be simple, with gold elements or gilt-washes sometimes offset against silver. However, the group are best-known for their textured surfaces, which were a reaction against the plain, unembellished surfaces of early and mid-century Modernism. Textures usually resemble bark, or many tiny slices.
- Learn about marks and look out for the style. Bargains are undoubtedly still out there at the back of dusty shelves in antiques shops, or in groups lots at small auctions.

An Edwardian silver box, in the form of a running pig, marks for Samuel Boyce Lambert, with hinged lid on his back, with Chester 1902 import mark.
1902 — *3.5in (9cm) long*
£600-800 — **TEN**

A Gerald Benney silver cufflink or stud box, with a textured 'bark' finish, and a hinged cover decorated with crimson enamel over a sun-ray ground, the interior lined with chamois leather, incised 'Gerald Benney London' with enameller's marks for Robert Vidal Winter, with hallmarks for London.
1972 — *3.5in (9cm) long 14.25oz (405g)*
£700-1,000 — **LC**

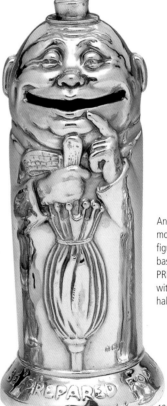

An Edwardian silver novelty money box, in the form of a figure with an umbrella, the base embossed 'ALWAYS BE PREPARED FOR A RAINY DAY', with a wooden bottom, with hallmarks for Birmingham.

An Elizabeth II silver model of a leopard, maker's marks for Wakeley & Wheeler, with remains of gilding, with hallmarks for London.
1975 — *5in (11.5cm) high 12.1oz (345g)*
£400-600 — **TEN**

A Victorian silver novelty cane handle, cast as multiple Classical bearded heads, marker's marks for John George Smith, with import marked for London.
1899 — *2.5in (6.5cm) high*
£450-550 — **TEN**

1913 — *5.75in (14.5cm) high*
£300-400 — **PC**

A silver candle extinguisher, with turned ebony handle, with hallmarks for Birmingham.
1993
£50-80 — **WHP**

A Victorian silver child's rattle, maker's marks for John Hilliard, with a chased baluster-shaped body, coral teether, whistle terminal, and five bells, with hallmarks for Birmingham.
1844 — *5in (12.5cm) long*
£180-220 — **LC**

QUICK REFERENCE

- As smoking becomes less fashionable in the West, memorabilia associated with it has grown in desirability and value. Of these, the most desirable objects are attractive and well-made pieces that can still be used today by enthusiastic smokers. Cigarette lighters are consequently one of the most popular collecting fields.

- Makers to look out for include Thorens, Ronson, and particularly the London-based Dunhill company. Founded in 1893, Dunhill has since produced some of the world's most luxurious lighter models, which have often been called the 'Rolls Royces' of cigarette lighters. They also introduced the legendary 'Unique' lighter in 1923. Look out for unusual features, such as built-in watches, novelty shapes, or lacquer decoration, as these add considerably to desirability and value.

- Due to prevalent fashions and trends, cigarette and cigar related memorabilia is currently more popular than that related to pipe smoking. This means that although many Victorian pipe-related pieces are finely made and appealing, they are generally not as desirable as pieces made during the early 20thC for wealthy cigarette or cigar smokers.

- Apart from the name of the maker, value is dependent on the quality of the materials and the complexity and style of the decoration. Also look out for special commissions, particularly for notable individuals. Marks, the style, and any variations in a mechanism can help to date a piece.

- Also consider the eye-appeal and humour of a piece, which can often add value. This applies particularly to pieces from the 1950s onwards, which are typically of lower intrinsic quality. A sought-after theme, such as erotic imagery or hunting, can help to make a piece more desirable.

A Dunhill 'Unique Giant' gold-plated brass table lighter, with engine-turned decoration.

The 'Giant' was first produced in 1929. Examples produced before the 1950s have an external vertical 'spring' made from a flap of metal mounted on the right hand side vertical snuffer arm support. You can see this on the crocodile skin covered lighter on the right.

4in (10.5cm) high

£120-180   **BELL**

A late 20th/early 21stC French Dunhill 'Unique' 18ct gold gas-filled pocket lighter, with engine-turned decoration, and stamped marks for Dunhill Paris.

Although this example still uses the characteristic Dunhill striking mechanism, it is filled with gas, not petrol, and is therefore modern. The shape is similar to the 'Sylph', which was introduced c1953.

2.5in (6.5cm) high

£320-380   **DN**

A Dunhill 'Unique B' 9ct gold pocket lighter, with plain finish and rubbed London import marks.

1.75in (4.5cm) high

£300-400   **GORL**

A 1930s Dunhill 'Unique Giant' table lighter, covered with crocodile skin, with silver-plated mounts, the base stamped 'PATENT NO. 143752'.

4.25in (11cm) high

£300-400   **WW**

A 1950s Dunhill 'Standard' chrome-plated table lighter, with engine-turned decoration.

Introduced c1948, the 'Standard' has a curved snuffer-spring mounting. The base is rounded and heavier than the similar 'Club' table lighter.

4in (10cm) high

£100-150   **GORL**

A CLOSER LOOK AT A DUNHILL LIGHTER

Dunhill's ingenious watch lighters (lighters incorporating watches) are very rare, particularly in precious metals.

Always flip down the front flap, fold out the watch housing, and check that the metal parts bear the same serial number as each other to ensure everything is original.

It bears London import marks for 1928, which was the first year that this model was produced, and only one year after the watch lighter was introduced.

This model is known as the 'Sports' as the vented chimney protects the flame from wind when used during outdoor pursuits.

A Swiss Dunhill 'Unique A' 9ct gold 'Sports' watch lighter, with 15-jewel lever movement, bimetallic compensation balance with overcoil hairspring, silvered dial with Arabic numerals, engine-turned decoration.

1928   *2in (5.5cm) high*

£1,500-2,500   **TEN**

A Dunhill 14k gold 'Rollalite' pocket lighter, the base stamped 'Dunhill 14K', with its original leather sheath.

2.5in (6.5cm) high 2.92oz (83g)

£350-450   **LHA**

A late 20thC French Dupont gold-plated gas-filled pocket lighter.

1.75in (4.5cm) high

£30-40   **SHAP**

A 1970s Dunhill silver-plated 'Rollagas' pocket lighter, with engraved decoration, and original blue fitted case.

The gas-filled 'Rollagas' superseded the petrol-filled 'Rollalite'. It is of little interest to most lighter collectors, who focus on earlier models. However, as examples are still comparatively affordable, and types and styles of surface decoration are so numerous, it would make an excellent area to look into if you're collecting on a budget but still seeking out quality.

2.5in (6.5cm) high

£30-40   **BELL**

A 1970s Dunhill gold-plated gas-filled ruler desk lighter, with brushed matt finish, in original fitted case, the base with stamped marks.

12in (30cm) long

£380-480   **WW**

A 1950s-60s Dunhill silver-plated 'Sylph Letter Knife' combination desk lighter and letter knife, with engine-turned decoration.

Introduced in 1954, this model was available in a wide variety of finishes. It originally came with a long rectangular leather sheath with a gilt-tooled ruler down one side.

8in (20cm) long

£150-200   **GORL**

A CLOSER LOOK AT A DUNHILL LIGHTER

These lighters were made by hand-carving and hand-painting the pattern onto the backs of cast blocks of colourless Lucite. The blocks were then glued to the metal lighter body.

The badly-worn plating on the metal decreases the value slightly.

This 'Miniature' size is rarer than the wider full size.

Dunhill's 'Aviary' lighters, which contain birds, are far rarer than the 'Aquarium' lighters, which contain fish. In 2010 an example containing a budgerigar sold for nearly £8,000 at auction.

That the birds are birds of prey increases the value further.

A 1950s Dunhill 'Aviary' 'Miniature' petrol table lighter, decorated with intaglio of birds of prey perched and in flight, the base with cast marks.

2.75in (7cm) high

£2,500-3,500   DN

An early 1950s English McMurdo 'Aquarium' table lighter, with silver-plating and carved and painted Lucite.

McMurdo was founded by an ex-Dunhill designer, and only operated between 1949 to 1955. As a result, its products can be rare, and this desirable 'Aquarium' style of lighter is particularly so. From the curving shape of the Lucite side panels, it appears they were sourced from the same producer who made those used by Dunhill.

3in (8cm) high

£800-1,200   BELL

An American Ronson chrome-plated cigar striker lighter, modelled as a seated mule, on a stepped rectangular base, lacks striker.

c1936   5.25in (13.5cm) high

£50-80   WHP

A late 19thC table lighter, in the form of a cold-painted spelter pheasant, the striker holder in the form of a tree trunk, striker missing, on rectangular base.

12in (30cm) long

£50-80   DA&H

A German erotic enamelled cigarette case, depicting Leda and the Swan.

Erotic subjects, here loosely veiled in Classical Greek myth, were highly popular around the turn of the 20thC, and continue to be so today. The better the enamelling and more titillating the scene, the higher the value. Solid silver or gold examples by noted makers are also usually more valuable.

c1900   3in (7.5cm) long

£400-600   TEN

A Namiki maki-e lacquer silver cigarette case, of square form with canted corners, the lacquered lid decorated with an ape, signed on base, the interior with presentation inscription, with maker's marks for William Neale & Son, with hallmarks for Birmingham.

The combination of an ape as subject matter and Namiki maki-e lacquer on silver is very rare. Most Namiki goods were retailed by Dunhill. For more information on Namiki, see p.162 and p.279.

1929   3.25in (8.5cm) high

£1,200-1,800   GORL

An Alfred Dunhill silver cigarette box, with cedar-lined interior, canted corners, and applied zoomorphic strapwork borders and feet, with hallmarks for London.

1938   *3.25in (8.5cm) long*

£350-450   **WW**

A 1970s-80s Dunhill walnut humidor, with cedar lining, lock, and built-in humidifier to the lid interior.

9.5in (24cm) wide

£100-150   **GORL**

A late 19th/early 20thC meerschaum pipe, carved as a bust length portrait of a Cavalier, the fitted case with Franz Hiess retailer's stencil.

Franz Hiess was a notable retailer of smoking accessories based on Kartner Strasse in Vienna. As well as being well-carved, the slightly sly expression of this Cavalier is very appealing.

A late 19thC carved meerschaum cheroot holder, the bowl carved as a man with flowing hair and a hat, with amber mouthpiece, the fitted case with Otto Schmidt retailer's stamp to lid interior.

10in (25cm) wide

£120-180   **CLV**

10in (25cm) wide

£850-950   **L&T**

An early 20thC meerschaum cheroot holder, the curving bowl carved with two owls, the silver band marked 'L. H. & S.', the fitted case stamped 'BBB', worn.

£60-80   **DS**

A late 19thC meerschaum pipe or cheroot holder, the bowl carved as a young girl near a plant, lacks mouthpiece, with fitted case.

£40-60   **DS**

QUICK REFERENCE - MEERSCHAUM PIPES

- Meerschaum pipes are hand-carved from a lightweight soft mineral deposit of magnesium silicate. Its dense but soft nature makes it ideal for intricate and deep carving. It has been used for pipes since the 18thC, but reached the peak of its popularity in the second half of the 19thC, with examples being produced in Germany, Austria and Switzerland. Today, nearly all meerschaum pipes are carved in Turkey where the mineral is most easily found.
- Meerschaum is German for 'sea foam'. The mineral was so-named because it was often found floating in lakes and, reputedly, its colour recalls the colour of sea foam on a sandy beach. As pipe production was focused in German-speaking countries, the German name stuck. When freshly carved, pipes are light in colour, like the example here. As they are used, they become darker, eventually reaching deep amber tones.

- The most common meerschaum pipes are carved with an old man's head, and values for undamaged pipes are typically less than £30. Instead, look out for deep and intricate carving, characterful expressions, erotic subjects, and especially rarer subjects that cross collecting markets. This very rare pipe is an excellent example. Not only is it deeply carved with a complex and realistic design, but it would also appeal to collectors of horse racing memorabilia.

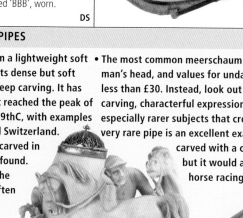

A very rare late 19thC cased silver-gilt mounted meerschaum pipe, carved in high relief to depict a jockey standing between two race horses.

12in (30cm) long

£2,000-3,000   **L&T**

An Everton v Manchester City F.A. Cup Final programme, for a game played on 29th April 1933.

1933

£450-550   GBA

An Austria v Wales international match programme, for a game played in Vienna on 9th May 1954.

1954

£180-220   GBA

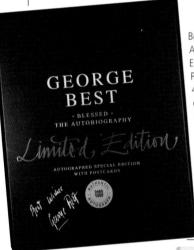

Best, George, 'Blessed: The Autobiography Limited Edition', published by Ebury Press, London, numbered 468 from a limited edition of 1,000, the leather-bound slipcase signed by Best in silver marker pen and inscribed 'Best Wishes', together with postcards.

This luxury edition sold out immediately after its publication.

2001

£250-350   GBA

A very rare programme for the postponed game between Arsenal and Everton on 27th February 1962, with a professional repair to pp.13-14.

£1,000-1,500   GBA

Busby, Matt, 'My Story', published by the Souvenir Press, London, signed on the two right-hand front papers 'With Best Wishes' by Busby, also signed by 24 of his Manchester United 'Busby Babes', with original damaged dust-jacket.

1957

£1,000-1,500   GBA

An official poster for the 1966 World Cup, designed by Carvosso, printed by McCorquodale & Co., London.

19in (48cm) high

£500-700   GBA

A yellow Brazil no.10 short-sleeved football jersey, worn by Ronaldinho (Ronaldo de Assis Moreira, b.1980) in the match versus the United Arab Emirates on 12th November 2005.

Played at the Sheikh Zayed Sports Complex in Abu Dhabi, the match was won by Brazil 8-0. Match-worn shirts, particularly those worn by famous players in notable games, tend to be the most valuable.

£450-550   GBA

A blue England v Argentina international cap, for a match played at Wembley on 22nd May 1974, from the 1973-74 season.

The game ended 2-2, with Mick Channon and Frank Worthington scoring England's goals, and Mario Kempes scoring both goals for Argentina. The England starting XI that day comprised Peter Shilton, Emlyn Hughes, Alec Lindsay, Colin Todd, Dave Watson, Colin Bell, Kevin Keegan, Channon, Worthington, Keith Weller, and Trevor Brooking, but the original recipient of the cap is unknown.

c1973

£800-1,200   GBA

A leather football signed on the occasion of the Brazil v Mexico international match 30th September 1970, signed by both the Brazilian and Mexican international teams, together with a black and white press photo of Pelé in action, signed and dedicated to the reverse, and with a cased Mexican silver 1970 World Cup commemorative medal.

This was Brazil's first international match following the team's victory at the World Cup match in Mexico in 1970. The game was a friendly played at the Maracanã in Rio, and gave the Brazilian public the first opportunity to hail their champions on the football field since the World Cup. Brazil won the game 2-1. The signatures were obtained by Pelé on behalf of his friend Reynaldo Renato Figueiredo, an airline pilot who had an apartment in the same block as Pelé in São Paulo.

1970

£800-1,200   GBA

An early 20thC green patinated spelter figure of a footballer, mounted on an oblong cream marble base.

12in (30cm) high

£150-200   GHOU

A 1990s bronze 'Goalkeeper' limited edition sculpture, by Auldwin Thomas Schomberg (b.1943), mounted on a black marble base.

Schomberg is perhaps best-known for his statue of 'Rocky', which was commissioned by Sylvester Stallone in 1981, and issued in a limited edition of three pieces.

24in (61cm) high

£600-800   GBA

A Gray's Sports China miniature urn, with a hand-coloured transfer-print of a footballer commemorating 'Woolwich Arsenal', marked with registered design number '588114'.

1911   *3.25in (8.5cm) high*

£250-350   GBA

QUICK REFERENCE

- Golf probably began with 12thC Scottish farmers knocking stones into rabbit holes, and developed into a fully-fledged sport with rules between the 15thC and 17thC. It's one of the oldest and most popular sports still played today and, due to its large international following, related memorabilia is highly sought-after.
- Most pieces sold and collected today will date from the 19thC or later. Pieces dating from the origins of the game until the turn of the 19thC are very rare. Clubs and balls occupy the upper regions of the market in terms of price but, away from equipment, most objects with a golfing theme are of interest. If a piece is decorative or connected to a famous player, course, or event, so much the better.
- Enthusiasm for the sport blossomed in the late Victorian era, leading to the production of many golf-themed ceramics, paintings, prints, silverware, and glass. Look out for pieces with eye-appeal, and those by well-known manufacturers such as Doulton and Shelley. Other items such as tournament tickets and programmes are also popular, and often more affordable. Signatures of attending players will typically increase value, particularly if it was a key event for them.
- In terms of equipment, look out for prestigious and high quality names, such as Tom Morris, Robert Forgan, Douglas McEwan, and Thomas Dunn. Most examples on the collectors' market will show signs of wear from play, so pieces in excellent condition will usually cost more. Nearly all modern equipment is of little or no interest to collectors.
- It was not until the 20thC that women began to participate in golf, so memorabilia relating to the female game is often scarcer and highly sought-after.
- The area is well-established, and some of the best shows and auctions are held around the time of the Open Championship.

An early 20thC D. Anderson of St Andrews light-stained socket-head driver, the head stamped with makers' mark and also stamped 'Robert Hughes Ltd Alexandria & Cairo' in gilt, and fitted with a full length hide, in apparently unused condition.

£50-70   MM

A William Park scared-neck driver, in light-stained golden persimmon, with maker's stamp to the crown and shaft, and original full-length hide grip.

c1895

£100-150   MM

An Alexander Patrick of Leven long-nose curved-face short-spoon, in dark-stained beech wood, with original tight-fitting three quarter length leather face-insert, and a period full-length hide grip with underlisting.

Long-nose clubs such as this generally date from before 1890. Patrick was a notable woodworker and craftsman, who also made spoked wheels and cabinetry.

c1870

£600-700   MM

A Gibson 'Westward Ho!' Sunday golf walking stick, fitted with a dark-stained socket-neck driver as a handle, complete with steel tip.

Although he had no interest in playing golf, Charles Gibson (1864-1932) was a notable and skilled clubmaker, who was born in Musselburgh, the heart of Scottish club-making. Following his apprenticeship, he was based at the Royal North Devon Golf Club at Westward Ho!, and took on five or six apprentices.

34.5in (88cm) long

£200-300   MM

A scarce George Brews patent 'Trusty' combination wood and brass mallet-head, with an integral brass sole plate and back weight forming part of the head, with partial stamp mark to brass plate, and replaced period hide grip.

£100-150   MM

SPORTING MEMORABILIA

A rare Forgan St. Andrews 'Gassiat'-style persimmon putter, with wide horn sole insert, with two large circular lead weights to the sole, with matching Forgan St. Andrews shaft stamp below the original full-length leather grip.

£400-500   MM

A rare unnamed off-set hosel blade putter, fitted with a smooth-faced symmetrical head, and with a green heart-shaft with original hide grip with under listing.

The design allows this club to be used by either left- or right-handed players. This rare design has not been seen at auction before.
c1895
£450-550   MM

A scarce James Gourlay of Carnoustie smooth-faced hosel iron, stamped with registered number '10745' for 1884, the head with a V-shaped valley between the face and the bottom of the hosel, vertical hand punched dot face markings, and stamped 'Auchterlonie St Andrews' to the shaft below the period full-length hide grip.

c1884
£100-150   MM

A CLOSER LOOK AT A GOLF CLUB

The button allows the angle of the head to be adjusted.

Urquhart's Ltd. of Edinburgh pioneered the adjustable golf club in the early 1890s, and won a number of patents for them before closing in c1909.

The mark stamped into the head is very crisp and clear, which is an appealing feature for collectors.

Urquhart's also produced similar adjustable clubs that have smooth faces without the maker's name. These are generally earlier in date, dating from c1895-c1903.

An Urquhart's Ltd. patent adjustable iron, stamped with the production number '1445' on the hosel and on the toe of the club next to the maker's bordered circular 'U' stamp mark, with thick full-length under listing.
c1904
£700-1,000   MM

A rare Charles L. Millar of Glasgow smooth-face rut niblick, fitted with an early wrapped cork grip, the head stamped with 'The Millar Thistle Brand' cleek mark.

£40-60   MM

A Standard Golf Co. 'Mills Patent "The Cleek" No. 1' alloy, model no.CB1, with sharp head stamps and details to sole, serial no.'175686', and fitted with a period full-length leather grip.
c1909
£70-100   MM

An American G. Spalding 'Schenectady Putter' alloy centre-shaft mallet-head putter, with deep crisscross face markings, fitted with a period full-length hide grip.

£100-150   MM

QUICK REFERENCE - GOLF BALLS

- The first golf balls were made from segments of leather sewn together and tightly stuffed with wet feathers. Known as 'featheries', they were used from the 16thC until c1848 when the 'feathery' was superseded by the 'gutty', a ball made from a tree resin known as gutta-percha. This resin was soft and pliable when heated, allowing it to be moulded, but resilient and hard when cool. More affordable and longer-lasting than the 'feathery', the 'gutty' revolutionised the game of golf as less-wealthy people could now afford to play. As gutties were more durable and could be hit further, clubs also had to become stronger, and courses longer.

- Patterned moulds were used from the 1870s onwards, after it was discovered that raised patterns made the ball 'fly' much better than smooth surfaces. In 1899 two Americans, Coburn Haskell and Bertram Work patented the 'Haskell' ball, which had a rubber core and a gutta-percha shell, and this became the default ball by 1910.

- Subsequently, a number of different variations and improvements were made including, in the 1960s, the development of a one-piece dimpled rubber ball.

- London-based Henley's Telegraph Works originally made insulated cable, but became one of the country's biggest makers of 'gutties' during the 1890s. With its moulded patriotic pattern, this is a rare ball in good condition.

A rare 'Agrippa' 27 1/2 'bramble'-pattern gutty golf ball, in good condition with prominent brambles to the surface.

'Brambles' are so-named as the raised nodules give the ball the appearance of a raspberry or blackberry. The' Agrippa' was the first bramble pattern golf ball to be produced.
c1886
£70-100   MM

An early machine-cut 'square mesh'-pattern gutty golf ball, lacking its paint and well-used.

£30-50   MM

A rare Henley's Telegraph Works 'Union Jack' gutty golf ball, retaining some of the original white finish, with some strike marks and discolouring, otherwise in good condition.
c1890
£700-900   MM

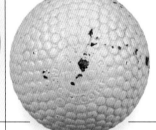

A Spring Vale 'Recovered Rubber Core' 'bramble'-pattern golf ball, in very good condition, retaining most of the original white finish.
c1910
£60-80   MM

An Avon 'Arc Green Dot Large Floater' 'bramble'-pattern golf ball, retaining all the original white paint finish, apparently unused.
c1910
£60-80   MM

A scarce 'The Wonder Ball' 'recessed diamond'-pattern golf ball, retaining all the original white finish, some strike marks, otherwise in fair condition.

The recognisable dimpled exterior finish became the standard pattern by 1930. During the preceding decades, all sorts of different patterns were moulded onto balls in order to make them fly 'truer' and better, from spirals to swirls, diamonds to stars, and concentric lines to grids. An extremely rare ball even bore a moulded map of the world!
c1920
£30-50   MM

A Dunlop 'V' 'recessed large flat circular'-pattern gutty golf ball, in re-painted fair condition with some wear.

c1910

£25-35 MM

A May & Malone 'Mesh' 'square mesh'-pattern golf ball, with its original black and silver label, and blue tissue wrapping, in good condition with some slight rubbing.

c1920

£70-100 MM

A Silvertown 'Silver Prince' 'square mesh'-pattern golf ball, with the original green and silver label, and paper wrapping, in good condition with some slight rubbing.

c1935

£30-40 MM

A Dunlop 'Blue Flash Mesh' golf ball, with the original blue and gilt label, and paper wrapping.

c1939

£30-50 MM

A boxed set of six rare American D. C. Albin 'Royce-Pro Tournament' golf balls, each in maker's original wrapping with flower labels, the lid interior with printed wording relating to their specifications and use, with slight wear and small split to the blue wrapper.

£150-200 MM

A Tiger Woods commemorative tin of golf balls, one of four, celebrating his 'Grand Slam' of 'Majors' in 2000, this one featuring an embossed removable lid depicting Woods kissing the US Open Championship trophy, played for at Pebble Beach that year, with each ball in the four cartons of four stamped 'Tiger' and 'No.1', in near mint condition.

These balls were produced by Nike Golf and were not approved for use in competition.

2000

£30-50 MM

A Tiger Woods commemorative tin of golf balls, one of four, celebrating his 'Grand Slam' of 'Majors' in 2000, this one featuring an embossed removable lid depicting Woods playing over the Swilken burn bridge on the 18th hole at St Andrews during the Open Championship (the British Open) of that year, with each ball in the four cartons of four stamped 'Tiger' and 'No.1', in near mint condition.

The 16 balls represent the 16 rounds Woods played to achieve his 'Grand Slam' of 'Majors'.

2000

£30-50 MM

A large French Siot-Decauville bronze statue of a golfer's caddie, by Fournier-Sarlovèze, mounted on a circular naturalistic base with the artist's signature moulded to the rim, the back stamped with the production number '2180' and 'Siot, Paris'.

Established in 1860, Siot-Decauville was one of the best known Parisian art foundries of the 19thC. It specialised in bronze reproductions of the works of renowned artists of the time including Jean-Louis-Ernest Meissonier, Marius-Jean-Antonin Mercie, Laurent-Honoré Marqueste, and François-Raoul Larche. (For more information see 'Miller's Antiques Handbook & Price Guide 2012-2013' p.571).

c1900   *17in (43cm) high*
£1,800-2,200   MM

An early 20thC spelter golfing figurine, depicted at the top of his swing, wearing plus fours and jacket, mounted on a square marble base.

Overall 11in (28cm) high
£120-180   MM

A 1930s silvered spelter figure of a lady golfer, awarded as a golf trophy, standing on an alabaster plinth, with some wear to the silvering.

Increasing numbers of ladies began playing golf in the 1920s and '30s. As such, most lady golfer statues or figurines show the fashionable bobbed haircuts and clothes of that period. The best also have some Art Deco stylisation.

11in (28cm) high
£150-200   CAPE

A Penfold golf balls papier mâché counter-top advertising figurine, in the form of a smartly dressed golfer, mounted on wooden rectangular base moulded with 'He played a PENFOLD', with later enlarged hole to mouth for pipe.

c1910
£500-600   MM

A brass 'Mr Punch' character golf caddie doorstop, stamped on the back 'Reg Pat no. 998912', mounted on brass rectangular base.

5in (13cm) high
£50-70   MM

A pair of 1920s bronze and marble golfing bookends, comprising a period golfer and his caddie on marbled bases.

Originally cast in the 1920s, these figurines have been widely reproduced. The caddy was produced as a 4ft (122cm) high concrete garden statue, and both have appeared on ashtrays and other similar items.

10in (25cm) high
£200-300   MM

A late 20thC Fairweather Collection moulded and painted resin figurine of a golfer, in a comic pose, on a circular wooden base.

7in (18cm) high
£50-80   GORL

SPORTING MEMORABILIA

A 52nd US Open Golf Championship official programme, played at the Northward Club, Dallas, Texas, comprising 102 pages including a précis of the championship from 1890 onwards, with stained cover and back pages, otherwise clean.

1952

£70-90　　　　　　　　MM

A 1987 US Open Golf Championship official sponsor's bound programme, signed by the winner Scott Simpson to the programme cover, bound with blue and gilt pictorial boards, issued by sponsor C. F. Airfreight US, complete with sponsor's covering letter.

1987

£60-80　　　　　　　　MM

Robert Browning, 'A History of Golf', first American edition, published by E. P. Dutton & Co., in original scarce dust-jacket, with colour plates and other illustrations, internally very clean, with minor tears to the jacket.

A comprehensive and well-written history of golf from its origins to the mid-1950s, this is often regarded as the first social history of the game.

1955

£60-80　　　　　　　　MM

A 1971 Walker Cup official programme, played at St. Andrews, in near fine condition, appears unread.

1971

£80-120　　　　　　　MM

A 1930s gouache artwork for an advertisement for waterproof golf shoes, showing a young man carrying a golf bag and umbrella in a thunderstorm, with the slogan 'GOLF SHOES GUARANTEED WATERPROOF AS WORN BY THE CHAMPIONS', signed 'Barbara Davies'.

11in (28cm) high

£100-150　　　　　　FLD

A signed Titleist golf balls advertising poster, with early photograph of Tiger Woods, signed by Tiger Woods, with slight crease folds.

Titleist signed Woods in 1996 after he turned professional upon winning his third consecutive US Amateur title. He was reputed to have earned $20m (£12.5m) from the deal.

c1997　　　　　　　*29in (74cm) high*

£250-350　　　　　　　MM

A rare signed press photograph of the Duke of Windsor (Edward VIII) at the top of his swing with Archie Compston looking on, signed in ink by Archie Compston.

Professional golfer Archie Compston (1893-1962) was perhaps the world's first celebrity golfer, and was coach to the Duke of Windsor during the 1930s.

9.5in (24cm) wide

£60-80　　　　　　　　MM

A rare 1937 Open Golf Championship gilt and enamel competitor's badge, for a game played at Carnoustie, Scotland won by Henry Cotton for the second time in four years, in very good condition.

Henry Cotton (1907-87) was a professional golfer who began his career aged 17. He reached the golden age of his career during the 1930s and '40s, winning the Open in 1934, 1937, and 1948. After retiring from being a professional player, he lived the 'high life' and designed a number of golf courses. It's Cotton's fame that makes this medal so valuable.

1937

£400-600   MM

Grand NATIONAL
Jugs for Collectors

BOOK FOR SALE

HEDGEHUNTER
Owner: Trevor Hemmings
Trainer Willie Mullins
Jockey Ruby Walsh

THE WINNER 2001 MARTELL GRAND NATIONAL

1st Edition

BINDAREE
★★★
Owner: Raymond Mould
Trainer Nigel Twiston-Davies
Jockey Jim Culloty

GRAND NATIONAL
Red Marauder, Jugs For Sale **Comply or Die etc**

GORDON
Let me know your "Wants!"

25 Stapenhill Road
Burton-on-Trent DE15 9AE **Tel: 01283•567•213**
Mobile: 07952•118•987 Email: gordon@jmp2000.com

A rare Haskell cast iron golfer's ashtray, featuring a red coated golfer with a movable 'bramble' golf ball head and hat, with the original spring-fitment, lacks one cigarette rest, and with slight wear.

7in (18cm) high   *c1900*

£350-450   MM

A silver vesta case, chased to the obverse with a golfing scene, the reverse inscribed 'C.S.G. C. Knock-Out First Prize 1907, J. Harris', in a very rare fitted soft leather carrying purse.

1.75in (4.5cm) wide

£600-800   L&T

A scarce American Keystone Mfg. Co. Bakelite golf ball sand tee mould, with spring-loaded plunger, in working order.

£150-200   MM

QUICK REFERENCE

- The first modern Olympic Games were held Athens in 1896. Initially most collectors were people who had been actively involved in the Games, such as athletes, but the public were encouraged to participate in the hype with a set of official stamps in 1896. Olympic coins were introduced in 1951, and the first official mascot was introduced in 1972.
- In general official merchandise is not as valuable as pieces made for use in the games. The most sought-after pieces of Olympics memorabilia are, of course, winner's medals and the famous torches. The now familiar convention of a gold medal for the winner, with silver and bronze for the runners up, only began at the 1904 games. Previously the winner had

been given silver, with second place receiving bronze. Value typically depends on age and rarity of the medal, the fame of the athlete, and the importance of the event.

- Other forms of medal can be a more affordable entry into collecting. Lapel badges have been produced since the games re-started and are usually easy to obtain. Participation medals are more desirable than lapel badges, but there are many on the market and they can be affordable.
- Posters are highly desirable, particularly those featuring a striking image by a well-known designer. Condition is crucial.
- Pieces from the earliest games tend to be scarce, and are therefore more likely to be sought-after and valuable. Look out for pieces connected to countries that no longer 'exist', such as East Germany or the Soviet Union, as historical interest can add to their desirability. Memorabilia from recent games may well appeal to collectors on a budget.

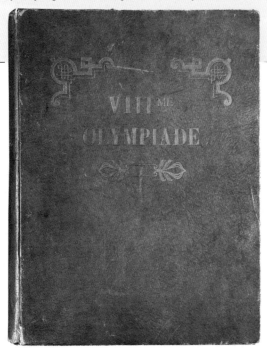

A copy of the official report of the 1924 Paris Olympic Games, published by the French Olympic Committee, the cover with gilt stamping, in good condition.
1924
£500-700   **GBA**

A copy of the official report of the 1932 Los Angeles Olympic Games, published by the Xth Olympiad Committee, Los Angeles, in good condition.
1933
£250-350   **GBA**

A copy of the American Olympic Committee's report of the 1936 Garmisch-Partenkirchen Winter Olympic Games, illustrated, with gilt-stamped blue linen-covered boards.
1936
£180-220   **GBA**

A magazine covering the equestrian events from the 1956 Melbourne/Stockholm Olympics, in very good condition.

The main Games were held in Melbourne in 1956, but, owing to Australian quarantine regulations, equestrian events were held five months earlier in Stockholm, Sweden.
1956
£20-30   **SAS**

A complete collector's set of 16 daily programmes for the 2000 Sydney Olympic Games, in mint condition, in original shrink-wrap packaging.
2000
£100-150   **GBA**

Harold Abrahams, 'Track & Field Olympic Records', published by Playfair Books Ltd., London, with damage to the front cover.
1948
£10-15   **PC**

'OLYMPIC GAMES' 'GERMANY BERLIN-1936', English language one sheet poster, designed by Franz Würbel, printed by Reiseverkehr, Berlin, with repaired areas, overpainting, and restored creases.

39.5in (100cm) high

£2,000-3,000   **SWA**

A CLOSER LOOK AT AN OLYMPIC GAMES POSTER

This was the first official poster ever produced for the Olympic Games.

The choice of naked figures is a reference to the original Olympic Games in which athletes competed in the nude. The word 'gymnasium' is derived from the ancient Greek 'gymnós', meaning naked.

The Swedish Olympic Committee found Hjortzberg's image too risqué, so the rather curious ribbon entering from stage right was added. Subsequently many have said that this motif has the opposite of its intended effect.

Olle Hjortzberg (1872-1959) was a Swedish artist and printmaker known for his church paintings, and illustrations for travel books.

'JEUX OLYMPIQUES STOCKHOLM 1912', French language one sheet poster, designed by Olle Hjortzberg in 1911, printed by A. Bortzells Tr. A.B., Stockholm, repaired tears in image and along vertical and horizontal folds.

1912   *41.5in (105cm) high*

£2,500-3,500   **SWA**

'XVIII OLYMPIC GAMES' 'TOKYO 1964', English language one sheet poster, designed by Yusaku Kamekura, Osamu Hayasaki, and Jo Murakoshi, printed by the Dai Nippon Printing Co., with tears in margins, creases, and abrasions.

1964   *41in (104cm) high*

£500-700   **SWA**

'Olympische Spiele München 1972', one sheet poster, designed by Allen Jones, unmounted, signed in the print.

1972   *39in (100cm) high*

£100-150   **WW**

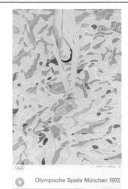

'Olympische Spiele München 1972', one sheet poster, designed by David Hockney, printed by Edition Olympia, framed, and signed within the print.

39in (100cm) high

£120-180   **WW**

'München 1972', one sheet poster, designed by Otl Aicher, depicting the hurdles in bright colours, slip mounted, framed, and glazed.

Aicher and his team designed a series of posters for the 1972 Olympic Games, each depicting a different sport, but all in the same colour-saturated style. The main poster showed the Olympic building, and another showed the schedule.

32.5in (82cm) high

£80-120   **FLD**

A 1900 Paris Olympic Games juror's badge, designed by L. Bottee, made by Christofle of Paris, inscribed 'JURY'.
1900
£700-1,000   GBA

A 1904 St. Louis Olympic Games official timer's badge, inscribed 'UNIVERSAL EXPOSITION, ST. LOUIS U.S.A. 1904', the ribbon inscribed 'INTERSCHOLASTIC MEET, MAY 14TH 1904', the brooch bar inscribed 'TIMER'.

Although similar examples are illustrated in Greensfelder's '1904 Olympic Games St. Louis, Missouri: Official Medals & Badge', this badge is believed to be unique. Examples of the Chairman's and President's Badges, identical except for the bar, are in the possession of the Missouri Historical Society. The Interscholastic Meet on May the 14th was the first athletic event at the 1904 Games, making this a rare and important piece of Olympic memorabilia.
1904
£5,000-6,000   GBA

A rare 1904 St. Louis Olympic Games 3rd place 'bronze' prize medal, for the 440 yards handicap swim, won by Marquard Schwarz of the USA, inscribed 'OLYMPIC HANDICAP GAMES, ST. LOUIS, 1904' '440 YDS SWIM, MARQUARD SCHWARZ'.

It is believed that the 1904 Handicap Games medal is the only Olympic prize medal to bear the words 'Olympic Games' to this day. This medal was awarded to American swimmer Marquard Schwarz (1887-1968), who also competed in the 1906 games in Athens. The name is sometimes misspelled Schwartz. This Olympic medal is listed in the official report by Spalding (p.231).
1904
£6,500-7,500   GBA

A 1912 Stockholm Olympic Games pewter participation medal, designed by Bertram Mackennal and Erik Lindberg, the obverse with Zeus seated on an Ionian column holding a figure of Nike, a view of Stockholm beyond, the reverse with a triumphant athlete in a chariot.
1912
£250-350   GBA

A rare 1936 Berlin Olympic Games silvered-bronze participation medal, designed by Otto Laczek.

Olympic Participation Medals (known as OPMS) are awarded to athletes, judges, and officials at each Olympic Games and act as a souvenir of their participation. As such, they are different from (and more common than) medals awarded to an athlete for winning a competitive event. The official reports state that 20,000 medals were made for the Berlin games by four foundries, and that they can be differentiated by their colour. Although they are known to exist, silvered and gilt medals are strangely not mentioned.
1936
£450-550   GBA

A 1964 Tokyo Olympic Games bronze participation medal, designed by Tar Okamoto, in original fitted wooden box.
1964
£200-300   GBA

A 1972 Sapporo Winter Olympic Games bronze participation medal, designed by S. Fukuda, in original presentation case.
1972
£300-500   GBA

A 1998 Nagano Winter Olympic Games participation medal, in original case of issue.
1998
£120-180   GBA

A CLOSER LOOK AT THE 'WALDI' OLYMPIC MASCOT

Waldi was designed by German graphic designer Otl Aicher (1922-1991), who designed Lufthansa's logo and founded the important Ulm School of Design.

This model was made by renowned company Steiff, which increases its value and desirability.

Waldi was the first ever official Olympic mascot. He was modelled on a real dachshund called Cherie von Birkenhof, and was meant to represent athletes' attributes of resistance, tenacity, and agility.

Representing the optimistic 'Rainbow Games', Waldi was made in a variety of colour combinations. The main scheme did not include red or black, as Aicher was concerned that these colours were associated with the Nazi party.

The marathon incorporated Waldi's shape in the design of its course.

A 1972 Munich Olympic Games Steiff 'Waldi' dachshund painted wood mascot, designed by Otl Aicher in 1971, with maker's label, and official label of the 1972 Olympic Games.

Interestingly, Waldi badges were not produced until a few years after the games.

1972   *5in (14.3cm) high*
£400-600   **QU**

A 1980 Moscow Olympic Games glass and steel paperweight, set with a print of the official mascot 'Misha'.
c1980
£10-15   **PC**

A 1988 Seoul Olympic Games silver tennis commemorative figurine, in the form of the official mascot 'Hodori' playing tennis, mounted on a turned wooden plinth and base, in original fitted case inscribed 'GAMES OF THE XXIVth OLYMPIAD, SEOUL 1988'.

5in (12cm) high
£50-80   **PC**

A 1964 Tokyo Olympic Games official Olympic rings flag.
1964   *75in (191cm) wide*
£200-300   **GBA**

A 2008 Beijing Olympic Games Union Jack flag, signed by 21 'Team GB' medallists, including Chris Hoy, Ben Ainslie, Victoria Pendleton, Zac Purchase, and Pippa Wilson, together with letters of authenticity, one confirming that the signatures were collected at the press conference to welcome the return of Team GB.
2008
£600-800   **GBA**

A rare Siemens-Schuckertwerke Bakelite three-dimensional model of the Reichsportfeld and Olympic Stadium, designed by Oskar Reich.

This model was originally sold in a card box, with the interior of the lid giving details about where certain competitions were held. Condition is vital. Boxed examples can sell for over twice this value.
1936   *11.75in (30cm) wide*
£150-200   **GBA**

A Jack Johnson autographed display, comprising a page from an autograph album signed by Johnson and inscribed 'former champ', below a black and white photograph of Johnson from 'The Ring', mounted, framed, and glazed, and with certificate of authenticity.

Known as 'The Galveston Giant', Johnson became the first black world heavyweight champion, reigning from 1908 to 1915. His most famous fight was against James L. Jeffries, known then as the 'Great White Hope', in 1910. Jeffries came out of retirement to fight Johnson saying, "I am going into this fight for the sole purpose of proving that a white man is better than a negro." Johnson knocked Jeffries down twice and won, causing widespread riots across the US. While many white people felt humiliated, black people were jubilant, and used the victory for the advancement of racial equality.

18in (46cm) high

£500-700   GBA

A Robert 'Bob' Fitzsimmons autographed display, comprising his signature on paper beneath a black and white photograph, mounted, framed, and glazed.

17in (43cm) high

£500-600   GBA

A Prince Naseem Hamed autographed display, comprising a signed colour photograph of the boxing champion, mounted above a miniature boxing glove in a shallow box, framed and glazed.

23in (58.5cm) high

£50-70   GBA

A left-hand Everlast boxing glove, signed by Joe Frazier in black marker pen.

18in (46cm) high

£120-180   GBA

A small early 20thC bowl, with transfer-printed decoration of a couple in period clothing playing tennis, the base impressed 'Gibson England'.

5in (12cm) diam

£50-80   FLD

A rare 1930s Dunlop Fort tennis ball advertisement display, modelled as an oversized tennis ball, set on a separate circular base moulded with the words 'DUNLOP THE BALL THE CHAMPIONS USE'.

Not only is this piece advertising a major brand, it's also very large in size, in superb condition, and in the desirable Art Deco style.

18in (46cm) high

£1,200-1,800   GBA

An early 20thC Kleenball boxwood tennis ball cleaner, with inset circular plaque and interior bristles.

4in (10cm) diam

£300-500   WW

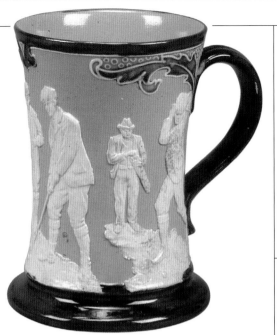

A rare Doulton Lambeth salt-glazed stoneware golfing mug, of waisted form, sprigged in white with golfers, the base with impressed marks.

6in (15cm) high

£1,000-1,500 DN

A Coalport 'Geoffrey Boycott' limited edition commemorative plate, commemorating ONE HUNDRED CENTURIES FOR YORKSHIRE', numbered 548 from an edition of 1,500, with box and certificate.

1985 *9in (23cm) diam*

£40-60 MOR

A large late 19thC painted cast-iron figure of a jockey, dressed in period jockey's clothing, mounted on a pedestal base with recessed panels.

37.5in (95cm) high

£400-600 FRE

A CLOSER LOOK AT A PAIR OF CUFFLINKS

Delvin G. Miller (1913-1996) was an important pioneer of harness racing in the US. He broke records, won 2,058 races, and bred and trained many successful horses.

Miller's most famous horse was Adios (1940-1965), who he acquired as a stud in 1948. Adios became the most famous horse in harness racing as he sired eight winners among his 589 offspring.

The cufflinks are well-cast with an excellent level of detail, and are made from solid gold and cobalt blue enamel.

Not only are these cufflinks prestigious objects that indicate Devlin's status, but they were also owned and worn by him, which raises their desirability.

A pair of mid-late 20thC American 10k yellow gold 'Grand Circuit Steward' cufflinks, in a horse harness racing design, engraved 'Delvin Miller', and stamped '10K'.

0.74oz (21g)

£180-220 LHA

An Aynsley 'Glorious Goodwood' limited edition commemorative loving cup, numbered 15, with a racing scene of the 'Grand Stand, Goodwood' in 1838 and gilt handles, the base with printed and painted marks.

1983 *5in (13.5cm) high*

£70-90 WW

A Victorian John Taylor & Sons oak billiard scoreboard, with trade label reading 'Billiard Table Makers, Edinburgh A6966'.

c1880 *42in (107cm) wide*

£200-300 DN

TAXIDERMY

QUICK REFERENCE

- Stuffed animals were popular decorative features during the mid-to late Victorian and Edwardian eras, but began to go out of fashion during the 1930s. By the 1970s, most commercial outlets had closed as tastes changed. Over the past fifty to sixty years, most people have associated taxidermy with bad taste tainted with cruelty.
- However, there has been a relative resurgence of interest in vintage pieces over the past few years, with interest being re-ignited among collectors, interior decorators, and those searching for unusual pieces to add to eclectic 'vintage' interiors or collections.
- Traditionally, animals were mounted in naturalistic settings in glazed cases or under glass domes to protect them from dust or other damage. Birds, alongside various head 'masks' mounted on plaques or shields, tend to monopolise much of the market. Fish have maintained consistent popularity and values, perhaps as fishing is generally held as being less cruel. They also appeal to anglers.

- Scarcer and more sought-after pieces include exotic animals such as tigers or giraffes. Animals with genetic, biological, or clear physical abnormalities can be rare and particularly valuable.
- General factors to consider when determining value include the type and precise species of animal, and its size. Also look at how realistically worked the animal is, and at the levels of quality and details of the mounting. Depending on the animal, a sense of drama (or even humour!) can also appeal and lead to higher prices.
- The maker is also very important, and labels bearing trade names can sometimes be found on the case or mount. Most towns and cities had at least one taxidermist until the mid-20thC, but key taxidermists include John Cooper, Peter Spicer, and Rowland Ward.
- Always examine the condition of the overall piece as it is difficult, and often very expensive, to make repairs. We do not condone the creation of modern examples. The sale and movement of many stuffed animals is strictly controlled, particularly with exotic or endangered species, so buyers and sellers should familiarise themselves with the relevant national and international laws.

A stuffed and shoulder-mounted eastern bongo (Tragelaphus eurycerus isaaci), with plaque noting its collection in the Sudan on '20/01/1977'.

Right horn 30in (76.5cm) long

£1,800-2,200   TEN

A green sea turtle (Chelonia mydas) shell, with wall mountings.

These shells have become popular with interior decorators. They are perceived by many as less concerning than other forms of taxidermy.

c1850   *25in (64cm) long*

£500-700   TEN

A stuffed and shoulder-mounted lion's head (Felis leo), in fierce, forward-thrusting pose, jaw agape revealing real teeth, with title plaques mounted to the chest reading 'Laibarua, 7.1.1973'.

This was collected before the Convention on the International Trade in Endangered Species (CITES) laws were passed in March 1973.

28in (70cm) high

£1,200-1,800   TEN

A stuffed and mounted wild boar (Sus scrofa), shown leaping over a fungi encrusted tree stump on a mount with ferns and mock oak leaves, with open snarling mouth, taken by Bill Brough.

62in (158cm) long

£500-700   TEN

A stuffed Nile crocodile (Crocodylus niloticus), with limbs outstretched and serpentine tail.

c1900   *58in (148cm) long*

£150-250   TEN

A stuffed and mounted stoat, in a naturalistic setting, contained in a glass-fronted display case.

The setting is very basic, which reduces the value.

£20-30   MAI

A stuffed and mounted stoat, on a bark base.

The bizarrely angled body of this stoat is very unrealistic and reduces the value.

£20-30   MAI

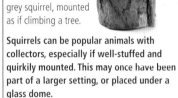

A stuffed and mounted grey squirrel, mounted as if climbing a tree.

Squirrels can be popular animals with collectors, especially if well-stuffed and quirkily mounted. This may once have been part of a larger setting, or placed under a glass dome.

£30-40   MAI

Mark Picks

As grimly ironic as a fox dressed as one of the people who hunted and killed him may seem, it's this sort of 'quirky' theme that is popular among a new breed of collectors. He's also very well-stuffed, mounted, and dressed, with plenty of detail, including a fob watch chain and suitably sized hunting horn. As fox hunting in the UK is now banned, he represents an interesting point in the history of the countryside. All of these factors combine to make him a good buy in the world of taxidermy.

A stuffed and mounted fox, standing upright and dressed in hunting clothes, holding a brass hunting horn, standing on a wooden base.

35in (89cm) high

£500-700   LC

A stuffed and mounted coney, in a naturalistic setting, contained in an octagonal glass-fronted display case.

£100-150   MAI

A stuffed and wall-mounted red deer stag's head, mounted on an oak shield.

£120-180   DN

TAXIDERMY

A fully-mounted white-throated toucan (Ramphastos tucanus), clinging to a branch with tail feathers upheld.

21.25in (54cm) high

£450-550   **TEN**

A fully-mounted blue and gold macaw (Ara ararauna), perched on a branch.

30in (76cm) high overall

£800-1,200   **TEN**

A CLOSER LOOK AT A PAIR OF BIRDS

The Resplendent Quetzal lives in the cloud rainforests of central South America, and was considered divine in Mesoamerican mythology because it was associated with the snake god Quetzalcoatl.

The setting is complete, detailed, and natural. The gilded and carved base, and large size indicate this was an important and expensive piece at the time.

Both birds are in excellent condition, and the mounting shows both the tail feathers, for which they are known, and the other extensive plumage.

This species is seriously threatened. Antique examples of rare species command a premium from collectors.

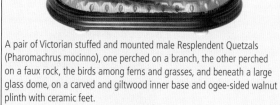

A pair of Victorian stuffed and mounted male Resplendent Quetzals (Pharomachrus mocinno), one perched on a branch, the other perched on a faux rock, the birds among ferns and grasses, and beneath a large glass dome, on a carved and giltwood inner base and ogee-sided walnut plinth with ceramic feet.

c1880   *33in (84cm) high*

£5,000-7,000   **TEN**

An early 20thC stuffed peregrine falcon, in a glazed case, mounted on a naturalistic rock setting with moss, the case with a label noting it was mounted by 'G. E. Lodge (died 1954 aged 94)'.

19in (47cm) high

£1,000-1,500   **DN**

An early 20thC stuffed and mounted pintail duck and kingfisher, set on a mossy and grassy naturalistic mount, and contained under a glass dome.

£80-120   **MAI**

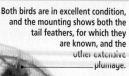

A stuffed and mounted barn owl, on a mossy perch in a naturalistic setting, contained in a three-sided, glass-fronted display case, bearing a label to the reverse reading 'This owl was caught by a German Prisoner of War (Ludwig Shaver) January 1919 - Reginald Wilson'.

£60-80   **MAI**

A stuffed and mounted jack pike, in a naturalistic setting, contained in a three-sided, bow-fronted glazed display case, bearing labels inscribed 'Birmingham Canal 4th November '48' and 'Specimen Fish preserved and mounted John Betteridge & Son...'.

1948

£150-250   MAI

A stuffed and mounted brown trout, in a naturalistic setting, contained in a three-sided, bow-fronted glazed display case, with a label reading 'Preserved by J. Cooper & Sons 28 Radnor Street, S Luke's London EC'.

Cooper was primarily a fish taxidermist, but did deal with other animals too. John Cooper founded the company in the 1830s, and died in 1872, leaving the business to his sons. Around 1896, the company name became 'John Cooper & Sons'. The company moved to Hounslow in the 1940s, before closing in the 1950s. In general with taxidermy, the style of the wording on a label can help to narrow down a period of manufacture.

£300-500   MAI

A stuffed and mounted pike and three small perch, in a naturalistic setting, contained in a bow-fronted, glazed display case, bearing a label inscribed 'Caught by Mr M Webb on River Kennet at Hintbury, 11th Nov. 1976, 16lbs 11ozs', also mounted with the original hook and sinkers it was caught with.

1976

£300-500   MAI

QUICK REFERENCE - ROWLAND WARD

- **Rowland Ward Ltd. was the largest and most renowned taxidermy company in the world. It was founded by James Rowland Ward (1847-1912), son of noted taxidermist Henry Ward, in Harley Street in 1872, and moved to Piccadilly a few years later. Ward became globally known for his big game trophies, but worked with most animals.**
- **His work is of extremely high-quality, and is realistically stuffed and posed. An innovator as well as a master practitioner of his art, he published over 30 books on big game animals and hunting between 1890 and 1911. He also claimed to have invented the transformation of animals into bizarre furniture, such as monkey lamps and crocodile dumb waiters, which he called 'Wardian Furniture'.**
- **His earliest known work is dated 1868, and was executed when Ward was only 20 years old and still used his first name 'James' on his work. Labels with a '158 Piccadilly' address date from the 1870s, and those reading 'Ward & Co. Ltd.' date from before 1898, when the business became known as 'Roland Ward Ltd.'. The company moved to Mayfair and then North London after World War II, and ceased selling taxidermy in the mid-1970s.**
- **'The Jungle' brand was strongly associated with Ward following his popular and complex jungle exhibits at major exhibitions in 1886 and 1895. His Piccadilly shop was also known as 'The Jungle'.**

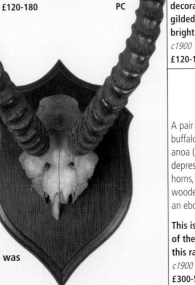

A pair of mounted springbok horns, on an oak shield mount, bearing a Rowland Ward label reading 'The Jungle'.

£120-180   PC

A pair of barasingha or swamp deer (Rucervus duvaucelii) antlers on a skull, mounted on a wooden shield.

Horns like this have become popular with some interior decorators. The skull is often gilded or the shield painted in a bright colour.

c1900   Horns 28in (72cm) long

£120-180   TEN

A pair of dwarf buffalo or lowland anoa (Bubalus depressicornis) horns, mounted on a wooden shield with an ebonised edge.

This is the smallest wild member of the Ox tribe. Little is known of this rarely seen animal.

c1900   Horns 6in (15.5cm) long

£300-500   TEN

QUICK REFERENCE

- The success of Dinky's 'Supertoys' (released in 1947) inspired Welsh toy company Mettoy to launch its own range of small model vehicles in 1956. The new Corgi toys included model cars, aircraft, farm vehicles, commercial vehicles, and boats.
- Corgi toys were the first model vehicles to have clear plastic windows, and models also featured opening doors and boots, as well as sprung 'Glidamatic' suspension from 1959.
- During the 1960s and 1970s a range of models were produced to tie-in with popular TV programmes and films, such as the James Bond series and Batman. These models were extremely popular at the time, and continue to be sought-after today.

- Variation is very important when determining value. Consider the colour, decals or stickers, and other features such as the interior or wheels that might differ from model to model. Some features or combinations may be rare and this is likely to increase desirability and value.
- Condition is also extremely important, with most collectors aiming to buy a model that looks like it did just after it had been purchased. These 'mint' condition examples will always command a premium. Look out for original boxes, which should also be in great condition, and remember that repainting a playworn model won't increase its value.

A Corgi 'BENTLEY CONTINENTAL SPORTS SALOON', no.224, in pale green with light metallic green lower sides and red interior, in very good condition, with box with minor wear.

There are a number of variations of this model, and all are worth roughly the same amount.

1961-65

£60-90 W&W

A Corgi '2.4 JAGUAR FIRE SERVICE CAR', no.213, in very good condition, with original box with minor wear.

£100-150 SAS

A Corgi 'SUNBEAM IMP POLICE CAR', no.506, with white body, black doors and bonnet, and brown interior, with figure driver, in near mint condition, Collectors Club folded leaflet.

There are three different variations of this model, all of which are worth roughly the same. Over 583,000 examples were sold.

1968-69

£60-90 VEC

Mark Picks

Based on a Vanwall car driven by the renowned Stirling Moss, this was the first racing car released by Corgi. Moss (with co-driver Tony Brooks) won the British Grand Prix at Aintree using this car the year the model was released, firmly planting it in the mind of every boy who wanted to grow up to become a racing driver.

The first examples were finished in a lighter green, and bore a racing number transfer '3'. Both the original and the model shown here were superseded by a red painted model with a '25' transfer, which was produced 1961-65, and is usually worth roughly the same as the earlier editions. The fact it's Corgi's first racing car, is connected with a famous racing driver, and is in great condition, makes this a superb buy.

A Corgi 'Triumph Herald Coupé', no.231, with red interior, in mint condition, with slightly warped box.

This is the earlier version with a white mid-stripe. Look out for the ultra-rare pale blue finish, which could fetch up to two or three times the value of this example.

1961-65

£120-180 W&W

A Corgi 'VANWALL' "FORMULA 1 GRAND PRIX' car, no.150, with 'Vanwall' and '20' transfers and promotional transfer to base, boxed, with some paint chips, box scuffed.

1957-61

£400-600 TOV

A Corgi 'FORD THUNDERBIRD - OPEN SPORTS' car, no.215S, finished in red, with original lightly creased and scuffed box.

This was also produced in white or blue, both without suspension, from 1959 to 1962. All versions are worth roughly the same.

1962-64

£60-90   TOV

A CLOSER LOOK AT A CORGI CAR

This model was released in November 1964. Over 977,000 examples were made and sold in its five year production run.

The standard colour was a metallic maroon. This brighter metallic red with its blue metallic roof may have been a factory trial piece.

It has an ingenious cam-driven mechanism, powered by the back wheels, for operating moving 'windscreen wipers' (actually moving clear plastic discs painted with 'wipers').

This colour is much rarer than the standard colour. Examples in maroon tend to fetch well under half this value in similar condition.

A Corgi 'MERCEDES BENZ 600 PULLMAN' car, no.247, in metallic red with a blue metallic roof, in very good condition, and boxed with paperwork.

1964-69

£100-150   W&W

A Corgi 'LOTUS MK11 LE MANS RACING CAR', no.151A, in mid-blue with red seats, lacking driver, with '3' racing number transfer to front, in very good condition, with box with minor wear.

1961-65

£70-100   W&W

A Corgi 'M.G.B. G.T.' car, no.327, in red with pale blue interior, in mint condition, with box with minor wear.

1967-69

£50-70   W&W

A Corgi Toys 'RILEY PATHFINDER POLICE CAR', no.209, with creased, scuffed, and repaired box.

1958-61

£40-60   TOV

A Corgi '1967 MONTE CARLO SUNBEAM IMP WINNER' car, no.340, in metallic blue with a cream interior and '77' transfers, in mint condition, in correct special issue box.

136,000 models were sold in the year of release. Look out for a similarly coloured model with 'WINNER' printed in a red panel on its box, as this is the most valuable version of this model. It usually fetches around 20% more than this example.

1967-69

£200-300   W&W

TOYS

QUICK REFERENCE - CORGI'S BEDFORD VANS

- Commercial vehicles with well-known brand names are a popular part of the diecast collecting market. The rarest examples can be very valuable. This Bedford van was the first light commercial vehicle model released by Corgi, and it went on to be released with five different colours and brands (plus variations) from 1956 to 1960.

- This 'Corgi Toys' version of the standard Bedford van was popular with collectors for obvious reasons, and 67,000 were made and sold. Along with the mid-blue finished version with 'Avro Bode' transfers, it tends to be the most valuable. Look out for the scarcer variations with either a blue body and yellow roof, or a blue lower half and yellow upper half. These can fetch over 50% more in similar or better condition.

- This van is important because it promoted Corgi's brand new corporate colours of blue and yellow.

A Corgi 'BEDFORD 12cwt. VAN', no.422, in yellow with mid-blue roof, with 'CORGI TOYS' transfers, in near mint condition, the box with minor wear.
1960-62
£350-450   W&W

A Corgi 'MAJOR' Bedford 'S' 'TANKER', no.1129, finished in light blue and white with 'Milk' transfers, in very good condition, with original box.
1962-65
£150-200   GORL

A Corgi 'BEDFORD AA ROAD SERVICE VAN', no.408, with divided windscreen and 'ROAD AA SERVICE' transfers, some minor paint chips and rubbing, with creased and scuffed box.

This is the earliest version of this model, and the most valuable. Later versions do not have a divided windscreen, and are generally worth around 25% less.
1957-59
£50-80   TOV

A Corgi 'BEDFORD 12cwt. VAN', no.403, finished in dark blue, with 'DAILY EXPRESS' transfers, in mint condition, with original box with minor wear.
1960-63
£100-150   W&W

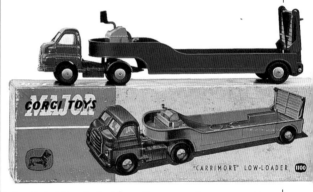

A Corgi 'MAJOR' Big Bedford S-type '"CARRIMORE" LOW-LOADER', no.1100, with red tractor unit and metallic blue low loader, in very good condition with some chips to the paint, with original box and internal packaging with some wear.
1958-63
£80-120   W&W

A Corgi 'COMMER "WALLS" REFRIGERATOR VAN', no.453, the cab and chassis in light blue, with cream rear body with 'Wall's ICE CREAM' transfers to sides, in very good condition with a few chips, with original box.

The cab can be found in either light or dark blue, the latter often fetches around 20% more. The value plummets if the transfers are worn.
1956-60
£150-200   W&W

A Corgi 'MAJOR' Bedford TK 'MOBILGAS PETROL TANKER', no.1140, finished in red with yellow interior, in near mint condition, the box with inner packaging and some wear.
1965-67
£120-180   W&W

A Corgi 'BATMAN' three piece gift set, no.GS40, comprising the 'Batmobile', 'Batboat on Trailer', and 'Batcopter', generally in excellent condition, with inner polystyrene tray in good condition, and fair condition outer striped window box.
1976-82

£200-300   **VEC**

A Corgi 'JAMES BOND' 'TOYOTA 2000GT', no.336, with driver, passenger, six rockets, badge, and instructions, in box with inner box, all in excellent condition.
1967-69

£100-150   **GORL**

A Corgi 'Charlie's Angels Custom Van', no.434, in excellent to mint condition, in original striped window box in very good to excellent condition.
1978-80

£50-70   **SAS**

A Corgi 'CHITTY CHITTY BANG BANG' car, no.266, original example complete with all figures and front and rear wings, in mint condition, the window box with minor wear.
1968-72

£200-300   **W&W**

QUICK REFERENCE - THE IMPORTANCE OF VARIATION

- Variation and completeness are important considerations with most diecast models, but they really count with this model. The first version of the "Thrush-Buster" was produced in white in 1966 only. It came with internal pictorial packaging and a plastic 'Waverley ring'. If the car is white, and the model is complete with all its packaging and the ring, then its value can leap to around five times the value of the example shown here! If any part is defective or missing, particularly the ring, then value falls dramatically.

A Corgi 'THE GREEN HORNET'S 'BLACK BEAUTY" car, no.268, in gloss black with hornet logo to roof, in mint condition, with display insert, radar scanners, missiles, paperwork, and box.
1967-72

£180-220   **W&W**

A Corgi 'THE MAN FROM U.N.C.L.E.' 'GUN FIRING' "THRUSH-BUSTER" car, no.497, finished in purplish-blue, in near mint condition, with original box in excellent condition.
1966-69

£80-120   **ECGW**

A Corgi 'Inspector Morse Jaguar Mk.II' car, no.96682, finished in maroon with a black roof, in mint condition, with first issue window box in near mint condition.

1993

£35-45   VEC

A Corgi 'SPIDER-MAN' 'Spidervan', no.436, in near mint condition, with original window box in excellent condition.

1979-80

£70-100   SAS

A CLOSER LOOK AT KOJAK'S BUICK

In 1977, the (rather stunted!) Kojak figurine gained a hat, and Crocker's jacket changed from blue to black. This 'second version' was produced until 1980 and is generally worth around 40% less than the first, perhaps because Kojak's baldness is so well-known and seen as iconic.

Always check that the model is complete with its self-adhesive New York Police Department Lieutenant's badge sticker.

As this example combines the blue-jacketed Crocker of the first version with the hatted Kojak of the second version, it must have been produced in 1977 as supplies changed over.

This model also hides a fun feature. The sound of gunfire can be heard by turning a wheel in the back bumper!

A Corgi 'KOJAK'S Buick', no.290, finished in bronze and complete with Crocker and Kojak figures, in excellent condition, with window box in very good condition.

1976-77

£70-90   AH

A Corgi 'Starsky & Hutch Ford Torino', no.292, finished in red with a white transfer, in near mint condition, in original window box in excellent condition.

The three figures included with this model were a novelty for Corgi. To avoid time-consuming and expensive hand-painting and still retain a crisply decorated figure, each part including the bases, legs, bodies, and heads was moulded separately. The scene of Starsky and Hutch arresting a suspect (who has his hands spread on the roof of the car) in front of a printed New York skyline was popular, with over 974,000 of these models being sold.

1977-82

£120-180   SAS

A Corgi 'THE MONKEES MONKEEMOBILE', no.277, finished in red, in mint condition, with window box in near mint condition.

Look out for the rare box variation with a 'clip-in' cardboard header that was used for shop display, as this can fetch around four times the value of the standard box.

1968-72

£100-150   BELL

A Corgi Juniors 'Scooby and his Friends' gift set, no.E3108, with five models in excellent to mint condition, with original window box in very good, but crumpled, condition.

£40-60   SAS

A Dinky 'Austin Devon', no.152. finished in cerise and green, with some playwear and scratches.

This was re-numbered from model no.40D. Look out for the version with a tan body and 'suede' green hubs, which can fetch over eight times as much as this one in mint condition.
1956-59
£60-80   TOV

A Dinky 'Austin' covered wagon, no.30S, finished in maroon with a red tinplate canopy, with some chipping to the paint.

Look out for the dark-blue body as this can fetch over twice the price of this version. This model was sold   unboxed.
1950-54
£70-100   TOV

SAS

Collecting or selling...we provide professional and sound advice for both large and small accumulations and collections (including a pick-up service) and hold regular auctions of Diecasts, Toys, Trains, Toy Figures, Dolls and Teddy Bears.

For free sample catalogue, information and valuations contact

SPECIAL AUCTION SERVICES
Tel: 01635 580 595
81 New Greenham Park, Newbury, Berkshire RG19 6HW
www.specialauctionservices.com
mail@specialauctionservices.com

A Dinky 'Austin' taxi, no.40H, finished in dark blue with light-blue wheels, with some chips to the paint.
1952-54
£70-100   TOV

An early Dinky 'Sports Tourer two-seater', no.24H, in red with green running board and wheel arches, with filled in windscreen and criss-cross chassis (second type), lacking headlights.
£60-80   CHT

A rare French Dinky 'Coffret Cadeau Tourisme' gift set . no.24-57, comprising five cars, 'Studebaker Commander', 'Simca Versailles', 'Renault Dauphine', 'Berline 403 Peugeot', and a 'Chrysler New Yorker', all in gift set box, vehicles in very good condition.
£1,500-2,000   W&W

TOYS

A Dinky 'Austin Devon Saloon', no.152, finished in deep blue with mid-blue hubs, in mint condition, with excellent condition box.

Blue is the second most sought-after and valuable version of this model after the slightly more valuable tan-bodied variation. This example is unusual, and additionally desirable, as the blue of the body does not match the hubs as is usual.

1954-59

£200-300   W&W

Andrew Clark Models

COLLECTORS TOYS

Est. 1981

WANTED NOW!

CHAD VALLEY

TOP PRICES PAID FOR:
- ○ Dinky
- ○ Corgi
- ○ Matchbox
- ○ Spot - on
- ○ Tin Plate Toys
- ○ Britains
- ○ Trains
- ○ White Metal
- ○ Minichamps
- ○ Polistil/Burago
- ○ Quality 1/18 Scale
- ○ Plastic Kits (Airfix etc)
- ○ Modern Collectables

Please post list, email, fax or phone with details
Andrew Clark, Unit 13, Baildon Mills,
Northgate, Baildon, Shipley, BD17 6JX
Office hours tel: 01274 594 552
Mobile: 077 5380 4232
Email: andrew@andrewclarkmodels.com

Selling models every week on www.ebay.co.uk
under andrewclarkmodels and andrewclarkmodels2

- Many auction prices beaten
- Anything considered, will collect
- Large collections a speciality
- Established in 1981

A Dinky 'Morris Mini-Traveller', no.197, finished in green with a yellow interior, in very good condition, with original box in good condition.

This is the second scarcest variation of this model. The scarcest and most valuable is in white with a yellow interior, and can fetch around 20% more in similar (or better) condition.

1961-71

£250-350   SAS

A Dinky 'Automatic Morris Mini-Minor', no.183, finished in bright metallic blue, in very good condition, in original fair condition box with 'COLOUR OF MODEL MAY DIFFER…' label, one flap-end detached.

1966-74

£40-60   SAS

QUICK REFERENCE - SOUTH AFRICAN DINKY TOYS

- Meccano, who produced Dinky, exported their products to many Commonwealth countries, of which South Africa was one of the most important. When the country withdrew from the Commonwealth in 1961, new import duties on 'luxury goods' threatened Dinky's market. 'Unfinished' goods were exempt from the tax, so Dinky chose to export unpainted models to be finished in the country. As a result, South African models are rare, and typically finished in unusual colours, for example, the standard colours for this model were pale blue or metallic blue. The base plates of South African models are also finished in a glossy paint, rather than the matt black of British models. It is said that only one batch of each model exported was sent, making South African models very rare.

- In 1966, parts were imported from Dinky's French factory to be assembled and painted in South Africa, and it is from this batch that this model dates. Boxes for these models were in Afrikaans and English, and also bore the name of the retailer. They are very, very rare, and increase value markedly. This box is the correct style for the period and model, but is a British replacement.

A rare South African issue Dinky 'Ford Consul Cortina', no.139, in mid-green with fawn interior, and spun hubs, in excellent condition, with English language box.

1966

£400-600   W&W

A Dinky 'Vauxhall Viva', no.136, finished in bright blue with red interior, in mint condition with good condition box.

There are two other colour variations in light blue and white. All three are usually worth roughly the same.

1965-68

£70-100   W&W

A CLOSER LOOK AT A DINKY LORRY

Foden trucks are among the most collectable and valuable models in the Dinky range. They were produced in an enormous variety of shapes and colours.

Always consider all the details, including the shape of the cab, the colour of the flashes on the cab, and the colours of the hubs, cab, chassis, and back. The combination on this example is the second rarest from the no.501 range.

The rarest combination, which can fetch up to around three times as much, was produced for the US market and has a red first issue cab, back, and hubs, a black chassis, no hook, and silver flashes on the cab.

As well as being in very good condition, it has its original 'Utility' style card box with printed label, which is another rarity.

A rare Dinky 'Supertoys' 'Foden Diesel 8-Wheel Wagon', no.501, with first type cab and chassis with unpainted hook, finished in dark blue with mid-blue flash to cab sides and mid-blue wheel hubs, in very good condition with light chipping to paintwork, complete with original box.

1948-52

£1,000-1,500 W&W

A Dinky 'Supertoys' 'Bedford Articulated Lorry', no.521, finished in yellow with red wheels, with some damage to the paint, with original box.

1950-54

£60-80 TOV

A Dinky restoration/copy 'Guy Van', no.514, finished in yellow with 'Weetabix' transfers, stamped 'V' and 'V001' to underside of chassis, in good condition.

£100-150 VEC

A Dinky 'Foden Flat Truck' with chains, no.905, with maroon cab, flatbed, chassis, and chain posts, and red hubs, in very good condition, with box lid only.

The same model in the same finish, but with matching maroon hubs, was produced for the same very short period of time. It is usually worth around 20% less than this variation.

1956-57

£100-150 GORL

A Dinky 'Guy Flat Truck' with tailboard, no.913, with deep blue cab and chassis, orange flatbed, and light blue hubs, in very good condition, with original box.

If the colours of the illustration of the model on the box match the colours on this model, then the value can more than triple. Collectors love to have the colours of the illustration matching the model, and boxes showing this colourway are very rare.

1954-56

£120-180 GORL

A Dinky 'Supertoys' 'Guy Van', no.918, finished in blue with red hubs and 'EVER READY' batteries transfers, with some scratches and chips, in a creased and scuffed box.

1955-58

£150-250 TOV

A Dinky Morris 'J' van, no.260, finished in red with 'ROYAL MAIL' transfers, in excellent condition, with lightly creased and scuffed box.

1955-61

£80-120 TOV

A Dinky 'Armstrong Whitworth "Whitley" Bomber', no.60V, finished in silver with RAF roundels, with original scuffed card box.
1937-41
£40-60   CHT

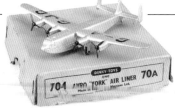

A Dinky 'Avro "York" Air Liner', no.704/70A, finished in silver with 'G-AGJC' registration transfer, in very good condition, with original yellow lidded box in fair to good condition.
1954-59
£50-80   SAS

A Dinky 'De Havilland Light Racer', No.60G, finished in yellow with red propellers and 'G-RACE' registration transfers, in excellent condition with re-touched propellers.
1945-49
£150-200   SAS

QUICK REFERENCE - DINKY METAL FATIGUE

- Pre-war Dinky toys were made from Mazac, a mixture of magnesium, zinc, and copper. While there was no problem with the alloy itself, the company soon began to add waste metal from various production processes (invariably including lead from lead figures) to the mixture. The addition of this lead and other metals made the alloy unstable, resulting in metal 'fatigue', 'sickness', or 'rot', with the metal cracking, crystallising, sagging, warping, and ultimately disintegrating. The process is irreversible, and a considerable part of the value of any Dinky model is dependent on whether it is affected, and how badly.

- Plane wings, like these, show the problem very clearly, but it can affect most models made by Dinky in the pre-war period. Some boys remember their models falling apart during their childhood, while other models still exist, completely unaffected, today. Recent research seems to indicate that models that seem to be unaffected at the moment are likely to remain unaffected, as a model was either made with unstable alloy, or it wasn't. However, if a model shows signs of the 'rot', it'll only get worse. To slow the process down, handle affected models as little as possible and keep their temperature as even as possible.

A Dinky '"Douglas D.C.3" Air Liner', no.60T finished in silver with 'PH-ALI' transfers, in fair to good condition, lacking one wheel, with original box in fair to good condition.
1938-41
£80-100   SAS

A Dinky 'H.L. Brook's Percival "Gull" Aeroplane', no.60K, finished in light blue and silver, with black 'G-ADZO' transfers, in very good condition, with original box in good condition.

This colour combination indicates that it is from the two later 'commemorative' releases of this plane, which was released as a standard model (No.60C) in different colours from 1934 to 1936. The second commemorative plane in the colourway shown is Amy Mollinson's 'Gull' plane, which is indicated by blue 'G-ADZO' wing transfers. It tends to be worth around the same as this model.
1936-41
£400-600   SAS

A Dinky General 'Monospar' plane, no.60E, finished in silver with blue wing tips and tail, with two single propellers, in good condition.
1934-36
£35-45   CAPE

A Dinky low wing monoplane, no.60D, finished in red, with black 'G-AVYP' registration transfers, small silver propeller, and pilot's head cast-in, in very good condition.
1936-41
£40-60   CHT

QUICK REFERENCE

- In 1902, American president, Theodore (Teddy) Roosevelt refused to shoot a bear cub on a hunting trip. The story led a Brooklyn shop owner, Morris Michtom, to produce a commemorative soft toy bear, which proved to be popular, and began a world-wide craze that's still with us today.
- German company Steiff (founded 1886) are considered the best maker. Other sought-after German makers include Gebrüder Hermann, Bing, and Schreyer & Co. (known by its trade name Schuco). British companies include Farnell, Merrythought, and Chad Valley, and American companies include Ideal, Gund, and Knickerbocker.
- The shape of a bear can often help identify the period it was made in, and which company it was made by. Before World War II, bears typically had long limbs with large, upturned paw pads, pronounced snouts, and humped backs. They were almost always made from mohair, and stuffed with wood shavings or kapock (wool), which makes them feel hard and solid. Post-war bears usually had shorter limbs, plumper bodies, rounder heads and shorter snouts. Synthetic materials were used from the 1960s onwards.
- Modern limited edition bears from notable makers, such as Steiff, are beginning to make good prices on the secondary market. Always keep your limited edition bear in mint condition, and retain the box and paperwork. Some limited editions are replicas of older bears, which should not be confused with the (more valuable) originals. If in doubt, smell your bear, as the scent of an old bear cannot be replicated.
- Even if not by a major maker, bears with cute, engaging expressions are likely to be popular. Whilst wear from years of love adds character, and much damage can be restored, most collectors prefer teddies to be in good condition. Tears, stains, replaced pads, and worn fur will reduce value.

A 1970s Steiff 'Minky Zotty' teddy bear, with jointed limbs, tipped art-plush fur, stitched nose, open mouth lined in felt, and growler.

Steiff's 'Zotty' bears take their name from 'zottig', the German word for shaggy. For more information, please see the Teddy Bear section of the 'Miller's Collectables Handbook 2010-2011'.

10in (25cm) high

£80-100   PC

A 1960s-70s Steiff gold mohair teddy bear, with jointed limbs, stitched nose, boot button eyes, and yellow Steiff tag in ear.

With his shorter limbs, plumper body, and more rounded head, he is typical of post-war teddy bears.

7.5in (19cm) high

£80-100   PC

A Steiff limited edition burgundy mohair teddy bear, no.659973, from the 'British Collectors' range, and from a limited edition of 3,000, complete with certificate and box.

1998   16in (40cm) high

£100-150   FLD

A Steiff limited edition grey mohair teddy bear, no.660047, from the 'British Collectors' range, and from a limited edition of 3,000, complete with certificate and box.

1999   16in (40cm) tall

£100-150   FLD

TOYS

A Steiff cinnamon mohair-plush 'replica 1903' 'Mr Cinnamon' teddy bear, no.000201, from the 'Classic Teddy Bear' range, with long mohair, squeaker, tag, and labels, in mint condition.

1993-2000   21.5in (55cm) high
£70-100   PC

A Steiff limited edition cinnamon curly mohair-plush 'Appolonia' teddy bear, no.667633, from a limited edition of 1,500, with lace collar and brooch, together with a felt bag marked 'The Toy Shoppe' (USA).

This bear was produced as an exclusive for The Toy Shoppe in the US. Her brooch shows a photograph of her 'husband' Maximillian, and the two of them are part of a 'family' of four bears, including son Little Max, and daughter Zoë.

2004   28in (71cm) high
£120-180   AH

A Steiff limited edition golden-brown and dusky-pink mohair-plush 'Club Millennium' teddy bear, no.420184, numbered 7,064 from a limited edition of 9,450, the paws embroidered '1999' and '2000', with porcelain Club medallion, box, and with certificate of authenticity.

Produced to commemorate the Millennium, the golden-brown mohair represents traditional Steiff bears of the past, and the pink mohair represents the new Steiff of the future.

12in (30cm) high
£100-150   AH

A Steiff limited edition gold mohair-plush 'Christopher' teddy bear, no.666681, from the 'Cherished Teddies' range, and from a limited edition of 2000, with ear button, amber eyes, pink sailor collar, and jointed limbs, in presentation box with certificate.

2002 12in (30cm) high
£80-120   AH

A CLOSER LOOK AT A STEIFF PANDA

In 2006, this bear was made exclusively for the US specialist retailer The Toy Shoppe as a limited edition of just 1,500 bears.

It is made from genuine alpaca. This was the first time in Steiff's long history that alpaca was used for a panda.

He should come with a special red and yellow mohair ball, Steiff buttons, and a white tag. He should also be numbered from a limited edition of 1,500.

He is much loved by collectors for his realistic, rounded form, which closely mimics real pandas. This was the first time that Steiff had made such a realistic looking panda.

A Steiff limited edition 'UK BABY BEARS 1994-1998' set, from the 'British Collectors' range, comprising pink, red, gold, cinnamon, and blond baby bears, numbered 0593 from a limited edition of 1,847, contained in an original fitted wooden case with certificate of authenticity.

Each 6.25in (16cm) high

1999
£150-200   AH

A Steiff limited edition black and white mohair-plush 'replica' 'Chub-Ling' giant panda, no.668302, from a limited edition of 1,500, together with a bag marked 'The Toy Shoppe' (USA).

2006   19in (48cm) high
£150-200   AH

A CLOSER LOOK AT A CHEEKY BEAR

The 'Cheeky' bear was introduced in 1957, and is still made today in different characters and colours, some produced as limited editions.

Earlier examples were made from silk-plush or mohair. Later examples tend to be made from acrylic or brightly coloured mohair.

The Cheeky is recognisable by his over-sized head and ears containing bells.

This type of label with a curving 'IRONBRIDGE SHROPSHIRE' was used from 1957 to 1991.

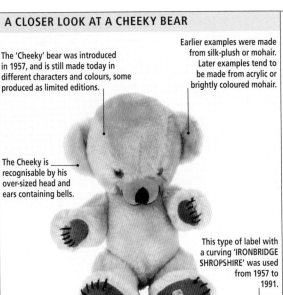

A late 20thC Merrythought gold plush 'Cheeky' teddy bear, with felt pads, stitched claws, and label to left foot, in excellent condition.

13in (33cm) high

£100-150   FLD

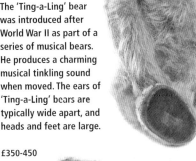

A small 1950s Chiltern 'Ting-a-Ling' teddy, with a bell in his tummy, velvet pads, and a mark to the right foot where a label was once stitched.

The 'Ting-a-Ling' bear was introduced after World War II as part of a series of musical bears. He produces a charming musical tinkling sound when moved. The ears of 'Ting-a-Ling' bears are typically wide apart, and heads and feet are large.

£350-450

12in (30.5cm) high

BEJ

A small 1930s Chiltern blond mohair teddy bear, with jointed limbs, glass eyes, stitched nose, and broken musical bellows in tummy.

10.5in (26.5cm) high

£250-300   BEJ

A large late 1950s Chiltern gold mohair teddy bear, with amber and black glass eyes, stitched nose, and jointed limbs with brown felt pads.

The floppy ears, large head, and pointy feet are typical of Chiltern's bears at this time. Glass eyes were soon superseded by plastic.

26in (65cm) high

£200-300   TOV

A 1930s-40s Merrythought blond mohair teddy bear, with jointed limbs, felt pads, stitched nose, glass eyes, and metal ear button.

19in (48cm) high

£150-200   GORL

A 1930s-40s Merrythought blond plush teddy bear, with jointed limbs, stitched nose, and Rexine paw pads, with metal button to left ear.

21in (54cm) high

£100-150   FLD

A 1950s Chad Valley faded-gold mohair teddy bear, with jointed limbs, stitched nose, black and amber glass eyes, tan felt pads, and label to right foot.

14in (36cm) high

£60-80   **AH**

A 1950s Chad Valley pale-gold mohair-plush teddy bear, with jointed limbs, stitched nose, amber and black glass eyes, rexine covered pads, and square label to right foot.

The form is typical of Chad Valley's post-war bears, with its shorter, stubbier limbs, rounded head, and plump body.

18in (46cm) high

£100-150   **AH**

A late 1950s/early 1960s Pedigree gold mohair bear, with jointed limbs, fixed head, and bells in the ears.

The design of this bear is very similar to Merrythought's popular and successful 'Cheeky' bear (see previous page), with his large head and ears containing bells.

14in (35.5cm) high

£50-80   **PC**

QUICK REFERENCE - WENDY BOSTON

• The Wendy Boston company was founded in Wales in 1954, and its bears (and those inspired by them) became familiar to a generation born in the 1960s and '70s. In 1954, the company introduced the first washable teddy bear, and pioneered safety 'lock-in' plastic eyes. Most of Wendy Boston's bears were unjointed, and so fixed in this seated position with welcoming, open arms. Many bears were produced using synthetic fur filled with rubber foam, and had ears integral to the head so they could be hung to dry on the washing line! Taken over by Denys Fisher in 1968, the company closed in 1976 having changed the way teddy bears looked and were made.

A 1950s Pedigree pink and white mohair teddy bear, with original stitching, eyes, and paw pads.

This is an unusual and scarce colour combination for this maker.

14in (35.5cm) high

£200-250   **PC**

A 1940s Pixie Toys blond mohair bear, with original stitching, eyes, and manufacturer's tag.

8in (20.5cm) high

£80-120   **LHT**

A Wendy Boston gold mohair-mix bear, unjointed, with original stitching and glass eyes.

16in (40.5cm) high

£50-80   **PC**

A 1930s German lavender-coloured bear, the colour hardly faded.

23in

£300-400   PC

A large 1920s-30s German dark-pink dual-tipped mohair bear, stuffed with wood wool, with original glass eyes, nose stitching, and three replaced paw pads.

34in (86cm) high

£600-800   PC

Mark Picks

Even though the maker of this bear is not known and would have been a minor maker, he has three features that make him desirable and a good bet for the future. Firstly, he is in excellent and original condition. Secondly, he has a quirky and appealing face - cute or characterful faces always attract collectors. Thirdly, he comes with an original photograph of his first owner. Provenance such as this not only makes a bear more desirable to collectors, it also makes him more valuable due to the rarity of this aspect. Without the provenance and the accompanying photo, he would be worth about half this price.

An early 20thC probably English gold mohair teddy bear, with jointed limbs, stitched claws, mouth and nose, felt pads, and glass eyes, together with a photograph of his original owner.

24in (61cm) high

£1,200-1,800   LHT

A CLOSER LOOK AT A FAKE OR REPRODUCTION TEDDY

With his long, curved arms, pronounced snout, humped back, and long chicken drumstick-like legs, he looks like German jointed bear made during the 1900s-1920s.

The wear to the fur on his snout is inconsistent with the rest of his body. He should show signs of wear from being carried around, hugged, and stroked.

If in doubt, sniff him, as the smell of decades of love and wear, or even careful display, cannot be reproduced.

Look closer. The pads are very clean, unworn, and are not replaced, and his fur is in similarly excellent, clean, and unworn condition - all are unusual for a bear nearly a century old.

A chocolate brown plush-covered teddy bear, with swivel head and limbs, wood-wool stuffing, black boot button eyes, a long shaven snout with vertically stitched nose, and woven fabric pads to the long arms and feet.

There's a difference between 'fake' and 'reproduction'. If the bear is being sold for the right price as a 'reproduction' of an older bear or as an 'artist's bear', then it's up to you to decide if you love him enough to add him to your collection. If he is being sold as a genuine early 20thC bear with an intention to deceive, then he is a fake.

13.75in (35cm) long

£20-30   PC

A 1950s European brown curly cotton-plush bear, with internal growler and original stitching and eyes, with some repairs.

18in (51cm) high

£50-80   PC

A 1970s British Gabrielle Designs 'Paddington' bear, designed by Shirley Clarkson in 1972, with original hat, duffel coat, luggage tag, and Wellington boots.

£100-150   LC

A 1920s-30s black plush 'Felix the Cat' soft toy, with wood-wool filling and wire skeleton, indistinct maker's pad to feet.

Like the Mickey also on this page, this toy has googly eyes, which are typical of the late 1920s and 1930s. Created by American illustrator Pat Sullivan in 1921, Felix the Cat is ever popular. Felix toys were made by Schuco and Steiff, but this example is probably English.

14in (36cm)

£180-200   GORL

A CLOSER LOOK AT A MICKEY MOUSE

A 1932 Dean's advertisement showed that these Mickeys could be clipped onto gramophone arms allowing him to 'Dance, Jazz, Shimmie, Fox Trot and execute quite a number of hitherto unknown steps' to music.

Known as 'Jazzers', they were the first Mickey Mouse toys produced by Dean's, originally cost 2 shillings, and were alleged to give 'endless amusement'.

His chin and neck is marked with a registered number, and he is dirty and worn, lacking his tail. Had he been in better condition, he could have fetched over twice as much.

Mickey was introduced in 1928 and Steiff also produced a (more valuable) version during the 1930s. The Deans' 'Jazzers' are among the earliest authentically licensed Mickey Mouse soft toys ever produced.

A Dean's velveteen 'Mickey Mouse' soft toy, with boot button eyes, and red shorts with buttons, worn and lacks tail.

8in (20cm) high

£120-180   TOV

A German ride-along white mohair donkey-on-wheels, on a metal frame, with four blue painted wheels with rubber tyres.

This is very similar to Steiff models. The lead's toggle has an aluminium 'Steiff' badge, but this was probably added later.

18in (44.5cm) high

£250-350   SAS

A 1930s-50s Steiff grey felt donkey-on-wheels, with boot button eyes, leather saddler, and green felt coat, with button to ear.

16in (41cm) high

£150-200   GORL

An early 20thC American or German stuffed hessian donkey pull-toy, on a metal frame with metal spoked wheels.

13.5in (34cm) long

£150-200   FRE

A 1950s-60s Steiff gold plush jointed lion cub soft toy, with metal Steiff button to ear.

13.5in (34cm) long

£80-120   **GORL**

A 1950s-60s Steiff seated tiger soft toy, with green and black glass eyes, striped fur, and button in ear.

13.75in (36cm) long

£40-60   **SAS**

A 1950s-60s Steiff mohair 'Xorry' fox soft toy, with graduated coloured fur and button in ear.

15in (38cm) long

£35-45   **SAS**

A Steiff green mohair 'Froggy' soft toy, no.2370/10, with button and yellow tag.

5.25in (13.5cm) high

£25-35   **SAS**

Judith Picks

Launched in 1996, Nintendo's 'Pokemon' has become the world's second most successful and financially lucrative computer game franchise ever, behind only Nintendo's other hit, 'Super Mario'. Beloved across the world by today's technology-focused children, 'Pokemon' merchandise may become the hot collectable of the future, as nostalgia is such a powerful driver behind collecting. Today's children will eventually grow up to be tomorrow's collectors, fondly remembering the games and toys of their childhoods. Although mass-produced, most merchandise will by then have become worn, damaged, dirtied, or all three. You should therefore look out for examples in mint or near mint condition, such as this large and appealing soft toy. Aim to buy classic character pieces, ideally items that were more expensive at the time, or were produced in smaller production runs, and those that still retain their tags or box if applicable. It may take a few decades for demand and prices to rise, but they should.

An American Play-By-Play giant-size light-green plush Pokemon 'Bulbasaur', with manufacturer's and Nintendo tag labels.

28in (71cm) long

£15-20   **SAS**

A 1930s Chad Valley 'Tom Webster's George' character soft toy.

12in (31cm) high

£150-250   **BELL**

TOYS

QUICK REFERENCE

- From the mid-19thC tin-plated steel replaced wood as the material of choice for toys. The metal sheets could be bent, embossed, fixed together, painted, and later decorated with coloured transfers. All this allowed toymakers to produce more intricately detailed models at an economic cost.
- Germany quickly became the epicentre of tinplate toy manufacture with major manufacturers including Gerbrüder Bing (1863-1933), Märklin (founded 1856), and Schreyer & Co. (1912-1978). Models from these makers are typically highly desirable and enthusiastically collected.
- From 1880 onwards the US became a secondary hotbed of tinplate toy production. Notable and prolific manufacturers include Louis Marx (1896-1912) and Ferdinand Strauss (c1914-1942), and their work is becoming increasingly sought-after.
- Following World War II production shifted to Japan, and the nature of the toys created changed. Battery-operated

features such as flashing lights and sound became common. Spacecraft and robot toys were very popular during this time, reflecting the excitement over the 'Space Race' in the 1950s and 1960s. Important and collectable Japanese manufacturers include Horikawa and Yonizawa.
- Early hand-painted pieces, produced before modern lithographic techniques were widely employed in c1910, tend to fetch the highest prices due to their rarity and high quality.
- Large, early ships or zeppelins by Märklin can fetch over £20,000. Models with humorous subjects are also sought-after. Post-war items are more numerous, and tend to be less expensive. Price depends largely on size, maker, and particularly condition so always check pieces carefully before purchasing as rust and scratched lithography are nearly impossible to restore. Reproductions of numerous toys have been made so always check colours against originals.

A German Distler tinplate clockwork limousine, finished in silver and black, with disc wheels and driver, fitted with headlights, with some wear and rust spotting.

£350-450   TOV

A German tinplate clockwork 'GK 547' saloon car, finished in yellow, green, and cream, with disc wheels and driver, with some wear and rust spots.

£150-200   TOV

An American Kingsbury tinplate clockwork model of the Napier-Campbell 'Bluebird', with rubber tyres, British and American flags to tail, and with wear to paint.

c1929   *18.5in (47cm) long*

£200-300   GORL

A German Märklin No.1092 tinplate clockwork Mercedes 300SL 'Gull Wing' car, finished in red, with opening door, steering, and battery-powered headlights, boxed, with certificate and key.

This is one of a series of annual re-releases from the Märklin Toy Museum, and was made using the original dies and moulds from the 1930s. It was only sold for a limited time during 1993.

A 1930s German tinplate clockwork 'Bluebird' speed car, lacks driver, in fair to poor condition.

12.5in (32cm) long

£250-350   AH

1993   *12in (30.5cm) long*

£150-200   TOV

A 1930s German Schuco 'Curvo 1000' tinplate military motorcycle, finished in blue and cream, the rider wearing a red jacket and brown trousers, the passenger with a mounted machine gun, with some wear to the printed finish.

£150-200   TOV

A French S.F.A. printed tinplate clockwork motorcycle and side car, with rider, in good condition.

c1950   *6.5in (17cm) long*

£50-80   AH

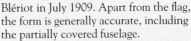

Mark Picks

Toys mirroring early forms of transport are enormously collectable. The most sought-after, and often most valuable, concern the development of the motorcar from the 'horseless carriage'. Zeppelins tend to be the most valuable form of air-travel toys, but early planes can be somewhat scarcer.

The form of this plane is based on the famous, ground-breaking Blériot XI monoplane, flown successfully over the English Channel by Louis Blériot in July 1909. Apart from the flag, the form is generally accurate, including the partially covered fuselage.

This model was undoubtedly expensive in its day, and has survived in very good condition. It's also impressively large, which adds further to the value. All these factors combine to make a model that should not decrease, and should only increase, in value.

A French hand-painted tinplate plane, with open cockpit, French flag, and pale blue painted finish.

c1910   *21.5in (55cm) long*

£800-1,200   GORL

A Lehmann 'Balky Mule' lithograph-printed tinplate toy, no.425, with clockwork action and articulated clown driver.

This comparatively common toy is also known as 'The Stubborn Donkey'. Watch out for bright colours, mules that are decorated with printed designs rather than covered with flock, and a lack of signs of age, as these usually indicate modern reproductions made in China.

c1910   *7.5in (19cm) long*

£100-150   AH

A rare and unusual early 20thC, probably German, tinplate toy, modelled as a swan on wheels towing a chariot, with flywheel mechanism.

4.7in (12cm) high

£500-700   BELL

A German Lehmann tinplate clockwork 'Paddy and the Pig' toy, no.500, depicting a man in cloth clothes riding a bucking pig, patented in 1903.

E. P. Lehmann, based in Nuremburg, is well-known for novelty toys with highly unusual and amusing forms. Only Gunthermann produced more bizarre creations.

c1908   *6in (15cm) long*

£500-700   FLD

A German Orobr tinplate clockwork battleship toy, with two funnels, masts, gun turrets, and lifeboats, finished in cream and red, with wheels to run along the floor, with some wear and rusting to the finish.

Although large and impressive at first glance, take another look as the quality and detailing aren't as good as ships by the best makers, such as Märklin. 'Orobr' was the brand of Brandenburg-based Oro Werke, who produced a number of inexpensive tinplate toys before World War I, and then again until 1922. Some records indicate that the company continued and took over competitor Greppert & Kelch in 1931, and grew to have a staff of around 500. Partners in the company included Reil, Blechschmidt, and Muller.

11in (29cm) long

TOV

A 1930s painted tinplate model of the 'Red Baron' Fokker DR.1 triplane, with suspension hooks.

£220-280   FRE   £300-500

A CLOSER LOOK AT A TINPLATE ROBOT

This is the rarest of four variations of Yoshiya's more common 'Chief Robot Man' toy. Three are simply variations of the same toy in different colours, but 'Mighty Robot' has a transparent head that lights up and contains moving gears.

He retains his original box (beware of replicas!), and he is in overall excellent condition with very little wear, and his transfers remain fresh.

Yoshiya is a well-known and much-collected maker.

A 1930s Fleischmann painted tinplate 'Columbus' two funnel passenger liner, with two loose suspended lifeboats, detachable masts fore and aft, each with ladder access to crow's nest, red and black hull with off-white upper desks, cream and red funnels, with working spring-driven motor operating the propeller.

16.5in (42cm) long

£800-1,200   CAPE

A 1930s German painted and lithographed tinplate 'Red Indian' canoeist, with spring-driven rowing action and two detachable oars, the canoe in pale green and blue.

8.25in (21cm) long

£200-300   CAPE

He has 'mystery action', a phrase used by the Japanese to describe a number of functions, but usually a 'bump n go' action.

This robot is large and in a skirted form that is typical of the period.

A Japanese KO Yoshiya battery-operated tinplate 'Mighty Robot', in original box.

1959   *11.5in (29cm) high*

£1,000-1,500   GORL

A Märklin painted tinplate 'Spinning Butterflies' parlour game, complete with three transfer-printed butterflies and a spinning holder, the box applied with 'Better Toys' distributor's label, in fair condition, box grubby.

£80-120   CAPE

QUICK REFERENCE

- Tootsietoys were made by Dowst Brothers Co., founded in Chicago in the late 19thC. The company began by casting shirt collar buttons and novelties for prizes with candy.
- The company's first diecast car was released in 1901. It was followed by others, but the success of the Model-T Ford released in 1915 ensured that the range grew in size and popularity in the 1920s and '30s. In 1926 Dowst merged with the Cosmo Manufacturing Co., and the range grew further.
- The Tootsietoys name was inspired by a young relation of the Dowst Brothers, whose nickname was 'Toots'. Registered in 1924, it was used on boxes from 1925 and on toys from 1926.
- In 1933 the company began producing its models in Zamac, an alloy of zinc, rather than lead. The new material was lighter and stronger. The quality of moulding also improved with models showing greater design sophistication, accuracy, and detail than ever before.

- The year 1933 also saw the introduction of the company's most successful and iconic line, a range of vehicles based on the 1932 Graham-Paige 'Blue Streak'.
- Millions of 'Grahams' had been produced before the 1929 stock market bankrupted many toy companies. Tootsietoys managed to survive this difficult period by simplifying its models, which reduced production costs and also made the models affordable to more buyers.
- Although Tootsietoys was largely eclipsed by Dinky, Matchbox, and Corgi after World War II, it continued and is still in business today. However, most collectors focus on pre-war designs and seek out scarce models with unusual variations in form or detailing, or those in rare colours.
- Always look for models in mint condition, and avoid pieces with repainting. Also look out for 'metal fatigue', where the Zamac begins to crumble as it degrades. This is irreversible.

A Tootsietoys 'Small Racer', no.23, finished in blue with grey driver, in fair to good condition.
Issued 1927
£15-20   AH

A Tootsietoys 'Model A Ford Coupe', no.4655, finished in beige, in excellent condition.
Issued 1928
£15-20   AH

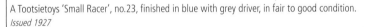

A Tootsietoys 'Mac 'LONG DISTANCE HAULING' Van Trailer', no.0803, with red tinplate roof, finished in yellow-orange, in good condition.
1933-36   *5.5in (14cm) long*
£20-30   AH

A Tootsietoys 'Greyhound Coach', no.1045, finished in gold and blue, in good condition.
1937-41
£10-15   AH

A Tootsietoys 'Model A Ford Coupe', no.4655, finished in beige, in excellent condition.
Issued 1928
£15-20   AH

TOYS

A Tootsietoys 'Hook and Ladder Truck', no.4652, finished in red and blue, with two ladders finished in gold, in good condition.

1927-33

£30-40   AH

A Tootsietoys 'Contractor' boxed set, no.0191, containing 'Mac Truck', and yellow, green, and blue side-tipping ratchet-operated dump trailers, box end flaps missing, in fair to good condition.

1933-41

£30-40   AH

A rare Tootsietoys 'Huber Star Farm Tractor', no.4654, finished in khaki-green, with red motor and green wheels, in good condition.

1927-32   *13in (33cm) long*

£10-15   AH

A rare Tootsietoys 'Huber Star Army Tractor', no.4654, finished in khaki-green with red wheels, the rear section inscribed 'USA W-1881', in good condition.

Note the ammunition box behind the driver, which differentiates this model from the other tractor shown on this page. This version is scarce as it was only produced 1931-32.

1931-32   *3in (7.5cm) long*

£30-40   AH

A Tootsietoys 'Mac Search-Light Truck', no.4644, finished in green, in excellent condition.

Issued 1931

£18-12   AH

A Tootsietoys 'Ford Tri-Motor' monoplane, no.04649, finished in silver, with rubber wheels, in fair to good condition.

1932   *4in (10cm) long*

£12-18   AH

A Tootsietoys 'Autogyro', no.4659, finished in green, with yellow tinplate main propeller, forward propeller blades missing, in fair condition.

Introduced 1934   *6in (15cm) long*

£30-40   AH

An American painted wood jigger toy, with jointed shoulders, hips, and knees, on a stencilled paddle and blue base with red stripes, with stencilled patent date of December, 1863, with wear commensurate with age, lacks stick.

Jigger toys were popular in the 19thC. The jointed figure 'dances' or 'jigs' manically when the paddle is flicked or moved. American examples tend to fetch more, particularly if they have a strong 'folk art' appeal as this example does.

An early 19thC turned ivory cup and ball game, thread worn, and cup with chips.

Ball 2.25in (5.5cm) diam

£100-150 WW

1863

£300-500 SK

A set of early 20thC Perry and Co.'s 'PATENT AUTOMATON DANCERS', comprising two carved wood figures with wire joints, a box containing a spring-driven movement to make them 'dance', and a wire connecting rod, the lid underside with printed paper label, one figure damaged.

Figure 8.75in (22cm) high

Box 7in (18cm) high

£150-250 CAPE

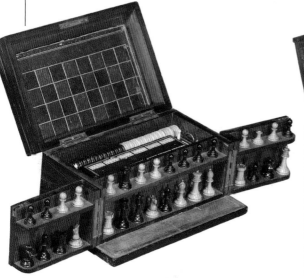

A mid-late Victorian coromandel games compendium, the fitted interior with a cribbage score marker and the playing pieces and boards for backgammon, steeplechase, and chess, two knights and two rooks with the red crown stamp of Jaques of London.

Box 13in (33.5cm) wide

£300-400 DN

An early 19thC Wallis's Manufactory jigsaw map of England and Wales, with details of railways, the wooden puzzle with printed paper, contained in a cedarwood box with printed paper label to lid.

£100-150 WHP

A late Victorian coromandel wood games compendium, enclosing an unmarked bone chest set, a draughts set, a brass-mounted cribbage board and other items, with registration marks for 1869.

12.5in (32cm) wide

£500-600 GORL

A rare Victorian horse racing game, retailed by T. Agnews & Sons of Manchester, with twelve cold-painted metal horses, two leather shakers, and bone markers and counters, with a leather-mounted mahogany racecourse board, contained in a plush-lined fitted mahogany case.

£700-1,000 GORL

TOYS

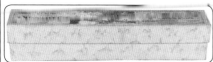

A 1930s Chad Valley 'TAKE TO PIECES' printed cardboard model of the R.M.S. 'Queen Mary', formed of thirteen layers of printed cardboard, with key chart, model and box damaged by damp.

In better condition, this ship with its box and instructions might have sold for over £80.

12in (30cm) long

£12-18   CAPE

A Meccano 'AEROPLANE CONSTRUCTOR' Outfit No. 1, including an Aero Clockwork Motor No. 1, additional parts, with box and instructions, and a No. 2 constructor instruction booklet, box, and contents play-worn.

£180-220   TOV

A 1930s Morris Scaleplanes 'Westland Wallace' red and green painted wood and tinplate biplane, with loose pilot and machine gunner, in near mint condition, with straw-coloured box, original label, and list of models.

£70-100   CAPE

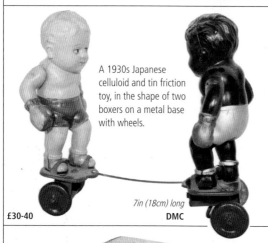

A 1930s Japanese celluloid and tin friction toy, in the shape of two boxers on a metal base with wheels.

7in (18cm) long

£30-40   DMC

A CLOSER LOOK AT A WOODEN MONKEY

Danish designer Kaj Bojesen (1886-1958) studied silversmithing under Georg Jensen, before being attracted by, and turning to, wood in the 1930s.

Between 1934 and 1957 he designed a whole menagerie of animals, of which this monkey was the best-loved. It was so popular in the 1950s that it was exhibited at the Victoria & Albert Museum.

Bojesen believed that his designs should radiate warmth, humour, and life, and also that lines should 'smile', which you can see in the monkey's face.

This is a period original rather than a modern re-issue, and it is also very large, which makes it desirable.

These monkeys are as popular with collectors of Scandinavian Modern design as they are with children.

An Adman 'GRANDSTAND TVG 3600' six-game colour television game console, with gun and original box.

1977

£10-15   CAPE

A large Kaj Bojesen teak articulated monkey, designed by Kaj Bojesen in 1951, stamped 'Kaj Bojesen Denmark'.

18in (46cm) high

£1,000-1,500   DRA

A Hornby 0-gauge clockwork 4-4-2 tank locomotive, No. 2221, finished in GWR green livery with gold and black lining, some playwear.

£100-150   TOV

A Hornby 0-gauge clockwork 2 4-4-4 tank locomotive, with 'LMS 4-4-4' transfers to side tanks, and lamps to buffer beam, in a lined Crimson Lake livery, in very good condition.

£200-300   W&W

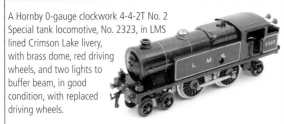

A Hornby 0-gauge clockwork 4-4-2T No. 2 Special tank locomotive, No. 2323, in LMS lined Crimson Lake livery, with brass dome, red driving wheels, and two lights to buffer beam, in good condition, with replaced driving wheels.

£120-180   W&W

A Hornby Dublo 3-rail EDL12 4-6-2 locomotive and tender 'Duchess Of Montrose', No. 46232, British Railways Brunswick green livery, 'L12' under cab roof, in very good condition, with original box with wear and damage to lid.

£60-90   W&W

A Hornby Dublo 3-rail 3226 4-6-2 locomotive and tender 'City Of Liverpool', No. 46247, in British Railways red Crimson Lake livery, in very good condition with minor wear, and with slightly worn box and packaging.

£300-500   W&W

A Hornby Dublo 2-rail 2224 2-8-0 8F freight locomotive and tender, No. 48073, in black LMR livery, in very good condition, and in slightly scuffed original box with two packing rings, with instructions, amended instructions dated June 1961, and guarantee slip.

£100-150   SAS

A Hornby Dublo 3-rail EDG 17 goods train set, comprising an 0-6-2 tank locomotive No. 89567 finished in BR black livery, a tanker truck, two other trucks, and a brake van, boxed, with track and a folding catalogue.

£80-120   TOV

TRAINS

A Bassett-Lowke 0-gauge 4-4-0 clockwork Standard Compound locomotive, No. 1082, in LMS lined Crimson Lake livery, with '1082' transfers to cab side sheets, the B-L standard tender with 'LMS' transfers to sides, with some wear and original box.

£220-280   W&W

A Bing 1-gauge clockwork 4-4-2 'Precusor' tank locomotive, No. 44, in L&NWR black livery, lined in red and white, with 'LNWR' transfers to tank sides, and running number '44' to bunker sides, in good condition with some restoration.

£550-650   VEC

A Bing 1-gauge modified live steam 4-6-0 'Experiment' locomotive and tender, in LNWR black livery, lined in white and red with Experiment over splasher, with running number '66', the tender finished in black with red and white lining, splasher gauge fitted to the top of the tender, in good condition.

£1,000-1,500   VEC

A rare Bing 1-gauge clockwork 0-4-0 tender locomotive, with brass dome and safety valve covers and non-connected outside cylinders, 'RN 1942' transfers to cab side sheets, in LNWR red lined black livery, with a 4-wheel tender, 'LNWR' transfers to sides, in very good condition.

£800-1,200   W&W

A mid-20thC Karl Bub clockwork model railway, with transfer-printed tinplate locomotive and carriages, slightly rusted track, and stained and damaged original card box.

7.5in (20cm) long

£40-60   PC

A 1930s Trix Twin 00-gauge passenger train set, No. 2/334, with two 0-4-0 locomotives and tender no.6200 in maroon and black LMS livery, rake of three twin bogey passenger coaches, two control units and track, the contents in good to fair condition, the box in almost mint condition.

£300-500   CAPE

A Wrenn W2227/A (ins) 4-6-2 'Princess Coronation Class' locomotive 'Sir William A Stanier S. R. S.', No. 6256, in LMS lined black livery, in near mint condition, in near mint condition box.

£350-550   VEC

QUICK REFERENCE - TREEN

- Treen is a generic term for small articles made from wood, such as beech, elm, and chestnut. Typically small, they were mostly intended for use around the home or farm, or in the professions or trades. Popular objects include drinking vessels, jars, bowls, measures, salts, utensils, and spice and snuff boxes.
- Most of the treen available to the collector will date from the late 17thC, with the most desirable pieces mainly dating from around 1720 to the end of the 18thC. During the 19thC, many lower- and middle-class homes replaced many wooden items with mass-produced earthenware or metal equivalents.
- A massive amount of treen was produced during the Victorian period. As the market is larger, mid-late 19thC treen can be more common than early pieces. It has often been ignored by collectors, but can still be interesting.
- Consider the quality of the carving, the wood used, and the age of the piece. Some types of item are more desirable than others, particularly if they are decorative. A warm and rich patination created by decades of daily use is also important to collectors.

A late 18thC turned lignum vitae goblet, with reeded bands to the bowl and spreading base, with knopped stem.

3.75in (9.5cm) high

£150-200   WW

A large 18thC treen salt, with a wide bowl and waisted stem, on a domed foot (foot repaired).

4in (10cm) diam

£150-200   WW

An early 18thC turned lignum vitae dipper cup, with two reeded bands on a collet foot, with small chip to the foot.

2.15in (5.4cm) high

£120-180   WW

An 18thC turned lignum vitae pestle and mortar, with old damages and splits.

Pestle and mortar sets are highly collectable. Lignum vitae is a tightly grained and resilient wood. The wear and damage is a good sign, as it shows authenticity.

10.5in (27cm) high

£300-500   WW

An early 19thC turned treen urn and cover, with a 'hive' finial, raised on a spreading foot.

This well-carved Classical form is desirable, both to treen collectors and interior decorators.

6.25in (16cm) high

£200-300   WW

A late 19thC carved fruitwood spice jar, of waisted cylindrical form, on flared base, the cover with turned knop.

5.5in (14cm) high

£50-80 DA&H

An early 20thC German treen spice box, with printed floral band and landscape depicting buildings in Wartenberg, the cover printed 'Korenka', containing seven lidded jars each with printed name to lid.

6.25in (16cm) diam

£120-180 WW

A CLOSER LOOK AT A PAIR OF BOOKENDS

Robert Thompson (1876-1955) was a notable British furniture maker based in Kilburn, North Yorkshire, whose hand-carved work was founded in the principals of the Arts and Crafts movement. The company is still running today.

As well as having very obvious mice, which is desirable, the colour on these bookends is rich and warm.

A late 18thC lignum vitae coffee mill, with a scrolled iron handle and turned knob, some restoration.

7in (18cm) high

£400-600 SWO

Every piece made is said to have a mouse carved on it somewhere, which is Thompson's signature and nickname. This reportedly came about after he took part in a conversation about being as being 'as poor as a church mouse'.

Bookends are practical objects, which still have relevance and use in today's houses. These two started out life as a pair, which is desirable.

A pair of Robert 'Mouseman' Thompson carved burr oak bookends, each with a single carved mouse.

6in (15cm) high

£650-750 TEN

A set of six 19thC turned lignum vitae coasters, with reeded decoration, contained in a cylindrical box and cover.

4.25in (10.5cm) diam

£150-200 WW

A Robert 'Mouseman' Thompson carved oak double pin-tidy, with carved mouse signature.

This was a gift to Eva Florence Cattle (née Soderquist), nursing sister and midwife, from Robert Thompson's daughter Elsie and his son-in-law Percy Cartwright during the 1930s.

5in (12.5cm) wide

£400-600 TEN

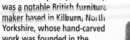

An early 19thC German carved coquilla nut snuff box, modelled as a lion, with damage to mouth.

The coquilla nut comes from the Brazilian feather palm, and is frequently carved into small functional or decorative objects, often by sailors. It begins life cream-coloured, and darkens over time and through use.

3.25in (8.5cm) long

£120-180 GORL

A late 19thC Scandinavian table snuff box, double-end carved in the form of a fish and a duck head, with inscribed and inked decoration in the form of roundels, feathers, and fish.

4.5in (11.4cm) wide

£120-180   TRI

A 19thC carved fruitwood inkwell, modelled as the head of a bearded man with bead eyes, with hinged cover to a brass hinged inkwell with glass liner.

Although not shaped like a dog's or bear's head, as is typical, this may have been a souvenir from the Black Forest, or the surrounding German or Swiss area.

5.25in (13.5cm) high

£80-120   WW

An early 20thC wooden box, the sliding lid with kingfisher terminals and chip-carved decoration.

4.75in (12cm) high

£60-80   WHP

A pair of probably late 19thC turned lignum vitae dumbbells, each with spherical weights connected by swollen handles.

10in (26cm) wide

£180-220   TEN

Miller's Compares

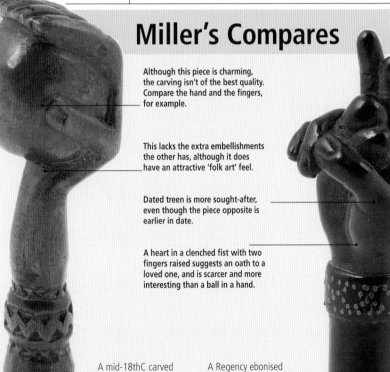

Although this piece is charming, the carving isn't of the best quality. Compare the hand and the fingers, for example.

This lacks the extra embellishments the other has, although it does have an attractive 'folk art' feel.

Dated treen is more sought-after, even though the piece opposite is earlier in date.

A heart in a clenched fist with two fingers raised suggests an oath to a loved one, and is scarcer and more interesting than a ball in a hand.

A mid-18thC carved wood pipe tamper, in the form of a clenched hand holding a ball, with knopped chip-carved handle, the end inscribed 'TT'.

3in (7.5cm) long

£200-250   WW

A Regency ebonised wood and piqué-work pipe tamper, in the form of a hand holding a heart with index and middle fingers raised, dated '1827'.

2.75in (7cm) high

£250-350   WW

An 18ct gold chronograph pocket watch, retailed by Sylvester L. Samuel, 484 Duke St., Liverpool, with gilt fusee lever movement, the white enamel dial with Roman numerals and outer fifths-of-seconds track, case with slide in the band to operate chronograph hand, the case with hallmarks for Chester.

1860 2in (5cm) wide

£550-650   **TEN**

An American Waltham 9ct gold hunter pocket watch, with black Arabic numerals on a white ground, second hand section, and personalised dust cover, on a short 9ct gold watch chain stamped '375'.

£500-600   **WHP**

A 19thC Swiss 10k gold pocket watch, with key-wind movement by Guinand, Genève, the white dial with subsidiary seconds dial, the curvette inscribed 'Examined by Hunt and Roskell, London', the back engine-turned, with key.

4.5in (11.5cm) diam

£300-400   **CAPE**

An American A. W. G. Waltham 14k gold 'William Ellery' hunter pocket watch, with white dial, Roman numerals, outer minute register, subdial for seconds, black spade hands, and set lever, with a gold-filled chain, the inner case stamped 'A.W.Co G5632 14K', the movement stamped 'Wm.Ellery. Pat Pinion Waltham, Mass. 2175131'.

Abraham Lincoln owned and used a Waltham 'William Ellery' model silver cased hunter pocket watch. Numbered '67613', and made in January 1863, it is now in the collection of the National Museum of American History at the Smithsonian in Washington DC.

1883

£350-450   **LHA**

A lady's 'Fine Silver' open-faced pocket watch, with key-wound movement, white dial with Roman numerals, engine-turned case, and key.

1.5in (4cm) diam

£20-30   **CAPE**

A French Art Nouveau Terma white metal pocket watch, with 8-day mechanical lever movement, the green coloured dial with Arabic numerals, the Art Nouveau case depicting a motor car on one side and a figure in robes on the other.

c1915   *2in (5.5cm) wide*

£400-600   **TEN**

A CLOSER LOOK AT A POCKET WATCH

An early 19thC silver pocket watch, with polychrome enamelled dial depicting a church in a landscape with two figures, the dial as a clock in the tower, with Roman numerals, the engraved back plate inscribed 'Nelson, London', numbered '1008'.

£700-1,000   **DUK**

The view shows the south side of the White House, designed by James Hoban, built from 1792-1800, and the official residence of every US President since then.

The heavily embellished case with its chased floral and 'snail' designs, all executed by hand, suggests this watch was made during the late 19thC.

The semi-circular South Portico was added in 1824 and Thomas Jefferson extended it again after moving there in 1801, adding colonnades to conceal stables and storage.

The watch is desirable itself, but the addition of the White House decoration makes this a sought-after piece of Americana.

A Savoye & Son gold open-face pocket watch, the engine-turned dial with raised Roman numerals, secondary dial, and with an engraved vignette of the White House, the case with chased decoration, the engine-turned back with vacant cartouche and elaborately decorated cuvette engraved 'Savoye & Son, Detached Lever Full Jeweled', with key-set and wound gilt movement engraved 'Savoye & Son, No. 1995'.

1.75in (4cm)

£400-600   **SK**

An early 19thC silver fusee verge pair-case pocket watch, the movement signed 'Rich'd Collis, Romford, no. 45386', the painted dial with scenes of silhouettes, a bridge, boats, and windmills, with matching outer cases, with hallmarks for London.

1828   *2.25in (6cm) diam*

£320-380   **GHOU**

An early 19thC silver fusee verge pair-cased pocket watch, the movement signed 'Willm King, London, no. 101919', the painted polychrome dial depicting St. Paul's Cathedral, with black Roman numerals, within plain outer cases, with maker's mark 'T.G.' and hallmarks for London.

1810   *2in (5.5cm) diam*

£320-380   **GHOU**

An early 20thC pocket watch, with key-less movement, base metal case, visible escapement, and dial decorated with a French aerodrome and planes in the sky, with gold-coloured monoplane automata.

£150-200   **GORL**

WATCHES

An early Rolex silver mid-size wristwatch, the white enamel dial with Arabic numerals and red '12', 15-jewel lever-movement, triple signed, with wire lugs and London import marks for 1918.

c1918   *1.25in (3cm) diam*
£150-200   **GHOU**

A Rolex 'Precision' 9ct gold wristwatch, with 17-jewel lever-movement, the silvered dial with applied baton markers, centre seconds, case with maker's mark 'DS&S', hallmarks for London, and stamped 'Rolex'.

1927   *1.25in (3.5cm) wide*
£800-1,200   **TEN**

A Rolex stainless steel wristwatch, with 17-jewel lever-movement and patented superbalance, overcoil hairspring, silvered dial with Arabic and dot markers, centre seconds, reference '4363', case with snap-on back numbered '4363 411387' and stamped 'Rolex 31 Victoires De Haute Precision'.

c1950   *1.5in (3.5cm) wide*
£650-750   **TEN**

A Rolex 'Oyster Quartz Datejust' wristwatch, with stainless steel case, the silvered dial with applied baton markers, date aperture under magnifier, centre seconds, and marked 'Superlative Chronometer Officially Certified', with quartz movement, reference number '17014', with Rolex stainless steel bracelet, original boxes, booklets, and guarantee.

c1994   *1.5in (3.5cm) wide*
£1,000-1,500   **TEN**

A CLOSER LOOK AT A ROLEX WATCH

This two colour 'Bubbleback' with hooded lugs was introduced in 1941, but was not popular and did not sell as well as the model without 'hoods'.

Hooded examples are consequently hard to find today, and generally fetch more than cases without hoods, which were produced from 1934 into the 1950s.

This watch is known as a 'bubble back' as the thick case has a domed back to accommodate Rolex's early automatic motor, which had a 360 degree winding rotor.

Other variations are known, including watches with Arabic numerals or luminous baton markers, a model with a milled bezel produced during the 1940s, and an early model with a subsidiary seconds dial.

A Rolex 'Oyster Perpetual' steel and rolled gold automatic centre seconds wristwatch, with 'Hooded Bubbleback' case, reference number '3065', the movement numbered '56695', the silvered dial with applied dagger markers, blued centre seconds, the case interior numbered '3065'.

c1950   *1.25in (3.5cm) wide*
£3,000-5,000   **TEN**

A Tudor 'Royal' 9ct gentleman's wristwatch, the dial with Arabic quarter numerals, baton markers and centre seconds, shock resisting 'Tudor 1156 ETA 1080' movement, Dennison case, with hallmarks for Birmingham.

Tudor are a less expensive sub-brand of Rolex.

1960   *1.25in (3cm) diam*
£200-300   **GHOU**

An Omega gentleman's gold wristwatch, with striped lever movement numbered '7317258', gold-coloured dial with luminescent Arabic numerals and numerals, subsidiary seconds dial, rectangular shaped case with hinged back numbered '6560674', stained and scuffed.

c1930-35   1.25oz
£650-750   DOR

An Omega 'Seamaster' 18ct gold wristwatch, the 17-jewel lever-movement adjusted to two positions, with silvered dial with applied baton and Arabic numerals, centre seconds, case with snap-on back, with hallmarks for Birmingham, and numbered '873 155312'.

1961   1.25in (3.5cm) wide
£700-1,000   TEN

An Omega 'Constellation' 18ct gold automatic chronometer wristwatch, the 24-jewel automatic lever-movement numbered '18310461', adjusted to five positions and temperature, micrometer regulator, silvered dial with applied baton markers, date aperture, and centre seconds, the case with screw back numbered '14393/4 SC 61', with strap and Omega buckle stamped '18k', together with Omega boxes and purchase receipt dated 1964.

The flagship 'Constellation' series was introduced in 1952, and is known for its very high quality construction and reliability. It was highly successful and, by 1958, 45% of all chronometers sold were 'Constellations'. You can tell this is an earlier model as the word 'Constellation' is not raised on the dial. This watch is in truly superb condition, has an 18ct gold case, and all its original paperwork and box.

c1964   1.5in (3.5cm) wide
£1,500-2,000   TEN

An Omega 'Automatic' 9ct gold gentleman's wristwatch, reference number '1061', numbered '1625422', the two-piece case with silvered dial, and raised baton numerals, hands, centre seconds hand, and date aperture, the jewelled Omega movement numbered '36194073', with hallmarks for London, on a tan strap.

1976   1.5in (4cm) long
£250-350   DN

Mark Picks

As men's fashion has become smarter, with an eye towards vintage styles, more men have begun sporting elegant watches like this one. It has simple and classic styling, typical of the 1950s and '60s, and is by renowned maker Omega, whose vintage watches are enjoying a Renaissance in interest. Along with the 'Constellation', the 'Seamaster' is the most important and notable range the company offered after World War II. Introduced in 1948, it has an automatic movement and combines strength, consistency, and accuracy. The 'De Ville' brand was applied to 'dress' watches, but the waterproof case makes this watch more widely practical. At prices like this for such a clean and appealing watch, why buy a new luxury watch when you can own an original classic?

An Omega 'Seamaster De Ville' gold-plated and stainless steel wristwatch, reference '135.020', with silvered dial, baton numerals, and hands, the 17-jewel 'Omega 501' movement numbered '26673902', on a black strap.

c1968   1.5in (4cm) long including lugs
£250-350   DN

A 1970s Omega 'De Ville' white metal wristwatch, the rectangular white dial with baton markers, movement reference '35189066', the case stamped '800', and the black leather strap with Omega buckle.

'White metal' is the term used to describe metals with a high silver content that do not bear English hallmarks and thus cannot be legally called 'silver' in the UK. Many bear silver marks used in other countries, for example, here the '800' refers to a silver alloy that contains 800 parts of silver to 200 parts other metals. Despite the current fashion for large watches, it's surprising that these late 1960s and '70s watches haven't risen in value yet, which may be due to the fact that most watch collectors don't yet see them as 'important' models. The current trend for these forms is exactly that - a fashion, and may change in the future.

1.75in (4.5cm)
£120-180   GHOU

QUICK REFERENCE - LONGINES

- Longines was founded by Auguste Agassiz in 1832, and is owned by the Swatch Group today. It created its first in-house movements in 1867, and went on to create a number of landmark designs and developments, including special watches for aviators. The Longines name is closely associated with the world of sport, and it has timed fourteen Olympic Games and had links with the Ferrari Formula 1 team. Its 1920s-30s manual, and 1950s automatic and manual watches tend to be more affordable than those by most other luxury Swiss brands, and so represent great value. As well as unusual or Art Deco styled cases, look out for notable ranges such as the 'Admiral' or the 'Conquest', particularly from the 1950s-60s.

A Longines mid-size 18ct gold wristwatch, reference '4310340', the 'cushion' shaped case with white enamel dial, Arabic numerals, arrow hands, and subsidiary seconds dial, the 15-jewel Longines movement calibre '1184N' numbered '4310340', on a later 9ct gold mesh bracelet.

c1935   Case 1in (2.5cm) long

£350-450   **DN**

A Longines military issue stainless steel gentleman's wristwatch, the black dial with Arabic numerals, luminous hands, and subsidiary seconds, with gilt lever movement, no '7434647', the cushion-shaped case with milled bezel.

Military dials were black to avoid light reflecting off a white or silver coloured dial and identifying a soldier's location. Note the Art Deco hands, and the 'cushion'-shaped case that was fashionable from the 1920s-30s.

c1940   1.5in (4cm) long

£700-800   **GHOU**

A Longines 14k gold gentleman's wristwatch, the dial with Arabic quarter numerals, gold baton markers, and subsidiary seconds, with 17-jewel calibre 23z movement, reference number '9892558'.

Produced for the American market, this watch had squared off lugs, which are extremely unusual.

c1955   1in (2.5cm) long

£300-500   **GHOU**

A Longines gentleman's wristwatch, reference number '6085-38', the stainless steel case with silvered dial, baton and Arabic numerals, dauphine hands, and arrow date hand, the 17-jewel Longines calibre 12682 movement numbered '7846370', on a tan leather strap.

c1950   1.75in (4.5cm) long

£300-500   **DN**

A Longines 9ct gold wristwatch, reference number '7132.1', the case with silvered dial, Arabic and baton numerals, and dauphine hands, the 17-jewel Longines calibre 280 movement numbered '11067273', on a green leather strap.

c1959   1.75in (4.5cm) long

£120-180   **DN**

An early 1980s Longines 18k gold 'Feuille D'Or' wristwatch, with plain gilded dial, reference number '19120296', and Longines calibre 'L975' quartz movement.

Although it may not be to everyone's taste, the styling of this watch is typical of the late 1970s and early 1980s. The true importance of the 'Golden Leaf' lies inside. Measuring an incredible 1.98mm in depth, this was the thinnest quartz watch in the world on its release in 1979. The record-breaking movement, which was integrated into the case, was developed by Longines and Ebauches SA (also known as ETA SA).

1in (2.5cm) long

£600-800   **GHOU**

A Longines 'Admiral' automatic stainless steel gentleman's watch, with sweep seconds, date aperture, and calibre L6651 movement.

c1972   1.5in (3.5cm) high

£120-180   **GHOU**

QUICK REFERENCE - BENRUS

- Benrus was founded in New York in 1921 by Romanian immigrant Benjamin Lazarus and his brothers. The name is a combination of the first letters of his forename and the last letters of his surname. Movements were made in Switzerland and cases in Connecticut, where the watches were also assembled.

- Benrus made watches for US servicemen, and built upon its pre-war success during the 1950s. In 1967, after an unsuccessful attempt to take control of its competitor Hamilton, the company was acquired by Victor Kiam. As cheap Far Eastern quartz watches flooded the market, assets were sold off and the name became primarily a brand. Benrus's glory days were over.

- With its high quality movement and solid gold case, this elegant and simple watch would have been expensive and near the top of the range in its day, during the golden age of this well-known American company.

A Bucherer stainless steel 'Green Berets' watch, with matt steel dial, applied block numerals, green baton hands, red second hand, date aperture, and stainless link bracelet, the case stamped '30 ATMS Waterproof Automatic Incabloc Stainless Steel'.

c1970   1.75in (4.5cm) diam

£100-150   LHA

A 1930s Claridge 'jump hour' or 'direct read' gentleman's wristwatch, with gold-filled case with engine-turned barleycorn panel and three apertures showing the hour, minutes, and seconds, with manual movement, on a brown leather strap.

£100-150   CHT

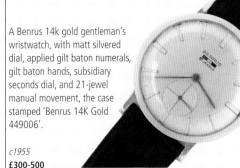

A Benrus 14k gold gentleman's wristwatch, with matt silvered dial, applied gilt baton numerals, gilt baton hands, subsidiary seconds dial, and 21-jewel manual movement, the case stamped 'Benrus 14K Gold 449006'.

c1955

£300-500   LHA

A Jaeger Le Coultre 9ct gold wristwatch, the textured silver circular dial with gilt Arabic numerals and red centre sweep seconds hand, with black leather strap.

c1955

£300-400   CAPE

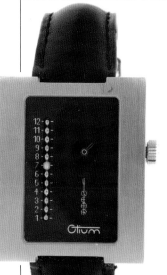

An Otium stainless steel automatic 'Linear' wristwatch, with matt black dial, linear chain-driven hour indication on left side aperture, Arabic numerals, minute subdial, modified Swiss ETA 2893 automatic movement, black leather strap, and original steel buckle, the case back stamped.

Founded by Dirk Hillgruber in 1999, Otium make a range of watches that use unusual indicators to tell the time. Here a series of coloured balls mounted on a chain indicate the hour, with the minutes being read on the dial to the right.

c2000

£650-750   LHA

A late 1960s Rado 'Manhattan' automatic stainless steel gentleman's wristwatch, the blue dial with sweep centre seconds, baton markers, and day and date aperture, with 17-jewel movement, and integral bracelet.

1.25in (3.5cm) wide

£100-150   GHOU

A late 1960s/early 1970s Swiss Rado stainless steel 'Diastar' watch, with matt black dial, silvered baton hands, date aperture, steel elastic bracelet, and manual mechanical movement, the back stamped 'Rado Water Sealed'.

The Rado 'Diastar' was launched in 1962 as the world's first scratch-proof watch. It has been in production ever since, and is now known as 'Diastar The Original'. Signs of wear and the layout of the face indicate vintage examples.

£70-100   LHA

WATCHES

A 1900s Schiaparelli oversized watch, with red face and shaped hands, the gold-plated bezel with large Roman numerals, stamped 'Schiaparelli SWISS MADE'.

Elsa Schiaparelli (1890-1973) was a famous Italian fashion designer, well-known for her hallmark colour, 'Shocking Pink'. Surprisingly, the face on this watch is red instead. Had it been in better condition, with less wear to the numerals and case, it could have fetched up to twice this price, as most watch-buyers buy to wear. Condition counts!

£80-120 LHA

A Tavannes Watch Co. rectangular stainless steel gentleman's wristwatch, the silvered dial with black Arabic numerals and subsidiary seconds, and with 15-jewel calibre 365k movement.
c1938   *1in (2.5cm) long*
£50-70 GHOU

A Universal Genève 18ct gold automatic wristwatch, the textured silvered dial with applied baton markers, with 25-jewel self-winding lever-movement adjusted to two positions and with micro-rotor, the case with snap-on back.
c1965   *1.5in (3.5cm) wide*
£400-600 TEN

An American Waltham Art Deco gentleman's wristwatch, with Arabic numerals and subsidiary seconds dial, with a 21-jewel movement, in a silver stepped case.
c1930
£120-180 PC

Mark Picks

The Swatch collectors market has been in decline since the height of the market during the 1990s. Interest is growing again, but it's highly variable, and unfortunately 'Pop Swatches' have never held the appeal to collectors that usual Swatches have.

Introduced in 1986, these funky watches had an elasticated fabric strap and a frame that the watch body could be clicked in and out of. This allowed the watch to be put into 'Pop Swatch' brooch frames, sweat bands, or pocket watch frames. I could be wrong, but they're so typical of the brash and bold late 1980s style that they could attract a fan base of buyers. My advice would be to go for those that best sum up the style and colours of the period, but the best bet would be to seek out pieces like this watch, which have been designed by top designers, such as Vivienne Westwood.

A Swatch 'Putti' 'Pop Swatch' watch, with original matching elasticated strap, designed in 1992 by Vivienne Westwood, in excellent condition, in original clear plastic case with original receipt dated '12/12/1992', together with instructions.
1992
£50-70 WHP

A 1960s Zenith 18k rose gold gentleman's wristwatch, the silvered dial with baton markers, sweep centre seconds, and date aperture, reference number '453934', with Zenith green leather band and buckle.
1.25in (3.5cm) long
£450-550 GHOU

A Swiss silver and green enamelled pendant watch, the white and blue porcelain dial with gilt accents, Roman numeral hour markers, outer Arabic minute register, and filigree hands, the enamelled case with an enamelled fleur-de-lys brooch, the case stamped 'J. G. Lady Racine Argent 0.800' 770405 Swiss', the movement stamped '788023 Prot'.

c1900   *1in (2.5cm) diam*

£150-200   **LHA**

A Concord 14k gold pendant watch, with matt white dial, applied gilt Roman and baton numerals, and gilt baton hands, the bow motif brooch stamped '14K', the inner case stamped 'Concord W Co S&W 14K Gold 903996', the movement stamped 'Concord Watch Co 17 Seventeen Jewels Swiss 334F unadjusted'.

The watch is mounted upside down so that it can be easily read when pinned onto a lady's jacket.

£80-120   **LHA**

A 1950s Egyptian Meyer Eliakim novelty lapel watch, modelled as a bird in a glazed cage, with eight cut- and rose-cut diamond accents, the copper dial with baton numerals and hands on the base of the cage, with a 17-jewel Pronto Watch Co. calibre GHX movement, signed 'Eliakim Cairo' and numbered '31516', with French control marks.

Based in Cairo, Meyer Eliakim was jeweller to the Egyptian royal family. This unique, bespoke piece was originally owned by an Egyptian racehorse owner.

1.5in (4cm) long

£600-800   **DN**

A rare and unusual Swiss Rolex 'Precision' 18ct gold pendant watch, in the form of a lantern, with a lever movement, 'Superbalance' patent escapement, guilloché dial with applied hour chevrons, and glazed casing.

c1950   *1.25in (3cm) high 0.6oz (16.8g)*

£2,000-3,000   **DOR**

A CLOSER LOOK AT A MOVADO CLOCK

The case slides open and closed to protect the watch face when travelling. This action also winds the watch mechanism.

This large 6in (15cm) wide model is scarce. Its size and the back strut indicates that it was meant to be used on a bedside table, rather than carried around.

Released by Movado in 1926, the model is known as the 'Ermeto', and was produced into the 1940s.

Look out for examples with added complications, such as moon phases, and days and months, or those in precious metal cases or with costly embellishments, such as Japanese maki-e lacquer.

A Swiss Movado oversized 'Pullman' travelling 'Frmeto' alarm clock, with black snakeskin covered case containing an 8-day mechanism, back-mounted strut support, alarm setting button to the winding crown, and numbered '711605', the whole face with Arabic numerals.

6in (15cm) wide

£600-800   **DN**

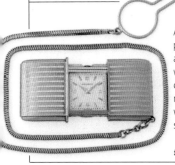

A Swiss Movado 18ct gold 'Ermeto' purse watch, the silvered dial with applied Arabic and baton markers, with sliding, ribbed decorated case to wind the mechanical lever-movement, the inside case back with engraved inscription, the case stamped '750'.

2in (5cm) wide

£1,000-1,500   **TEN**

An Art Deco Vacheron & Constantin for Finnigans 18ct gold purse watch, with signed 15-jewel lever movement numbered '410447', adjusted to five positions, bimetallic compensation balance (winding stem missing), silvered dial with applied Arabic numerals, the case numbered '11647', with front-opening shutters operated by depressing the sides of the case.

Finnigans were a high-end, luxury maker and retailer, founded in 1875. It grew to have stores in London, Manchester, and Liverpool.

1.75in (4.5cm)

£550-750   **TEN**

QUICK REFERENCE

- Glass wine bottles were introduced in the early 17thC, and were sealed with wooden pegs. Before that, wine was kept in ceramic vessels or casks. Corks were introduced to seal bottles in the late 17thC, and corkscrews were developed shortly after. Today the corkscrew is one of the most widely sought-after and valuable wine-related collectable.
- Corkcrews can be divided into two broad categories: the 'straight-pull', where the brute force of the user draws the cork out, and the 'mechanical', where a mechanism helps to draw out the cork. The latter type tends to be the most desirable and valuable, and saw its 'golden age' of variety and invention during the Victorian era.
- Thomason-types, with their ingenious double helix mechanism, and rack-and-pinion operated King's screws are among the more valuable mechanical types. Look out for names such as Dowler, Lund, and Robert Jones.

- Do not ignore novelty forms, as these can be sought-after, especially if they are witty or amusing. The same applies to other wine and drinking accessories or memorabilia, which saw their heyday between the 1920s and the 1950s.
- Born in Prohibition America, the cocktail shaker is still with us today. Look out for novelty shapes such as zeppelins, planes, and even polar bears, as such pieces can fetch high sums if from a desirable period. The quality and materials of the shaker, as well as its date, will affect value. The name of the maker or retailer will affect value too, with names such as Asprey, Revere, and Chase being highly sought-after. Some were by notable designers, and this too can increase value.
- Novelty shakers and bar accessories made during the 1950s to 1970s can be collectable, but most pieces are not valuable. Typically brightly coloured with jaunty patterns, the sense of fun is more important than the quality, which is usually low.

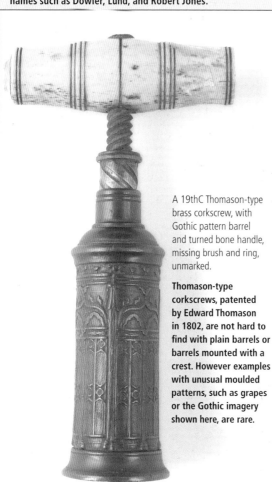

A 19thC Thomason-type brass corkscrew, with Gothic pattern barrel and turned bone handle, missing brush and ring, unmarked.

Thomason-type corkscrews, patented by Edward Thomason in 1802, are not hard to find with plain barrels or barrels mounted with a crest. However examples with unusual moulded patterns, such as grapes or the Gothic imagery shown here, are rare.

£1,200-1,800   WW

A 19thC Thomason-type brass corkscrew, with turned rosewood handle, lacking brush.

£180-220   DA&H

A 19thC Thomason-type brass corkscrew, with a bone handle, mounted with a Royal crest.

7in (18cm) long

£150-200   LC

A small 19thC Thomason-type brass corkscrew, with ringed barrel and horn handle.

6.5in (17cm) long

£50-80   ECGW

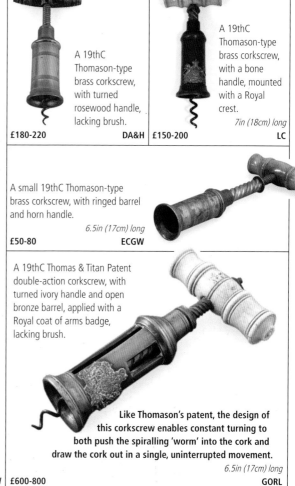

A 19thC Thomas & Titan Patent double-action corkscrew, with turned ivory handle and open bronze barrel, applied with a Royal coat of arms badge, lacking brush.

Like Thomason's patent, the design of this corkscrew enables constant turning to both push the spiralling 'worm' into the cork and draw the cork out in a single, uninterrupted movement.

6.5in (17cm) long

£600-800   GORL

WINE & DRINKING

A late Victorian brass and steel corkscrew, the turned ebony handle lacking a brush.

8in (20cm) high

£100-150   **CAPE**

A 19thC 'King's Screw'-type Patent brass corkscrew, with a bone handle and brush, worm damaged.

£150-200   **LC**

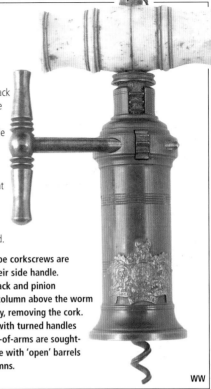

A 19thC narrow-rack 'King's Screw'-type corkscrew, with a turned bone handle lacking its brush, the barrel with an applied tablet with the Royal coat of arms, marked 'Patent', traces of gilt, with grooved wire helix, reduced.

A 19thC cast iron mechanical 'King's Screw'-type corkscrew, the column stamped 'LUND PATENT LONDON', the turned wooden handle with brush, with signs of rust and wear.

£150-200   **TEN**

'King's Screw'-type corkscrews are recognised by their side handle. Operating on a rack and pinion mechanism, the column above the worm is raised vertically, removing the cork. Large examples with turned handles and ornate coats-of-arms are sought-after, as are those with 'open' barrels made up of columns.

£250-350   **WW**

WANTED BOTTLES

ALL PURCHASES MADE IN CONFIDENCE
RARE ITEMS PURCHASED FROM OVERSEAS
COLLECTION NATIONWIDE
BREWERIANA & WHISKIANA

WANTED: Full Bottles of Whisky + Spirits, Labels, Advertising, Enamels, Figures, Mirrors, Posters, Ephemera, Dispensers, Doulton - Artware Flagons plus KINGSWARE

GORDON
the 'OLD BOTTLEMAN'
25 Stapenhill Road
Burton-on-Trent DE15 9AE
Tel: 01283·567·213
Mobile: 07952·118·987
Please Telephone between 9am and 7pm

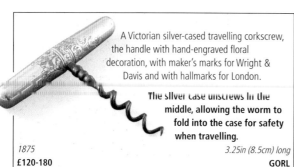

A Victorian silver-cased travelling corkscrew, the handle with hand-engraved floral decoration, with maker's marks for Wright & Davis and with hallmarks for London.

The silver case unscrews in the middle, allowing the worm to fold into the case for safety when travelling.

1875
3.25in (8.5cm) long
£120-180
GORL

A late 18th/early 19thC straight-pull pocket corkscrew, with a turned horn handle, the worm with a grooved helix, the silver sheath initialled 'E. V.' within a shield with wriggle-work borders, unmarked, handle chipped.

Smaller examples of this form, with similar tapering cylindrical silver sheaths, are often Dutch in origin.
3.5in (9cm) long

£450-550
WW

A CLOSER LOOK AT A CORKSCREW

This was effectively the 19thC equivalent of a 'Swiss army' pocket knife and includes a number of tools such as a button hook, corkscrew, and pick. This sort of device is collectable today.

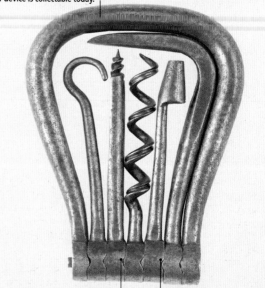

Each tool folds out for use, with the protecting bow frame acting as a practical handle. The larger the piece and the more tools there are, the higher the value.

Holtzapffel, founded in 1792 in London, are the best and most desirable maker of this type of object. They became renowned for their complex tool benches and lathes.

Holtzapffel pieces also attract tool collectors, which helps to push the price up on pieces like this. Without the name, this piece would be worth a fraction of its current value.

A 19thC Holtzapffel steel folding bow, stamped 'HOLTZAPFFEL', with five tools including a corkscrew with a grooved helix.
£400-600
WW

A late 19th/early 20thC champagne bottle-shaped corkscrew, with ivory panels, faintly marked 'P. Millot, Eperney', with a wire helix, master blade, and foil cutter.
£150-200
WW

A left handed combination pocket knife and corkscrew, with a grooved helix and three blades, two marked 'Hubert. M. Fawsitt & Co., Sheffield'.
£120-180
WW

A 20thC brass novelty corkscrew, modelled as a revolver, the barrel covering the wire helix.
£15-20
WW

A 1930s pair of Asprey & Co. silver-plated novelty cocktail shakers, modelled as dumbbells, the bases marked 'Asprey London, 3138, pat. applied for 20510/35'.

10.5in (27cm) high

£800-1,200 **GORL**

A 20thC silver-plated 'One & Half Pint' novelty cocktail shaker, in the form of a handbell, with turned wooden handle.

Certain parts of the US were under Prohibition (in which the production, sale, and transportation of 'intoxicating liquors' was prohibited) from 1920 until 1933. As well as creating a strong black market, this period saw the golden age of cocktails made using illegally created alcoholic drinks, nicknamed 'moonshine' or 'hooch'. Many cocktail shakers were disguised as everyday objects, with bells being popular. This novelty form continued to be produced long after Prohibition ended.

£150-250 **TOV**

A CLOSER LOOK AT A COCKTAIL SHAKER

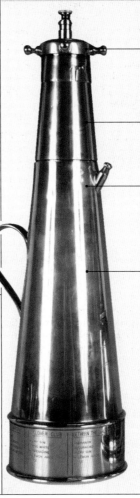

Made by high quality maker John Turton & Co. of Sheffield, this piece was retailed by Asprey & Co., who added it to their range in 1932.

Wittily themed, novelty shaped cocktail shakers from the glamour of the inter-war period are the most popular - and expensive - category of cocktail shakers.

Shaped like a 1930s fire extinguisher, this cocktail shaker has a base that revolves to reveal the ingredients for eight classic cocktails.

Its popularity on the vintage market has meant that Asprey have reintroduced it with a current retail price of £4,500. The marks on the base of modern examples are different to vintage examples.

A 1930s Asprey & Co. silver-plated 'The Thirst Extinguisher' novelty cocktail shaker, of conical form with inscribed shield-shaped label and loop handle, the rotating base section inscribed with eight various cocktail ingredients, the base marked 'A & Co, Asprey, London 3212' and with registered number '233773' for 1894.

15in (37.5cm) high

£800-1,200 **TOV**

An early 20thC Continental electroplate Zeppelin-shaped cocktail shaker, in a leather carry case, unsigned.

Beware, as this popular form has been reproduced in modern times, as have aeroplane-shaped examples. Authentic examples will show signs of age and wear, and are typically not silver-plated.

12in (30cm) wide

£1,000-1,500 **WW**

A 20thC silver-plated cylindrical cocktail shaker, with a scalloped mushroom-shaped lid, together with six silver-plated conical cocktail goblets, three shown.

£70-100 **CAPE**

An early 20thC Chinese silver cocktail shaker, of tapering form with detachable lid and filter, the textured ground with plain banding.

8.75in (22cm) high 10.6oz

£150-200   **AH**

A 1930s Japanese cocktail shaker and five matched conical goblets, decorated in black lacquer and gilt paint with a cockerel seated on a flowering blossom bough.

£30-50   **FLD**

A mid-20thC silver cocktail shaker, with plain finish and a knurled border around the cover, stamped with maker's mark 'P&S', and with hallmarks for Birmingham.

1960   *9in (23cm) high 18oz*

£300-500   **LC**

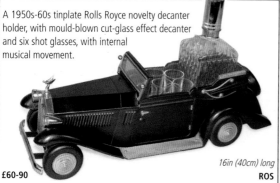

A 1950s-60s tinplate Rolls Royce novelty decanter holder, with mould-blown cut-glass effect decanter and six shot glasses, with internal musical movement.

16in (40cm) long

£60-90   **ROS**

QUICK REFERENCE - CHASE

- Chase are a highly sought-after and important name in vintage American metalware. Founded in 1876, the company's initial production was largely created for industrial or military use.
- The company began producing homewares during the 1930s and early 1940s. A number of key designers were hired to work on the new range, including Russel Wright, Walter von Nessen, and Howard Reichen. Its in-house designer was Harry Laylon.
- Designs were strongly Art Deco in style, matching the fashions of the day. This smart and glamorous set captures that look perfectly. The chrome-plated finish, the clean, geometric lines, and bold blue glass shout out the style, and the cocktail shaker even mimics one of the skyscrapers that were being built at the time.

A 1930s American Chase 'Blue Moon' Art Deco cocktail set, designed by Howard Reichen, comprising eleven goblets with blue glass bowls, a cocktail shaker, matching tray, and four bottle coasters.

£300-500   **DRA**

A 1920s-30s travelling cocktail set, the brown leather suitcase fitted with compartments containing a cocktail shaker, four metal mounted glass bottles, and a box, with a mixing spoon to the lid.

Late Victorian and Edwardian fitted travelling dressing cases filled with a myriad of bottles can be hard to sell, even if the bottle tops are in silver and the set is by a great maker. It's down to practicality - what do we do with them now? The opposite is true of this set, which could easily be used today for picnics or glamorous visits to events such as horse races. Had the condition been better (look at the handle) the price might have been higher, and it certainly would have been higher if this set had been by a notable maker or in silver.

£500-700   **WW**

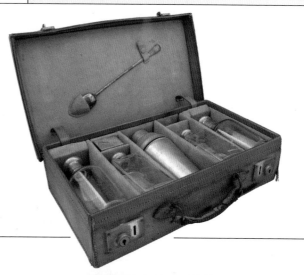

A 1930s bottle opener, with carved Catalin handle.

6.25in (16cm) long

£20-30   P&I

A 1930s P. H. Vogel & Co. Catalin dice and silver-plated cocktail shot measure, stamped 'P.H.V. & Co. EPNS MADE IN ENGLAND'.

4.25in (11cm) high

£60-70   BEV

A CLOSER LOOK AT A CLASSIC COCKTAIL BOOK

Harry Craddock left Prohibition America to join London's world famous Savoy hotel in 1920. Within a few years he had become renowned for his cocktails and, among a wealthy clientele, one of the best-loved barmen in the world.

Craddock's name is legendary. He is said to have popularised the dry martini, and invented the Corpse Reviver.

Although the book has never gone out of print, this is a first edition from the first year it was published, and so is highly desirable to cocktail cognoscenti.

The striking and dramatic cover artwork is typical of the Art Deco style.

If this copy had been in better condition, it would have fetched more.

Harry Craddock, 'The Savoy Cocktail Book', first edition, published by Constable & Company, London.

1930

£250-350   WW

A French silver-gilt combination cocktail spoon and sugar crusher, the reverse of the bowl with oak leaf decoration, with maker's mark of 'J.D.' in a lozenge.

7in (17cm) long

£120-180   WW

A modern latticework wine bottle cradle, with 'JHL' makers' marks and hallmarks for London.

1970   *10.75in (27.2cm) long, 10.5oz*

£200-300   WW

A large 19thC pottery wine barrel, decorated with a brown glaze and bearing the inscription 'John + Gould his bottle'.

8in (21.5cm) high

£350-450   WW

QUICK REFERENCE - RHINO TAXIDERMY

- The few years prior to 2011 saw rhinoceros taxidermy fetching increasingly large sums of money at auction. Some examples that had been forgotten in country house collections for decades were selling for over £100,000 as the predominantly Chinese buyers vied to own the largest examples. These horns were not for display, but for use, as the rhinoceros horn is deemed to have medicinal properties by the Chinese, South Koreans, and some other nationalities.
- In early 2011, the British government introduced new laws banning the sale of horns that have not been 'worked', or those where the artistic merit is unclear. As such, mounted horns or heads are now banned from sale. A carved libation cup worked before 1947, or rhino horns with more decorative treatments can be sold.
- Whilst undoubtedly helping conserve living rhinos, the ban led to a spate of thefts of these carved and mounted rhino horns from museums, auction houses, and country houses.

A taxidermy mounted white rhinoceros (Eratotherium simum) horn, on a specially prepared chamfered and angled raised skin pad, the whole mounted on an original oak shield.

c1900   *Lower horn 24.75in (63cm) long*

£20,000-30,000   **TEN**

A 18thC/19thC whalebone fid, crudely monogrammed to the top 'JAL'.

I've heard loads of suggestions for what this spike might be used for, the most outlandish of which is that it's a stake to kill a vampire! That may be possible, but a fid is actually a sailmaker's tool, used for a variety of tasks such as opening holes or knots in canvas. The term is also used as a unit of measurement for rope, and is used by the Canadian Navy to describe a stupid person. A fid is sometimes mounted decoratively to make an abstract sculpture, which is sometimes classed as folk art.

13in (33cm) long

£800-1,200   **SWO**

A fossilised mammoth tooth.

7.5in (19cm) long

£200-250   **DOR**

A group of nine prehistoric coprolites.

Coprolites are fossilised animal dung! They are useful for paleontologists as they indicate what food dinosaurs ate. When they were discovered in the abdominal areas of dinosaur skeletons, scientists initially believed they were swallowed stones!

Largest 6in (15cm) diam

£150-250   **GORB**

A rare early 19thC brass cannon ball shot gauge, comprising fourteen rings ranging from sizes 1 to 42.

10in (25cm) diam

£2,200-2,800   **GORL**

A late 19thC/early 20thC air gun walking cane, with a black painted metal shaft and turned wood knop, lacking pump.

Concealed weapons, such as sword sticks and this air gun, are illegal in many states or countries, and cannot be carried in public. Similarly many countries or states ban their sale.

39.5in (100cm) long

£300-500   **GHOU**

A silver mechanical cucumber slicer, with maker's marks for Roger Sparrow and hallmarks for London, the open frame with rods supporting a screw-thread with a moveable back plate, the steel rotating blade with a wooden handle.

This rather unneccessary and luxurious kitchen applicance fetched as much money as it did primarily because of the quantity and value of the raw material it's made from. At the time of its sale, the price for an ounce of silver had risen dramatically, reaching a high of £30.16 in April 2011.

1989   *9.75in (25cm) long 18.5oz (576g) gross*

£400-600   **DN**

A 19thC decalcomania vase and cover, with chinoiserie motifs.

Decalcomania was developed in the mid-18thC and saw the height of its popularity in the mid-19thC. The design of a print or painting is transferred in ink to a surface, typically of a vessel like a vase. In some instances, the print itself is applied, almost like découpage with Victorian 'scraps'. It led to the more widely understood term, 'decal', which is still in use today.

20in (51cm) high

£700-1,000   **LC**

A 19thC 'potichomania' witch's ball, internally applied with numerous decals of flowers, birds, insects, and sea shells, featuring green tinted metal.

Potichomania is the term used to describe glass vessels that have been decorated on the inside with engravings or paintings to imitate painted porcelain. Witches' balls were hung in British homes during the late 18thC and 19thC to ward off witches and evil spirits. They are typically green or blue in colour, and can be as large as 7in (18cm) in diameter.

5.75in (14.5cm) diam

£400-600   **TEN**

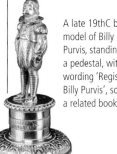

A late 19thC brass model of Billy Purvis, standing on a pedestal, with wording 'Registered Billy Purvis', sold with a related book.

Billy Purvis (1784-1853), known as the 'Jester of the North', was a well-known clown and illusionist who owned a travelling theatre, which was based in Newcastle and performed at races and fairs across the North. Despite his fame in the area, he died in poverty while travelling, and is buried at St. Hilda's in Hartlepool.

£120-180   **A&G**

A Sun Fire Office cast lead fire insurance fire mark, with a raised sun face, numbered '421858'.

These 'fire marks' were hung on the outside of houses and related to the fire insurance company that the home owner had a policy with. There were many such companies, and they were highly competitive before they began to amalgamate into larger corporations. The Sun Fire Office company was active 1706-1959.

6.75in (17cm) high

£200-250   **ECGW**

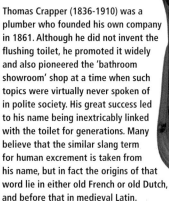

A late Victorian Thomas Crapper & Co. 'Invictas Washdown Closet' ceramic lavatory bowl, transfer-printed with floral decoration, with registered number '155245' for 1890.

Thomas Crapper (1836-1910) was a plumber who founded his own company in 1861. Although he did not invent the flushing toilet, he promoted it widely and also pioneered the 'bathroom showroom' shop at a time when such topics were virtually never spoken of in polite society. His great success led to his name being inextricably linked with the toilet for generations. Many believe that the similar slang term for human excrement is taken from his name, but in fact the origins of that word lie in either old French or old Dutch, and before that in medieval Latin.

1890   *17in (43cm) high*

£30-40   **ECGW**

Every item illustrated in the Miller's Collectables by Judith Miller and Mark Hill has a letter code that identifies the dealer, auction house or private collector that owns or sold it. In this way the source of the item can be identified. The list below is a key to these codes. In the list, auction houses are shown by the letter A, dealers by the letter D, and private collectors by the letters PC. Inclusion in this book in no way constitutes or implies a contract or a binding offer on the part of any of our contributors to supply or sell the goods illustrated, or similar items, at the prices stated.

A&G Ⓐ
ANDERSON & GARLAND
Anderson House, Crispin Court,
Newbiggin Lane, Westerhope,
Newcastle upon Tyne NE5 1BF
Tel: 0191 430 3000
info@andersonandgarland.com
www.andersonandgarland.com

AH Ⓐ
ANDREW HARTLEY
Victoria Hall Salerooms,
Little Lane, Ilkley LS29 8EA
Tel: 01943 816 363
info@hartleysauctions.co.uk
www.andrewhartleyfinearts.co.uk

AMER Ⓐ
AMERSHAM AUCTION ROOMS
Station Road,
Amersham-on-the-Hill HP7 0AH
Tel: 01494 729 292
info@amershamauctionrooms
.co.uk
www.amershamauctionrooms
.co.uk

ANT Ⓓ
THE ANTIQUE GALLERY
8523 Germantown Avenue,
Philadelphia. PA 19118, USA
Tel: 001 215 248 1700
www.antiquegal.com

BAD Ⓓ
BETH ADAMS
Stands G023-25/28-30
and SO59-60,
Alfies Antique Market,
13-25 Church Street,
Marylebone, London NW8 8DT
Mob: 07776 136 003
www.alfiesantiques.com

BEJ Ⓓ
BÉBÉS ET JOUETS
Tel: 01289 304 802
bebesetjouets@tiscali.co.uk

BEL Ⓓ
BELHORN AUCTION SERVICES
9387 South Old State Road,
Lewis Center, OH 43025, USA
Tel: 001 614 921 9441
auctions@belhorn.com
www.belhornauctions.com

BELL Ⓐ
BELLMANS AUCTIONEERS
Newpound, Wisborough Green,
Billingshurst,
West Sussex RH14 0AZ
Tel: 01403 700858
enquiries@bellmans.co.uk
www.bellmans.co.uk

BER Ⓓ
BERTOIA AUCTIONS
2141 De Marco Drive
Vineland, NJ 08360, USA
Tel: 001 856 692 1881
www.bertoiaauctions.com

BEV Ⓓ
BEVERLEY ADAMS
No longer trading

BGL Ⓟ
BLOCK GLASS LTD
blockglss@aol.com
www.blockglass.com

BH Ⓓ
**BLACK HORSE ANTIQUES
SHOWCASE**
2180 North Reading Road,
P.O. Box 343, Denver, PA 17517,
USA
Tel: 001 717 336 844/
www.blackhorselodge.com/
Antiques.asp

BLNY Ⓐ
**BLOOMSBURY AUCTIONS
NEW YORK**
No longer trading.
Enquires to Bloomsbury, London

BLO Ⓐ
BLOOMSBURY AUCTIONS
24 Maddox Street W1S 1PP
Tel: 020 7495 9494
info@bloomsburyauctions.com
www.bloomsburyauctions.com

BPH Ⓓ
BATTERSEA PEN HOME
P.O. Box 6128,
Epping CM16 4GG
Tel: 01992 578 885
orders@penhome.co.uk
www.penhome.co.uk

BR Ⓓ
BEYOND RETRO
110-112 Cheshire Street,
London E2 6EJ
Tel: 02076 133 636
www.beyondretro.com

CA Ⓐ
CHISWICK AUCTIONS
1 Colville Road, London W3 8BL
Tel: 02089 924 442
info@chiswickauctions.co.uk
www.chiswickauctions.co.uk

CANS Ⓓ
CANDY SAYS
Tel: 01277 212 134
www.candysays.co.uk

CAPE Ⓐ
CAPES DUNN
The Auction Galleries, 38 Charles
Street, Manchester M1 7DB
Tel: 0161 273 1911
capesdunn@googlemail.com
www.capesdunn.com

CARS Ⓓ
**THE LALIQUE MASCOT
COLLECTORS' CLUB**
The White Lion Garage
Clarendon Place, Kemp Town,
Brighton BN2 1JA
Tel: 01273 622 722 or
07890 836 734
laliqueclub@virginmedia.com
www.carsofbrighton.co.uk

CAT Ⓓ
CATALIN RADIO
5439 Schultz Drive
Sylvania, OH 43560, USA
sales@catalinradio.com
www.catalinradio.com

CBA Ⓓ
COMIC BOOK AUCTIONS LTD
P.O. Box 58386
London NW1W 9RE
Tel: 02074 240 007
www.compalcomics.com

CHT Ⓐ
CHARTERHOUSE
The Long Street Salerooms,
Sherborne DT9 3BS
Tel: 01935 812 277
www.charterhouse-auction.com

CLV Ⓐ
CLEVEDON SALEROOMS
Kenn Road, Kenn, Clevedon,
Bristol BS21 6TT
Tel: 01934 830 111
info@clevedon-salerooms.com
www.clevedon-salerooms.com

CWD Ⓓ
COLLECTORS WORLD
118 Wollaton Road, Wollaton,
Nottingham NG8 1HJ
info@collectorsworld-nottingham.
com
www.collectorsworld-nottingham.
com

DA&H Ⓐ
DEE, ATKINSON & HARRISON
The Exchange, Exchange Street,
Driffield YO25 6LD
Tel: 01377 253 151
www.dahauctions.com

DCP Ⓓ
THE DUNLOP COLLECTION
PO Box 6269, Statesville,
NC 28687 USA
Tel: 001 871 2626
dunloppaperweights@mac.com

DMC Ⓐ
DUMOUCHELLES
409 East Jefferson Avenue,
Detroit, MI 48226, USA
Tel: 001 313 963 6255
www.dumouchelles.com

DODA Ⓓ
DODA ANTIQUES
434 Richards Street Vancouver, BC,
Canada
Tel: 001 604 602 0559
www.dodaantiques.com

DOR Ⓐ
DOROTHEUM
Palais Dorotheum, Dorotheergasse
17, 1010 Vienna, Austria
Tel: 0043 1 515 600
www.dorotheum.com

DN Ⓐ
DREWEATTS
Donnington Priory, Donnington,
Newbury RG14 2JE
Tel: 01635 553 553
donnington@dnfa.com
www.dnfa.com

DRA Ⓐ
DAVID RAGO AUCTIONS
333 North Main Street, Lambertville,
NJ 08530, USA
Tel: 001 609 397 9374
info@ragoarts.com
www.ragoarts.com

DS Ⓐ
DUNBAR SLOANE
7 Maginnity Street, Wellington
6011, New Zealand
Tel: 04 472 1367
info@dunbarsloane.co.nz
www.dunbarsloane.com

DSC Ⓟ
DOLL SHOWCASE
squibbit@ukonline.co.uk
www.britishdollshowcase.co.uk

DUK Ⓐ
DUKE'S
The Dorchester Fine Art Saleroom,
Weymouth Avenue, Dorchester
DT1 1QS
Tel: 01305 265 080
enquiries@dukes-auctions.com
www.dukes-auctions.com

ECGW Ⓐ
**EWBANK CLARKE GAMMON
WELLERS**
Burnt Common Auction Rooms
London Road, Send, Woking
Surrey GU23 7LN
Tel: 01483 223 101
antiques@ewbankauctions.co.uk
www.ewbankauctions.co.uk

EG Ⓓ
EDISON GALLERY
900 South Clinton, Chicago,
IL 60607, USA
Tel: 001 312 832 9800
glastris@edisongallery.com
www.edisongallery.com

FIS Ⓐ
DR. FISCHER
Trappensee-Schlösschen
74074 Heilbronn, Germany
Tel: 0049 7131 15557 0
info@auctions-fischer.de
www.auctions-fischer.de

FLD Ⓐ
FIELDING'S
Mill Race Lane, Stourbridge,
West Midlands DY8 1JN
Tel: 01384 444 140
info@fieldingsauctioneers.co.uk
www.fieldingsauctioneers.co.uk

FRE Ⓐ
FREEMAN'S
1808 Chestnut Street,
Philadelphia, PA 19103, USA
Tel: 001 215 563 9275
info@freemansauction.com
www.freemansauction.com

GAZE Ⓐ
T. W. GAZE
Diss Auction Rooms,
Roydon Road, Diss IP22 4LN
Tel: 01379 650 306
sales@dissauctionrooms.co.uk
www.twgaze.com

GBA Ⓐ
GRAHAM BUDD AUCTIONS
P.O. Box 47519,
London N14 6XD
Tel: 020 8366 2525 or
07974 113 394
gb@grahambuddauctions.co.uk
www.grahambuddauctions.
co.uk

GC Ⓟ Ⓒ
GRAHAM COOLEY COLLECTION
Tel: 07968 722 269
gc@itm-power.com

GCHI Ⓓ
THE GIRL CAN'T HELP IT!
Alfies Antiques Market,
Stands G80/90 & 100,
13-25 Church Street,
London NW8 8DT
Tel: 020 7724 8984 or
07958 515 614
sparkle@sparklemoore.com
www.thegirlcanthelpit.com

GHOU Ⓐ
GARDINER HOULGATE
9 Leafield Way, Corsham,
Bath SN13 9SW
Tel: 01225 812 912
auctions@gardinerhoulgate
.co.uk
www.gardinerhoulgate.co.uk

GORB & GORL Ⓐ
GORRINGES
Garden Street, Lewes BN7 1XE
Tel: 01424 478 221
gardenst@gorringes.co.uk
www.gorringes.co.uk

H&C Ⓐ
HISTORICAL & COLLECTABLE
Kennetholme, Midgham
Reading RG7 5UX
Tel: 01189 712 420
www.historicalandcollectable.com

H&G Ⓐ
HOPE & GLORY
No longer trading

H&L Ⓐ
BEARNES, HAMPTON &
LITTLEWOOD
St Edmund's Court, Okehampton
Street, Exeter, Devon EX4 1DU
Tel: 01392 413100
info@bhandl.co.uk
www.bhandl.co.uk

HERR Ⓐ
HERR AUCTIONS
Friesenwall 35, 50672 Cologne,
Germany
Tel: 0049 221 25 45 48
kunst@herr-auktionen.de
www.herr-auktionen.de

HSR Ⓓ
HANS VINTAGE FOUNTAIN PENS
www.hanspens.com

IMC Ⓐ
I. M. CHAIT
9330 Civic Center Drive
Beverly Hills, CA 90210, USA
Tel: 001 310 285-0182
chait@chait.com
www.chait.com

JDJ Ⓐ
JAMES D JULIA INC
203 Skowhegan Road,
Fairfield, ME 04937, USA
Tel: 001 207 453 7125
info@jamesdjulia.com
www.jamesdjulia.com

JPC Ⓟ Ⓒ
JINDRICH PARIK COLLECTION
http://www.webareal.cz/
ceskoslovenskesklo

KAU Ⓐ
AUKTIONSHAUS KAUPP
Schloss Sulzburg, Hauptstraße 62
79295 Sulzburg, Germany
Tel: 0049 76 34 50 38 0
auktionen@kaupp.de
www.kaupp.de

KT Ⓐ
KERRY TAYLOR AUCTIONS
Unit C21, Parkhall Road Trading
Estate, 40 Martell Road, London,
SE21 8EN
Tel: 020 8676 4600
info@kerrytaylorauctions.com
www.kerrytaylorauctions.com

L&T Ⓐ
LYON AND TURNBULL LTD.
33 Broughton Place,
Edinburgh EH1 3RR
Tel: 0131 557 8844
info@lyonandturnbull.com
www.lyonandturnbull.com

LC Ⓐ
LAWRENCES
The Linen Yard, South Street,
Crewkerne, Somerset TA18 8AB
Tel: 01460 73041
enquiries@lawrences.co.uk
www.lawrences.co.uk

LHA Ⓐ
LESLIE HINDMAN AUCTIONEERS
1338 West Lake Street, Chicago,
IL 60607
Tel: 312.280.1212
www.lesliehindman.com

LHT Ⓟ Ⓒ
LEANDA HARWOOD
Private collector

LOC Ⓐ
LOCKE & ENGLAND
18 Guy Street,
Leamington Spa CV32 4RT
Tel: 01926 889 100
info@leauction.co.uk
www.leauction.co.uk

LSK Ⓐ
LACY SCOTT & KNIGHT
10 Risbygate Street, Bury St
Edmunds, Suffolk IP33 3AA
Tel: 01284 748 623
fineart@lsk.co.uk
www.lskauctioncentre.co.uk

M20C Ⓓ
MID20THC
No longer trading

MA Ⓓ
MANIC ATTIC
Alfies Antiques Market, Stand
S48/49, 13-25 Church Street,
London NW8 8DT
Tel: 020 7723 6066
ianbroughton@hotmail.com
www.memoriespostcards.co.uk

MAI Ⓐ
MOORE, ALLEN & INNOCENT
The Norcote Salerooms, Burford
Road, Norcote, Nr Cirencester,
Gloucestershire GL7 5RH
fineart@mooreallen.co.uk
www.mooreallen.co.uk

MAR Ⓐ
FRANK MARSHALL
Marshall House, Church Hill,
Knutsford, Cheshire WA16 6DH
Tel: 01565 653284
antiques@frankmarshall.co.uk
www.frankmarshall.co.uk

MDM Ⓓ
M&D MOIR
manddmoir@aol.com
www.manddmoir.co.uk

MGT Ⓓ
GLITZ GURU
enquiries@glitzguru.com
www.glitzguru.com

MHT Ⓓ
MUM HAD THAT
No longer trading

MM Ⓐ
MULLOCK'S
Ludlow Racecourse
Bromfield, Ludlow,
Shropshire, SY8 2BT
Tel: 01694 771771
auctions@mullocksauctions.co.uk
www.mullocksauctions.co.uk

MOR Ⓐ
MORPHETS
6 Albert Street, Harrogate
North Yorkshire HG1 1JL
Tel: 01423 530030
enquiries@morphets.co.uk
www.morphets.co.uk

MTB Ⓓ
THE MAGIC TOYBOX
210 Havant Road, Drayton,
Portsmouth PO6 2EH
Tel: 02392 221 307
magictoybox@btinternet.com
www.magictoybox.co.uk

ON Ⓐ
ONSLOWS
The Coach House, Manor Road,
Stourpaine DT11 8TQ
Tel: 01258 488 838 or
07831 473 400
www.onslows.co.uk

P&I Ⓐ
PAOLA & IAIA
Stand S057, Alfies Antiques Market,
13-25 Church Street,
London NW8 8DT
Tel: 07751 084 135
paola_iaia_london@yahoo.com
www.alfiesantiques.com

PC Ⓟ Ⓒ
PRIVATE COLLECTION

POOK Ⓐ
POOK & POOK
463 East Lancaster Avenue
Downingtown, PA 19335, USA
Tel: 001 610 269 4040
info@pookandpook.com
www.pookandpook.com

PSA Ⓐ
POTTERIES SPECIALIST
AUCTIONS
271 Waterloo Road,
Cobridge, Stoke On Trent ST6 3HR
Tel: 01782 286 622
enquiries @ potteriesauctions.com
www.potteriesauctions.com

QU Ⓐ
QUITTENBAUM
KUNSTAUKTIONEN
Theresienstrasse 60,
D-80333 Munich, Germany
Tel: 0049 89 2737021-25
www.quittenbaum.de

RBJ Ⓟ Ⓒ
ROBERT BEVAN-JONES
COLLECTION
Private collector

RCC Ⓓ
ROYAL COMMEMORATIVE CHINA
Paul Wynton & Joe Spiteri
Tel: 02088 630 625
Mob: 07930 303 358
royalcommemoratives@hotmail.com

RET Ⓓ
RETROPOLITAN
Tel: 07870 422 182
enquiries@retropolitan.co.uk
www.retropolitan.co.uk

RM Ⓓ
RETROMINDED
www.retrominded.com

ROS Ⓐ
ROSEBERY'S
74-76 Knights Hill,
West Norwood SE27 0JD
Tel: 020 8761 2522
auctions@roseberys.co.uk
www.roseberys.co.uk

RTC Ⓓ
RITCHIES
No longer trading

RW Ⓐ
RICHARD WINTERTON AUCTIONEERS
The Old School House, Hawkins Lane, Burton On Trent, Staffordshire DE14 1FT
Tel: 01283 511224
burton@richardwinterton.co.uk
www.richardwinterton.co.uk

SAS Ⓐ
SPECIAL AUCTION SERVICES
81 New Greenham Park, Newbury RG19 6HW
Tel: 01635 580 595
www.specialauctionservices.com

SHAP Ⓐ
SHAPES
1 Bankhead Medway, Sighthill Edinburgh, EH11 4BY
Tel: 0131 453 3222
admin@shapesauctioneers.co.uk
www.shapesauctioneers.co.uk

SK Ⓐ
SKINNER INC
63 Park Plaza, Boston, MA 02116, USA
Tel: 001 617 350 5400
www.skinnerinc.com

SWA Ⓐ
SWANN GALLERIES
104 East 25th Street, New York, NY 10010, USA
Tel: 001 212 254 4710
swann@swanngalleries.com
www.swanngalleries.com

SWB Ⓓ
SWEETBRIAR GALLERY
No longer trading

SWO Ⓐ
SWORDERS
Cambridge Road, Stansted Mountfitchet CM24 8GE
Tel: 01279 817 778
auctions@sworder.co.uk
www.sworder.co.uk

TCM Ⓓ
TWENTIETH CENTURY MARKS
www.20thcenturymarks.co.uk

TDG Ⓓ
THE DESIGN GALLERY
5 The Green, Westerham, Kent TN16 1AS
Tel: 01959 561 234
www.designgallery.co.uk

TEN Ⓐ
TENNANTS
The Auction Centre, Leyburn DL8 5SG
Tel: 01969 623 780
enquiry@tennants-ltd.co.uk
www.tennants.co.uk

TGM Ⓐ
THE STUDIO GLASS MERCHANT
Tel: 020 8668 2701
info@thestudioglassmerchant.co.uk
www.thestudioglassmerchant.co.uk

TOV Ⓐ
TOOVEY'S
Spring Gardens, Washington RH20 3BS
Tel: 01903 891 955
auctions@tooveys.com
www.rupert-toovey.com

TRI Ⓐ
TRING MARKET AUCTIONS
Brook Street, Tring Hertfordshire HP23 5EF
Tel: 01442 826 446
sales@tringmarketauctions.co.uk
www.tringmarketauctions.co.uk

TWF Ⓓ
TWICE FOUND
608 Markham Street, Mirvish Village, Toronto, Ontario M6G 2L8, Canada
Tel: 001 416 534 3904
www.twicefound.com

VEC Ⓐ
VECTIS AUCTIONS LTD
Fleck Way, Thornaby, Stockton on Tees TS17 9JZ
Tel: 01642 750 616
www.vectis.co.uk

VZ Ⓐ
VON ZEZSCHWITZ KUNST UND DESIGN GMBH & CO KG
Friedrichstrasse 1a, 80801 Munich, Germany
Tel: 0049 89 38 98 930
www.von-zezschwitz.de

W&L Ⓓ
W&L ANTIQUES
Stand G060, Alfie's Antiques Market, 13-25 Church Street, London NW8 8DT
Tel: 0207 723 6066
Mob: 07788 486 297
teddylove@blueyonder.co.uk

W&W Ⓐ
WALLIS & WALLIS
West Street Auction Galleries, Lewes BN7 2NJ
Tel: 01273 480 208
auctions@wallisandwallis.org
www.wallisandwallis.co.uk

WAD Ⓐ
WADDINGTON'S AUCTIONEERS
111 Bathurst Street, Toronto, Ontario, M5V 2R1, Canada
Tel: 001 416 504 9100
www.waddingtons.ca

WES Ⓐ
WESCHLER'S
909 E Street, NW Washington, DC 20004, USA
Tel: 001 202 628 1281
info@weschlers.com
www.weschlers.com

WHP Ⓐ
W & H PEACOCK
26 Newnham Street Bedford MK40 3JR
Tel: 01234 266366
info@peacockauction.co.uk
www.peacockauction.co.uk

WW Ⓐ
WOOLLEY & WALLIS
51-61 Castle Street, Salisbury SP1 3SU
Tel: 01722 424 500
enquiries@woolleyandwallis.co.uk
www.woolleyandwallis.co.uk

ZI Ⓓ
ZEITGEIST INTERIORS
Tel: 07522 680 827
info@zeitgeist-i.com
www.zeitgeist-i.com

If you wish to have any item valued, it is advisable to contact the dealer or specialist in advance to check that they will carry out this service and whether there is a charge. While most dealers will be happy to help you with an enquiry, do remember that they are busy people with businesses to run. Telephone valuations are not possible. Please mention the Miller's Collectables by Judith Miller and Mark Hill when making an enquiry.

ADVERTISING

Huxtins
David Huxtable
P.O. Box 325,
WV 245, USA
david@huxtins.com
www.huxtins.com

Junktion Antiques Ltd
New Bolingbroke, Boston,
Lincolnshire
PE2 7LD
Tel: 01205 480 068 or
07836 345 491
junktionantiques@hotmail.com
www.junktionantiques.co.uk

Rex and Lisa Rixon
(Formerly of 'The Tin Shop')
Tel: 01723 351 089 or
07977 587 011

Dan Tinman
Focus on the Past
25 Waterloo Street
Clifton Village,
Bristol BS8 4BT
Tel: 01761 462 477 or
07768 166 808
dan@dantinman.com
www.dantinman.com

ANIMATION ART

Art You GREW Up With
Tel: 0800 098 8743
gallery@animaart.com
www.artyougrewupwith.com

ART DECO

Art Deco Etc
Tel: 01273 202 937
johnclark@artdecoetc.co.uk or
decojohn@hotmail.com

AUTOGRAPHS

The Autograph Collectors Gallery
7 Jessops Lane,
Gedling, Nottingham
NG4 4BQ
Tel: 0115 961 2956
graham@autograph-gallery.co.uk
www.autograph-gallery.co.uk

Special Signings
Tel: 01438 714 728
sales@specialsignings.com
www.specialsignings.com

AUTOMOBILIA

Automobilia Planet
P.O. Box 321, Hartlepool,
TS24 4EL
Tel: 01429 286 146 or
07960 795 038
www.automobiliaplanet.com
(Written enquiries can be
submitted through website)

Finesse Fine Art
Tel: 07973 886 937
tony@finesse-fine-art.com
www.finesse-fine-art.com

Junktion Antiques Ltd
New Bolingbroke, Boston,
Lincolnshire PE22 7LD
Tel: 01205 480 068 or
07836 345 491
junktionantiques@hotmail.com
www.junktionantiques.co.uk

The Lalique Mascot Collectors' Club
The White Lion Garage
Clarendon Place, Kemp Town,
Brighton BN2 1JA
Tel: 01273 622 722 or
07890 836 734
laliqueclub@virginmedia.com
www.carsofbrighton.co.uk

BANKNOTES, BONDS & SHARES

Banknotes, Bonds & Shares
Colin Narbeth & Sons Ltd,
20 Cecil Court,
Leicester Square,
London WC2N 4HE
Tel: 020 7379 6975
colin.narbeth@btinternet.com
www.colin-narbeth.com

Intercol London
43 Templars Crescent,
Finchley, London N3 3QR
Tel: 020 8349 2207 or
07768 292 066
sales@intercol.co.uk
www.intercol.co.uk

BOOKS

Zardoz Books
20 Whitecroft, Dilton Marsh,
Westbury, Wiltshire BA13 4DJ
Tel: 01373 865 371
enquiries@zardozbooks.co.uk
www.zardozbooks.co.uk

BREWERIANA

Junktion Antiques Ltd
New Bolingbroke,
Boston,
Lincolnshire PE22 7LD
Tel: 01205 480 068 or
07836 345 491
junktionantiques@hotmail.com
www.junktionantiques.co.uk

Gordon Litherland
25 Stapenhill Road,
Burton on Trent,
Staffordshire
DE15 9AE
Tel: 01283 567 213 or
07952 118 987
gordon@jmp2000.com

CERAMICS

A1 Collectables
Kingston Antique Centre,
29 Old London Road,
Kingston Upon Thames,
Surrey KT2 6ND
Tel: 020 8977 7230
www.a1-collectables.co.uk
(Written enquiries can be
submitted through website)

Beth Adams
Stands G023-25/28-30
and SO59-60,
Alfies Antique Market,
13-25 Church Street,
Marylebone,
London NW8 8DT
Mob: 07776 136 003
www.alfiesantiques.com

China Search
4 Princes Drive,
Kenilworth,
Warwickshire CV8 2FD
Tel: 01926 512 402
info@chinasearch.co.uk
www.chinasearch.co.uk

Cornishware.biz
Vintage-Kitsch,
1 Crown & Anchor Cottages,
Horsley, Newcastle
NE15 0NG
Tel: 01661 852 814 or
07979 857 599
info@cornishware.biz
www.cornishware.biz

Gallery 1930
18 Church Street,
London NW8 8EP
Tel: 020 7723 1555
gallery1930@aol.com
www.gallery1930.co.uk

Adrian Grater
Stand 26,
Admiral Vernon Arcade,
141-149 Portobello Road,
London
W11 2DY
Tel: 020 8579 0357 or
07814 286 624
adriangrater@tiscali.co.uk

Tony Horsley
P.O. Box 3127,
Brighton,
East Sussex
Tel: 01273 550 770 or
07711 987 633
enquiries@tonyhorsley.co.uk
www.tonyhorsley.co.uk

KCS Ceramics
Tel: 020 8384 8981
www.kcsceramics.co.uk
(Written enquiries can be
submitted through the website)

Sue Norman
The Bourbon Hanby Arcade,
151 Sydney Street,
London
SW3 6NT
Tel: 07747 654 354
sue@sue-norman.demon.co.uk
www.sue-norman.demon.co.uk

Past Caring
76 Essex Road,
Islington,
London N1 8LT

ReMemories Antiques
74 High Street,
Tenterden,
Kent TN30 6AU
Tel: 01580 763 416

Retroselect
info@retroselect.com
www.retroselect.com

Rick Hubbard
(Mode Vogue)
Tel: 07767 267 607
www.modevogue.com

Geoffrey Robinson
Alfies Antiques Market,
Stands GO77/78 & GO91/92,
13-25 Church Street,
London
NW8 8DT
Tel: 07794 085 723
www.robinsonantiques.co.uk
(Written enquiries can be
submitted through website)

Rogers de Rin
76 Royal Hospital Road,
Paradise Walk,
London
SW3 4HN
Tel: 020 7352 9007
rogersderin@rogersderin.co.uk
www.rogersderin.co.uk

Undercurrents
28 Cowper Street,
London
EC2A 4AS
Tel: 020 7251 1537
shop@undercurrents.biz
www.undercurrents.biz

Richard Wallis Antiks
Tel: 020 8523 8127 or
07721 583 306
info@richardwallisantiks.co.uk
www.richardwallisantiks.com

CIGARETTE CARDS
Pat O'Connell
8 Rosemount Close,
Honiton,
Devon EX14 2RP
Tel: 01404 41953
info@cardstocollect.com
www.cardstocollect.com

COINS & MONEY
British Notes
P.O. Box 257,
Sutton,
Surrey SM3 9WW
Tel: 020 8641 3224
pamwestbritnotes@aol.com
www.britishnotes.co.uk

Coincraft
44 & 45 Great Russell Street,
London WC1B 3LU
Tel: 020 7636 1188
info@coincraft.com
www.coincraft.com

Intercol London
43 Templars Crescent,
Finchley,
London
N3 3QR
Tel: 020 8349 2207 or
07768 292 066
sales@intercol.co.uk
www.intercol.co.uk

Colin Narbeth
Colin Narbeth & Sons Ltd,
20 Cecil Court,
Leicester Square,
London
WC2N 4HE
Tel: 020 7379 6975
colin.narbeth@btinternet.com
www.colin-narbeth.com

COMICS
The Book Palace
Jubilee House,
Bedwardine Road,
Crystal Palace,
London SE19 3AP
Tel: 020 8768 0022
info@bookpalace.com
www.bookpalace.com

Phil's Comics
P.O. Box 3433, Brighton,
East Sussex BN50 9JA
Tel: 01273 673 462 or
07739 844 703
phil@phil-comics.com
www.phil-comics.com

COMMEMORATIVE WARE
Commemorabilia
15 Haroldsleigh Avenue,
Crownhill, Plymouth PL5 3AW
Tel: 01752 700 795
ron_smith@commemorabilia.
co.uk
www.commemorabilia.co.uk

Royal Commemorative China
Paul Wynton & Joe Spiteri
Tel: 020 8863 0625
Mob: 07930 303 358
royalcommemoratives@hotmail.
com

COSTUME & ACCESSORIES
Linda Bee
Grays Antiques Market,
Stands L18-20,
1-7 Davies Mews,
London W1K 5AB
Tel: 020 7629 5921
info@graysantiques.com
www.graysantiques.com

Beyond Retro
110-112 Cheshire Street,
London E2 6EJ
Tel: 020 7613 3636
(and two further stores in Soho,
London and Brighton, East
Sussex. See website for details)
info@beyondretro.com
www.beyondretro.com

Cad van Swankster at The Girl Can't Help It
Alfies Antiques Market,
Stands G80/90 & 100,
13-25 Church Street,
London NW8 8DT
Tel: 020 7724 8984 or
07958 515 614
sparkle@sparklemoore.com
www.thegirlcanthelpit.com

Decades
20 Lord Street West,
Blackburn BB2 1JX
Tel: 01254 693 320

Fantiques
Tel: 07056 242 460
paula.raven@ntlworld.com

Old Hat
66 Fulham High Street,
London SW6 3LQ
Tel: 020 7610 6558

Rokit
101 Brick Lane, London E1 6SE
(and other London locations)
Tel: 020 7375 3864
www.rokit.co.uk
(Written enquiries can be
submitted through website)

Sparkle Moore at The Girl Can't Help It
Alfies Antiques Market,
Stands G80/90 & 100,
13-25 Church Street,
London NW8 8DT
Tel: 020 7724 8984 or
07958 515 614
sparkle@sparklemoore.com
www.thegirlcanthelpit.com

Steptoe's Dog Antique & Vintage Online Store
Tel: 01132 748 494
www.steptoesantiques.co.uk
(Written enquiries can be
submitted through website)

Kerry Taylor Auctions
Unit C21, Parkhall Road
Trading Estate, 40 Martell
Road, London, SE21 8EN
Tel: 020 8676 4600
info@kerrytaylorauctions.com
www.kerrytaylorauctions.com

Vintage Modes
Grays Antiques Market,
1-7 Davies Mews,
London W1K 5AB
Tel: 020 7409 0400
info@vintagemodes.co.uk
www.vintagemodes.co.uk

Vintage to Vogue
28 Milsom Street, Bath,
Avon BA1 1DG
Tel: 01225 337 323
contact@vintagetovoguebath.
co.uk
www.vintagetovoguebath.co.uk

Wardrobe
51 Upper North Street,
Brighton, East Sussex BN1 3FH
Tel: 01273 202 201

COSTUME JEWELLERY
Crested China
The Crested China Company,
Highfield, Windmill Hill,
Driffield, East Riding of
Yorkshire YO25 5YP
Tel: 0800 980 2089
dt@thecrestedchinacompany.com
www.thecrestedchinacompany.
com

Cristobal
26 Church Street,
London NW8 8EP
Tel: 020 7724 7230
sminers@aol.com
www.cristobal.co.uk

Eclectica
Tel: 020 7607 6327
enquiries@eclectica.biz
www.eclectica.biz

Richard Gibbon
Tel: 07958 674 447
neljeweluk@aol.com

William Wain
Tel: 07971 095 160 hello@
williamwain.co.uk
www.williamwain.com

DOLLS
British Doll Showcase
squibbit@ukonline.co.uk
www.britishdollshowcase.co.uk

Glenda O'Connor
Grays Antique Market
Stands A18-A19 and MB026,
1-7 Davies Mews, London
W1K 5AB
Tel: 020 8367 2441 or
07970 722 750
glenda@glenda-antiquedolls.
co.uk
www.glenda-antiquedolls.co.uk
www.graysantiques.com

Victoriana Dolls
101 Portobello Road,
London W11 2BQ
Tel: 01737 249 525
www.heatherbond.co.uk
(Written enquiries can be
submitted through website)

FIFTIES, SIXTIES & SEVENTIES
20th Century Marks
Oak Lodge, Rectory Road,
Little Burstead,
Essex CM12 9TR
Tel: 01474 872 460
michael@20thcenturymarks.co.uk
adam@20thcenturymarks.co.uk
www.20thcenturymarks.co.uk

Ian Broughton
Alfie's Antiques Market,
Stands S48/49 & 59/60,
13-25 Church Street,
London NW8 8DT
Tel: 020 7723 6066
ianbroughton@hotmail.com
www.alfiesantiques.com

Fragile Design
14-15 The Custard Factory,
Digbeth,
Birmingham B9 4AA
Tel: 0121 224 7378 or
07766 770 920
info@fragiledesign.com
www.fragiledesign.com

InRetrospect
37 Upper St. James Street,
Kemptown, Brighton,
East Sussex BN2 1JN
Tel: 01273 609 374

Luna
139 Lower Parliament Street,
Nottingham NG1 1EE
(also a London Outlet)
Tel: 0115 924 3267
info@luna-online.co.uk
www.luna-online.co.uk

The Modern Warehouse
3 Trafalgar Mews,
Hackney, London E9 5JG
Tel: 020 8986 0740 or
David: 07747 758 852
Rob: 07930 304 361
info@themodernwarehouse.com
www.themodernwarehouse.com

Multicoloured Timeslip
Tel: 07971 410 563
dave_a_cameron@hotmail.com

Planet Bazaar
Arch 68, The Stables Market,
Chalk Farm Road,
London NW1 8AH
Tel: 020 7485 6000
info@planetbazaar.co.uk
www.planetbazaar.co.uk

Retropolitan
Tel: 07870 422 182
enquiries@retropolitan.co.uk
www.retropolitan.co.uk

FILM & TV

Prop Store
Great House Farm, Chenies,
Rickmansworth,
Herts WD3 6EP
Tel: 01494 766 485
stephen@propstore.com
www.propstore.com

GLASS

**Andrew Lineham
Fine Glass**
Tel: 01243 576 241
Mob: 07767 702 722
andrewlineham@talktalk.net
www.antiquecolouredglass.com

**Antique Glass at
Frank Dux Antiques**
33 Belvedere, Lansdown Road,
Bath, Avon BA1 5HR
Tel: 01225 312 367
m.hopkins@antique-glass.co.uk
www.antique-glass.co.uk

Artius Glass
Tel: 07860 822 666
wheeler.ron@talktalk.net
www.artiusglass.co.uk

Cloud Glass
info@cloudglass.com
www.cloudglass.com

Francesca Martire
First Floor,
Alfies Antiques Market,
13-25 Church Street,
London NW8 8DT
Tel: 020 7724 4802
info@francescamartire.com
www.francescamartire.com

Glass etc
18-22 Rope Walk, Rye,
East Sussex TN31 7NA
Tel: 01797 226 600
andy@decanterman.com
www.decanterman.com

Grimes House Antiques
High Street, Moreton in Marsh,
Gloucestershire GL56 0AT
Tel: 01608 651 029
grimeshouse@gmail.com
www.cranberryglass.co.uk

**Jeanette Hayhurst
Fine Glass**
32A Kensington Church Street,
London W8 4HA
Tel: 020 7938 1539 or
07831 209 814
jeanettehayhurstantiqueglass@
btinternet.com
www.antiqueglass-london.com

**Nigel Benson
20th Century Glass**
Mob: 07971 859 848
nigelbenson@20thcentury-
glass.com
www.20thcentury-glass.com

Past Caring
76 Essex Road, Islington,
London N1 8LT

Pips Trip
13 Pyne Road,
Surbiton,
Surrey KT6 7BN
sales@pips-trip.co.uk
www.pips-trip.co.uk

**The Studio Glass
Merchant**
Tel: 020 8668 2701
info@thestudioglass
merchant.co.uk
www.thestudioglass
merchant.co.uk

KITCHENALIA

Appleby Antiques
67-69 Portobello Road,
London W11 2QB
Tel: 01453 753 126 or
Mike: 07778 282 532
Sue: 07775 797 620
mike@applebyantiques.net
www.applebyantiques.net

**Below Stairs of
Hungerford**
103 High Street,
Hungerford,
Berkshire RG17 0NB
Tel: 01488 682 317
hofgartner@belowstairs.co.uk
www.belowstairs.co.uk

Jane Wicks Kitchenalia
Country Ways, Strand Quay,
Rye, East Sussex TN32 7DB
Tel: 01424 713 635
janes_kitchen@hotmail.com

Jennifer's Cutlery
P.O. Box 9201
Nottingham NG1 9DJ
Tel: 0115 925 6418
Jenniferlwallis@hotmail.com
www.jenniferscutlery.co.uk

The Talking Machine
30 Watford Way,
London NW4 3AL
Tel: 020 8202 3473
Mob: 07774 103 139
davepauled2@yahoo.com
www.thetalkingmachine.eu

MILITARIA & MEDALS

Jim Bullock Militaria
P.O. Box 217, Romsey,
Hampshire SO51 5XL
Tel: 01794 516 455
jim@jimbullockmilitaria.com
www.jimbullockmilitaria.com

The Old Brigade
Tel: 01604 719 389
mail@theoldbrigade.co.uk
www.theoldbrigade.co.uk

West Street Antiques
63 West Street,
Dorking,
Surrey RH4 1BS
Tel: 01306 883 487
weststant@aol.com
www.antiquearmsand
armour.com

MODERN TECHNOLOGY

Junktion Antiques Ltd
New Bolingbroke, Boston,
Lincolnshire
PE22 7LD
Tel: 01205 480 068 or
07836 345 491
junktionantiques@hotmail.com
www.junktionantiques.co.uk

PAPERWEIGHTS

Alan and Helen Thornton
Tel: 01935 822 316
alan.thornton@physics.org
www.pwts.co.uk

Weights-n-things
Tel: +49 (0)221 940 3350
www.weights-n-things.com
(Written enquiries can be
submitted through website)

PENS & WRITING

Battersea Pen Home
P.O. Box 6128,
Epping
CM16 4GG
Tel: 01992 578 885
orders@penhome.co.uk
www.penhome.co.uk

Hans's Vintage Pens
Tel: 07850 771 183
hans.seiringer123@btinternet.com
www.hanspens.com

Henry The Pen Man
Admiral Vernon Antiques
Market,
141-149 Portobello Road,
London W11 2DY
(Saturdays only)
Tel: 020 8530 3277
www.henrysimpole.com
(Written enquiries can be
submitted through website)

PLASTICS & BAKELITE

Paola & Iaia
Stand S057,
Alfies Antiques Market,
13-25 Church Street,
London NW8 8DT
Tel: 07751 084 135
paola_iaia_london@yahoo.com
www.alfiesantiques.com

POSTCARDS

PC Postcards
Rear No.12,
Worcester Road,
Malvern,
Worcestershire
WR14 4QU
Tel: 01886 832 195
info@pcpostcards.co.uk
www.pcpostcards.co.uk

POSTERS

At The Movies
Tel: 07770 777 411 (Liza)
info@atthemovies.co.uk
www.atthemovies.co.uk

Barclay Samson
Tel: 020 7731 8012
www.barclaysamson.com
(Written equiries can be
submitted through website)

DODO
Alfies Antiques Market,
Stand F071/3,
13-25 Church Street,
London NW8 8DT
Tel: 020 7706 1545
liz@dodoposters.co.uk
www.dodoposters.com

Limelight Movie Art
313 King's Road,
London SW3 5EP
Tel: 020 7751 5584
sales@limelightmovieart.com
www.limelightmovieart.com

The Reelposter Gallery
Central London
(Visits by appointment only)
Tel: 07970 846 703
info@reelposter.com
www.reelposter.com

Rennies Seaside Modern
47 The Old High Street,
Folkestone, Kent CT20 1RN
Tel: 01303 242 427
info@rennart.co.uk
www.rennart.co.uk

POWDER COMPACTS

Phoenix Antiques
Squires Holt,
Church Street,
Petworth,
West Sussex, GU28 0AD
Tel: 01798 343 344 or
07759 697 108
sara@sneak.freeserve.co.uk

Mary & Geoff Turvil
Vintage compacts, small
antiques & collectables
enquiries@glitzguru.com
www.glitzguru.com

RADIOS

On the Air Ltd
The Vintage Technology Centre,
The Highway,
Hawarden,
Deeside CH5 3DN
Tel: 01244 530 300 or
07778 767 734 info@
vintageradio.co.uk
www.vintageradio.co.uk

Junktion Antiques Ltd
New Bolingbroke, Boston,
Lincolnshire PE22 7LD
Tel: 01205 480 068 or
07836 345 491
junktionantiques@hotmail.com
www.junktionantiques.co.uk

Philip Knighton
(For repairs)
Tel: 01823 661 618 or
07734 014 860
philip.knighton@btconnect.com

ROCK & POP

**Briggs Rock & Pop
Memorabilia**
Loudwater House,
London Road, Loudwater,
High Wycombe HP10 9TL
Tel: 01494 436 644
music@usebriggs.com
www.usebriggs.com

Collectors Corner
P.O. Box 8,
Congleton,
Cheshire, CW12 4GD
Tel: 01260 270 429
dave.popcorner@gmail.com

More Than Music
P.O. Box 3091,
Eastbourne,
East Sussex BN21 9HB
Tel: 01293 543 157
www.mtmglobal.com
(Written enquiries can be
submitted through website)

**Sweet Memories
Vinyl Records**
101 Fratton Road,
Portsmouth,
Hampshire PO1 5AH
Tel: 02392 837 730
vinylrecordsuk@aol.com
www.vinylrecords.co.uk

Tracks
P.O. Box 117,
Chorley,
Lancashire PR6 0QR
Tel: 01257 269 726
sales@tracks.co.uk
www.tracks.co.uk

SCIENTIFIC, TECHNICAL, OPTICAL & PRECISION INSTRUMENTS

Arthur Middleton
Tel: 01279 876 984
Mob: 07887 481 102
arthur@antique-globes.com
www.antique-globes.com

Branksome Antiques
370 Poole Road,
Branksome,
Dorset BH12 1AW
Tel: 01202 763 324 or
07773 911 974
www.branksomeantiques.co.uk

Charles Tomlinson
Tel: 01244 318 395
charlestomlinson@tiscali.co.uk
www.fleaglass.com

SMOKING

Richard Ball
'The Antique Lighter Shop'
Shop4.Contact@Lighter.co.uk
www.lighter.co.uk

SPORTING MEMORABILIA

Bob Gowland
Tel: 01367 850 020
bob@bobgowland.com
www.bobgowland.com

Manfred Schotten
109 High Street,
Burford,
Oxfordshire OX18 4RG
Tel: 01993 822 302
admin@schotten.com
www.sportantiques.co.uk

Rhod McEwan Golf
Ballater,
Royal Deeside,
Aberdeenshire AB35 5UB
Tel: 01339 755 429
teeoff@rhodmcewan.com
www.rhodmcewan.com

Sporting Antiques
St. Ives,
Cambridgeshire
Tel: 01480 463 891 or
07831 274 774
johnlambden@
sportingantiques.co.uk
www.sportingantiques.co.uk

Graham Budd
P.O. Box 47519,
London N14 6XD
Tel: 020 8366 2525 or
07974 113 394
gb@grahambuddauctions.co.uk
www.grahambuddauctions.co.uk

TELEPHONES

Candlestick & Bakelite
P.O. Box 308,
Orpington,
Kent BR5 1TB
Tel: 020 8467 3743
candlestick.bakelite@mac.com
www.candlestickand
bakelite.co.uk

**Retrofones
(Mobile Phones)**
Tel: 08707 117 711
www.retrobrick.co.uk
(Written enquiries can be
submitted through website)

Telephone Lines
304 High Street,
Cheltenham,
Gloucestershire GL50 3JF
Tel: 01242 583 699
info@telephonelines.net
www.telephonelines.net

TOYS & GAMES

The House of Automata
Seapark,
Kinloss,
Forres IV36 3TT
Tel: 01309 691 212 or
07790 719 097
07811 827 357
magic@thehouseofautomata.com
www.automatomania.com

**Collectors Old Toy Shop
(John & Simon Haley)**
89 Northgate,
Halifax,
West Yorkshire HX1 1XF
Tel: 01422 360 434
collectorsoldtoy@aol.com
www.collectorsoldtoyshop.com

Andrew Clark Models
Unit 13, Baildon Mills,
Northgate,
Baildon,
Shipley BD17 6JX
Tel: 01274 594 552 or
07753 804 232

Dave's Classic Toys
Gloucester Antiques Centre,
99a High Orchard Street,
Gloucester Quays,
Gloucester GL1 5SH
Tel: 01452 529 716
david.grounsellsky.com
www.gacl.co.uk

Donay Games
Tel: 01444 416 412
info@donaygames.com
www.donaygames.com

Garrick Coleman
75 Portobello Road,
London W11 2QB
Tel: 020 7937 5524
garrickcoleman@aim.com
www.antiquechess.co.uk

Hugo Lee-Jones
Tel: 01227 375 375 or
07941 187 207
electroniccollectables@
hotmail.com

**Intercol London
(Playing Cards)**
43 Templars Crescent, Finchley,
London N3 3QR
Tel: 020 8349 2207 or
07768 292 066
sales@intercol.co.uk
www.intercol.co.uk

The Magic Toybox
210 Havant Road, Drayton,
Portsmouth PO6 2EH
Tel: 02392 221 307
magictoybox@btinternet.com
www.magictoybox.co.uk

Metropolis Toys
Metropolis Toys,
41b Smith Street,
Warwick CV34 4JA
Tel: 01926 400 311
chris@metropolistoys.co.uk
www.metropolistoys.co.uk

Mike Delaney
Tel: 01993 840 064 or
07979 910 760
mail@vintagehornby.co.uk
www.vintagehornby.co.uk

Mimififi
27 Pembridge Road,
Notting Hill Gate,
London W11 3HG
Tel: 020 7243 3154
www.mimififi.com

**Sue Pearson Dolls &
Teddy Bears**
147 High Street, Lewes,
East Sussex BN7 1XT
Tel: 01273 472 677
sales@suepearson.co.uk
www.suepearson.co.uk

Teddy Bears of Witney
99 High Street, Witney,
Oxfordshire OX28 6HY
Tel: 01993 706 616
alfonzo@witneybears.co.uk
www.teddybears.co.uk

Toydreams
sales@toydreams.co.uk
www.toydreams.co.uk

**The Vintage Toy &
Train Shop**
Nigel Grinstead
Tel: 07710 915 934

Vintage Toy Box
contact@vintagetoybox.co.uk
www.vintagetoybox.co.uk

Wheels of Steel (Trains)
Grays Antiques Market,
Stands B10-11,
1-7 Davies Mews,
London W1K 5AB
Tel: 020 7629 2813
willia198@aol.com
www.graysantiques.com

WATCHES

Kleanthous Antiques
144 Portobello Road,
London W11 2DZ
Tel: 020 7727 3649
antiques@kleanthous.com
www.kleanthous.com

70s Watches
Tel: 01603 741 222
graham@70s-watches.com or
graham.wilson@ymail.com
www.70s-watches.com

The Watch Gallery
129 Fulham Road,
London SW3 6RT
Tel: 020 7581 3239
help@thewatchgallery.co.uk
www.thewatchgallery.co.uk

INDEX TO ADVERTISERS

The following list of general antiques and collectables centres, shops and markets has been organised by region. Any owner who would like to be listed in our next edition, space permitting, or who wishes to update their contact information, should email info@millers.uk.com.

LONDON

Alfie's Antiques Market
13-25 Church Street,
NW8 8DT
Tel: 020 7723 6066
info@alfiesantiques.com
www.alfiesantiques.com
(Closed Monday)

Bermondsey Antiques Market
Bermondsey Square,
Crossing of Long Lane &
Bermondsey Street, SE1
Every Friday morning 5am-2pm

Camden Passage Antiques Market
Camden Passage, Angel,
Islington, N1
www.camdenpassage
islington.co.uk
(Wednesday & Saturday mornings)

Covent Garden Antiques Market
Jubilee Hall,
Southampton Street,
Covent Garden, WC2
Tel: 020 7240 7405
http://www.jubileemarket.
co.uk/antiques
(Mondays from 5am-4pm)

Grays Antiques Market
58 Davies Street &
1-7 Davies Mews W1K 5AB
Tel: 020 7629 7034
info@graysantiques.com
www.graysantiques.com
(Closed Sunday)

Kensington Church Street Antiques Centre
58-60 Kensington Church
Street,
London W8 4DB

Northcote Road Antiques Market
155a Northcote Road,
Battersea, SW11 6QB
Tel: 020 7228 6850
antiques@spectrumsoft.net
www.spectrumsoft.net/nam
.htm

Palmers Green Antiques
482 Green Lanes,
Palmers Green N13 5PA
Tel: 020 8350 0878

Past Caring
76 Essex Road,
Islington N1 8LT
(Opens 12pm)

Portobello Rd Market
Portobello Road, W11 2QB
Tel: 020 7229 8354
info@portobelloroad.co.uk
www.portobelloroad.co.uk
(Every Saturday from 6am)

Spitalfields Antiques Market
Lamb Street/Commercial Street,
E1 6BG
www.oldspitalfieldsmarket.com
(Thursdays from 10am-4pm)

BEDFORDSHIRE

Ampthill Antiques Emporium
6 Bedford Street,
Ampthill MK45 2NB
Tel: 01525 402 131 or
07831 374 919
info@ampthillantiques
emporium.co.uk
www.ampthillantiques
emporium.com
(Closed Tuesday)

Woburn Abbey Antiques Centre
Woburn Abbey,
Woburn, WK17 9WA
Tel: 01525 292 118
www.woburnantiques.co.uk
(Written enquiries can be
submitted through website)

BERKSHIRE

The Collectors Centre
14&15 Harris Arcade,
Station Road,
Reading RG1 1DN
Tel: 01189 588 666
all@collectorscentrereading.co.uk
www.collectorscentrereading.
co.uk

Great Grooms at Hungerford
Riverside House,
Charnham Street,
Hungerford RG17 0EP
Tel: 01488 682 314
hungerford@greatgrooms.co.uk
www.greatgrooms.co.uk

BUCKINGHAMSHIRE

Antiques at... Wendover
The Old Post Office,
25 High Street,
Wendover HP22 6DU
Tel: 01296 625 335
antiques@antiquesat
wendover.co.uk
www.antiquesat
wendover.co.uk

CAMBRIDGESHIRE

Cambridge Antiques Centre
1-2 Dales Brewery,
Gwydir Street, Off Mill Road,
Cambridge CB1 3NГ
Tel: 01223 356 391
www.cambsantiques.com

Waterside Antiques Centre
The Wharf,
Ely CB7 4AU
Tel: 01353 667 066
waterside@ely.org.uk
www.ely.org.uk/waterside.html

DERBYSHIRE

Alfreton Antique Centre
11 King Street,
Alfreton DE55 7AF
Tel: 01773 520 781
www.alfretonantiquescentre.com

Bakewell Antiques & Works of Art
(G. W. Ford & Son Ltd)
1-4 King Street,
Bakewell DE45 1DZ
Tel: 01629 812 496
ian@gwfordantiques.co.uk
www.gwfordantiques.com

Heanor Antiques Centre
1-3 Ilkeston Road,
Heanor DE75 7AG
Tel: 01773 531 181
sales@heanorantiques
centre.co.uk
www.heanorantiques
centre.co.uk

Matlock Antiques & Collectables
7 Dale Road,
Matlock DE4 3LT
Tel: 01629 760 808
info@matlockantiques.co.uk
www.matlockantiques.co.uk

DEVON

The Quay Antiques Centre
The Quay, The Strand,
Topsham,
Exeter EX3 0JB
Tel: 01392 874 006
office@quayantiques.com
www.quayantiques.com

ESSEX

Debden Antiques
Elder Street, Debden,
Saffron Walden CB11 3JY
Tel: 01799 543 007
info@debden-antiques.co.uk
www.debden-antiques.co.uk

GLOUCESTERSHIRE

Gloucester Antiques Centre
99a High Orchard Street,
Gloucester Quays,
Gloucester GL1 5SH
Tel: 01452 529 716
info@gacl.co.uk
www.gacl.co.uk

Durham House Antiques
Sheep Street,
Stow-on-the-Wold
GL54 1AA
Tel: 01451 870 404
durhamhouseGB@aol.com
www.durhamhousegb.com

Top Banana Antiques Mall
1 New Church Street,
Tetbury GL8 8DS
Tel: 0871 288 1102
enquiries@topbananaantiques
.com
www.topbananaantiques.com

HAMPSHIRE

Squirrels Collectors Centre
9a New Street,
Basingstoke RG21 7DE
Tel: 01256 464 885
ahs@squirrelsuk.fsnet.co.uk.

HEREFORDSHIRE

Hereford Antique Centre
128 Widemarsh Street,
Hereford HR4 9HN
Tel: 01432 266 242

The Secondhand Warehouse & Antique Centre
The Granary,
New Street,
Leominster HR6 8DR
Tel: 01568 614 114
secondhandwarehouse@mail.com
www.secondhand-warehouse.co.uk

HERTFORDSHIRE

By George Antique Centre
23 George Street,
St Albans AL3 4ES
Tel: 01727 853 032

Riverside Antiques Centre
The Maltings,
Station Road,
Sawbridgeworth CM21 9JX
Tel: 01279 600 985

IRELAND

Archives Antiques Centre
88 Donegall Pass,
Belfast,
County Antrim BT7 1BX
Tel: 02890 232 383

Powerscourt Centre
59 South William Street
Dublin 2
Tel: +353 (0)1671 7000
www.powerscourtcentre.ie

KENT

Burgate Antiques Centre
23A Palace Street,
Canterbury CT1 2DZ
Tel: 01227 456 600
vkreeves@burgate1.fsnet.co.uk

Castle Antiques
1 London Road,
Westerham TN16 1BB
Tel: 01959 562 492

Otford Antiques and Collectors Centre
26-28 High Street,
Otford TN14 5PQ
Tel: 01959 522 025
info@otfordantiques.co.uk
www.otfordantiques.co.uk

Tenterden Antiques Centre
64 & 66A High Street,
Tenterden TN30 6AU
Tel: 01580 766 116 (no.64) or
01580 765 655 (no.66a)

LANCASHIRE

GB Antiques Centre
Lancaster Leisure Park,
Wyresdale Road,
Lancaster LA1 3LA
Tel: 01524 844 734
www.gbantiquescentre.com

Heskin Hall Antiques
Heskin Hall, Wood Lane,
Heskin,
Chorley PR7 5PA
Tel: 01257 452 044
www.heskinhallantiques.co.uk
(Written enquiries can be submitted through website)

Karlen Antiques Centre
Bank Hall Works,
Off Colne Road,
Burnley BB10 3AT
Tel: 01282 431 953
www.antiquesshipper.co.uk
(Written enquiries can be submitted through website)

LINCOLNSHIRE

Hemswell Antique Centres
Caenby Corner Estate,
Hemswell Cliff,
Gainsborough DN21 5TJ
Tel: 01427 668 389
enquiries@hemswell-antiques.com
www.hemswell-antiques.com

St Martins Antiques Centre
23a High Street,
St Martins,
Stamford PE9 2LF
Tel: 01780 481 158
info@st-martins-antiques.co.uk
www.st-martins-antiques.co.uk

NORFOLK

Tombland Antiques Centre
Augustine Steward House,
14 Tombland,
Norwich NR3 1HF
Tel: 01603 619 129

Old Granary Antiques Centre
King Staithe Lane,
King's Lynn PE30 1LZ
Tel: 01553 775 509

NORTHAMPTONSHIRE

Brackley Antique Cellar
Drayman's Walk,
Brackley NN13 6BE
Tel: 01280 841 841
antiquecellar@tesco.net
www.brackleyantiquecellar.co.uk

NOTTINGHAMSHIRE

Castlegate Antiques Centre
55 Castlegate,
Newark NG24 1BE
Tel: 01636 700 076

Newark Antiques Centre
Regent House, Lombard Street,
Newark NG24 1XP
Tel: 01636 605 504
thephoenixexperi@btinternet.com
www.newarkantiquescentre.com

OXFORDSHIRE

Deddington Antiques Centre
Laurel House, Bull Ring,
Deddington OX15 0TT
Tel: 01869 338 968
www.deddingtonantiquecentre.co.uk
(Written enquiries can be submitted through website)

The Lamb Arcade Antiques & Lifestyle Centre
High Street,
Wallingford OX10 0AA
Tel: 01491 835 166
info@thelambarcade.co.uk
www.thelambarcade.co.uk

The Quiet Woman Antiques Centre
Southcombe,
Chipping Norton OX7 5QH
Tel: 01608 646 262
quietwomanantiq@aol.com
www.quietwomanantiques.co.uk

The Swan at Tetsworth Antiques Centre
High Street,
Tetsworth OX9 7AB
Tel: 01844 281 777
antiques@theswan.co.uk
www.theswan.co.uk

SCOTLAND

Now and Then
9 West Crosscauseway,
Edinburgh EH8 9JW
Tel: 0131 668 2927 or
07772 420 279
nowandthen@btconnect.com
www.oldtoysandantiques.co.uk

Rait Village Antiques Centre
Rait,
Perthshire PH2 7RT
Tel: 01821 670 379
val.eassonmilne@btopenworld.com

Scottish Antiques & Arts Centre
Abernyte,
Perthshire PH14 9SJ
Tel: 01828 686 401
and
Doune,
Stirling, FK16 6HG
Tel: 01786 841 203
www.scottish-antiques.com

SHROPSHIRE

Stretton Antiques Market
36 Sandford Avenue,
Church Stretton SY6 6BH
Tel: 01694 723 718

SOMERSET

Old Bank Antiques Centre
14-17 Walcot Buildings,
London Road,
Bath BA1 6AD.
Tel: 01225 469 282/338 818
alexatmontague@aol.com
www.oldbankantiquescentre.com

STAFFORDSHIRE

Compton Mill Antique Emporium
Compton,
Leek ST13 5NJ
Tel: 01538 373 396
kelly.butler@ntlbusiness.com
www.leekonline.co.uk/shopping/antiques/compton

Curborough Hall Antiques
Watery Lane,
Lichfield WS13 8ES
Tel: 01543 417 100

Potteries Antique Centre
271 Waterloo Road,
Cobridge,
Stoke-on-Trent ST6 3HR
Tel: 01782 201 455
enquiries@potteriesantiquecentre.com
www.potteriesantiquecentre.com

SUFFOLK

Melford Antiques Warehouse
Hall Street,
Long Melford,
CO10 9JA
Tel: 01787 379 638

Snape Maltings Antiques & Collectors Centre
Saxmundham
IP17 1SR
Tel: 01728 688 038

SURREY

Kingston Antiques Centre
29 London Road,
Kingston-upon-Thames
KT2 6ND
Tel: 020 8549 2004
johncobbold1@yahoo.co.uk
www.kingstonantiques
centre.co.uk

Pilgrims Antiques Centre
7 West Street,
Dorking, RH4 1BL
Tel: 01306 875 028

SUSSEX (EAST)

**The Brighton Lanes
Antiques Centre**
12 Meeting House Lane,
Brighton BN1 1HB
Tel: 01273 823 121
peter@brightonlanes
antiques.co.uk
www.brightonlanes
antiques.co.uk

Brighton Flea Market
31a Upper St. James's Street,
Brighton BN2 1JN
Tel: 01273 624 006
www.flea-markets.co.uk

**Church Hill Antiques
Centre**
6 Station Street,
Lewes BN7 2DA
Tel: 01273 474 842
churchhilllewes@aol.com

Lewes Antiques Centre
20 Cliffe High Street,
Lewes BN7 2AH
Tel: 01273 476 148

Snooper's Paradise
7-8 Kensington Gardens,
Brighton
BN1 4AL
Tel: 01273 602 558
nic@internetdropshop.co.uk
www.northlaine.co.uk/
snoopers-paradise/

SUSSEX (WEST)

Arundel Antiques Centre
6 High Street,
Arundel
BN18 9AB
Tel: 01903 884 164
info@arundelantiques.co.uk
www.arundelantiques.co.uk

WALES

Afonwen Antiques
Afonwen, nr Caerwys,
Mold, CH7 5UB
Tel: 01352 720 965
www.afonwen.co.uk/antiques
(Written enquiries can be
submitted through website)

**Offa's Dyke Antiques
Centre**
4 High Street, Knighton,
Powys LD7 1AT
Tel: 01547 528 635

WARWICKSHIRE

**Stratford-upon-Avon
Antique Centre**
59-60 Ely St,
Stratford-upon-Avon CV37 6LN
Tel: 01789 204 180
www.stratfordshops.wobc
com/antiquescentre.htm

WEST MIDLANDS

Yoxall Antiques
68 Yoxall Road, Shirley,
Solihull B90 3RP
Tel: 0121 744 1744
sales@yoxallantiques.co.uk
www.yoxallantiques.co.uk

WORCESTERSHIRE

Foley House Antiques
28 Worcester Road,
Malvern WR14 4QW
Tel: 01684 575 750
www.foleyhouseantiques.com
(Written enquiries can be
submitted through website)

YORKSHIRE

The Antiques Centre York
41 Stonegate,
York YO1 8AW
Tel: 01904 635 888
enquiries@
antiquescentreyorkeshop.co.uk
www.antiquescentreyorkeshop.
co.uk

Cavendish Antiques
44 Stonegate, York YO1 8AS
Tel: 01904 621 666
info@cavendishantiques.com
www.cavendishantiques.co.uk

The Collectors' Centre
35 St Nicholas Cliff,
Scarborough YO11 2ES
Tel: 01723 365 221
www.collectors.demon.co.uk
(Written enquiries can be
submitted thorugh website)

**The Ginnel Antiques
Centre**
Off Parliament Street,
Harrogate HG1 2RB
Tel: 01423 508 857
Info@theginnel.com
www.theginnel.co.uk

DIRECTORY OF AUCTIONEERS

The following list of auctioneers who conduct regular sales by auction is organised by region. Any auctioneer who would like to be listed in the our next edition, space permitting, or to update their contact information, should email info@millers.uk.com.

LONDON

Bloomsbury Auctions
24 Maddox Street W1S 1PP
Tel: 020 7495 9494
info@bloomsburyauctions.com
www.bloomsburyauctions.com

Bonhams
101 New Bond Street W1S 1SR
Tel: 020 7447 7447
info@bonhams.com
www.bonhams.com

**Christies (South
Kensington)**
85 Old Brompton Road,
SW7 3LD
Tel: 020 7930 6074
info@christies.com
www.christies.com

Chiswick Auctions
1 Colville Road (off Bollo Lane),
Chiswick W3 8BL
Tel: 020 8992 4442
info@chiswickauctions.co.uk
www.chiswickauctions.co.uk

Criterion Auctioneers
53 Essex Road,
Islington N1 2SF
Tel: 020 7359 5707
islington@criterion
auctioneers.com
and
41-47 Chatfield Road,
Wandsworth, SW11 3SE
Tel: 020 7228 5563
wandsworth@
criterionauctioneers.com
www.criterionauctions.co.uk

Graham Budd Auctions
P.O. Box 47519, N14 6XD
Tel: 020 8366 2525 or
07974 113 394
gb@grahambuddauctions.co.uk
www.grahambuddauctions
.co.uk

Lots Road Auctions
71-73 Lots Road,
Chelsea SW10 0RN
Tel: 020 7376 6800
info@lotsroad.com
www.lotsroad.com

Rosebery's
74-76 Knights Hill,
West Norwood SE27 0JD
Tel: 020 8761 2522
auctions@roseberys.co.uk
www.roseberys.co.uk

Sotheby's
34-35 New Bond Street
W1A 2AA
Tel: 020 7293 5000
www.sothebys.com

BEDFORDSHIRE

W. & H. Peacock
Bedford Auction Centre,
26 Newnham Street,
Bedford
MK40 3JR
Tel: 01234 266 366
info@peacockauction.co.uk
www.peacockauction.co.uk

BERKSHIRE

Dreweatts
Donnington Priory, Donnington,
Newbury RG14 2JE
Tel: 01635 553 553
donnington@dnfa.com
www.dnfa.com

Special Auction Services
81 New Greenham Park,
Newbury RG19 6HW
Tel: 01635 580 595
www.specialauctionservices.com
(Written enquiries can be
submitted through website)

BRISTOL

Dreweatt's
St. John's Place,
Apsley Road,
Clifton, BS8 2ST
Tel: 0117 973 7201
bristol@dnfa.com
www.dnfa.com/bristol

BUCKINGHAMSHIRE

**Amersham Auction
Rooms**
Station Road,
Amersham-on-the-Hill HP7 0AH
Tel: 01494 729 292
info@amershamauction
rooms.co.uk
www.amershamauction
rooms.co.uk

CAMBRIDGESHIRE

Cheffins
Clifton House,
1&2 Clifton Road,
Cambridge CB1 7EA
Tel: 01223 213 343
fine.art@cheffins.co.uk
vintage@cheffins.co.uk
www.cheffins.co.uk

CHANNEL ISLANDS

Martel Maides Auctions
Cornet Street,
Street.
Peter Port
Guernsey GY1 2JX
Tel: 01481 722 700
auctions@martelmaides.co.uk
www.martelmaides.co.uk

CHESHIRE

Bonhams
New House,
150 Christleton Road,
Chester CH3 5TD
Tel: 01244 313 936
chester@bonhams.com
www.bonhams.com

CLEVELAND

**Vectis Auctioneers
(Toys & Dolls)**
Fleck Way, Thornaby,
Stockton on Tees TS17 9JZ
Tel: 01642 750 616
www.vectis.co.uk
(Written enquiries can be
submitted through website)

CORNWALL

W. H. Lane & Son
Jubilee House,
Queen Street,
Penzance TR18 4DF
Tel: 01736 361 447
info@whlane.co.uk
www.whlane.co.uk

David Lay FRICS
Penzance Auction House,
Alverton,
Penzance TR18 4RE
Tel: 01736 361 414
david.lays@btopenworld.com
www.davidlay.co.uk

CUMBRIA

**Mitchells Antiques &
Fine Art Auctioneers &
Valuers**
47 Station Road,
Cockermouth CA13 9PZ
Tel: 01900 827 800
info@mitchellsfineart.com
www.mitchellsantiques.co.uk

Penrith Farmers' & Kidds
Skirsgill Saleroom,
Penrith CA11 0DN
Tel: 01768 890 781
info@pfkauctions.co.uk
www.pfkauctions.co.uk

DERBYSHIRE

Bamfords Ltd
The Old Picture Palace,
Dale Road, Matlock DE4 3LT
Tel: 01629 57460
bamfords-matlock@tiscali.co.uk
and
The Derby Auction House,
Chequers Road,
off Pentagon Island,
Derby DE21 6EN
Tel: 01332 210 000
sales@bamfords-auctions.com
www.bamfords-auctions.co.uk

DEVON

**Bearnes Hampton &
Littlewood**
St Edmund's Court,
Okehampton Street,
Exeter EX4 1DU
Tel: 01392 413 100

and
Dowell Street,
Honiton EX14 1LX
Tel: 01404 510 000
info@bhandl.co.uk
www.bhandl.co.uk

Bonhams
The Lodge, Southernhay West,
Exeter EX1 1JG
Tel: 01392 425 264
exeter@bonhams.com
www.bonhams.com

DORSET

Charterhouse
The Long Street Salerooms,
Sherborne DT9 3BS
Tel: 01935 812 277
www.charterhouse-auction.com
(Written enquiries can be
submitted through website)

Duke's
The Dorchester Fine Art
Saleroom, Weymouth Avenue,
Dorchester DT1 1QS
Tel: 01305 265 080
enquiries@dukes-auctions.com
www.dukes-auctions.com

Onslows
The Coach House, Manor Road,
Stourpaine DT11 8TQ
Tel: 01258 488 838 or
07831 473 400
www.onslows.co.uk
(Written enquiries can be
submitted through website)

Semley Auctioneers
Station Road,
Semley,
Shaftesbury SP7 9AN
Tel: 01747 855 122
enquiries@semley
auctioneers .com
www.semleyauctioneers.com

ESSEX

**Sworders Fine Art
Auctioneers**
Cambridge Road,
Stansted Mountfitchet
CM24 8GE
Tel: 01279 817 778
auctions@sworder.co.uk
www.sworder.co.uk

GLOUCESTERSHIRE

Chorley's
Prinknash Abbey Park,
Cranham GL4 8EX
Tel: 01452 344 499
enquiries@simonchorley.com
www.simonchorley.com

**The Cotswold Auction
Company**
Chapel Walk, Cheltenham,
Gloucestershire GL50 3DS
Tel: 01242 256 363
info@cotswoldauction.co.uk
www.cotswoldauction.co.uk

**Mallams Fine Art
Auctioneers & Valuers**
26 Grosvenor Street,
Cheltenham GL52 2SG
Tel: 01242 235 712
cheltenham@mallams.co.uk
www.mallams.co.uk

Moore, Allen & Innocent
The Norcote Salerooms,
Burford Road, Norcote,
Cirencester GL7 5RH
Tel: 01285 646 050
fineart@mooreallen.co.uk
www.mooreallen.co.uk

HAMPSHIRE

Andrew Smith & Son
The Auction Rooms,
Manor Farm, Itchen Stoke,
Nr Winchester SO24 0QT
Tel: 01962 735 988
auctions@andrewsmith
andson.com
www.andrewsmithandson.com

**Jacobs & Hunt
Fine Art Auctioneers**
26 Lavant Street,
Petersfield GU32 3EF
Tel: 01730 233 933
auctions@jacobsandhunt.com
www.jacobsandhunt.com

HEREFORDSHIRE

Brightwells
The Fine Art Saleroom,
Easters Court,
Leominster HR6 0DE
Tel: 01568 611 166
info@brightwells.com
www.brightwells.com

HERTFORDSHIRE

Tring Market Auctions
Brook Street, Tring HP23 5EF
Tel: 01442 826 446
sales@tringmarketauctions.co.uk
www.tringmarketauctions.co.uk

ISLE OF WIGHT

Shanklin Auction Rooms
79 Regent Street,
Shanklin PO37 7AP
Tel: 01983 863 441
shanklin.auction@tesco.net
www.shanklinauction
rooms.co.uk

KENT

Dreweatts
10 Mount Ephraim,
Tunbridge Wells TN1 8AE
Tel: 01892 544 500
tunbridgewells@dnfa.com
www.dnfa.com/tunbridgewells

Gorringes
85 Mount Pleasant Road,
Tunbridge Wells TN1 1PX
Tel: 01892 619 670
tunbridge.wells@gorringes.co.uk
www.gorringes.co.uk

LANCASHIRE

Capes Dunn
38 Charles Street,
Manchester M1 7DB
Tel: 0161 273 1911
capesdunn@googlemail.com
www.capesdunn.com

LEICESTERSHIRE

Gilding's
64 Roman Way,
Market Harborough LE16 7PQ
Tel: 01858 410 414
sales@gildings.co.uk
www.gildings.co.uk

LINCOLNSHIRE

Golding Young
Old Wharf Road, Grantham,
Lincolnshire NG31 7AA
Tel: 01476 565 118
enquiries@goldingyoung.com
www.goldingyoung.com

MERSEYSIDE

Cato, Crane & Company
6 Stanhope Street,
Liverpool L8 5RF
Tel: 0151 709 5559
www.cato-crane.co.uk
(written enquiries can be
submitted through website)

NORFOLK

T. W. Gaze
Diss Auction Rooms,
Roydon Road,
Diss IP22 4LN
Tel: 01379 650 306
sales@dissauctionrooms.co.uk
www.twgaze.com

**Keys Auctioneers &
Valuers**
Keys Aylsham Salerooms,
off Palmers Lane,
Aylsham NR11 6JA
Tel: 01263 733 195
auctions@keys24.com
www.keysauctions.co.uk

**Knights Sporting
Auctions**
Cuckoo Cottage,
Town Green,
Alby
Norwich NR11 7PR
Tel: 01263 768 488 or
07885 515 333
tim@knights.co.uk
www.knights.co.uk

NOTTINGHAMSHIRE

Mellors & Kirk
The Auction House,
Gregory Street,
Nottingham
NG7 2NL
Tel: 0115 979 0000
enquiries@mellorsandkirk.com
www.mellorsandkirk.com

T. Vennett-Smith
11 Nottingham Road,
Gotham
NG11 0HE
Tel: 0115 983 0541
info@vennett-smith.com
www.vennett-smith.com

OXFORDSHIRE

Mallams
Dunmore Court,
Wootton Road,
Abingdon, OX13 6BH
Tel: 01235 462 840
abingdon@mallams.co.uk
www.mallams.co.uk
or
Bocardo House,
St. Michaels Street,
Oxford OX1 2EB
Tel: 01865 241 358
oxford@mallams.co.uk
www.mallams.co.uk

SHROPSHIRE

Halls Fine Art
Welsh Bridge,
1 Frankwell,
Shrewsbury SY3 8LA
Tel: 01743 284 777
fineart@halls.to
www.hallsestateagents.co.uk
/fine-art

Mullock's
The Old Shippon,
Wall under Heywood,
Church Stretton
SY6 7DS
Tel: 01694 771 771
auctions@mullocks
auctions.co.uk
www.mullocksauctions.co.uk

SOMERSET

Clevedon Salerooms
The Auction Centre,
Kenn Road, Kenn,
Clevedon BS21 6TT
Tel: 01934 830 111
info@clevedon-salerooms.com
www.clevedon-salerooms.com

Lawrences Auctioneers
The Linen Yard, South Street,
Crewkerne TA18 8AB
Tel: 01460 73041
enquiries@lawrences.co.uk
www.lawrences.co.uk

STAFFORDSHIRE

**Potteries Specialist
Auctions**
271 Waterloo Road,
Cobridge,
Stoke-on-Trent ST6 3HR
Tel: 01782 286 622
enquiries@potteriesauctions.com
www.potteriesauctions.com

**Richard Winterton
Auctioneers**
The Lichfield Auction Centre,
Wood End Lane, Fradley Park,
Lichfield WS13 8NF
Tel: 01543 251 081
lichfield@richardwinterton.co.uk
www.richardwinterton.co.uk

Wintertons
Uttoxeter Auction Centre,
Short Street, Uttoxeter ST14 7LH
Tel: 01889 564 385
enquiries@wintertons.co.uk
www.wintertons.co.uk

SUFFOLK

Diamond Mills
117 Hamilton Road,
Felixstowe IP11 7BL
Tel: 01394 282 281
nigel.papworth@
diamondmills.co.uk
or
edna.boon@diamondmills.co.uk
www.diamondmills.co.uk

Neals
26 Church Street,
Woodbridge IP12 1DP
Tel: 01394 382 263
enquiries@nsf.co.uk
www.nsf.co.uk

SURREY

Barbers
The Mayford Centre, Smarts
Heath Road, Woking GU22 0PP
Tel: 01483 728 939
www.invaluable.com/Barbers

**Ewbank Clarke Gammon
Wellers Auctioneers**
Burnt Common Auction Rooms,
London Rd, Send,
Woking GU23 7LN
Tel: 01483 223 101
antiques@ewbankauctions.co.uk
www.ewbankauctions.co.uk

Dreweatt Neate
Baverstock House, 93 High St,
Godalming GU7 1AL
Tel: 01483 423 567
godalming@dnfa.com
www.dnfa.com/godalming

EAST SUSSEX

Burstow & Hewett
Lower Lake, Battle TN33 0AT
Tel: 01424 772 374
auctions@burstowandhewett. co.uk
www.burstowandhewett.co.uk

**Dreweatt Neate
(Eastbourne)**
Tel: 01323 410 419
eastbourne@dnfa.com
www.dnfa.com/eastbourne

Gorringes
Garden Street, Lewes BN7 1XE
Tel: 01424 478 221
gardenst@gorringes.co.uk
www.gorringes.co.uk or 1
5 North Street, Lewes BN7 2PD
Tel: 01273 472 503
clientservices@gorringes.co.uk
www.gorringes.co.uk

Raymond P. Inman
98A Coleridge Street,
Hove BN3 5AA
Tel: 01273 774 777
r.p.inman@talk21.com
raymondinman.bttradespace.com

Wallis & Wallis
West Street Auction Galleries,
Lewes BN7 2NJ
Tel: 01273 480 208
auctions@wallisandwallis.org
www.wallisandwallis.co.uk

WEST SUSSEX

Bellmans
Newpound, Wisborough Green,
Billingshurst RH14 0AZ
Tel: 01403 700 858
enquiries@bellmans.co.uk
www.bellmans.co.uk

Denhams
Dorking Road, Warnham,
Horsham RH12 3RZ
Tel: 01403 255 699
enquiries@denhams.com
www.denhams.com

Toovey's
Spring Gardens,
Washington RH20 3BS
Tel: 01903 891 955
auctions@tooveys.com
www.rupert-toovey.com

TYNE & WEAR

Anderson and Garland
Anderson House,
Crispin Court,
Newbiggin Lane,
Westerhope,
Newcastle upon Tyne
NE5 1BF
Tel: 0191 430 3000
info@andersonandgarland.com
www.andersonandgarland.com

Corbitts (Stamps)
5 Mosley Street,
Newcastle upon Tyne NE1 1YE
Tel: 0800 525 804
collectors@corbitts.com
www.corbitts.com

WARWICKSHIRE

Locke & England
18 Guy Street,
Leamington Spa CV32 4RT
Tel: 01926 889 100
info@leauction.co.uk
www.leauction.co.uk

WEST MIDLANDS

Bonhams
The Old House, Station Road,
Knowle, Solihull B93 0HT
Tel: 01564 776 151
knowle@bonhams.com
www.bonhams.com

Fellows Auctioneers
Augusta House,
19 Augusta Street,
Birmingham B18 6JA
Tel: 0121 212 2131
info@fellows.co.uk
www.fellows.co.uk

WILTSHIRE

Finan & Co
Tel: 01747 861 411
post@robertfinan.co.uk
www.robertfinan.co.uk

Gardiner Houlgate
9 Leafield Way, Corsham,
Bath SN13 9SW
Tel: 01225 812 912
auctions@gardinerhoulgate.co.uk
www.gardinerhoulgate.co.uk

Henry Aldridge & Son
Unit 1,
Bath Road Business Centre,
Bath Road,
Devizes SN10 1XA
Tel: 01380 729 199
andrew@henry-aldridge.co.uk
www.henry-aldridge.co.uk

Woolley & Wallis
51-61 Castle Street,
Salisbury SP1 3SU
Tel: 01722 424 500
enquiries@woolleyandwallis.co.uk
www.woolleyandwallis.co.uk

WORCESTERSHIRE

Andrew Grant
Tel: 0844 984 9617
fine.art@andrew-grant.co.uk
www.andrew-grant.co.uk

G. W. Railwayana Auctions
'The Willows',
Badsey Road,
Evesham WR117PA
Tel: 01386 760 109
master@gwra.co.uk
www.gwra.co.uk

Phillip Serrell
The Malvern Saleroom,
Barnards Green Road,
Malvern WR14 3LW
Tel: 01684 892 314
serrell.auctions@virgin.net
www.serrell.com

EAST YORKSHIRE

Dee Atkinson & Harrison
The Exchange Saleroom,
Exchange Street,
Driffield YO25 6LD
Tel: 01377 253 151
info@dahauctions.com
www.dahauctions.com/
auctionhome.aspx

NORTH YORKSHIRE

David Duggleby
The Vine Street Salerooms,
Scarborough YO11 1XN
Tel: 01723 507 111
auctions@davidduggleby.com
www.davidduggleby.com

Tennants
The Auction Centre,
Leyburn DL8 5SG
Tel: 01969 623 780
enquiry@tennants-ltd.co.uk
www.tennants.co.uk

SOUTH YORKSHIRE

A. E. Dowse & Son
Cornwall Galleries,
94 Scotland Street,
Sheffield S3 7DE
Tel: 0114 272 5858
aedowse@aol.com
www.toyauction.info

BBR Auctions
Elsecar Heritage Centre,
Barnsley S74 8HJ
Tel: 01226 745 156
sales@onlinebbr.com
www.onlinebbr.com

Sheffield Railwayana
4 The Glebe, Clapham,
Bedford MK41 6GA
Tel: 01234 325 341
sheffrailwayana@aol.com
www.sheffieldrailwayana.co.uk

WEST YORKSHIRE

Hartleys
Victoria Hall Salerooms,
Little Lane,
Ilkley LS29 8EA
Tel: 01943 816 363
info@hartleysauctions.co.uk
www.andrewhartleyfinearts.co.uk

**Thomson Roddick &
Medcalf**
Coleridge House,
Shaddongate,
Carlisle, Cumbria CA2 5TU
Tel: 01228 528 939
auctions@thomsonroddick.com
www.thomsonroddick.com

SCOTLAND

Bonhams Edinburgh
22 Queen Street,
Edinburgh EH2 1JX
Tel: 0131 225 2266
edinburgh@bonhams.com
www.bonhams.com

Lyon & Turnbull
33 Broughton Place,
Edinburgh EH1 3RR
Tel: 0131 557 8844
info@lyonandturnbull.com
www.lyonandturnbull.com

Lyon & Turnbull
182 Bath Street,
Glasgow G2 4HG
Tel: 0141 333 1992
glasgow@lyonandturnbull.com
www.lyonandturnbull.com

WALES

Bonhams Cardiff
7-8 Park Place,
Cardiff CF10 3DP
Tel: 02920 727 980
cardiff@bonhams.com
www.bonhams.com

Peter Francis
Towyside Salerooms
Old Station Road,
Carmarthen SA31 1JN
Tel: 01267 233 456
enquiries@peterfrancis.co.uk
www.peterfrancis.co.uk

Welsh Country Auctions
2 Carmarthen Road,
Cross Hands,
Llanelli SA14 6SP
Tel: 01269 844 428
www.welshcountryauctions. co.uk
(Written enquiries can be
submitted through website)

IRELAND

Mealy's
Kilkenny Road,
Castlecomer,
County Kilkenny
Tel: 00 353 56 44 00942
info@mealys.com
www.mealys.com

MAJOR FAIR & SHOW ORGANISERS

Arthur Swallow Fairs
Donington Park (Derbyshire),
Lincolnshire Show Ground
www.arthurswallowfairs.co.uk

Clarion Events
Antiques for Everyone,
Birmingham
www.antiquesforeveryone.co.uk

**Winter Fine Art &
Antiques Fair Olympia**
www.olympia-antiques.co.uk

**IACF (International
Antique & Collectors Fair)**
Newark (Nottinghamshire),
Ardingly (Sussex), North Weald
(Essex), Newbury (Berkshire),
Redbourn (Hertfordshire),
Swinderby (Nr. Lincoln) and
Shepton Mallet (Somerset)
www.iacf.co.uk

Nelson Fairs
Alexandra Palace (London),
Gresham's School (Norfolk),
Newmarket Racecourse
(Suffolk)
www.nelsonfairs.com

The following list is organised by the type of collectable. If you would like your club, society or organisation to appear in our next edition, or would like to update your details, please contact us at info@millers.uk.com.

ADVERTISING

Antique Advertising Signs
The Street Jewellery Society,
6 Crossley Terrace,
Arthur's Hill,
Newcastle-Upon-Tyne NE4 5NY
Tel: 0191 241 5196
info@streetjewellery.org
www.streetjewellery.org

AUTOGRAPHS

Autographica
6 St Winifreds Road,
Biggin Hill,
Kent TN16 3HR
Tel: 01959 573 792
dave.moviestar@btinternet.com
www.autographica.co.uk

AUTOMOBILIA

**Brooklands Automobilia
& Regalia Collectors'
Club,**
The White Lion Garage
Kemp Town,
Brighton,
East Sussex BN2 1JA
Tel: 01273 622 722 or
07890 836 734
www.brmmbrmm.com/barcc

BAXTER PRINTS

The New Baxter Society
c/o Reading Museum
& Art Gallery,
Blagrave Street,
Reading,
Berkshire RG1 1QH
newenquiries@newbaxter
society.org
newbaxtersociety.org

BOOKS

The Enid Blyton Society
tony@enidblytonsociety.co.uk
www.enidblytonsociety.co.uk

The Followers of Rupert
www.rupertthebear.org.uk

BOTTLES

British Bottle Review
www.onlinebbr.com/mag

BREWERIANA

**The Association
for British Brewery
Collectables**
www.breweriana.org.uk

CERAMICS

**Carlton Ware Collectors'
International**
CWCI Ltd,
Carlton Works,
Copeland Street,
Stoke-upon-Trent,
Staffordshire ST4 1PU
cwciclub@aol.com
www.lattimore.co.uk/deco/
carlton.htm

**Clarice Cliff Collectors
Club**
www.claricecliff.com
(Written enquiries can be
submitted through website)

**Collecting Doulton &
Beswick**
P.O. Box 310,
Richmond,
Surrey TW10 7FU
editor@collectingdoulton.com
www.collectingdoulton.com

**Fieldings Crown Devon
Collectors Club**
P.O. Box 462,
Manvers,
Rotherham S63 7WT
Tel: 01709 874 433
fcdcc2003@talktalk.net
www.fieldingscrowndevclub
.com

**Friends of Blue Ceramics
Society**
P.O. Box 122,
Didcot D.O.,
Oxford OX11 0YN
www.fob.org.uk

Goss Collectors' Club
www.gosschina.com

**Hornsea Pottery
Collectors' & Research
Society**
128 Devonshire Street,
Keighley,
West Yorkshire BD21 2QJ
hornsea@pdtennant.fsnet.co.uk
www.easyontheeye.net/
hornsea/society.htm

M.I. Hummel Club
www.mihummelclub.com
(Written enquiries can be
submitted through website)

Mabel Lucie Attwell Club
Abbey Antiques,
63 Great Whyte,
Ramsey, Huntingdon,
Cambridgeshire PE26 1HL
Tel: 01487 814 753
www.mabellucieattwellclub.com

**Moorcroft Collectors'
Club**
www.moorcroft.com/Site/
Collectors

Myott Collectors Club
www.myottcollectorsclub.com

Pendelfin Collectors Club
www.xystos.co.uk

**Poole Pottery Collectors'
Club**
infopoolepotterycollectors
club.co.uk
www.poolepotterycollectors
club.co.uk

**Potteries of Rye
Collectors' Society**
2 Redyear Cottages,
Kennington Road,
Ashford, Kent TN24 0TF
www.potteries-of-rye-society
.co.uk

**Royal Winton
International Collectors'
Club**
www.royalwinton.co.uk/
club.htm

The Shelley Group
7 Raglan Close,
Frimley,
Surrey GU16 8YL
Tel: 01483 764 097
shelley.group@shelley.co.uk
www.shelley.co.uk

Sylvac Collectors Circle
174 Portsmouth Road,
Horndean,
Waterlooville,
Hampshire PO8 9HP
admin@sylvacclub.com
www.sylvacclub.com

**Official International
Wade Collectors Club**
PO Box 3012
Stoke-on-Trent ST3 9DD
Tel: 0845 246 2525
club@wadecollectorsclub.co.uk
www.wadecollectorsclub.co.uk

CIGARETTE CARDS

**Cartophilic Society of
Great Britain**
Pubrelations@csgb.co.uk
www.csgb.co.uk

COINS, BANK NOTES &
PAPER MONEY

**British Numismatic
Society**
c/o The Warburg Institute,
Woburn Square,
London WC1H 0AB
secretary@britnumsoc.org
www.britnumsoc.org

Royal Numismatic Society
c/o The British Museum,
Department of Coins and
Medals,
Great Russell Street,
London WC1B 3DG
Tel: 020 7636 1555
info@numismatics.org.uk
www.numismatics.org.uk

**International Bank Note
Society**
www.theibns.org

**International Bond and
Share Society**
www.scripophily.org

COMMEMORATIVE WARE

**Commemorative
Collectors Society
& Commemoratives
Museum**
Lumless House,
77 Gainsborough Road,
Winthorpe,
Newark,
Nottinghamshire NG24 2NR
Tel: 01636 671 377
commemorativecollectorssociety
@hotmail.com
www.commemoratives
collecting.co.uk

COMICS

**The Beano & Dandy
Collectors' Club**
PO Box 3433,
Brighton BN50 9JA
phil@phil-comics.com
www.phil-comics.com/
collectors_club.html

COSTUME &
ACCESSORIES

**The British Compact
Collectors' Society**
P.O. BOX 64, Langford,
Biggleswade SG18 9BF
www.compactcollectors.co.uk

The Costume Society
28 Eburne Road,
London N7 6AU
Website@CostumeSociety.org.uk
www.costumesociety.org.uk

The Hat Pin Society of Great Britain
PO Box 1089,
Maidstone ME14 9BA
www.hatpinsociety.org.uk
(Written enquiries can be submitted through website)

DISNEYANA

Walt Disney Collectors' Society
wdccduckman@aol.com
www.wdccduckman.com

DOLLS

The Doll Club of Great Britain
2 Palace Green, Ely,
Cambridgeshire CB7 4EW
dollclubgb@yahoo.co.uk
www.dollclubgb.com

The Fashion Doll Collectors Club of Great Britain
postmaster@fashiondoll collectorsclubgb.co.uk
www.fashiondollcollectorsclub gb.co.uk

EPHEMERA

The Ephemera Society
P.O. Box 112, Northwood,
Middlesex HA6 2WT
Tel: 01923 829 079
info@ephemera-society.org.uk
www.ephemera-society.org.uk

FILM & TV

The James Bond International Fan Club
P.O. Box 21, York YO41 1WX
Tel: 01347 878 837
davidblack@007.info
www.007.info

Fanderson – The Official Gerry Anderson Appreciation Society
query@fanderson.org.uk
www.fanderson.org.uk

GLASS

The Carnival Glass Society
PO Box 14, Hayes,
Middlesex UB3 5NU
www.thecgs.co.uk
(Written enquiries can be submitted through website)

The Glass Association
150 Braemar Road,
Sutton Coldfield B73 6LZ
info@glassassociation.org.uk
www.glassassociation.org.uk

Isle of Wight Studio Glass Collectors' Club
Old Park,
St Lawrence,
Isle of Wight PO38 1XR
www.isleofwightstudioglass.co.uk

Jonathan Harris Studio Glass Collectors Club
www.jhstudioglass.com/Collectors-Club

KITCHENALIA

National Horse Brass Society
www.nationalhorsebrasssociety.org.uk
(Written enquiries can be submitted through website)

The Old Hall Club,
Sandford House,
Levedale, Stafford ST18 9AH
Tel: 01785 780 376
oht@gnwiggin.freeserve.co.uk
www.oldhallclub.co.uk

The British Novelty Salt & Pepper Collectors Club
www.communigate.co.uk/london/bnspcc/index.phtml
(Written enquiries can be submitted through website)

MECHANICAL MUSIC

Musical Box Society of Great Britain
www.mbsgb.org.uk
(Written enquiries can be submitted through website)

The City of London Phonograph & Gramophone Society
www.clpgs.org.uk
(Written enquiries can be submitted through website)

METALWARE

Antique Metalware Society
vin@oldcopper.org
www.oldcopper.org.uk

MILITARIA

Military Historical Society
john.chapman@purley.eu
www.militaryhistsoc.plus.com

The Orders & Medals Research Society
P.O. Box 248, Snettisham,
King's Lynn, Norfolk PE31 7TA
membershipsecretary@omrs.org.uk
www.omrs.org.uk

PAPERWEIGHTS

Paperweight Collectors Circle
PO Box 941, Comberton,
Cambridge PDO, CB23 7GQ
info@paperweightcollectors circle.org.uk
www.paperweightcollectors circle.org.uk

Caithness Glass Paperweight Collectors Members Society
www.caithnessglass.co.uk/collectors

PENS & WRITING

The Writing Equipment Society
membership@wesonline.org.uk
www.wesonline.org.uk

PERFUME BOTTLES

International Perfume Bottle Association
www.ipba-uk.co.uk

PLASTICS

Plastics Historical Society
general@plastiquarian.com
www.plastiquarian.com

POSTCARDS

Postcard Club of Great Britain
www.postcard.co.uk

POTLIDS

The Pot Lid Circle
enquiries@thepotlidcircle.co.uk
www.thepotlidcircle.co.uk

QUILTS

The Quilters' Guild of the British Isles
St Anthony's Hall,
Peaseholme Green,
York YO1 7PW
Tel: 01904 613 242
info@quiltersguild.org.uk
www.quiltersguild.org.uk

RADIOS

The British Vintage Wireless Society
www.bvws.org.uk

RAILWAYANA

Railwayana Collectors Journal
www.prorail.co.uk

SCIENTIFIC & OPTICAL INSTRUMENTS

Scientific Instrument Society
90 The Fairway,
South Ruislip,
Middlesex HA4 0SQ
www.sis.org.uk
(Written enquiries can be submitted through website)

SEWING

International Sewing Machine Collectors' Society
www.ismacs.net

The Thimble Society
Shop 72,
The Admiral Vernon Arcade,
141-9 Portobello Road,
London W11 2DY
antiques@thimblesociety.com
www.thimblesociety.com

SMOKING

The Lighter Club of Great Britain
www.lighterclub.co.uk

SPORTING

International Football Hall of Fame
info@ifhof.com
www.ifhof.com

Programme Monthly & Football Collectable
P.O. Box 3236,
Norwich NR7 7BE
Tel: 01603 449 237
theeditor@pmfc.co.uk
www.pmfc.co.uk

British Golf Collectors Society
secretary@golfcollectors.co.uk
www.golfcollectors.co.uk

Rugby Memorabilia Society
P.O. Box 57, Hereford HR1 9DR
RugbyMemorabiliaSociety@googlemail.com
www.rugby-memorabilia.co.uk

STAMPS

Postal History Society
www.postalhistory.org.uk

CLUBS & SOCIETIES

Royal Mail Stamps & Collecting
www.royalmail.com/portal/stamps

STANHOPES

The Stanhope Collectors' Club
jean@stanhopes.info
www.stanhopes.info

STAINLESS STEEL

The Old Hall Club,
Sandford House, Levedale,
Stafford ST18 9AH
Tel: 01785 780 376
oht@gnwiggin.freeserve.co.uk
www.oldhallclub.co.uk

TEDDY BEARS & SOFT TOYS

Dean's Collectors Club
P.O. Box 217,
Hereford HR1 9AB
www.deansbears.com

Merrythought International Collectors Club
club@merrythought.co.uk
www.merrythought.co.uk
Steiff Club
www.steiff.com

TOYS

The British Model Soldier Society
www.btinternet.com/~model.soldiers

Corgi Collector Club
www.corgi.co.uk/collectors-club/corgi-collector

Hornby Collectors Club
www.hornby.com/hornby-collectors-club

The Matchbox Club
P.O. Box 120, Deeside,
Clwyd CH5 3HE
Tel: 01244 539 414
help@matchboxclub.com
www.matchboxclub.com

Collectables are particularly suited to online trading. When compared with many antiques, most collectables are easily defined, described and photographed, whilst shipping is relatively easy, due to average sizes and weights. Collectables are also generally more affordable and accessible, and the internet has provided a cost-effective way of buying and selling without the overheads of shops and auction rooms. A huge number of collectables are offered for sale and traded daily over the internet, with websites varying from global online marketplaces, such as eBay, to specialist dealers' sites.

• There are a number of things to be aware of when searching for collectables online. Some items being sold may not be described accurately, meaning that general category searches, and even purposefully misspelling a name, can yield results. If something looks, or sounds, too good to be true, it probably is. Using this book should give you a head start in getting to know your market, and also enable you to tell the difference between a real bargain, and something that sounds like one. Good colour photography is absolutely vital – try to find online listings that include as many images as possible, including detail shots, and check them carefully. Be aware that colours can appear differently between websites, and even between computer screens.

• Always ask the vendor questions about the object, particularly regarding condition. If no image is supplied, or you want to see another aspect of the object, ask for more information. A good seller should be happy to cooperate if approached politely and sensibly.

• As well as the 'e-hammer' price, you will very likely have to pay additional transactional fees such as packing, shipping and possibly regional or national taxes. Ask the seller for an estimate of these additional costs before leaving a bid, as this will give you a better idea of the overall amount you will end-up paying.

• In addition to large online auction sites, such as eBay, there are a host of other online resources for buying and selling. The internet can also be an invaluable research tool for collectors, with many sites devoted to providing detailed information on a number of different collectables.

INTERNET RESOURCES

Miller's Antiques & Collectables
www.millersonline.com
Miller's new website is the ultimate one-stop destination for collectors, dealers, or anyone interested in antiques and collectables. Join the Miller's Club to search through a catalogue containing many thousands of authenticated antiques and collectables, each illustrated in full colour and accompanied by a full descriptive caption and price range. Browse through practical articles written by Judith Miller, Mark Hill, and a team of experts to learn tips and tricks of the trade, as well as learning more about important companies, designs, and the designers behind them. Read Judith's daily blog, and order the full range of Millers books direct. You can also search the best fully illustrated A-Z of specialist terms on the internet; a dealer, appraiser and auctioneer database; a guide to silver hallmarks; and learn about care and repair of your antiques and collectables. The site is continually updated, so check back regularly to see what's new.

Live Auctioneers
www.liveauctioneers.com
A free online service which allows users to search catalogues from selected auction houses in Europe, the USA and the United Kingdom. Visitors to the site can bid live via the Internet into salerooms as auctions happen. Registered users can also search through an archive of past catalogues and receive a free e-mail newsletter.

The Saleroom.com
www.the-saleroom.com
A free online service that allows users to search catalogues from selected auction houses in Europe, the USA and the United Kingdom. Visitors to the site can bid live via the internet into salerooms as auctions happen. Registered users can also search through an archive of past catalogues and receive a free e-mail newsletter.

eBay
www.ebay.com
Undoubtedly the largest and most diverse of the online auction sites, allowing users to buy and sell in an online marketplace with over 52 million registered users from across the world.

ArtFact
www.artfact.com
Provides a comprehensive database of worldwide auction listings from over 2,000 art, antiques and collectables auction houses. User can search details of both upcoming and past sales and also find information on a number of collectors' fields. Basic information is available for free, access to more in depth information requires a subscription. Online bidding live into auctions as they happen is also offered.

The Antiques Trade Gazette
www.antiquestradegazette. com
The online edition of the UK trade newspaper, including British auction and fair listings, news and events.

Maine Antique Digest
www.maineantiquedigest. com
Online version of America's trade newspaper including news, articles, fair and auction listings and more.

La Gazette du Drouot
www.drouot.com
The online home of the magazine listing all auctions to be held in France at the Hotel de Drouot in Paris. An online subscription enables you to download the magazine online.

Auction.fr
www.auction.fr
An online database of auctions at French auction houses. A subscription allows users to search past catalogues and prices realised.

Go Antiques/Antiqnet
www.goantiques.com
www.antiqnet.com
An online global aggregator for art, antiques and collectables dealers. Dealers' stock is showcased online, with users able to browse and buy.

INDEX

INDEX

INDEX